Control for Life Extension

A Personalized Holistic Approach

by

Valery Mamonov, Ph.D.

Disclaimer

The information in this book is accurate to the best of the author's knowledge. All the procedures and suggestions in this book are based on the personal experiences and research of the author. This book is written and sold for informational and educational purposes only and is not intended as a substitute for medical advice from a trained medical professional. Some of the therapies (such as dry fasting) described in this book are very intense and, if used improperly, may cause adverse effects. Because people, their circumstances, and health conditions are very different, there is always some risk involved. Neither the author nor the publisher takes any responsibility for possible damages, loss, expense, or any other consequences from the use of any therapy, exercise, and suggestions described herein. Readers, especially those with health problems, are advised to consult a physician or other qualified health-care provider before implementing any of the dietary or other approaches presented in this book, and to attempt to have their support and cooperation in the quest for a healthier and longer life.

All poems by the author, unless otherwise noted.
Outside and inside cover art and design by the author and Nancy Jacob.
Exercises are demonstrated by Xu Fang, Steve McDonald, and the author.
Photographs by the author, except those of Steve McDonald by James McDonald, Jr.

Long Life Press, Co., 3 Hoyts Lane, Rome, Maine 04963
(207) 397-2624

Printed in the United States of America

Library of Congress Catalog Number: TXu 909-920

Mamonov, Valery, 1941–
    Control for Life Extension: A Personalized Holistic Approach

    608 p.   22.8 cm.

    Includes selected bibliography and index
    1. Self-help. 2. Health. 3. Longevity. II. Title. [1. Self-help. 2.
        Health.   3. Longevity–Popular works.]
    RA776.75.M263   613'.0438   909-920
    ISBN 0 – 9710654 – 0 – 3   TXu

Dedication

*This book
is dedicated to
my mother, Anna Danilovna,
guardian
throughout my life,
who continues
to guide me
from heaven
even still.*

Table of Contents

ACKNOWLEDGMENTS

Many people have helped shape my perception of the world, acquire experience, and become health-conscious. Without their teaching, sharing of ideas, and help, it is difficult to imagine that I would have been able to write this book and to conduct the research upon which it is based.

I am forever indebted to my yoga teacher, Eugene Bazh, who now lives in Moscow. My first thought of writing a book of this kind came to me about twenty years ago when I witnessed his forty-day-long fasts. I learned various exercises, diets, meditation, body-cleansing methods, and mind-body-connection from him. His ideas and practices have inspired me to think of fasting in the broadest terms. The restriction of our basic biological needs and encouragement of our emotional, intellectual, and spiritual activities is the most expedient means of achieving good health and longevity.

My first experience with yoga was with my friend Vladimir Samol, to whom I want to express my great, although belated, gratitude. His experiments on himself at near-death states and his sudden death at the age of forty-six (caused by his going too far--using a special technique to stop his heart beating and failing to revive it again) became the most pivotal turning point of my entire life. I was then thirty-seven years old, and it has changed my life completely ever since. It's a pity that he never met Eugene Bazh, who appeared in my life only one year later. I believe that these two enlightened yoga teachers would have become great friends had they known each other.

I must also give special thanks to eighty-nine-year-old Vladimir M. Kuznetsov. He is one of the health pioneers in Russia who developed an original holistic system, which combines embryology and oriental horoscope.

The illustrations in the *Exercise* chapter of the book are possible as a result of the photographs of Xu Fang of Shanghai, a mysterious Chinese beauty who has abstained from food for the last thirteen years, and Steve McDonald of Woburn, Massachusetts. I express my utmost gratitude to them for their great contribution.

I am especially grateful to both Demetrios Antonopoulos, forty-seven, of Boston, and Brenda Bernard, sixty-seven, of Woburn, Massachusetts, who took great pains to answer all the questionnaires necessary for drawing profiles of their centenarian fathers. Demetrios gave me much encouragement in the writing of this book and made English language corrections in the first part that were very helpful. Mary Moscaritolo of Stoneham, Massachusetts read several parts of the manuscript and I am very thankful for her corrections as well.

I am not sure whether this book will be regarded as popular, but writing this kind of book has been a wonderful venture for me. My previous writing was limited to scientific papers and I have enjoyed immensely the new experience of this kind of research and writing. I give thanks to my editors and collaborators in the publishing of this book.

I thank Jeanne Bradley, my first editor, who began editing the manuscript. Most of the editorial work, however, was done by Constance Burt of TechEdit Services, who made the editing process enjoyable and exciting. We had many discussions and I am grateful for her support of my vision. It was Connie's critical guidance that made the book more readable.

I am greatly indebted to my family members and friends for their steady, loving support and help. My daughter Victoria and her husband Stephen Mourousas hosted me in Woburn, Massachusetts, and provided me with the best of living and working conditions. Stephen also had the courage to utilize some recommendations of the book for himself.

I am thankful to my old friend Boris Klovsky, who encouraged me by saying, "You are writing the book on health and medicine, but you are not a physician to begin with. You will have to deal with stuff like author's rights, too." It was he who first influenced me in my decision to keep away from medical issues--which are entirely in the realm of medical doctors--and stick to the health and life extension themes.

I want also to thank my dear friend Vladimir Ostrov, who helped me to emigrate from Russia. He encouraged me by saying that he believed that I could write this book because I was living it in practice.

My Japanese friends Yasuhide Kawasaki, Jiro and Masako Tokawa, Yasuko Asawa, Kaori Yamane, and many others deserve my heartfelt thanks. They helped me to find relevant information on Japanese centenarians and even hosted me in Japan while I was working on the research for this book. My young friend Andreas Renfer of Switzerland helped me with much valuable information on the Internet and with computers in general.

My meetings with centenarians could hardly be possible without the help of Vennes Sundaram of Singapore, my Russian colleague Lyudmila Vasilievna of Nakhodka City, Japanese physician Professor Okuyama, and others. The relatives of American and Russian centenarians provided me with much important information: Jean Casey of Belgrade, Maine (a niece of Frank Shomo, 108), and Vera Zhukova of Nakhodka, Russia, (daughter of Nataliya Yusova, 101).

I apologize to those whom I have neglected to mention in my praise and thanks. This is not due to lack of my gratitude to them, but rather because of my inadequate memory.

INTRODUCTION

It is your lucky day.
You found a fountain of youth,
Especially if you are blood type A.
You will unearth the truth.

Your thick blood's an inner time bomb,
If you eat for your type wrong.
If you can't resist the grill,
You must think about the will.

Your age is short, and hard to lengthen,
If you continue your way.
To make your life long, I have to say,
Read the *Control for Life Extension.*

This book will give you a great hope,
It will be for you a salvation rope.

It is the most significant day in your life. It is the day of your enlightenment: it is the day of your conversion, of your transformation into a centenarian. You will never remain the one you were before. All your dreams of being extremely healthy and living a long life have become true, with incredible physical, mental, emotional and spiritual health. A new life of super-health unfolds for you from now on. Never in your life were you as healthy as you will soon become. With every passing day, you will become more vital, vigorous, robust, aware, and enlightened. For the first time in your life, you will experience an extreme happiness--a happiness of supreme health.

Today is your birthday. You are born twice. You have already one, the birthday of your past. Today is the birthday of your future. This is your real birthday. Celebrate it; mark it on the calendar. Your birthday present is your birthright to enjoy a vibrant health lasting many, many more years. Today is the day of your departure from all misfortunes, illnesses, and frustrations.

You made the right choice. You won a one-hundred-year vibrant-health diamond star. You bought the book, which shows a clear way of becoming a super-healthy centenarian. It does not matter who you are and what your age is. An unprecedented health improvement, money back, is guaranteed. The only thing you need to do is just read this book. Your innate urge for freedom through self-control will be supported and reinforced while reading it. Having read it, you will be charged with a desire and energy to change. You will see immediate positive results by application of the information in this book. I thank you for becoming my companion, and I will not leave you alone in this transformation. I have also chosen this path, and we will go together.

All blood types or other constitutional types will benefit from this book, but especially people with blood type A. Their average life expectancy is the shortest, only sixty-two years, a full quarter of a century shorter than that of blood type Os. This book is of tremendous significance for blood type As. Although blood type Os have every chance to reach one hundred in a relaxed way, blood type As can extend their life span and gain the same goal only through self-discipline and very hard work. This book contains everything you need to know to reach a century mark, despite your unfavorable blood chemistry or heredity and all the odds of life.

When we hear the word "centenarian," we seldom associate it with good health. The image of a centenarian--frail-looking, with a wrinkled face framed by thin, snow-white hair, sunken cheeks accentuated by toothless gums, usually almost blind and deaf, and often sitting quietly in a wheelchair not recognizing anyone--is not appealing to you. You don't want to become as fully dependent on others as a newborn child--a burden to family members, without a future or any hope of becoming healthy and fit again. To merely exist is surely boring, and not your ideal. The ideal life for you and me is to live long, stay healthy and self-sufficient, and die abruptly in our sleep.

Of course, all centenarians are not like that description. There are centenarians who are healthy and fit and who often lead active lives. They keep busy and occupied with their interests, skills, and hobbies, but these people are few and far between. As a whole group of long-lived people, however, centenarians are very rare. If you ask someone whether they know of a centenarian, the usual reply is no.

The ratio of centenarians in the population is minute. In the entire country of Iceland--reputed to have the longest life span in Europe--there were only twenty-seven centenarians in the 1995 population of 267,958 people (i.e., one person in 10,000). In the United States, there are about two centenarians for every 10,000 people. In Okinawa, Japan, world famous for long–living people, there are 3.25 centenarians for every 10,000 people. Perhaps only 20 percent of these individuals are healthy and fit, about one in 100,000. This is an extremely small percentage.

Even these very rare champions of longevity are still an unexplained phenomenon. Why they live so long, nobody knows. Much research has been devoted to the science of gerontology and related areas, but the mystery is still there. Centenarians themselves do not know either and often are very surprised that they have lived so long. It seems that they occasionally did everything right, although others around them did wrong. More than a hundred factors affect longevity. These particular people exercised the special talent of avoiding negative factors, achieving a ripe old age despite all the odds of life. Sounds like magic; well, it really is. It is magic unexplained at present, but I strongly believe that science will find the key to unlock the mysteries hiding behind the door of longevity.

If you are in your twenties and thirties today, you have a chance to live to be one hundred, according to David Mahoney and Richard Restak, M.D. In their book, *The Longevity Strategy,* they rely on the advances of science--especially in the field of brain research--that make the hundred-year life span possible. The "exceptional" longevity of some people who become centenarians is no longer exceptional, they say. The perspective of relaxing and waiting for future scientific achievements is attractive, but what if you are in your fifties or sixties? I am not inclined to wait until the life span of humans on the whole will be increased; rather, I want to explore opportunities to extend an individual's life through a holistic approach and one's own efforts.

I do share the popular idea that everyone can reach a hundred and more–including blood type As–even if longevity does not run in one's family. My confidence is based on recent scientific achievements, the world's holistic traditions, more than twenty years of my own research in this field, and many examples of self-made centenarians who adopted a healthy diet and lifestyle.

One of these centenarians is Dr. Paul Bragg, an American health pioneer and life-extension specialist. He is a living proof of exceptional longevity. He gained such a fitness level that he could surf at the age of ninety-five, and he made his body ageless. I am, and forever will be, a big fan of Paul Bragg. I fasted "after Bragg," I have chosen a diet and lifestyle "after Bragg," and I became health-conscious "after Bragg."

I am also an admirer of Dr. Souren Arakelyan, the Russian biologist who has experimented on himself with caloric restriction combined with a raw-food diet for the last thirty-four years. His goal is to prove that a diet of raw, enzymes-rich, live foods consisting of fruits, vegetables, grains, and nuts, moderate fasting, and exercise are the vehicles to achieve a super long life of 125 years. He is seventy-two years old now, but he looks as if he is forty, and he enjoys incredible health. In his research, he experimented with fasting on domestic animals such as hens, pigs, cows, and horses--and **tripled the life span** of his hens. No other researcher in the world has attained such an outstanding result. In his raw-food-diet approach to longevity, Dr. Arakelyan is supported by Dr. Norman W. Walker, an American scientist who studied enzymes and the principles of living on raw food for more than a half-century. Dr. Walker ate raw fruits and vegetables, and lived to be a healthy and active 109 years old, proving his theory.

Dr. Arakelyan's raw-food journey began at the age of thirty-eight after reading the book *On the Traces of Raw Food Diet,* by Aterov (Arshavir Ter-Ovanesyan). This Iranian author ate meat and other cooked foods until the age of fifty-two, when he became so sick that he would be short of breath after climbing only two steps. He also suffered from heart failure, chest pains, constipation, indigestion, insomnia, chronic bronchitis, chronic hemorrhoids, and frequent colds. After complete abstinence from cooked food and eating only raw foods for eight years, Aterov was vibrantly healthy and strong at the age of sixty (when he wrote his book), and could easily climb to the top of hills and walk fifteen miles without getting tired. At the age of ninety in 1985, he still enjoyed perfect health and vitality.

I also admire George Burns, an American comedian and the author of *How to Live to Be 100 and More: The Ultimate Diet, Sex, and Exercise Book.* He was living proof of his book and actually lived to be a hundred. With his wonderful attitude, sparkling sense of humor, and healthy diet and lifestyle (except for the habit of smoking), he is an excellent model to follow.

You will find in this book many cases of vigorous centenarians and ageless celebrities--inspirational stories that offer hope to everyone. However, you can get the impression, especially from George Burns' story, that it is easy to reach one hundred while drinking martinis and coffee, smoking cigars, and dating young girls. If we are dreamers, it is acceptable to believe that we can also do that; but, as realists, we know it is not. Yes, you have a great chance to live to be one hundred (regardless of your blood type, body constitution, and heredity) if you use the information contained in this book for your *awareness*, as a theoretical basis, using it to take *control* over your own life, as a practical action. This book will not give you a "magic pill" or golden key that instantly unlocks the gate of longevity. There is no such pill or key in Nature--Nature expects you to follow her laws in the first place. This book is about a radical change of your lifestyle and habits, self-discipline, commitment, and hard work for the rest of your life. You will find in this book everything you need to know about *regaining youth and vigor, prolonging your life span far beyond average, and living a "life that's full,"* as Frank Sinatra sings.

For me as an author, coming to the point of writing a book on life extension was neither simple nor a one-way street. Until the age of thirty-seven, I was leading the life of an ordinary intellectual in Moscow, Russia, and lacked knowledge about health. My career was quite successful: I received my Ph.D. degree in engineering in 1969, worked in Russia for twenty-six years, then in Israel and Japan for six years, until 1996. I was granted several awards, including governmental, and my profile was included in *Marquis' Who Is Who in Finance and Industry*, 1998-1999. In Russia, I worked for more than twenty years in the Research Institute of Bases and Underground Structures in Moscow. My job involved site experiments that required significant physical activity. I often went on missions to the remote regions of the former USSR and stayed in the field for months.

Although my health was quite good, my lifestyle was far from what one would regard as healthy. I was merely deducting from my inherited health account, and doing nothing to replenish it. I even smoked for a few years and drank vodka occasionally, though always in moderation and without excess. Although self-destructive traits have never ruled in my life, I would not define my state at that time as "health-conscious."

My experience with healthy diets, holistic methods, and yoga exercises stems from my close friend Vladimir Samol. I first met him through my work and we had a few talks, which revealed that we shared the same philosophy. He had an incredible charisma and was a powerful magnet to me. Although he was the very model of fitness--marathon runner and avid health enthusiast--he unfortunately overestimated his own abilities. He experimented on himself at near-death states and died suddenly at the age of forty-six (using a special technique, he stopped his heart from beating, but failed to revive it again). His death struck me very deeply and became a turning point in my life. I was 37 years old and it has completely changed my life ever since. In trying to figure out the specific cause of his death, I met people involved in yoga, folk medicine, and holistic therapies. I joined groups of people with channeling abilities, attended yoga classes, and read many related books, among them those of Paul Bragg and Herbert Shelton, both American health pioneers. My life at that time had split into two major activities: working in a research institute and occupying my leisure hours with learning about holistic cures, as well as yoga exercises, fasts, diets, and other alternative health doctrines.

The idea of writing a book on life extension came to me in the early 1980s, while I was practicing fasts in Russia under the guidance of my yoga teacher, Eugene Bazh. He is forty years old now and lives in Moscow. He has extraordinary abilities in terms of extrasensory perception, and his healing power is great. People's auras are visible to him and he is even able to see bodies of thought. Although young and healthy, he practices spiritual forty-day-long fasts. I learned about various exercises, diets, meditation, body-cleansing methods, and mind-body-connections from him. It was delicious and tantalizing food for my thought.

My life changed dramatically once again in 1990 when I emigrated from Russia. I worked in Israel for more than a year, then found a job in a Japanese company in Tokyo, where I worked for the next five years. By that time my daughter had married an American and moved to the United States. I often visit and stay with her family in the United States.

After retiring from the corporate life at the age of fifty-five, I decided to dedicate myself to research in the field of longevity, the primary subject of interest to me. I left my successful career as a consulting engineer in geotechnics in 1996 to concentrate full-time on creating a program that would offer a new approach to longevity.

Personally, there were a few reasons for me to be concerned about my overall health and life span. First, I am blood type A, which live the shortest. Heart disease, stroke, and cancer kill blood type As early in life. My heredity traits, although not great, are not too bad. My paternal grandfather and maternal grandmother died when they were in their early nineties. My father died at the age of seventy-eight of colon cancer and he suffered from a prostate disorder. My mother died of pneumonia when she was seventy-three.

My father's constitution was strong and, for most of his life, he was active and healthy, but my mother was born with quite a weak constitution. In the course of her life, she was highly spiritual, but did nothing to improve her physical health. I inherited the weaknesses of vital organs from my mother. In addition, I am very tall (6 feet, 4 inches); most long-living people are usually short. Tall people have relatively weak hearts and circulation systems, and are also vulnerable to cancer. Being mindful of my unfavorable blood chemistry and inherited weaknesses, I felt that I needed to acquire knowledge about maintaining health and to achieve longevity through my own efforts.

For the last two decades and especially since my retirement, I have tried to practice a healthy lifestyle. I eat lots of raw vegetables and fruits, and try to abstain from foods inappropriate for my blood type. I exercise (Ayurvedic dosha and Yin-Yang), practice fasts, and engage in many intellectual and spiritual activities. At my age of sixty, I am rather strong (I can do one-arm pushups and the peacock yoga pose) and flexible (I can bend forward and put my palms on the floor and sit in the padmasana pose), and my heart is quite conditioned (currently, I do 1,200 knee bends in one session).

While in Japan, I was very impressed to learn that the book, *A Great Revolution in the Brain World,* by Dr. Shigeo Haruyama, became a national bestseller, with three million copies sold. It showed that the Japanese public is much interested in health and longevity topics. The same health-conscious trend was revealed in the United States when the book, *Life Extension,* by Durk Pearson and Sandy Show, was ranked the runaway #1 national bestseller. Thus, I learned that in both the East and the West, people are eager to know how to become healthier and live longer. For many, health even becomes the first priority in their life–and so it became in my life too. All of my life, I have had a strong feeling that what I learned about health through self-education, careful study, and personal experience may be useful for other people. Now I am given a chance to offer you my thoughts and share with you my knowledge on health and life extension. I have not the slightest doubt that you will benefit by discovering a wealth of valuable information about yourself and the direction to move in your life, although you may have a different philosophy.

It is not necessary for you to have the same background I have to understand the information in this book. There are some subjects that you may not be familiar with, such as doshas, chakras, or egregores, which require a sort of open-mindedness to comprehend. If they sound disturbing or fearful to you, perceive them as metaphors. However, along with the simple explanation given, you may find something intriguing and even helpful in them. I also do not expect you to believe that it is possible to live for years without food and still be healthy and active; it is difficult for me to accept as well. Although these cases are well documented, they overturn all existing knowledge and common sense, which is really difficult for the intellect to accept.

Most of the factual material for this book was gathered within the last four years. My self-supported research project included travels to Japan, Singapore, Iceland, Russia, and the United States, where I interviewed both long-living people and centenarians. One of my most fruitful and interesting sojourns was my trip to China to meet the then 29-year-old Xu Fang. She is the Chinese beauty-mystery who has not eaten for the last 13 years. I learned about her while staying in Japan and instantly wanted to meet her. In history, there are cases of non-eating religious devotees, such as Teresa Neumann of Germany and Giri Bala of India. A great kriya-yoga teacher, Paramahansa Yogananda, the author of *Autobiography of Yogi,* interviewed both of them. However, Xu Fang lives now, not in the past, and I became excited to meet and interview such a wonder. I found her to be healthy, flexible, fit, and vigorous. Her eyes and skin emitted a radiant health and vitality.

Although she allegedly has lived completely without food for more than a decade, she is leading an active life. As is common among non-eating people, she is a deeply religious Buddhist. I also met one of the Chinese military scientists who had done extensive research about her, but some of his ideas sounded doubtful to me. Other researchers in China have studied Xu Fang, but still her case remains a scientifically unexplained phenomenon. Many just do not believe that it is possible. Even Chinese physicians, who confirmed with ultrasound tests that she had no digestive juices in her stomach, said they do not believe it is possible to survive without food.

The ideas and information that I have gathered during the past twenty years culminated in my book, which shows that for most people, a healthy lifestyle, rather than heredity, affects their longevity most of all. The main theme of this book is that basic human biological needs for food, air, water, sleep, and sex, if satisfied with *restriction* and *moderation*, result in many noticeable benefits for health and longevity. The book demonstrates how to control each of these basic needs, as well as one's thoughts and emotions. A six-stage cleansing of one's internal organs, alternate dry fasting, water and juice fasting, a raw food diet for detoxification and rejuvenation, various approaches to longevity, and a life extension program are also described.

As a result of my own experience and research efforts, I developed a *Restriction–Abundance* approach to longevity. The longevity seeker is advised to choose a personal health program through understanding his or her unique body constitution and personality. Good health and longevity may be achieved if one:

• restricts basic biological needs for food, water, oxygen, and sleep, taking inside the body a minimum necessary just for survival

• takes good care of the body, supplying it with nutrition-rich live foods and exercise, and adheres to a healthy lifestyle

• chooses a diet, activity, and lifestyle appropriate to individual type

• takes control over emotional and mental states and learns to cope with stress to achieve peace of mind

• cultivates and lets bloom in abundance individual talents, creativity, skills, and crafts

• exercises the brain and strives for intellectual development and spiritual growth

Major features of lifestyle are discussed in detail, along with many other factors affecting longevity. I herein stress that conscious effort and hard work are absolutely necessary to achieve lifelong fitness and longevity. The reader will find in the book much helpful information about the main aspects of life. I elaborate on the thirteen diagnostic systems (i.e., eight Western and five Oriental) related to longevity and provide questionnaires with most of them that allow one to draw his or her own unique profile. This renders a theoretical basis and a direction in which to move to achieve a balanced state of physical and emotional health. To test their workability, I applied these thirteen systems to two American centenarians, as well as to myself. As a result of self-assessment by these diagnostic systems, I now know myself much better than before and it is my hope that longevity-seekers also will benefit from a better understanding of themselves. Because each diagnostic system is linked to longevity, I believe their use gives further insight into the secrets of longevity and may be applied in future gerontological studies.

The *personalized holistic approach to longevity* is what makes this book different from other books. Adult readers of both genders will find herein several revolutionary ideas about basic aspects of life. For instance, it seems that *carbon dioxide* enhances longevity, not oxygen, as once commonly thought. The benefits from drinking less water also are explained. The information presented in this book about the role of oxygen and water in particular--which are of a primary importance for survival--is almost entirely unknown in this country. Some very efficient exercises described in this book will also be unfamiliar to most people. Longevity-enhancing exercises are detailed and illustrated by photographs of Xu Fang, the Chinese non-eating woman, and the author. Readers will also find food charts appropriate to their type, including longevity foods and drinks.

Each part begins with a sonnet, which summarizes that particular part poetically. You will certainly find the quality of poetry far below high standards. I am not much of a poet and I admit that sometimes the meaning is first difficult to understand. It may be because I did not choose proper words, which may leave the impression that they are used for the sake of rhythm rather than sense (even the rhythms are not always good). Although your reaction likely will be negative, still, I dare to include them. It is my hope that you will find some lines sounding not bad at all.

Each sonnet consists of fourteen lines that are arranged in four verses: three of four lines each and one of two lines. The rhythm pattern is consistent through all seven sonnets. Employing this particular pattern, I mimicked Alexander Pushkin, a great Russian poet and the pride of his country. Since I am a Russian soul myself, I was born with love for Pushkin in my blood. His novel in verses, *Eugene Onegin*, consists of 390 sonnets with fourteen lines each. *Eugene Onegin* is known to classical music amateurs through the opera (based on Pushkin's novel) of Peotr Tchaikovsky, a great Russian composer. It is a pity that Pushkin is virtually unknown in the Western world because all attempts to translate his poetry into English have failed. The melody of verses and their beauty are largely lost in the translation.

I consider this book a self-help book, which is actually a blend of reliable scientific, holistic, metaphysical, and hard-to-believe (yet documented) information like that about the Chinese non-eating beauty-mystery. I spent ten days in China two years ago with her and have included an illustrated journal of our time together.

You will most probably consider some ideas in this book, such as the raw food diet, protein restriction diet, dry fasting, and carbon dioxide accumulation, as extreme. They may sound "unnatural" or even shocking in the first encounter; however, the results for health improvement reaped from them may also be extremely beneficial. Indeed, they are very powerful and, **if applied without great caution**, may even be harmful. I discuss what I learned from other people who used them with obvious benefit in achieving supreme health and extraordinary longevity, and I applied these ideas to myself, seemingly without harm.

I have learned not only from individuals such as Paul Bragg, Herbert Shelton, Arshavir Ter-Avanesyan, Porphiry Ivanov, Norman Walker, and many others, but also from entire long-living populations, including the Hunza, Vilcabamba, and Abkhasia. Consciously (i.e., pioneering individuals) or unconsciously (i.e., populations with a naturally healthy lifestyles), these people achieved the goals that we all desire; therefore, they are trustworthy. They leave us clues.

Still, the longevity seekers are mostly longevity researchers who experiment on themselves to prove their theories. Each believes that he or she found a key to longevity, whether it is fasting, a natural way of living, or following a raw-food diet. They are very knowledgeable people, aware of the dangers of self-experimentation. Each became a philosopher and teacher of his or her own approach to longevity, the leader of a school with hundreds and sometimes thousands of followers. The teachers could study a history of a follower and impart the necessary guidance and instruction, thus protecting them from mistakes. Although the likelihood of mistakes is reduced in this way, it still exists to some extent because no one knows all the answers regarding longevity.

Readers like you, who are distant from those circles, need to become researchers yourselves in order to avoid possible harm. Reckless self-experimentation can be very **dangerous**; therefore, be **very careful** when applying information from books, including this one. You need to be informed, but do not hurry. To be on the safe side, always think twice before you try something. Implement your changes very slowly, one step at a time. You have an eternity ahead, and you find time for all your endeavors. When it comes to longevity, quick fixes do not work. It may result in the loss of health and shortening rather than a lengthening of life.

Rather than telling you to do it this way or that (as medical doctors and nutrition specialists would), I am going to demonstrate a range in many aspects of health and longevity. Rather than instructing you, I provide options that you can choose from, according to your own values and goals. The options are not many, though, because many things are predetermined for you with your inherited body type, blood type, and biochemical individuality. It is possible, however, to decrease your dependence on your type through fasting or adopting a raw-food diet. They are powerful means, not alone for rejuvenation and life extension, but also for one's liberation.

Along with providing various information related to your health and longevity, I also try to increase your awareness, freedom, and enlightenment. Armed with knowledge, you will feel self-confident and you can achieve the goals of your "impossible" dreams. The more you know, the more conscious and free you are. The more conscious you become, the more you progress in spiritual evolution, which is the very meaning of life itself. In this way, your raised consciousness is beneficial to you and those around you.

It is entirely up to you whether you choose to increase your self-awareness, but it is my hope that you will. Access to a higher consciousness and awareness is easier if you take control of your own life. Relative to this theme, control means the power of self-restraint. Self-control, discipline, and hard work are the keys to the transformation of one's body, mind, and spirit, and the acquisition of true freedom, which is the quintessence of life.

Any path to self-improvement in terms of health and longevity begins with an interest in one's own health. People are obsessed with achieving their personal goals, pursuing their hobbies, building their houses, being engaged in relationships, and almost all other life activities except the most important one: **their health**. They do not realize--until they loose it--that their health is the most important objective in life; when person is healthy, then he or she is really happy. In many cases, people belong to their company, their family, their friends, but not to themselves. They may take many social and family responsibilities, but fail to take the responsibility for their own health. As Frank Sinatra sang in *My Way*, "...For what is a man, what has he got, if not himself then he has naught." It is my hope that the information in this book will provide food for your mind and the inspiration to find enough time for yourself. You can discover a new joy, the joy of being in control of your own unique and unrepeatable life. It is all in your own hands to make yourself healthier and more fit, to increase the quality of your life, and to make it longer and happier.

PART ONE: BODY TYPES

To be around a long time,
A strong and fit body is a must.
It's better if the face will often shine,
And wisdom is not left in the dust.

If you enjoy research and freedom,
And don't let in offense or boredom,
The blood in you is of type B or O,
You burn your food neither fast nor slow,

You live your days in a healthy manner,
And strive to increase the Kapha dosha,
And being concerned with the Yin-Yang ratio,
Were granted at birth the longevity banner,

If you were born in winter or spring,
You have on your finger a centenarian ring.

We Are All Unique

Every person is unique. There are no two equal people, including identical twins; they may have a similar physical build, but they will certainly have wide diversities of emotional and thinking processes. It was God's plan to create us to be different from one another. God must be happy that all His creatures are unique. If people were all alike, it would probably bore God and He would leave us to go elsewhere. Because each of us is so unique, He is interested in us, so He stays with us.

Every individual has a unique bodily constitution, blood type, and metabolic type (i.e., fast and slow oxidizers), personality, temperament, instincts, and ancestry. Although there are only four blood types, there are no two identical blood samples within one blood type. The blood of every individual has unrepeatable and varying characteristics. To these Western categories that describe an individual we must add various Oriental categories, including the Ayurvedic dosha type, Yin-Yang type, Five Elements type, Chakra characteristics, and horoscope. Each of these features also has a specific range of qualities; therefore, ultimately, the variations and permutations are endless.

Each person is unique because of physiological, psychological, external, and internal (including cellular level) differences; therefore, one has a unique set of needs. The only way to satisfy these needs is to correctly address all the recommendations for each particular individual. In other words, diet, exercise, personal growth, and any other plan must be *personalized*. Good health and longevity can be achieved through better self-understanding, better comprehension of what is good and what is bad for each individual, and self-control as a means to avoid harmful influences on one's body, mind, and spirit.

A personalized approach to medicine and nutrition is not a new concept--it was developed centuries ago by Egyptian, Greek, Arabian, and Chinese physicians. In modern times, many researchers acknowledged the concept of **biochemical individuality**, a term first introduced by biochemist Dr. Roger Williams. Among others to explore this approach are Dr. William Sheldon (author of the somatotype theory), Dr. Henry Bieler and Dr. Elliot Abravanel (who classified individuals by the dominance of one of their glands), Dr. Peter D'Adamo (who employs a four-blood-type concept), Dr. William Kelley and William L. Wolcott (who stress a person's metabolic type), and Ann Louise Gittleman (who considers ancestry, blood type, and metabolic type).

Because we are so unique, we need to know ourselves better to be able to understand the causes of both our health and our infirmity. This involves some knowledge of medicine, physiology, psychology, and the origin of a person's self. This is the first step in achieving and maintaining health, the second is taking personal responsibility, and the third is taking appropriate action to achieve the desired results. There is currently an ocean of information available about basic principles of good health, including a healthy diet, exercise, positive mental attitude, the avoidance of bad habits, and stress-management skills. The difficulty is in choosing from the numerous recommendations those that will work for you in practice. How can this be accomplished if one knows little or nothing about oneself? Actually, this knowledge greatly affects the total culture of the individual as well. Without basic knowledge of medicine and oneself, contemporary man cannot be considered cultured, according to one prominent scientist. My task is to at least help you to become closely acquainted with yourself.

Survival of the Fittest, Wisest, and Calmest

Long-living people live in different countries and on different continents, with a wide range of climatic and environmental conditions. The food they eat, water they drink, even the air they breathe may differ significantly. Centenarians of Iceland live in a cold climate, eat food that is rich in animal proteins, and enjoy unpolluted water and air. Centenarians in Singapore live in a hot and moist climate, and eat lots of vegetables and fruits, but the air in that metropolis is not very clean. The lifestyles and daily physical activities also differ greatly among countries.

However, there is something common to all of them that allows these people to live so long: their unflappable health and fitness. This is not the sort of super-fitness possessed by people such as the winners of the Boston Marathon or the male and female models smiling from the front pages of the *Men's Fitness* or *Health* magazines. Rather, it is merely a healthy fitness--taking all things in moderation--that is the motto of most long-living people of the world. Moderate health and fitness are enough to survive all the odds of life--crossing the finish line of a super marathon run where the distance is measured not in miles, but in years.

Fitness and health are what is necessary for people to achieve their lifetime goals, fulfill their particular mission, and move toward actualization of their potentials, talents, and spirituality. Even survival of the species and natural selection is dependent on the level of fitness possessed by an animal. The sound physical condition of a particular animal is what allows it to survive and to be selected. For instance, if an organism is better able to escape a predator, it is more likely to have offspring. That is what Charles Darwin (1809 - 1882) in his theory of evolution meant by "natural selection" and what British philosopher Herbert Spencer (1820 - 1903) called "survival of the fittest."

In other words, fitness is one of the most important principles in the evolution of both animals and humans. It is equally important for centenarians to survive to one hundred years or more. Centenarians are very rare: one or two, often fewer, in ten thousand people. Many think of them as exceptional people who somehow managed, through no effort of their own, to reach that old age; many of the oldest do not themselves understand how they did it. For most centenarians, it was the good genes with which they were born that helped them reach or surpass the century mark. For an ordinary person without great genes, the likelihood of living to 100 is a mere 0.01 percent or less.

Centenarians possess other qualities that, in addition to fitness and heredity, support them though their long journey. These qualities include the gift of wisdom and a calm and sober mind, which navigates them through the rough seas of life. They have the wisdom to follow the laws of Nature, and not violate them. Again, it is not a super-wisdom or super-calm mind; rather, they are wise enough to cooperate with Nature, not compete with it. Wasn't it with a wise and sober-mind that Nina Rust from Roseburg, Oregon (106 years old at the time of the interview in 1987) managed to deal with worries while raising her twelve children? When Jim Heynen, who profiled her in his book *One Hundred Over 100,* asked whether she lost sleep worrying about all her children, she replied, "No, I figured that if something bad was going to happen, I had better get a good night's sleep so that I'd be better able to deal with it." A simple wisdom of an ordinary centenarian--she is just one example among many other centenarians who display a true everyday life wisdom. Later in this book, you will find other examples of how wisdom and a calm mind helped people survive under severe circumstances.

Centenarians obviously can be regarded as living proof of being the fittest, wisest, and calmest. However, within the broad aspects of this fitness, wisdom, and calm mind, there is something concrete that centenarians do right that the remaining 99.99 percent of humanity does wrong. It is not a single thing, but rather a combination of many factors. Among them are the kinds of activity that comprise their life; what and how they eat and drink; how they work and rest; how they cope with stress and deal with others; how they perceive life; their emotions and thoughts; and so on. Certainly, their genetic predisposition, physical nature, and personality traits must also be considered. As we systematically analyze the influencing factors, we may be able to better understand the mystery of longevity.

1

SOMATOTYPES

In our attempt to explore factors affecting longevity, we begin with the classification of an individual by body and personality type. Body-typing also may be useful in drawing a person's unique profile. According to some experts, an individual's body type may to some degree influence his or her life span. Although it seems that the influence of body type is not a strong one and that very old age can be achieved with any body constitution, the soundness or weakness of a particular vital organ may be associated with body type, or *somatotype*.

The first person to classify people by body shape was the ancient Greek physician, Hippocrates. In modern times, German psychiatrist Ernst Kretschmer proposed the classification of three basic human body builds as follows: *pyknic* (plump), *athletic* (muscular), and *asthenic* (frail and linear), as well as *dysplastic* (a combination of the first three basic types).

Widely known is the somatotype theory developed by American psychologist William Sheldon in the 1940s. His theory was based on a careful examination of forty-six thousand photographs of nude male bodies and body measurements. More than one thousand of those pictures are displayed in his book, *Atlas of Men: A Guide for Somatotyping the Adult Male at All Ages*. He divided individuals into three categories relative to their body constitution: fat, muscular, or slender. Sheldon's somatotype is a measure of body shape, not of size; any somatotype can be of any stature. The three basic body types (i.e., somatotypes) are as follows:

- *Endomorph*: heavy and fat, with a soft body and poorly developed muscles, round in shape, and known as a barrel type
- *Mesomorph*: husky, with a hard and muscular body (a kind of athletic type), rectangular in shape, and known as wineglass type

• *Ectomorph*: tall and slim, lightly built, with flat chest and poorly muscled limbs, and often shaped like a test tube.

Very rarely, though, does any male belong to a single, extreme somatotype. People often have the features of two or even three of the types. According to Sheldon, an individual's tendency toward each body type is assessed with scores of 1 to 7 that are plotted on a triangle graph, with the three sides representing the three somatotypes. A person who is an extreme endomorph would score 711, an extreme mesomorph would score 171, and an extreme ectomorph would score 117. An average person who has some ectomorphic tendencies would score 446, endomorphic tendencies would score 644, and mesomorphic tendencies would score 464.

Physical performance of each body type is assessed in five categories: strength, power, endurance, body support, and agility. The endomorphic type is low in all categories, the mesomorphic type is high in all categories, and the ectomorphic type is high in endurance, bodily support, and agility but low in strength and power.

Sheldon, however, did not confine somatotypes to just physical performance. He assumed that the body frame of each individual was interrelated with one's behavior and temperament. Features of one's psyche (i.e., mind) are related to those of the soma (i.e., body), and the general relationship between the two may be as follows:

• *Endomorphs* tend to be sociable, easygoing, leisure-loving, relaxed, and convivial.
• *Mesomorphs* are often physically active, strong, athletic, and aggressive.
• *Ectomorphs* are more sensitive, self-conscious, restrained, introspective, and quiet.

The features of the physique and personality traits are listed in Table 1-1.

Table 1-1. Personal Features for Somatotype Assessment

Features	Endomorph	Mesomorph	Ectomorph
Physical Build and Characteristics			
1. Body build	Short, thick-set, heavy, fat	Medium, strong, athletic	Tall, thin, delicate build
2. Body shape	Pear-shaped	Rectangular–shaped	Rail-shaped
3. Muscles	Soft, underdeveloped muscles	Hard, muscular body	Lightly muscled
4. Bones	Large	Medium	Small
5. Head, face, and neck	Round head, short neck	Massive cubical head, thick neck	Thin face, receding chin, high forehead, thin neck

Features	Endomorph	Mesomorph	Ectomorph
6. Chest and abdomen	Large, fat chest and abdomen	Broad shoulders and chest, medium abdomen	Thin, narrow chest and abdomen
7. Limbs	Weak penguin like arms and legs, with heavy upper arms and thighs but slender wrists and ankles	Heavy muscular arms and legs	Long, slender, poorly muscled arms and legs
Total			
Personality Traits			
Personality type	Sociable, loving	Physical, adventurous, love of risk and chance	Intellectual, restrained, self-conscious
Emotions	Evenness of emotions	Emotionally alert	Emotionally restrained
Desire	For affection	For power and dominance	For privacy
Character by nature	Secure	Courageous, assertive, bold	Fearful, often nervous
Lifestyle	Love of food and comfort	Zest for physical activity	Introverted
Coping with others	Relaxed, easy-going	Competitive, active, and noisy	Inhibited, quiet
Social tendencies	Tolerant	Indifference to what others think or want	Socially anxious, artistic

To correctly assess your body type, compare your photographs--front, side, and back views--to those shown in Dr. Sheldon's book, *Atlas of Men*. If you have difficulty finding it (which is available in many libraries throughout the United States), the upper part of Table 1-1 entitled "Physical Build and Characteristics" can be used for a *rough* assessment. For each line, mark the entry that best describes you at present or as you have been most of your life. If you fall equally between two descriptions, highlight both. Total the scores for each somatotype and plot them on the graph shown in Figure 1-1 b. If the total score for any particular somatotype is 0, add 1.

If it is difficult to choose an appropriate description, consult with your relatives or friends because they may see you better than you see yourself. The body shapes shown in Figure 1-1a can also be useful for a general idea of the particular somatotype to which you belong. The photographs are adapted from Dr. Sheldon's book *Atlas of Men*; the graphical display of somatotypes in Figure 1-1b is adapted from the book, *The Human Body*, published by the Running Press Gem, which I modified by adding zones and dots.

As shown in Figure 1-1b, the two large shaded circles represent the longevity zone, according to Dr. Sheldon's assessment, and are discussed later in more detail. The famous American comedian George Burns, who lived to the age of one hundred, was of the mesomorphic–ectomorphic type, according to my assessment score of 135. Another centenarian (also a comedian), Hal Roach, who was barrel-chested in stature and very robust, was probably of the mesomorphic type.

a).   b).

Endomorph (711)   Mesomorph (171)   Ectomorph (117)

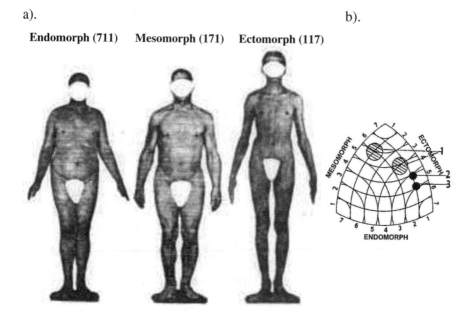

Figure 1-1. Somatotypes and Their Graphical Display
a. Body Shapes of the Three Extreme Somatotypes
b. Examples of Graphical Display for Certain People:
1. Longevity zone; 2. George Burns; 3. Author

> When I tried to assess myself by comparing my own photographs with those in Dr. Sheldon's *Atlas of Men*, I came up with a score of 146; therefore, I am of the mesomorphic-ectomorphic type. My height is 6 feet, 4 inches (191 cm) and my weight is 170 pounds (77 kg). Compared to an average sized person, I always have been quite tall and slightly underweight. I inherited my body constitution primarily from my maternal grandmother, who was 5 feet, 4 inches (173 cm) tall; however, my father, with his height of 6 feet, 1 inch (185 cm), was not a short man. My grandmother lived to the age of ninety-three and my father died when he was seventy-eight years old.

It has been observed that people of the endomorphic type are healthy and that all of their systems are very efficient and work well in the younger years. However, after the age of fifty, these people slow down and their bodies show the effects of wearing out. He or she is a good starter but a poor finisher. In contrast, people of the ectomorphic type often enjoy their best health after the age of fifty. Their endurance and sustained good health is often a pleasant surprise, not only to others, but also to themselves. Although an ectomorph has the problem of gaining weight, sports trainers claim that with intense workouts and proper nutrition, some ectomorphic clients were able to gain 15 to 30 pounds. They conclude, therefore, that a somatotype is more a tendency than a destiny.

Another observation reveals a link between somatotype and both mental and physical illness. According to Kretschmer, thin (i.e., asthenic) types seem more likely to be schizophrenic, while stocky (i.e., pyknic) types are more prone to manic-depressive illness. Vermont folk medicine holds that endomorphs have higher blood pressure than ectomorphs. An ectomorph frequently is more vulnerable to sickness in the springtime of the year; they are advised to watch their diet and have a yearly medical check-up in that season. The heavy endomorphic types usually become sick in the fall, and they must be careful in that season.

Without doubt, body types have certain influences on personality, primarily through the limits they impose upon personal abilities. Generally, mesomorphs are physically stronger than ectomorphs, and endomorphs are usually poor performers in sports in which endurance is crucial, such as long-distance running. A good example is the Boston Marathons that I have observed: most of the runners were slim ectomorphs, a small percentage was muscular mesomorphs, and only a few were fat endomorphs (even the fat runners were just slightly overweight).

As people age, their muscular strength, endurance, and body weight change, depending on lifestyle and diet. A common tendency is to gain weight and reduce physical performance. The most susceptible body type to weight gain is the inactive endomorph. The normally tall and slim ectomorph, if overweight, usually shows it around the waist, the first area of the body to respond to over-eating. His or her arms and legs might remain slender, but there is a noticeable bulge in the middle of the torso. The overweight endomorph simply blows up like a balloon, becoming fat and flabby all over. The mesomorph, who is the least susceptible to weight problems, shows excess weight around the middle, which is composed of a layer of flab over the normally firm, tight muscles.

All three somatotypes can be recognized among sumo wrestlers in Japan, who work hard at both exercising and eating in order to gain extra weight. Akebono, with his great belly and relatively slender legs, seems to be of the ectomorphic type; Takanohana and Musashimaru are surely of the endomorphic type; and the muscular Terao and Kirishima are of the mesomorphic type.

Regarding the link between body type and longevity, Dr. Sheldon found that **excessively long-lived people, specifically centenarians, usually belong to the endomorphic-mesomorphic type,** with scores of 261, 361, and 362 (see the left-shaded circle in Figure 1-1b). Although people of this somatotype are most prone to coronary artery disease and diabetes, the longest living individuals are those who inherited an exceptionally strong cardiovascular system for a firm foundation of their good health. Another group of long-living people seems to be the ectomorphic–mesomorphs, who have scores of 254, 244, 354, and 344 (see the right-shaded circle in Figure 1-1b). The dot marked 2, which shows the position of George Burns on the graph, is close to this longevity zone.

It seems apparent that most long-living people are of the ectomorphic and mesomorphic types. Despite the adage, "There is no fat centenarian," in practice, there are.

Consider the case of the overweight endomorph centenarian, Albert W. Holmgren, who was one hundred years and nine months old when Jim Heynen interviewed him in 1987. He weighed 245 pounds most of his life. Although he was tall, with a height of 6 feet, 2.5 inches, he was nevertheless markedly overweight by 37 percent above his ideal weight. Some of his personality traits, such as spending much of the day reading and socializing, along with his relaxed character, further suggest that he would probably be of the endomorphic somatotype.

He is definitely an exception to the usual trend; that is, the overwhelming majority of centenarians are neither seriously overweight nor underweight.

2

PERSONALITY TYPES

Our behavior traits significantly affect our health condition and longevity. When the *Bonn Longitudinal Study* was conducted in 1932, Lehr found that along with genetic, physiological, and lifestyle factors affecting longevity, personality characteristics also seemed to be almost as important.

Studies of centenarians and the oldest elderly conducted by Gallup and Hill in 1960 (i.e., 164 people aged 100 to 117) and Jewett in 1973 (i.e., 79 people aged 87 to 103) showed that centenarians are generally relaxed, easygoing, cheerful, self-confident, independent, and active. They are convivial and enjoy other people, are tolerant of frustration, and feel that they have spent their lives well. In 1977, Woodruff found that people who are calm, happy, relaxed, flexible, and content with their lives have a tendency to live longer. Conversely, aggressive, repressive, stubborn, dogmatic, and adventurous people live fewer years than the average life expectancy. Therefore, this chapter discusses the personalities of particular people categorized by their behavior, of which there are three types: Type A, Type B, and Type C. These personality types were first introduced in the 1960s after prolonged research, and gained popularity afterwards.

Type A. Type A is characterized as highly competitive, keenly ambitious, always in a hurry, and easily annoyed. Other characteristics of a Type A personality include a sense of being under constant time pressure, a suspicious nature, chronic impatience, and excessive. Type A's tend to become easily upset, often for little reason. Although Type A's are frequently successful in their professions, they are never satisfied. They often try to do more than one thing at a time: they talk on the phone while working on the computer or driving the car, or they read while eating.

Many people who have heart attacks fit this behavioral description; therefore, doctors believe that having a Type A personality is a risk factor in heart disease. This belief is based on the *Western Collaborative Group Study (WCGS)* conducted in 1961, in which 3,500 healthy men were assessed and then followed for more than eight years. The study found that Type A men were nearly three times more likely to develop heart disease as compared with their "healthy" Type B counterparts. The *Framingham Heart Study* found that for working women, heart disease is four times more prevalent in Type A's than in Type B's.

Recent research at Duke University discovered that the hostility most often associated with Type A's is the **real** risk factor. "People who are merely ambitious or driven aren't the ones at risk for heart disease," according to Redford Williams, M.D., director of Duke's Cultural Behavioral Medicine Research Center. "But people who are hostile--not just irritable, but rude, abrasive, cynical, vengeful, manipulative, or condescending--are," he adds.

Type B. A Type B is noncompetitive, less driven, patient, easygoing, and never has outbursts of rage, out-of-control temper tantrums, or hostile episodes, as Type A's do. They are perfectly relaxed, at peace with themselves and their environs; their lack of anger stems from a sense of inner peace. Type B's, unlike Type A's, are able to express their emotions appropriately. Characteristics such as a pleasant demeanor, the conscious control of anger, and temporary fearlessness in the face of trauma allow them to cope with stress effectively. Although they are not driven over-achievers, Type B's are often as successful in their professions as Type A's.

Type C. A Type C is unfailingly pleasant and appeasing, but unable to express his or her emotions, especially anger. Type C's often are oblivious to the feeling of anger. From an early age, they have denied their own needs by internalizing anger or displeasure and suppressing their emotions. Another characteristic of a Type C personality is a profound sense of hopelessness and despair, caused by a loss of hope or a loved one. These people feel lonely; their loneliness starts at an early age and progresses into adulthood. We all feel these emotions at certain times in our lives, but if we chronically suppress our needs and emotions, it may cause serious disease and illness. Type C's have the same behavioral patterns that people at risk for cancer usually have. "Strongly associated with cancer," as Lydia Temoshok, Ph.D., and Henry Dreher say in their book, *The Type C Connection*. According to Dr. Temoshok, patients who were emotionally constricted, passive, withdrawn, or appeasing tended to have thicker tumors.

The reason that people with a Type A personality are at higher risk for heart attack is that their anger and hostility put a burden on their cardiovascular system. Similarly, Type C's are at greater risk of cancer because their unexpressed negative emotions keep the bad hormones inside and weaken their immune system. In contrast with coronary-prone Type A's and cancer-prone Type C's, Type B's are healthy, with a decreased risk for heart disease and cancer. Personality type can be evaluated using Table 2-1.

Table 2-1. Evaluation of Behavioral Traits of Types A, B, and C People

Nos	Type A	Type B	Type C
1	Very competitive	Noncompetitive	Passive
2	Quick to anger, easily irritated	Consciously controls anger	Suppresses anger
3	Copes through hostility, competitiveness	Expresses emotions appropriately	Tends to appease, doesn't show negative feelings
4	Self-centered on own needs	Capable to meet own needs and to respond to others	Self-sacrificing, denying own needs
5	Always rushed	Never feels rushed, even under pressure	Lethargic
6	Wants good job to be recognized by others	Cares to satisfy self, no matter what others think	Tries to please others, avoids conflict
7	Impatient	Patient	Obedient even when manipulated by others
8	Fast (e.g., eating, walking, speaking)	Normal speed	Slow in doing things
9	Hard-driving	Easygoing	Bland
10	Struggling	Confident and content	Easily gives up
11	Few interests outside work	Many interests	Puts interests of others over own
12	In control	Self-supportive	Helpless
13	Emphatic in speech (may pound desk)	Slow, deliberate speaker	Lost voice, does not speak about own needs
14	Pursues opportunities the world offers	Moderately ambitious	Hopeless
15	Rejecting	Offering	Accepting

In compiling this table, I used the nonverbal characteristics of Type A and Type C behaviors that were proposed by Dr. Temoshok in her book, *The Type C Connection* (developed with Bruce Heller). I relied also on the *Bortner Type A Rating Scale*, published in the *Journal of Chronic Diseases* (1969, vol. 22).

Everyone possesses some features of all three behavioral types, and no one embodies all of them. Most people can be described as falling somewhere along the *continuum of coping styles*, as Dr. Temoshok termed it. The competitive, aggressive, and anxious Type A's and the never-angry, passive, and appeasing Type C's are at the pathological extremes of the continuum.

The relaxed, self-assured, and contented Type B's dwell healthily in the middle region. On one-axis scale of the continuum, the three types are the fixed points on the edges and in the center. Some people, however, fall into the space between Types A and B or between Types B and C.

Table 2-1 is designed to elicit responses that are based on self-perceptions. Some responses may be difficult to admit; for example, one would probably rather characterize himself or herself as assertive rather than hostile and angry. If you think that some of the descriptions used in the questionnaire do not apply, substitute more pleasant-sounding synonyms or antonyms. The table has not been perfected; if you dislike some of the descriptions, please do not get angry or frustrated--spare your nerves and cardiovascular system, for the sake of life extension! To assess your personality type, highlight the descriptions that most closely fit you. If you fall equally between two neighboring descriptions, highlight them both. Then count the total score for each type. I explain this evaluation technique using myself as an example.

While going through this table, I highlighted a few double descriptions in one row. For instance, I fall somewhere between "always rushed" and "never feels rushed, even under pressure," so I included them both. Furthermore, I consider myself both "easygoing" and "bland," so I marked both of them as well. My self-evaluation resulted in a Type A score of 3, a Type B score of 10, and a Type C score of 7. Because one has to belong to one category on the coping continuum scale, a further evaluation would be as follows: I definitely tend to be somewhere between Type B and C, but I am closer to Type B. Having a few scores in Type A puts me even closer to Type B than Type C. It will probably be correct if we assign two points to each Type A score and then find the proportion on the Type B and C part of the scale. This results in 3 x 2 + 10 = 16 for a score on the Type B side; therefore, the proportion is 44 percent from Type B toward Type C. The scale with my behavioral type point on it is shown in Figure 2-1.

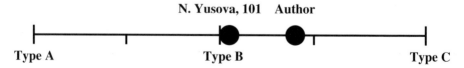

Figure 2-1. The Continuum Scale of Behavioral Types

Another point represents the profile of Russian Nataliya Yusova, age 101. As we now understand, the best seat (as in the theater) is always in the center. In my case, it is somewhat to the right of center, but not too much. The encouraging news is that we are not chained to one location forever, but can consciously work to move to the center. The risks associated with Type A behavior and the related stress can be modified.

Regarding the lack of anger expressed by Type C's, psychiatrist Alice Miller in her book, *For Your Own Good,* offers the following advice: "Everyone must find his own form of aggressiveness in order to avoid letting himself be made into an obedient puppet manipulated by others. Only if we do not allow ourselves to be reduced to the instrument of another person's will can we fulfill our personal needs and defend our legitimate rights. But this appropriate form of aggression is unattainable for many people who have grown up with the absurd belief that a person can have nothing but kind, good, and meek thoughts and at the same time be honest and authentic."

In dealing with people, the rule is that if you do not demand of others, they will demand of you. This rule is especially true with demanding extroverts.

> I tested this approach on one of my demanding friends to see whether it worked. I entered the room where he was working with his co-workers and asked him, "Why is the window closed? Open it and let some fresh air in." He was slightly surprised because it was not my usual way of treating him. He shrugged his shoulders, stood up without any words, took a stick with a handle used to open the window, and then opened it. I started to talk to him about our common job; after a few minutes, I purposely said: "It is too cold today and perhaps it will be harmful to the coffee tree. Close the window, it may freeze up." Again, he mumbled something, but stood up and closed the window. It was so unusual for him, who was the very model of being demanding of others, to obediently submit to someone's order. His co-workers obviously were quite surprised as well. For me, it was the proof that the rule regarding demand or be demanded of works quite well.

This simple exercise may help extra-shy Type C's to learn how to assert themselves.

The findings of researchers that many centenarians are easygoing, happy, and relaxed actually reveal that most of them are Type B's. A study of eighty-two centenarians in Tokyo conducted by Yoshiko Shimonaka, Katsuharu Nakazato, and Akira Homma in 1986 - 1989 found that **Type B behavior promotes longevity**; therefore, there were more Type B centenarians. People in their sixties may display Type A behavior, but as they age, they begin to display more Type B tendencies. Although gender difference in personal behavior may be controversial, the Japanese study of both men and women found that Type B behavior was most prevalent in the eldest of both sexes. Conversely, a 1968 study conducted by Neugarten and Gutmann in the United States suggested that women grow more aggressive and domineering as they grow older, while men become more nurturing and complacent with age.

An image of a centenarian is often associated with the wise, calm, and generous great-grandfather or great-grandmother. However, sarcastic, selfish, stubborn, unsociable, and even aggressive individuals are also found in this group. When I was in Singapore in 1997, I happened to meet one of these "aggressive" female centenarians. My Singaporean friend, Vennes S., accompanied me during my visit to the Nightingale Nursing Home. Madam Ang Leng, 106 years old, had resided in this facility since November 1996. The photograph in Figure 2-2 (see p.269) shows Madam Ang Leng with Vennes S. and the author. Before moving to the nursing home, she lived with her family until September 1996, when she was hospitalized suffering from pneumonia and injuries resulting from a fall.

I was shown a copy of her ID with the date of her birth: 1891 in Singapore. Madam Ang Leng had nine children: four sons and five daughters. One of her sons had already passed away.

When I met her, she sat in an ordinary chair and looked extremely gaunt. She sometimes walked with a walker. Her physical condition was good and no serious disease had been found during her last medical checkup two months prior. Her blood type was AB positive, her blood pressure was 120/90, and her resting heart rate was 98. She was diagnosed with senile dementia, her sight and hearing were impaired, and she had difficulty in recognizing people. Her doctor showed me part of her medical record, which read as follows: "aggressive behavior, restless." According to her nurses, she complained non-stop, day and night. Indeed, when I saw her, she murmured something in Chinese in a grouchy voice.

In the nursing home, she had been receiving good care, including five changes a day, physical therapy, and massage. Her regular diet consisted of oats or milo (grain sorghum) porridge with milk and black coffee for breakfast; soy beans, potatoes, and vegetables for lunch; and soup with pork, rice, fish, or chicken for dinner. She also was given a multivitamin/multimineral formula as a supplement.

When I was back in the United States in March of 1998, I received a letter from Vennes S. informing me that Madam Ang Leng had passed away in February 1998, just three months after I met her.

Many centenarians are reputed for their "my pace" attitude and for not paying much attention to what others say or think. They freely express their feelings and negative emotions without much concern for how others will react. A shining example of such a personality is 103-year-old Lydia Pavlovna Vesselovzorova, who was born in Russia and lived in Japan. I first learned about her in Japan from an NHK TV program about centenarians, and then I visited her on March 1, 1999, during a trip to Japan.

Two qualities that she possessed that promote longevity were stressed in the program: her custom of freely expressing her thoughts and emotions regardless of whether they are pleasant to the ears of others, and her habit of drinking wine. The latter contradicts the trend in Russia of the decreasing average life span in the last decade due to excessive drinking (and a stressful life caused by economic turmoil). Mr. M. Okamura, a producer in the Entertainment Programs Division of NHK, put me in touch with Professor Okuyama, the therapist and ophthalmologist who was taking care of Lydia Vesselovzorova and who helped me arrange a meeting with her.

She was born into a Russian noble family in Sankt-Petersburg on June 26, 1896. Her father was a teacher of mathematics (a service nobleman) and her mother was a land noblewoman. Lydia Vesselovzorova escaped from the Russian Revolution in 1918 and immigrated to China. There she married Suhorukov, a White Army officer who belonged to an ancient Russian noble family. She told me that she loved him, but he died five years after their marriage, leaving her all alone. She worked as a professor of Russian language and literature in Harbin, northern China, and then moved to Japan in 1957. She liked her work and life in China and she valued the Chinese people very highly; however, she hated the Communist regime and Mao Tse-tung, and could not tolerate staying in China any longer.

In the TV program, when she was asked whether she liked her life in Japan (she had been living there for the last forty years), she replied: "I don't like it here, the climate is terrible." Asked about her life in China, she became angry and used swear words when she talked about Mao Tse-tung and his wife, who also took an active part in the Cultural Revolution. When asked whether or not the Japanese at the university were good students, she replied: "They didn't work like the Chinese, who studied hard. They preferred to go to the cinema, they didn't work at all."

When I visited her, Lydia Vesselovzorova lived in a nursing home in the city of Machida, about two hours by train from Tokyo. She was sitting on the bed when I first came into her room, and she said she was glad to see a Russian face and to hear the speech of a native Russian. She complained to Professor Okuyama (who was also fluent in Russian) about how the bed was very uncomfortable for her. Professor Okuyama studied in Russia for seven years, graduated from the medical school at Moscow University, and then received his Ph.D. degree there under the supervision of Professor S. Fedorov (a world-famous Russian eye surgeon). He had an appointment and was in a hurry to leave, but before he left we had a photograph taken of the three of us (Figure 2-3, see p.269).

L. Vesselovzorova had impaired vision and hearing, so I sat very close to her and spoke directly into her ear in a loud voice. She could distinguish the faces when I showed her the photographs of my daughter and her children. When she realized that my daughter was married to an American, she said that she was happy for her. Going to America had always been her dream and she complained that she had missed a chance to go there. "I am a fool for staying here in Japan, though I had an American visa and didn't go there. They deceived me by saying there is an age limit in America and I would not find a job. It is our noble's pride to live on the earned money and I was told that here I can work until I die. I am a fool, a big old fool," she complained.

We talked about famous Russian writers and poets. Although she liked Leo Tolstoy and Dostoevsky most, nobody was an authority to her, not even Tolstoy or Alexander Pushkin (a poet of genius and the fame of Russia). "He was bad with his family, an egoist, but he was gifted and hence he had a right to be an egoist," she commented about Tolstoy. She recited a verse about Tatiana from *Eugene Onegin*, Pushkin's novel (English translation by Douglas Hofstadter):

> Tatiana, Russian deep in spirit
> (Though as to why, she had no clue),
> Adored our Russian winters. Here it
> Is good and cold, lovely and blue.

"Why did Tatiana, this fool, not know why she loves the cold and snowy Russian winter? It's ridiculous. She was simply born there and loved winter, therefore," Lydia Vesselovzorova said, criticizing Pushkin for losing sense for the sake of verse. "For me, the sense is important, but I don't know, perhaps I'm wrong," she added.

She did not like anything about Japan or the nursing home: the food, her bed, or the doctor who had performed surgery on her leg when she fell and broke her hipbone a few years ago. She claimed that she had some medical knowledge that she acquired while translating medical literature from English into Russian, and she argued with the Japanese doctor and accused him of bad treatment. She even rejected their blood pressure measurements, claiming that they were harmful to her. She also complained that her knee was mistreated and she couldn't walk thereafter. Despite her exceptionally old age, her mind was quick and sharp, but she was very suspicious and exaggerated her fears that others had harmed her intentionally.

She was also concerned about the fate of Russia and believed the writings of Russian philosopher Vladimir S. Soloviev (1853 - 1900)[1], who foretold of a Third World War in which both Russia and Japan would be annihilated. I told her that I just had come from Russia and that many people were starving due to poverty. The newly rich Russians have millions, but the majority is on the edge of starvation. Her former students read the Japanese newspapers to her and she knew about the bad situation in Russia. She commented that people in Russia have destroyed their own country. "New rich" acquire great money, but they do not pay any taxes. "No government in the world can survive without tax collection. This is very bad," she told me.

Her complaints seemed to give her more energy than the food she was given. "The food is disgusting. It's a sort of jelly made of soybeans; I hate it. My major food is bread with coffee, sometimes a potato croquette. I love to eat fruits like oranges and persimmons. Also, I eat meat and chicken stewed with potatoes that Alex Chromov of the Fedorov Foundation cooks and brings to me. I eat until I am full, then," she continued to complain.

In the TV program, when asked where her longevity comes from, Lydia Vesselovzorova replied: "It's my heredity. My great-grandfather lived to the age of ninety-four years. He wasn't a good man at all, he loved wine and women in excess, but he was very old when he died while holding a glass of wine at a drinking party. He was making a speech and suddenly fell dead. He was very happy to die like that." She also drinks wine, as it was shown in the TV program. When I asked her about the age of her parents, she told me that

---

[1] Vladimir S. Soloviyev, the greatest Russian philosopher of the 19th century. He perceived himself as a prophet destined to find the way to universal regeneration. According to Soloviyev, Russia's mission in universal history was in the unification of the Christian Churches and the establishment of a theocratic Kingdom of God on Earth.

her father died at the age of seventy-two and her mother at a much younger age, but she couldn't recall how old she was when she died.

Lydia Vesselovzorova's blood type was O; among blood types, people with type O have the longest average life span–eighty-seven years. Although she did not appear to do anything special to support her longevity, such as engaging in healthy diet or exercising, I believe her favorable blood chemistry combined with good genes gave her very many years. Her ancestors lived quite long lives, given that the average life span in Russia was a mere thirty-two years in 1896-97 and forty-four years in 1926-27. The average life span was even shorter a century earlier in her great-grandfather's lifetime. Not long ego, Professor Okuyama informed me that Lydia Vesselovzorova passed away on April 4, 2000, at the age of 103 years and nine months.

Although the average life span was short, there were cases of exceptionally long-living Russians by the end of the nineteenth century, as evidenced by the following excerpt from *Apple Fragrance,* a short story by Russian writer and Nobel Prize winner Ivan Bunin (1870 – 1953):

"...Moreover, our Viselki has always been known for a prosperous village since the beginning of time, since grandfather's day. Viselki people lived to a ripe old age - which is the first sign of a prosperous village - and all these old people were tall and big-boned, with hair as white as snow. You were always hearing someone say: "Look at Agafya there, she's eighty-three if she's a day!" Or conversations like this:

"And when are you going to die, Pankrat? You must be nearly a hundred by now?"
"What's that you say, your honor?"
"I'm asking how old you are."
"That I couldn't tell you, your honor."
"D'you remember Platon Apollonich?"
"Of course I do, I remember him well."
"You see! That means you can't possibly be less than a hundred."

The old man, standing rigidly before his master, would smile a humble and guilty smile. What could he do? He had outlived his day, he felt. And probably he would have outlived it even longer if he had not eaten too much onions on St. Peter's Day." There's moral in this story: "Be moderate while eating onions on St. Peter's Day."

As studies show, a "centenarian personality" is not limited to the wise, quiet, and content character, but also includes selfish, sarcastic, and unsociable behavior. The Japanese comedian Koasa began "Koasa ga mairimashita" ("Koasa arrived"), a TV program in Japan about centenarians. Every Sunday for three years, he invited a centenarian onto his show and interviewed him or her on the stage. He met a total of 157 people aged from 100 to 105. According to his analysis, most Japanese centenarians have Blood Type B, and most are selfish people by nature. They have difficulty dealing with their families, but they don't care.

Some American centenarians are also like that.

> Sarah Delany, in her book *On My Own at 107, Reflections on Life Without Bessie*, her words addressed to Bessie (her younger sister and a century-long companion who died in 1995 at 104) were, "I am the one who was paying bills, writing letters, and getting the taxes for the accountant. Things like that. You'd say, 'Sadie, you do it, would you? I just don't feel like it.' It kind of annoyed me, because I had to do everything, but you had this philosophy that since you'd lived past a hundred, you didn't have to do anything you didn't want to. Oh, you were a naughty old gal!"

> Both sisters achieved their extreme age due to great heredity, a healthy lifestyle (including yoga exercises), and possibly their Type B behavior; although Sarah (obedient and responsible) would definitely be placed to the right of Type B on the continuum scale and Bessie (naughty) would definitely be to the left.

That the Type B person has more chances of becoming a centenarian is further evidenced by case of Nataliya Ya. Yusova. She lived in the city of Nakhodka (in the Far East region of Russia), where I met with her a few times from November of 1998 through February of 1999. I first came to Nakhodka as a member of the World Bank Study team involved in a project to improve the water supply and wastewater system of the city. This four-month job was offered to me by Pacific Consultants International, Co., a Japanese company.

In the Russian Primorsky region, Nakhodka has the second largest population (after Vladivostok), with its economy supported by a harbor with ship-repairing and fishery industries. The attractions for newcomers to Nakhodka are the numerous Japanese cars on the roads, the climbing uphill cottages of new-rich Russians, and the many beautiful women in the offices and outdoors. All four women on our local staff could be described as either beautiful or very pretty, as shown in Figure 2-4 (see p.270).

The international study team consisted of eleven members: two Japanese, five Americans, three Russians, and one Israeli (myself). We also hired a local staff of two engineers, three interpreters, a computer engineer, and a typist. The project manager, fifty-one-year-old Norihiro Noda of Japan, was an expert in ecology who had received his Ph.D. degree in Germany. Noda had also worked in the World Bank in Washington for five years. I was assigned as the assistant project manager, with responsibilities that included preparing Russian versions of the reports and managing various day-to-day needs such as housing, transportation, organizing the working space, interpreting for and communicating with local authorities, and supervising the local staff's work.

Without any doubt, longevity and beauty are closely interrelated. Appreciation of beauty is a feature of many centenarians and a strong incentive for those who want to become a centenarian. Russia is known for its beautiful women; in cities such as Moscow, Sankt-Petersburg, Vladivostok, and especially Minsk in Byelorussia, one encounters many beauties. Nakhodka is not exceptional in this respect, and Vodokanal of Nakhodka (the municipal enterprise for water supply and wastewater services) employs many beautiful young women--among them Veronica and Olga, two secretaries of Vodokanal's director. In the research institute in Moscow, where I worked for twenty-six years before emigrating from Russia, there were some extraordinarily beautiful women.

> The most stunning among them was Nina Ekimyan, who had a Ph.D. in engineering. She was so beautiful that men involved in both related and non-related research at other engineering institutes and organizations made unnecessary special trips to see her. We worked together in the "pile foundations" laboratory, and I was deeply in love with her too. Imagine Marilyn Monroe but with bigger blue eyes, larger breasts, perfectly shaped full lips, and much taller: that was Nina.
>
> She looked so sexy that the director of our institute nearly had a heart attack when he saw her come running inside after a sudden rain shower, with her big breasts distinctly outlined under her wet blouse. She was also a clever engineer and researcher, and had the gift of a melodious voice. Although she took singing lessons when she was a student, she never sang in public. Her singing taboo was a mystery and nobody knew about her talent; however, I once had the great fortune of hearing her wonderful voice for myself.
>
> We were sitting under the bright sun on fine white sand of the beach in Yalta, the Black Sea resort where Nina and I were on our summer vacation. She was suffering from a minor stomach ulcer that year and agreed to go far away from Moscow with me because she regarded me as a reliable and trustworthy friend. I never told her about my love for her so she felt comfortable with me. We were sitting close to each other; she was grasping her bent knees and was deep inside her own thoughts, when she suddenly started singing in a low voice. Her song was short, less than a minute, but I was nearly breathless the entire time. More than twenty-five years have passed since then, but I can still hear the song in my head: "It is good to love the one who values love that

high." It was a Russian song with a beautiful tune that has been one of my favorites ever since.

Most of the top-ranked and renowned Russian scientists in the field of soil mechanics and foundation engineering were her fans. Her private life was quite complex--she endured three unhappy marriages, but eventually married Alexander, a very handsome engineer, and they continue to enjoy a happy marriage.

While working on this book in the last four years, beautiful women and centenarians comprised the range of my interests during trips to Iceland, Singapore, Japan, China, and Russia. Although pretty girls are not rare in Nakhodka, centenarians are extremely so. Local people whom I asked about centenarians told me that in the entire city of 190,000, there was only one woman who celebrated her hundredth birthday, in August 1998. The local TV station did a program about her; the newspaper *Nakhodkinsky Worker* published an article entitled *Grandma Nataliya's Heart Is Young*; and she received congratulations from Victor S. Gnezdilov, Mayor of Nakhodka, who personally presented her with a large bouquet of flowers and souvenirs.

She was born on August 21, 1898, in Dudovtschina village in the Kirovsk region of Russia, about a thousand kilometers (about 620 miles) northeast of Moscow. Her father lived to seventy-five, her mother to seventy-three, and her paternal grandmother to ninety--a respectable heredity for a Russian, where the average life span in the 1920s was only forty-four years.

Nataliya Yusova had eleven children, four of whom died very early and the other seven reaching adulthood. Her oldest daughter, Anna, was born in 1921 and died at the age of fifty; the youngest, Vera, was born in 1941. Her husband and their oldest son were killed during World War II. Three older children became terminally ill due to overwork and bad conditions during the war and post-war years, and they also died quite young. Only three of her children are still alive. She lived with fifty-eight-year-old Vera and her husband Anatoly in a small three- room apartment. Her thirty-eight-year-old granddaughter Lyudmila, and eighteen- year-old great-granddaughter Victoria, a college student, lived in a separate apartment nearby and visited her often. A photograph of the four generations started by Nataliya Yusova is shown in Figure 2-5 (see p. 270).

All her long life, Nataliya Yusova was a hard worker, most often as a milkmaid on a collective farm. Her workday usually started as early as 3 a.m. and lasted until sunset. At work, she often moved around 40-liter milk churns and sometimes carried 70-kg bags of grain on her shoulders. "I was a strong woman," she said, although she was only 4 feet, 10.5 inches (148 cm) tall and weighed 106 pounds (48 kg). This was her weight when I met her, but she was never much heavier than that. During the war, although many people around her died of starvation, she and her children survived thanks to the cow that she was keeping. However, they were able to use only a small portion of the cow's milk and dairy products because every household was required to give most of it to the state. Their chicken's eggs and the wool and even skin of their sheep were also subjects of severe taxation; almost nothing was left to the collective farmers for private use. Her family's main food source was potatoes and edible grass, but they somehow survived nonetheless.

Diet was definitely not the key to Nataliya's longevity. Her breakfast was always small: a cup of tea with sugar and a piece of plain bread or small roll. She never ate them with butter, however. Lunch and dinner were ordinary, eaten together with the whole family. Sometimes the main dish was a cutlet or "pelmen,"--a Russian type of ravioli with ground meat--vegetables, or seafood salad with vegetable oil or mayonnaise. She often ate potatoes stewed with meat or sausages, fish, pickled tomatoes, cucumbers, and cabbage.

Many female centenarians had many children; it seems that giving birth when in their early forties had a rejuvenating effect on their bodies. Nataliya Yusova's younger daughter Vera was born when she was forty-three. "I never knew her when she was young, that is why she didn't seem that old to me," said Vera.

About twenty years ago, a growth appeared on Nataliya's right cheek below the eye, which later was diagnosed as skin cancer. Although development was very slow, the wound became bigger and deeper. It started to bleed at night and she experienced pain in her eye. In December 1998, she was hospitalized and underwent a course of radiotherapy, which worked well for her. I saw her wound when she was back home after spending only one month in the hospital. The wound had stopped bleeding, had become much shallower, and a cork-type growth had appeared on it. Her doctors were surprised; they never expected such success for a woman of that age.

She experienced side effects from the radiotherapy, including dizziness, weakness, and loss of appetite, so she stayed mostly in bed for a week or so, being afraid of falling and trying to avoid even short walks around the room. She then gradually recovered from the side effects and her appetite returned to normal. During my last visit in early February 1999, she was sitting on her bed and we had quite a long talk. This had been only the second time in her long life that she was hospitalized. The previous year, a visiting physician came to check her and found that her heart was as strong as that of a young woman. I brought a heart-rate monitor and measured her pulse; it averaged seventy-six beats a minute in a sitting position.

At the age of 100, she was still physically active and helped at home, washing dishes and clothes; she even cooked meals for the family and cleaned the apartment. Her activities declined because she suffered from constipation and had a bowel movement only once a week. I bought a purgative herb for her and asked her daughter Vera to give it to her.

According to Vera, she had a quiet and content nature. She was lively and friendly, with kindness, generosity, and hospitality being the chief features of her personality. She had a strong will, though, and insisted on doing things in her own way, without giving much regard to pleasing others.

Her strong heart, good health, and the positive outcome of the skin-cancer treatment rendered hope that she may have had several more years of life, but sadly, she died shortly after her 101st birthday after having a minor stroke and being bedridden for four months. She passed away on January 17, 2000. According to Vera, she did not suffer any more from skin cancer and her face was free from it when she died. She did well to live over a span of three centuries.

At my request, her daughter Vera answered the personality questionnaire (see Table 2-1) for her mother. Nataliya Yusova's evaluation scored 2 points for Type A, 14 points for Type B, and 3 points for Type C; therefore, she was overwhelmingly a Type B and on the scale of personality types, she is immediately to the right of the central B point (see Figure 2-1). Her case confirms the conclusion of Japanese researchers who linked longevity with Type B behavior.

3

INSTINCTS

Why are some people healthy--living long lives--yet others are not? Without searching for the nature of these long-living persons, their individuality, personality, and level of adaptability, it is impossible to find one correct answer. We have already discussed how bodily constitution affects one's behavioral pattern, but the modes of behavior of an individual are determined by his or her instincts, which can be regarded as basic needs.

The dictionary defines "instinct" as an innate pattern of behavior in most animals in direct response to certain stimuli. Instinct is an inborn drive or innate urge that is characteristic of a species, that is necessary for self-preservation, and that satisfies basic biological needs. In human beings, it similarly means an innate impulse or propensity to act without conscious intention. Instinctive reactions are unlearned responses that are apparently unconscious or automatic. In addition to innate character, instinct is specific to a certain species and appears in the same form in all members of the species.

Human instincts are defined as the elements in behavior that are inborn in an individual or develop later in life as a result of the individual's own constitution. Instincts are congenital behaviors. They appear or develop in a definite order and regularity in the life of an individual as he or she progresses from childhood to maturity. Instinctive behavior is usually contrasted with intelligent or "learned" behavior that is acquired on the basis of the individual's experience. Instinct seems to set limits on what could be acquired by learning; therefore, the capability of controlling one's instincts ranks among the highest basic human needs in the personal development of our fullest potential.

Animal studies show that the behavior of lower organisms is predominantly instinctive, dictated by physiological needs--life-preservation, nutrition, reproduction, and pain avoidance. Behavior in higher organisms is largely determined by learning. In human behavior, intelligent behaviors prevail and purely innate tendencies are fewer in number.

For our purposes, I note Sigmund Freud's duel instinct theory that human behavior grows out of expression of two contrary sets of instincts: *life instincts*, which enhance life and growth; and *death instincts*, which are hostile, aggressive, sadistic behaviors that draw us toward destruction. Life instinct represents the universal urge to maintain life: the self-preservative impulses and the sexual impulses. Death instinct manifests the tendency to lead organic matter back to the inorganic state (i.e., the entropy principle). In his earlier works, Freud distinguished two groups of instincts: the ego (self-preservation) and the sexual instincts. Later, he combined these opposing instincts into one, the life instinct as opposed to the death instinct. Freud admitted, however, that the death instinct is seldom found in its pure state and is very elusive. More often, it expresses itself by fusing with the life instinct; an example is the strange feeling of love and hate toward the same person or object that we sometimes experience.

In its theory of instincts, yoga has many similarities to Freud's life/death instincts. According to yoga, it is the supreme will to live that manifests itself in the self-preservation, fear of death, and destructive impulses toward those who might thwart one's life. In the yoga interpretation of instincts, the will to live doesn't confront the desire for sexual gratification; rather, it states that sexual impulse makes continuance of life pleasurable. Instead of the death instinct, yoga considers the instinct of liberation as a deep urge that is inherent in all life. It is known as the "nirvana principle," which does not signify death, but rather liberation from the wheel-of-rebirth existence. In this sense, nirvana is not an entirely negative concept like death.

These theories of instincts are important from the longevity standpoint because, as we will see, long-living people are--for the most part--driven by life instincts, lead with the strong will to live, and successfully avoid self-destructive tendencies.

The dictionary lists "instinct" as having the following seven characteristics: (1) aggressive, (2) death, (3) ego, (4) herd, (5) life, (6) sexual, and (7) social. One contemporary instinct theory that is applicable to longevity is the *Seven-Instinct Concept*, developed by V.I. Garbuzov, M.D., of Sankt-Petersburg, Russia, and described in his book *Man, Life, and Health.* According to Dr. Garbuzov, the seven basic human instincts are: (1) self-preservation, (2) reproduction, (3) altruism, (4) research, (5) dominance, (6) freedom, and (7) preservation of dignity.

1. **Self-preservation** is the basic instinct in humans and animals to preserve their own life and safety. It represents the endeavor to maintain the

integrity and survival of the organism in facing all the odds of life and even the disruptive threats. The instinct of self-preservation is not one of cowardice, but rather of preservation of the self, of one's integrity and self-value.

2. **Reproduction** is the instinct, drive, or ability of all living creatures to create new life, thus making possible the continuous existence of a species or race. With the process of reproduction, nature replaces old and wearied beings with vital and fresh ones. Nature supplies us with many recuperative powers, but it sets limits on our healing and reparative powers. To economize energy, nature scraps spent individuals and organisms, and gives life to new ones. The instinct to reproduce overshadows the self-preservation instinct; innately, all animals would sacrifice themselves for the sake of fostering their offspring.

3. **Altruism** is a principle of action and is defined as a concern or regard for others, unselfishness. It is the instinctive behavior performed for the benefit of others without regard to the possible detrimental effect on the performer. According to *Webster's International Dictionary*, "altruism" is an ethical term--the opposite of individualism or egoism–that embraces those moral motives that induce an individual to regard the interests of others. In the course of evolution, in order that a particular group could survive, the members of that group must overcome a certain amount of aggression and hostility to cooperate with one another. Nothing could save any group, nation, or even humanity itself if individuals did not become altruistic. The wisdom of survival has taught individuals to treat others in the way that they themselves would like to be treated (i.e., "The Golden Rule").

There are scientific examples of altruistic behavior among animals as well. Sylvia S. Mader, in her book *Inquiry into Life* (5th edition), notes a report about chimpanzees that live in the Kibale Forest in East Africa. They usually forage in groups of three or four. The group spreads out, and when one spots a tree with fruit, it calls to the others. Another example of animals acting altruistically is the behavior of ants and bees. Only the queen lays eggs--all female workers (comprising most of the hive) do not have any offspring of their own.

As a moral motive, altruism is usually a feature of humans, not animals. It is the instinct of altruism that comes into play when a person rushes to rescue someone in trouble, stops to help a fallen person, or calls for an ambulance at an automobile accident. While it may seem as if members of an animal group are altruistic, it can be shown that their motives are more likely to be selfish and their behavior serves to increase their own fitness, according to sociobiology (i.e., the science that studies social behavior).

Some people also deny the possibility of altruism in humans. "If you blindly and recklessly risk your life for a total stranger, you have made the decision--spur of the moment as it may be--that you will feel better risking your life, knowing you tried to rescue a stranger, than having to live with the thought that another human being died whom you might have been able to save," said Robert J. Ringer in his best-selling book, *Looking Out For #1*. "...There's no such thing as altruism in the so-called unselfish sense. There is only rational or irrational selfishness. ...Be especially wary of those who actually believe they're altruistic, for they are the most vain and dangerous of all people," he added. However, be it rational or irrational, a person acts when driven by an instinctive urge to help. I do not believe it is a matter of decision, for there is no time to think in an emergency.

In the hierarchy of instincts, altruism ranks higher than self-preservation or reproductive instincts. People often risk their lives for others and give up their marriages--even the possibility of having children--for their relatives or because of spiritual devotion.

4. **Research** is defined as an endeavor to discover new facts and reach new conclusions. For the survival of both kin and other individuals, it was necessary for some powerful motive to induce a person to search for education, knowledge, creativity, and self-development. Life dictates a need to discover new means of labor and defense, new ways of hunting, and alternate and new ways to search for shelter. Thus, the instinct to research was forged out of necessity. Driven by the instinct of research, humankind ignored the self-preservation and reproduction instincts. Many scientists and explorers in the past were so involved with their research that it cost them their lives. Greek philosopher Diogenes (412? -323 BC); English philosopher, physicist, and mathematician Sir Isaac Newton (1642-1727); and German philosopher Immanuel Kant (1724-1804) devoted their lives to science, and none ever married. Each of these individuals lived to be quite elderly, considering that the average life span of people in their era was less than forty years.

5. **Dominance** means to have a commanding influence on someone or exercising control over others. Dominance exists in both animals and humans. It comes from competition among members of the same population for food, territory, and mates. The stronger male animal takes the dominant position among males within a given society and receives food and his choice of mates before weaker animals do. He leads the group, maintains the order, and fights

for a female or with a leader of another group for territory, as in the case of elephant seals. Among humans, some are born with a talent to be gifted leaders and some are not. The former individuals are called the "genetical nobles" who others obey and acclaim as their leaders. For them, the dominance instinct is stronger than the instincts of self-preservation and reproduction.

6. **Freedom** implies a condition of being free or unrestricted as well as the state of being free to act. Every living creature strives for freedom. Some animals are not able to raise offspring if they are behind bars in a zoo. The individual becomes deeply unhappy, sick, and degraded with the loss of freedom. There is a Latin saying: "Vita sine liberate--nihil" (Life without freedom is nothing). Many people have given up their lives for freedom and faced death with the pride of knowing that "It was better to die standing than to live kneeling." The instinct of freedom is the culmination of all other instincts. Freedom is a condition for the survival of offspring because there is no sense of continuing a family in slavery. Creativity is not possible without freedom, and altruism cannot exist without it.

7. **Preservation of Dignity**. Dignity is the state of being worthy of honor or respect. Dignity together with freedom is the highest instinct of humans and stands among the highest values of civilization; dissent, freedom of thought and speech, justice, honor, human dignity, and self-respect reign supreme. The sense of human dignity is the cement of society of equal persons and it sustains any true society. Society is governed by the rule that respect for others must be founded in self-respect. Again, dignity is often valued more than life itself, even more than freedom. Giordano Bruno was burned alive for his cosmology on the Campo de' Fiori in 1600, but his self-dignity would not allow him to save his own life.

Instincts manifest to different degrees in each individual; one or more instincts may be expressed more than others. Prevailing instincts, as well as inherited tendencies, determine personality type and vocation. If a person has one prevailing instinct, he or she belongs to a pure type. If a few instincts are equally strong, he or she is a combined type. According to Dr. Garbuzov, everyone belongs to one of the following seven major instinct types: (1) egophylum (phylum--type), (2) genophylum (genus--family), (3) altruistic, (4) research, (5) dominance, (6) liberophylum, or (7) dignitophylum. According to these predominant instincts, people are characterized as the following types:

1. **Egophylum type**. People of this type are careful and sober-minded; tend to be distrustful, suspicious, and egocentric; avoid risk; are unadventurous; and prefer stability. They are highly predisposed to worry and hypochondria and they are afraid of height, water, and high speed. They are not racers, mountain climbers, or navigators. They mostly value their security and well-being. Being judicious to avoid risk, they preserve themselves and their family, and appear to be the keepers of the genealogical fund of their kin.

However, if by self-affirmation they overcome their fears and become, for instance, a racer, they fight their own fears, torture themselves, and end up with diseases of the heart and blood vessels. People of the egophylum type are very sensitive to insult; they are proud of themselves and, therefore, quite vulnerable to hurt.

2. **Genophylum type**. It is common for people of this type to substitute the concept of "I" with the concept of "we," meaning family. Everything in their life is placed under the interests of family and children; for them, family is above all other things. Their motto is "My house is my fortress." They are super-fathers and super-mothers. They are the keepers of their family and the gene fund of their kin.

3. **Altuistic type**. People of this type are kind, responsive, and compassionate. In their childhood, if they were attacked by a bully, they would not fight in order to spare the aggressor any pain, while stoically bearing their own pain. Altruistic people experience the calamities of others more they do their own misfortunes.

They are selfless people and devote their lives to helping others, protecting the weak, and taking care of the sick and elderly. They are often missionaries, or nurse the terminally ill in hospitals, or are the soldiers of the Salvation Army; "Kindness above all" is their motto. Albert Schweitzer, Mother Teresa, and Andrei Sakharov are included in the altruistic type.

4. **Research type**. People of this type are creative, desirous of knowledge, inventive, seek to understand the essence of all things, and strive to find cause and effect connections. Scientists, researchers, travelers, inventors, and creators are included in the research type. They even risk their lives for the cause of science, and often forego the comforts of life and family. People of the research type gave to humanity power from the nucleus; helped to master the sea, sky, and space; and found ways to double the life span and shorten the work day. Actually, the work of scientists has liberated humankind, enabling personal fulfillment to the highest potential. "Creation, research, and progress above all" is their motto.

5. **Dominance type**. People of this type are genetic leaders; that is, they are born to be leaders. They are logical thinkers, self-critical and critical; and they have the ability to foresee the development of events, to accept new ideas, and to pick out the essentials. People of the dominance type are responsible, efficient, and practical; understand other people; and are emotionally restrained and steadfast. Career is the first priority for them. They know what they want to achieve and how to achieve it; they are persistent and purposeful in the achievement of their goals. People of this type are egocentric, but they allow social interests and values as expedience necessitates. They adhere to rules of play, laws, and the necessity of reforms, but in an evolutionary way, without revolution. They are open to calculated risk without adventure. They think in the category of "millions" and are inclined to ignore the interests of the individual. "Business above all" is their motto. They are as necessary as order and leadership are.

6. **Liberophylum type**. The people of this type are freedom-loving, with an intolerance for restriction, compliance, routine, bureaucracy, and conservatism. They are predisposed to travel, including many business trips; to work independently; and to not be controlled from above. People of this type are optimistic, rely only on themselves, and live for today. The statement "God will give a day, God will give food too," comprises the primary principle of their lives. They are genetically revolutionary, the overthrowers of authority, and anarchists by nature. The whole world is their home and "Freedom above all" is their motto.

7. **Dignitophylum type**. People of this type are proud, intolerant to any form of humiliation by an individual or entity, and are ready to give up their position, possessions, family, and even their own life in the name of dignity and honor. Nothing can force them to bend their proud heads. "Honor above all" is their motto. Tyrants in all times and nations cut off the heads of dignitophylumous and liberophylumous people. Dignitophylums are not arrogant like egophylums and the extreme of the dominance type; their pride is noble. Together with liberophylums, they naturally counterbalance any form of authoritarian power.

These seven instincts are divided into two groups that somehow oppose each other. According to Dr. Garbuzov, the first two instincts, self-preservation and reproduction, comprise the group of Yin, characterized as passive, inhibitive, egocentric, and centered on self and family problems. This is the feminine group of instincts, which generally tends to reflect the innate necessity of security (family), stability, peace, and harmony with nature. The other group, the dominance, research, freedom, and dignity instincts, comprises the group of Yang, characterized as active, socially centered, outwardly oriented toward self-realization among other people and society, with social interests in general. This is a masculine group of instincts, which generally tends to reflect the innate necessity of self-affirmation, activity, search for the new, freedom, and preservation of dignity. Each person has one or the other group of prevailing instincts.

To thoroughly understand the nature of an individual, his/her profile by instinct may be helpful. The degree to which each instinct manifests itself can be scored: one point assigned to the less expressed instinct and seven points to the most; therefore, the predominant instinct will have a score of seven. A highly expressed instinct will score six points, well expressed will be five, and so on.

For an example, I will draw from my own instinct profile. The predominant instinct in my case is freedom. Throughout my life, I have valued freedom most of all. I realized how important freedom was for me when I got married at the age of twenty-four. After a few years of married life, I found myself so restrained, so confined and bound, that I could scarcely tolerate it. My wife was good and kind and loving; the root of my unhappiness was my lost freedom. I made a poor husband, and we divorced after four years of marriage; I realized that married life was not for me. I know some people consider this a stupid independence. In being unwilling to admit "need" for bonding and intimacy, a person may hide in the excesses of work, play, drink, drugs, pornography, and meaningless sex. This may be true but, in my case, I just feel comfortable being alone. Twenty-eight years have passed and, although there were a few opportunities, I have never remarried. Whenever I even got close to marriage, the freedom instinct--being stronger than my love--stopped me cold.

My scientific career was quite successful. I earned a Ph.D. in engineering at the age of twenty-eight, was promoted to the position of senior researcher, and worked in the leading research institute in Moscow. In the eyes of my friends and co-workers, I was a big success. I had a comfortable apartment close to the center of Moscow and all the material things I needed. I was unsatisfied, though, mostly with the environment of daily life, and I suffered emotionally from the stupidity of rules and norms established in the USSR under Communist rule.

Every day I felt a heaviness on my heart. I was overwhelmed with many whys: Why are the rules so inhuman? Why are there lies everywhere, in the newspapers and mass media programs? Why is a person treated so badly in all the institutions? Why are individuals deemed worthless wherever they go? Why is it so easy for the authorities and other people to humiliate a person? Why can't people admit their slavery? Answers to all these questions were quite clear to me: people in Russia were used to tolerating the conditions that government had set for them, so there was no need for the government to change anything. People deserve their government and the government deserves its people; this is a universal law. Later, after the collapse of the Soviet Union and the Communist Party in 1991, not only did the government changed it was replaced with another government entirely.

I was not, however, a revolutionary or fighter for human rights. This is not my nature; I am not that altruistic. All I could do was escape alone. I defected in 1990, seeking political freedom. Nobody could have predicted that just one year later, the almighty Communist Party, which seemed to rule forever, would be destroyed and banned by the new democratic revolution. I enjoyed freedom and my new life in Israel, despite my lack of money. I soon found a job, but later got a better paying one in Japan. My next step was to acquire financial freedom, so I worked hard for five years in a Japanese company and saved money. Upon retiring four years ago, I finally had both freedoms that I had been seeking. I also felt free of the need to work for someone else for money. I eventually had the opportunity to act on what had been my dream for years: I started my life-extension research project in order to write this book. This is why I consider *freedom* to be my predominant instinct.

After freedom, I rank self-preservation highest among all my instincts. More than twenty years ago, I tried to choose healthy habits, diet, and lifestyle. My heredity is quite good on my father's side, but a son inherits the strength or weakness of his vital organs from his mother. Spiritually, my mother was deeply involved, but her physical constitution was rather weak. That is why I could not rely on my genes alone and had to earn and maintain my health and fitness through my own efforts. This does not mean that I always do the right thing; sometimes I make the wrong choices. However, in general, I am concerned about my health; therefore, self-preservation scores six points in my instinct profile. I deeply believe that we all have to make our own health number one among our priorities, taking all possible responsibility for being healthy and fit. Unfortunately, many people do not control their health adequately because they pay more attention to their hobbies and other interests in life; they leave their health to doctors to maintain.

The research instinct is number three in my case. In my research work, I was not gifted enough to be an academic scientist; my work was more experimental than theoretical. I preferred site work, and about half the time was away from Moscow, working in various regions of the USSR. As a geotechnical engineer, I was involved in field tests on pile foundations in big constructional projects, and I sometimes risked my health and even my life for my work. In many field experiments, to install load cells and various gauges in the bored piles before they were cast with concrete, I sometimes descended into large-diameter boreholes to depths of 100 to 200 feet. Once I was working in a borehole on-site in Tadjikistan. The mixer trucks that brought liquid concrete were casting it into a neighboring borehole. Exhaust fumes from the trucks filled up the hole that I was in--the air-ventilating system was not properly built and, consequently, my lungs were filled with highly polluted air. For a couple of days afterwards, I still felt the bitterness in my throat. I did not become sick at that time, but it definitely did not enhance my health. In all my travels to boreholes, they transported me in a crane in a cage; I recall many life-threatening moments.

I admit that I acted stupidly in risking my life and health and that it was "irrational efforts," as Robert J. Ringer says. However, that is what happened in my life. Equally stupid was my emigration alone, without money or any possible means of support. Nevertheless, my curiosity and research instincts were stronger than my fears of becoming sick or even dying. I am not saying that I am such a brave man and fear nothing—far from it. Perhaps it can be judged as irrational stupidity, but all my life I have been like this. Destiny was really kind to me and I have been lucky to survive. For these reasons, I assign a score of five points to my research instinct.

To proceed further with constructing my instinct profile, at this point, I would rather shift to the end of the list of instincts because it is easier to assign the appropriate scores to them. I am quite confident that it is the dominance instinct that I lack most. My career or a higher rank in position was never important to me. Moreover, I even risked my position when I refused to cooperate with the KGB when they asked me to become its spy in the city of Krasnoyarsk in Siberia, where I worked after graduation from college. I was twenty-two years old, a brand-new engineer who was then preparing to enter the Ph.D. phase of education.

I understood the potential threat to my future career, but I couldn't accept the offer to cooperate with the KGB. Later, I put an end to any possibility of future promotions in the research institute in Moscow (where I worked for twenty-eight years) when I refused to join the Communist Party. They were very angry with me when I refused. It was not an act of heroism and there were no negative consequences; I am only trying to show that dominance was not my vehicle.

My leadership and organizational abilities are less than average. As a senior researcher, I was head of a small group of three or four engineers and technicians. Often I could not organize their work properly, and my assistants were sometimes bored, with no work to do. Although they helped me with simple tasks in preparation for experiments and data processing, the data analysis and writing of reports were my tasks. I felt bad that I did not teach them to do analysis or to write reports. Due to my lack of leadership and organizational abilities, the dominance instinct is under-expressed in me and it would score merely one point.

Next to the worst is my reproductive instinct. My first and only marriage produced one daughter, my only offspring. Before marriage and after divorce, I had love affairs and girlfriends, but no more children were ever born. That was because of me; so far, no more souls have chosen me as a father for rebirth. However, there is a Russian saying: "It's not evening yet"; so I have not lost all hope for future possibilities. Under these circumstances, I would assign a score of two points to my reproductive instinct.

A little better but still bad is my altruistic instinct. I do not mean to imply that I am so mean that I won't help others; I am selfish, but not to the extent that I care only about myself. I would gladly help others in trouble. I readily share with others what I have learned from my life extension research, and sometimes people find it helpful. However, I am not prepared to give all of my possessions (rather scarce) to charity. It is one of my many shortcomings; I have to work to develop my altruistic instinct. So far, I would give it a score of only three points.

The last remaining instinct is dignity. In me, it definitely outweighs reproduction and dominance. It is painful for me to see one person humiliate another. Scenes of humiliation that happened decades ago in my presence have cut deeply into my memory. I remember being on the tram in Moscow, when a couple stood close to me. The middle-aged woman was angry, yelling at the man and scolding him badly. He humbly tolerated all her shouts, not responding or trying to stop her, and I felt great pity for that poor fellow. Then she moved to the front of the tram to pay a fee; he was alone for a few moments and I had a strong desire to approach him and say: "Man, get out at the next stop. Take a taxi home, pack quickly, and buy a one-way railway ticket to **any** destination. You will feel yourself to be human again." Unfortunately, I did not do that and I regret it even still.

There are also times when my own dignity was offended. Saleswomen in Russia could easily yell at you, feeling confident that an intelligent person wouldn't yell back. They also knew that you were dependent on them since they had in their hands the goods you needed. If you gave up and went to another shop, you would be in line again for at least an hour. I experienced a few such attacks when I tried to show a saleswoman that she was wrong. Whenever I tried to argue back, I was a complete failure; they were professionals and I was just an amateur. Those humiliations added to my desire to leave that wonderful country. The dignity instinct is certainly present in me, but it is not as strong as my freedom, self-preservation, and research instincts. Therefore, I rank it number four with a score of four points.

With all of my instincts now scored, we can draw my instinct profile, which is shown in Figure 3-1.

The left side of the figure shows the pyramid of instincts, suggested by Dr. Garbuzov; at the right is my personal profile. My readers must know the instinct profile of their author. I liked this exercise; probably you will like it too--you will know yourself a little better than you did before. It is apparent to me that sometimes it is difficult to see the prevalence of one instinct over another. If it is difficult for you to rate your instincts, then consult with people who most often experience the expression of your instincts--those who observe you and know you well. Perhaps you will have a unique profile like mine.

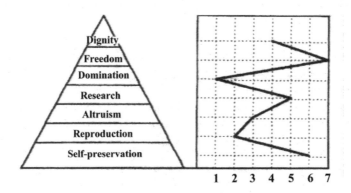

Figure 3-1. Pyramid of Instincts and the Author's Instinct Profile

Actually, the instincts of long-living people and centenarians (not mine) are of primary interest in our search for a long and healthy life. Centenarians are the sparkling examples with regard to expressing their instincts. The fact that they have managed to live a hundred years ranks them as great masters of survivorship and leaders of the self-preservation instinct. They share all the qualities of the egophylum type, which represent the self-preservation instinct: careful, egocentric, suspicious, unadventurous, and sober-minded. Together with good genes and decent health, these are very important components of successful survival. So many people die prematurely because of their adventurous character; for example, mountain and rock climbers, swimmers, scuba divers, and skiers.

These are very challenging sports and activities, but they put a person at high risk of losing their life. Paul Bragg, an American health pioneer and life extensionist, died in a surfing accident at the age of ninety-five. I was a big fan of his and feel badly about his death. Even if a person feels young at heart and has a very fit, strong, and robust body, he had better not forget the reality of his age. My yoga teacher Eugene Bazh told me that with each passing life cycle of twelve years, we have to move more slowly. All physiological functions of our body slow down with age and so must we. To behave in accordance with one's age is the wisdom of centenarians. "Don't bend the elbow too much," advised Frank Shomo of Robinson, Pennsylvania, who lived to the age of 108.

Health consciousness in centenarians is often not a declared life principle, but instead is comprised of good habits that are incorporated naturally into their lifestyle. The necessity of self-preservation and health consciousness gradually gained societal awareness; however, there were many times and societies that entirely rejected them. For instance, during the Communist era in Russia, it was considered very bad if someone was health conscious. Official propaganda ingrained the idea of giving life up to the very last drop of blood for the sake of revolution and Communism--considered a privilege to live under--as the great accomplishment. People believed this lie and treated each other accordingly. The Soviet poet Nikolay Dorizo expressed this belief in his verse *On Egoism* (the translation from Russian is mine):

> Since he preserves himself in such a way,
> God punishes him with the long life,
> That he is living long no one would say
> But rather that he is long dying.

However, Communist Party leaders did not share the same beliefs established for the masses. Top party officials were not embarrassed with "long dying" at all and enjoyed longevity. Lazar Kaganovich, an aide of Stalin, lived to 98 years of age, Vyacheslav Molotov, a foreign minister in Stalin's era, lived to the age of 96; and Georgy Malenkov, a Prime Minister after Stalin's death, reached age 86. Their lives were very stressful and each lived in deadly fear of Stalin, but they managed somehow to preserve themselves, even under the severe circumstances of "Joe the Terrible's" rule.

The second instinct, reproduction, is very strong in most centenarians. In both the West and the East, more than a few centenarians had as many as twelve children.

Kin Narita (who died in January 2000 at the age of 107) of Japan had eleven children and her twin sister, Gin Kanie, 108, had five children.

Four American centenarians interviewed by Jim Heynen--namely Dora Davis, 107, Nina Amanda Rust, 106, Russell Williams, 104, and Maria Prisciliana Salazar, 104--each had twelve children.

Madam Ang Leng, 106, whom I met in Singapore (and mentioned previously), had nine children. Among men, 100-year-old To Megoro of Japan fathered and raised eleven children.

Many centenarians attributed their longevity to living with their families, in which they were highly respected. In a study of eighty-two centenarians living in Japan and aged from 100 to 106, seventy-one (86 percent) lived at home with their families.

The altruism instinct is what fostered the longevity of many centenarians, as evidenced by these examples of American centenarians from the book *One Hundred Over 100*, by Jim Heynen:

(1) 100-year-old Ann Berdahl led a life of service to others as a nurse, modeling her life after Florence Nightingale, the greatest woman in nursing history;

(2) 100-year-old Esther Henrickson said that she always kept busy caring for others; and

(3) in sharing his secrets, 100-year-old Philip Thomas McGough said, "And try to please everybody. If you see somebody having trouble, try to help them. I started helping people when I was a little boy."

In Singapore, 100-year-old Teresa Hsu lives an active life helping the poor and elderly. "Why are we on this world if not to care for others? I feel a sister to all," she said, as reported by the *Straits Times* newspaper on November 7, 1997.

The research instinct, driven by curiosity, is a characteristic of many centenarians. "It's her curiosity," said the daughter-in-law of 101-year-old Alice Maud Thomas, in response to the question of how her mother-in-law got so old. "She's always been interested in everything. If she saw a flower along the road, she would have to stop and look at it," she added. Koasa, a Japanese comedian who ran the TV program about 100-year-old people and who had met 157 centenarians, maintains that many of them were born under the astrological sign of Sagittarius. The characteristic feature of this sign is curiosity, he said.

The dominance instinct, which makes people leaders, decreases in men and becomes stronger in women as they age. Neugarten and Gutmann obtained this finding in 1968. Some centenarians were managers. Male Takeuchi Masaro of Japan, 101, is still acting president of a chocolate factory with two hundred employees. With age, ambitions that were more prevalent at middle age slow down. Men do not completely give up on dominance; they are assertive and forceful, as shown in a study by Martin et al.

The freedom instinct is quite strong among long-living people. They knew what they wanted, how to maintain their independence, and how to express their strong will. Koasa says that 100-year-old people are often quite naughty and their families have difficulties in dealing with them.

Preservation of dignity, which is equal to freedom of thought and speech, definitely manifests itself in some centenarians. Self-confidence and self-respect are among traits found in men and women of a hundred years and over. A shining example was Lydia Vesselovzorova (who died in April 2000 at the age of 103), who was born in Russia and spent the second half of her life in Japan. She always said what she thought, although her words of truth were sometimes painful to the sensitive Japanese who took care of her. Frank Sinatra, in his song "My Way," sang "To say the things he truly feels, and not the words of one who kneels." It is life of glory if one can keep their virtue.

4

TEMPERAMENTS

One more characteristic that may be helpful in understanding why centenarians are healthy and managed to live long lives is their difference in temperament. The dictionary defines "temperament" as a person's distinct nature and character, especially influenced by physical constitution and permanently affecting behavior. For example, one surely has heard the expression "nervous" or "artistic" temperament.

Differences in responses appear very early in life. There are quiet children, but some cry a great deal. Some babies are fussy and "difficult," but others are easily soothed and are "content" kids. One infant shows a readiness to laugh, yet another (the shy one) averts his/her eyes. There is little doubt among researchers that temperaments are determined exclusively by heredity, and that temperamental differences persist to some degree throughout childhood.

The researchers, however, are certain that a child's temperament is changed according to the environmental influences of his/her surroundings. "Inborn temperament predisposes an infant to react in a certain way, but temperament and life experiences interact to mold personality," say Rita L. Atkinson, et al., in their book, *Introduction to Psychology*. Still, some people carry their innate qualities throughout their entire life. Surely, the centenarians possess this characteristic; many state that they were always as they are now.

Temperament types were known in ancient India, China, and Tibet; the Greek physician Hippocrates (c. 460 - c. 377 BC) also knew and studied them. He identified four basic individual temperament types: *choleric*, *phlegmatic*, *sanguine*, and *melancholic*. Each temperament related to the predominant liquid substance ("humour") flowing in the body: *chole* means bile, in the Greek language; *phlegma* means lymph; *melas chole* means black bile; and *sanguis* means blood in Latin. Another Greek physician and scholar, Galen (c. 129 - c. 199 AD), based on Hippocrates' theory, acknowledged these four temperament types and postulated that there were six others. In the following description of temperaments, I relied on the books *How to Understand Others by Understanding Yourself Personality Plus*, by Florence Littauer, and *Man, Life, Health* (in Russian), by V.I. Garbuzov, M.D.

Choleric Temperament. A person of this temperament has innate leadership qualities and is goal-oriented. The Choleric is a dynamic person who is always aiming, reaching, succeeding, and achieving. "All or nothing" is their motto. They are fighters and take any risk for the sake of goal achievement, for getting it "all." It is impossible to distract or persuade them, for they know everything better than anybody else. Their golden rule is: "Do it *my* way, now!"

The Choleric usually exhibits a leadership attitude very early in life; s/he takes control over the family very soon. To solidify control, s/he will use a loud voice and demand his/her rights immediately. Strong-willed children who won't do anything they are told are a great difficulty for their parents. One of my friends has such a child. He was born saying "no" immediately to whatever he was asked or told to do. If he wants something, he wants it furiously and *never* gives up. He is seven years old now, but he has always been this way. Four years ago, he was very attached to the "Barney and Friends" TV program for children. He wanted to watch it twenty-four hours a day; when the videotape came to the end, he couldn't wait until it was rewound. He would cry non-stop until "Barney and Friends" was on the screen again. One year later, it was the same story with the "Teletubbies" program. "Grandma, be very quiet in the library," he often would instruct his grandmother.

The Choleric person has the only idea, the only passion, and the only love. They never get tired. They do not undo the knots--they cut them, as Alexander the Great cut off the Gordian knot with his sword. They usually rise to the top in whatever career they choose. The majority of political leaders are primarily Choleric. The Russian tsars Ivan the Terrible and Peter the Great were Cholerics. In modern times, Margaret Thatcher is an excellent example of a Choleric woman.

Phlegmatic Temperament. The Phlegmatic was created to provide others with stability and balance. S/he refrains from the extremes or excesses of life; s/he chooses the middle road and walks steadily, avoiding conflicts. S/he is slow in his/her actions, but does everything without fuss, patiently, and honestly. His/her ability to get along with everyone is outstanding and, if properly motivated, s/he can achieve the highest of positions. By his/her nature, s/he is just, trouble-free, does not grumble, and patiently waits for the better things to come. Whatever idea is suggested, s/he readily agrees with it.

People like that are usually pleasant and inoffensive, and have a low-key personality; one wants to keep them around.

The Phlegmatic's ability to stay calm in the face of a storm is one of the most admirable qualities. When Rudyard Kipling, in his famous *If* poem, said: "If you can keep your head when all around you are loosing theirs, and blaming it on you," he probably wanted others to model the Phlegmatic person. S/he is not overwhelmed with emotions and his/her heart is not host to anger; s/he simply does not think it is worth getting upset. If the pressure on them becomes too tough, they just go silently away. When this happens, the best workers and the best family men or women are lost. His/her power is great, but is not designed to be hasty. This is not the power of a racecar, but rather the power of a bulldozer. S/he is reliable, prefers to stay at home, and settles for peace--but is also steadfast in war.

Sanguine Temperament. A person of this temperament is quick in everything: s/he thinks and speaks quickly, is quick-witted, sharp-minded, and finds the proper word immediately. The person in a group who is the loudest and chats non-stop is definitely the Sanguine. S/he prefers to tell stories, while others merely talk.

One of my former colleagues at the research institute in Moscow, Dr. Christopher Djan, has that temperament. He was always the center of attention, telling colorful stories and anecdotes. This trait makes him the life of any party--people invite the charming and witty Christopher to their parties to ensure success. He is a close friend of mine and we have spent many days together; I am his fan too. He is very animated and lively, a fountain of energy.

Dr. Djan could immediately relax in any situation, regardless of what it was. I enjoyed his ability to fall asleep during the very heart of a conversation. He would ask someone a question and then fall asleep while the other person was answering it. This obviously was confusing for his counterpart. After a while, he suddenly would awake and go on with another question, as if nothing had happened. There were attempts to laugh at him, but each time his sharp-minded response was so rapid and annihilating that his counterpart was always at a complete loss for words.

Our Sanguine Christopher is quite successful in his scientific career and is an author of many writings and more than a dozen inventions in the field of pile foundations. He has three children from two marriages and takes good care of all of them. His second wife Lena (Helen) holds a Ph.D. in food-processing science. He joked and told stories about her research while she was in her doctoral program.

Helen's research subject for her Ph.D. thesis was "Russkie blyny," Russian pancakes designed to be fried in an automatic machine from a soft type of wheat. Traditionally, only hard and more expensive wheat was used for pancakes, which were as thin as a veil (i.e., about 1 millimeter thick). She added ground carrots to the batter in order to preserve the texture and strength of the mix, which was an essential part of the frying process, especially when a pancake is turned over inside the automatic machine without access of the operator. She studied the physical and mechanical properties of the batter with carrot as an additive. At the presentation of her thesis, each member of the scientific counsel was given a pancake to test. They found them tasty and her research data to be convincing, and she received her Ph.D. degree.

Another researcher studied a new technique of stuffing macaroni with meat. In Russia, there were rumors that this dish, known in the Russian language as "macaroni-po-flotsky" (which means macaroni served to the naval fleet), was a favorite food of Mikhail Gorbachev. The researcher developed a vacuum method in which the ground meat was sucked automatically inside the macaroni tubes. At his presentation, the scientists were delighted with both the process and the product's taste, and they approved both the macaroni and the results of his Ph.D. research.

The ease with which Christopher could solve an embarrassing situation is illustrated by the following example. One day we were on our way home after work. Christopher had an agreement to meet his wife Lena at the metro station at a certain time. Because it was rush hour, we were late by about a quarter of an hour when we met her. She did not like to wait and looked upset. Their conversation went like this:

CHRISTOPHER: Hi, my birdie, you look somewhat upset.
LENA: I was worrying that something happened.
CHRISTOPHER: What do you mean? No, nothing happened at all.
LENA: I was waiting here for half an hour. Where were you?
CHRISTOPHER: Oh, my love, I've been waiting for you all my life, and you couldn't wait for me just half an hour?
LENA (*smiling, disarmed*): You *always* know what to say.

A Sanguine person works quickly and makes work into fun. S/he sees excitement in each experience. In everything, s/he sees the flowers, rather than the weeds. Even though s/he may not have more talent or opportunity than the other temperaments, s/he always has more fun. S/he is optimistic and outgoing, emotional and demonstrative. A Sanguine individual is enthusiastic in almost everything; s/he has many ambitions and many ideas. If his/her target, however, is too difficult to achieve, s/he easily gives up. S/he is like a sunny day when the sun and rain occur together. S/he cried a while ago, but s/he is already laughing now.

To be the center of attention comes from the Sanguine's childhood, when family and teachers doted on him/her; s/he wants it to last a lifetime. His/her desire to be helpful and popular makes him/her volunteer without hesitation. People love the Sanguine. Without them, the world would be dull and without spark and prime, which are the very foundation of the Sanguine temperament.

Melancholic Temperament. The Melancholy thinks deeply, even as a baby. The never-smiling child analyzes everyone who passes by. As a teenager, s/he is serious and reliable, and often annoyed by the lighthearted attitude of others. S/he works out the best plan of his/her life rather than searching for excitement upon reaching adulthood, s/he is dedicated to order, and is serious in his/her purpose. Getting to the heart of the matter is what the Melancholic person wants and does. It is not important to them how fast they can do something, but rather how well. They do their best to achieve perfection and high standards.

His/her appreciation of beauty and intelligence is an innate characteristic. Music, art, poetry, literature, and philosophy would be absent without the Melancholy. Aristotle said, "All men of Genius are of Melancholic temperament." Petr Tchaikovsky, the Russian composer, is a shining example of a Melancholic musician. Mankind needs them very much: they are the heart and soul, mind and spirit of the world. They appreciate gifted people, admire talents, and can cry easily when overwhelmed with emotions.

By his/her nature, the Melancholic person can't afford to be wasteful and uses money thriftily. Getting a bargain and using money-saving coupons is fun for them. At times they overdo it, becoming stingy. To avoid waste, a Melancholic sometimes eats leftovers, although this is not a healthy habit.

Every temperament is great and has its own place; each has advantages and disadvantages. Some people, however, take the negative sides of the Melancholy too seriously. According to Dr. Garbuzov, features of the Melancholy such as pessimism, depression, indecision, apathy, and focusing just on his/her own problems are unnatural. These traits are not inborn, but instead are acquired as a result of a bad environment, he states. On these grounds, he discounts the Melancholic temperament altogether and acknowledges only the other three. What temperament shall we assign then to the classic Melancholy Petr Tchaikovsky, the world-famous Russian composer? Except for leftovers, I find nothing wrong with the Melancholic temperament; I would rather say that some stubborn and demanding Choleric people who ignore others have been spoiled by their family (i.e., the influence of environment). However, nobody doubts that these people are Choleric; therefore, I stand on the four-temperament approach.

Perhaps the description of four temperaments lacks some features, but I hope I have given a general idea of their differences. To learn more about each temperament in order to be fully prepared to assess your own profile, Table 4-1 summarizes the characteristics of the four temperaments.

Table 4-1. Qualities of the Four Temperaments

Nos.	CHOLERIC	PHLEGMATIC	SANGUINE	MELANCHOLY
	Innate Abilities			
1	Leadership qualities, but is quick-tempered	Low-key personality, but fearful and worried	Appealing, charming, but dwells on trivia	Thoughtful, deep, but has low self-image
2	Dynamic and active, but too impetuous	Easygoing and relaxed, but selfish	Talkative and a storyteller, but is compulsive talker	Analytical, but too introspective
3	Compulsive need for change, but impatient	Calm, collected, and cool, but indecisive	Life of the party, but scares others off	Serious, but tolerates being hurt
4	Take-charge attitude, but comes on too strong	Adaptable to any situation, but too shy	Looks for fun and games, but has too loud a voice and laugh	Talented and creative, but moody and depressed
5	Strong will, but won't give up when losing	Avoids conflicts, but too compromising	Inquisitive and cheerful, but can't remember names	Undemanding and calm, but keeps the negative in mind
6	Decisive, good planner, but is inflexible	Tolerates a flexible schedule, but avoids responsibility	Good sense of humor, but blusters and complains	Follows any schedule, but off in another world
7	Must correct wrongs, but loves to argue	Thirst for knowledge, but unenthusiastic	Sincere at heart, but gets angry easily	Reliable, but has false humility
8	Exudes confidence, but dislikes emotions	Patient and balanced, but self-righteous	Innocent, but naive, gets taken in	Conscientious, but self-centered
9	Independent and self-sufficient, but bossy	Hides emotions, but is strong-willed	Emotional, but often exaggerates and elaborates	Sensitive to others, but has selective hearing
10	Unemotional, but not complimentary	Consistent life, but is lazy and careless	Lives in the present, but controlled by circumstances	Self-sacrificing, but has guilt feelings
	Qualities at Work			
11	Goal-oriented, but may make rash decisions	Competent and steady, but not goal-oriented	Charms others to work, but by themselves would rather talk	Perfectionist, but gets depressed over imperfections
12	Sees the whole scene, but doesn't analyze the details	Peaceful and agreeable, but lacks self-motivation	Starts in a flashy way, but forgets obligations	Persistent and thorough, but slow to start work
13	Organizes well, but is manipulative	Has administrative ability, but is hard to get moving	Inspires others to join, but wastes time talking	Orderly and organized, but deep need for validation
14	Seeks practical solutions, but is bored by trivia	Finds the easy way, but discourages others	Thinks up new activities, but doesn't follow through	Schedule-oriented, but not people-oriented

Nos.	CHOLERIC	PHLEGMATIC	SANGUINE	MELANCHOLY
15	Moves quickly to action, but always justifies the means	Mediates problems, but resents being pushed	Has energy and enthusiasm, but is undisciplined	Detail-conscious, but prefers analysis to work
16	Can run anything, but may work too much	Avoids conflict, but may give up and quit a job too easily	Creative and colorful, but decides by feelings	Finds creative solutions, but is self-deprecating
17	Delegates work, but is demanding of others	Makes right decisions, but would rather watch	Volunteers for jobs, but is easily distracted	Economical, but spends too much time planning
18	Stimulates activity, but may be rude or tactless	Good under pressure, but lazy and careless	Looks great on the surface, but confidence fades fast	Likes figures, lists, but can't cooperate with others
19	Achieves the goal, but has little tolerance for mistakes	Just and agreeable, but seems to be insensible	Has many aims and ideas, but can easily give up if they are not realized at once	Needs to finish what s/he starts, but often sets standards too high
20	Stimulates activity, but demands loyalty	Quiet and witty, but may become furious	Sees right direction, but his/her priorities are out of order	Sees the problems, but is too skeptical

Qualities as a Parent

21	Exerts sound leadership, but tends to over-dominate	Makes a good parent, but is lax on discipline	Makes home fun, but keeps it in a frenzied manner	Keeps home in good order, but may be too meticulous
22	Establishes goals, but is often too busy for family	Takes time for the children, but doesn't organize the home	Turns disaster into humor, but is disorganized	Sets high standards, but often plays the martyr
23	Motivates family to action, but is impatient with poor performance	Can take the good with the bad, but takes life too easily	Is the circus master, but doesn't listen to the whole story and often acts hastily	Wants everything done right, but sulks over disagreements
24	Organizes household, but won't let children relax	Doesn't get upset easily, but is bored by arguments	Is liked by children's friends, but forgets children's appointments	Sacrifices own needs for others, but puts guilt on children
25	Knows the right answer, but gives answers too quickly	Is not in a hurry, but tries to avoid responsibilities	Settles down family tension, but doesn't see the signs of boredom in others	Encourages scholarship and talent, but puts goals beyond reach
26	Delegates responsibilities to children, but may send them into depression	Has a willingness to help family members, but needs to be motivated	Turns mistakes into party game, but often exaggerates	Picks up after children, but may discourage them

Qualities as a Friend

27	Has little need for friends, but is possessive of friends and mate	Easy to get along with, but dampens enthusiasm	Makes friends easily, but looks for credit	Makes friends cautiously, but is suspicious of people

Nos.	CHOLERIC	PHLEGMATIC	SANGUINE	MELANCHOLY
28	Will work for group activity, but dominates others	Pleasant and enjoyable, but not exciting	Doesn't hold grudges, but interrupts and doesn't listen	Content to stay in the background, but is withdrawn and remote
29	Will lead and organize, but decides for others	Inoffensive, but sarcastic and teasing	Thrives on compliments, but wants to be popular	Deep concern for other people, but is antagonistic and vengeful
30	Loves to argue and to prove that s/he is right, but can't say, "I'm sorry"	Good listener, but stays uninvolved	Talks in colorful extremes, but repeats stories	Accepts complaints, but dislikes opponents
31	Excels in emergencies, but tends to use people	Has compassion and concern, but judges people	Apologizes quickly, but is fickle and forgetful	Can solve other's problems, but holds back affection
32	Is always right, but unpopular	Dry sense of humor, but keeps his/her mouth shut	Prevents dull moments, but dominates conversations	Faithful and devoted, but unforgiving

Each person does not belong to just one temperament, but rather is a combination of a few. To draw your own temperament profile, see Table 4-2. In Table 4-2, entries in italics describe the author. Using a marker, highlight the words that describe you best. This table was compiled by Fred Littauer, and is organized in such a way that the words in each line start with the same letter. Each line, therefore, does not describe one quality, but may reflect different qualities, and some of the same qualities are described in different words. For example, although the words "animated" and "lively" are synonymous, they are used in different lines as characteristics of the Sanguine temperament. "Animated" is defined as lively, vigorous, having life; "lively" is defined as full of life, vigorous, energetic.

Personality characteristics such as calm, imaginative, and assertive-- which belong to long-living people and centenarians--are not used in this table. Nevertheless, I preserved the original form of this table, but reshuffled the rows putting them in alphabetical order and making some minor corrections. For instance, because the word "reluctant" was used twice, I substituted its synonym "disinclined" (reluctant = unwilling or disinclined; disinclined = unwilling or reluctant) to avoid repetition.

Table 4-2. Features for Evaluation of a Person's Temperament

Nos.	CHOLERIC	PHLEGMATIC	SANGUINE	MELANCHOLY
		Strengths		
1	*Adventurous*	*Adaptable*	Animated	Analytical
2	Bold	Balanced	Bouncy	*Behaved*
3	Chief	*Contented*	Cute	Chart-maker
4	Competitive	*Controlled*	Convincing	*Considerate*
5	Confident	Consistent	Cheerful	*Cultured*
6	Daring	Diplomatic	Delightful	Detailed
7	Decisive	Dry humor	Demonstrative	Deep
8	Forceful	*Friendly*	Funny	Faithful
9	*Independent*	Inoffensive	Inspiring	Idealistic
10	Leader	*Listener*	Lively	Loyal
11	Mover	Mediator	*Mixes easily*	Musical
12	Outspoken	*Obliging*	*Optimistic*	Orderly
13	Persuasive	*Peaceful*	Playful	*Persistent*
14	Positive	*Patient*	Promoter	Planner
15	Productive	*Permissive*	Popular	Perfectionist
16	Resourceful	*Reserved*	Refreshing	*Respectful*
17	*Self-reliant*	Satisfied	*Spirited*	Sensitive
18	Strong-willed	Submissive	Sociable	Self-sacrificing
19	Sure	Shy	*Spontaneous*	Scheduled
20	Tenacious	*Tolerant*	Talker	Thoughtful
		Weaknesses		
21	Argumentative	Aimless	Angered easily	Alienated
22	Bossy	Blank	Brassy	*Bashful*
23	Crafty	*Compromising*	*Changeable*	Critical
24	Domineering	*Doubtful*	*Disorganized*	Depressed
25	Frank	*Fearful*	*Forgetful*	Fussy
26	Headstrong	*Hesitant*	Haphazard	Hard to please
27	*Impatient*	*Indecisive*	Interrupts	*Insecure*
28	Intolerant	*Indifferent*	*Inconsistent*	*Introvert*
29	Lord over others	Lazy	Loud	*Loner*
30	Manipulative	Mumbles	Messy	Moody
31	Nervy	*Nonchalant*	Naive	Negative attitude
32	Proud	*Plain*	*Permissive*	Pessimistic
33	Rash	*Reluctant*	Restless	Revengeful
34	Resistant	*Disinclined*	Repetitious	Resentful
35	Short-tempered	Sluggish	*Scatterbrained*	Suspicious
36	Stubborn	*Slow*	Show-off	Skeptical
37	Tactless	Timid	Talkative	Too sensitive

Nos.	CHOLERIC	PHLEGMATIC	SANGUINE	MELANCHOLY
38	Unaffectionate	Uninvolved	*Unpredictable*	Unpopular
39	Unsympathetic	Unenthusiastic	Undisciplined	*Unforgiving*
40	Workaholic	*Worrier*	Wants credit	Withdrawn
	Strengths Totals: 3	11	3	6
	Weakness Totals: 1	12	7	5
	Combined Totals: 4	23	10	11

The author of this temperament table advises that you choose one word in each row that is most applicable. In assessing my own temperament type, there were rows in which all four words were not applicable to me, and other rows had two or even three words that seemed to fit. This is why I think it is better to highlight the appropriate words, regardless of how many are in a single row. Then assign the total combined score for all four temperaments to equal 100 percent. Finally, calculate the percentage of each temperament. Figure 4-1 shows a temperament profile after the percentages had been plotted and graphed.

Another example of the temperament assessment is the case of Spiros Antonopoulos (March 10, 1897 - November 19, 1996), who lived to the age of ninety-nine years and eight months. He was the father of my American friend, forty-seven-year-old Bostonian Demetrios Antonopoulos; we will analyze his temperament profile as well. According to Demetrios' assessment, his father's scores were as follows:

	Choleric	Phlegmatic	Sanguine	Melancholy
Strength:	16	0	1	5
Weakness:	12	1	5	2
Totals:	28	1	6	7

The combined total score is 42 and the percentage of each temperament in Spiros Antonopoulos is 67 percent Choleric, 17 percent Melancholic, 14 percent Sanguine, and 2 percent Phlegmatic. These figures show that almost 100-year-old Spiros was mostly Choleric, much less Melancholic and Sanguine, with a tiny portion of Phlegmatic temperament within him.

The temperament of both his son Demetrios and the author (the author's descriptions are in italic in Table 4-2) were also evaluated. All three temperament profiles are shown in Figure 4-1 in graphical format.

As shown in this figure, the profile of the long-living Spiros is much different from that of his son, Demetrios. However, the profiles of Demetrios and the author are quite close. Perhaps this is one of the reasons why we became friends.

Here we have a person who lived to nearly 100 years of age, with a Choleric temperament. What are the temperaments of other long-living people and centenarians? Studies such as the Bonn Longitudinal Study of 1932, the Georgia Centenarian Study in 1991, and others revealed that qualities such as being easy-going, relaxed, friendly, contented, peaceful, selfish, and even worried--associated with the Phlegmatic temperament--promote longevity.

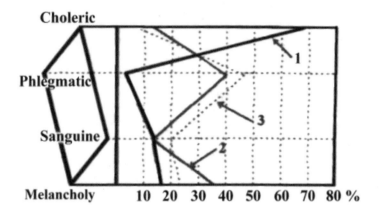

Figure 4-1. The Temperament Profile

1. Spiros Antonopoulos, 99.7

2. Demetrios Antonopoulos, 47

3. Author, 60

Aggressive, adventurous, repressive, and stubborn people of the Choleric temperament tend to live a less-than-average life span; however, other qualities of this temperament--such as forcefulness, dominance, and self-confidence--are traits found to increase longevity. The Choleric temperament, therefore, has both self-destructive and life-supportive features. In the case of Spiros Antonopoulos, the life-shortening qualities such as adventurousness, competitiveness, short-temperedness, and stubbornness were offset by the longevity-promoting features, such as forcefulness, independence, self-reliance, dominance, and a strong will. Due to the influence of self-destructive qualities, his life was shortened to nearly 100 years. Without those features, he probably could have become one of the champions of longevity.

Centenarians are also of the cheerful, inspiring, optimistic, and lively Sanguine type. They often have a "life-of-the-party" attitude. For example, 102-year-old Anselmo Medina, of Denver, Colorado, is called "Mr. Party" by his family members. He never misses a birthday, wedding, or anniversary, reported *Newsweek* in the August 11, 1997, issue.

Centenarians also possess the qualities of Melancholic people who often are faithful and suspicious, but their resentful and unforgiving qualities harm their health and decrease their longevity.

5

BLOOD TYPES

The next variable that greatly adds to the uniqueness of our biochemical individuality is blood type. Blood type is an individual's genetic blueprint that determines his/her biochemistry and susceptibility to disease and environmental conditions, and also dictates diet and lifestyle choices. Not only are we different because of our blood type, but also it directly affects our health and longevity. "Your blood type is the key that unlocks the door to the mysteries of health, disease, longevity, physical vitality, and emotional strength. Your blood type determines your susceptibility to illnesses, which foods you should eat, and how you should exercise," according to Dr. Peter J. D'Adamo in his landmark book, *Eat Right for 4 Your Type*. His book is based on forty years of research by the author and his father. They successfully applied their blood-type approach to thousands of patients.

All people are divided by their blood qualities into four types: O, A, B, and AB. "The blood type reflects the body's internal chemistry and determines the way the body absorbs nutrients. What foods you absorb well and how your body handles stress differ with each blood type," further states Dr. D'Adamo. Thus, knowing one's blood type, which is always important to know in case of an emergency, has one more area of application. Of all systems of the body, the most influenced by different blood types are the digestive and immune systems, says Dr. D'Adamo. Blood type is associated not only with physiological differences, but also with personality variations and the ability to cope with stress. Even the speed of aging can be changed with proper adjustment of diet for blood type.

A primary study of blood types began in 1918 when Ludwik Hirszfeld and his wife, both physicians, conducted blood-group tests of many races and nationalities. Since that time, blood banks have accumulated data on blood types of more than twenty million individuals worldwide. The combined findings show that blood type O is the most common in the Western world, accounting for 50 percent in the United States and 46 percent in England; it decreases in the Eastern world to 31 percent in India and Japan. The next most common blood type is A, which is not ruled by the West-East orientation. It is most prevalent in Japan at 46 percent, 43 percent in England, and 40 percent in the United States; it is the least prevalent in India at 19 percent. Blood type B is as low as 7 percent in the United States and 8 percent in England, increases to 19 percent in Japan, and soars to 41 percent in India. Blood type AB, which has the lowest prevalence in the world, displays a trend similar to Blood type B; that is, merely 2 percent in the United States, 3 percent in England, 4 percent in Japan, and significantly higher with 8 percent in India. Other nations fall between these extremes.

The application of blood types was greatly enlarged due to the recent landmark research of Steven M. Weissberg, M.D., and Joseph Christiano, A.P.P.T. (graduate of The Academy of Professional Personal Trainers). They found a distinct connection between blood types and life span, as well as work and sexual compatibility of individuals. In their book, *The Answer Is in Your Blood Type,* based on a survey of 5,114 subjects both living and deceased, they state that the average age of death of people with Blood type A in the United States is only 61.6 years. Living significantly longer--by a full quarter of a century--are people with Blood type O, who achieve an average age of 86.7 years. People with Blood type AB survive to 69.5 years and with Blood type B to 78.2 years. According to the mortality statistics shown in their book, the two life extinguishers for type A and AB are cancer and heart disease. The authors attribute the vast difference in the age at death to diet in this country, where the meat that type As and ABs do not tolerate well is a staple food. People with Blood type O and B, with their strong stomach acid, digest meat much easier.

At the crux of Dr. D'Adamo's theory are lectins, food proteins with agglutinating properties that affect the blood. Lectins perform different functions in our bodies and have both positive and negative effects. The lectins on the surface of our liver and gallbladder bile ducts contain the passing bacteria and viruses and are, therefore, beneficial for our bodies. However, some food lectins escape digestion in the stomach and may stick to the lining of the intestinal tract causing inflammation, or may enter the bloodstream, where they react with red and white cells, agglutinating them. Lectins are found in virtually all foods and are especially abundant in meat, dairy products, grains, vegetables, legumes, and seafood.

Dr. D'Adamo believes that certain lectins are compatible or incompatible with different blood types. For example, the lectins from lima beans are incompatible with Blood Type A, but do not do any harm to Blood Type B. However, buckwheat lectins agglutinate cells of Blood Type B, but the cells of Blood Type A are not affected. The lectins of dairy products are incompatible with all blood types, except for the newest Blood type, AB, which can tolerate dairy foods. Therefore, to avoid the harmful effects of lectins, one must eat as appropriate for his/her blood type, according to Dr. D'Adamo.

Lectins are also responsible for the aging process due to their agglutinating damage to kidneys and brain cells. Kidney failure and deterioration of brain function are common conditions in elderly people. Cellular damage in these organs can be reduced by decreasing the intake of lectins from food.

The major difference between Blood types O and A is that Os have high stomach-acid content (i.e., their digestive juices are high in acidity), and As have low stomach-acid content (i.e., their digestive juices lack acidity). This is because the ancestors of Type O were hunters and were used to high animal protein and low-carbohydrate foods. Type As, however, descended from agrarian ancestors who lived mostly on high-carbohydrate, low animal protein foods. Type Bs, whose ancestors descended from steppe dwellers, evolved relatively recently (i.e., about twelve thousand years ago); they resemble Type Os in their ability to digest meat. Type ABs are the newest (since about two thousand years ago), and they resemble both Blood Types A and B, having inherited their genes. Type ABs also lack stomach acid similar to Type As, but to a lesser degree; they can digest meat a little better than Type As. In general, people of both Blood types B and AB, being the most recent in existence, are considered to have the most tolerant, evolved digestive systems.

The major physiological and psychological characteristics and dietary and lifestyle recommendations for people with the four blood types, as defined by D'Adamo, Weissberg, and Christiano, are listed in Table 5-1.

In his book, Dr. D'Adamo makes general recommendations (listed in Table 5-1) and specifies foods relative to each blood type (called the Blood Type Diet). "I've tested virtually all common foods for blood-type reactions, using both clinical and laboratory methods," states Dr. D'Adamo. He divided foods into three groups: highly beneficial, neutral, and foods to avoid. The food charts that I compiled from his book are shown in Appendix A. To list the foods according to the Food Pyramid, I arranged them in six categories and fourteen subcategories. I further modified the chart by subdividing each group into "yes" or "no" subgroups according to my Vata Dosha type (described in detail in the Ayurvedic Dosha chapter). Further modification involved foods listed according to their Yin-Yang properties as described in the Yin-Yang Principle chapter. The modified table is in Appendix B.

Table 5-1. Characteristics and Diets of the Four Blood Types

Type O	Type A	Type B	Type AB
Characteristics			
Meat eater	Vegetarian	Balanced, dairy eater	Composite of A and B
Robust digestive tract, efficient metabolism. Strong immune system, but can attack itself, becoming overactive	Sensitive digestive tract, vulnerable immune system, open to microbial invasion	Tolerant digestive tract, strong immune system, flexible adaptation to a new diet and environment	Sensitive digestive system, overly tolerant immune system, but the tendency for over-tolerance
Poor tolerance to new diet and environment	Good adaptation to settled diet and environment	Most flexible adaptation to new diet and environment	Chameleon's response to new diet and environment
Responds best to stress with intense physical activity	Inherently high-strung and less emotionally hardy. Responds best to stress with calming action	Responds best to stress with creativity	Responds best to stress spiritually, with physical verve and creative energy
Prefers physically vigorous sex	Prefers slow and easy sex	Prefers physically moderate sex	Prefers slow and easy sex
Ulcers, blood-clotting disorders, arthritis, hypothyroidism, allergies	Heart disease, cancer, anemia, liver and gallbladder disorders, Type I diabetes (reaps what he sows)	Auto-immune disorders, multiple sclerosis, chronic fatigue syndrome, Type I diabetes	Heart disease, cancer, anemia
Diet and Lifestyle			
High-protein, low-carbohydrate diet: meat, fish, vegetables, fruit. Restrict grains, legumes, beans	Vegetarian diet (high carbohydrate, low fat): grains, legumes, beans, vegetables, tofu, seafood, fruit	Varied diet: meat (no chicken), dairy, grains, legumes, beans, vegetables, fruit	Mixed moderate diet: meat, dairy, grains, legumes, beans, vegetables, fruit, tofu, seafood
Supplements: vitamins B and K, calcium, iodine, licorice, kelp	Supplements: vitamins B-12, C, and E; folic acid, hawthorn, echinacea, quercitin, milk thistle	Supplements: magnesium, licorice, ginkgo, lecithin	Supplements: vitamin C, hawthorn, valerian, echinacea, quercitin, milk thistle
Exercise – vigorous: aerobics, running, contact sports, martial arts	Exercise – calming, centering: golf, Tai chi, yoga, relaxation techniques	Exercise – moderate physical, with mental balance: swimming, tennis, cycling, hiking, walking	Exercise – calming, centering combined with moderate physical: yoga, Tai chi, tennis, cycling, hiking
Weight loss plan: restrict wheat, corn, beans, cruciferous vegetables; add red meat, salt, liver, seafood, kale, spinach, broccoli, kelp	Weight loss plan: restrict wheat, meat, dairy, kidney and lima beans; add soy foods, vegetables, olive oil, pineapple, green tea	Weight loss plan: restrict wheat, corn, buckwheat, lentils, peanuts, sesame seeds; add eggs, salt, venison, liver, licorice, tea	Weight loss plan: restrict red meat, corn, buckwheat, seeds, kidney and lima beans; add seafood, tofu, kelp, dairy, greens, pineapple

From Dr. D'Adamo's book, I learned that with my own Blood Type A, I am susceptible to heart disease, cancer, liver and gallbladder disorders, Type I diabetes, and anemia. Consequently, I tried to adjust my diet to Dr. D'Adamo's recommendations. I do not, however, follow the Blood Type Diet plan to the letter because of my personal lifestyle history, my dietary experience, and other considerations of what is good and bad for me.

I grew up in Russia, where white wheat bread and potatoes were the traditional staple foods in our diet. A traditional salad of raw tomatoes, cucumber, and onion was often served in the summer and autumn. The Russian dish "bortsch," made of beets, cabbage, tomatoes, potatoes, and meat, was frequently eaten in my family. The latter three vegetables and wheat are foods to avoid for a person with Blood Type A. It was easy for me to give up cabbage because it produces gas and tomatoes because of their high purines, but I still eat potatoes because they are very rich in potassium. Brazil nuts are also a food I should avoid. However, Brazil nuts contain a large amount of selenium, a mineral that is very necessary for our bodies. Therefore, I eat one or two Brazil nuts a day and believe that the possible harm from them is offset by their nutritional value.

Further modification in my diet occurred when I learned that the average life span of a person with blood type A is sixty-two years; I am now approaching that age. I heeded the warning of Weissberg and Christiano on the absolute necessity for type As to seriously follow a Blood-type diet. Comparing D'Adamo's and Weissberg's dietary recommendations, I decided to eat more raw food (in compliance with my Blood type A) and restrict protein intake (contrary to Weissberg's and Christiano's advice to eat more protein than carbohydrates). I understood that Blood Type As are so vulnerable to life-threatening diseases and so endangered that only by exercising an *optimal* nutrition and *proper* lifestyle can they extend their life.

Optimal nutrition implies an intake of all necessary nutrients in the amounts that are efficiently metabolized and used for tissue repair and energy. Protein is an inefficient energy source and is necessary only in limited amounts for tissue repair. The most harmful foods for people with Blood type A are protein sources such as meat and dairy products; therefore, a small quantity of plant protein is their best choice. More information on the optimal nutrition is in the chapter entitled "Food Intake Control."

Blood-type differences have attracted public attention for many decades in Japan. Rather than physiological differences, blood types were always linked to personality types and behavioral traits. The leading researcher of the blood-type - personality connection, Toshinaka Nomi, together with Alexander Besher, published a book entitled, *You Are Your Blood Type*. It became a bestseller and sold six million copies. The personality profiles described in that book are according to blood type, as are the lifestyle recommendations, such as marriage advice and what a kind of profession to choose.

In 1996, after Dr. D'Adamo's book appeared in the United States, other related human-health and well-being topics such as diet, disease, aging, and longevity drew the attention of Japanese researchers. Dr. D'Adamo's book received so much publicity in Japan that surveys in hospitals were conducted in order to find the correlation between blood type and disease.

The Japanese people demonstrate how they can handle unfavorable blood chemistry with the proper diet. Although Blood type A prevails (46 percent of the population), the Japanese have the longest life expectancy for females of 83.6 years, and the second longest (after Luxemburg) life expectancy for males of 77.0 years. The secret of their longevity is in the traditional diet, which is consistent with their blood type, with staple foods such as rice, tofu and miso (bean curd), fish, seaweed, and green tea.

Observation of the Japanese people shows that many of their centenarians have Blood type B, although some Blood type Os and As also are among them. This was the conclusion of Koasa, a Japanese comedian who initiated and ran for three years a TV program about centenarians, and who met 157 people aged 100 and older. It is interesting to note that Blood type Bs (19 percent of the population) prevail in this centenarian group over Blood type Os (31 percent of the population), which have the longest life span in the United States. Either this group, which accounts for about 2 percent of more than ten thousand Japanese centenarians, is not representative or the trend in Japan is different than that in the United States. Further studies on centenarians will perhaps cast more light upon the Blood type–longevity connection.

While biochemical reactions of the blood with food are very evident, I want to describe a case where a person seemingly breaks the eating rules set by Dr. D'Adamo and nevertheless stays in good health.

> His name is Kazue Takagi, 82, and he is the father of my Japanese company co-worker. The most striking fact about Takagi-san is that thirty years ago, he had stomach cancer and his stomach was completely removed. He changed his lifestyle after surgery and adopted a "my pace" attitude, to which he attributes his relatively good health.

> Takagi-san wakes up at 4:30 each morning and does morning exercises. He steps barefooted on bamboo and practices an imitation of a golf stroke. At 5:30, he has his breakfast: a slice of white-bread toast with melted cheese, a glass of cold milk or instant coffee with skim milk and white or brown sugar. Each morning he also eats one umeboshi--a pickled plum with boiled water,

one Ca-biscuit, and one piece of banana. At 6:45, he goes to work, walking 1.5 kilometers to the station. He works until noon and then goes for lunch outside like any other salaried worker. He eats ramen (a wheat-noodle soup), tempura (seafood and vegetables fried in oil), and soba (wheat noodles) with rice and miso soup. He returns home at about 6 p.m. and takes a Japanese bath. He then has his dinner: natto (fermented beans), a bowl of rice, one raw egg, one Ca-biscuit, and one piece of banana. He does not eat much meat or fish. Unlike other Japanese, Takagi-san does not like sushi or sashimi (i.e., raw fish on a rice ball).

The point is that Takagi-san has Blood Type A, and the milk, banana, and wheat are foods that he should avoid. Furthermore, his diet, with outside lunches that include foods deep-fried in oil, does not seem to be healthy. Nevertheless, he has survived more than thirty years without a stomach, and he is healthy and still working at the age of eighty-two. Perhaps his "my pace" attitude offsets all his dietary downfalls.

I mentioned previously that many Japanese centenarians have Blood Type B. At this point, I want to note that sweet potatoes, which in China are regarded as a longevity vegetable, are also common in Japan. It is a highly beneficial food for Type Bs and it complies with the Blood Type Diet.

Foods such as corn, pumpkin, radish (daikon in Japan), tempeh, and tofu (the plant source of all essential amino acids) are foods to avoid for people with Blood type B. It is impossible to imagine the traditional diet in either China or Japan without those foods. The question is, therefore, whether the Blood Type Diet works for all people. My view is that it is better if everyone tries this diet and determines its workability for him/herself. It is important that any changes in one's current diet, in terms of both including new kinds of food and excluding others, be made gradually, which avoids physiological stress and harm to the body, especially in the elderly.

A one-axis scale, with Blood Types O and AB of three centenarians and the author's Type A, is shown in Figure 5-1.

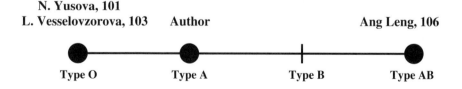

Figure 5-1. Blood Type Scale

Among the centenarians that I have met, Ang Leng (who died in 1998 at the age of 106) was Type AB, and both Lydia Vesselovzorova (who died in April 2000 at the age of 103) and Nataliya Yusova (who died in January 2000 at the age of 101) were Type O.

Although the extensive research of Dr. Peter J. D'Adamo, his father Dr. James D'Adamo, and Dr. Steven M. Weissberg is marked with reliability and credibility of modern science, the mainstream medical establishment has not yet recognized the importance of the Blood-type approach to people's health. Only recently has it appeared on the TV health programs on a par with high-protein and fat-burning diets. In studies of American centenarians, the Blood-type survey has not been incorporated thus far. Unfortunately, books or articles about centenarians do not contain data on Blood type. The medical institutions that sponsor longitudinal studies will probably realize the necessity to survey the Blood-type connection in the near future.

Many American centenarians call themselves "meat and potatoes" people, although potatoes are to be avoided for both Blood types O and A (the majority of the U.S. population).

A prime example is John J. Beatty (profiled on page 149) from Woburn, Massachusetts, who lived to 100, and who had Blood Type O. Among his dietary preferences were beef (highly beneficial for his blood type), potatoes, cream, milk, coffee, and ice cream (foods to avoid for his blood type). Because he achieved the one-century mark, he seemed to be correct about his diet; his good genes and favorable blood chemistry also probably helped him to reach this age.

Spiros Antonopoulos, from Lorain, Ohio, is another centenarian (profiled on page 154) who was Blood type O and who ate potatoes with his veal, chicken, and turkey. He even drank coffee with a half and half dairy product (foods to avoid for his Blood type) for breakfast, but he gave up coffee after his angina attack at the age of sixty-eight. He definitely benefited from the healthy eating habits that he adopted at that time, which allowed him to live another thirty-two years.

Two of the women centenarians that I met, Lydia Vesselovzorova (who lived to 103) and Nataliya Yusova (who lived to 101) both had Blood type O, which--combined with their good heredity--brought them over the century mark. However, the third centenarian, Madam Ang Leng (who lived to 106) had Blood type AB, which is very surprising because an ABs' average life span is seventy years (in the United States). Although she was Chinese and lived in Singapore, it does not help to understand the secret of her extraordinary longevity. Her case only confirms the fact that longevity is mysterious and locked under "seven seals," with which medical science has to deal.

Among the many factors affecting longevity, Blood type seems to be the most influential, which is why I used it as the dominant factor to determine the personalized diet. Other factors, including metabolic type, Ayurvedic Dosha type, Yin-Yang type, ancestral heritage, and--to a lesser degree--the Five Elements type and horoscope type, are used as modifying factors, and are discussed in detail in the following chapters of this part.

6

METABOLIC TYPES

Centenarians of any nation, due to the mere fact that they have lived extraordinarily long lives, prove one important longevity rule: Eat right. Eating right has recently been associated with blood type and metabolic type. As with anyone else, centenarians belong to different metabolic and blood types. Nevertheless, they managed to nourish their bodies in the right way for their type, thereby enhancing the benefits of their good heredity in achieving a ripe old age.

Metabolism is the conversion of food into energy, which the body needs for running all of its processes and for sustaining life itself. The water, air, and light that we take in are also metabolized. Oxidation activity (i.e., metabolic rate) is either fast or slow according to our unique metabolism. Therefore, metabolic type is one of the important characteristics of a person's biochemical individuality.

How many metabolic types are found among people? The number ranges from two (slow oxidizer and fast oxidizer, as introduced by Dr. George Watson) to ten types (from fast-oxidizing meat-eaters to slow-oxidizing vegetarians, as identified by Dr. William D. Kelly). The most commonly used theory among researchers, however, is that there are three metabolic types: slow, fast, and mixed.

The diet must be different for each type. Slow oxidizers are advised to eat low-protein, low-fat, and high-carbohydrate food, as recommended in the diets proposed by the U.S. Government and Dr. Dean Ornish. The best diet for fast oxidizers includes low-carbohydrate, high-protein, and high-fat foods, such as recommended in the Atkins' diet. Mixed oxidizers do better with relatively equal amounts of protein, carbohydrates, and fat, such as cited in the Zone Diet.

Probably the most comprehensive analysis of metabolic types was conducted by William L. Wolcott of Winthrop, Washington, in his recently published book *Metabolic Typing Diet*. According to Wolcott, thousands of life-supporting processes and biochemical reactions of bodily metabolism take place under the direction of Fundamental Homeostatic Controls. Good health is only possible through these controls, which provide continuous homeostatic balance, adaptation to environmental changes, and metabolic efficiency.

Wolcott introduced the principle of metabolic dominance, which states that each individual, depending on his/her constitution, has a ruling, or dominant, system that governs bodily reactions to specific foods. Gabriel Cousens, M.D., in his book *Conscious Eating* states that the oxidative system is dominant in 60 percent of the population and the autonomic nervous system in 40 percent. Different researchers emphasize one or another fundamental control in evaluating metabolic type.

In his assessment of metabolic types, Wolcott employs both the oxidative and autonomic nervous systems. He identified three basic metabolic types: Protein Type, Carbo Type, and Mixed Type. The Protein Type needs to eat more proteins (at every meal and heavier in kind), as well as a moderate amount of carbohydrates; whereas, the Carbo Type usually thrives on a low-protein, low-fat diet and needs a larger amount of carbohydrates. Furthermore, each individual may fine-tune his/her diet to fit specific needs as influenced by age, gender, stress level, daily activities, exercise, seasonal and climate changes, and so on.

The oxidative system is the central part of Ann Louise Gittleman's, M.S., assessment of metabolic type. In her book *Your Body Knows Best,* she identifies two types of people who do not burn energy efficiently and thus have weight problems: slow burners and fast burners. The metabolism of each specific type can be slowed or hastened with the appropriate foods. For slow burners, she suggests a diet "that is lighter on fatty foods and heavier on both complex (not processed) carbohydrates and protein." For fast burners, "a diet that has a higher fat and protein content" is advised. The metabolism of some people is neither fast nor slow: they burn food for energy at just the right speed. They are often slim and healthy, and seldom have weight-gain problems.

Taking the oxidative system as a dominant factor, Gittleman uses two more modifying factors: ancestral heritage and blood type. Knowing about and eating the food our ancestors ate will prevent us from missing out on the specific nutrients that gave them good health and fitness.

Similarly, Dr. Cousens regards the oxidative system as the most influential among the homeostatic controls. He defines slow and fast oxidizers based on questionnaires that he developed. For fast oxidizers, he recommends a diet composed of 50 to 55 percent protein, 30 to 35 percent carbohydrates, and 20 to 25 percent fat. For slow oxidizers, the proportions of these nutrients would be 30/55/15, and for mixed oxidizers (who score between the two extremes), it would be 40/40/20. Dr. Cousens stresses that giving our body the correct amounts of macro- and micronutrients specific to each type allows us to enter our personal "zone" (i.e., the homeostatic state in which the food we eat is converted into the maximum amount of energy).

The endocrine system is at the core of metabolic typing proposed by Henry Harrower, M.D., Henry Bieler, M.D., and Elliot D. Abravanel, M.D. They found that certain foods stimulate the endocrine glands, including the pituitary, thyroid, adrenals, and gonads. One of these glands is usually dominant and, if overstimulated, becomes responsible for excess body weight. Dr. Abravanel and Elizabeth A. King, in their book *Dr.Abravanel's Body Type Program for Health, Fitness, and Nutrition,* define three metabolic types in men: adrenal, pituitary, and thyroid; and four in women: the same three plus gonadal. Dr. Abravanel provides a personalized plan for each type. For example, a high-protein, low-carbohydrate diet suits a thyroid type, but is wrong for a gonadal type, which does better on a low-protein, high-carbohydrate diet.

Kenneth Baum, a sports performance expert at the Biodynamics Institute in San Capistrano, California, also proposed personalized diet plans in his book, *Metabolize!: The Personalized Program for Weight Loss.* He identifies five metabolic types (i.e., Types A through E). Type A has slow metabolism, is governed by the pituitary gland, and requires a high-carbohydrate diet with plenty of vegetables, poultry, and fish. The opposite is true for Type E, which has fast metabolism with a body chemistry dominated by the hormone adrenaline, which is produced by both the adrenal and thyroid glands. They must eat a diet rich in protein with some fat, but low in carbohydrates. Types B, C, and D are transitional between A and E, with Type C being the most balanced of the five. A Type C's diet is composed of one-half carbohydrates, one-third of protein, and the rest of fat.

Define your own metabolic type using the questionnaire in Table 6-1 that I compiled based on these works. Highlight the characteristics that fit you most closely and count the total score under each column. With any particular entry, if you fall between fast and slow metabolism, highlight both. In choosing the answers, keep in mind that you are assessing your current actual condition, not a past or desired one.

Table 6-1. Self-Assessment of a Person's Metabolic Type

Nos	Fast Metabolism	Slow Metabolism
	Body build, appearance, and physiological functions	
1	Broad shoulders, full-chest, and good strength	Pear-shaped, curvy, with weaker upper body or small and very slim
2	Ears are pink or red, darker than the skin of the face	Ears are pale, lighter than the skin of the face
3	Eyes are very moist, even tears appear	Eyes are dry
4	Eyes are often itching, even though there is no cold or allergy	Eyes are rarely itching, if there is cold or allergy
5	Face color is pink, ruddy, flushed	Face color is pale, sallow
6	Face complexion is bright, shiny, radiant	Face complexion is pasty, chalky, dull
7	Nose often is too moist, even tends to run	Nose often is too dry
8	Pupil's diameter is equal to or smaller than the width of the iris ring around it	Pupil's diameter is larger than the width of the iris ring around it
9	Fingernails are thin, even weak and brittle, can be easily bent over	Fingernails are thick, strong, and hard
10	Skin, more often in the winter, especially on fingertips and heels, cracks for no reason	Skin on fingertips and heels, even in the winter, never cracks
11	Skin itches often, especially the scalp, arms, or calves	Skin itches rarely, even the scalp, arms, and calves
12	Goosebumps, even on the arms and legs, rarely appear	Goosebumps, especially on the arms and legs, appear easily and often
13	Dandruff on the scalp often forms, especially after eating animal fats	Dandruff on the scalp never forms, even after eating animal fats
14	Weight is usually gained in the upper body	Weight is usually gained in the belly
15	Saliva in the mouth is too much in quantity, with a tendency for drooling	Saliva in the mouth is too little in quantity, often dry mouth
16	Dislikes the heat, does best in cool or cold weather	Often feels cold, does best in warm or hot weather
17	Coughs easily and often, especially soon after eating or at night, even when not sick	Does not cough, unless when sick
18	Strong reaction to insect bites or stings, including swelling, pain, itching, bruising, redness, and takes long time to go away	Weak or mild reaction to insect bites or stings, and goes away quickly
19	Easily and often gags	Rarely or never gags
20	Brief sneezing attacks, especially after eating, not associated with colds or allergies	Almost never sneezes, unless having cold or allergies
	Psychological characteristics and behavioral traits	
21	Hard-driving, hyperactive, and ambitious personality	Laid back, even-tempered, and easy-going personality
22	Often is impatient, irritable, anxious, in a state of nervousness, excitability	Often experiences depression, apathy, fatigue, exhaustion
23	Deals with many things at once	Approaches problems one at a time
24	Extroverted, socializes easily with people, loves company	Introverted, feels awkward at social gatherings, prefers being alone

Nos	Fast Metabolism	Slow Metabolism
25	Loves to eat; food is a big or central part of life	Rarely thinks about food; eats more because has to than because wants to
26	Eating sweets before bed interferes with sleep or even causes insomnia	Eating sweets before bed does not interfere with sleep or cause insomnia
27	Eating heavy food like meat, fowl, and cheese improves sleep	Eating heavy food like meat, fowl, and cheese disrupts or worsens sleep
28	Has insomnia caused by the need to eat something before going to bed or after waking up in the middle of the night	Rarely or never experiences that kind of insomnia
29	Skipping meals causes negative symptoms like feeling worse, getting irritable, jittery, weak, tired, with a lack of energy	Skipping meals does not bother much, can easily forget to eat
30	Often wants to snack between meals (typically three meals a day)	Rarely or never wants or needs snacks
Dietary preferences and food reactions		
31	Strong appetite, out of control	Poor appetite, under control
32	Does not feel thirsty, unless after eating salty foods	Gets thirsty easily and often, even if salty foods were not eaten
33	It is hard to fast on juice or water	It is easy to go a long time without food, even fast
34	Loves salty foods, even craves them	Foods salted only lightly are best
35	Loves sweet foods, even craves them	Sweet foods seem too sweet, eating them may even throw out of balance
36	Likes sour foods such as pickles, sauerkraut, lemons, yogurt, even craves some of them	Generally does not care for sour foods
37	Going four hours without food results in a jittery or weak feeling	Can easily go more than four hours without food
38	A high-protein meal gives a sense of increased energy and well-being	A high-protein meal results in a sleepy or lethargic feeling
39	A high-carbohydrate meal with fruits, vegetables, pastry, or candy results in feeling worse and does not satisfy	A high-carbohydrate meal with fruits, vegetables, pastry, or candy satisfies and gives sustained energy
40	Prefers fatty foods over sweets	Has aversions to fatty foods
41	Drinking coffee results in a jittery, nervous, hyper, nauseated, and shaky feeling	A cup of coffee starts the morning off just right
42	Feels good or better after eating red meat	Eating red meat decreases energy and well-being
43	Gaining weight is due to eating many carbo-hydrates like bread, pasta, fruits, and vegetables	Eating meats and fatty foods leads to weight gain
44	Eating sweet foods gives a quick lift followed by a sudden drop of energy	Eating sweet foods gives a feeling of sustained well-being and lasting energy
45	Fruit juice between meals can make light-headed, jittery, shaky, and hungry soon after	Fruit juice between meals satisfies and nourishes well until next meal
	Total score:	Total score:

After adding the two totals, subtract the lower score from the higher one; then divide the result by the number of questions answered and multiply by 100 percent. If the result was less than 33 percent, your metabolism is moderate, if you came up with more, it is either fast or slow, depending on which score was higher. For example, my score in the "fast" column is 24; in the "slow" column it is 37. Therefore, it yields: $(37-24)/45 \times 100\% = 29\%$. My metabolism is moderate, bordering on slow. It corresponds with the Mixed Type of Wolcott's metabolic typing.

This brief review of metabolic-type approaches and diets shows that a customized nutritional plan has distinctive advantages over one-dimensional diets and continues to gain popularity. It strongly supports my own attempt to explore biochemical individuality. So far, I cannot find any information linking metabolic types to longevity. To the best of my knowledge, no studies on centenarians involving metabolic type have been done to date. Metabolic typing--a product of the 20th century, is a developing nutritional science involving much of the current biochemical and endocrinological research. "Modern research is still fairly young in the area of biochemical individuality: we are all pioneers," opines Gittleman. Increased efforts in research and application of metabolic typing to life extension will help in the discovery of more secrets to human longevity.

The metabolic-type approach helps us to better understand certain traits of long-living people, such as drinking and smoking. These habits are universally regarded as unhealthy, but they seem to do no harm to some centenarians. A good example is American comedian George Burns, who lived to 100 years of age. He had been smoking cigars and drinking as many as four or five martinis daily, while going without food on Sundays. He was small, slim, and easygoing, all features of a slow metabolism. Thus, his alcohol, cigars, exercises, and sexual activity (if he was not joking) increased his metabolic rate and were beneficial to his health. His Sunday fasts, which slowed down his metabolism, were balanced by accelerating it with martinis.

Another example is world-longevity champion Jeanne Calment, of France, who lived to be 122. She drank a glass of port wine at each meal and smoked cigarettes until the age of 117. She was relaxed and, therefore, most likely also a slow oxidizer. Her wine-drinking and smoking, which increased her metabolism, were as good for her as they were for George Burns. It is highly likely that both of them had blood type O, which allowed them to get away with unhealthy habits--but the rest of us shouldn't count on it.

7

LIFESTYLE

Currently, many people admit that heredity and lifestyle are the factors that most significantly affect longevity. We all know that science is unable--thus far--to predict whether someone will reach a hundred years of age, but it seems that these two factors alone aren't the entire answer. It is extremely rare that anyone in a centenarian family was also a centenarian. If there were another centenarian in the same family, it was usually not an immediate relative. For example, Russian-born Lydia Vesselovzorova, who lived to the age of 103, had a great-grandfather who lived to the age of 94.

Lifestyle in itself is not the answer to longevity either. Only a few of the many thousands of centenarians who were born by the end of the 19th century had healthy lifestyles throughout their lives. For the majority, their lives were filled with wearing and grinding physical labor. For others, life was hazardous, like Belle Odom (who lived to 109 years of age), a black woman who was born and raised in rugged Texas farm country. She lived alone in a cabin without running water until she reached the age of 100. By the way, in the state of Maine where I currently live, there is a joke about running water that goes like this:

A man is visiting his friend who has built a new house. "Boy, what a beautiful house you have--such a big area, lots of sun, a nice view from the window. Do you also have running water?" asks the visitor.

"Yeah," replies the host, "It's here," as he points to the window, where his wife appears bringing a bucket of water from the well.

Who do you think will live longer, the friend or his wife? Probably his wife because she includes exercise in her lifestyle. Perhaps the absence of running water also added more years to Belle Odom's life.

Let's return to the two factors of heredity and lifestyle. The promising news is that medical science currently doubles its knowledge about human beings every four years. Numerous research projects and studies are conducted on a daily basis worldwide. Unlike the elderly among us, those who are now in their twenties and thirties can just sit back and wait. Perhaps in the near future, we will have the answers that we seek to the mysteries of longevity, but those who are in their sixties and seventies (approaching an average life span)--who are not eager to leave this wonderful life--must rely chiefly on themselves.

Heredity is difficult to deal with because it is already too late to change anything about it. This is the way of thinking in the Western world. In books on longevity, heredity is usually regarded as a factor that is beyond human control. In India, however, they look at heredity with a wide-open "third eye." For instance, Dr. Shantha, in his book *The Handbook of Ayurveda,* says that there are three conditions required for achieving a long, healthy, and happy life:

- balanced inheritance (in other words, choose your parents with care)
- good quality of spirit (one free of envy, anger, resentment, and ego)
- healthy lifestyle and a good diet

It is surprising that lifestyle is last on the list. As we see from the list, a person must first control his/her birth; it is his/her personal responsibility to be born with strong longevity genes. Another condition is to believe in reincarnation, which embodies the idea that a waiting soul somehow slips into a body when the body has reached a certain stage of development. This sort of thinking is not an exclusive feature of the exotic Orient. American centenarian Stella H. Harriss, a former teacher of chemistry at Kansas State University, when asked how she got to be so old, replied, "I picked my ancestors carefully."

Heredity definitely plays an important role in achieving a ripe old age; this axiom has never been denied. The case of Japanese identical twins Gin Kanie, 108, and Kin Narita (who died in January 2000 at the age of 107) is a good example of this. According to *The Guinness 1999 Book of World Records*, the oldest twins ever were Americans Eli Shadrac and John Meshak Phipps, who were born in 1803 in Affigton, Virginia. Eli died first, at the age of 108, in 1911. Identical twins (i.e., developed from the same egg) have more propensity toward longevity than fraternal twins (i.e., developed from separate eggs, who may differ distinctly from one other).

The heredity of many if not most people, however, is not the best. Is there any chance for those who were careless in choosing their parents? How much can we count on lifestyle? According to Everett L. Smith, director of the biogerontology laboratory at the University of Wisconsin, "...about 50 percent of the average aging decline is self-induced by lifestyle, and the other 50 percent is due to the genes or the makeup of the individual biological system." Not bad--at least half; our efforts will not be in vain.

Good news that a healthy lifestyle can do miracles in achieving health and a long life comes from the Japanese. Dr. Yukio Yamori, a professor at Kyoto University, studied people from Okinawa who were reputed for their longevity. The Okinawian diet--low in salt; low in calories; rich in seaweed, vegetables, fish, and some pork--is gaining popularity in Japan. Aged Okinawians are often featured in TV programs and the newspapers and magazines often write about them.

At the beginning of the 20th century, many Okinawians emigrated (together with their longevity genes) to Hawaii, Brazil, and other countries. They adopted the local lifestyle and a diet that is rich in white-flour products; with an excess of sugar, meats, cheese, and fats; an overabundance of salt; and a lack of green vegetables. Professor Yamori traced some of them and discovered that their life span was 16-17 years shorter than that of the average Okinawian still living in Okinawa. Many of the immigrants suffered from arteriosclerosis, stroke, and diabetes, and died prematurely. Professor Yamori concluded that lifestyle prevails over heredity in living a long and healthy life.

There are distinct uncertainties in using the term "lifestyle." According to the dictionary definition, "lifestyle" means the practical way of life of a person or group. Some authors, including Harvey and Marilyn Diamond, confine lifestyle to only diet and eating habits. Dr. Stuart M. Berger defines lifestyle as habits including drinking, smoking, sleeping, wearing seatbelts, getting exposure to the sun, coping with stress, and taking prescription drugs--but excludes diet and exercise.

The results of the Southern California study on aging patterns of almost seven thousand people are well known. Their health status and lifestyle were assessed by a twenty-three-page lifestyle questionnaire. Factors found to affect health the most were not income, physical condition, or genetic inheritance, but rather the following healthy lifestyle habits:

1. Sleeping seven or eight hours a night
2. Eating breakfast almost every day
3. Not eating between meals
4. Normal weight– (i.e., not more than 5 percent underweight and not more than 10 to 20 percent overweight (the lower number for women, the higher number for men)
5. Regular physical activity– (i.e., engaging often in active sports, long walks,

gardening, or other exercise)

6. Moderate drinking– (i.e., drinking no more than two alcoholic drinks a day)

7. Never smoking cigarettes

We can see from this list that exercise and eating habits, not diet, are included in the meaning of lifestyle. The Southern California study showed that lifestyle affects health even more than heredity does.

American medical science values lifestyle very highly for its influence on healthy living and life extension. "For all its extraordinary complexity, the human body requires surprisingly little special care," says C. Everett Koop, M.D., former U. S. Surgeon General, in his book *Dr. Koop's Self-Care Advisor*. He adds, "...the basics of a healthy lifestyle are known, non-controversial, and uncomplicated. If you follow these eight proven steps, you will not only enhance your prospects of a long and fulfilling life; you'll also add spring to your step right now:

1.	Get some exercise	5.	Be careful out there
2.	Maintain a healthy weight	6.	Stay involved
3.	Eat well	7.	Relax
4.	Put out the smoke	8.	Take care of your teeth."

Nearly the same list of lifestyle habits that help maintain good health in later years--with one more very essential addition--is in *A Consumer's Guide to Aging*, by David H. Solomon, M.D., et al. They maintain that "Along with not smoking, exercising regularly, eating a balanced diet, reducing stress, and maintaining a social network, another important influence on our well-being--largely overlooked and too often scorned--is exercising our sensuality and sexuality."

In the East, similar principles of lifestyle are considered to promote longevity. According to a survey of 548 male and 2,303 female centenarians in Japan, as published in the *Diet Data Book* in 1995 (in Japanese), the following lifestyle habits enhanced longevity (figures indicate the percentage of respondents):

	Men	Women
1. Paid attention to diet	50.2	38.3
2. Followed right rules and lived regular life	45.4	36.6
3. Did not take things too seriously	42.0	38.2
4. Got enough sleep and rest	42.0	31.5
5. Did appropriate exercise	32.8	20.0
6. Was moderate in smoking	24.5	4.9
7. Was moderate in drinking wine	21.9	4.8

	Men	**Women**
8. Early diagnosis and quick cure of an illness	8.8	14.3
9. Many hobbies, lived each day to the fullest	18.6	13.9
10. Did not pay special attention to anything	15.7	25.5
11. Was careful to avoid obesity	8.6	4.8
12. Other	13.5	11.8

The factors revealed in this Japanese survey are well known, namely that proper diet is the first priority, followed by regularity in life, a "take-it-easy" attitude, and sufficient sleep and rest. Moderate exercise, drinking and smoking in moderation, regular medical checkups, and being involved with hobbies are also very important. These rules seem to be universal throughout the world's populations.

From the short review cited previously, we can see which everyday actions and habits constitute lifestyle. My objective is to graph the lifestyle profile of a person similar to the way body constitution, personality type, instinct, and temperament were graphed. Again, the profile is drawn based on a questionnaire. First, the dominant parts of one's lifestyle must be chosen and then each part with appropriate entries on the questionnaire must be filled in. The dominant parts are the components that most affect health and longevity, such as diet and eating habits, work, rest, leisure, sleep, activities, exercise, and the way one treats his/her body, mind, and spirit.

To draw your lifestyle profile, read the questions in Table 7-1 and highlight one of the three possible answers. Then total the ten scores shown at the right of the answer for each of the four lifestyle parts. Your lifestyle profile will be composed of the calculation of the four totals. This table contains important lifestyle factors that most affect health and longevity. I compiled it myself, but I was inspired by a similarly designed health-assessment questionnaire called the *Type of Your Health Level*. This health assessment--as used in Japan--is based on twenty-four questions in three areas: diet, exercise, and rest; a three-angle diagram then is drawn from this information. A few of the questions in the Japanese table are related to lifestyle, so I used them (with some modifications) in Table 7-1:

It will probably be difficult to quickly answer the questions that fit you most. Some of the entries, such as number of calories, amount of protein and fat, and number of foods to avoid for your blood type, need preliminary calculations or reference to the food charts included in Appendix A.

Table 7-1. Assessment of Lifestyle of a Person

Diet and Eating Habits					
1. How many calories do you consume every day?	More than 3,000 kcal	0	From 1,600 to 3,000 kcal	1	Less than 1,600 kcal	2
2. How many kinds of food to avoid for your blood type do you eat every day?	More than 10	0	From 4 to 10	1	Less than 4	2
3. How much salt do you consume every day?	More than 15 g (3 teaspoons)	0	5 to 15 g (1 to 3 teaspoons)	1	Less than 5 g (1 teaspoon)	2
4. How much animal fat and margarine do you eat every day?	More than 100 g	0	From 50 to 100 g	1	Less than 50 g	2
5. How much animal protein do you eat every day?	More than 100 g	0	From 50 to 100 g	1	Less than 50 g	2
6. What amount of food do you eat at one sitting?	100 % of stomach volume	0	90 to 80% of stomach volm.	1	70% of stomach volume	2
7. How many times do you chew before swallowing a mouthful?	Less than 10 times	0	From 10 to 30 times	1	More than 30 times	2
8. Do you eat icecream or have icy drinks after your meal?	Yes, each time; they are so refreshing	0	Sometimes, if I eat out	1	No, never; my stomach is not that strong	2
9. Do you eat raw fruits and green vegetables?	No; they are good, but chicken is better	0	Sometimes, if I don't forget to serve them	1	Every day; I can't live without them	2
10. Do you eat leftovers?	Every day, they are tasteful	0	One or two times a week	1	Never; I cook proper amount	2
Work, Rest, and Leisure					
11. Level of stress at your work?	High	0	Moderate	1	Low	2
12. How many hours do you work a day?	10 hours and more	0	7 to 10 hours	1	Less than 7 hours	2
13. Do you move during working hours?	Not really	0	Sometimes	1	A lot	2
14. How many hours do you sleep at night?	Less than 7 hours	0	More than 8 hours	1	7 to 8 hours	2
15. What is the quality of your sleep?	Interrupted	0	Awaken 1 to 2 at night	1	Deep, sound	2
16. How many times do you wake up to urinate at night?	More than 2 times	0	1 to 2 times	1	No wake ups	2
17. What are your sexual relations?	Not satisfying	0	Some areas need help	1	Satisfying and positive	2
18. How much alcohol do you drink a day?	A few bottles of beer or glasses of wine, or 1 glass of whisky	0	2 to 3 glasses of beer, 1/2 to 2 glasses of wine, 50 to 150 cc of whisky	1	1 glass of beer, or 1/2 glass of wine, or 30 cc of whisky or less	2
19. Cigarettes that you smoke a day?	More than 10	0	From 3 to 10	1	Less than 3	2
20. Do you have an interest (hobby) in anything?	No, not at all	0	Not sure, I do sometimes	1	Yes, in many things	2

Physical Activity and Exercise						
21. How many times a week do you exercise to the degree of perspiring?	Not one, it's not for me	0	1 to 3 times	1	More than 3 times	2
22. How long do you walk every day, including going to work and back?	Less than 10 minutes	0	From 10 to 30 minutes	1	More than 30 minutes	2
23. Do you go upstairs or use a lift?	Always lift	0	Sometimes lift	1	Never use lift	2
24. How many times a week you do aerobics, stretches, strength exercise?	Do not exercise	0	From 1 to 3 times	1	More than 3 times	2
25. When was the last time you did any strenuous exercise or activity when you got out of breath?	One month ago	0	Two weeks ago	1	Within the last week	2
26. Do you force yourself beyond your strength and endurance in exercises?	Often I do	0	Sometimes	1	Never	2
27. Do you include warming up and cooling down while exercising?	No	0	Sometimes	1	Always	2
28. Do you exercise during illness such as cold, an acute infection, or flu?	Yes, as usual	0	A little	1	No	2
29. Do you exercise regularly or occasionally?	Occasionally	0	Quite often skip exercises	1	Regularly	2
30. Do you check your maximum heart rate at the peak of exertion?	No	0	Sometimes	1	Often	2

Life Habits, Emotions, and Mental and Spiritual Activities						
31. Do you wear seatbelts in the car?	Never	0	Sometimes	1	Always	2
32. How often do you brush your teeth and floss?	Every other day or two	0	Once a day	1	After each meal	2
33. Do you often worry about events or relations with people?	Often	0	Sometimes, not usually	1	Just a little bit	2
34. What emotional state are you in quite often?	Irritated, quick to anger	0	Sometimes bored and depressed	1	Calm, content, satisfied	2
35. How often do you joke and laugh?	Very rarely	0	Quite often	1	Every day	2
36. How often are you engaged in mental activities such as studying, playing musical instruments, and painting?	Very rarely	0	A few times a week	1	Every day	2
37. Do you often enjoy meeting with friends, going for entertainment, making trips, etc.?	Very rarely	0	Once a month	1	Every weekend	2
38. Do you feel you are in control of your life?	Not really	0	Maybe yes, maybe no	1	Under full control	2
39. How active you are in your spiritual life, including personal spiritual growth, religious devotion?	No spiritual life at all	0	Sometimes, like going to church	1	Active spiritual life	2
40. Are you conscious about your health and motivated to live a healthy and long life?	No, it is not for me to pay such big taxes; no thank you	0	Perhaps, but all those boring diets, exercises	1	Yes, I want to, I want it now; please teach me how	2

Take your time and don't be concerned about the effort involved--and prepare yourself for even more work because there are more questionnaires in the following chapters. As the English proverb says, "Don't be frustrated, all your troubles are ahead."

The lifestyle questionnaire is sensitive to changes in one's lifestyle.

> My current lifestyle--retired and living in Rome, Maine--is much different than it was four years ago when I worked for a Japanese company and lived in Tokyo. My present lifestyle is less stressful; I exercise more, am better able to watch my diet, and so on.

If you have recently changed your lifestyle, look through the questionnaire twice; assess your former and latter lifestyles, and compare in which direction (healthier or not) you have moved.

Each group of ten questions in the questionnaire results in a maximum score of 20. In my case, my scores were 18, 16, 16, and 15 in all four groups of questions. My lifestyle profile is shown in Figure 7-1.

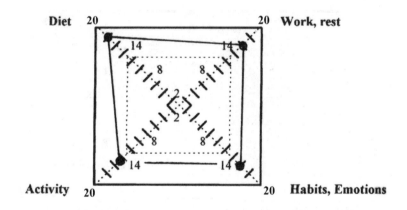

Figure 7-1. Lifestyle Profile of the Author

If you scored at least 13 in each group of ten questions (i.e., the dotted line inside the graph), your lifestyle is healthy and promises longevity. If your score is less than 13 in any group, you should make changes toward a healthier lifestyle.

Many centenarians attribute their longevity to a healthy lifestyle, a "clean life," as they say. The following examples illustrate this belief.

> In an interview in 1987, Charles Bickner, of Brookings, Oregon, then a hundred years old, revealed the secrets of his longevity: "The main thing is what you eat. Regular exercise is also important." For the last twenty years of his life, he took ten minutes every morning to exercise with 10-pound dumbbells before going on his daily one-mile roundtrip walk to the post office, reported Jim Heynen in his book, *One Hundred Over 100*.

> Mary Frances Annand, of Pasadena, California, another centenarian profiled in his book, said: "I always walked several miles a day."

> A hundred years old in 1987, Esther Henrikson, of Chula Vista, California, also gave some insight into the secrets of longevity: "Well, I had a good start-- lived on a farm, had pretty good food. And I lived a clean life. No smoking or drinking and never ate between meals."

We cannot say that these centenarians lived to the age of a hundred or more just because of a healthy lifestyle--their heredity definitely also played a role. Good genes seem to run in the family of Esther Henrikson--her brother lived to be 102 years old and her sister lived to the age of 94. However, without doubt, a clean life helped her and other centenarians to live that long.

8

HEREDITY

Although heredity is said to be beyond human control, followers of the reincarnation theory believe that one can choose his/her parents and hence his/her heredity, although it is not clear thus far how this can be accomplished. What is quite clear is that each of the personality-profile features discussed previously is largely affected by heredity, as is the duration of one's life. Genetics influences bodily constitution to the extent that twins are alike whether they are extraordinarily tall, short, or heavy. Here are a few examples from the *The 1999 Guinness Book of World Records* showing the striking power of genes:

> "The tallest male twins in the world are Michael and James Lanier of Troy, Michigan, who were born in 1969 and are both 7 feet, 4 inches tall.
> The tallest female twins are Heather and Heidi Burge of Palos Verdes, California. Born in 1971, they are 6 feet, 4 ¾ inches tall."

> "The shortest twins were Matyus and Bela Matina of Budapest, Hungary (later of the United States), who were both 2 feet, 6 inches tall.

> The shortest living twins are John and Greg Rice of West Palm Beach, Florida, who are both 2 feet, 10 inches tall.

> The world's heaviest twins were Billy and Benny McCrary (alias "The McGuires") from Hendersonville, North Carolina. Normal in size until they were six years old, Billy and Benny weighed in at 744.77 and 724.88 pounds, respectively, in November 1978, when each had a waist measurement of 7 feet."

As for longevity, many people think that heredity plays an overwhelming role; therefore, our years on earth are predetermined and there is not much we can do to increase them. Others are not inclined to give up so easily, putting their lives entirely in the hands of destiny. They combat poor heredity by undertaking a healthy lifestyle and utilizing exercise programs or employing other achievements of modern science. The third group combines both of these approaches, giving some credit to heredity factors, but also relying on a healthy diet and exercise. In discussing this issue, David Seidman, author of

The Longevity Sourcebook, asks the question: "Heredity or environment? Nature or nurture? Genetics or diet and exercise? Both," he replies. I agree with him.

Data on the role of heredity in achieving a ripe old age is quite controversial. On one side, a great number of experts believe in the predominant role of heredity in a human's life span. The facts supporting this belief are numerous. In some families, youthfulness lasts much longer than it does in others. Indian author M.S. Kanungo, in his book *Genes and Aging,* says that "the offspring of long-lived parents have longer-than-average life spans."

Dr. Leonard Hayflick, a prominent longevity researcher and the author of *Why and How We Age,* states: "Clearly, having long-lived parents and grandparents increases the likelihood of achieving great longevity, although it is no guarantee." According to Dr. Hayflick, "when both parents survive to age seventy or older, the likelihood that their children will reach ninety or a hundred is almost twice as great as that found for the general population." This is good news for me, because my father lived to the age of seventy-eight and my mother to seventy-three.

Many researchers have undertaken studies in an attempt to search for longevity genes. Thomas Moore, in his book *Life Span: Who Lives Longer and Why*, says: "It is likely there are longevity genes." Long-living twins are the best example of the power of heredity.

The twin sisters Kin-san (who died in January 2000 at the age of 107) and Gin-san, 108 (known as Mrs. Gold and Mrs. Silver), are the longevity icons of Japan. They have often appeared in the mass media advertising healthy foods.

According to *The 1996 Guinness Book of World Records*, American twins Mildred Widman Philippi and Mary Widman Franzini of St. Louis, Missouri, celebrated their 104th birthdays on June 17, 1984. Mildred later died on May 4, 1985; however, they both look great in the photograph, about thirty years younger.

Sarah L. Delany, 108, of Mount Vernon, New York, enjoyed a century-long relationship with her sister Dr. Annie Elizabeth Delany (two years younger), who died on September 25, 1995, at the age of 104. The Sisters Delany are known for their book, *Having Our Say: The Delany Sisters' First 100 Years.* The hundred-plus-year-old sisters are also reputed for their healthy habits of eating garlic and practicing yoga exercises.

According to a 1996 TV program in Japan, **heredity plays a dominant role in a person's longevity**. Japanese author Mizuno Hajime says that a person's chances to live to the age of one hundred are predetermined by 80 percent at the time of his/her birth. In a 1993 Japanese survey of 2,851 centenarians (548 men and 2,303 women), 21 to 26 percent of the respondents' fathers lived to between 70 and 79 years of age and their mothers lived to between 80 and 89 years of age. Parental ages exceeding ninety years were found in the case of both male and female centenarians, accounting for 7 percent of the fathers and 13 percent of the mothers. The total percentage of parents who lived more than seventy years averaged 56 percent for male centenarians and 52 percent for female centenarians.

In the book, *One Hundred Secrets of 100-Year-Old People*, by Japanese Tomio Sato, Editor, which was based on interviews with 103 centenarians, researchers used a twenty-four-entry questionnaire. One of the questions was, "Do you know whether among your neighbors there are people of a ripe age or not?" The ripe age referred to was seventy or more, to which sixty-nine people replied "yes" and thirty-four replied "no." This shows that people of average life span or older are present in both families of centenarians and in those of the neighborhood.

However, gerontological authorities, including Dr. Walter M. Bortz II (past president of the American Geriatrics Society) and Dr. John Rowe, estimate that genes account for one third of the factors affecting one's life span. Chinese scientists calculated that life span is determined by 25 percent genetic factors and 75 percent lifestyle factors. **Diet, rather than heredity, influences a person's duration of life**, says Professor Yukio Yamori at Kyoto University in Japan, contradicting the role that heredity plays in life span. His findings were discussed in the previous chapter.

Jim Heynen, who interviewed a hundred American centenarians in 1987-89, proposed additional data that supported the idea of the minor influence of heredity. Only sixteen centenarians were reported to have family members who lived ninety to a hundred years of age. The fathers of centenarians in six cases and the mothers in four cases lived that long; only in one case—that of Otto Burthus of Granite Falls, Minnesota--did both father and mother live longer than a hundred years. Ten centenarians had sisters and seven had brothers who reached very old age, although there is only one case of both parents and siblings living very long. The ratio of centenarians whose parents lived long lives was much lower in the United States than in Japan, which may be a result of the age range (70+ in Japan, 90+ in America) rather than either lifestyle or heredity.

A person's heredity is definitely worth knowing because, armed with this knowledge, he/she can more easily prevent family diseases. Awareness of the danger is half the battle against it. If heart disease runs in the family, a person must work hard to strengthen his/her heart muscle, choose the proper diet, and adjust lifestyle in the prevention of or treatment for arteriosclerosis, high blood pressure, and so on. Whether stroke or cancer, much can be done to fight the odds of becoming ill with these diseases.

The heredity profile of the author, shown in Figure 8-1, lists the ages of my parents and grandparents on both sides.

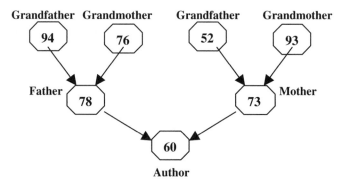

Figure 8-1. Heredity Profile of the Author

As shown in this figure, my father lived to the age of seventy-eight and my mother to seventy-three. Although these are not extremely old ages, they both nearly equal (my mother) or surpass (my father) the average life span in Russia, which in 1990 was 64.2 years for men and 73.8 for women. My paternal grandfather lived to ninety-four years of age and my maternal grandmother to ninety-three years of age. These quite old ages may increase my chances to live longer than the average life span, even beyond my parents' ages. My maternal grandfather died at fifty-two, but his premature death was caused by an accident; he fell from a boat in winter and died from hypothermia.

9

AYURVEDIC DOSHAS

Many of us know that Oriental medicine and philosophy have significantly influenced Western medicine. In ancient times, the Greek physicians Hippocrates (4th-century B.C.), the founder of Western medicine, and Galen (2nd-century A.D.) learned it from the East. During the European "Dark Ages," the 10th-century Persian physician and scientist Avicenna, the father of Arabic medicine and a follower of Galen, passed it to the West.

Both Oriental and ancient Western physicians categorized patients according to their type. Based on the evaluation of a person, they prescribed an appropriate diet or therapeutic treatment. Healing in the hands of the ancient, highly skilled practitioners was an art, relying more on empirical observations than on science. The Oriental healing tradition includes as the major medical systems Ayurvedic medicine, Traditional Chinese Medicine, and Yoga philosophy and medicine. In this part, we discuss these major systems and their relation to health and longevity.

Ayurveda, India's traditional medicine with a five-thousand-year history, is considered the world's oldest and the most complete medical system with a deep spiritual basis. The Ayurvedic healing tradition, which is holistic at heart, addresses the individual and seeks to identify the unique patterns of each patient. Ayurveda regards the human being as a trinity of body, mind, and spirit. It evaluates a full range of physiological, psychological, and behavioral characteristics and traits of a person with the physical symptoms they manifest. The major purpose of Ayurveda is to preserve youthfulness and achieve longevity. Its diagnostic methods are metaphysical rather than quantitative and objective. The Ayurvedic diagnosis and treatment relies on understanding vital forces known as *doshas,* which control our bodily functions. Deepak Chopra, M.D., who incorporates Ayurvedic principles into

Western medicine, calls doshas "metabolic principles." The three doshas are *Vata, Pitta,* and *Kapha.*

If one knows his/her dosha, s/he can change his/her lifestyle and diet so that it will help him/her live a healthier, happier, and longer life. Acquiring this knowledge serves as a theoretical basis for change in the right direction. One can also see what bodily constitution s/he received from his/her parents and what s/he has done with his/her body in the course of life. In his book *Perfect Health,* Dr. Chopra stresses that knowledge of your body type enables you to evolve to a more ideal state of health. Being familiar with doshas, a person can better judge which factors are most important for his/her body.

In the following description of the three doshas, I relied on the following books: *Encyclopedia of Indian Medicine,* by Professor S. K. Ramachandra Rao (Editor); *Perfect Health,* by Deepak Chopra, M.D.; *The Ayurvedic Cookbook,* by Amadea Desai; *Ayurveda,* by Scott Gerson, M.D.; *The Book of Ayurveda;* by Judith H. Morrison; and *A Woman's Best Medicine,* by Melanie Brown, Ph.D., Veronica Butler, M.D., and Nancy Lonsdorf, M.D.

A person of the **Vata** type is slender, too small or too tall, and ill-nourished by constitution, but strong. People of this type have prominent joints, veins, and features; their skin is rough, hard, dry, cracked, and cool. Their hair is brownish in color, thin, coarse to the touch, and curly or wavy. Body weight is slight and movements are quick, unsteady, light, and changing. They speak fast and indistinctly. They do not eat much food and their eating habits are irregular. Sweet, sour, and salty are the tastes they like, and they prefer steamed foods and hot drinks. They sleep few hours and they fly in their dreams.

The Vata-type person is enthusiastic, imaginative, and moody. S/He quickly comprehends but just as quickly forgets. S/He loves outdoor exercise, games, music, dance, and travel, but s/he is easily fatigued. Changeability is a primary characteristic of the Vata type, and their mood and actions are unpredictable and variable. S/He is easily excited and upset and unable to control his/her senses. His/her sexual urges are poor. S/He is greatly susceptible to diseases of the nervous system and mental abnormalities.

A person with the **Pitta** constitution is average in body build, strength, and endurance. His/her body is well proportioned and moderately nourished, and s/he easily maintains a stable weight. S/He has loose joints, flabby muscles, and warm hands and feet with good circulation. His/her skin is soft, fair, light yellowish or reddish, lustrous, and warm, often with freckles and several moles. The face is heart-shaped with high cheekbones and a pointed chin. His/her hair is fair or reddish, slow growing, easily falls out, and turns gray early. His/her eyes are medium in size, active, and with an intense luster.

The Pitta type's digestion is rapid and s/he enjoys a good appetite with frequent feelings of hunger and thirst. S/He prefers sweet, bitter, and astringent tastes, and likes chilled foods and cold drinks. His/her sleep is moderate, with red-colored or frightening objects possibly appearing in dreams. S/He is moderate in sexual desires, has no great sex appeal, and has limited popularity with the opposite sex. His/her memory is good, with logical thought processes and great intelligence. This type of person takes initiative, has a sense of responsibility, is rapid in decision-making, and is consistent in handling affairs. What s/he says is reasonable, clear, and to the point, but s/he can also have a quick temper and be very jealous. S/He is vulnerable to illnesses such as disorders of the blood, digestive disturbances, ulcers, and urinary ailments.

A person of the **Kapha** type is solid, heavy, strong, and enduring. His/her body is short, stout, large, and well nourished with well-proportioned limbs and strong bones and muscles. S/He tends to be overweight with a slow metabolism. S/He moves slowly, with a dignified gait, avoids inessential movements, and is content to just sit quietly. S/He talks slowly but distinctly. S/He is slow in everything--in how s/he thinks, acts, and eats. These people sleep long and heavily, and their dreams pertain to rivers and lakes, flowers, and aquatic birds. Their appetite is reduced and they seldom feel very hungry or thirsty. Their favorite dishes are bitter, pungent, and astringent in taste. Food assimilation is very efficient in this type of person, and they need small amounts of food in proportion to their body size and strength.

The Kapha person enjoys well-developed intelligence and his/her conclusions are well thought out; however, it takes more time for him/her to arrive at them. S/He doesn't have many desires, takes control over his/her senses, and is slow to get emotionally upset or irritated. His/her voice is pleasant sounding, with clear and deliberate enunciation. This type of person has a great aptitude for sexual activity and a corresponding capacity for sensual enjoyment. These people are prone to high cholesterol, obesity, allergies, respiratory disorders, and sinus problems. However, if they choose a healthy diet and lifestyle, their life expectancy is enhanced.

Each person is not one extreme type as described previously, but rather a combination of two or even three types. Only one of the dosha types, however, will be prevalent. These descriptions, together with Table 9-1, show how dosha characteristics relate to other systems of body/personality-type evaluation, and provide a general idea of each dosha type.

To evaluate your own dosha type, use the entries in Table 9-2, which is helpful in self-assessment. In contrast to other evaluations--which are undoubtedly useful for acquiring a better understanding of your individuality--this dosha-type assessment, together with blood type and Yin-Yang type, directly influences the food that is appropriate for your type. As in other evaluations, highlight the words that fit you best. Count the total points of each dosha and its percentage, first in Section 1 (inherited constitution) and then in Sections 1 through 3 (current dosha state).

Table 9-1.   Relation between Dosha Type and Other Systems

Features	Vata	Pitta	Kapha
Dominant Element	Wind	Fire	Earth and Water
Humor	Wind	Bile	Phlegm
Galen Type	Sanguine	Choleric	Phlegmatic
Kretschmer Type	Asthenic	Athletic	Pyknic
Sheldon Type	Ectomorph	Mesomorph	Endomorph
Life Expectancy	Reduced	Normal	Good

Table 9-2. Evaluation of a Person's Dosha Type

Features	Vata	Pitta	Kapha
Section 1. **Body Build and Physical Characteristics**			
1. Body build	Thin and always have been, tall, can be unusually tall or short	Medium build, strength and endurance, well-proportioned frame	Heavy set, solid, strong, broad, strong chest, supple muscles, lean limbs
2. Child-age body	Thin as a child	Medium build as a child	Plump or a little chunky as a child
3. Weight	Light, cannot easily gain weight	Portly, easily maintains a stable weight	Heavy, cannot easily lose weight
4. Bones	Light, prominent	Medium bone structure	Heavy bone structure
5. Joints	Cracking, dry, prominent	Loose, well proportioned	Big, well formed, and lubricated
6. Muscles	Slight, prominent tendons	Medium, firm	Solid, well-developed
7. Hair	Medium or light brown, thin, dry, curly, wavy, shiny, brittle, lifeless	Light, blond, reddish, or early gray, straight, fine, oily, slow growing	Dark brown or black, thick, wavy, slightly oily, full of body
8. Skin	Dry, rough, cracked, and numb, color turns dark, skin feels cold	Soft and looks smooth, light reddish, shining, yellow and red patches	White, greasy, plump, cool, smooth, not very sensitive
9. Face	Long, angular, chin is often underdeveloped; dark, dull, fearful	Heart-shaped, chin is often pointed; red, ruddy, anxious, and restlessness	Large, rounded, full; pale, whitish, unconcern, apathy, and self-pity

Features	Vata	Pitta	Kapha
10. Eyes	Small, dark, lack of moisture, not shining, restless, blink often, contracted pupils	Sharp, penetrating, light green, gray, or amber, with red venules, inflamed, yellow whites	Large, clear, attractive, charming, white-looking whites, large pupils, thick eyelashes
11. Teeth	Irregular, fragile, liable to plaque, dental decay	Medium size, yellowish	White, big, and regular
12. Lips	Thin, narrow, tight, dark	Medium, soft, pink	Thick, large, smooth, firm
13. Tongue	Dry and furrowed, from bluish to blackish	Red and swollen	Furred (white) and swollen
14. Voice	Dry, rough, hoarse, sore vocal cords, dry cough	Sounds angry , "heated," tendency to shout at others	Sounds pleasant, low, soft and sweet, clear enunciation
15. Nails	Small, dry, rough, darkish	Medium size, pink, soft	Large, smooth, white, hard

Section 2. Physiological Functions

Features	Vata	Pitta	Kapha
16. Pulse	Fast, thin, variable, "like a movement of a snake"	Strong and full, more rapid than usual, "like a jumping frog"	Steady, slow, rhythmic, "like a swan swimming in a pool"
17. Urine	Clear, scanty, frequent	Clear and hot, yellow to reddish, abundant, feel scalding when urinating	Pale, moderate, concentrated, turbid
18. Stools, elimination	Hard, dry, verging on black feces, tendency to constipation, gas	Loose to watery, yellow or blood-stained, abundant, tendency to diarrhea	Pale, slimy to loose, oily, cause irritation, regular daily bowel movements
19. Energy	Low level, fluctuates	Moderate level	Abundant vitality
20. Appetite	Variable, sometimes very hungry	Good, cannot tolerate missing a meal	Constant, likes to eat, but can easily skip a meal
21. Food quantity	Irregular	Eats too much	Small quantities of food are required
22. Favorite food	Hot, sweet, sour, pungent, salty, heavy, oily foods; likes to snack, nibble	Warm, sweet, light, bitter; likes high-protein food, chicken, fish, eggs, beans	Loves dry, low-fat, sweet, spicy, salty food, bread, starchy food
23. Meal time	Irregular	Eats too often	Punctual meal times are not important
24. Eating habits	Eats in a rush	Moderately fast	Eats slowly
25. Diges-tion	Alternatively good and not good	Usually good	Fine, sometimes a little slow
26. Thirst	Variable	Usually thirsty	Rarely thirsty
27. Circu-lation	Poor; cold hands and feet	Good; warm hands and feet	Perfect; cool hands, hot feet
28. Sweat	Scanty, no odor	Profuse, especially when hot; strong fleshy or sour odor	Moderate, but present even when not exercising; cold, pleasant odor
29. Endur-ance	Expends energy quickly, and sinks until recovered	Manages energy well	Good stamina
30. Climate preference	Hates cold, prefers warm climate, sun, and moisture	Prefers cool, well-ventilated places	Any climate is fine, but without extreme humidity

Features	Vata	Pitta	Kapha
31. Sleep	Interrupted, 5-7 hours, insomnia	Sound, 6-8 hours	Deep, heavy sleeper, slow to waken
32. Dreams	Flying, running, climbing mountains and trees, fear, nightmares	Anger, violence, sun, fire, lightning flashes, battles, fights, passionate	Romantic, sentimental, water, clouds, lakes with lotus flowers and swans
33. Sexual interest, capacity	Low to moderate, strong when romantically involved	Moderate to strong sexual desires and capacity	Slow to awaken but sustained, generally strong
34. Way of speaking	Talkative, fast, interrupts, imaginative or excessive	Clear, sharp, precise, detailed, convincing	Slow, monotonous, singing, with moments of silence
Section 3. **Psychological Traits**			
35. Physical activity	Fairly active, but dislikes competitive activities	Enjoys physical activities, prefers competitive ones	Loves leisurely activities, content just sitting quietly
36. Exercise	Feels more mentally relaxed when exercising	Exercise helps keep emotions under control	Exercise and diet help keep weight down
37. Leadership	Creative thinker	Good initiator and leader	Good at keeping an organization running smoothly
38. Relationships	Brief, easily adapts to different people	Often chooses friends on the basis of their values	Slow to make new friends, but forever loyal
39. Routine	Dislikes routine	Enjoys planning, routine	Works well with routine
40. Money	Easy to spend, impulsive, poor, spends on trifles	Careful in spending, spends on luxuries	Tends to save, accumulate, wealthy, spends on food
41. Mood and emotions	Mood changes easily, highly responsive	Intense, quick-tempered, forceful in expressing feelings	Even, steady, relaxed, slow to anger
42. Reaction to stress	Anxiety, fear, worry	Anger, jealousy, irritable	Complacent, steady, slow
43. Most sensitive to	Noise	Bright light	Strong odors
44. Thinking	Superficial with many ideas; more thoughts than deeds	Precise, logical; good planner and gets plans carried out	Calm, slow, cannot be rushed; good organizer
45. Work	Creative	Intellectual	Caring
46. Way of learning	By listening	Reading or using visual aids	Associating with another memory
47. Reactions	Hesitant and procrastinating	Angry, judgmental	Not easily upset or irritated
48. Deep beliefs	Changes these frequently, according to latest mood	Strong convictions that may govern behavior	Deep steady beliefs that are not easily changed
49. Decisions	Hasty and ill-considered	Rapid decision-making, consistency in affairs	Slow in reaching conclusions
50. Lifestyle	Erratic	Busy, but plans to achieve too much	Steady and regular; may be stuck in a rut
Total score, Section 1	8	4	3
Total score, Sections 1-3	23	19	8

The total score in Section 1 (i.e., the first fifteen entries) of the questionnaire represents an individual's balance of doshas. It also depicts his/her constitution, which s/he was born with and which s/he inherited from his/her parents. Section 2 (physiological functions) and Section 3 (psychological traits) contain entries that can be affected by diet and lifestyle; therefore, they represent a person's current dosha state. For example, let's look at the results of my own evaluation.

> The evaluation of my constitutional type resulted in 8 points (53 percent) of Vata, 4 points (27 percent) of Pitta, and 3 points (20 percent) of Kapha. The Vata dosha is most prevalent in my case, with Pitta as the secondary dosha and some proportion of the Kapha dosha. The figures representing my current doshas state are as follows: 23 points (46 percent) of Vata, 19 points (38 percent) of Pitta, and 8 points (16 percent) of Kapha. The Vata part is somewhat decreased, the Pitta part is increased, and the Kapha is only slightly decreased. My current dosha state is more balanced than my original constitutional pattern. Not bad--perhaps my recent healthy lifestyle is responsible for this harvest.
>
> Actually, this is my second dosha self-evaluation; the first time was in May 1997. The corresponding figures for my three doshas at that time were 80, 14, and 6 percent. So, what happened? There were reasons for the decrease in my Vata dosha and the increases in my Pitta and Kapha doshas. (The part associated with my body build that I inherited from my parents did not change.)
>
> In August 1997, I undertook a month-long alternate dry fasting (described in the *Alternate Dry Fasting* chapter of Part 4). At the end of the month, I had lost 15 pounds and looked very thin and gaunt. As a positive effect of fasting, about one third of an ounce of brown sand came out of my kidneys through my urine. The pain on the left side of my lower back that had lasted for a half year before fasting vanished. Two months later, while I was in Singapore, I visited a practicing Ayurvedic doctor who was stationed in the "Little India" district in Singapore. The reason for my visit was a dull pain that I had been experiencing in my liver region for about a week. During my visit, Vennes S., a Singaporean friend who had accompanied me, helped as an interpreter.
>
> The doctor, who was in his fifties, briefly examined my face and performed a pulse diagnosis. His assessment indicated a decrease in the liver and pancreatic functions. He prescribed two Ayurvedic tonics for me: Dasamoolarishtam and Kumaryasavam. When I asked him about my dosha, he replied that I belonged to the Vata dosha by about 80 percent. It was surprising to me that his evaluation was determined merely from a pulse diagnosis and examination of my face (which I also arrived at using the previous questionnaire)--which supports my inclusion of the questionnaire in this book.

It would be better, however, to see an Ayurvedic doctor for your dosha assessment. I agree with Judith H. Morrison, who states in her book, "Ideally, you should ascertain this (your dosha constitution) from an expert Ayurvedic physician, who has been trained in Ayurvedic pulse diagnosis. Your constitution can also be assessed by accurate observation. However, as yet there are few people in the West who have had sufficient training to assess constitution accurately." In any case, self-evaluation with the use of the questionnaire may help you to understand your dominant dosha and body type. For the most accurate self-assessment, be self-critical while choosing the options describing your features and qualities. "Be honest and observant, judge how you are, not how you would like to be. Look for trends that endure," advises Morrison. If you are doubtful of some of your traits, ask a relative or friend who knows you well. "We do not see ourselves as others see us" the old adage implies.

Everybody has his/her unique constitutional balance of doshas and current ratio of doshas. The combination of constitutional doshas may be good or poor. A person whose doshas are well combined (i.e., about one third of each dosha) will experience excellent health under most circumstances. However, if the doshas are poorly combined and only one predominates, that person will suffer illnesses more often.

The results of self-assessment can be illustrated on the graph shown in Figure 9-1. The round dot reflecting the ratio of all three doshas represents the Ayurvedic profile, or *constitution*. In Figure 9-1, the round dot depicts my constitution and the square dot represents my *current ratio* of doshas. The length of the arrow indicates the distance from the constitutional balance to the current dosha state. The most balanced state of health for a particular individual with his/her particular heredity is near the point of his/her constitutional ratio. An ideal balance of doshas is at the center of the plot, with each dosha having a ratio of 33 percent. Lucky is the person who has this balance.

The plot in Figure 9-1 gives a theoretical basis for the way to a healthier and longer life. In my case, I need to decrease the excessive Vata dosha within me and increase both the Pitta and Kapha doshas. According to Table 9-1, the life expectancy of a person of the Vata type is reduced compared to the other two doshas. Increasing the proportion of my Pitta and Kapha doshas also increases my chances of living longer; this is very significant for me, and adopting the Vata pacifying diet and lifestyle is a way to achieve it.

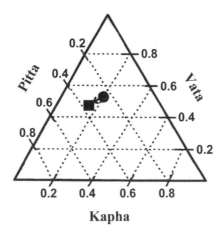

Figure 9-1.   Author's Ayurvedic Doshas Profile (Example)

The most important part of our diet is what kind of food we eat because, together with the physical form of food and its chemical substances, we ingest the *prana* (life force) and subtle influences attached to the food. These subtle parts affect elements of the doshas directly.

The Ayurvedic classification of foods is different from the classification of foods for blood types; however, it provides more insight to what is appropriate for an individual's specific dosha. Dr. Vasant Lad, Director of the Ayurvedic Institute in Albuquerque, New Mexico, developed the food charts that were used by Morrison in *The Book of Ayurveda.* Based on these charts, I modified the blood-type food charts shown in Tables 1 through 4 in Appendix A. I subdivided each column of "highly beneficial foods," "neutral foods," and "foods to avoid" into two subcolumns. In the Ayurvedic approach, they are called "yes" and "no" lists of foods.

The foods defined as "yes" were placed in the left subcolumn, the "no" foods in the right subcolumn. Thus, I modified the food chart for my blood type (A) and my predominant Vata dosha, as shown in Table B-1 in Appendix B. Six subcolumns in this table were assigned the following headings, from left to right: *Super, Very Good, Good, So-So, Bad,* and *Very Bad.* I can now see that the foods in the three left subcolumns are appropriate for me, the rest are not. The best foods matching both my blood type and Vata dosha are under the heading of "Super" in the extreme left subcolumn.

The highlighted foods in Table B-1 of Appendix B are low in Vata and high in Pitta and Kapha; therefore, they are good for me, especially rice and oats. I lived the first half of my life without eating much of those grains. In the last twenty-five years, however, I have eaten a lot of rice, and now eat lots of oats as well.

Rice is a major ingredient of the Asian pilaf dish. I enjoyed it in Tadjikistan and Uzbekistan, where I worked for many years on engineering projects. It is prepared there so deliciously that there were reportedly casualties due to overeating it (according to the rumors). The other main ingredients of pilaf are lamb, carrots, onion, cottonseed oil, sheep's fat, and local spices. While it is very rich and heavy, it is the most delicious food that I have ever tried. I have traveled to thirteen countries and enjoyed many dishes of local cuisines, but pilaf is my favorite. When I lived in Japan for five years, I ate rice every day. Just as wheat bread is a common side dish in Russia, rice is present in each meal in Japan, China, and other Oriental countries.

Oats are also an excellent grain for the *Vata* type. In both young and old, it makes the system stronger and fortifies the brain and nerves, according to Ayurvedic medicine. Oatmeal gruel (e.g., Quick Oats) is very nutritious and called "spare food" in stomach and bowel disorders. A half-cup serving of dry cereal yields 140 calories, 5 grams of protein, 16 percent daily value (PDV) of dietary fiber, and 10 percent PVD of iron. Oatmeal reduces *Vata* and *Pitta* and strengthens *Kapha*.

In the vegetable category, carrots, garlic, red onions, parsnips, leeks, and okra fall under my "Super" subcolumn.

> I call myself a "garlic man" because I eat it both raw and cooked every day. Every other day in the morning, I grind one clove of garlic and swallow it on an empty stomach in order to kill the bad bacteria found in the intestine and keep the digestive tract healthy. I couldn't eat it while I was working among other people in Russia, Israel, and Japan because of the bad odor; however, it doesn't bother anyone now.

In my practice of eating garlic, I am supported with "heavy artillery"--none less than the world champion of longevity herself.

> Jeanne Calment, of Arles, France, who died in 1997 at the age of 122. Her diet of garlic, olive oil, and fish is thought to have been critical in achieving her record age.

The famous American centenarian sisters, Sarah L. (who died in 1997 at the age of 104) and A. Elizabeth Delany, 108, ate garlic regularly. They wrote in their book *Having Our Say: The Delany Sisters' First 100 Years*, "Every morning, after we do our yoga, we each take a clove of garlic, chop it up, and swallow it whole."

The long-living people in Abkhasia reportedly consume large daily quantities of garlic, both cooked and raw. Abkhasians believe it has healing properties and enjoy its taste.

Carrots are also a favorite vegetable of mine. I go nowhere without carrots, eating them every day. Carrot juice or a raw salad is usually my first food after breaking a fast; my coworkers in Moscow nicknamed me "Hare" because of my habit. Some centenarians attribute their longevity to eating carrots.

"I've been very fond of carrots, and that's it," said 100-year-old Ethel Noel in 1989, as quoted by Jim Heynen in his book *One Hundred Over 100*.

Returning to the food charts, the number of combinations of four blood types, three predominant doshas, and two Yin-Yang types (discussed in the next chapter) results in twenty-four charts, three pages each, for a total of seventy-two pages. I am unable to list all the charts in this book; therefore, I present as an example the food charts for my case (i.e., blood type A, predominant Vata dosha, and predominant Yin type). To determine other combinations, I refer you to *The Book of Ayurveda*, by Judith H. Morrison, in which the Ayurvedic food charts for all three doshas are presented. You can then modify the blood--type food charts (see Tables 1 through 4 in Appendix A) for your specific predominant dosha. Further modification according to Yin-Yang type is discussed in the *next* chapter of this book.

Morrison makes many other recommendations about daily activities and lifestyle in *The Book of Ayurveda*. Some valuable advice for my Vata type is as follows:

• *Daily routine*. Introduce regularity to your life and maintain it.
• *TV*. Avoid watching too much TV, which overstimulates eyes and ears. Avoid listening to fearful news.
• *Computers*. Avoid spending too much time working with the computer. Take frequent breaks away from the computer, preferably in fresh air.
• *Leisure*. Spend time in calm, gentle, and creative pursuits. A sauna, with its warm and moist qualities, is most beneficial.
• *Exercise*. Vigorous aerobic exercise may damage the joints, which are weak in the Vata type; therefore, a regular amount of gentle exercise like yoga or stretching every day is preferable.

• *Vacation*. Have a vacation in a single destination with plenty of sun and warmth. Find a beautiful place and enjoy being idle.

Knowing your dosha type and applying the principles of Ayurveda to yourself increases your chances of living a healthier and longer life. Many centenarians possess the following habits: getting up early in the morning, going to bed early at night, eating well-cooked food, enjoying light and pleasant activities in the day time, and walking or engaging in moderate exercises. I believe in the importance of these principles from my own experience, although I cannot say that I am deeply involved in Ayurveda. In mapping a person's unique profile, the Ayurvedic dosha type seems to me to be both helpful and necessary. These are the principles of the Ayurveda daily routine and healthy lifestyle. Followers of Ayurveda adhere to these healthy rules, which are universal throughout all holistic systems.

As a holistic medical tradition with the primary goal of preservation of youth and life extension, Ayurveda has much to offer a longevity seeker. According to classic Ayurvedic treatises, one hundred years free of infirmity or disease is a normal life span for humans. To achieve this, Ayurveda allots an important role to diet, exercise such as yoga, daily and seasonal routines, and meditation, as well as various healing and rejuvenating techniques such as aromatherapy, purification, fasting, herbal therapy, and massage or self-massage. In addition to *The Book of Ayurveda*, I refer you to an excellent book, *Perfect Health*, by best-selling author Deepak Chopra, M.D., who was trained in conventional Western medicine and adopted Ayurveda in his practice. He has treated more than ten thousand of his patients with Ayurveda therapies in this country, and his book contains a wealth of valuable information about Ayurveda techniques and approaches to longevity.

10

YIN – YANG PRINCIPLE

Oriental body-type classification and health-condition diagnosis involves the *Yin-Yang* principle, which is fundamental in Chinese philosophy and medicine. An interdependence of all elements in nature is explained in the Yin-Yang terms. The occurrence of these two Chinese terms is increasing throughout Western literature. The concept of Yin and Yang comes from the great ancient Chinese treatise, *I Ching* (*The Book of Change*), written by the legendary Taoist philosopher Lao-Tzu around 1250 B.C. The Yin and Yang duality is considered a basic concept of life. Widely known is the Yin-Yang symbol, a circle divided into two parts--usually black and white--by a curved line; each part has a small circle inside filled with the opposite color. The symbol represents the wholeness much valued in Oriental traditions. It also symbolizes united opposites, each containing a seed of the other. By their nature, Yin and Yang forces are dualistic but complementary.

Yin represents the negative and passive force. Its qualities are darkness, coldness, weakness, and hollowness. It is also considered female in nature and is symbolized by water. *Yang* represents the positive and active force. Its qualities are light, heat, strength, and solidity. It is considered male in nature and is symbolized by fire. A *balance* between these two fundamental cosmic forces is a key factor in all life processes and natural forms.

The dualistic Yin and Yang forces persist throughout various aspects of an individual: the person's constitution and the nature of any disease, foods eaten, personal characteristics, attitude, perception of life, and so on. Chinese medicine considers an imbalance in the amounts of Yin and Yang energy as the root of pathology and cause of all diseases. Predominance of one of the forces in constitution and present condition results in disease. An individual's good health and well-being can be achieved if these contrasting aspects of the body and mind are balanced, so says Yin-Yang theory.

Each person is born with either a Yin or a Yang constitution. "All body types can be seen according to the theory of Yin and Yang," states Shizuko

Yamamoto in her book, *Barefoot Shiatsu*. Your mother's constitution and her diet during pregnancy mainly determine the quality of your basic physical constitution, states Naboru Muramoto in his book, *Healing Ourselves*. In addition to a person's constitution, there is present condition; both situations must be considered when thinking about a person's condition. A person's general condition is determined to a great extent by the food he/she has eaten recently, adds Muramoto.

Yang Person. A Yang person has a large, strong, muscular, and stocky body; broad shoulders; enjoys a good appetite and can eat a lot; is capable of doing more activities; his/her voice is strong and loud; and he/she needs fewer hours of sleep and rest. His/Her stamina seems to be unlimited and his/her immune system easily resists any harmful effects. If he/she becomes sick, he/she feels very bad but recovers very quickly. There are two kinds of Yang person: fat and thin. The Hollywood heroes Arnold Schwarzenegger and Silvester Stalone are Yang fighters and winners. Most sumo wrestlers of Japan are of the fat Yang type. One of my former Japanese colleagues is of that Yang type. He is bigger than average size, a bit fat. He is a fountain of energy: he does everything very rapidly, moves like a meteor, and usually runs--not walks--in the office. When he caught a cold once, he looked terribly ill. He had a severe headache and running nose. Nevertheless, he stayed in the office until the end of the day. He was already fully recovered by the next morning--as if there had been no sickness at all. I was greatly surprised by the strength of his immune system.

Yin Person. A Yin person's body is small or slender, with narrow shoulders, small bones, soft muscles and sinews, and protruding joints. His/her voice is weaker than normal. His/Her capacity for food, work, and entertainment is limited. He/She cannot stand a stressful situation for a prolonged period. He/She needs more time for rest, to restore energy, and to recover from an illness. He/She tends to lead a calmer, quieter, and less stressful life. He/She is more thoughtful, conservative, and quite effective in his/her accomplishments. Yin people are also subdivided into fat and thin. The Yin hero of the Orient is a modest sage with hidden powers of philosophy and wisdom.

Our physical characteristics, tendencies, activities, and likes and dislikes can all be seen as either Yin or Yang. Although this classification is very simple, it is sometimes very difficult to accurately assess each condition. Is your constitution Yin or Yang? What have you done with the constitution that you have been given at birth? Table 10-1 contains forty-two entries that help estimate a person's Yin or Yang constitution and condition. It can be done qualitatively by simply assessing which force dominates; it also can be done quantitatively by highlighting each entry that describes you best and then counting the total Yin and Yang points.

Table 10-1.   Assessment of a Person's Yin-Yang Type

Nos.	Yang	Yin
	Physical Build	
1	A skinny person who is very muscular and whose skin is dark	A skinny person
2	A fat person who is very muscular and whose skin is light	A fat person with full, rounded face, whose muscles are flabby
3	The head is small, smaller than one-seventh the size of the body	The head is large, larger than one-seventh the size of the body
4	Person stands erect	Person slumps
5	Person walks with toes pointing inward ("pigeon-toed")	Person walks with toes pointing outward
6	Person walks on toes leaning forward	Person walks on heels
	Physical Characteristics	
7	The face shape is round, square, or forms a triangle with base down; it is fleshy. The jaw is wide. The chin is somewhat flattened, can be with cleft	The face shape is long and narrow or forms a triangle with base up. Forehead is large and chin is pointed. Face has less flesh than average.
8	The facial features are small in size and located toward the center of the face. The nose is contracted and almost flat.	The facial features are larger. Eyes are rounder and located toward sides. The nose is long and expanded.
9	The distance between the eyes and mouth is relatively short. The distance between the inside corners of the eyes is very narrow. The eyes are small and narrow ("folded").	The distance between the eyes and mouth is rather long. The distance between the outside corners of the eyes is rather wide. The eyes are large and round.
10	Irises turn toward the nose	Irises turn toward the ears
11	Irises are shifted down from the center. The whites show at the top.	Irises are shifted up from the center. The whites show at the bottom.
12	Eyebrows are broad	Eyebrows are thin
13	Eyelashes are short	Eyelashes are long
14	The eyes emit strong life force. The pupil is contracted. The complexion is clear in the areas above and below the eyes.	The eyes have no life force and are very weak. The pupil is expanded or very large. The areas above and below the eyes are sometimes darkly colored.
15	Short nose pointing upward	Long nose starting high up on the face
16	The mouth is small	The mouth is large
17	The lips are thick	The lips are thin

Nos.	Yang	Yin
18	The teeth angle toward inside of the mouth	The teeth angle toward outside of the mouth
19	Low, long ears that lie flat against the head, with full lobes	High pointed ears that stick out from the head, with reduced lobes
20	The color of face, nose, cheeks is red	The color of face is pale
21	The skin is clear and smooth, neither dry nor too moist. It radiates life and energy. Skin color is light rose to red.	The skin is sallow, yellowish, rough, and may be excessively dry. Skin color is dark, dirty-looking, pale or yellow.
22	Feet and hands are hot and dry	Feet and hands are cool and wet
23	Nails are short, wide, and flat	Nails are long, narrow, and bulging
24	Hair is wavy or curly	Hair is straight
25	With age, the hair turns white	With age, this person will go bald
	Physiological Functions	
26	The digestive system is strong. The appetite is good.	The digestive system is weak. The appetite is irregular.
27	Person likes animal food: meat, poultry, fish, eggs, cheese, butter, and salt	Person likes sweet tastes such as fruit and desserts, and sour tastes such as citrus and vinegar. Cannot tolerate salt.
28	Person can eat green vegetables or their juice and feel no discomfort	Green vegetables or their juice cause the intestines to blow up and diarrhea
29	Person can eat tomato, eggplant, and watermelon and feel good	If person eats these vegetables, he/she feels weak
30	If this person takes drugs, such as aspirin or antibiotics, they are not harmful for digestive system	If he/she takes drugs, the reaction will be very strong. Sometimes the digestive system is damaged.
31	The bowel movement is regular and the stool holds together. The person is prone to constipation, but a laxative brings relief.	Person often goes to the toilet; the stool is soft and loose. When constipated, there will be no relief even after taking a laxative.
32	The pulse is strong, rhythmical, and even	The pulse is weak, irregular, and usually slow; sometimes the pulse cannot be felt
33	Person can drink much liquid or alcohol without great effect	Cannot drink much or feels dull, the body swells. The person loses energy and generally does not feel good.
34	Person can smoke cigarettes without too much effect	Cannot tolerate smoking
35	Woman has regular menstruation, lasting from five to seven days. The blood is excessive and thick.	She has irregular menstruation, with a short period and thin blood.
36	Person likes cold climates and weather.	Person likes warm climates and weather.

Nos.	Yang	Yin
37	Person can take a hot bath every night and feel good.	Person feels tired after taking a hot bath.
38	The voice is strong and lively. The speech is clear. He/She has stamina even when speaking for a long time, such as lecturing.	The voice is weak and the expression is unclear. He/She speaks in short sentences with many pauses.
39	Person does not sleep much and recovers from fatigue quickly.	Person sleeps many hours and still is tired; recovers from fatigue slowly.
40	The abdomen is resilient, somewhat thick and bouncing. Above and below the navel is evenly warm. The navel is deeply indented.	The abdomen is flabby and lacks resiliency. There may be cold spots around the navel. The navel itself indents only slightly.
	Psychological Aspects	
41	The nature is positive and aggressive. This person is very active, works hard, and recovers easily.	The nature is pessimistic. This person tires very easily and has a poor recovery rate.
42	The movements are quick and the reactions are fast due to a strong autonomic nervous system.	This person moves and reacts slowly because the autonomic nervous system does not function properly.

If you fall equally between two descriptions, highlight both. This information will help you better understand your unique individuality. You will then be able to apply the diet and lifestyle recommendations in order to balance the Yin-Yang forces.

Let's look at the Yin-Yang-type assessment of Xu Fang, 31, a Chinese mystery who has not eaten for the last thirteen years. In March 1998, while visiting her in Beijing, I found her to be perfectly balanced, with 51 percent Yang and 49 percent Yin. Her Yang-Yin ratio is close to 1, an ideal balance. Her profile is shown in Figure 10-1; detailed information about Xu Fang is in the *Food Intake Control* chapter.

My own personal evaluation results in 13 *Yang* and 31 *Yin* points (a few entries were highlighted for both). Totaling them and assigning a sum to 100 percent results in 30 percent Yang and 70 percent Yin. The Yin-Yang scale is shown in Figure 10-1. The Yang-Yin ratio in my case is Yang-Yin = 13/31 = 0.42 < 1.0. This shows that the Yin force dominates my constitution and condition. In other words, only until recently have I sought to improve my weak inherited constitution; I need to undertake special efforts to correct the Yin-Yang imbalance. These measures include proper diet–mostly rich in

Yang foods–exercise, cleansing body organs and systems, and a relaxed lifestyle.

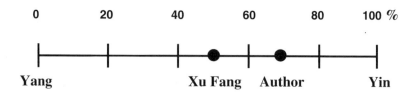

Figure 10-1. Yin-Yang Type Scale

How is the Yin-Yang principle related to longevity? The younger ages, with the exception of childhood and middle age, are governed by Yang, while Yin forces rule old age. Together with our inherited Yang or Yin constitution, there are relative changes in these energies and body shape throughout our lives. "The Yin-Fat type represents morning, spring, and the very young stage of development up to the age seven. The Yang-Fat type represents the time around noon, summer, and the teenager of development, from the ages of seven to eighteen. The Yang-Thin type represents the evening, the autumn season, and the ages between thirty-five and fifty-five. The Yin-Thin body type represents night, winter, and the old-age years," say Shizuko Yamamoto and Patrick McCarty in their book, *Whole Health Shiatsu*. To achieve good health and long life, we need to balance the excess Yin energies of old age through an increase of Yang energies by proper nutrition and Yang lifestyle. "The secret of longevity is not to fight nature but to slow down the aging process with appropriate foods, which balance Yin and Yang," says Ng Siong Mui in her book, *The Chinese Health, Beauty, and Rejuvenation Cookbook*.

Just as people are divided into two types--Yang and Yin--so are foods. The principles of food classification were set by the founder of the modern Macrobiotic Movement, George Ohsawa (1893-1966). It is based on the potassium (K) and sodium (Na) ratio (K/Na) and the difference (K - Na). In his time, Ohsawa was inspired by Dr. Sagen Ishizuka (1851 - 1910), a founder of the Japanese macrobiotic medicine and diet. He became famous in Japan after his book, *The Chemical Diet for Longevity,* was published. Dr. Ishizuka treated his patients using dietary suggestions. He prescribed potassium-salt type foods or sodium-salt type foods, depending on their diseases. He was an advocate of eating whole grains--especially brown rice--various vegetables, and daikon (i.e., Japanese radish).

A smaller K/Na ratio and K - Na difference indicate Yang food, a bigger ratio and difference indicate Yin food. The major foods listed as follows are classified as Yang and Yin, with more Yang or Yin quality in the beginning of each list. I compiled this list using the following books: *Macrobiotic Zen and the Art of Rejuvenation and Longevity*, by George Ohsawa; *Acid and Alkaline*, by Herman Aihara; and the illustrated chart in *Yin-Yang Foods*. The latter book, published by the Japanese CI Society, is sold in natural food stores in Japan.

Grains	(Yang): buckwheat, millet, rice, wheat; (Yin): corn, oats, barley, rye
Vegetables	(Yang): dandelion root, water buttercup, burdock and burdock root, carrot, lotus root, pumpkin, onion, leek; (Yin): potato, eggplant, tomato, shiitake mushroom, cucumber, sweet potato, spinach, asparagus, celery, cabbage, garlic, daikon, turnip
Fruits	(Yang): strawberry, apple, cherry, chestnut, mulberry; (Yin): pineapple, orange, lemon, banana, mango, peach, pear, melon, watermelon, plum, avocado
Dairy foods	(Yang): Roquefort cheese, goat's cottage cheese, goat's milk; (Yin): kefir, yogurt, ice cream, buttermilk, processed cheese, sour cream, margarine, butter, milk, Camembert cheese, Swiss cheese, soft cheeses
Fats, oils	(Yang): "egoma" butter; (Yin): animal fats, lard, margarine, butter, coconut oil, peanut butter, peanut oil, olive oil, sunflower oil, sesame oil
Sugars	(Yang): malt; (Yin): honey, white sugar, brown sugar, molasses
Poultry, meat	(Yang): fertilized eggs, pheasant, turkey, duck, pigeon, partridge, mutton, lamb; (Yin): frog, pork, veal, beef, horsemeat, red meat, rabbit, hare, chicken
Fish, seafood	(Yang): caviar, shrimp, tuna, mackerel, whale, lobster, sardine, anchovy, herring, yellowtail, sea bream, horse mackerel, salmon, catfish, kombu, wakame; (Yin): oyster, shellfish, octopus, eel, crab, clam, flatfish, carp, pikeperch, crawfish, trout, pike, flounder

Beans   (Yang): azuki beans;
(Yin): soybean; green, white, and black beans; pinto and kidney beans

Nuts, seeds   (Yang): sesame seeds, fried pumpkin seeds, squash seeds, chestnut;
(Yin): cashews, peanuts, almonds, filberts, nutmeg

Drinks, juices   (Yang): ginseng tea, Yang-Yang tea, mu tea, bancha tea, dandelion root, coffee, kokkoh, chamomile;
(Yin): coffee, cola, cocoa, fruit juices, sugared drinks, wine, beer, dyed tea, mineral water, soda water, water, lime-tree-leaves concoction, peppermint tea, vodka, whiskey

Condiments, spices   (Yang): unrefined sea salt, salt, soy sauce, miso, dill, pickled plum, celery, cilantro, burdock, saffron, wild chicory, cinnamon, chervil, rosemary;
(Yin): ginger, red pepper, capsicum, lemon, vinegar, mustard, clove, vanilla, laurel, anise, caraway

The contemporary leader of the international macrobiotic community, Michio Kushi, divides all foods into three main categories in his book, *The Cancer Prevention Diet*:

• *Strong Yang Foods*: refined salt, eggs, meat, cheese, poultry, fish, seafood

• *Balanced Foods*: whole-grain cereals; beans and bean products; sea vegetables; roots; round and leafy vegetables; seeds and nuts; spring and well water; non-aromatic, non-stimulant teas; natural sea salt

• *Strong Yin Foods*: temperate-climate fruit; white rice; white flour; tropical fruits and vegetables; milk, cream, and yogurt; oils; spices (e.g., pepper, curry, nutmeg); aromatic and stimulant beverages (e.g., coffee, black tea, mint tea); honey, sugar, and refined sweeteners; alcohol; foods containing chemicals, preservatives, dyes, and pesticides; drugs (e.g., marijuana, cocaine); medications (e.g., tranquilizers, antidepressants).

Some discrepancies will be found when comparing these two lists. For instance, white rice is regarded as Yang food in Ohsawa's list and as a strong Yin food in Kushi's list. Natural sea salt is Yang in the first list and a "balanced" food in the second list. This shows that the Yin-Yang classification of foods is not absolute, merely relative. Regarding discrepancies in the macrobiotic diet and medicine, Yamamoto and McCarty say in their book, *Whole Health Shiatsu*, "Remember that these systems are created by people as models to understand natural, universal forces. No system perfectly describes reality."

The best perception of Yin-Yang principles is as tools that help to better understand a person's own nature, the food he/she eats, and the environment he/she lives in. Also, the Yin and Yang foods can be understood--to some extent--in terms of their warming and cooling properties: Yang is warming and Yin is cooling. Just as we feel thirsty in warm weather, salt has the same effect, which is Yang. After we eat salty food, we want to drink water, which is Yin. The Yin and Yang qualities of food are altered with cooking. Potatoes, which are Yin, cooked with salt become more balanced. Similarly, a Yin person, who is actually Yang-deficient, needs more Yang warming foods. They can be either in their natural form or cooked with salt and Yang spices, which would cover the Yang deficit. Conversely, a Yang person who has excess warmth in his/her body may crave a cold beer or ice cream, which are Yin, to achieve the balance. However, the warming and cooling origins of food can be easily altered with preparation. Let's take ginger tea as an example. First I grind ginger, then pour boiling water over it. When I drink it hot, I feel a very warm sensation in my stomach, although ginger itself is a Yin food.

Now we have three factors that affect the foods we eat: blood type, Ayurvedic dosha type, and Yin-Yang type. An example of the food chart that considers all three factors--namely, my blood type A, dominant Vata dosha, and Yin type--is shown in Table B-1 of Appendix B. For each food category in this table, the Yang foods are placed at the top of the list and the Yin foods at the bottom.

> I belong to the Yin type, therefore, I try to reduce Yin foods and include Yang foods in my diet. The most beneficial for me are the foods in the upper parts of each list. It is worth mentioning that particularly strong Yang foods, such as caviar, eggs, coarse sea salt, and ginseng, are good for me. I should avoid or reduce to a minimum the very strong Yin foods, such as honey, sugar, kefir, coffee, cola, wine, fruit juice, and water.

The macrobiotic diet and medicine associates many diseases with people's ignorance of their diets, whether or not they eat in accordance with the principles of Yin and Yang. For instance, Ohsawa considered heart diseases and cancer to be caused by eating too many Yin foods. As a remedy for these diseases, he recommended a diet composed of 100 percent grains. Herman Aihara, a well-known expert at the George Ohsawa Macrobiotic Foundation in San Francisco, agrees. In his book, *Acid and Alkaline,* he says that cancer-causing foods are very Yin, both acid- and alkaline-forming foods (i.e., virtually all Yin foods), and Yang, acid-forming foods such as chicken, beef, pork, fish, and dairy products.

There are cases in which people achieved significant improvement and even cured themselves of disease through the use of a macrobiotic diet. A person named Benedict cured the tumor in his prostate gland with a macrobiotic diet; Lois Armstrong reported this in the October 10, 1983, issue of *People Weekly*. Basically, the macrobiotic diet is composed of 50 to 60 percent whole grains and their products, 20 to 30 percent locally grown vegetables, 5 to 10 percent beans and sea vegetables, 5 to 10 percent soups, and 5 percent condiments and supplementary foods, including beverages, fish, and desserts. In terms of basic nutrients, the diet includes 12 percent proteins, 15 percent fat, and 73 percent complex carbohydrates.

Depending on the Yin or Yang type of person, environment and lifestyle adjustments are important too. Usually, Yin-type people prefer warmer climates and seasons; dress in warm clothes during cold weather; and eat hot soups, food, and beverages. Yang people seek the opposite. A Yin person can increase his/her energy and enhance brain functioning by taking a cold shower after a hot bath, according to Aihara. Deep diaphragm breathing, holding one's breath after exhaling, singing, and chanting allow an increase in the carbon dioxide and oxygen content in the blood. This helps Yin people increase their energy level and strengthen their immune system.

Who is healthier, a Yang or Yin type? Although the Yang person is a model of vitality, it does not mean that in the long run he/she is healthier than his/her Yin counterpart. **Yang people seem to burn themselves too fast, while Yin people can smolder longer until a ripe old age.** As they age, all people slow down in activities and body movements; in this respect, one becomes more Yin. Age-induced changes lead to the transformation of a Yang type into Yin, accompanied by losses and emotional discomfort. However, for the Yin inborn type, it will be a smooth continuation of his/her natural processes and tendencies.

The skinny person is generally regarded as a Yin type. However, he/she is a Yang type if his/her body is muscular and skin is dark. Elderly people who keep active increase the Yang part in themselves. Long-living people in the "longevity valleys" of Hunza, Vilcabamba, and Abkhasia are skinny and muscular, with dark skin due to long exposure to the sun. Although they are very old, they are of the Yang type.

It seems that many centenarians belong to the Yin type with quite a large proportion of Yang type as well.

In 1987, Susie Pittman, 103, a small woman from Marble Valley, Alabama, weighed a little more than 100 pounds. However, she was riding a self-propelled lawnmower when she was 100. In her 90s, she landscaped the yard after a big rain, using a shovel. In his book, *One Hundred over 100,* Jim Heynen reported that she was able to propel herself and lift shovelfuls of dirt.

Another centenarian, Albert W. Holmgren, 100 when interviewed, was overweight most of his life, weighing 245 pounds. However, he worked physically hard as a painting contractor throughout his entire working life. He seemingly belonged to the Yang type, which never changed.

George Burns, a famous American comedian who lived to a hundred, was diminutive and probably belonged to the Yin type by his inborn constitution. In his life, he smoked cigars and drank martinis, which increased the Yin. However, he regularly walked and exercised, thereby increasing the Yang component in him.

Another famous comedian, centenarian Hal Roach--barrel-chested and very robust at the age of a hundred--seemed to be a Yang type by his constitution.

The longevity champion, Jeanne Calment of Arles, France, who lived to 122, was described as very skinny with bony legs. Her diet included garlic and olive oil, and she drank port wine, which are all Yin. She was known to ride a bicycle at the age of one hundred. She played the piano, painted, and hunted, thereby increasing the Yang force in herself.

The Japanese centenarian, Genkan Tonaki, who was 108 in 1993, worked in sugar-cane fields until he retired at eighty-five. This physical labor sustained a Yang force in him.

In the Western world, we are not used to the Yin-Yang terms, and they seem alien to us. However, some health advocates rely heavily on this system.

My second teacher, Vladimir M. Kuznetsov, 89, from Moscow, incorporated the Yin-Yang principle in his health system, which combines embryology and the Oriental horoscope. He considers the month after our conception, when the internal organs were formed in our embryonic stage. Kuznetsov advises treating each of our vital organs using the Yin-Yang principle, with particular care in the months of their formation.

Because the Yin-Yang philosophy is part of Traditional Chinese Medicine, people in China seem to be more prepared to take it seriously. Luo, 32, a boyfriend of Xu Fang, was very interested in it. When we had our meals together he often asked me, whether the particular food we ate was Yin or Yang. Xu Fang, because she does not eat at all, treated all the food the same: "Food is bad," she told me a few times. She is lucky in her neglect of food.

However, we have to eat to survive. Thus we should eat right and the Yin-Yang approach is another tool to achieve this.

The person who understands the principles of Yin and Yang will consciously perceive what's going on in his every day life and why. He will be able to control his desires for food, drink, and satisfy them just to the extent that is absolutely necessary for his survival. He will not let them overshadow his wisdom. His wisdom will stop him from excessive consumption as soon as the basic need is met. Any excess will disturb the balance between Yin and Yang, which is one more key to health and longevity.

11

FIVE ELEMENTS THEORY

Another organizing principle for determining a person's constitutional type is the Five Elements Theory. This theory, used together with the Yin-Yang diagnosis, enables one to obtain important supplementary information about an individual. According to Chinese Traditional Medicine, the five basic elements that our bodies are composed of are fire, earth, metal, water, and wood. According to this concept, everything in the world and the human body contains these five elements. The five elements or properties are interdependent and can promote or restrain one another. Each element influences our physical tendencies and personality type.

Relative to physiology, each element is linked to the internal functional relationships of vital organs, which are categorized in terms of Yin-Yang. Fire is associated with the heart and small intestine; earth with the spleen, pancreas, and stomach; metal with the lungs and large intestine; water with the kidneys and bladder; and wood with the liver and gallbladder. The energy of these vital organs gives rise to five emotions: the heart governs joy, the spleen governs sorrow, the lungs govern melancholy, the kidneys govern fear, and the liver governs anger. If a person does not control his/her anger or joy, the "life" force of the liver and heart will suffer; if all five elements exist in good balance, the person is healthy and full of vitality. Therefore, through vital organs and emotions, each element assigned to a person helps describe his/her individuality and character. In the following description, I referred to these books: *Man, Life, Health* (in Russian), by V.I. Garbuzov, M.D.; and *Asian Health Secrets*, by Letha Hadady.

The Fire Person. Fire symbolizes the highest activity, greatest fullness and joy of life, and extreme passions--both love and hatred. The people of this type can be hyperactive, anxious, and emotionally unstable. The major organ of the fire element is the heart, and the "window" of this element is the tongue. "Fire symbolizes the mind of the heart," says Dr. Garbuzov, explaining the fire element; that is where the saying "My tongue is my enemy" originates. Modern man doesn't express what he has in his heart and hides his emotions. This is unnatural and he is punished with diseases of the heart and small intestine, says Dr. Garbuzov.

Also, over-sensitivity and sentimentality come from the heart of the Fire person. He/She can cry and then laugh soon after. Fire people usually have a small head and a pointed chin. Their hands are long, with long flexible fingers and oval-shaped nails. They sometimes talk with their hands, expressing passion. They are Sanguine by temperament: quick, resourceful, and light-minded. They do not last long; they are like dry hay--quickly inflamed and quickly burned down. Their downfalls include a life without joy, the cold reasonableness when demands of the heart are suppressed, and the failures and misfortunes that they take as catastrophes. The Fire person needs to relax and learn to cope with stress. Overwork and stimulants such as caffeine are harmful to him/her. What he/she really needs is to pacify his/her passion. However, an impassiveness that is over-controlled by the mind is equally bad for him/her. Because a Fire person is not merely passions and emotions, but also mind and reason, he/she can take control of his/her life to make it healthier and to live longer.

The Earth Person. The Earth-type person is associated with reflection, sadness, quietness, and non-hastiness. The major organs of the earth element are the spleen, stomach, and pancreas. Ancient healers believed that the strength and vitality of these organs determined a person's health, resistance to disease, and longevity. The mirror of an Earth person's health is the mouth. If his/her teeth are healthy, the gums are clean and pink in color, and the smell is fresh, he/she is young and healthy regardless of chronological age.

The Earth person has a massive head, round face with fleshy cheeks and chin, muscular torso, and short limbs. He/She tends to become fat. His/her hands are massive, with short fingers. He/She is emotionally reserved, but impressionable and easily injured. The loss of hope, the fury of passions, and living against his/her nature and age can all be detrimental for him/her. An Earth person likes to think, but his/her thoughts are far from reality. He/She is more of a philosopher than a person of action is, and he/she speaks more than he/she acts. In sex, as in all other things, he/she is calm and debates more than acts. He/She is an optimist, but susceptible to sadness; there is a sad smile on his/her face. As a child, he/she was big, plump, good-natured, gluttonous, lazy, and loved to sleep.

The Earth person likes sweets and craves cake, candy, and ice cream. Without a healthy diet and lifestyle, the stomach, pancreas, mouth, joints, and sex organs become weak. Poor digestion may result in diabetes, heart disease, lung trouble, and even tumors. Exercise, such as sit-ups and yoga especially for the abdominal region, is very helpful for this type of person. Exercise helps balance his/her blood sugar, adds vitality to the center of the body, and lifts his/her spirits.

The Metal Person. This type of person is restrained, susceptible to pondering, and pessimistic. These people are cute, deeply involved with their profession, and can be successful whether experts in their profession or clerks. The major organs for the Metal people are their lungs, and their windows are the nose (sense of smell), skin, and hair. The condition of their skin and hair reflects the condition of the metal element in their body and their overall condition. Premature aging is a fatal consequence of the chronic pathology of systems comprising the metal element. Therefore, smoking is bad and harmful to their skin, youthfulness, and attractiveness, especially for women--it aggravates their complexion, sex appeal, and ability for childbirth.

Metal people are usually tall, narrow-shouldered, and often stooping. They have a small head and their nose is long and wide. Their hands are long, with longer palms. They have long, crooked fingers and rectangular fingernails with vertical lines. They have little endurance--easily exhausted-- and their ability to work is limited. Knowing this, they are slow–moving and expend their energy economically. As children, they were slim and pale, quickly got tired, and had a bad appetite. They are vulnerable to asthmatic bronchitis, constipation, skin diseases, and tooth problems; they are permanent patients of dentists. Cleansing and a healthy diet rich in fiber and green vegetables help with constipation. They dislike being cold and always wear a cap. They prefer hot, spicy food and dairy products.

Metal people like solitude and feel comfortable when isolated from others. They are Phlegmatic by temperament. Being alone is never boring for them; it protects their energy and inspiration, allowing them to do intellectual or spiritual work, which they love. These people find it difficult to regularly write letters and telephone others, but are surprised when accused of coldness. Although sadness is their characteristic, it is a light sadness. What is really bad for Metal people is depression, darkness, and hopelessness. However, their innate urge for freedom and independence gives them inspiration to wish for and achieve their goals.

The Water Person. Water is the source of life. The Atkharvaveda, an ancient Indian treatise, says: "Waters are full of healing, waters keep the disease away." Threats to the Water person produce fear, which shortens their life. The kidneys are the major organs of the water element, and play a key role in health and longevity. Ears are the window for this element; consequently, impaired hearing means that the Water person is becoming weak. In childhood, this element controlled the growth of bones and their condition in adults.

The condition of the skeletal system reflects the strength or weakness of the water element. If this element is strong, the person is flexible and young despite chronological age. The legendary flexibility exercises of the ancient Orient aim at strengthening joints and bones, which prolong youth and increase longevity. Strong muscles are necessary for good health; however, flexibility in the spine and joints is even more important.

As a rule, a Water person has a big head, a lean face with vertical wrinkles, and a nose that is often hooked, and is susceptible to bags under the eyes. Their hands are short and fleshy, with fingernails that are short and thin, and turn under with weakness. Water people usually have a strong body; however, if the water element is weakened at birth, they are fragile. Their trunk is long and their limbs are short. If their kidneys are healthy from birth, their intellect and sexual system are strong; otherwise, they are weak both intellectually and sexually. There is cunning in their character, and they prefer trade, business, or mediation as a profession.

If the water element is weak or becoming weak, a person is susceptible to fear, attacks of despair, and depression. He/She can lose interest in life and become sad and withdrawn. Fear, intolerable annoyance, and offense are destructive for Water people. They are sensitive to the cold, which results in sore throats and cold hands and feet. In the winter, Water people do not live; they merely exist. The Water person likes salty food; food is tasteless if it is not sprinkled with salt. Often, the Water person tends to work hard until he/she is exhausted, then needing a long time to recover. Adrenal exhaustion can cause poor memory, sexual problems, and a weakened immune system. To strengthen the kidneys and adrenal glands, yoga exercises and herbs are helpful.

The Wood Person. The personal characteristics of this type are courage, initiative, and unbending will. Movement is supported with the emotional energy of the wood element. Wood people hate being stopped, delayed, or frustrated. They look for constructive ways to fulfill their goals. They love to move, exercise, dance, and travel. In their urge to create that which they also love, they can be impatient and demanding. Their "king organ" is the liver, but it can be easily hurt as well. All the troubles of these people are related to the liver: they have been intolerant of chocolate and eggs since childhood, and they are vulnerable to allergies and vomiting.

Wood people are usually tall, broad-shouldered, with strong arms. They can be characterized as toilers. Their eyes, big and wide open, are the "flower of the liver." Good eyesight and the clean and shining whites of their eyes embody the youth and health of this element. The hands of wood people are evenly proportional in size and shape. Their fingernails are fragile or horizontally grooved, which indicates poor calcium absorption. They are "night owls," usually going to bed late. Their golden time is the spring, when they feel a surge of vitality; however, they can be easily hurt in this season. These people prefer sour and bitter foods: vinegar, horseradish, mustard, pickled mushrooms, yogurt, and sharp cheese. However, the important point in this description is that the weakest organs of Wood people are the liver and gallbladder, although they are the dominating organs in this type as well.

By their temperament, Wood people are Choleric. The suppression of anger, an intolerable humiliation, a wounded dignity, and the necessity to give up can all be disastrous for them. With a weak wood element, they have poor circulation and joint problems, and they suffer from headaches. The weakened liver can cause high blood pressure, allergies, and vision problems. It is better for Wood people to avoid excessively fatty and rich foods and drinks. Movements occupy much of their vital energy. However, with wise use of their personal strengths, they can gain insight and achieve their mountain-high goals.

The five elements symbolize the energies that are either prevalent or insufficient in our vital organs. Typically, people don't have the energy of only one element, but rather a combination of two or more. For example, one can belong mostly to the metal type, but also have manifestations of the wood and fire elements. The objective of this exercise is to build the five-element profile to show which elements are involved and in what proportions.

Table 11-1 is a questionnaire designed to help assess a person's five-element type. Read the entries in the table and highlight the descriptions that fit you best. This table was compiled by Tom Williams and is organized in such a way that, in most entries, it describes the quality or feature in one word. After you count the total points for each element, assign 4 percent to each score and calculate the percentage of each element.

Table 11-1. Assessment of a Person's Five-Element Type

#	Fire	Earth	Metal	Water	Wood
			Archetype		
1	Wizard	Peacemaker	Alchemist	Philosopher	Pioneer
			Affinities: Desires and Values		
2	Small head and pointed chin	Massive head, round face with fleshy cheeks and chin, muscular torso, short limbs	Tall, narrow-shouldered, and often stooping. Small head, nose is long and wide	Big head, lean face with vertical wrinkles, often has hooked nose with bags under eyes	Tall, broad-shouldered, with strong arms. The eyes are big and wide open
3	Long hands, with longer flexible fingers and oval-shaped nails	Hands are massive, with short fingers	Long hands, with long, crooked fingers, rectangular nails with vertical lines	Short and fleshy hands, with fingernails that are short, thin, and turn under with weakness	Proportional size and shape of hands. Nails are fragile or horizontally grooved
4	Sensuality	Family	Reason	Continuity	Arousal
5	Spontaneity	Stability	Aesthetics	Originality	Practicality
6	Expression	Harmony	Definition	Mystery	Uniqueness
7	Intimacy	Loyalty	Simplicity	Self-sufficiency	Challenge
8	Merging	Commitment	Quality	Privacy	Achievement
9	Excitement, Passion	Relationships, Diplomacy	Order, Correctness	Solitude, Anonymity	Struggle, Agility
10	Self-exposure	Involvement	Standards	Caution	Independence
11	Performing, Yielding	Sharing, Interdependence	Purity, Precision	Toughness, Conservation	Action, Contest
			Aversions: Fears and Difficulties		
12	Inactivity	Separateness	Intimacy	Sharing	Slowness
13	Separation	Disloyalty	Complexity	Rashness	Clumsiness
14	Confusion	Conflict	Chaos	Vulnerability	Ambiguity
15	Roughness	Change	Nonsense	Ignorance	Interference
16	Boundaries	Aloneness	Spontaneity	Dishonesty	Authority
17	Deliberation	Impermanence	Carelessness	Superficiality	Compromise
18	Dullness	Greediness	Impropriety	Faith	Frustration
19	Ordinariness	Insecurity	Intemperance	Exposure	Constancy
20	Conservation	Emptiness	Vagueness	Waste	Submitting
			Challenges, Contradictions, Knots		
21	Wants contact, intimacy, but needs solitude	Wants to be at the still point, but feels stuck	Wants relationship, but needs distance	Yearns for truth, but fears exposure	Wants to lead, but misses companionship of equals
22	Loves sensation, but fears excess intensity	Wants to be full, but feels weighted down and overwhelmed	Knows what is right, but accepts what is safe	Yearns for connection, but intolerant of contact	Yearns to do, to act, but subject to uncontrollable impulse

#	Fire	Earth	Metal	Water	Wood
23	Loves to say yes, but can't say no	Seeks emptiness, but fears that there is nothing at the core	Aspires toward beauty, but settles for utility	Likes to be squeezed, but scared of being squashed	Makes rules, but likes to break them
24	Yearns for fusion, but dreads dissolution	Desires change, but wants things to stay the same	Wants joy, but fears spontaneity	Wants to penetrate inside, but detests being absorbed	Demands freedom, but needs to struggle
25	Lives in the moment, but dreads future	Wants to be needed, but wary of being absorbed, losing the self	Likes creativity, ingenuity, but intolerant of disorder, dissonance	Enjoys being left alone, but dreads being abandoned	Feels invincible, but fears vulnerability and loss of control

My personal evaluation resulted in 9 points (36 percent) of the metal element, 6 points (24 percent) of the wood element, 6 points (24 percent) of the water element, 2 points (8 percent) of the fire element, and 2 points (8 percent) of the earth element. A quite complicated character, aren't I? My five-element profile is shown in Figure 11-1.

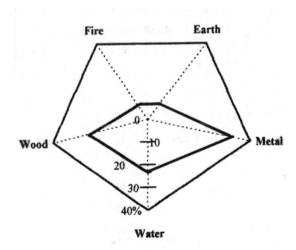

Figure 11-1. Five-Element Profile of the Author

Centenarians surely bear the features of these five elements, depending on their personality, temperament, attitude, and so on.

> Elizabeth Delany, who died at the age of 104 in 1995, had wood characteristics such as courage and unbending will. Sarah Delany, 108, in her book *On My Own at 107: Reflections on Life Without Bessie*, addressed her passed-away sister this way: "I always avoided confrontation. Sometimes I think that's a smart way to be. ...But you were fearless. You stood up against adversity no matter the cost, Bessie. I don't think there are too many people like that in this world."

> Sarah was a worrier and optimist at the same time, which is a sign of the earth element.

Just as the food one eats is associated with his/her blood type, Ayurvedic dosha type, and Yin-Yang type, so it is linked to the energy of the five elements. In turn, they are associated with the five flavors and govern functions of the internal organs. The food chart shown in Table 11-1 is based on information adapted from *The Complete Book of Chinese Healing and Health*, by Daniel Reid.

Table 11-2. Foods Appropriate to the Five Element Types

Element	Organ	Flavor	Food				
			Meats Fish	**Grains**	**Beans**	**Vegetables**	**Fruits**
Fire	Heart, Small Intestine	Bitter	Lamb, Shrimp	Corn	Red lentils	Kale, mustard greens, endive, bitter greens, tomatoes, scallions	Apricots, strawberries
Earth	Spleen-Pancreas, Stomach	Sweet	Tuna, Sword-fish, Wild birds	Millet	Chick-peas	Winter squash, yams	Sweet fruits
Metal	Lungs, Large Intestine	Pungent	Cod, Flounder, Beef, Turkey	Rice	Navy and soy beans, tofu	White onion, cabbage, turnip, radish, cauliflower, celery	Pears
Water	Kidneys, Bladder	Salty	Bluefish	Buck-wheat	Kidney, black, pinto, azuki	Seaweed	Blackberries, blueberries, black grapes, watermelon
Wood	Liver, Gall-bladder	Sour	Chicken	Wheat, rye, oats, barley	Lentils, green peas, string beans	Bean sprouts, salad greens, green peppers, broccoli	Citrus fruits

The flavors associated with elements are used in the Taoist "Five Element" cooking that aims to nourish weak organs. For instance, sour wood-energy foods are beneficial for a weak liver, but they should be avoided with an overactive liver. The lungs and large intestine can be stimulated with pungent metal-energy foods. As a natural diuretic, salty water-energy foods may provide good service to the kidneys and bladder. Whole-grain brown rice, although difficult to digest, contains all five-element energies in proper proportion and is regarded as the most perfectly balanced food.

The flexible joints and bones are associated with the strong water element, which prolongs youth and longevity.

Matniaz Olobergenov, 107, from Uzbekistan, who was said to be as flexible as a young man.

Spiros Antonopoulos from Lorain, Ohio, lived to the age of 99 years and 8 months; with his Choleric temperament, he had the metal and wood element features.

Solitude, the trend of the metal element, was present in Redden Lee Couch who, in 1987 at the age 104, decided to stop living with his daughter and lived by himself, according to Jim Heynen in his book, *One Hundred Over 100*.

The personality characteristics of each element and physiology, both "based on energy, which bridges the gap between body and mind," as Reid says, may be useful in strengthening or pacifying energies of vital organs. For instance, as shown in Figure 11-1, I lack fire and earth energies, and my heart is hypoactive. I need warming fire- and earth-energy foods, bitter and sweet in flavor; stimulating foods and even a little alcohol are good for me. On the other hand, a large percentage of metal energy makes me vulnerable to respiratory ailments. I should restrain myself from metal-energy foods, take good care of my lungs, do breathing exercises, and cultivate deliberation.

The Five-Element Theory provides insight to the personality traits of an individual and indicates how to avoid self-destructive tendencies and achieve the energy balance that promotes health and longevity.

12

CHAKRA SYSTEM

Having met and talked with people from various countries, I noticed that many don't have the slightest idea about *chakras*. Those interested in yoga had heard this word, but they usually didn't know more than that. Many people were surprised that I knew the Sanskrit names of the seven chakras in the human body. People generally find something mystical and fearful in the talk about charkas; it's not common knowledge. However, I believe that it fits quite well with our purpose—to understand more deeply the personality differences of individuals. Moreover, of all the different typologies discussed in this book, I deem the chakras the central role because they enable us to clearly understand the ways to a longer and healthier life.

The language of the chakras is useful in explaining many phenomena that can't be explained through common knowledge. For instance, there is a Russian saying regarding the behavior of a drunken person: "He went out of his mind." Its sense is clearly understood if the explanation is in terms of chakras. Mind control associated with the sixth chakra is lost and the person descended to one of the following lower chakras, namely:

- the first one, if he behaves violently
- the second one, if he rushes to grab women
- the third one, if he starts saying how important his occupation is
- the fourth one, if he expresses extreme love or hatred for others
- the fifth one, if he sings, dances, or recites poems

Each case is a descent to either the basic instincts or behavioral patterns, which in a sober state are kept in check with mind control.

Short descriptions of chakras are found in most books on yoga; however, the following special books discuss them in every possible detail: *Chakras, Energy Centers of Transformation*, by Harish Johari; *Autobiography of a Yogi*, by Paramahansa Yogananda; *Ayurveda: Secrets of Healing*, by Maya Tiwari; *The Elements of the Chakras*, by Naomi Ozaniec; *The Only Dance There Is*, by Ram Dass; *Hands of Light*, by Barbara Ann Brennan; and *Chakra Workout*, by Blawyn and Jones.

Chakras are psycho-energetic centers, the centers of activity of subtle energy (i.e., the vital force termed *subtle prana*). Just as everyone has a physical body, so everyone also has a subtle body (energy) as well. It consists of seven layers (or bodies) that surround our physical body, and it is called an *aura*. The seven major chakras connect physical body to auric bodies. There are also twenty-one minor chakras, dozens of lesser chakras, and a few hundred acupuncture points in the body. These are the gates through which the physical body exchanges energy with the aura and outer space. As Brennan puts it, we are like sponges in the Energy Sea around us. People who can visualize chakras describe them as swirling vortexes of energy.

Chakras are thought to be responsible for receiving, processing, and transmitting energy from the Universal Energy Source. The subtle energy flows into the body through chakras and within the body through "Chinese" channels or meridians. All seven chakras are connected through a vertical channel in the spinal cord, where energy flows up and down. This flow is not confined to the physical body, extending beyond it above the head and below the coccyx. The seven chakras are viewed as swirling cone-shaped vortexes with their tips pointed into a vertical channel of energy. They entrain or suck cosmic energy, operating the same way that cyclones and whirlpools do in the air and in the water. Energy flows into the chakra cones swirling clockwise.

Each chakra with its open end or cone base is attached to a corresponding layer of auric body. Tips of chakra cones--called roots or hearts of the chakras--are connected to the spinal energy channel. Within these roots are seals that control energy flow. Chakras act as transmitters of the universal energy (i.e., *prana, ch'i*) from its cosmic source to the physical body via the *nadis* (i.e., energy channels), nervous system, endocrine system, and blood.

Chakra is a Sanskrit word that means wheel, often associated with wheels of the mind that dwell in a forest of desires. Throughout life, a person dwells in this forest of desires, and thinks and understands life's situations from the standpoint of the chakra in which he/she normally feels most comfortable. Typically, one of the seven chakras in every individual is better developed than the others and can be used to characterize the person's individuality.

"Gross man seldom or never realizes that his body is a kingdom, governed by Emperor Soul on the throne of the cranium, with subsidiary regents in the six spinal centers or spheres of consciousness," says Paramahansa Yogananda about the role of chakras in his book, *Autobiography of a Yogi*. Chakras are also called *lotuses* or *padmas*. This beautiful symbol tells us a great deal about the nature of the chakra as a living force. The exquisite flower blooms upon the water, but its roots are deeply buried in the mud far below the surface. Just like a lotus, a chakra can be closed, in bud, blossoming, active, or dormant. The Sanskrit names of the seven chakras and their location in the body are as follows:

- *Muladhara,* the first (base or root) chakra: at the bottom of the spine, in the perineum, the area of the body between the anus and the genitals
- *Svadhisthana,* the second (sacral or navel) chakra: in the area just above the genitals; very roughly, the so-called Mount of Venus, or *mons veneris*--the area that in adulthood is covered with pubic hair
- *Manipura,* the third (solar plexus) chakra: a little above the navel, in the area of the solar plexus, as its physical analogue
- *Anahata,* the fourth (heart) chakra: in the heart region; sometimes called the cardiac plexus
- *Vishuddha,* the fifth (throat) chakra: at the bottom of the throat, or carotid plexus
- *Ajna,* the sixth (brow or third eye) chakra: on the lower forehead between the eyebrows, as its projection on the face--but often believed to correspond with the pineal gland and medulla plexus, in the middle of the head
- *Sahasrara,* the seventh (crown) chakra: on the top of the head, at the cerebral plexus; a sort of crown to the physical body.

The seven major chakras are located along the spine near the major nerve plexuses of the body (Figure 12-1).

The first chakra has one cone opening directed downward, which pumps energy from the earth up the spine. The seventh chakra receives energy from the universe through one cone that is opened up. The second through sixth chakras have two cones each: one on the front and another on the back of the body. They are called the front and rear aspects of a particular chakra. Each chakra corresponds to certain physical systems and related organs. Chakras are interrelated with the autonomous nervous system (i.e., parasympathetic and sympathetic branches) as well.

Because chakras absorb and metabolize the universal energy that vitalizes body systems and organs, they have physiological functions. At the same time, each chakra is also connected with psychic states and behavioral characteristics of an individual, including instinct, vitality, emotions, memory, creativity, and spirituality. The cosmic energy is often associated with consciousness; therefore, chakras are also considered the body's primary centers of consciousness and have psychological functions.

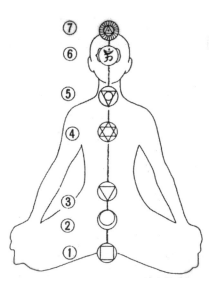

Figure 12-1. Seven Chakras and Their Locations in the Body
(The drawing is adapted from the book, *Yoga and Meditation*, by Akiyo Naito.)

The physiological and psychological functions of the chakras are shown in Table 12-1.

The first, or **Muladhara,** chakra is related to survival, security, the material world, and stability, and can be characterized roughly as survival of the individual as a separate being. It is what Herbert Spencer and then Charles Darwin called "survival of the fittest." Spencer ranked the "how to survive" knowledge as number one in its importance to be acquired by every individual. According to the Darwinian motivations of human beings, the strongest motivation of a person in life is to protect his/her integrity. The Muladhara chakra is directly related to the self-preservation instinct, and is associated with fulfilling the basic needs--such as food, water, air, and sleep-- that are absolutely necessary for our survival and maintenance of health. Its basic psychological block is the fear of death.

The Muladhara chakra is our base in the physical world. Matters that are related to the material world include shelter, stability, success, individuality, trust, courage, patience, activity, and senses. The motto of this chakra is "I have." It means that a person is grounded in his/her being--that he/she is secure and comfortable in whom he/she is, and that he/she patiently achieves his/her goals with courage. As part of this world and nature, we share many instincts and functions with other living creatures. The will to survive represented by this chakra is the most fundamental drive; the willingness to battle against adverse circumstances of life and to adapt to new situations could not be possible without it. The glands associated with our most primitive instincts and drives are the adrenals, which are responsible for the "fight or flight" response through the discharge of adrenaline. The aspects of the first chakra that are fundamental to human existence are anger, greed, delusion, avarice, illusion, and sensuality. The people whose profession is to protect others and who are trained to fight (e.g., policemen, military personnel, and bodyguards) are those with a high energy level in the Muladhara chakra.

Table 12-1. Physiological and Psychological Functions of Chakras

Nos.	Name of Chakra	Physiological Functions (Area of the Body Governed)	Psychological Functions
1	Muladhara	Spinal column, legs, blood, adrenal glands, kidneys, bladder, and colon	Quantity of physical energy, will to live
2	Svadhisthana	Reproductive organs, genitals, prostate, gonads, and spleen	Quality of love for the opposite sex; giving and receiving physical, mental, and spiritual pleasure. Quantity of sexual energy
3	Manipura	Stomach, pancreas, liver, and gallbladder	Awareness of belonging to the Universe. Spiritual wisdom, will, control of emotions and imaginations. Striving for health, healing abilities
4	Anahata	Heart, circulatory system, blood, arms, hands, and thymus gland	Love to other human beings, openness, and sensuality. Ego will, will toward the outer world.
5	Vishuddha	Throat, mouth, and thyroid gland	Self-sufficiency, taking in what life offers and assimilating. Sense of self, satisfaction with social and professional life
6	Ajna	Lower brain, left eye, ears, nose, and pituitary gland	Ability to comprehend mental ideas and concepts, to visualize. Capacity to implement ideas in practice
7	Sahasrara	Upper brain, right eye, and pineal gland	Spirituality, religiousness, integration of personality with life

The **Svadhisthana** chakra is related to procreation, sensual gratification, and sexual desires. Its aspects are procreation, family, passion, and fantasy. After one's life is protected and earthly security in the form of monetary wealth in the first chakra are attained, then a person can be concerned with the next matters, which are reproduction, sensual desires, and sexual life. This chakra also governs creativity at all levels. According to some suggestions, the continuous activity of the sex hormones in humans results in an increased alertness in the brain. This idea may confirm the traditional belief that this chakra and the mind are directly linked to one another.

Still, the major function of the Svadhisthana chakra is reproduction and sexuality, which are inactive until puberty. Together with sensuality, desire, pleasure, passion, giving, and receiving, the second chakra is also associated with health, vitality, tolerance, hospitality, assimilation of new ideas, and cooperation in working with others. The motto of the second chakra is "I feel." In a balanced state of the Svadhisthana chakra, a person experiences fulfillment of sexual expression. He/She enjoys being male or female and is comfortable with him/herself sexually. He/She is successful, fruitful, and reproduces with ease, and flows smoothly with the changes of life.

In the physical body, the Svadhisthana chakra rules all liquids: blood and lymph circulation, the production of urine and seminal fluids, and menstrual flow. If imbalances or blockages occur in this chakra, all these systems will suffer. Because of its profound influence on the mind, the second chakra can cause an altering of certain states. If the chakra is excessively active or overly Yang, a person can become sexually overactive and have undue fantasies. The excessively Yin chakra can cause impotence or other sexual problems. If a person wants to be balanced and to maintain good health, he/she must regulate diet, sleep, and sex to attain a harmonious, peaceful state of body and mind. Sex professionals or those who use sex to achieve their goals are people with the increased energy of the Svadhisthana chakra.

The **Manipura** chakra corresponds to the digestive system. This chakra is a power center, which relates to the storage of prana or vital force, and also is called a reservoir of physical and spiritual energy. It is also known as the solar plexus and is dominated by the fire element, which aids in the digestion and absorption of food. Similar to the digestive system, which breaks down food and aids in the extraction of the energy needed for survival, the solar plexus extracts and stores prana. All living creatures need prana, and all are receivers and storers of it. We absorb prana from live food, spring water, fresh air, beautiful natural landscapes, or any kind of beauty around us; these are all great sources of prana. When we ingest them or are in contact with them, we feel a surge of rising energy, as if our batteries are charged. The role of live food such as fresh fruits and vegetables with their juices, grains, seeds, and nuts cannot be overemphasized. Overcooked and processed foods that have no prana left in them can be destructive to our body. "Don't bring inside your body dead cells," says Russian life-extensionist Dr. Souren Arakelyan.

In the modern world, a Manipura chakra person is one of power, the one who acquired the power to command and organize. The third chakra is like Wall Street and Washington and London, says Ram Dass. Its primary connection is with power, mastery, and ego control. Our boss is stronger by the energy of this chakra than we are, which is why he/she is our boss. If we accumulate more power than he/she has, we will replace him/her and become the boss. If he/she is a general manager, there is a president of the company who is superior to him/her in terms of the third-chakra energy. A person of power can be the boss in the company, but in his/her family, the spouse or one of the children can possess the higher power, and he/she will be inferior to them. Those in power--the leaders, executives and managers, presidents of companies, bankers, politicians, and strong spouses--are the people with the highest energy in the Manipura chakra.

The Manipura chakra is also a seat of long and healthy life. Without strong and healthy digestive organs, a long life is hardly possible. Eating and digestive disorders are often linked to imbalances in the third chakra. The stomach is very vulnerable to stress; ulcers are a classic disorder of this center. This stress can be due to unexpressed--especially negative--emotions, which remain lodged in this chakra until they are freed (if their cause is found). Anger is often trapped in this chakra and can remain there for years. However, if the energies of this chakra are balanced and active, the person is in good health and enjoys well-being.

The solar plexus chakra is a center of free will, logic, personal power, mastery of desire, efficiency, flexibility, and self-control. Radiance, warmth, humor, and laughter also belong to this center. The motto of a third-chakra person is "I can." He/She lives in harmony with his/her digestive organs and acknowledges feeling in them. He/She avoids absorbing negative energies by controlling negative emotions. He/She has a clear sense of personal determination and works to make his/her personal power grow stronger with each passing day.

The *Anahata* chakra is a center of unconditional love, understanding, forgiveness, acceptance, and compassion. The heart chakra unites our heart's love energy with cosmic wisdom. In many cultures, the heart and love are not thought of one without the other. If someone loses his/her love, he/she feels pain in his/her heart--the heart is broken. When someone is in love, his/her love goes together with cherishing, caring, protecting, supporting, and many other qualities. At this time, a particular quality of energy pours from the heart center. However, the love of the heart center is associated more with universal love than with personal love that we usually experience. For most people, the true-love experience does not happen often, and only rare individuals live their entire lives with such a love. Theresa Neumann, Mother Theresa, and many Christian saints were the embodiments of the love force. They were channels for the love of Jesus Christ that flowed through them to others, and their love had the power to heal and change.

The heart chakra is governed by the air element. Air is filled with prana and we take it in with the air we breathe. The energy of the Anahata chakra aids in the functions of the lungs and the heart, which provide oxygen and life force to all organs and systems. In the physical body, this chakra is associated with the heart, circulatory system, blood, and thymus gland; the sense of touch is also controlled by the heart chakra. The motto of a heart-chakra person is "I love." He/She knows and understands love and accepts love from others. Through our hands, we offer love in loving caresses and express our feeling of tenderness with loving touches. The heart meridians go down the arms into the hands; people who have hand power radiate their healing energy through their hands.

The *Vishuddha* chakra is related to creativity and self-expression, the gateway to communication with the unknown. This chakra is associated with the power of the spoken word, with the clear verbal communication that employs sound located in the throat. Poets, writers, singers, orators, comedians, and storytellers all know the power of the word and of sound, and use them in communication with the public. All these talented people have a high-level energy of the Vishuddha chakra. Great orators and political leaders are able to inspire the group mind--history is full of examples of those who could lead the group mind into madness. Mass communication also would be impossible without words. Our lives are filled with many words and various sounds. The need to speak freely--to express thoughts and feelings with words--is a psychological need of all human beings.

Sound is a form of vibration, which carries the energy. All religious traditions use prayers or mantras that aid in shaping the spiritual state of believers. Each chakra has also its own mantra or seed sound, which is said to have the power to increase the energy of the chakra. The "Om mane padme hum" mantra is one of the most well-known Buddhist mantras. In the physical body, the function of hearing is assigned to the Vishuddha chakra. More than the ordinary physical hearing of our everyday life, it refers to a subtle quality of inner hearing; it is like the "third ear"--the ability to hear with the mind rather than with physical ears. The process of creativity is linked to that development of inner hearing.

Great composers undoubtedly heard music inwardly. Beethoven had this inner hearing of music even when he became deaf later in his life. Mozart, Paganini, Mahler, and other great musicians were often tuned to that inward "music of spheres." Alexander Skryabin, a Russian composer, had the rare ability of both hearing and seeing colors associated with the sound of music. His symphonic poem "Prometheus" was created as color music. Its performance was designed as a combination of music played with an orchestra and colors projected on a screen. I once had the opportunity to watch a performance of "Prometheus" in Moscow. The performer responsible for the color part played a type of organ with his hands and feet and this special device produced the colors displayed on a big screen.

Activation of the Vishuddha chakra brings increased telepathy--the ability to communicate directly mind-to-mind without words. Tophik Dadashev of Azebraijan, known in Russia for his channeling powers, was said to understand the thoughts of foreigners without knowing their language. Some poets and writers experience a kind of inner dictation. Alexander Pushkin, a Russian classical poet known for his poem-novel "Eugene Onegin," never corrected his drafts--they were perfect at the first writing. How could it be possible without divine inspiration? Mozart and Pushkin were called "God-made geniuses," while other great artists were called "self-made geniuses." Richard Bach, an American writer, is said to have created his famous *Jonathan Livingston Seagull* by listening to the inner voice that dictated the story to him.

A person with an open Vishuddha chakra acquires knowledge of what is true and the understanding of the past, present, and future. He/She can even live without food or drink, like Therese Neumann, Giri Bala, and Xu Fang. Xu Fung's sister, who is sometimes called by name Nadya, told me that after one year in the non-eating state, Xu Fang was able to know the previous lives of her family members.

The **Ajna** chakra is called the "third eye," a center related to intuition, self-awareness, clear thinking, wisdom, and paranormal powers. When awakened, this center certainly acts as a third eye--the eye of the mind, of the soul. The meaning of the name *ajna* ("to know") refers to the means of direct knowing beyond the ordinary senses. Our two physical eyes can see the present and the past; the third eye reveals insight to the future. The person established in the Ajna chakra goes beyond all kinds of desires that motivate life and induce him/her to move in many directions. Instead, he/she now becomes one-directed, and he/she will be able to know the past, present, and future. In this state of consciousness, contact with the inner teacher--the source of wisdom within--becomes possible. We are all familiar with the outer teachers--we need them because the self of our personality is limited. However, the inner teacher is the higher self, and experiences such as that of the Holy Guardian Angel are essentially contacts with sources outside the limited self.

Relative to the physical organs, the Ajna chakra is the first one that is connected to the brain rather than the body. The mind governs the body and has no restrictions in time and space such as a body has. Thoughts have wings and they fly not only in the present and to the past, but also to the future. With activation of the Ajna chakra, a person discovers new ways of using his/her mind. The increasing power to see with the mind's eye brings the power of visualization, the facility for creating images. Most of us had a vivid imagination in our childhood, but for the majority of us, it vanished with adulthood and education. Visualization as a powerful tool is a key factor in certain kinds of meditation, self-healing, and expansion of consciousness. Just as speech is governed by the throat chakra, so visualization is an attribute of the third-eye chakra.

A person who enters the Ajna chakra acquires wisdom, the insight into clear understanding of the most basic laws of the universe. Egyptians were very concerned with this knowledge, and it is the primary subject of Plato's pure ideas. The realm of pure ideas is where all great philosophers, thinkers, and metaphysics belong. The individual who establishes him/herself in the brow chakra realizes that he/she is an immortal spirit in a temporal body. He/She no longer identifies him/herself with the body, only with ideas. His/Her motto is "I see." Clear thinking, perfect concentration, peace of mind, devotion, and being in the "here and now" are all qualities and attributes of those who have entered the Ajna chakra.

The *Sahasrara* chakra is related to universal love and unity, divine wisdom and understanding, and liberation into the cosmic realm and bliss. The Sahasrara chakra is like the ocean where the union of individual raindrops is achieved, where the yogi realizes that he is one with the cosmic principles that govern the entire universe within the body. This is a person's gateway to the universe where the union is achieved. It is said that this chakra is even beyond all laws and ideas. The word *Sahasrara* means thousandfold, which reflects its image in the form of the lotus with one thousand petals. It also symbolizes the totality of creation--the idea of wholeness, completion, and realization. The yogi who enters the crown chakra becomes illuminated like the sun and his aura of light is continually radiant. In the Christian tradition, the saints are always depicted in icons and paintings with a halo of golden light above their head--this is an accurate depiction of the awakened crown chakra of the saints.

Awakening of the Sahasrara chakra is at the heart of the extension of consciousness in every spiritual system. Union is an ultimate goal and final point of yoga, a liberation called *moksha* in Hinduism and *nirvana* in Buddhism. The *baga*, which means union with God, is the goal in Sufism too. Yogananda said, "The seventh center, the 'thousand-petal lotus' in the brain, is the throne of the Infinite Consciousness. In the state of divine illumination, the yogi is said to perceive Brahma or God the Creator as Padmaja, 'the One born of the lotus'." For each person, the awakening of this chakra is the highest possible achievement of human life. Hiroshi Motoyama of Japan, the Shinto priest who personally experienced an awakening of the crown chakra, describes the benefits and changes that it brings: "When the center begins to awaken, it can bring unusually sensitive mental states. These are normally short-lived and pass. The physical body becomes healthy. The powers of concentration improve; discernment becomes deeper and more reliable. The mind is freed from attachments; insight deepens. The ability to take effective action toward the fulfillment of goals increases. Psychic abilities strengthen. The resulting freedom of mind makes it possible to exist in the realm of enlightenment while living in the world." It is said that the person who experiences this enlightenment is *sat-chit-ananda*, or truth-being-blessed, or he/she is his/her own real self.

We all possess the potential for enlightenment represented by the crown chakra. However, it is almost impossible for most of us to achieve the awakening of the Sahasrara or any other chakra without the guidance of a Teacher, because a teacher gives oral instructions that eliminate the chances of abuse or misunderstanding. The chakra workout if done improperly can do more harm than good and even become life threatening. Vladimir Samol was my friend who died while practicing deep meditation, which involved stopping his heart from beating. The awakened chakras give super powers and sound so attractive that for some it is difficult to resist the temptation to give it a try. However, all things worth obtaining must be paid for; everything in life has a price. The price of unconsidered playing with chakras can be one's health or even life.

There are a few ways or methods to increase the energy level of the chakras. Some yoga exercises described in the exercise chapter are helpful for this purpose. Color-therapy eyeware, created and designed by Terri Perrigoue-Messer, uses the effect of light energy in colors on the chakras. This therapy offers eyeglasses of seven different colors and claims that a blast of energy will be felt if the glasses are worn for thirty to sixty minutes a day. There are also training courses for chakra workouts available in many cities in the United States; some people even go to India to attend the Yoga schools.

Of the seven chakras described herein, the three lower chakras connect us to the earth, the three upper chakras connect us to the universe, and the seventh Anahata chakra combines the divine and earthly nature in us humans. We are created in the image of God and we are semi-gods who walk in the lower layer of divine space on the surface of Earth. The overall goal of our life is spiritual evolution. We are given a chance to take this step and to get closer to God.

Chakra Profile

Every person has a certain amount of energy stored in each chakra, and each chakra is open, more or less. Open means able to receive the energy from the space around us, open for the energy to flow in. If a chakra is open to the degree that it functions normally, we enjoy health and vitality in the organs and parts of the body related to it. If a chakra is nearly closed and malfunctioning, we suffer from related disorders.

The distribution of energy over the different chakras in each of us is uneven. Some chakras can be more developed or open than others. The most developed chakra, with the higher energy level, can be called dominant or prevailing. For instance, someone craves food and drink and consumes them in excess; even when aware that this is harmful to him/her, he/she cannot stop. The result is that he/she is obese and sedentary, and his/her spine and joints are not flexible. In this case, we say that much of his/her energy is attached to the first chakra. The more energy attached or consumed in any particular chakra, the less there is left for other chakras or for other activities in the same chakra. Another person may perfectly control his/her diet and can even fast on juice or water easily. He/She often exercises and leads an active life. In this case, we say that this person consumes little and the amount of energy left in the first chakra is quite significant.

People whose chakras are harmonically developed are very rare. Heredity plays an important role and determines which chakras will be well functioning after we mature. If a person becomes an accomplished pianist, it means that he/she was gifted with this talent and received a well-developed fifth chakra at birth. We can achieve much if we work hard to develop one or another ability in ourselves; however, if we have not been gifted with it, the achievement will be modest. The cases of people being gifted in all seven chakras are very rare. Most people have one or two developed chakras, with their other chakras underdeveloped. Consider the case of Emmanuel Kant, a great philosopher with a wide-open sixth chakra. He never married, though, and left no offspring, which means that his second chakra was not strong.

Of all the people I have met, the only person with all seven chakras highly developed is my yoga teacher, Eugene Bazh. He was born in the city of Sukhumi, a Black Sea port and the capital of Abkhasia, located south of the former USSR and now the Republic of Georgia. By the age of five, he was under the care of a Chinese man who spent most of his life in India and became a yoga guru. Eugene stayed with him until the age of seventeen and acquired many skills, including Hatha Yoga technique, Indian dances, Chinese martial arts, Sanskrit language, massage, fortunetelling, and many others. I first met him when he moved to Moscow at the age of eighteen--he rented a room in my apartment and stayed with me for about seven years.

To start, he opens the *Muladhara* chakra; his body is very flexible and he performs Yoga asanas (i.e., postures) perfectly. When he demonstrates the martial arts, he completely controls the movements of his legs and arms, and never hurts his partner. Any element of kata exercise done with the right arm or leg, he can precisely repeat with the left ones.

Eugene follows a diet rich in whole grains, green salads, and dairy products, with some meat and poultry. Most of all, he likes cooked buckwheat with butter and cheese. Twice I witnessed him undertaking a water fast for as long as forty days. He explained that he aimed for spiritual growth during these fasts. Usually quite well fed, he became very thin by the end of the fasts--his nose looked like the blade of a knife. The beverages he drinks are milk, kefir, green and herb teas, and--very rarely--wine or vodka. Born in May and being a Taurus by horoscope, he does not like fish and never eats it.

The *Svadhisthana* chakra is the very strong center of Eugene Bazh. His reproductive ability is great. At the age of forty, he has one son from his first marriage and four children--three sons and one daughter--in his current second marriage. He claims also to have one pre-marriage daughter. When I called him two years ago from Japan, he told me that she has a child already and he called himself a "young grandpa." In Moscow, most people usually have one child, rarely two.

In Figure 12-2, Eugene Bazh is shown performing the Tai Chi kata.

Figure 12-2. Eugene Bazh Performing the Tai Chi Kata

Equally strong is the energy of Eugene's *Manipura* chakra. In Moscow, he often was an instructor for karate classes, Tai Chi sessions, and recreation groups; I attended his classes a number of times. His students were both men and women, aged from ten to seventy, and he always perfectly managed them. It is worth noting that in his pre-Moscow period, he was a karate trainer of large groups of police officers in the city of Sukhumi, the capital of Abkhasia. These people are reputed to be very short-tempered and controlling them is almost impossible. At present, he is a vice-president of a recreation company in Moscow, a type of health and fitness club for children and adults.

The *Anahata* chakra is highly developed in Eugene Bazh. His heart is always open to people and he is tremendously popular. He has an outstanding ability to diagnose diseases and heal with massage, acupressure, and dietary suggestions. He never refuses to help people and has cured many of almost incurable diseases such as scoliosis (curvature of the spine), impaired sight and hearing, and arthritis. When I had a problem in my left knee, he started the treatment by adjusting the subtle body (i.e., the aura) of the knee first. He manipulated with his hands 3 feet away from my knee, in front of it and to the left. It felt like he was actually applying the real massage to my knee. Then he did a few real massages on it, which helped me a lot. He never accepted money for his treatments; if people gave him gifts, he never kept them for himself--he usually distributed them among his apprentices.

The talents, which are associated with the *Vishuddha* chakra, are blooming in Eugene Bazh. He writes verses, paints (his father is a painter) spiritual paintings, performs Indian dances, and recently wrote a book entitled *Alone with God*. He told me about his book in our telephone conversation and I wonder whether it has been published in Russia.

The *Ajna* chakra, which is related to creativity and philosophical thinking, is well developed in him. For meditation purposes, he created original and very complicated yantras (i.e., charts) of visible and invisible energies, personality states, emotions, and so on. From his sketch, I drew it on the wall of my apartment in Moscow. He always has an unusual perspective on common things and never sticks to a particular idea; rather, he places it in dialectical relation to other ideas. My friends, many of them professors and Ph.D.s, have been happy to talk to him and to witness his wisdom. I spent many nights listening to his excursions into a creation of the universe. After my emigration in 1990, he became famous in Moscow because of his lectures on religious and supernatural themes.

The spiritual awakening, supernatural abilities for telepathy, the ability to see aura, even an ability (rare among channelers) to *see thoughts*--to know the present, past, and future--all these are associated with the *Sahasrara* chakra, and are just a few of Eugene's talents. The crown chakra is definitely awakened in him. His body is strong, extremely flexible, and healthy. His yoga postures are perfectly correct and beautiful. His senses have a broader range than those of an ordinary person. His knowledge and wisdom are phenomenal. In everything that happens around him, he sees the core and deeply understands the causes and effects.

Although he never reads books, he receives his knowledge through the "direct channel" from the "universal source," and it strikes with its depth and universal order. He told me that in his meditations, he usually receives the teachings from his spiritual teachers, who are visible and audible in his mind. His freedom is close to absolute; I never saw as free a man as he is, regardless of the circumstances. The yoga principle of non-attachment is his innate characteristic. He taught me this principle and, when I emigrated ten years ago, I ended up with a non-attachment to him; I've missed him ever since.

Chakra System and Longevity

This book discusses how to stay healthy and live a long life. Knowledge of the chakras can give insight to deeper understanding about how to do that. The three lower chakras--Muladhara, Svadhisthana, and Manipura, the earthly chakras--are responsible for our survival, both physical as an individual and psychological as a member of a family and society. The three upper chakras--Sahasrara, Ajna, and Vishuddha, the heavenly chakras--are associated with our intellectual and spiritual development and they are of divine origin within us. The central Anahata chakra, which unites our divine and earthly origins, is linked to our emotional development.

My idea is that for achieving good health and longevity, a person needs to control his/her basic biological needs including food, water, air, sleep, sex, and personal power. The word "control" is used here in the sense of restraint, limitation, and consuming only what is necessary for survival and maintaining good physical health: less food, less water, less oxygen, fewer orgasms, less idleness (more exercise), and sleep in moderation. Then there is control of emotions and thoughts, where "control" means command over these states necessary to gain and maintain mental and psychological health. The third requirement is to develop all of a person's talents, gifts, skills, intelligence, and spirit as much as possible--to fully blossom. These activities support both physical and mental health. If all three requirements are fulfilled, a person can enjoy good physical and mental health and longevity, even if personal heredity is not the best.

With this approach, I am not advocating for the Spartan life or self-flagellation for the sake of prolonging life. Gratification of the senses is a great motivation in life in general; however, I am advocating for **higher intellectual and spiritual gratification rather than gratification of basic instincts**. Yogi devotees say that we have to give up many things in order to receive all in return.

Everything that we take from the outside world for pleasure must be paid for, and all the efforts that we produce inside are rewarded--this is a universal law. Actually, with limiting food, drink, sleep, and sex (a big effort), one begins to appreciate and enjoy them more, thereby increasing gratification even with just the basic needs. To gain a "life that is full," a person needs to work on it, and work hard. As a Russian poet said, "The soul ought to toil day and night, day and night." Mastering self-control is time consuming process and chances to accomplish it are greater if one lives a long life.

The chakra profile shown in Figure 12-3 assesses the **energy expenditure** at each chakra level for three people.

As can be seen in the chakra profiles for three people and the longevity profile, there is a distinct difference between them. The assessment of energy level of each chakra is relative and is based on my personal impression and other considerations.

Miss Xu Fang has not eaten for the last thirteen years, drinks only a little water, and sleeps six to seven hours; therefore, she does not spend much energy on the lower Muladhara chakra associated with biological needs. She is not married yet and has no children, so her second chakra is at a lower level of energy expenditure as well. She runs her own business, which is why her third chakra spends more energy than the first two. She loves people so much and helps them a lot; therefore, she acts at the high energy level in her Anahata chakra. She can play the piano a little (she said), her "third eye" is open, she knows the present and the past of people, and she deeply believes in Buddha and loves to meditate. Therefore, I assessed the energy of her three upper chakras as relatively increasing from the Vishuddha to the Sahasrara chakra.

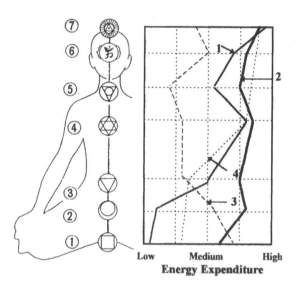

Figure 12-3.   Chakra Profile
1. Xu Fang
2. Eugene Bazh
3. Author
4. Longevity Profile

The detailed characteristics of Eugene Bazh's chakra energy discussed previously result in his profile being at the high energy level of all but the Muladhara chakra, which is moderate. My chakra profile is more modest and I need to work hard to change the level of energy of all my chakras. The ideal distribution of chakra energies for achieving a long and healthy life is shown on line 4; the profiles of Miss Xu Fang and Eugene Bazh are much closer to the ideal than mine is. I need a lot of time to catch up with them.

There are many examples of centenarians who achieved that kind of fulfilling life.

The queen of longevity, Jeanne Calment of France, who lived to age 122, had always watched her diet, including in it garlic, olive oil, and fish, the reputed promoters of health. She exercised (hunted, rode a bicycle at age 100); enjoyed playing the piano, painting, and singing (she released a rap CD at 121); and liked chocolate, port wine, and cigarettes (in moderation, just for pleasure). She retained her sense of humor to the end and was "never bored."

Frank Shomo of Robinson, Pennsylvania, who lived to the age of 108, worked for forty-two years. After his retirement when he was in his seventies, he used his skills to make leather wallets, belts, and handbags. He deeply believed in God, was a member of the Masons Lodge for forty-seven years, and Bible study became a daily ritual in his later years.

The American sisters Sarah, 108, and Elizabeth Delaney (who died at 104 in 1995), did stair-climbing and yoga exercises, ate garlic, wrote a book entitled *Having Our Say: The Delany Sisters' First 100 Years*, and enjoyed reading poetry and literature, listening to music, and looking at paintings.

These people are just a few examples of the "upper chakras" life.

13

ORIENTAL HOROSCOPE

The position of the stars and planets on the day of a person's birth allegedly affects his/her longevity. Whether there is a link between a person's duration of life and the horoscope type or sign that he/she was born under is questionable. However, some observations show that such a link probably exists. The first observation is that of Koasa, the Japanese artist who hosted a TV program about centenarians. He met 158 centenarians within three years and found that many of them were born under the constellation of Sagittarius (November 22 – December 21). The group of Japanese researchers who interviewed 103 centenarians also traced the link between longevity and horoscope sign at birth. Those born under the Pisces sign (February 19 – March 20) were in the majority (twenty-two people), followed by twenty people born under the Aquarius sign (January 20 - February 18), and sixteen people born under the Aries sign (March 21 – April 19). The third observation is mine: I analyzed the dates of birth of American centenarians written about in the book *One Hundred Over 100*, by Jim Heynen, relative to their horoscope signs. Table 13-1 shows the number of centenarians in the United States and Japan born under different horoscope signs.

As can be seen from this table, the **majority of centenarians in both countries were born in the winter and spring seasons**, with few born in the summer and fall. Certainly, the statistical array is too small to draw any definite conclusion; however, at first glance, there seems to be a relation between month of birth or horoscope type and longevity. The following discussion includes personality characteristics, health, and dietary choices of different horoscope types.

The following description of horoscope types is based on these sources: *Practical Astrology*, by Jerry L. Keanne, Ph.D. (Russian edition); and *Collins Pocket Reference Astrology*, by Diagram Books. The examples of centenarians whose features match the characteristics of certain horoscope types are taken from the book, *One Hundred Over 100*, by Jim Heynen.

Table 13-1.   Centenarians in the United States and Japan
Born Under Different Horoscope Signs

Nos.	Horoscope Sign	Months - Days	Ruling Element	USA	Japan
1	Aries	Mar. 21 – Apr. 19	Fire	10	16
2	Taurus	Apr. 20 - May 20	Earth	11	3
3	Gemini	May 21 – Jun. 21	Air	10	6
4	Cancer	Jun. 22 – Jul. 22	Water	7	4
5	Leo	Jul. 23 – Aug. 22	Fire	4	3
6	Virgo	Aug. 23 – Sep. 22	Earth	7	4
7	Libra	Sep. 23 – Oct. 23	Air	6	6
8	Scorpio	Oct. 24 – Nov. 21	Water	6	4
9	Sagittarius	Nov. 22 – Dec. 21	Fire	7	6
10	Capricorn	Dec. 22 – Jan. 19	Earth	11	14
11	Aquarius	Jan. 20 – Feb. 18	Air	12	18
12	Pisces	Feb. 19 - Mar. 20	Water	9	19
	Total			100	103

Oven or Aries (the Ram), March 21 - April 19

The Oven sign symbolizes activity, and it controls the head. The positive Oven has an active, straightforward personality and he/she has many features of a creator. Rather than profoundly, he/she acts quickly and resolutely. The typical Oven is fiercely competitive, takes initiative, and expects others to follow. They have very clear goals and use their wits and brains to get what they want. They love to be in command, to order others about, and to rush into the rough sea of activity. These were the features of Albert Starr, 105, a rancher from Mullen, Nebraska, who was born under the Oven sign. "He ran the ranch like a benevolent dictator. He assigned every (of his seven sons) his task; one broke horses, all milked but were assigned their own cows, one ran hay sled, one checked the cattle, and so on," Heynen wrote about him.

The negative side of an Oven is a sign of destruction--a precursor of an accident, fire, or disaster. He/she serves as an expression of dictatorship and destruction. Whether positive or negative, an Oven is a person of action rather than a thinker. The direction of their activity, whether creative or destructive, is a matter of individual choice through the freedom of will.

Health. A typical Oven person is healthy and fights illnesses and diseases with sheer willpower. Good health is the feature that promotes long life. An Oven may suffer emotionally when life teaches him/her a hard lesson and his/her pride is hurt. Common disorders for the Oven sign include those of the head, such as acne, epilepsy, neuralgia, headaches, and migraines.

In both the United States and Japan, those born under the Oven sign are the next to highest number of centenarians, as shown in Table 13-1. The American centenarians of this sign who were interviewed by Heynen in 1987-1989 are listed as follows:

> • Geraldine Pringle, 101, a governess from Oakland, California. "Geraldine Pringle could never lie, steal, or hurt anyone…. She has never been bothered by grudges, envy, greed, or selfishness," said Frank Tinney, Jr., who knew her for many decades.

> • Sarah Silvers, 100, a drugstore operator and community volunteer from Los Angeles, California. "Her life is characterized by guts. She is a tall rock. Her courage and dignity are an inspiration to those who know about her," said her close friend.

Taurus (the Bull), April 20 - May 20

Stability and certainty are the features of the Taurus sign, which controls the neck and throat. A person born under this sign is practical, down to earth, target-oriented, persistent, and artistic.

The positive Taurus is a wide-open, serious person who thinks and acts slowly. Their steady way of thinking and conservative outlook is difficult to change. They can be dependable and offer enduring loyalty. Calm, patient, thorough, attentive, gentle, and placid, he/she is only interested in the very best of everything. He/she is open to others and values their talents. Contrary to the Oven, who listens to nobody, Taurus listens often, but rarely agrees. Patronage of Venus makes him/her an admirer of beauty and harmony in the best sense of these words.

The negative Taurus is stubborn, obstinate, and steadfast, with a big strength hidden in him/her. He/she resists any changes, even if they bring him/her profit. Furthermore, he/she can be reserved, greedy, and pompous. Their intellect is confined, but their instincts are pronounced. Tendencies to be self-indulgent, to delay action by lengthy pondering, to be easily embarrassed, and to be insensitive are also among their negative features.

In general, a Taurus is a decisive and persistent individual, and the direction of the expression of his/her character--positive or negative--is a matter of individual choice through the freedom of will.

Health. Taureans are healthy and robust people, although they may become a little overweight. Even if they had health problems in early years, they can later become healthy again.

> That is what happened to Philip S. Eastburg, 101, from Seattle, Washington. At the age of nineteen, he had a "heart leakage" that nearly killed him. However, one day while doing light work on the family farm, a miracle recovery happened to him. Because of that experience, he believes in guardian angels. Ever since then, he has been healthy; when he was one hundred years old, his legs were the only trouble for him.

Swollen glands and laryngitis are typical sicknesses of Taureans.

It is said that when a typical Taurus makes love, it is the most physical and natural pleasure in the whole world.

> This can be applied to Russell Williams, 104 (at the date of the interview in 1987), of Chimacum, Washington. He seemed to be a master of making love. He had twelve children, with his last child born when he was seventy-two years old.

> Russell worked hard all his life, first as a boy in the cotton fields, then farming in Oklahoma, and finally at a smelter for thirty-one years before retiring. "If hard work could open the doors to the Kingdom of Longevity, Papa Williams would be St. Peter," wrote Heynen. However, his daughter-in-law revealed another of his secrets for being around so long: "Good booze, good cigars, good food, and a lot of love." His drinking ability was fabulous: at the age of 100, he could drink a half-gallon of vodka in four or five days.

Although Taurus is reputed to be earthy and materialistic, there are profound spiritual devotees among Taureans too. Bessie Hubbard, 100, from Stanwood, Washington, is one of them. "She's a woman who seems to run on high-octane spiritual power, someone who hates TV, who has never had any hobbies, and who loves to work," wrote Heynen.

Reading the horoscope books can be fun, but sometimes it is a real inspiration.

> I was excited when I encountered the description of health for people born on May 11 (my birthday): "As adults, May 11 people are usually more than capable of taking care of themselves, even tending to be exceptionally long-lived, but may exhibit hypochondriac behavior. They often have extreme dietary preferences, but nonetheless manage to remain remarkably healthy," said Gary Goldschneider and Joost Elffers in their book, *The Secret Language of Birthdays*. Taking good care of myself is definitely a habit of mine and thus

this description suits me quite well. What inspires me the most is the long-living promise, which I hope will work for me. Luckily, the hypochondriac behavior is not my feature, at least so far. Also, I do not have dietary preferences that could be hazardous to my health. If there were any, I believe I could control them.

Gemini (the Twins), May 20 - June 20

This sign symbolizes quickness and personality. It controls the shoulders, arms, and lungs. On the negative side, someone born under this sign is a frivolous person who rushes endlessly from here to there. Being unreliable, he/she is not only badly organized, but also brings disorder all around him/her. Conversely, the positive counterpart of Gemini is a person of creativity, punctuality, and organization. These features are expressed in them as strongly as the opposite ones in the negative type. Their head and hands are smart; and they are quick in both perception and action.

Geminis are full of life, generally enjoy spontaneous activities, and are always eager to be off on a new adventure.

Even a mother of twelve children, as was Nina Rust, 105 (in 1987), of Rosenburg, Oregon, was not restrained from getting thrilling experiences-- sometimes dangerous and even life-threatening. She was a fearless woman throughout all her long life. "Nina was…the kind of person who would sit in the tops of trees when her brothers cut them down so that she could have the thrill of falling with the tree and landing in the creek. Another time, she ran off to kill a rattlesnake for the pleasure of showing it to her friends," Heynen wrote about her. She was shown on national TV riding an elephant at the Oregon Wildlife Safari when she was a hundred years old. When she was 106, she took a motorcycle ride with her grandson.

In any case, Gemini can be everything opposite to the slow and ponderous Taurus. Whether their quickness is brilliant in the positive sense or a sign of cunning and adroitness in the negative sense is entirely a matter of individual choice and the way of self-expression.

Health. In general, Geminis are healthy if they have enough room to breathe and space to explore. Nervous exhaustion can occur if they fail to cope with stress. The Geminian maladies are coughs, colds, bronchitis, laryngitis, and other respiratory-system complaints.

Cancer (the Crab), June 21 - July 22

This sign symbolizes mother and controls the stomach and chest. The negative Cancer is tenacious, imperious, demanding, and proprietary, although at the same time, he/she is as weak and as changeable as the moon-- their governor--in its various phases. The positive Cancer protects, secures, and creates the hearth and home comforts, and sympathizes with as only a mother does. Cancers are generous, magnanimous to the extent that they can sacrifice themselves, and they are always within reach if they are needed.

In general, the Cancer person is tenacious, and never lets him/herself despair. However, the manifestation of their positive or negative side is a matter of individual choice through the freedom of will.

Health. The Cancer person can withstand sickness quite long, provided that he/she is secure and receives affection from surrounding people. They may suffer from indigestion, anemia, and low vitality. However, watching their diet, they can enjoy good health.

> Pearl Rombach, 101, of Melbourne, Florida. At the age of fifteen, she was overweight, weighing 155 pounds; however, at 101, her weight was only 115 pounds because of poor digestion. Despite two surgeries for colon and breast cancer, she was active and had been feeling fairly well.

Leo (the Lion), July 23 - August 21

This sign symbolizes life force and controls the heart and upper part of the back. The negative Leo is egotistic, knowing nothing but his/her own personal likes and dislikes. He/she shows off, always plays a role, and is an actor to the degree that a distinct border between personality and play becomes obscure.

The positive Leo is a self-confident person, benevolent, self-expressing, impulsive, and unrestrained, but also open and never surrendering. No one can imagine him/her to be quiet and calm.

> Giving up was not in the character of Harry Wander, 100, of Boise, Idaho, when at the age of twenty-nine he was told by doctors that he would live at best just another six months. Because of a bad heart condition, both the Dutch and U.S. armies turned him down. He started an exercise program of boxing and wrestling, however, and lived another seventy-one years.

In any case, a Leo must always "shine," never despair, and support and encourage others, even if the situation turns hopeless. The manifestation of a

Leo's positive or negative qualities also depends on individual choice and personal will.

Health. People born under the Leo sign are energetic and healthy, but they need to be loved to stay happy and healthy. Their ill-health conditions are high fevers, sudden illnesses, and accidents. When becoming sick, they do not stay in bed long enough; therefore, a health problem often recurs.

> Charles Bickner, 100, of Brookings, Oregon, attributed his longevity to receiving a lot of love and affection. "My wife gets the credit," said Charles, meaning her home cooking. "The main thing is what you eat," he added.

Virgo (the Virgin), August 22 - September 22

Virgo symbolizes the beginning of a harvest season, and controls the solar plexus and intestines. The negative side of a Virgo person is so self-centered that he/she can become mean, very pedantic, niggling, caustic, sarcastic, and cunning. He/she tries to avoid responsibilities, escape from difficulties, and seek advantage by any means. A person born under the Virgo sign will use intrigue to achieve his/her mercenary purposes. His/her mind can be well developed, but with a defective way of thinking.

The positive Virgo is a serious, diligent, humble, and conscientious man or woman, prepared to serve others to the point of self-sacrifice, having no thought of profit for themselves, seeking no award, and not because of vanity. His/her mind is clever and the way of thinking is clear. "I just like everybody. I have nothing against anybody," was the motto of Mary Annand, 100, of Pasadena, California. The Virgo person can become a politician, a profound researcher who serves the people or one who completely loses the trust of others. Which side of the Virgo's character--the positive or the negative--will be developed is an entirely personal choice of the individual.

Health. The typical Virgo person is careful about his/her body and is quite healthy; however, Virgos are vulnerable to hypochondria if they are unhappy or worry too much. If a Virgo becomes sick, he/she usually has disorders of the digestive and lymph systems, such as diarrhea, malnutrition, appendicitis, indigestion, and hernias. If they take good care of themselves, a healthy diet allows Virgos to live long.

> Birdie Jordan, 100, of Corsicanna, Texas. "Mother taught us about good food. We always had a vegetable and meat and either stewed or fresh fruit," said Birdie.

Libra (the Scales), September 23 - October 22

This sign symbolizes the beginning of maturity and the peak of harvest season. It controls the kidneys, ovaries, and lower back. On the negative side, Libra--although not criminal—may be very unbalanced. Librans have extremely emotional personalities and fail to control his/her emotions at all. The actions of an adult are as impulsive as those of a child; in his/her urge for physical, mental, and emotional excitement, he/she is unaccountable and irresponsible.

On the positive side, a Libra--being highly emotional--assimilates the lessons of childhood quite well, and displays good balance between his/her physical and emotional life. Reasonable and calm, this sign in its positive manifestation controls what is practically uncontrollable: him or herself. He/she is sober-minded, pleasant and full of life, and well balanced.

> "He's always been a very slow, calm, and quiet person," said his daughter-in-law about Wallace Bostwick, 100, of Fullerton, California.

The balance takes place in any case; however, whether the negative or positive scale of Libra's character will outweigh the other fully depends on the individual.

Health. Librans are generally healthy people. They become ill if they are left alone for a long time. They quickly recover from sickness. The types of sickness common to Librans are diseases of the kidneys, liver, and skin.

Scorpio (the Scorpion), October 23 - November 21

This sign is a symbol of reincarnation. It governs the bladder and sexual organs. The negative Scorpio is lustful, stupid, and concentrates only on satisfaction of his/her physical needs. Nothing can stop Scorpios from achieving their aims, and they prefer to create a disagreement between people in order to govern them. In treating their subordinates this way, they bluntly manifest their despotism, and they can be psychologically ill. The positive Scorpio consciously accepts the value of physical and material life, but is equally aware of the reality of the non-physical world. Sharp-minded and a profound thinker, deeply sympathetic to other people, he/she will struggle to do the right thing despite becoming unpopular.

In any case, Scorpios have a passionate, strong-willed, and furious character, but the direction of their expression--right or wrong--is a matter of individual choice.

Health. Although a typical Scorpio is rarely ill, his/her burning desire to finish a job and too much hard work can destroy health. The most common Scorpio illnesses are those of the bladder and reproductive organs, as well as nose and throat problems. However, even when hard work is done with love, it seems to not be hazardous to a Scorpio's health.

> Jacob Kirchmer, 101, of Belleair, Florida. He said about his hard work, "Nobody worked the way I did.... I worked at different places in my life, but I always enjoyed it. If something needed to be done, I would do it."

The Scorpio is a problem sign for me, being a Taurus (born on May 11); astrology books usually state a complete incompatibility between these two signs. My ex-wife Larisa, a Scorpio born on November 13, is an example of this incompatibility; after five years of marriage, we eventually divorced. Unfortunately, at the time of my marriage (at the age of twenty-four), I had no idea of the horoscope signs and their compatibility.

However, I have found that it is not all Scorpios, only the negative ones, with whom I fail to get along with smoothly. A case of complete incompatibility that I encountered was with Ivan Mudov, 53, of Specific Consultants International, Inc., and a wealthy descendant of Russian emigrants to Australia. He was interested in investing in gold mines in Tajikistan and hired a few engineers, technicians, and me to conduct a feasibility study. Born on October 26, he has many positive features of the Scorpio sign, including being responsible, investigative, dynamic, unshakable, hard-working, able to concentrate intensely, enjoying a good fight, and always determined to win. Intending to invest his own money, he did a detailed study and our small team produced a comprehensive report for him in a very short time.

However, on the other side of his nature are the features of the negative Scorpio. He exploited the six study-team members intensively; most of the time, we worked from 8 a.m. to 6 p.m. with only a fifteen-minute lunch break, as well as Saturdays and some Sundays. As it is probably a common practice in some private hard-working companies, no overtime payment or even verbal appreciation was given to the study-team members. The working environment that he created was very stressful and filled with unnecessary pressure on and humiliation of his subordinates. It continued during our leisure time because we lived in the same hotel and often had our dinner together.

I was assigned as his assistant and experienced his worst treatment on a daily basis, as assessed by one member of our team. Next to worse treated were Denis Pamphilov of Kiev and Nikolay Fibrov of Moscow, both financial analysts. His best treatment was enjoyed by Lala Kotova, a typist. Two other team members were between these two extremes.

As a bright representative of the negative Scorpio family, Mudov had an outstanding ability to bite others before even thinking that it could hurt them. One day in the middle of June, after dinner and talk afterwards, we were about to leave for our rooms. We were working then on the final report and everybody was very busy. The deadline was near and Nikolay Fibrov had to submit his part of the report to Mudov before going back home to Moscow. He was determined to work late at night and before saying "good–bye," Mudov and I spoke briefly to him:

> Mamonov: Nikolay, don't work too hard.
> Mudov: Work too hard.
> Mamonov: Don't crash from overworking.
> Mudov: Crash in the plane, not here.

We were all petrified and speechless--unable to say anything else after these terrible words. Even Lala seemed to feel ashamed of her boss and ex-countryman; only Mudov alone did not understand how outrageous his remark was. More than that, he seemed to have fun with his deadly joke. Insulting and humiliating people are among the likes of Mudov. "He pretends to be intelligent, but he is not, because an intelligent person will never humiliate others," said one team member about Mudov.

Another Scorpio, but a positive type, is Richard Nakahashi, a consultant in planning, management, and communication, of Boston, Massachusetts. Although he has a Japanese family name, after three generations in America, he does not speak Japanese and visited Japan for the first time in 1998. His birthday is November 14, and he seems to have none of a Scorpio's negative features. He is very kind, respectful to everyone, perfectly avoids any obstacles; is wise, generous, compassionate, and concerned; and has an easygoing personality. I met him in Nakhodka, a city in Russia where we were working together on a water-supply project. We became friends and spent a few evenings talking after dinner, while cracking the local cedar nuts. He invited me to visit him in the United States and I had dinner with him and his family after my return to Boston.

The possible explanation of these two opposite Scorpios, negative and positive, in addition to the personal choices, can be attempted using the chakra theory. Mudov's strongest chakra is the Manipura chakra, a center of power on a social level. In Australia, he occupies the position of vice president and co-owner of the company, and he probably restrains himself from expression of his negative features in order to not undermine his business. In Russia, he was at the top of a small pyramid of power and he enjoyed the opportunity to use unrestrained power with all his might.

A positive Scorpio, Nakahashi is governed mostly by the Anahata chakra, a center of love. He told me once that with his wife and two sons, he enjoys a family life full of love and affection. Also, he perceived his mission to Nakhodka as an opportunity to talk to local people and officials (fifth chakra) and to exchange thoughts (sixth chakra), rather than just write the report. He has a talent for getting along perfectly with all kinds of people. In December 1998, before he and the other people departed, our boss (in an attempt to save money) insisted on bringing five people and their luggage to the airport in a four-passenger car, which was both inconvenient and even dangerous on the snowy road. Nakahashi asked him directly, "Do you want to experiment on me?" The boss was unable to reply, and immediately gave up his idea.

My incompatibility as a Taurus seems to occur with just negative Scorpios rather than the sign as a whole. However, usually it is my problem, not my counterpart's. I failed to find the key to my ex-wife and I failed to do the same with Mudov. He definitely feels comfortable with himself; he is proud of himself and seems to enjoy his life in his own way. The problem throughout my life is that I am a bad actor; if I do not like someone, I do not hide it. I showed Mudov that I did not like him; I often opposed him, argued with him when I thought he was wrong, and did not demonstrate the loyalty that he demanded of me. Our relationship was not bad at first, but gradually worsened. Although I have had certain losses, I have no regrets; hopefully, I have acquired some experience. Whether this experience will help me the next time I encounter a negative Scorpio or any another sign is still an unanswered question.

Sagittarius (the Archer), November 22 - December 21

This sign is symbolized by the arrow in its flight. It controls the liver, hips, and blood. A negative Sagittarius is miserly, very egotistic, and idle, and he/she is a poor thinker, interpreting current events as merely a reflection of the viewpoint of others. His/her cruelty is not the cruelty of a dictator, struggling to retain power, but rather that of an invader, who strikes quickly, takes everything he/she wants, and moves to new conquests, leaving chaos behind them. The positive Sagittarius is generous, frank, strong-willed, and always giving themselves to others without any thought of reward. Sagittarians generously share with others whatever they possess. "Abundance for all" is their motto.

All these characteristics can be applied to Maria Salazar, 100, of Denver, Colorado, a mother of twelve children. "She's always been a brave and sturdy woman. She has been a very well person, usually the only one who could take care of everyone else," said one of her daughters.

In any case, the Sagittarius mind is quick and clear, but whether they are directed to good or bad actions is a question of their own choice and freedom of their will.

Health. The Sagittarius person is usually energetic and healthy. Even if they become sick, their positive attitude and optimism help them to overcome illnesses quickly. Illnesses of the joints such as arthritis, rheumatic problems, and diseases of the legs and hips are common in them.

Capricorn (the Goat), December 22 - January 20

The Capricorn sign symbolizes going uphill and the broad opportunities to observe what becomes visible. It controls the spleen and ankles. Negative Capricorns are career-focused; nothing can stop them and they can "walk over corpses" to achieve their aim. However, often after having achieved it, they do not use their success and keep going forward, ignoring the pain of their efforts. Positive Capricorns find their way through the obstacles and earn their position working hard. They control themselves more than others and realize the necessity to treat others with understanding and compassion. Ideally, the positive Capricorn is a practical person, and people of this sign embody a father, just as people of the Cancer sign (the sign opposite to Capricorn) embody a mother.

In general, Capricorn is full of an attack power; he/she unbendingly leads their way to the top. Whether their efforts bring positive or negative fruits is a matter of individual choice.

Health. Unlike other signs, the Capricorn person tends to be healthier when he/she grows older. Although they are not very robust in their younger years, if sober and temperate, they often live to a ripe old age. Typical illnesses are rheumatism, damage to their legs and knees, other bone diseases, and depression. More than medicines, their remarkable positive attitude makes them healthy and helps them to last long.

Faith Linsley, 100, of Barre, Vermont, said: "I never went to a hospital until I was eighty-four years old. I didn't take medicines—they upset my stomach—and I think that's one reason why I'm so old. But attitude is the main thing--be positive. And I think my sense of humor has protected me from stress."

Aquarius (the Water-Carrier), January 21 - February 19

Aquarius is symbolized by the outflow of invigorating water above the soil, which enables future life to appear on the surface of the earth. It controls the calves, ankles, and circulation of fluids in the body. Negative Aquarians are people who more or less become a burden for society, often because of their antisocial actions. Under the mask of freedom and love, they reveal unruliness, and although they appeal to society for help, they help nobody but themselves. Positive Aquarians are like statesmen and humanists, fighting for freedom not for themselves but for others, participating in the commitments of the country. They induce people to strive for progress, leading and showing the way. In any case, Aquarians seek public rather than private activities; however, whether their actions will be directed to good or evil depends on their personal choices.

Health. Typical Aquarians cannot take their health for granted; they have to make efforts to earn it. Regular exercise and plenty of sleep and fresh air are necessary for them to be healthy. At a young age, Aquarians are usually very healthy and naturally robust, but in later years, they may suffer from diseases of the nervous and blood systems.

> Exercise and a regulated lifestyle helped Brother Adelard Beaudet, 103, of Harrisville, Rhode Island, to achieve his great age. He played hockey when he was young and was a swimmer in his very ripe old age. At nineteen, he joined the Brotherhood of the Sacred Heart, where he was a member for eighty-three years. "Brother Adelard always disciplined himself and tended to his own affairs, but his life was never stressful," said another Brother.

Pisces (the Fish), February 20 - March 20

The Pisces sign is symbolized by the attraction to counteraction, by the desire to travel simultaneously in different directions. It controls the soles of the feet and mental and physical abilities.

In a negative sense, the one born under the Pisces sign is weak-willed, directed in his behavior, and impressed by the opinion of others. He/she is a weak imitator, with a lack of initiative, which means that he/she fails to control both his/her emotions and private affairs.

In a positive sense, although tending to fluctuate between two attachments, he/she manages to govern them both with love and understanding. The Pisces person offers help to everyone without prejudice and demanding a response. They are rarely strong-willed, but always reliable.

> These are precisely the features of Leo Roncco, 104, of Thermopolis, Wyoming. He was a softhearted man who, even at his advanced age, visited the sick every day. "Everybody I talk to tells me you're a do-gooder, Mr. Roncco," Jim Heynen said to him in the interview. Mr. Roncco replied, "I'll help anybody. If you can't help your fellow man, what the hell are you good for?"

Of all the signs, Pisces enjoys adaptability the most; whether it is directed to good or bad actions depends on individual choice through the freedom of will.

Health. If Pisces people are loved and happy, they are healthy; if not, they may turn to alcohol or drugs to escape from emotional insecurities. They are vulnerable to disorders of the feet and toes, such as corns, boils, and foot deformities.

The graphical representation of the horoscope type is very simple—simply put a mark in the appropriate sector of the Zodiac chart shown in Figure 13-1.

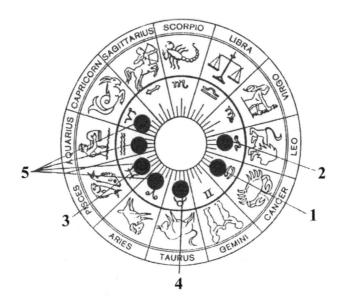

Figure 13-1. Horoscope Type of Four People and Longevity Zone
1. Lydia Vesselovzorova, 2. Nataliya Yusova,
3. Spiros Antonopoulos, 4. Author, 5. Longevity Zone

(The Zodiac chart is adapted from the *Random House Unabridged Dictionary*, 2nd Edition.)

As shown in this figure, two women centenarians that I interviewed were born in the summer and do not belong to the longevity zone. This proves that there is no rule without exceptions and that the "rule" that I am trying to establish (i.e., a correlation between horoscope type and longevity) is probably not strong enough. The influence of horoscope sign is definitely weaker than that of heredity or lifestyle. Therefore, any person, regardless of his/her Zodiac sign, can use a healthy diet and lifestyle to try to live far beyond the average life expectancy.

Food for Horoscope Types

The Zodiac sign that a person is born under affects his/her destiny, general health state, and personality characteristics. According to Rana Rickmeier, it affects their diet as well. "Just as each sign of the Zodiac is linked to one of the four cardinal elements—earth, air, water, fire—so too is each sign linked to a particular *nouriture*, or primal form of nourishment. Just as each of the twelve signs is ruled by a specific planet, so too is there a specific cornucopia of fruits of the Earth that are related to each of the signs by way of the ruling planets," says Rickmeier in her book, *The Astrological Cookbook.*

People of the signs that are ruled by the water element, such as Cancer, Scorpio, and Pisces, are advised to eat fish or crabs. Meat may serve as a major nouriture for other signs, specific types corresponding to particular sign—mutton for Oven, beef for Taurus, veal for Virgo. Other categories of food, such as grains, vegetables, fruits, and herbs, also vary for different signs. Food appropriate for each horoscope type is listed in the chart included in Appendix C.

According to my Taurus sign, I am supposed to eat beef; however, my thin stomach acid (blood type A) does not allow me to digest beef properly. There is a discrepancy in my case between these two recommendations, and I gave preference to my blood type over my horoscope type. In my diet, I eat beef very rarely, perhaps once a month or so. Years ago, even when I had no idea about blood types (relative to diet), I never liked meat; poultry and fish were my main sources of animal protein. At present, I am becoming a vegetarian and do not eat meat at all.

However, another Taurus, my yoga teacher Eugene Bazh, likes meat and never eats fish. This does not mean that he is more attached to the Zodiac sign than I am. If one's favorite food, however, is different from what is suggested for his or her sign, it only means that personal food likes and dislikes may overrule the menu, even if it is recommended by the stars.

14

PERSONALITY PROFILE

Two objectives of the *Body Types* part of this book are to draw a unique personality profile, especially of centenarians, and to try to find a link between the person's characteristics and longevity. In the previous chapters, we compiled a dozen charts concerning particular characteristics of a person. Combined with the person's photographs at different ages, these charts depict his/her personality profile. For an example, my own Five Elements profile is shown in Figure 11-1. Similarly, in other charts, my particular profiles are shown. Self-assessment is a difficult and time-consuming job, and it is one reason why I did myself. However, I am only sixty years old and my age does not fit for a longevity discussion. It would be more interesting to have similar profiles of "ripe-old–age" people who could serve as models of longevity.

The problem is that the approach proposed in this book involves specific knowledge about topics such as chakras or doshas, which are new concepts for many people. Also, a great amount of information about a person (including medical data) is necessary to answer all the questionnaires. The assessment of centenarians, based on published books or articles, is almost impossible because it lacks specific data. The only people who can provide the necessary information are the oldest ones themselves or their relatives.

Actually, relatives could be more helpful because the answering process needs a sound memory and reasoning abilities, which centenarians might lack. Also, it is a time-consuming job that would be difficult for them to accomplish. In addition, the quality of answers might be compromised because people tend to avoid revealing the negative features of their character. I was fortunate to find a few families whose relatives lived beyond one hundred years, including those whom I interviewed.

One of the respondents was Demetrios Antonopoulos, forty-seven, of Boston, Massachusetts. He is the son of Spiros Antonopoulos, one hundred (actually, he died in 1997 at the age of ninety-nine years, eight months), and answered all the questionnaires about his father and himself. Another respondent who agreed to do this difficult job was Brenda Bernard, sixty-seven, of Woburn, Massachusetts. She is the daughter of John J. Beatty, who lived to one hundred years (he died in 1995). The profiles of Brenda and her husband Frank Bernard, seventy-two, are also included. The graphed profiles and photographs of Spiros Antonopoulos and John J. Beatty at four different ages are shown following the texts about these two centenarians.

The twelve-system profile (i.e., seven Western and five Oriental systems) has been tested on a total of six people, including the author. Overall, the questionnaires and descriptions seem to be readable. There were some difficulties in drawing the Chakra profile (there is no corresponding questionnaire). To overcome this problem, I provided additional explanations to Demetrios and Frank and Brenda. However, I think that the Chakra profile evaluation still needs to be refined.

Answers were followed by calculations. While I did them myself (the calculation of percentages in most cases), a person can easily do them on his/her own; placing dots on the graphs is not very difficult either. Perhaps some difficulties might be encountered in filling out the somatotype and Ayurvedic doshas three-axis graphs. Referring to the author's examples and comparing his scores with their graphical representation may be helpful.

For the Five-Elements profile, the five-axis graph is used; however, the scale is shown only for the Water element; the other axes use the same scale. If the maximum score of any particular element is less than 40 (as in my case; see Figure 11-1), it is simpler to put the dots on a 10-point scale. In the cases of John J. Beatty and Brenda Bernard, the Earth score exceeded 40; therefore, the maximum 50-percent scale was used. Although none of elements exceeded 40 percent for Spiros Antonopoulos, the same 50-percent scale was used to make the comparison between the two centenarians easier.

John J. Beatty

John J. Beatty (May 20, 1894 – January 8, 1995) was born, educated, and lived all of his life in Woburn, Massachusetts. He served in the U. S. Navy during World War I. He worked in the Park Division and Water Department of the Metropolitan District Commission for more than thirty years, and retired at the age of sixty-two. He had four children--one son and three daughters--fourteen grandchildren, and fifteen great-grandchildren.

Physical Characteristics. His height was 5 feet, 8 inches and his weight was 175 pounds for most of his life. His Body Mass Index (BMI) was equal to 27.3. He was slightly overweight.

Typical Diet. John was a "meat and potatoes" man. Among his favorite foods were steak, tomatoes, milk, cream, coffee, candy, and ice cream. Following is his typical diet:

Breakfast. Cereal (1 cup) with cream (1/4 cup), banana (1 piece), and coffee (I cup) with milk mixed with cream and sugar (2 teaspoons).

Lunch. Soup (1 cup), tomato (1 piece, boiled), hamburger (6 ounces) or chicken sandwich (2 slices between 2 slices of bread), and chocolate cake (1 slice).

Dinner. Roast beef, turkey, or chicken (4-5 ounces); mashed potatoes with milk (1 cup); mashed turnip or squash (1 cup); and coffee (1 cup) with milk mixed with cream and sugar (2 teaspoons).

John was not a great fruit or vegetable eater and only a few kinds were in his diet. He was a meat- rather than fish-eater. Surprisingly, he ate many foods--such as potatoes, coffee, milk, and cream--that are among those to avoid for his blood type O. The food-combining experts would not use him as an example of their philosophy either: proteins, carbohydrates, and fats were well mixed in his meals.

The clue is in his strong digestive system: he never had any problems with his stomach. He had a "cast-iron" stomach, as family members used to say. His immune system was equally strong--he never got sick. The fact that he lived to one hundred is the best proof of the rightness regarding his diet, habits, and lifestyle. His diet was definitely appropriate for him, which confirms once again that current dietary recommendations are not suitable for all people.

The following body constitution and personality features of John J. Beatty were assessed by his daughter, Brenda Bernard, of Woburn.

Somatotype. In the Physical Build and Characteristics Assessment, John scored 2, 5, 3 and belonged to the ectomorphic mesomorph type. On the graphical chart, his dot is located between two longevity zones, closer to the eastern zone.

Personality Type. In his behavioral traits, he scored 7 points of Type A, 9 points of Type B, and 1 point of Type C personality. On the continuum scale, his dot is closer to Type B, at 61 percent from Type A.

Instincts. The dominant instinct in John was freedom, followed by self-preservation, dignity, reproduction, altruism, domination, and research.

Temperaments. The percentage of each temperament in John was 34% Choleric, 17% Phlegmatic, 32% Sanguine, and 17% Melancholy.

Blood Type. John belonged to blood type O.

Lifestyle. The scores of the four components of his lifestyle were as follows:

Diet and eating habits	10
Work, rest, and leisure	17
Physical activity and exercise	8
Life habits, emotions, mental and spiritual activities	10

Except for the second component, John's lifestyle underscores to be overly healthy.

Heredity. John's father lived to the age of sixty-two and his mother until ninety-seven--he definitely inherited longevity genes from his mother. Compared to diet and lifestyle, heredity seemed to play an overwhelming role in his longevity.

Ayurvedic Doshas Type. The constitutional doshas type of John J. Beatty consisted of 0.12 of Vata, 0.69 of Pitta, and 0.19 of Kapha (round dot on the chart). His overall Ayurvedic doshas type included 0.20 of Vata, 0.45 of Pitta, and 0.35 of Kapha (square dot on the chart). In general, he improved his inherited doshas proportions, making them more balanced.

Ying-Yang Type. John's Yang-Yin score is 32 to 9; therefore, his Yang part of 78% prevails over his Yin part of 22%.

Five-Elements Type. The five elements in John scored 23% Fire, 41% Earth, 9% Metal, 9% Water, and 18% Wood. The Earth element prevailed in him, followed by the Fire element.

Chakra Profile. The energy expenditure at the third and two upper chakras is slightly more than medium. At the two lower and two upper chakras, John's profile is close to the longevity chakra profile. However, in the fourth and fifth chakra regions, it is quite distant, with a lack of energy in these chakras.

Horoscope Type. Born on May 20, John was a Taurus by horoscope type. Good genes, a diet appropriate for his type, healthy habits such as not smoking and not drinking, a positive attitude, and features such as a lack of dominance and adventure--which saved him from stress--promoted John's longevity.

24 years old   49 years old

73 years old   100 years old

John J. Beatty   Western Systems

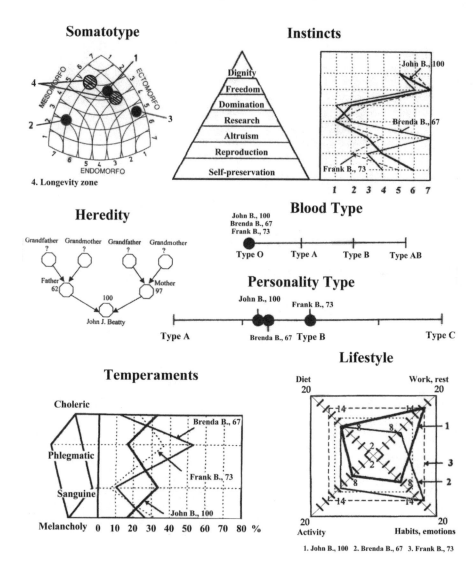

Somatotype

4. Longevity zone

Instincts

Dignity
Freedom
Domination
Research
Altruism
Reproduction
Self-preservation

John B., 100

Brenda B., 67

Frank B., 73

1 2 3 4 5 6 7

Heredity

Grandfather Grandmother Grandfather Grandmother
?   ?   ?   ?

Father 62   Mother 97

100

John J. Beatty

Blood Type

John B., 100
Brenda B., 67
Frank B., 73

Type O   Type A   Type B   Type AB

Personality Type

John B., 100   Frank B., 73

Type A   Brenda B., 67 Type B   Type C

Temperaments

Choleric

Phlegmatic

Sanguine

Melancholy 0 10 20 30 40 50 60 70 80 %

Brenda B., 67

Frank B., 73

John B., 100

Lifestyle

Diet
20

Work, rest
20

Activity
20

Habits, emotions
20

1. John B., 100 2. Brenda B., 67 3. Frank B., 73

John J. Beatty   Oriental Systems

Ayurvedic Doshas

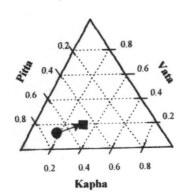

Five Elements Profile

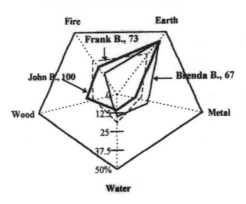

Yin - Yang Type

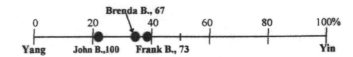

Chakra Profile

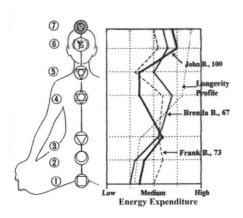

Horoscope Type

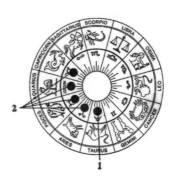

1. John B., 100   2. Longevity zone

Spiros Antonopoulos

Spiros Antonopoulos (March 10, 1897 - November 19, 1996) was born in Greece, where he lived until the age of nineteen. He then immigrated to the United States, the only one in his family of seven to do so. He lived the majority of his life in Lorain, Ohio, where he worked in a steel mill for more than thirty years, retiring at the age of sixty-five. He also worked as a helper at a Holiday Inn for about fifteen years until the age of ninety. He married at the age of forty-five and had six children--three sons and three daughters--and fourteen grandchildren.

Physical Characteristics. He was 5 feet, 6½ inches tall and his weight was between 155 and 160 pounds for most of his life. His BMI is equal to 25.6.

Typical Diet. Spiros was quite a health-conscious man. He watched his diet, especially after an angina attack at the age of sixty-eight. His typical diet before the attack was as follows:

Breakfast. Coffee (1 cup) with half-and-half and toast. He quit coffee in later years due to a bladder problem (i.e., urinary incontinence).

Lunch. Veal stew (3-4 ounces), fish, chicken, or ground lean turkey meatballs; sweet potato; and steamed vegetables in season (1 cup). Lunch was his largest meal of the day.

Dinner. Leftovers from lunch with rice, corn, or other vegetables in season (1.5-2 cups) and fruit (1-2 pieces).

After his angina attack, he avoided coffee and his diet was, as follows:

Breakfast. Oatmeal (1 cup) or corn flakes with low-fat milk.

Lunch. About the same as before, but the amount of food was reduced.

Dinner. Salad of fresh vegetables or cooked greens (1 cup), potato salad with olive or canola oils, and fresh lemon juice diluted with water(1 glass).

Work and Rest. Spiros worked three shifts, rotating between 7 a.m. – 3 p.m., 3 p.m. – 11 p.m., and 11 p.m. – 7 a.m. There were life-threatening incidents at his place of work, but he was lucky to escape from injuries. He used to nap for 1½ to 2 hours, depending on the shift he was working. After his retirement from the steel mill, he mostly napped after lunch for about 2 hours. He loved to go to the coffee shop to talk politics and play cards with his Greek peers.

Somatotype. In the Physical Build and Characteristics Assessment, Spiros scored 1, 7, 4, belonging to the ectomorphic mesomorph type. On the chart, his dot is located close to the eastern longevity zone.

Personality Type. In his behavioral traits, Spiros scored 8 points of Type A, 8 points of Type B, and 0 points of Type C personality. On the continuum scale, his dot is located exactly in the middle of Type A and Type B.

Instincts. The dominant instinct of Spiros Antonopoulos was self-preservation, followed by freedom, dignity, reproduction, domination, altruism, and research.

Temperaments. The percentage of each temperament in Spiros Antonopoulos is 68% Choleric, 3% Phlegmatic, 12% Sanguine, and 17% Melancholy. The Choleric part of his temperament prevailed over the other temperaments.

Blood Type. Spiros belonged to blood type O.

Lifestyle. The scores of the four components of his lifestyle are:

Diet and eating habits	11
Work, rest, and leisure	15
Physical activity and exercise	13
Life habits, emotions, mental and spiritual activities	11

Although the first and fourth components are 2 points short of a healthy mark of 13, his overall lifestyle could be regarded as relatively healthy.

Heredity. Spiros' father and mother died when they were in their early seventies. He did not seem to inherit longevity genes from his parents.

Ayurvedic Doshas Type. The constitutional doshas type of Spiros Antonopoulos consisted of 0.18 of Vata, 0.82 of Pitta, and 0 of Kapha. It is greatly unbalanced with a prevalence of Pitta. His overall Ayurvedic doshas type included 0.11 of Vata, 0.68 of Pitta, and 0.21 of Kapha. In the course of life, his Vata and Pitta decreased and Kapha increased. In general, Spiros improved his inherited doshas proportions, making them more balanced.

Ying-Yang Type. Spiros' Yin-Yang score is 26 to 14, so the Yang part of 65% prevails over the Yin part of 35% in him.

Five-Elements Type. The Five Elements in Spiros scored 12% Fire, 16% Earth, 28% Metal, 20% Water, and 24% Wood. The Metal element prevailed in him, followed by the Wood element.

Chakra Profile. The dominant chakra in Spiros was the sixth one; he was somewhat of a philosopher. Personal spiritual devotion was quite important to him as well. He was a little self-centered and used to rely on himself. When compared to the chakra longevity profile, his profile looks similar to it, except in the fourth and fifth chakras region where the energies are lower.

Horoscope Type. Spiros was born on March 10; thus, his horoscope type is Pisces. Rather then heredity, his physical activity, healthy lifestyle, respect among family members, and intellectual and spiritual involvement seemed to promote Spiros' longevity.

45 years old   56 years old

74 years old   95 years old

Spiros Antonopoulos   Western Systems

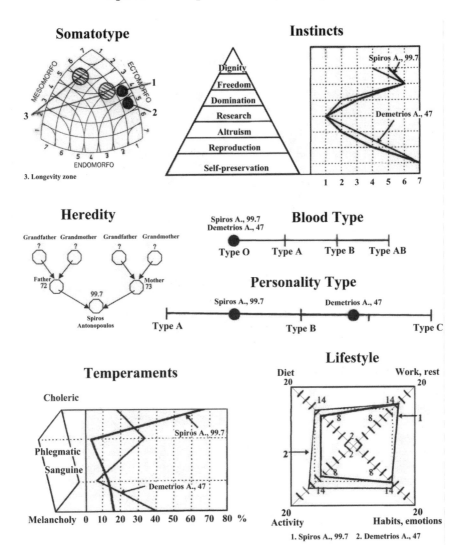

Somatotype

3. Longevity zone

Instincts

Dignity
Freedom
Domination
Research
Altruism
Reproduction
Self-preservation

Spiros A., 99.7
Demetrios A., 47

1 2 3 4 5 6 7

Heredity

Grandfather Grandmother   Grandfather Grandmother
?   ?   ?   ?

Father
72

Mother
73

99.7

Spiros
Antonopoulos

Blood Type

Spiros A., 99.7
Demetrios A., 47

Type O   Type A   Type B   Type AB

Personality Type

Spiros A., 99.7   Demetrios A., 47

Type A   Type B   Type C

Temperaments

Choleric

Phlegmatic

Sanguine

Spiros A., 99.7

Demetrios A., 47

Melancholy 0 10 20 30 40 50 60 70 80 %

Lifestyle

Diet   Work, rest
20   20
        14   14
            8   8   1
2
            2
            8   8
        14   14
20   20
Activity   Habits, emotions

1. Spiros A., 99.7   2. Demetrios A., 47

Spiros Antonopoulos   Oriental Systems

Ayurvedic Doshas

Five Elements Profile

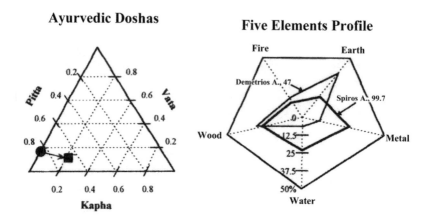

Yin - Yang Type

Chakra Profile

Horoscope Type

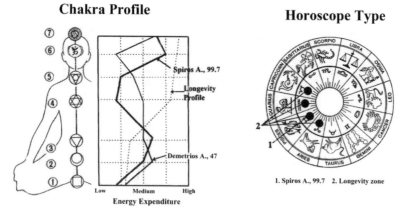

1. Spiros A., 99.7   2. Longevity zone

Let us now compare the data on these two centenarians to determine how their characteristics relate to longevity. Regarding body size, they both were of medium height, as are most long-living people. Their BMIs were within a healthy range, although John J. Beatty was slightly overweight. Both of them were engaged in physical labor and were active for most of their life. Their exercise was confined to walking alone. There was nothing noteworthy about their diet and food likes, although John--who followed a typical American diet--seemed to eat larger amounts of food. Spiros Antonopoulos ate large amounts of green vegetables and a lot of garlic; otherwise, he ate an average amount of food. He watched his diet more carefully after his angina problem.

By somatotype, both men belonged to the ectomorphic mesomorph type. On the chart, their dots are located very close to the longevity zone.

Their personality type falls between Type A and Type B behavior, which correlates quite well to longevity. Most centenarians are Type B personalities, as the study in Japan showed.

Two of their dominant instincts were self-preservation and freedom. The outlines of their Instinct profiles look so similar as to merit special note. In both cases, their lowest scores were the domination and research instincts, followed by altruism. My guess is that the lack of adventure in their characters prevented them from accidents and premature death. The case of Paul Bragg always comes to my mind. He was so fit and strong that he participated in challenges reserved for younger people. He died in a surfing accident at the age of ninety-five. Also, my close friend Vladimir Samol died at the age of forty-six while doing dangerous yoga exercises, such as stopping his heart from beating. They both were victims of too much research instinct. My research instinct (see Figure 3-1) is also quite high; I have mentioned previously the life-threatening commitments I had in the past. I must learn from these cases about the dangers of being too adventurous and the benefits of being careful.

Temperaments are seemingly different in the two men: Spiros was mostly Choleric with small portions of the other three temperaments; in John, the Choleric and Sanguine parts were bigger than the Phlegmatic and Melancholy parts; however, all four parts were more evenly distributed in him. Despite the dangers of a hot-tempered Choleric temperament for health and longevity, Spiros survived to a hundred years of age. His son, Demetrios, is very different than his father regarding temperament (prevailing Phlegmatic and Melancholy), but is very similar in the Instincts profile.

Both centenarians were blood type O. They did not suffer from indigestion (with lowered stomach-juices acidity) as do blood type A's and elderly people.

There were minor differences in their lifestyles, with Spiros' scores somewhat higher (except in Work, Rest, and Leisure) in the lifestyle assessment. John was a heavy smoker for about thirty years and drank sometimes, but he quit these habits at the age of fifty. Spiros smoked sometimes, but not excessively. He drank a glass of wine at lunch and supper.

Heredity definitely played a bigger role in the case of John J. Beatty. The longevity of Spiros Antonopoulos was the result of a relatively healthy lifestyle rather than great genes.

Regarding the Ayurvedic doshas type, the constitutional part in particular, both men were born with a larger portion of the Pitta dosha. Within the course of their lives, they increased the Kapha dosha and achieved a more balanced state of all three doshas. Pitta and Kapha doshas are associated with increased longevity.

The Ying-Yang type in both Spiros and John is quite similar – their Yang part prevails over the Yin part. The Yang type is more common in younger people; as we grow older, our Yin part usually increases.

They are quite different in regard to the Five Elements. The Metal element associated with the urge for freedom and eagerness for intellectual and spiritual activities prevailed in Spiros Antonopoulos. A Metal person is also linked to a Phlegmatic temperament and a preference for solitude. However, Spiros was different, with a Choleric temperament and enjoying the company of his friends. In John, the Earth element, which governs the spleen, stomach, and pancreas, was dominant. His stomach was strong, proving the ancient belief that the strength and vitality of the digestive organs promote a person's health, resistance to diseases, and longevity. Optimism, associated with the Earth element, was the second nature of John J. Beatty. His determination to live to a hundred was very strong, which helped him to reach the century mark. The Five Elements profile of his daughter, Brenda Bernard, is quite similar to his.

The dominant chakra in both centenarians was the sixth one; they were philosophers. Personal spiritual devotion was quite high in them as well. The centers of altruistic love and talents (i.e., the fourth and fifth chakras) are the lowest in energy expenditure for both centenarians. Comparing to the chakra longevity profile, their profiles look similar except for the fourth and fifth chakra regions. This coincides with Japanese research that showed that centenarians are often egotistical people. Jim Heynen, who interviewed a hundred American centenarians, also concluded that the common feature is "tough love." They are somewhat self-centered and rely mostly on themselves; many had no specific talents or gifts.

Regarding horoscope type, John was a Taurus and Spiros was a Pisces; both signs are linked to longevity.

We can see from their profiles that these two American centenarians are somewhat different in regard to their heredity, body type, and personal characteristics such as temperaments and the Five Elements. John J. Beatty was born in the United States and lived most of his life in one place. Spiros Antonopoulos was born in Greece and changed continents when he came to America. There are certain similarities in both, however, concerning blood type (O), personality type (between A and B), Yin-Yang type (more Yang than Yin), instincts (freedom and self-preservation dominate), dominant chakras, and general outline of their chakra profiles.

Obviously, no definite longevity correlation can be concluded; the statistical array of the database is too small. However, if hundreds of cases were compiled, it would provide more insight into which personality profile features are most common in centenarians. If their workability is proved in mass tests, the profiles could probably be used in further gerontological studies. At this stage, my intention is to introduce a new approach to the analysis of the body/personality type – longevity connection, and to test its workability on centenarians (and their relatives). I am going to continue the this research, and my readers are invited to help me draw the personality profiles of their relatives who are a hundred years old and older, if any.

After finishing this part, I believe you know yourself better than before. However, not all people get excited about the possibility of knowing themselves better. "I am not sure that I want it," said Frank Bernard, seventy-two, of Woburn, when I suggested he could learn more about himself from this part. If you are inclined, though, your personality profile will allow you to better apply the factual information in this book and/or in other books of this kind. **If you feel you need an improvement program, you can design it according to the body constitution, psychological traits, and intellectual and spiritual needs of your unique personality.**

PART TWO: HEALTHY AND LONG-LIVING BODY

Should you ask me what's best to eat,
I'll tell you: eat right for your type, you should
Eat raw fruits, veggies, not milk and meat,
And don't stuff your face with food.

Chinese Xu Fang does not eat at all,
Food does not charge her body a toll.
Drinking just water and breathing air,
She radiates health with her skin and her hair.

To spare your kidneys, don't drink much water.
Your friend is carbon dioxide, not oxygen.
Have enough quality sleep, snooze, and then
Exercise more than your son or daughter.

Enjoy your sex, but avoid frequent ejaculation.
Yours then is good health, long life, and liberation.

Foundations of Health

"The only way to keep your health is to eat what you don't want,
drink what you don't like, and do what you'd rather not."
--Mark Twain

"Self-control is the basic law of health."
--Henry Lindlahr, M.D.

Letting philosophers argue about the old question--that is, whether reality is of the nature of thought (mind over matter) or whether all phenomena, including those of the mind, are due to material agencies (matter over mind)-- we will go straight to our objective: in achieving longevity, both body and mind must be equally healthy. It is a widely accepted hypothesis in biology that a human is "...not mind and body, but body and mind in one. Body is one aspect of this unity, mind is another," said H.G. Wells, et al., in their book, *The Science of Life*. "Man, in this hypothesis, is not Mind plus Body; he is a

Mind-Body," they added. It is only for convenience that we distinguish between body, mind, and spirit, and separately study physiological and psychological aspects of the unity, which is a single universal human being.

Which constituents are essential for a healthy and sound body, mind, and spirit? Both Western and Oriental thought share similar ideas in this respect. The great Greek physician Hippocrates (c. 460 – c. 377 BC), the father of Western medicine, taught that good health can be attained and maintained only through the proper balance of physical, mental, and spiritual energies. It was natural for him and other ancient physicians to acknowledge the importance of a *holistic* approach, which incorporates body, mind and soul.

According to Leon Chaitow, N.D., D.O., of London, England, positive health depends on three factors, which are interconnected. The first of these is the body's structural system, including all of the muscles, bones, ligaments, nerves, blood vessels, and organs, and their functions. The second factor is the body's biochemical processes, which involve the absorption and utilization of nutrients, and the elimination of wastes, along with the complicated biochemical relationships that are the key to cellular function and health. The third factor consists of the mind and emotions, as well as the spiritual dimension of each person.

The modern Oriental approach to good health and longevity holds that body, mind, and spirit have to be well balanced and in good harmony with nature. "Genetic inheritance, education, and job activities throughout life build not only one's character, but also one's body. Food, drink, emotions, stress, and what we think add to the body chemistry and make us who we are. We are a combination of our family genes and environment," say Shizuko Yamamoto and Patrick McCarty in their book, *Whole Health Shiatsu*. "You may want to carefully observe how you think, breathe, eat, move, sleep, and maintain relationships, for these are the six fundamentals of health," they add.

Therefore, in order for all body systems to function properly, we need to fulfill the basic biological needs for food, water, air, sleep, movement, and sex. Our emotions, thoughts, and spirits, which affect our mental and physical health, need our attention as well. To achieve perfect health and long life, we need to earn them with our own efforts, taking control and responsibility over our life. The way to attain this is to become a master of our body, mind, and spirit–that is, to take conscious control over our biological needs; over life-threatening degenerative diseases such as heart disease, cancer, and stroke; to control our emotions and thoughts; and to let our talents, intelligence, skills, interests, and hobbies bloom in abundance. We will discuss all these aspects in the following chapters, starting with basic biological needs.

15

NUTRITION AND DIETS

"Thy food shall be thy remedy."
--Hippocrates

Everybody eats--eating is a part of everyone's life. Everybody needs food to live. Food gives us life, and food is life itself. All living creatures need food. Air and sunlight are food for plants. Plants are food for animals. Plants and animals are food for humans. It wouldn't be an exaggeration to say that food is absolutely necessary for our survival and health. Ordinary people in ordinary conditions can't live without food. There are cases in the history of mankind and even today in which people abstained from food for years and even decades. However, these few people achieved special spiritual states that are unattainable for most people. Modern science still fails to explain the phenomenon of surviving long term without food and being alive and healthy. I believe that we will have many discoveries in this field in the future.

A deep understanding that food and health are closely interrelated is one of the fundamental ideas of ancient medical systems, such as the Indian Ayurveda and Traditional Chinese Medicine. Ayurveda has taught for thousands of years that our health is largely determined by what we eat. The Yellow Emperor of China (2698 - 2589 BC) is known for his appreciation of the idea that a balanced diet is absolutely essential for maintaining one's health and avoiding illnesses. Modern scientific research, especially nutritional discoveries of the last two decades, gave credit to many kinds of healing foods that can improve our health, sometimes even better than drugs.

Plants use the energy of the sun to combine substances from the soil and air to produce complex substances that make up living matter. We are not able to do that and must rely on food by eating plants or the animals that ate plants. According to Western science, food--solid or liquid--functions for our body primarily in two ways--nutritional and energetic--as follows:

1. Food provides substances needed to build and renew our cells, bones, muscles, and tissues, and for our growth, maintenance, repair, and reproduction.

2. As a fuel, food produces body heat and energy necessary for performing physical and mental work.

These two functions are fulfilled by the substances in food called *nutrients*, which are divided into the following two major types:

• macronutrients (proteins, carbohydrates, and fats) that contain calories
• micronutrients (vitamins and minerals) that have no caloric value

To maintain good health, all these nutrients (a total of fifty) must be supplied to the body in sufficient quantities, fine quality, and proper proportions. Nutrients have existed in food since the beginning of time, but scientists discovered them only within the last hundred years or so. Sometimes four more vital substances--water, fiber, oxygen, and light--are considered nutrients; however, fiber (insoluble) is composed mostly of complex carbohydrates that are not digested in the small intestine. Water as a nutrient is overshadowed by the food we eat, but it comes to light under certain circumstances: fasting with water can last up to three months, but dry fasting can last only about eighteen days. Oxygen and sunlight are essential for all vital processes in the body. Nutrition is the way our body assimilates and utilizes food ingredients to maintain proper functioning.

Oriental medicine has a somewhat different approach to food--it holds that solid, liquid, particle, and vibration forms of food are essential to our body. Although solid, liquid (macronutrients), and particle (minerals and vitamins) forms of food are all the same, it is the vibration food that contrasts with the Western approach. Vibration foods are sunshine, weather, cosmic radiation, smell, prana, magnetic fields, and even the rotation of the earth. All life on earth is dependent on these powerful vibrations.

Air that contains nitrogen, oxygen, and carbon dioxide must also be considered as a source of food for our body. There are many types of food for the mind as well: thoughts, dreams, meditation, study, investigation, research, creation, watching movies and TV, listening to music and the radio, conversations with others, internal dialogues with ourself, fantasies, and many others are examples of food for the mind. Everything around us feeds our five senses too. Sensitive people can feel the vibrations coming from places, objects, things, and people; this is called extra-sensory perception (ESP). Again, I am trying to show the full range of all possible kinds of food. You may think that I am exaggerating when I talk about smell or prana as a kind of food; probably you would be right, but who knows?

The three basic kinds of food that our bodies can use as sources of building materials and energy are *proteins, carbohydrates,* and *fats.*

Proteins constitute our muscles, tendons, blood, and organs. They comprise our bones, skin, hair, teeth, cartilage, and fingernails. They also are an essential part of the connective tissues, blood, lymph and tissue cells, hormones, *enzymes*, antibodies, and other body elements. Proteins are complex molecules, mainly formed of carbon, nitrogen, and oxygen in various combinations as amino acids (i.e., *amine* = containing nitrogen), which are considered the proteins' building blocks. Our digestive system breaks down proteins into amino acids so that cells can assimilate them. The most important function of amino acids is to maintain and build muscle mass-- proteins in food provide these needed amino acids for muscle-building.

There are more than twenty (some authors indicate twenty-three and even twenty-six) amino acids needed to maintain health, eight of which (some say nine and probably ten) are known as *essential amino acids*. It is widely accepted nowadays that essential amino acids cannot be manufactured in the bodies of animals and humans; therefore, in order to survive, they have to get them from food. The eight essential amino acids are isoleucine, leucine, lysine, methionine, phenylalanine, threonine, tryptophane, and valine. Some authors add two more--cystine and tyrosine--to this list.

Essential amino acids are originally produced by plants during the process of *photosynthesis*. Nonessential amino acids can be produced in our bodies from various substances. Proteins containing sufficient amounts of all eight essential amino acids are present in animal foods, such as meat, poultry, fish, eggs, and dairy products, and one plant food--soybeans. Proteins lacking or having insufficient quantities of one or more essential amino acids are present in plants: beans, peas, lentils, grains, seeds, nuts, vegetables, and fruits.

Contrary to frequent statements in textbooks and popular books on health, all eight essential amino acids can be obtained in adequate quantities from virtually *any* vegetable or whole grain, as recent research has shown. For instance, plants such as white (baked) and sweet potatoes, brown rice, tomatoes, pumpkins, whole wheat flour, corn, rolled oats, white beans, asparagus, and broccoli contain *all* essential amino acids and in amounts much higher than people need. Even if some of them were missing in one particular plant, no one is going to live exclusively on a just one kind of grain or vegetable throughout his/her life; therefore, there is no danger of losing any particular essential amino acid. Moreover, there exists an amino-acid pool in the body and, when needed, amino acids are pulled from it for protein synthesis or energy needs. The condition when supply and expenditure of amino acids is balanced is called "nitrogen balance." An intake greater than output puts one into "positive nitrogen balance"; "negative nitrogen balance" occurs when output of amino acids exceeds intake.

Even people on a strictly vegetarian diet get their "quality protein" by eating a *variety* of plant foods. It is worth noting that the best and only food designed by nature to meet human amino-acid needs is human breast milk. Among existing diets, a pure vegetarian diet is the closest to it. For those concerned about getting essential amino acids, a supplement like *Bragg Liquid Aminos* (sold in natural food stores) is a possible solution. This delicious, all-purpose seasoning is produced from soy protein and contains 16 essential and non-essential amino acids. The serving size is only a half-teaspoon (2.5 ml); therefore, the 946-ml bottle can last as long as one year.

Although essential amino acids are necessary, not all of them are beneficial to our health and longevity. A few studies have shown that two acids– phenylalanine and tyrosine – were found to strengthen the immune system and inhibit tumor growth when they were *restricted* in the diet. This probably applies to a vegetarian diet as well. Plants with a low or moderate content of these amino acids include apples, cabbage, collard greens, mustard greens, and dried figs. Lentils have a very high content of these two amino acids. Definitely, much more research must be done on this subject.

Proteins are not used for energy when it can be derived from carbohydrates, if they are available in sufficient amounts. In addition, the almost 100 percent efficiency of carbohydrate conversion into energy is much higher than the 58 percent efficiency of proteins. Proteins that give the same 4 kcal per 1 gram as carbohydrates are an expensive fuel to afford.

Regarding protein quality, many authors acknowledge that animal proteins are better than plant proteins. However, because animal proteins contain undesirable substances, such as fat and cholesterol, it is better to limit or completely exclude them from the diet. A great choice of a high-quality plant protein is soybeans and their products. Soybeans contain all the macronutrients and are a good source of calcium, phosphorus, and other minerals and vitamins. Tofu, a soybean curd, is even called "the cow of China." The Chinese proudly consider its invention a great achievement in their history.

Carbohydrates are organic compounds of carbon, hydrogen, and oxygen, which derive mainly from sugar and starch and provide our body with energy for rapid use. Carbohydrates are virtually of plant origin, although they also are present in milk. They are divided into two categories: simple (refined) carbohydrates or sugars, and complex carbohydrates. *Simple carbohydrates* are abundant in white bread, white pasta, white rice, sugary cereals and snacks, cookies, and cakes. Plant sources of sugars include sugar beets, sugar cane, fruits, and honey. *Complex carbohydrates* come from fruits and vegetables, whole grains, breads, pastas, cereals, and legumes.

The best carbohydrates for good health and longevity are complex carbohydrates, although some kinds are superior to others. Some experts even call complex carbohydrates life-extenders, because they largely prevail in the diet in the world's longevity centers. Fruits are always on the top of the list, and they are even called rejuvenating carbohydrates, followed by vegetables. However, starchy vegetables such as potatoes and corn can cause a sudden rise in blood sugar, as do simple carbohydrates, which have a detrimental effect on our health and are reputed to be age accelerators. Any carbohydrates eaten in excess lead to weight gain; therefore, weight-reducing high-protein diet proponents fight an unceasing war against them.

Fat (lipids) is a white oily substance in the body that stores and provides us with energy (long-term energy source), cushions vital organs, and protects the body against cold. Fat also helps in the body's absorption of the fat-soluble vitamins A, D, E, and K. Fats are either saturated or unsaturated. Saturated fats, which as a rule are solid at room temperature, come from meat, eggs, and dairy products, but they also are present in lesser amounts in vegetable oils and in significant amounts in coconut and palm oils. Unsaturated fats, which are liquid at room temperature, predominate in vegetable oils and fats, and are represented by mono-unsaturated and polyunsaturated fats. Unsaturated fats come from edible oils, seeds, nuts, and some fruits including olives, avocados, sesame seeds, and coconuts.

As with proteins, there are essential fatty acids that must be a part of a person's diet: omega-3, omega-6, linoleic, and linolenic. Omega-3 comes from fish oil and fatty fish, such as salmon, tuna, herring, halibut, cod, sardines, trout, mackerel, shark, swordfish, and bluefish; or shellfish, such as shrimp, lobster, oyster, crab, and scallops. The plant sources of omega-3 include olives and flax seeds and their oils. Omega-6 polyunsaturated fatty acids are predominant in safflower, sunflower, regular, and corn oils. In lesser amounts, they are present in the oil from soybeans, walnuts, sesame seeds, peanuts, and macadamia nuts, as well as canola, flax seed, and extra virgin olive oil; the last three oils are regarded as the healthiest. Overall, omega-6 polyunsaturated fatty acids are found to be unhealthy and to speed up the aging process, especially in the hydrogenated form as in margarine, salad oil, and shortening. Polyunsaturated fats are subject to rapid oxidation (becoming peroxidized) and the subsequent free-radical oxidative attack on our cells. Peroxidized fats are regarded as mutagenic, carcinogenic, clot-forming, and suppressants to our immune system. Antioxidants that prevent their damaging effect are the vitamins A, C, E, B-1, B-5, and B-6; the minerals zinc and selenium; and the amino acid cysteine.

Fats are very difficult to digest and assimilate, and the body treats them with caution. The initial stage of digestion occurs first in the stomach, with the aid of the gastric enzyme lipase. Partly digested fats are released from the stomach very slowly, at a speed of about 10 grams an hour. Then, with bile from the liver and the enzyme lipase from the pancreas, the thorough and complete digestion of fats takes place in the duodenum. Before entering the bloodstream, fats sit for several hours in the lymph system, and then are released very slowly to prevent obstruction of the blood.

As an energy source, fats are expected to provide 9 calories per gram; however, some estimations indicate that only 41 percent of palmitic acid (i.e., one of the fatty acids) is converted into energy. This means that the efficiency of fats as fuel can be even less than that of proteins. About 10 percent of fats taken with food may appear in the feces undigested. Metabolism of fats requires more than twice as much oxygen as for carbohydrates and protein, which entails the increased formation of free radicals that are overly hazardous for all body systems.

Fiber is undigestible plant substances that provide bulk, which helps in moving food and waste quickly through the intestines and can prevent constipation. The common sources of fiber include stems, twigs, and the inner bark of plants. Fibers are divided into two types: soluble and insoluble. *Soluble fibers* include pectin, barley, rye, and oat fiber; guar gum; and locust bean. Other sources of soluble fiber are black-eyed peas, kidney beans, pinto beans, navy beans, lentils, split peas, oat bran, all-bran, oatmeal, prunes, pears, apples, corn, sweet potatoes, zucchini, cauliflower, and broccoli. They play an important role in lowering blood cholesterol levels and reducing the speed of glucose entering the bloodstream, thereby reducing the secretion of insulin. *Insoluble fibers,* which largely pass unchanged through the intestines, are present in beans, celery, cereals, wheat bran, and many wholesome foods. Eating too little fiber causes insulin resistance, diabetes, and premature aging.

Vitamins are organic (i.e., contain carbon) substances that participate in regulating metabolic and other biochemical processes of the body. They are derived from plant and animal sources, and we need them in small amounts. Vitamins are essential to our body's functioning and for maintaining good health. They are fifteen in number, nine of which--C and the eight B vitamins--dissolve in water and pass out of the body in the urine; therefore, they must be replenished daily. Four vitamins--A, D, E, and K--dissolve in fat and are stored in body fat cells for weeks, months, or even years, and are released as the body demands. Three vitamins of the B complex--B5, biotin, and folic acid--and choline, an amino acid related to the B-complex family, are considered essential micronutrients for humans. By improving nerve transmission, choline is good for memory enhancement and thinking; it is found in animal foods such as fish, egg yolks, cheese, and liver. The plant sources of choline are green leafy vegetables, cabbage, cauliflower, beans, peas, peanuts, and seed oils. Vitamins A, C, E, B-1, B-5, and B-6 are powerful antioxidants, which protect our cells from free-radical attacks.

Minerals are inorganic chemical elements that are necessary for proper functioning of the body, and which are obtained exclusively from the food we eat. Taken by plants from the ground, they are incorporated into the plant's organic compounds, and we either consume the plants or the animals that ate the plants. Minerals serve as constituents of cells and body fluids, and as structural components of muscles and bones. Minerals needed in daily gram amounts are called *macro-minerals*; those needed in daily microgram amounts are called *micro-minerals,* or trace elements. Macro-minerals include calcium, chloride, magnesium, phosphorus, potassium, sodium, and sulfur; trace elements include chromium, copper, fluoride, iodine, iron, manganese, molybdenum, selenium, and zinc. The minerals zinc and selenium have very strong antioxidative properties and help our cells in fighting free radicals.

Enzymes are special protein molecules that act as catalysts in speeding up numerous chemical reactions in our body. All metabolic reactions in cells occur in an orderly, highly structured pattern. Each multi-step reaction requires a specific enzyme that controls the rate at which the specific reaction occurs. The number of enzymes in our body is as numerous as the number of chemical reactions. So far, scientific research has identified more than five thousand enzymes. The key enzymes are the metabolic (e.g., respirative, antioxidation, and alcohol-breaking), digestive, and food enzymes. Metabolic and digestive enzymes are secreted by our body; food enzymes are supplied by the food we eat.

• Metabolic enzymes, a vital part of the constantly occurring numerous chemical reactions in cells, are collectively termed *metabolism.*

• Respirative enzymes help with collecting oxygen in the alveoli, which then enters the bloodstream and is delivered to different body parts. They also help in transporting the nitrogen and the oxygen for its use in protein synthesis and in releasing carbon dioxide in the alveoli.

• Antioxidation enzymes such as *superoxide dismutaze (SOD)* and *glutathione peroxidase* protect the body from the damage caused by superoxide free radicals.

• The alcohol-breaking enzyme called *alcohol dehydrogenase* converts alcohol into the harmful chemical *acetaldehyde,* which is detoxified by another enzyme, *aldehyde dehydrogenase,* which oxidizes acetaldehyde into a harmless acetate (i.e., vinegar).

• Digestive enzymes start acting in the mouth, working all along the digestive tract to help break down food into simpler compounds that can be assimilated by cells for energy production and for building body tissues. The enzyme *amylase,* which contributes to the digestion of carbohydrates, is present in saliva and pancreatic juices. The enzyme *protease,* which helps break down proteins, is secreted by the pancreas. The enzyme *lipase,* which helps break down fats, also is secreted by the pancreas, but in lesser concentrations than protease and amylase.

• Food enzymes are contained in all uncooked foods in proportions that allow for their proper digestion. Carbohydrates in grains such as wheat or oats contain higher amounts of amylase and lesser concentrations of protease and lipase. Meats have sizable amounts of protease and lesser amounts of lipase (lean meats) and amylase. Fat-containing oils, seeds, nuts, and dairy products are loaded primarily with lipase. Low-protein fruits and vegetables contain lesser amounts of the protein digestive enzyme and higher amounts of the enzyme *cellulase,* which is necessary for fiber digestion. Enzymes are sensitive to high temperatures and die at 118° F (48° C); therefore, prolonged cooking such as boiling, frying, and stewing--which is usually done at much higher temperatures--destroys them.

Phytochemicals are compounds found in plants that protect them from environmental stresses and infections. They are equally protective for people against heart disease, cancer, and other degenerative illnesses, and even from aging itself. They are abundant in green leafy vegetables, yellow, orange, and red fruits, and sprouts, and soybeans. Researchers have so far identified several hundred phytochemicals, the most important of which and the plants containing them are allicin (garlic), ellagic acid (cherries and strawberries), liminoid (lemongrass, peels of citrus fruits, dill, and caraway), lutein (kale and collard greens), lycopene (tomatoes, raw and cooked), quercetin (red and yellow onions), sulforaphane (broccoli, Brussels sprouts, and kale), xanthophyll (spinach and collard greens), and zeaxanthin (green leafy vegetables).

How Much Food Do We Need?

The amount of food we need ranges very broadly and depends on many factors: body constitution, metabolic rate, expenditure of energy, climate, condition of the body, mind and spirit, emotional state, and stress level, to name just a few. Let's look at the average body demands and at extremes of food consumption, keeping in mind how all this affects longevity.

A widely accepted system of measuring a person's need for food is the system of calories. To start with, the U.S. Food and Agriculture Organization (FAO) and World Health Organization recommend a daily consumption of 2,600 calories per capita, although requirements vary considerably due to occupation, climate, age, and other factors. Actual daily per capita consumption in 1995, as presented in *The Illustrated Book of World Rankings* for 162 countries and based on the *UN Statistical Yearbook,* ranges from 3,951 calories in Ireland to 1,699 calories in Ethiopia; the United States ranks sixth, with 3,642 calories. Experts at the U.S. Department of Agriculture (USDA) estimate that the right amount for many *seniors* and sedentary women is 1,600 calories per day. For active women, children, and teenage girls, the requirementis approximately 2,200 calories; active men and teenage boys may need 2,800 calories.

For maintenance of body mass, the calorie input and output has to be in balance. In his book *Weigh Less, Live Longer,* Louis J. Aronne, M.D., provides a table of daily calorie intake for achieving or maintaining desired weight depending on a person's height. The taller the person, the greater is his/her calorie intake. I found in his table that for my height of 6 feet, 2 inches (191 cm), the corresponding desired weight and calorie intake is as follows:

75.0 kg (165 lb.): 2,755 kcal
77.3 kg (170 lb.): 2,790 kcal
79.5 kg (175 lb.): 2,824 kcal
81.8 kg (179 lb.): 2,858 kcal

According to Dr. Aronne's table, to maintain my standard weight of 81.8 kg, I have to consume as much as 2,850 kcal. My calorie intake also can be calculated using the Basal Metabolic Rate (BMR), as suggested in the

Reader's Digest *Live Longer Cook Book*:

BMR = weight in pounds x 10 = 180 x 10 = 1,800 kcal

Everyday activities like deskwork, shopping, housework, and cooking require an additional 30 percent more calories:

BMR x 1.3 = 1,800 x 1.3 = 2,340 kcal

In Japan also, calorie intake depends on both a person's height and level of activity. Yoshihiko Suzuki and Kazuko Shiozawa in their book, *Food Guide Based on 80 Kcal* (in Japanese), provide a formula for determining calorie intake. The calculation involves the following three steps:

1. Standard weight = (height, cm - 100) x 0.9 (for people shorter than 150 cm, the coefficient of 0.9 is not applied)
2. Number of calories per 1 kilogram of standard weight is determined based on activity level:
    a. Non-active (sedentary, elderly)   20-25 kcal
    b. Low activity (office workers, managers,
clerks, housewives without breast-fed children)   25-30 kcal
    c. Medium activity (salesmen, shop and factory
workers, jobs that involve standing on their feet)   30-35 kcal
    d. High activity (farmers, fishermen, construction workers) 35-40 kcal
3. Multiply standard weight by number of calories.

For people with an expenditure of 25 kcal per 1 kilogram of body weight (i.e., low activity), the recommended food intake depends on height:

143-158 cm: 1,200 kcal
153-168 cm: 1,400 kcal
163-178 cm: 1,600 kcal
173-188 cm: 1,800 kcal

The calculation for my height of 191 cm results in the following:

1. (191-100) x 0.9 = 81.9 kg
2. 25 kcal is my activity level
3. 81.9 kg x 25 = 2,047 kcal

We can see from these three calculations that in America, I am advised to eat from 2,340 to 2,850 kcal, while in Japan it is a little more than 2,000 kcal. I thank my dear Japanese friends for your consideration; in Japan, I would eat less to save money because food is distinctly more expensive than in the United States.

Diets

To obtain these calories, what kinds of food and how much of them should we eat? This involves another measuring system of grams and ounces of particular foods, aside from calories. This is the realm of *diets* that specify the percentage of proteins, carbohydrates, and fats; kinds of food; and amounts of servings of food groups such as bread, vegetables, fruits, dairy, meat, and fats. Most diets fall into one of six categories, depending on whom they are targeted for or the goal to achieve:

• General population: such as the USDA Food Guide Pyramid diet of the U.S. Government, Mediterranean, Healthy, and Andrew Weil's Optimum Health Plan

• Customized: for metabolic types such as the Wolcott, Cousens, D'Adamo, Gittleman, and Abravanel diets

• Weight loss: high-protein and high-fat diets such as Atkin's, the Zone, and DiPasquale's diets

• Therapeutic: low-fat, low-protein, high-carbohydrate diets for prevention of heart disease and diabetes, such as the American Heart Association (AHA), National Institutes of Health (NIH), American Diabetic Association (ADA), Pritikin, Ornish, Macrobiotic, and food-combining diets

• Specific population groups: such as vegetarians, raw foodists, exercisers, athletes, and centenarians

• Life-extension and rejuvenation diets: such as the Paul Bragg, Souren Arakelyan, and David Wolfe diets.

A brief review of popular diets is shown in Table 15-1.

Table 15-1   Popular Diets

No s.	Diet	Diet Plan	Author	Percentage			Notes
				Prt	Car	Fat	
1	For general population	USDA Food Guide Pyramid	Recommended by the U.S. Government	12	58	30	Recommended well-balanced, healthy diet
2		Typical Western Diet	USA actual	15	42	43	Protein: 91 g/day Carbo: 243 g/day Fat: 114 g/day
3		Healthy Diet*	USA	15	70	15	*referred to in the B. Sears' book *Enter the Zone*

No s.	Diet	Diet Plan	Author	Percentage			Notes
				Prt	Car	Fat	
4	For general population	Typical Chinese Diet	Rural Chinese	10	80	15	Protein: 64 g/day Carbo: 524 g/day Fat: 43 g/day
5		Mediterra-nean	Italy, Greece, Crete	10 - 18	46- 50	35 - 40	Grains, fruits, green vegetables, lean meat, nuts, olive oil, red wine
6		Optimum Health Plan	Andrew Weil	25	50- 55	20 - 25	Fish (salmon) as major source of protein, whole grains, broccoli, fruits
7	Custo-mized	Metabolic Type	William L. Wolcott	40 25 30	30 60 50	30 15 20	Protein type Carbo type Mixed type
8		Metabolic Type	Gabriel Cousens	50- 55 30 40	30- 35 55 40	20- 25 15 20	Fast oxidizer Slow oxidizer Mixed oxidizer
9		Blood Type	Peter D'Adamo	% vary by blood type			Type O: high protein, Type A: high carbohydrates
10		Body Type, Metabolism	Elliot Abravanel	% vary by body type (1,200 kcal)			Male types: Adrenal Pituitary, Thyroid Female types: above three + Gonadal
11		Ancestry, Blood Type, Metabolism	Ann Louise Gittleman	% based on variety of factors			Fast Burner: more protein and fat; Slow Burner: more carbohydrates + protein
12	Wei-ght Loss	High-protein, high-fat, low-carbohydrates	Robert Atkins	45	10	45	Carbohydrates restricted to 15-60 g/day
13		The Zone, High-protein	B. Sears	30	40	30	Favorable carbs: fruits, vegetables
14		High-fat, high-protein, low-carbohydrates	Mauro Di Pasquale	40 - 50 15 - 30	4 - 10 35 - 60	40 - 60 20 - 40	Weekdays (30g carbohydrates) Weekend (carbohy-drates loading)
15		Dean Ornish's Program	Dean Ornish	20	70	10	For weight loss and prevention of heart attacks
16	Thera-peutic	Pritikin	Natan Pritikin	10 - 15	75- 80	10	For weight loss and prevention of coronary heart disease

Nos.	Diet	Diet Plan	Author	Percentage Prt	Percentage Car	Percentage Fat	Notes
17	Thera-peutic	Low-protein	AHA, NIH	10	60	30	Heart health, overall health
18		ADA	ADA	20	60	20	American Diabetes Association
19		Macrobiotic	George Ohsawa	10 - 15	70-75	10 - 20	50% whole grains; 25% land and sea vegetables; 10 to 15% beans and bean products; 15% animal foods
20		Food-combining	Herbert Shelton	Combinations of proteins, fats, and carbohydrates rather than their daily %			Good: fat + carbohydrates Bad: protein + carbohydrates
21		Vegetarian		10 10	80 83	10 7	Vegetarians, Tara-humara Indians, New Guineans
22	Athle-tes		Frank Melfa	25	65	10	Bodybuilding
23	Exer-cisers	In-Sync Diet Plan		33	50	17	Average
				% based on 6 daily metabolic phases			6 levels of daily activity or exercise
24	Anti-Aging	Anti-Aging Zone	Barry Sears	30	40	30	1,200 kcal females; 1,500 kcal males
25		Shed 10 Years	Julian Whitaker	15 - 20	70	15	Complex carbs, soy, organic food
26		Age-Defying	Robert Atkins	50-75% protein and fat			10% simple + 25% - 50% complex carbohydrates
27		Anti-Aging	Art Mollen	20	60	20	One animal protein food per day
28		Biomarkers	Evans & Rosenberg	10-20	60	30 or less	Limited saturated fat
29	Long-Living People	Hunza Valley, Pakistan	Survey of Dr. S. Maqsood	10	73	17	1,923 kcal Protein: 50 g/day Carbo: 354 g/day Fat: 35 g/day
30		Vilcabamba Valley, Ecuador	Survey of Dr. G. Vela	14	71	15	1,200 kcal Protein: 39 g/day Carbo: 200 g/day Fat: 19 g/day
31		Abkhasia, Georgia	Survey of Kyucharyants	–	–	19	1,800 kcal Fat: 40-60 g/day

No s.	Diet	Diet Plan	Author	Percentage			Notes
				Prt	Car	Fat	
32	Long-Living People	Balanced	Italian Centenarians	20	60	20	Study of 70 centenarians (17 males and 53 females) aged 100 to 108
33	Life Extension	Bragg Life Extension Plan	Paul Bragg, Patricia Bragg	20	–	7	60% raw fruits & vegetables; 7% cereals & legumes; 7% dried fruits, honey, molasses
34		The Anti-Aging Plan	Roy Walford	15	75	10	1,800 kcal caloric restriction
35		Very Low Calorie Diet	Stuart Berger	20	60	20	1,600 kcal females; 1,600+ kcal males
36		Raw Food Diet	Souren Arakelyan	Raw plant foods, fasting for 3 days/month			1,000 kcal
37		Extremely Low Calorie and Protein Diet	Galina Shatalova	11	53	36	700-1,000 kcal Protein: 20 g/day Carbo: 100 g/day Fat: 30 g/day
38	Elderly	Sunfood Diet (raw plant foods)	David Wolfe	Green leafy vegetables: 40%, sweet fruits: 20%, fatty*: 40%			*Fatty fruits, nuts, coconuts, seeds

Diets for the general population, such as the USDA Food Guide Pyramid diet, are based on well-established dietary advice that is mostly supported by scientific research and studies. They are regarded as **well-balanced diets**: low in protein, moderate in fat (up to 30 percent), with carbohydrates making up the bulk of the diet (50 to 60 percent). These diets recommend eating whole grains and other complex carbohydrates; more fish, beans, fruits, vegetables, and plant oils; and less animal protein, refined carbohydrates, and saturated fat. These guidelines are broadly recognized as healthy and are accepted by health experts and leading American health organizations. Other diets, such as the Chinese rural, Mediterranean, and Andrew Weil's diets, are also regarded as healthy and well balanced. These diets, however, are "one-size-fits-all" diets and do not consider the fact that people are very different. Customized diets are still in the minority, but their popularity is gradually increasing.

Metabolic diets, such as those of Wolcott and Cousens, are individual-centered. They emphasize the variety of metabolic processes occurring in different people when they utilize food. Most of them classify people by three metabolic types: fast oxidizer, mixed oxidizer, and slow oxidizer. Dr. D'Adamo's blood-type diet stresses that blood chemistry and its reactions to food are different for each blood type. Therefore, people of the four different blood types (i.e., O, A, B, and AB) must eat different foods. Ann L. Gittleman takes this a step farther, adding to these two factors a person's ancestry and genetic heritage. The personalized diets are very appealing to me, and I include Ayurvedic dosha types (similar to metabolic types), blood type, and Yin-Yang type when I search for a proper diet for each of us to attain longevity.

Therapeutic diets, especially the macrobiotic diet, are high in carbohydrates and low in protein and fat. The proportions of main macronutrients in these diets are close to those of vegetarian diets. A food-combining diet implies that to enhance digestion and assimilation, different kinds of food must be compatible with each other. General rules include not eating proteins and starches, meat and milk, fruits and flesh foods, raw fruits and vegetables, or citrus fruits and starches in the same meal. Some of these diets are introduced for the prevention and cure of major degenerative diseases, such as heart disease and cancer. Diets for athletes require higher protein intake for building muscles and performing strenuous exercises. It is interesting to note that Italian centenarians also eat more protein (20 percent) than Americans typically consume (12 percent). A study in Japan also showed that its centenarians eat more protein than the average Japanese does.

Diets for weight loss attract much public attention and are currently hotly debated. As studies show, half of American adults are overweight and interested in weight reduction. You can lose weight quickly and stay slim forever, even without reducing the amount of food you eat, claim Nathan Pritikin and Dr. Dean Ornish, advocates of low-fat, high-carbohydrate diets. These diets are based on the belief that excessive fat consumption is the primary cause of obesity, heart disease, and some cancers. In the United States, a 20 to 30 percent reduction in mortality rates from heart disease in the past twenty-five years is attributed to a decrease in fat intake.

Exactly the same claims about weight loss and health benefits come from the proponents of **high-protein, low-carbohydrate diets**. A few of the best-selling books recommending the shift to these diets are *Dr. Atkins' New Diet Revolution*, by Robert Atkins, M.D.; *Enter the Zone*, by Barry Sears, Ph.D.; *Protein Power*, by Michael and Mary Eades; and *Healthy for Life*, by Richard and Rachael Heller. The common belief in these books is that the only real enemy is carbohydrates, which make you obese, and that eating them is dangerous to your health. According to Dr. Atkins, in a high-carbohydrate diet, the body produces excess insulin, which converts carbohydrates into body fat. The logic follows that restricting carbohydrates as a source of fuel pushes the body to burn stored fat. The intake of carbohydrates ranges from less than 10 percent in Dr. Atkins' diet to 40 percent in the Zone diet. Breads, pasta, cereals, fruits, vegetables, and legumes are all restricted in both diets. The Zone diet considers carbohydrates such as rice, potatoes, pasta, bread, lima beans, carrots, bananas, and apple juice to be dangerous for health.

People on these diets lose some weight quickly; however, it is mostly water and muscle mass, rather than fat. This happens mostly to sedentary people. The reason for weight loss seems to be a negative calorie balance induced by eliminating calories from carbohydrates. It sounds paradoxical to lose muscle protein by eating about 1 pound a day of protein-rich foods such as chicken (6 ounces), ribeye steak (6 ounces), tuna salad (1 cup), and almonds (1 ounce) (typical in the Atkin's diet). The point is that all these diets are rich in fat too, and fat together with protein becomes a main fuel for the body. As a result, ketone bodies are produced in excess from the breakdown of food fats and some stored body fats. With low blood sugar, the body enters a state of ketosis (as in fasting) and starts to convert protein from muscles into glucose. This paradox is apparently similar to Barry Sears' admonition, "You have to eat fat to lose fat."

On the other hand, excessive protein consumption (i.e., 30 to 45 percent) in the long run can be hazardous to a person's health. It entails loading the body with the toxic end products of protein metabolism; uric acid buildup; and the risk of gout, kidney stones, liver and kidney failure, arteriosclerosis, diabetes, and a depletion of calcium stores--resulting in osteoporosis and risk of bone fractures.

Vegetarian diets are as old as the world is. Among strict vegetarians of the past were Plato and Pythagoras, Buddha and Mahatma Ghandi, Nitzsche and Leo Tolstoy. Many claim that a vegetarian diet results in a host of health benefits, including better protection against heart disease, stroke, and cancer. The restriction or complete elimination of animal products is the heart of a vegetarian diet. Vegans are the strictest toward animal products, and do not allow any meat, fish, eggs, or dairy products. Lacto-vegetarians permit dairy products, and ovo-lacto-vegetarians also permit eggs. Meat-eaters often warn vegetarians to carefully plan their diets in order to avoid a deficiency of key nutrients, such as calcium, iron, zinc, vitamin B_{12}, vitamin D, and essential amino acids. Eating soybeans or tofu--which provide high-quality vegetable protein--and selecting complementary proteins help overcome this pitfall.

The biggest issue regarding vegetarian diet is vitamin B_{12}, which is believed to be found only in animal products in quantities sufficient to meet human needs. Vitamin B_{12} helps to synthesize DNA, carry oxygen in the blood, isolate nerve fibers from each other, and grow new tissue and skin. The Recommended Daily Allowance (RDA) requirement (1995) of vitamin B_{12} is 2.0 micrograms for both males and females; pregnant and nursing females need 2.2 and 2.6 micrograms, respectively. The required amounts seem to increase over time and, in the year 2000, the Daily Value indicated in the *Hannaford All-Purpose Multivitamin & Multimineral Supplement* is 6.0 micrograms for adults; what the body actually needs is apparently much less. According to research conducted back in 1968 by Victor Herbert, if a conventional diet is eaten, individuals need a mere 0.1 microgram of vitamin B_{12} per day. The plant sources of vitamin B_{12} include soybeans, tempeh, olives, green leafy vegetables, roots of cruciferous vegetables, seaweed, and alfalfa, as well as leaves of kohlrabi. It is said, however, that non-animal sources of vitamin B_{12} are not constant. I refer the reader to *Nutrition for Vegetarians*, by Drs. Agatha and Calvin Thrash, who include a compelling discussion on vitamin B_{12} in their book. To be on the safe side, vegetarians-- especially vegans--are advised to take vitamin B_{12} supplements.

Long-living people's diets, based on the surveys and **life-extension diets** of certain scientists experimenting on themselves, all have in common a low-calorie, low-protein, low-fat, and high-carbohydrate intake with emphasis on wholesome or raw plant foods. Some of the diets, such as Dr. Galina Shatalova's diet with its mere 20 grams/day of protein, 100 grams/day of carbohydrates, and 700 to 1,000 kcal/day intake, may seem to be an extreme, semi-starvation diet. However, Dr. Shatalova, a scientist who was involved in the Russian astronauts' nutrition research and enjoys her own good health being now in her nineties, is a living proof of the workability of her diet.

> A 100-year-old Singaporean, Teresa Hsu, also lives on very little food. Her breakfast usually consists of a glass of water (0 kcal) or milk (150 kcal). She often has milk (150 kcal) and salad for lunch, or food that people sometimes bring her (probably 300 to 400 kcal). Dinner is milk or yogurt (150 kcal). The daily total is about 800 kcal. "You waste energy digesting unnecessary food!" she was reported as saying in the November 7, 1997, issue of *The Straits Times,* a Singapore newspaper.

A raw-food diet means that all the foods a person eats are raw, uncooked plant foods. It is considered an extreme diet and people who engage in eating only raw foods are regarded as experimenting on themselves. Almost every nutritionist and physician will tell you about numerous dangers, including bacteria and germs; indigestion; a deficiency of essential amino acids, minerals, and vitamins D and B_{12}; the hazards of surviving on low-calorie raw food in winter, and many others. The people who have lived on a raw-food diet for years and even decades will tell you instead that eating cooked food is the fastest way to acquire many degenerative diseases, age rapidly, and die prematurely. The most powerful argument in a favor of eating raw foods is the preservation of digestive enzymes in food, which otherwise are easily destroyed in cooking. The raw-food diet is discussed in more detail later in this chapter.

How Much Protein Do We Need?

The other question is about the amount of protein we need. Many physicians and nutritionists believe that too much protein is harmful. Excessive protein intake for a prolonged period is linked to serious degenerative illnesses such as heart disease, cancer, stroke, kidney failure, diabetes, and many others. To the contrary, Peter W.R. Lemon, Ph.D., a prominent expert in the field of protein and exercise research in the Applied Physiology Research Laboratory at Kent State University in Ohio, believes that a high-protein diet is not as hazardous as many fear. Indeed, two or three times the RDA requirements for protein (i.e., 54.4 grams/day for a 150-pound or 68-kg male) perhaps is not harmful for a normal, healthy, and exercising individual, but would be a burden for elderly people, in whom kidney function is reduced.

On the other hand, too little protein consumption leads to malnutrition, a condition also dangerous to our health. The healthy amount, if established, cannot be a fixed amount, because it is very dependent on a person's body constitution, blood type, lifestyle, and activities, as well as climate, season, environmental conditions, and other factors.

The scientific estimation of protein requirements for a human body is based on measurements of nitrogen losses (i.e., in the urine and feces, through the skin, perspiration, and internal body structure) in experimental subjects who are put on a protein-free diet, according to Frances Moore Lappe, author of the book, *Diet for a Small Planet*. The total daily nitrogen loss must be replenished with dietary protein. The protein requirement for body maintenance is determined to be an average of 0.34 gram of protein per 1 kilogram (2.2 pounds) of body weight per day, or 25 grams for a 160-pound (73-kilogram) male. To obtain the protein allowances, the Committee on Dietary Allowances of the National Academy of Sciences, Food and Nutrition Board, based on these amounts, made a few adjustments for the following:

• the individual differences and to cover 97.5 percent of the population (30 percent up)

• the less efficient use of protein in an ordinary eating pattern as compared with the experimental conditions (30 percent up)

• the usability of dietary protein (actually used as compared with what is eaten), which in the United States is estimated to be 75 percent

With these adjustments, the Committee came up with the 0.84 gram of protein per 1 kilogram (2.2 pounds) of body weight per day, or 61 grams for a 160-pound (73-kilogram) male. The U.S. RDA is 0.8 gram of protein per 1 kilogram (2.2 pounds) of body weight per day, or 58 grams for a male of the same body weight, or 60 grams of protein for a 2,000-kcal diet; these amounts are very close to the previous estimates.

For comparison, the minimum daily requirement established by the World Health Organization is 0.47 gram of protein per 1 kilogram (2.2 pounds) of body weight per day, or 34 grams for a 160-pound (73-kilogram) male. The Japanese recommend 70 grams of protein in a 2,550-kcal diet. For achieving longevity, they advise that 50 grams of meat, one slice of fish, one egg, and one to two cups of milk be eaten daily, which results in 60 to 73 grams of protein. Dr. Roy L. Walford and Lisa Walford recommend about the same amount. In their book, *The Anti-Aging Plan,* they state that a person requires about 0.015 ounce of "complete" protein per pound of body weight per day, which comes to 70 grams for a 160-pound (73-kilogram) male. The Russian balanced-nutrition guidelines advise 100 grams of protein for adults. American bodybuilders who pack on muscle mass daily consume 1.5 to 2.0 grams of protein per 1 kilogram of body weight; for example, 120 to 160 grams of protein per 80 kilograms (176 pounds) of body weight.

Natural-health advocates are much stricter when it comes to protein consumption. Their sole concern is the amount of dietary protein necessary for the replacement of body protein, which is lost daily with dead cells and broken down in the metabolic processes. Protein is not considered to be an energy source. According to Dr. Galina Shatalova of Moscow, Russia, the daily protein intake necessary to maintain the body weight of an adult human is estimated to be 0.25 gram per 1 kilogram of body mass. For the adult with a body weight of 160 pounds (73 kilograms), this means 18.3 grams of protein a day. A somewhat higher figure is stated in the book *Fit for Life* by Harvey and Marilyn Diamond, who say that to maintain weight, the human body needs to replenish a daily loss of 23 grams of protein, which is very close to the previously mentioned scientific estimate. The protein is lost through the feces and urine, from growing hair and nails, sloughed-off skin, and perspiration. According to H. & M. Diamond, the human body recycles 70 percent of the protein that is contained in waste.

The recycling of amino acids is the key to understanding why we need so little protein. Back in 1964, a researcher named Rose estimated that 18 grams of protein a day would be sufficient. In 1971, Hegsted suggested that we need a mere 10 grams of protein a day, considering that our body is very efficient in recycling amino acids. An amount close to this figure is stated in *The Optimum Nutrition Bible*, by Patrick Holford, one of Britain's leading nutritional authors and the founder of the Institute for Optimum Nutrition in London. He states, "At the low end of the scale are reports of protein sufficiency when 2.5 percent of total calorie intake comes from protein." For a 2,000-kcal diet, it recommends 50 kcal or 12.5 grams of protein. Actually, it is very difficult to design a 2,000-kcal diet with this tiny amount of protein, because protein is in everything. A person must eat only low-protein plants such as apples and cucumbers. For instance, twenty apples (80 kcal each) and six cucumbers (40 kcal each), which comprise 12.5 grams of protein, would total only 1,840 kcal.

For therapeutic purposes, amounts as low as 0.2 gram per kilogram of body weight reportedly have been used with significant effects in the treatment of patients with kidney failure for a prolonged period. For a 160-pound (73-kilogram) male, this translates into 14.6 grams of protein per day.

Animal protein is a real test for our digestive system. The point is that, biologically, we are not as suited for eating meat as are carnivorous animals. They have a short intestine, very strong digestive juices (ten times stronger than ours), and the meat they eat passes in 3 to 4 hours. Our intestine is three times longer, our digestive juices are weak, and for most people it takes 24 to 48 hours for meat to pass. The acid environment favorable for the breakdown of meat exists only in the stomach, where meat stays only a few hours. Therefore, very little meat (i.e., about 2 ounces for blood type A and 6 ounces for blood type O) can be properly digested at one time; any larger amounts pass through the intestines only partly digested.

Animal protein, like our muscle protein, has a very complex structure and a significant amount of energy is necessary to break it down to molecules that can be utilized in the cells. A small part of them is used to replenish dead cells; the bigger part is burned for energy. It is commonly known that meat is a heavy food for digestion. It is quite an energy-consuming process and we must first take in calories in order to have enough later after metabolism of the meat. Digesting meat is like an internal workout and our body must sweat a lot to do the job. This is probably one of the reasons why people on a high-protein diet lose weight--they do not need to go to the gym because they have one inside. Their bodies are already engaged in strenuous exercise digesting the meat.

Vegetable protein can serve as an alternative to animal protein for blood type A's, who are advised to keep close to a vegetarian diet. Among vegetable sources of high-quality protein are quinoa, brown rice, broccoli, pumpkin, and sunflower seeds, as well as soybeans, including tofu, miso, and tempeh. The protein in spinach, peas, and lentils is not of a high quality; however, combined with grains such as rice, they result in complete protein. Discussing a healthy amount of vegetable protein intake, Drs. Agatha and Calvin Thrash, in their book *Nutrition for Vegetarians,* state, "Men and women can live without apparent harm on protein intakes of 25 to 40 grams from vegetable foods." Living proof that an individual can survive taking the lowest level of that range is Dr. Norman Walker, who daily consumed 25 grams of protein by eating exclusively raw fruits and vegetables and nuts; he lived to 109 years of age. I do not know what his blood type was, but his case shows how little dietary protein we actually need.

As far as exercise is concerned, it is good for our health; however, in the case of meat-digesting exercise, the problem is with the byproducts of meat metabolism. It is not carbohydrates that have just water and carbon dioxide as metabolism end products. Carbon dioxide is exhaled with air and water is expelled with the urine. The byproducts of protein metabolism (from meat and other sources) are uric acid and urea. With proper elimination, they do not harm us--but often our elimination system does not work perfectly. If accumulated in the body due to excessive protein consumption, uric acid and urea cause numerous diseases, including kidney stones, gout, gallbladder stones, and arthritis. Too much protein eaten at one meal overloads the bloodstream with amino acids and leads to the excessive production of insulin to process them. As a result, excess protein is converted into body fat.

Consider the Japanese, who traditionally eat little meat, mostly fish, rice, and sea and land vegetables. They are slim and rarely have heart disease. On the contrary, sumo wrestlers (by their profession) are the models of obesity. For centuries, their diet was based on rice and vegetables; however, in the last fifty years, meat has been added. They have become heavier and heavier with every passing decade. A wrestler's average weight of 317 pounds in 1953 is now 412 pounds, and the life span is sixteen years less than that of an average Japanese male. The same happened to Japanese from Okinawa who immigrated to Brazil at the beginning of the twentieth century. They relocated with their great longevity genes, but adopted a local lifestyle with abundant meat (as much as 2 pounds a day) in the diet. As a result, 25 percent of the transplanted Japanese suffered from diabetes and lived fifteen to seventeen years less than their peers in Japan.

Excessive Protein Consumption and Cancer

A diet containing too much protein, especially animal protein, can lead to cancer, says Dr. A. Vogel in his widely recognized book, *Swiss Nature Doctor*. Excessive protein intake leads to constant irritation of the cells, thus encouraging abnormal cell growth, adds Dr. Vogel. The publication *Diet, Nutrition, and Cancer* of the National Academy of Sciences suggests that high protein intake may increase the risk of cancer of the breast, colon, rectum, pancreas, prostate gland, and kidneys. Michio Kushi, in his book *The Cancer Prevention Diet,* ascribes animal protein to the primary high-risk factors in the development of many types of cancer. The countries with high protein consumption have higher death rates from cancer, as Figure 15-1 shows.

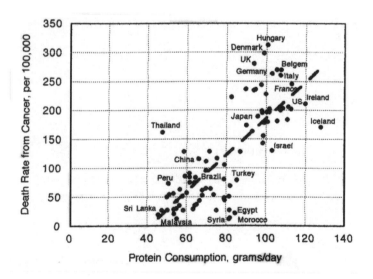

Figure 15-1. Death Rate from Cancer versus Protein Consumption
in 87 Countries

Although the scatter in Figure 15-1 is quite large, the correlation between protein consumption and death rate is quite distinctive. The highest death rate is found in Hungary; Denmark, with its protein consumption of approximately 100 grams per day, is second. Other European countries with high protein consumption, including the United Kingdom, Belgium, France, Italy, and Germany, are shown in the upper left-hand corner of the graph, above the approximation line. Although protein consumption is among the highest in the United States, Ireland, and Russia, the death rate from cancer is close to the approximation line. Although its protein consumption is the highest (127.9 grams per day), Iceland enjoys a lower than average death rate. Among the countries with low protein consumption, Thailand is way above the line because of air pollution in Bangkok and extremely spicy foods that irritate the digestive tract, which contribute to the development of lung and colon cancers. China is close to the line and Malaysia is below it. The group of Arab countries including Egypt, Syria, and Morocco enjoy the lowest death rate despite a medium protein consumption of about 80 grams per day-- perhaps because of fasting during the Ramadan month.

In this discussion, I am not trying to claim that excessive protein causes cancer; rather, combined with other risk factors, it may promote the development of cancer. Research studies show that ill-absorbed protein, such as when protein enters the colon, may cause flatulence and, in extreme cases, colon cancer.

Excessive Animal Fat Consumption and Heart Disease

A high-fat, low-fiber diet, the intake of excessive calories, and a sedentary lifestyle are linked to the high incidence of coronary heart disease in developed Western countries. Animal fats have a high content of cholesterol and free radicals, which impose a damaging effect on the blood and body cells. The over-consumption of food rich in animal fats loads the blood with fatty acids, which adhere to the walls of arteries. This speeds up the arterial thickening and formation of plaque deposits, which results in many disorders including high blood pressure, enlarged heart, and kidney trouble. The fatty plaques and streaks on the arterial walls may narrow or even close the artery, causing a heart attack or stroke.

Of the three main groups of fats in food--saturated, mono-unsaturated, and polyunsaturated--the saturated fats tend to increase the level of cholesterol in the blood. Saturated fats are found mostly in animal food products such as lard, butter, meat, whole milk, cream, and cheese, as well as in palm and coconut oil. It seems that in developed countries, high animal-fat consumption is related to higher death rates from ischemic heart disease, as Figure 15-2 shows.

The data on death rates in twenty-three selected countries for 1987-1990 were obtained from the *Gale Country & World Rankings Reporter*; the data on fat consumption in these countries for 1990 was obtained from the U.S. *FAO Quarterly Bulletin of Statistics*, Vol. 7, 1994.

As shown in Figure 15-2, there is a distinct correlation between animal-fat consumption and the death rate from ischemic heart disease, although the scatter is rather large. The highest death rate is found in the Czech Republic, although its fat consumption of 93.5 grams per day is moderate; other factors increase the death rate in that country. New Zealand is ranked second in death rate, with its animal-fat consumption of about 116.5 grams per day. Other European countries with high death rates, such as Finland, Hungary, and Bulgaria, are above the approximation line.

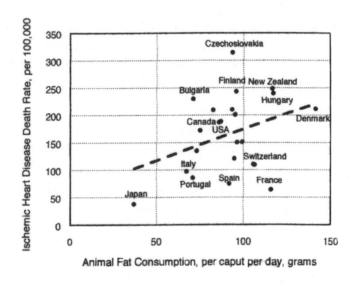

Figure 15-2. Death Rate from Ischemic Heart Disease versus
Animal-Fat Consumption in 23 Developed Countries

In the United States and Canada, both animal-fat consumption and death rates are moderate. In Denmark, although protein consumption is among the highest, the death rate from ischemic heart disease is near the mean line.

Despite its high animal-fat consumption (115.6 grams per day), France enjoys a much lower than average death rate. This is called the "French paradox"--the key is found in the habit of drinking red grape wine in that country. Mediterranean countries including Italy, Spain, and Portugal, which are known for a diet rich in olive oil, show low death rates together with moderate animal-fat consumption. The Japanese consume the lowest amount of animal fat (i.e., 37.3 grams per day) and enjoy the lowest death rate from ischemic heart disease among developed countries.

It would be incorrect to claim that excessive consumption of animal fat alone causes heart disease; however, combined with other risk factors, it may contribute to the development of heart disease. Many factors associated with lifestyle and diet are responsible for heart disease; excessive consumption of saturated fat is among them. Small amounts of saturated fats are not harmful to the heart--the problem starts when they are consumed in excess; that is, more than 30 percent of calories from fat or more than 67 grams of fat in a 2,000-calorie diet.

Because an excessive intake of protein may be detrimental for a person's health, the global question is whether food is the only source of protein for our bodies, or are there other sources? We will discuss this matter in the next chapter.

16

FOOD CONSUMPTION AND LONGEVITY

Protein Synthesis

Proteins are produced in plants by a process called *protein synthesis* in which nitrogen is extracted from the soil and carbon dioxide is extracted from the air with the use of sunlight energy. Animals manufacture proteins from the plants they eat (herbivorous animals) or from the flesh of animals that ate plants (carnivorous animals). Either way, all kinds of proteins in our food--whether they are vegetable or animal proteins--originate from plants. Plants build their structural fibers utilizing nitrogen not only from the soil, but also from the air, which contains 78 percent nitrogen.

If protein synthesis takes place in plants, is it possible in animals and humans? Russian scientist-physiologist I.M. Setchenov, who studied the problem of transformation of nitrogen in air into proteins, stressed that the nitrogen content in human arterial blood that is enriched with air gases is larger than in the venous blood that passes through the body's tissues. This means that nitrogen gas from air can be utilized for building the structure of an organism not only in plants, but also in the human body.

Another Russian scientist, M.I. Volsky, discovered two ways to transform nitrogen gas into proteins in the human body: (1) by bacteria contained in the upper respiratory system and in the large intestine of a human body; and (2) by blood cells in the body's circulatory system. He estimated that in 100-volume units of arterial blood, there is 1.60 percent nitrogen; however, in venous blood it is 1.34 percent. The daily amount of nitrogen inhaled by the human body is 14.5 liters, or 18 grams, which is enough to produce 112 grams of protein in the body.

The possibility for the human body to utilize atmospheric nitrogen was suggested in the United States by Dr. Norman Walker. In his book *Raw Vegetable Juices,* Dr. Walker says that when the air reaches tiny sacs called *alveoli*, two kinds of enzymes found in the lungs come into play. The first is an oxide enzyme, which secretes oxygen; the other is a nitrous enzyme, which helps to "fix the nitrogen" (explained in the next subchapter) from the air. The enzymes help to collect the oxygen, which is transported throughout the entire body. They also help to transport nitrogen, which is further used in the body for protein production.

Is nitrogen fixation also possible in animals? The theory of the Russian academician Guly holds that nitrogen from air can be absorbed and utilized by animals. American scientists E. Franzblau and K. Poppa also found in their research that nitrogen compounds can be produced from lightning that strikes a hundred times per second in the earth's atmosphere. During electric discharges in the air, as in lightning, some gaseous nitrogen is converted into active nitrogen, which is a mixture of molecules and atoms of nitrogen with an increased energy level. Active nitrogen, in contrast to ordinary atmospheric nitrogen, is highly reactive and easily forms compounds with oxygen, hydrogen, phosphorus, sulfur vapors, and some metals. These nitrogenous compounds can be absorbed by living organisms directly from the air.

Amino acids were synthesized in many experiments by passing an electrical discharge (S. Miller, 1953, United States) and by ultraviolet radiation (A.G. Pasynski and T.E. Pavlovskaya, 1956, Russia), and in other experiments that used heat energy and ionizing radiation. Thermonuclear processes that occur within the sun and stars are the primary source of these forms of energy.

Nitrogen Fixation

Nitrogen is a gaseous chemical element with a density of 1.25 grams per liter. Although the atmospheric air is 78 percent nitrogen, free gaseous nitrogen cannot be utilized by humans, animals, or high plants. Modern medicine implies that nitrogen, which makes up about 16 percent of protein, comes into the human body from protein-rich foods through digestion. Now the question is, how does it enter protein? To be absorbed by living systems, nitrogen must be "fixed"; that is, combined with oxygen or hydrogen to form compounds such as nitrates or ammonia.

Nitrogen fixation is the biological process of the conversion of inorganic atmospheric nitrogen (N_2) into organic nitrogenous compounds. It is achieved with nitrogen-fixing bacteria, including yeast, fungi, Rhizobia, blue-green algae, and actinomycetes that populate the soil and water basins including seas, oceans, rivers, and lakes. Research on nitrogen fixation started more than a hundred years ago, in 1894, when S.N. Vinogradsky, a Russian scientist, suggested that ammonia could be formed by nitrogen fixation.

The condition when nitrogen intake and nitrogen output are equal is called *nitrogen balance*. If an amount of protein taken into the body is less than a degraded amount, a negative nitrogen balance takes place. This happens when some body protein is burned as a fuel to produce energy, but the protein supply is inadequate. Elderly people gradually lose their lean body mass if they don't consume enough protein. In growing organisms or in athletes such as bodybuilders, a positive nitrogen balance exists when their protein intake exceeds protein degradation. But how is the nitrogen balance maintained in non-eating people?

Non-Eating People

Going without food within a certain period of time, or *fasting,* was widely used for centuries throughout the world for religious purposes. Only recently, in the twentieth century, has fasting been used for therapeutic purposes as well. How long can abstinence from food last? Dr. Herbert Shelton of Florida (United States) reports that one patient fasted under his supervision for three months. After abstaining from food for ninety days in 1904, Tanaka Morihei of Japan developed spiritual powers at the age of twenty.

A person can last much less time if going without both food and water. Under no-food, no-water conditions, people lose much of their weight, or even die. The case of Andreas Mihavecz of Bregenz, Austria, who was left by mistake without food and water for seventeen days, was included in *The 1997 Guinness Book of World Records* as the world's longest deprivation of food and water. He was close to death when he was discovered. In a voluntary dry fast of ten days, Russian Leonid Aleksandrovich lost 20 kilograms of his weight. Another year, he fasted without water for eighteen days and claims that it is longer than the *Guinness Book* of records. These are cases with a happy ending; however, there is a well-investigated but unfortunate case of a Welsh girl named Sarah Jones, who died from fasting without water and food for eight days.

Some people, however, can live without food for years, even decades. Doctors nowadays all say that it is impossible without a miracle. There are well-authenticated cases in history, as Catholic writers insist, of these unique people, some of whom are currently still alive. In the past, there were

Christian saints who had lived for several years without food or drink but had received Holy Communion during their fast. Most of them were also stigmatic people. Dr. Imbert-Goueyre, in his book *La Stigmatization,* mentions a few of the most remarkable cases:

- In the fifteenth century, Nicholas von Flu (Bruder Klause, a hermit who saved the Swiss Confederation with his impassioned plea for union) lived for twenty years on the Blessed Sacrament alone, which he received once a month.
- St. Lidwina of Schiedam lived without food for twenty years.
- In the sixteenth century, Venerable Dominica dal Paradiso lived for twenty years without food.
- Blessed Elizabeth von Reute lived for fifteen years without food.
- Catherine Emmerich lived for twelve years without food.
- In the nineteenth century, Louise Lateau lived for fourteen years without food.
- St. Catherine of Siena lived for eight years without food.

Regarding Louise Lateau, an Indian criya Yogi, Paramahansa Yogananda, in his book *Autobiography of a Yogi,* says that she abstained from food for twenty years. He mentions two other cases: Dominica Lazarri and Blessed Angela of Foligno, who also lived without food. In the twentieth century, a few people were reported to survive in a non-eating state for many years. The most famous among them is Teresa Neumann, who lived solely on the Holy Communion for thirty-one years and whose case was thoroughly investigated.

Osanami Toshie. According to a report of the Japanese Psychics scientific meeting held in 1930, Osanami Toshie (October 26, 1863 - October 29, 1907) abstained from food and sometimes water for fourteen years. "Japan Gave Birth to an Outstanding Medium" was the title of the report compiled about her. While she was still eating, she was very lean and ate about two eggs a day, said her landowner Chiba. In her non-eating state, there was an occasion when she ate a piece of a grape, but she immediately vomited blood. According to Takano, very rarely did she eat a very small piece of apple or pear, but each time she did not like the food. Her physiological functions, such as elimination of feces and urine, completely vanished, and in her entire life she never had her monthly menstruation. She was completely devoted to God and had an ability to communicate with the souls of dead people. When she died at the age of forty-four, she looked very young, like a twenty-year-old girl.

Giri Bala. The most incredible case of going without food and water for fifty-six years is that of Giri Bala, and the only source of information about her is the book, *Autobiography of a Yogi*, by Paramahansa Yogananda. Yogananda is a famous criya yoga master who established a community in California (United States). He went to India to visit Giri Bala and talked to her about her unique ability to live without food and water. He writes the following about Giri Bala: "Giri Bala of India has not eaten food or taken liquids from the age of twelve years for over fifty-six years. Her nourishment was derived from the finer energies of the air and sunlight, and from the cosmic power that recharged her body through the medulla oblongata. Giri Bala used to sleep very little, as sleep and waking were the same for her. She was meditating at night, attending to her domestic duties in the daytime. She has never been sick or experienced any disease. She had no bodily excretions. She could control her heartbeat and breathing. In visions she often saw her guru and other great souls," described Yogananda of this unique woman. If all that was really possible, then Giri Bala was certainly a person supported by a divine life force.

It is also known that she was forced by her parents to marry at the age of twelve and she was given to the care of her husband's family. Her abstaining from food started because of her mother-in-law, who scolded and humiliated her because she was a gluttonous and well-fed girl. Giri Bala prayed to God to teach her how to eat less and God heard her prayers.

In an attempt to explain the cases of abstaining from food and water for decades, Paramahansa Yogananda said in his book, "Man's body battery is not sustained by gross food (bread) alone, but by the vibratory cosmic energy (Word, or Aum). The invisible power flows into the human body through the gate of medulla oblongata. This sixth bodily center is located at the back of the neck at the top of the five spinal chakras (Sanskrit for "wheels," or centers of radiating life force)." Only rare people like Giri Bala can utilize this power.

Teresa Neumann. Teresa Neumann (April 8, 1898 - September 18, 1962) of Konnersreuth in Bavaria, Germany, abstained from food for thirty-one years. She not only survived, but also maintained an active, even vigorous existence without earthly food, nourished only by the Blessed Sacrament. Even more remarkable is that the Blessed Sacrament usually gave her strength and vigor in a quite apparent manner. When asked how could she live without food, she replied, "I do not live on nothing, but on the Savior. He said, 'My flesh is meat indeed.' Why shouldn't this be the case when He wants it to be?" Father Fahsel and other people witnessed the immediate effect after the Sacred Host was given to her: "First, a distinct strengthening of the body is immediately noticeable. She was often found in a pitiable state of weakness before receiving, especially if one of her mystical vicarious states of suffering preceded the reception of Holy Communion. At these times her face is sunken, dark rings appear under her eyes, she can hardly sit on the chair behind the altar. All these signs of weakness disappear as soon as she has received Holy Communion."

At the age of eighteen, she had severe back pains after a few falls and became blind. She was cured of these illnesses by a miracle, but her life of suffering included a stigmatism that continued until her death. She was chosen by God to fulfill her vocation through suffering.

Through prayer, Teresa had the curing power to work out on her own body the ailments of others. The saint's abstinence from food dates from 1923, when she prayed that the throat disease of a young man of her parish-- then preparing to enter holy orders--be transferred to her own throat. She used to sleep only 1 or 2 hours at night. In spite of the many wounds on her body, she was active and full of energy. She loved birds, looked after an aquarium of fish, and worked often in her garden. Catholic devotees wrote her for prayers and healing blessings. Many seekers were cured of serious diseases through her.

Martha Loban. Martha Loban (? - February 1981) of France abstained from food for fifty-three years, from 1928 until her death in 1981.

Xu Fang. She is called the Chinese mystery and she now lives in Shanghai. She is 170 centimeters tall and weighs 50 kilograms--a thirty-one-year-old beauty with all the features of a super-model. She is quite wealthy and she runs her own garment shop. According to a Japanese Fuji TV program that was shown on December 20, 1997, her three-room apartment with expensive furniture looks luxurious, but it has no kitchen and no refrigerator; they are of no need because Xu Fang has not eaten for the last twelve years. She drinks water and sometimes mineral water, but eats no food at all--for twelve years!

She was born on June 25, 1969, in the city of Uragai in Northern China, and she belongs to the Dauer nationality. Her father and mother are university professors and she has younger twin sisters and a younger brother. According to her sister Xu Qua, she was a good eater up to the age of eighteen--among the four children, she used to eat the most. And the wonder about her is that her transfer to a non-eating state happened overnight.

In the article about her published in the December 1996 issue of the Japanese journal *Borderland*, she explains how it happened to her: "It was just before the university entrance exams in February 1988, I was at the age of eighteen years old then. I attended a Qigong seminar; it was the fourth session. In the middle of training, when Qigong teacher was explaining the exercises, a woman appeared in front of me. Until now I do not clearly understand, was that a vision or daydream, but I had a feeling as if she descended from heaven. She had a bottle in her right hand and a branch of willow in her left hand. (This description depicts the Goddess of Mercy, one of the cosmic power and order deities.) Then she held up the bottle over my chest and stroked with the branch on my head. In an instant, I felt as if I was showered with water, and a feeling of happiness aroused in me. Strange, but my appetite gushed out and I was craving for something tasteful to eat.

"However, when I was back home and put into my mouth a piece of my favorite food that my father cooked for me, I couldn't swallow it and spit it out. My appetite was completely gone. After some time, I was feeling that my body and mind became light. Even an ability to learn seemed to increase. But when other people were asking me to teach them 'my way,' I knew that my 'Pi Gu' [non-eating] state has started not by my will, but this was a will of God," she explained.

After Xu Fang entered the non-eating state at the age of eighteen, she continued to grow and her height increased from 167 to 170 centimeters. At the same time, her many physiological functions such as bowel movements and monthly menstruation ceased. She urinates a little but she has had no feces ever since. When it rains, she urinates more often, although she does not drink water on rainy days. However, there were many doubts about whether Xu Fang really does not eat or if she eats something. The journalist who interviewed her for the *Borderland* article found an apple in her apartment. Xu Fang said with a laugh that she likes apples, but just to smell them. And she feels full after she smells an apple. The Japanese TV team searched for traces of food in her apartment, but found nothing. A female Japanese announcer stayed with her for 72 hours to watch her day and night, but Xu Fang did not eat. In the morning, she brushed her teeth; the announcer became suspicious and asked her about it. Xu Fang replied that after she drank a cola, she brushes her teeth, but if she drinks just water, she does not brush them. The physician in the hospital who conducted the ultrasound test on her and proved that there is no digestive juice in her stomach said, "But I do not believe that she can live without food for nine years."

A lot of research was conducted on Xu Fang in the Chinese Military

Research Center. Ryu Shin-tyu, a researcher who has known her from the times she was a child, says that the blood flow in her capillaries is a few times faster than that of ordinary people, and her breathing rate is much slower than in others. There is no saliva in her mouth and no acid in her stomach. The content of metabolic substances such as acetone and ketone bodies in her blood is increased, which usually is caused by prolonged starvation or in the case of diabetes. In any case, it manifests in the abnormal condition, but Xu Fang's body is very healthy and in a sound condition.

Trying to find out the mechanisms of her survival without food, researcher Ryu Shin-tyu suggested that due to the Qigong influence, some cells in Xu Fang's body became capable of producing organic substances from inorganic matter and energy from the sun's radiation. Furthermore, protein can be produced from those organic substances. If the amount in those cells is sufficient, the non-eating state can be continued for a long time.

Another hypothesis comes from Ka Un Ro, a Chinese best-selling author who wrote about Xu Fang in a few of his books. He suggests that in her digestive system there is a bacterium that is able to fix the nitrogen from the air. It is known that the azotic bacteria found in soil and vegetables such as legumes is capable of fixing nitrogen from the air, then converting it into ammonia, further producing amino acids, and finally making proteins. Ka Un Ro says that this can occur in some people as well. There are Papua people who mostly live on sweet potatoes and do not eat any proteins, yet they are healthy and fit. Over a long period, their intestinal bacteria acquired the ability to fix nitrogen from the air. Perhaps humans also had this ability but it was lost in us in the course of time, hypothesizes Ka Un Ro. However, Mitsuoka Tomosabi, a Japanese professor, says that the bacteria in the Papua people are different from the azotic bacteria in the soil. He denies the possibility of humans to convert ammonia into amino acids. Anyway, somehow Xu Fang produces all the substances necessary for her survival from the air, water, and light.

Actually, it is difficult to believe that a human being is able to go without water and food for more than fifty years. For modern people living in industrial societies, who need to eat three times a day and intake food with a certain number of calories, it sounds like a fairy tale.

If we accept that such a thing is possible, then this is definitely a phenomenon. Is there any explanation to this phenomenon? Yogananda explains it in this way: "The non-eating state attained by Giri Bala is a yogic power mentioned in Patanjali's Yoga Sutras III: 31. She employs a certain breathing exercise that affects the *Vishuddha chakra*, the fifth center of subtle energies located in the spine. The *Vishuddha chakra,* opposite the throat, controls the fifth element, *akash* or ether, pervasive in the inter-atomic spaces of the physical cells. Concentration on this chakra ("wheel") enables the devotee to live by etheric energy." Thus, it is cosmic energy that these special and rare people dwell upon.

Can anyone do that? It seems not. Non-eating is not a person's choice; rather, the person is chosen. "The explanation is hidden in the complexities of personal karma. Many lives of dedication to God lie behind a Teresa Neumann and Giri Bala, but their channels for outward expression have been different," says Yogananda. Well, we all have heard about karma and reincarnation, but perhaps not all of us will be satisfied with this explanation. Moreover, not everyone believes in reincarnation--even the prominent Indian philosopher Krishnamurti denied it at all.

The Japanese author Nakaya Shinichi, in his book *Secrets of Food and Sages That Can Save Mankind*, published in 1997, attempts to find a scientific explanation for the non-eating state of Giri Bala and Teresa Neumann. He relies on the theory of Dr. George Krail from Cleveland, Ohio, who declared it at the medical conference of the Memphis Scientific Society back in 1933: "Electrons of the food taken inside the body discharge their energy at the protoplasm of cells and it becomes again the chemical energy supplied to the whole body like an electric current."

In other words, the human body itself and the food that we need for fuel are all made of tiny suns (i.e., electrons). Our food and our bodies provide storage for sun energy, for sunlight. The matter that captures sunlight is *chlorophyll*, which gives the green color to grass and trees. On how important chlorophyll as a keeper of sun energy is for all of us, William Lorenz wrote in the *New York Times*: "At present in nature, chlorophyll is the only known matter that is able to capture the sun energy. This matter captures energy contained in sunlight and stores it in plants. This energy is absolutely necessary, indispensable for all living creatures." We can see from these words what an important job chlorophyll does for us. Even our earth, which astronauts call the "green planet," received this romantic name because of chlorophyll.

We are talking about the nutritional value of food, how many calories it contains, and so on. But where do these calories come from? They also come from the sun. Dr. Michael Colgan wrote the following on this subject in his article *You Need Oxidation* in the August 1997 issue of *Man's Fitness*:

"Starches and sugars, the structural fibers in wood, and the structural proteins in flesh, all store about 4 calories of energy per gram. All fats and oils, including fuel oil, store about 9 calories per gram. But where does this energy come from? *It comes from the sun.*"

How is the sun energy fixed and stored in plants? Dr. Colgan explains it this way: "Plants capture the energy of sunlight by combining particles of light with the gas carbon dioxide, extracted from the air, and the gas nitrogen, extracted from the soil, in order to build their structure. Plants are simply containers for the life force of sunlight." As discussed previously, it is possible to fix nitrogen directly from the air, which is more than three-quarters nitrogen.

My explanation of the non-eating phenomenon involves both traditional Oriental medicine and modern science. Ayurveda says that our bodies, our food, and everything around us are built from five basic elements: earth, water, air, fire, and ether. As we eat, we bring inside our body the solid (physical) form of the food, as well as prana and aura, which are the subtle influences attached to the food. Solid food is constituted mostly from the earth, water, and fire elements; prana is from the air and aura is represented by ether. *Prana* means life force and fresh natural food is full of it. Food production, processing, and packaging reduce prana in food, or even may destroy it completely if, for example, food is cooked in a microwave. The aura or subtle influences are the emotions and attitudes of people who grow and cook food. It is said that a sensitive yogi will fall sick if he eats food cooked without love. Therefore, food prepared with love is good for our health. Our digestion can be badly affected on a subtle level by food cooked in anger.

Non-eating people are those who do not take solid food--by no means do they not take in other kinds of food. Remember the discussion about light and air? Because the non-eating people could stay alive and healthy for decades, we are left with the impression that they took their food from the air. Yes, the air that ordinary people breathe provides *oxygen* to burn the solid foods we eat. However, the biochemical reactions of non-eating people are different from ours. Because they do not have ready-made food to be burned for energy, they have to produce it first. How can they produce food? The answer is through protein synthesis, utilizing nitrogen gas and oxygen from the air and carbon dioxide and hydrogen from their own tissues. Nitrogen gas to be used in protein synthesis–specifically, amino-acid synthesis--is fixed by bacteria in our lungs and digestive tract. The carbon dioxide that we breathe out as a waste is utilized by non-eating people as a building material.

You may remember the Russian physiologist Setchenov, who discovered that arterial blood has more nitrogen than venous blood. In his investigation, he tested ordinary people who eat three meals a day. They have a sufficient supply of nitrogen from the proteins in food they eat, and do not need much from the air. However, non-eating people do not have nitrogen taken with food and they must get it all from the air. That is why the percentage of nitrogen in their venous blood must be less than 1.34 percent, as measured by Setchenov. I wonder if researchers will have the opportunity to take these measurements on non-eating people in the future.

What promotes nitrogen to be fixed and then utilized in the amino-acid synthesis that occurs in non-eating people? Do you remember the discussion of lightning, the discovery of American scientists? Lightning in the atmosphere fixes nitrogen gas from the air to be used by living creatures, and the enlightenment state of non-eating people is like continuous numerous tiny lightning flashes in them. Therefore, nitrogen gas from the air is fixed in them in two ways: with internal bacteria and by means of internal lightning. I believe that these processes occur in non-eating people in the most effective way of all nature.

Do non-eating people burn proteins produced by protein synthesis as a fuel to maintain their body temperature and heat? I think they do not. If you remember, Osanami Toshie and Giri Bala had no bodily excretions. From that we can conclude that there were no solid wastes in their bodies at all. The dead cells of the body tissues that usually compose a part of the wastes are fully utilized in their case. As dead cells decompose, they supply the material to the amino-acid pool, which becomes a source for the new amino-acid synthesis. This synthesis and further protein production cover all the body's need for protein, including the inevitable protein loss from dead skin cells, dandruff, growing and falling hair, growing nails, perspiration, tears, and other secretions.

Furthermore, it means that no fuel would be burned in their bodies and they would receive the heat necessary for biochemical functions directly from outer space. Other than heat, they receive life force from the etheric energy of cosmic nature. I believe that to repair their tissues, the non-eating saints manufacture amino acids from nitrogen gas in the air, and that to maintain body temperature, they get heat and etheric energy from space. It sounds far-fetched, does it not? But wait a moment, please.

First let us discuss the amino acids and then the heat issues. You know that the eight essential amino acids cannot be manufactured in our bodies and, in order to survive, we have to get them from food. The best source is animal protein. However, there are many people--complete vegetarians--who never tasted meat in their entire life and lived extraordinarily long lives. The Russian scientist Dr. Souren Arakelyan, seventy-three, says that his uncle Marut Arakelyan, who lived to the age of 102, ate very little and in his entire life never knew the taste of meat. Among centenarians, about 10 percent are vegetarians. We know that essential amino acids also can be derived from plant sources. I think the existing knowledge about essential amino acids, which is drawn for ordinary people dependent on food, cannot be applied to non-eating people.

Our Body Cells Are Tiny Biothermonuclear Reactors

The amino acids issue puts forward a question: Are all the chemical elements necessary to produce amino acids in the air? Of course not--we have in the air nitrogen, oxygen, hydrogen, carbon dioxide, and inert gases such as argon, xenon, and others. However, the point is that we can produce missing elements in our cells because *human body cells are biothermonuclear reactors where the processes of transmutation of chemical elements are underway.* We think of thermonuclear process as a reaction at the highest temperatures, which will burn all living matter. However, it has been proven that even at low temperatures, elements change their structure. The discovery of *biological transmutation* by Professor Louis Kervran proves the possibility, for instance, for calcium to change into magnesium and vice versa, for potassium to change into sodium, and so on, thereby supporting the analogy to a thermonuclear reactor with biological transmutation.

Biological transmutation means that if there is a lack of certain substances, they can be produced from others that are in excess. When analyzing the diets of centenarians, a full set of fifty essential macro- and micronutrients, vitamins, minerals, enzymes, and so on is never found in their food. Most centenarians never took any supplements at all. Do they take a daily dose of 200 micrograms of selenium, which has been found to be absolutely necessary for retarding the aging process? No, most of them have never heard about selenium. So how have they survived without selenium? The only possibility is that their biothermonuclear reactor produced it from other substances.

The workability of the cell reactor is dependent on a person's spiritual state or level of consciousness. If a person lives just to satisfy his/her primary biological needs such as shelter, food, water, and sleep (i.e., on a basic survival level) and employs merely his/her physical body, we would say that their first (Muladhara) chakra is dominant. In this case, their reactor works only in a low-capacity regimen, if at all. These people need a full range of nutrients, vitamins, and minerals to be taken with food and are fully dependent on a supply of nutrients from outside. However, it is difficult to imagine an individual operating merely on a low chakra, even in the primitive societies. Humans care about their loved ones, fulfill their duties in the family and community, do some crafts, believe in God, and so on, thereby employing the upper chakras as well.

The higher the level of consciousness, the bigger is the capacity with which a biothermonuclear reactor operates. For example, a person is the president of a company and much involved in intellectual and spiritual activities in his/her personal life (i.e., the third through seventh chakras), such as Mr. Toshio Doko, who became president of the Toshiba Corporation of Japan at the age of sixty-nine. His working day was from 7 a.m. to 11 p.m., and he was so busy with his numerous responsibilities that he sometimes skipped lunch or dinner. For the last forty-five years of his life, he slept only 4 hours at night. However, upon awakening, he would read the Buddhist scripts for 1 hour. He seemed to take his energy not from food and rest, but from his overwork and prayers. Still, he was healthy and lived to the age of ninety-one; the biothermonuclear reactors of his cells were largely involved. Or think of Bessie Hubbard, 100 (in 1987) from Stanwood, Washington, who was characterized as "...a woman who seems to run on high-octane spiritual power, someone who hates TV, who has never had any hobbies, and who loves to work." This characteristic supports the idea that *spiritual* and *intellectual powers* are the energy source for biothermonuclear reactors.

Non-eating people are usually deeply involved religiously. They belong to the highest--seventh level--of consciousness, the Sahasrara chakra, and their thermonuclear reactor works with the full capacity. They derive their food from the air and ether, and their reactor provides their cells and tissues with all the necessary substances by converting one element into another. They survive independently of food, and they are in absolute control of food intake; as for solid food, they take in nothing. They are free from earthly matters and they fully devote themselves to God. Although their life duration is not long, their lives are bright and glorious.

Regarding scientific knowledge, it is worth noting that nowadays, due to intense research work all around the world, all medical knowledge that ever existed up to the present time is doubled every four years. In four years or less, we will know two times as much about the human body and health that we do now. And what will we know in twenty or thirty years? There will be thousands of new discoveries and an ocean of new information. Many paradoxes and unexplained phenomena of modern science will become common knowledge.

The next question is: how do these non-eating saints keep warm? Giri Bala lived in Calcutta, India, in a tropical and humid climate. Although the air temperature was usually lower than her body temperature, the difference was just a few degrees. Osanami Toshie lived in Japan, where four-season weather changes from hot in summer to chilly in winter. Still, there are no such susceptible frosts that happen in Germany, where Teresa Neumann lived. There is another unique person, Porphiry Ivanov from Russia, who trained himself to bear the cold to a degree that he could sleep naked in the snow, and wear just shorts in the winter when the frosts were severe. His tolerance to cold can help us understand how our non-eating heroes got their heat.

Porphiry Ivanov. Porphiry Ivanov (1901 - 1986) was famous as a living saint because of his outstanding healing powers and supernatural wisdom before he died in 1986 at the age of eighty-five. His appearance was unique: he looked like Poseidon, the mythical God of the Sea, with long white hair, a tanned, massive body, and rounded shoulders. He always went barefoot and throughout the year wore nothing but long shorts. He had been trained as an engineer and was leading the life of an ordinary person when at the age of thirty-five, he started to train himself to tolerate the cold. His idea was that if our face can tolerate a severe frost, why cannot we train other parts of the body, gradually revealing them in winter? He succeeded to the degree that in a few years, he did not wear any clothes at all.

During World War II, the German invaders captured him when they saw him nearly naked walking along the snow-covered road. They suspected him to be fleeing from a concentration camp. When they realized that he never wore any clothes, they still could not believe it and wanted to test him. They put him on a military motorbike and, while riding at a high speed, they poured cold water on him, thereby exposing him to both frost and wind. After a few runs, they got frozen themselves, but Ivanov appeared unaffected, with just steam rising from his body. Ivanov passed their test and they released him.

This unique tolerance of Porphiry Ivanov to cold attracted the attention of many journalists, medical doctors, and scientists. Agajanyan, M.D. and Katkov, in their book *Reserves of the Human Organism,* compared him with Tibetan monks, who appeared in a contest of drying sheets soaked in icy water and then squeezed on their naked backs. The winner was the one who dried the most sheets. When asked how they do it, they explained that they imagine a cord kept burning along their spine. In addition to his legendary tolerance to cold, Porphiry Ivanov acquired other supernatural abilities, such as sitting underwater for dozens of minutes, and fully abstaining from food and water for more than a week. He was a renowned guru of dry fasting for 42 hours; I partly became his follower and fasted "after Ivanov" several times. He cured many people, including his wife, from tuberculosis with the cold and fasting. Many followers treated him like a god and called him "teacher."

How is Porphiry Ivanov related to self-heating, non-eating people? His ability to sleep naked in the snow drew two people, a scientist-physicist and a journalist, to investigate the case. They came from Moscow and stayed in his house in the Rostov region for a week during winter. On their return, they published an article about Ivanov in which they reported their dialogues with him. Asked whether he feels the cold or not, Ivanov answered, "Yes, pretty much." He also told them that he feels as if he *gets warmth from the cold.* They discussed in the article that it is impossible according to the Second Law of Thermodynamics, which holds that in closed systems, heat only can be transferred from warm to less warm objects, not backwards. They mentioned, however, the forgotten hypothesis of Konstantin Tsiolkowsky, the father of Russian aeronautics, which states that in some systems, the transfer of heat from cold to warm objects is possible.

I was much impressed and wanted to test whether I could have this feeling. In my apartment in Moscow, there was quite a long bathtub, and I started to take cold baths on winter mornings when the tap water is the coldest. At first, I would submerge myself for 10 seconds, then gradually increase the time in the water: the next day I stayed in the bathtub for 15 seconds, then 20 seconds, and so forth. After two weeks, my tolerance to the cold water increased and I added 10 seconds to the previous session. When I had built up to 2 minutes, I found myself able to relax even though I was submerged in very cold water. It seemed like a miracle when I realized that I felt warmer and warmer with every passing second. After getting out of the bathtub, instead of a chilly sensation, I felt filled with energy. I can assure you that it worked for me; if you do not believe me, check it out for yourself!

Now we can understand how non-eating people get their heat: they take it from the space around them regardless of the source of energy--the sun, moon, stars, or wind--or how big the difference is between the air temperature and their body temperature. Vibration foods were discussed previously, and this is an example of universal energy fields that become a source of energy for non-eating people.

Overeating People

At the other extreme of food abstainers are food over-consumers. Overeating and obesity are features of rich Western nations. About one third of the adult white population in the United States and Canada is defined as medically obese, with many extra pounds over standard weight. I personally have observed in Boston, the state of Maine, and other places many extremely fat people. Among the rich nations, only Japan and the Scandinavian countries have small percentages of obese people in their population. However, all these fat people are merely amateurs. They spend a lot of money on extra food and have no benefits from their overweight, only health problems. There are professionals who eat a lot to gain weight and to benefit from it: the sumo wrestlers, traditionally from Japan but recently in other countries as well. Although they number only a few hundred, they are a good example for this discussion of food-consumption extremes.

Body weight is a weapon in sumo wrestling and the *sumotori* (i.e., wrestler), in addition to daily exercises and wrestling itself, has one bigger job: to eat to gain or maintain weight. Their daily meal is chanko nabe, a potluck sort of stew containing fish, fowl, red meat, tofu, and various vegetables. Chanko nabe is a nutritionally balanced and high-calorie main dish, consumed in huge amounts. A sumotori also eats side dishes such as rice, noodles, fried chicken, grilled fish, Chinese dumplings, Western-style salads, omelets, and so on. Just looking at the size of sumo wrestlers, one can imagine how much they eat. However, sumotoris who have already reached their working weight do not eat as much as the apprentices--*wakamono*--who are at the stage of gaining weight. They eat really legendary amounts of food, such as eight giant bowls of rice, 150 pieces of sushi, and twenty-five portions of barbecued beef at one sitting, according to Lora Sharnoff in her book, *Grand Sumo: The Living Sport and Tradition*. I was very impressed with that amount of food and attempted to count the number of calories. According to Yoshihiko Suzuki and Kazuko Shiozawa, authors of the book *Food Guide Based on 80 kcal* (in Japanese), each giant bowl of rice (300 grams) provides 444 kcal; each piece of sushi provides 50 kcal on average (i.e., 20-gram rice ball equals 30 kcal plus various kinds of fish ranging from 7 kcal for cuttlefish, 16 to 22 kcal for tuna, salmon, and sea eel, to 60 kcal for egg covers); and each piece of barbecued beef provides 100 kcal. Accordingly, the total calorie amount of an average meal is calculated by the following equation:

$$444 \times 8 + 50 \times 150 + 100 \times 25 = 13{,}552 \text{ kcal}$$

Because sumo wrestlers eat twice a day, their daily calorie intake is even more then that. Unusual even among Japanese sumo wrestlers, with their weights of up to 350 to 420 pounds (160 to 190 kilograms), is the case of Konishiki, an American from Hawaii, who was reported to eat 30,000 calories a day to maintain his weight of 615 pounds (280 kilograms).

When I first watched a sumo tournament on TV in Japan in 1991, I thought, "What ugly sportsmen are these obese people, they look so unhealthy, especially Konishiki with his folds of fat bulging and dangling everywhere on his huge body." Later, I was gradually intrigued--even becoming a fan of sumo wrestling--and I found that some of them, like Kirishima, Terao, and Kyokudozan, had very muscular and well-shaped bodies. One feature of sumo wrestlers is that although they look so fat, they have big lean muscle mass due to their strenuous exercises; the proportion of fat to lean muscles is about the same as in ordinary people.

The lifestyle of a sumotori has some healthy features including exercising on an empty stomach and going without food until noon, a nutritionally well-balanced diet, and drinking freshly squeezed juices of green vegetables as a natural vitamin supplement. However, the habits of overeating, napping after a huge lunch, and exercising at an excessively strenuous level are destructive to their overall health. The life span of a former sumotori is only in the early sixties; that is, about sixteen to seventeen years shorter than for average Japanese men. Sumo doctors are concerned that the recent tendency toward increased heaviness will lead to further health deterioration of the sumotori.

Food Consumption Scale

If we consider the range of food consumption (i.e., caloric scale) in humans, we find Giri Bala and Teresa Neumann at the lower extreme and wakamono sumo wrestlers at the higher extreme. In between these two extremes, there are the native people of the "longevity valleys," centenarians, and ordinary people of different nations with varying daily caloric consumption.

Another type of range is the food intake in different diets relative to animal protein density (i.e., the animal-protein scale). At one end of this range are the non-dairy fruitarians and vegans, who do not eat any animal products; followed by lacto-vegetarians, whose diets include dairy products; and ovo-lacto vegetarians, who include eggs and dairy products in their diets. Next to vegetarians are those who eat balanced food, fish- and meat-eaters, who range from those who eat animal proteins rarely--once a week--to those who eat meat at every meal. The Eskimos of North America and the Yakuts of Russian Siberia, who live above the Polar Circle, eat mostly meat and fish; the latter people are at the other end of the protein range.

Sumo wrestlers who consume a variety of foods in huge amounts are at the higher extreme on the caloric scale and somewhere in the middle of the animal-protein scale. Some other ranges, such as diets that focus on the consumption of fats, carbohydrates, salt, and other nutrients, give us yet another perspective. Depending on their nutrient content, various diets more or less do affect longevity, but first let's discuss how calorie intake affects longevity.

Lifetime Energy Consumption

Max Rubner found that for mammals of different body size, from small to large, the unit energy consumption within a life span does not vary much. For instance, guinea pigs (with a life span of six to seven years) burned about 260 kcal per 1 gram of body tissue during their lives; horses (with a life span of fifty years) burned about 280 kcal. However, humans expend a much larger amount, about 800 kcal per lifetime. Assuming for simplicity that body weight is constant throughout life, a person weighing 80 kilograms will expend in his/her life:

$$80,000 \times 800 = 64,000,000 \text{ kcal}$$

This means that the *life energy limit* of an individual is about 64 million kcal. A somewhat smaller figure of 50 million kcal for a human's lifetime is found in the Russian book, *The Healing Nutrition,* by Dr. Galina Shatalova. She says that this figure is derived by the promoters of balanced nutrition, who recommend a daily intake of 2,500 to 3,000 kcal for Russian people.

According to the evaluation of Jules Hirsch, M.D., at Rockefeller University Hospital, each person consumes in his/her lifetime an average of 3 tons of fat, 3 tons of protein, and 8 tons of carbohydrates. All that food that can be carried by a big truck is burned in our body using 10 million quarts of oxygen, resulting in energy equal to:

$$3,000,000 \times 9 + 3,000,000 \times 4 + 8,000,000 \times 4 = 71,000,000 \text{ kcal}$$

It is difficult to say what is the right figure and it can't be the same for all. It greatly depends on age, sex, level of activity, climate, a person's metabolic rate, and his/her ability to utilize energy from food. Under the same environmental conditions, some people utilize food more efficiently than others. They eat just a little and it is enough for them to maintain or even gain weight, while others eat a lot and do not gain weight at all. Stress and worry play a role in food utilization too. Some of my friends and I easily lose weight under stressful conditions, while other people eat "comfort food" to release stress, and gain weight. A person's state of mind and spirit greatly affect food metabolism; recall the cases of highly spiritual sages in India, who ate small quantities of plants that enabled them to stay alive.

Whatever the correct figure, the main idea is this: the amount of energy from food that we consume throughout our lives seems to be *limited*. The sooner one consumes this limited amount, the earlier he/she dies. According to the calculation of Dr. Shatalova, based on a 50-million-calorie limit, if one consumes 2,500 calories a day, he/she will live about fifty-eight years; however, if the intake is reduced to 1,000 calories throughout his/her life, he/she will live 137 years. Definitely, the way of attaining longevity is not that simplistic. A person's life duration depends on many factors, including heredity, blood type, and ability to resist diseases, rather than just what food he/she eats. Nonetheless, it is clear that the fewer calories we consume, the more chance we have to reach a ripe old age.

Calorie Intake Estimate

The purpose of this estimation is to find out how calorie intake correlates to the duration of life. There is a small amount of calorie-intake data regarding centenarians in literature; however, it is lacking for non-eating people, sumo wrestlers, and a few more centenarians, who I attempted to assess myself. Because of the absence of factual material, my assessment includes some assumptions.

Osanami Toshie. She lived to the age of forty-four, abstaining from food for her last fourteen years. As a child and teenager, she averaged about 300 kcal. As an adult, before she started her non-eating life, she reportedly ate about two eggs a day (156 kcal) and was very thin. While abstaining from food, she reportedly ate very rarely (let's assume once a week), perhaps an apple (73 kcal) or a pear (51 kcal, Asian type). With these assumptions, her average daily intake throughout her life results in 155 kcal.

Giri Bala. Giri Bala of India lived to sixty-eight years and completely abstained from food and water for fifty-six years. She *ate a lot* until she was twelve, then she suddenly stopped eating. Assuming that to that age she consumed the same number of calories as American girls, then her lifetime average is 350 kcal.

Teresa Neumann. This German woman lived to the age of sixty-four and she consumed no food except Holy Communion for thirty-one years (1928 - 1959). In her childhood, she was accustomed to continuous and heavy labor on her parent's farm, and she grew tall and strong. Perhaps she was eating well then, so we can assume again that the American diet for girls (i.e., from 1,290 kcal at the age of one year to 2,375 kcal at fourteen years old) is applicable for her.

At the age of fourteen, she started to work and she earned her bread by hard work on the land for four years. After an accident at the age of eighteen, she became ill and suffered for seven years. In those four years, she was consuming perhaps the average amount for young girls--2,380 kcal. Until the age of thirty, when her abstinence from food started, she was ill, fasted sometimes, and did not consume more than 600 kcal a day, which we also assume for her last three years. Her lifetime daily average is estimated to be 734 kcal.

Sumo Wrestlers. The average wrestler starts his career at the age of about twelve. Until this age, it is assumed that he is consuming the average American diet for boys (i.e., from 1,315 kcal at the age of one year to 2,770 kcal at twelve years old). Then he doubles his consumption for the next three years and, from fifteen to eighteen, when he gains weight, he eats the enormous amount of 13,550 kcal described previously. His sports career lasts on average until he is thirty-two; at that time, he maintains his working weight, consuming about 10,000 kcal a day. After retirement, he slows down with food, but still it is 5,000 kcal until he is forty. The last twenty-three years, his intake is probably 3,500 kcal. With these assumptions, the average daily intake of a sumo wrestler is 5,434 kcal.

Centenarians. Although diet and nutrition are major factors affecting longevity, there is little information on what and how much centenarians eat. A significant contribution in this field is a study conducted by Italian researchers on a group of seventy centenarians. In their article, *Dietary Patterns in Centenarians*, published in the *Geriatria e Gerontologia* journal, researchers Golosio, et al., from La Sapienza University of Rome, investigated the role of dietary factors in the oldest old. The ages of the seventy centenarians (seventeen males and fifty-three females) surveyed ranged from 100 to 108 years, with a mean age of 101.6. Dietary information regarding the present life of the elderly and their past was collected in a questionnaire using a *dietary history method.* Colored photographs were included to assess the actual nutrition of centenarians. Qualitative dietary patterns were assessed using a *food frequency* questionnaire. Researchers also included in the questionnaires information about the most important factors such as socioeconomic status, living arrangements, mobility impairment, chewing efficiency, taste and smell sensitivity, swallowing function, and so on, which may affect the quantity or quality of food.

This study showed that the average daily calorie intake was 1,608 kcal among males and 1,427 kcal among females. Proteins constituted 19.2 percent of their food, carbohydrates 59.6 percent, and total fats 21.2 percent. Average protein intake per day was 54 grams in males and 52 grams in females; total fats in both males and females were about 56 grams; and carbohydrates were 176 grams in males and 162 grams in females.

Centenarians attract much attention in Japan and many studies were conducted there. The data from a few studies appeared in the special centenarian issue of *Youth* magazine in March 1998. Based on the findings of a 1972-1973 study of centenarians, Hiroshi Shibata, the director of the Research Institute of Olds in the Tokyo region, reports that the average daily calorie intake of people aged 100 and more is 1,073 kcal for men and 939 kcal for women.

As for a diet of individual centenarians, we are fortunate to have a couple of sources: (1) "The George Burns Seven-Day Diet," which is described in detail in his book, *How to Live to Be 100 - Or More*; and (2) the diet of the Japanese identical twins, Kin Narita (died in January 2000 at the age of 107) and Gin Kanie, 108. George Burns (January 20, 1896 - March 9, 1996) published his book when he was eighty-six years old and went on to prove the promise given in the title--he died in 1996 when he was a hundred years and fifty-two days old.

Using *The Complete Book of Food Counts*, by Corinne T. Netzer, I attempted to count the calories George Burns ate in a week's time. He ate well-balanced food with green salads, rich in vitamins and minerals, but it was not a purely natural diet. He drank coffee quite often and often indulged in cookies, English muffins, ice cream, and crackers. If we assume that he was not joking (professionally) about going without food on Sundays, one fasting day a week--even with a martini--gave a good boost to his health.

Wine consumed in moderation is no longer considered harmful to health since the reports about the longevity world champion Jeanne Calment, 122, who took a glass of port wine with each meal. George Burns' daily intake was about 1,400 to 1,500 calories on weekdays, about 1,000 calories on Saturdays, and about 330 calories (just the martini) on Sundays; therefore, his weekly and daily intakes were 8,684 kcal and 1,240 kcal, respectively. Assuming that he had that kind of diet throughout his life, his total lifetime calorie intake was 45.4 million calories.

The diet and calorie estimate of Susie Pittman, 103, was published in the book *One Hundred Over 100*, by Jim Heynen. She ate the following three meals a day:

> • Breakfast: toast, 1 slice; 1 egg, scrambled; 3 ounces of orange juice; coffee
> • Lunch: 1 vegetable serving (4 tablespoons); 4 ounces of meat (three times a week) or vegetables only (four times a week); 1 cookie or small slice of cake
> • Dinner: 1 glass of milk, 1 small slice of cake

"A high estimate of her caloric intake would put her at about 800 calories four days a week, and 1,200 calories three days a week, for a total of about 6,800 calories a week," concluded Jim Heynen. Thus, her average daily intake is 971 kcal. This is the smallest amount among centenarians, but Susie Pittman is a small woman and she weighs just a little more than 100 pounds.

The diet of the Japanese longevity icons Kin Narita (died in January 2000 at the age of 107) and her twin sister Gin Kanie, 108, consisted of well-balanced traditional foods, including tofu, fish, seaweed, cooked vegetables, and rice. Their daily diet and calorie estimation is shown in Table 16-1.

Table 16-1. Daily Diet of Kin Narita and Gin Kanie

Meal	Kin Narita		Gin Kanie	
	Food	Kcal	Food	Kcal
Breakfast	Taro	65	Fried liver	4
	Miso soup with daikon and fried tofu	42	Miso soup with seaweed and leek	20
	Pickled plum	4	Pickled plum	4
	Fish, hard-boiled	95	Rice	120
	Rice porridge, hot	128	Green tea	0
Lunch	Eggplant, hard-boiled	60	Pickled cucumber, 2 slices	20
	Eel	203	Horse mackerel	137
	Spinach, steamed	20	Sea bream sashimi	50
	Tomato	26	Rice	120
	Plain hot water with medicine	0	Japanese tea	0
Dinner	Miso soup	40	Flatfish	110
	Potato, boiled	116	Sea bream sashimi	60
	Eggplant, hard-boiled	60	Hamburger	200
	Eel	203	Potato salad	128
	Tuna, raw (sashimi)	90	Rice	120
	Plain hot water	0	Japanese tea	0
	Total	1,152	Total	1,093

As shown in the table, the amount of food was quite large for their small body size. The daily calorie intake is about 1,152 kcal for Kin Narita and about 1,093 kcal for Gin Kanie. Kin Narita ate umeboshi (pickled plum), fresh raw tuna (maguro sashimi), and eel (twice a day). Other than the tuna, which she received free from a neighbor who owned a fish shop, her diet was quite expensive, especially eel fish; therefore, this was not her lifelong diet, perhaps just for the last five or ten years. People in Japan say that the twin sisters became wealthy after they appeared on TV on the occasion of their 100-year jubilee; before their fame, they could not afford such luxury food.

As we can see from the calorie intake range, some people--like sumo wrestlers--who belong to the first (i.e., Muladhara) chakra, live mostly on physical food, while Giri Bala and Teresa Neumann--with their high spiritual devotion (sixth and seventh chakras)--could stay alive on spiritual food. It seems that the higher level of consciousness (chakra) involved, the less solid food is necessary for an individual. It is as if highly spiritual people can utilize the cosmic energy—prana on a subtle level and nitrogen gas from the air on a physical level—more effectively to live on and produce all necessary nutrients for their body.

Calorie Intake and Longevity

Extensive research and experiments on animals for about sixty years have shown that a scientifically proven method of life extension is calorie restriction, which we have been discussing in this book. It is not proven on humans yet, because the maximum life span of humans is approximately 120 years and more time is needed. However, researchers like Dr. Roy Walford and Dr. Souren Arakelyan of Russia, who experiment on themselves, are now in their seventies; under favorable circumstances, we will know how their theory worked on humans in forty or fifty years. The next question is: What is the optimum calorie intake that promotes longevity? The answer is found in the relationship between daily calorie intake and life span (Figure 16-1).

Actually, this graph is a scale showing the full range of calorie intake and its relation to duration of life. Four groups of dots on this plot represent different categories of people, as follows:

• Dots with daily intake less than 750 kcal represent non-eating people.
• Dots with a life span of 100 years and more represent individual centenarians and groups of centenarians from Japan (total number of 495 in 1973) and Italy (seventeen men and fifty-three women). The data on calorie

intake of centenarians was either obtained from published sources or estimated by the author.

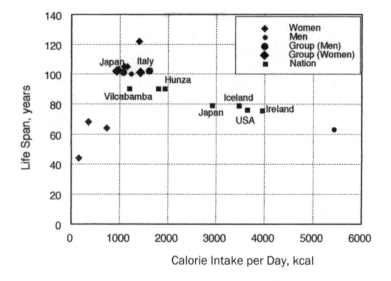

Figure 16-1. Relationship between Daily Calorie Intake
and the Life Span of Humans

• Square dots that represent nations are subdivided into two sets: one set of three dots represents the oldest old in the world's three "valleys of longevity"--Vilcabamba in Ecuador, Hunza in Pakistan, and Abkhasia in Georgia (located between the former two). The average calorie intake among the elderly in Vilcabamba is 1,200 kcal (from the survey of Dr. Guillermo Vela of Quito); in Abkhasia, it is 1,800 kcal (from the survey of Vladimir Kyucharyants); and in Hunza, it is 1,923 kcal (from the survey of Pakistani nutritionist Dr. Magsood Ali). The life span of long-living people in these three regions is reduced to ninety because of the possibility of age exaggeration (discussed previously). The other set of four dots represents the countries with either the world's longest life span (Japan in the world, Iceland in Europe) or highest calorie intake (Ireland). These data reflect average calorie intake per capita and average overall life expectancy in 1994-1995 in these countries. Although the United States consumed somewhat fewer calories than Ireland five years ago, recent data indicate that the United States--consuming an average 3,699 kcal per capita--became the leading country among the top ten world calorie consumers, followed by Portugal (3,667 kcal), Greece (3,649 kcal), Belgium and Luxembourg (3,619 kcal),

Ireland (3,565 kcal), Austria (3,536 kcal), Turkey (3,525 kcal), France (3,518 kcal), Italy (3,507 kcal), and Cyprus (3,429 kcal). Ireland is now ranked fifth in this list.

• One dot at the extreme right represents the sumo wrestlers of Japan.

As shown on this plot, the daily calorie intake of individual centenarians and groups ranges from 940 kcal (women in Japan) to about 1,600 kcal (men in Italy). The plot peaks at about 1,400 kcal, where both centenarians and long-living people from "longevity valleys" meet each other. Fewer calories in the cases of non-eating people do not promote longevity, and non-eating women lived just forty-four to sixty-eight years. The overeating sumo wrestlers, who consume about 5,500 kcal a day, live sixty-odd years, which is about seventeen years less than average Japanese men.

The plot also shows that the Japanese centenarians and the nation as a whole consume fewer calories than the people in European countries with high life-expectancy rates. The Japanese are smaller in body size than Europeans and Americans, and need fewer calories. The world's highest calorie intake puts Ireland closer to sumo wrestlers, with a life expectancy rate of 3.5 years less than that of Japan. Furthermore, Japanese and American centenarians consume only one third of the average calorie amount per capita in those countries.

White dots on the plot represent calories required per day by "typical" American males and females, depending on their age, who live in temperate climates. The upper white dots correspond to an average life span of seventy-seven to seventy-nine years. These data were taken from the book, *The Human Body*, published by Running Press Gem.

Black dots reflect calories consumed by individual or groups of centenarians surveyed and people from "longevity valleys." The average age of long-living people from these valleys, including Hunza, Vilcabamba, and Abkhasia, is assumed to be ninety years; scientists began to doubt their supreme longevity because of cases of age exaggeration.

Data on calories consumed by George Burns and the Japanese twins were obtained by my own calculations based on their diets. We also can see from Figure 16-1 that **a lifelong intake of about 1,400 to 1,600 kcal for both men and women is the key that opens the gate to the longevity garden**. It is recommended in the United States that 2,000 kcal for women and 2,670 kcal for men between the ages of twenty-three and fifty are too high and seem to lessen the chances for living more than an average life span. If a person wants to reach a very ripe old age, it is worth taking control of calorie intake and limiting consumption to the longevity champion's level.

17

FOOD INTAKE CONTROL

"Delicious food destroyed mankind."
--Nickolai M. Amosov, M.D., Russian academician of medicine

"Don't bring dead cells inside your body."
--Souren Arakelyan, Ph.D.

Cooked and Raw Food

The overwhelming majority of this planet's population eats cooked food. Many people do not suspect that there is another way of eating. Even vegans, the strictest of all vegetarians, cook their beans, grains, and vegetables. The contemporary medicine and nutrition science paradigm implies that to render foods digestible and easier to assimilate, they must be cooked. Indeed, it is difficult to digest raw rice, wheat, or oats, and vegetables such as broccoli, cauliflower, and pumpkin--if lightly cooked--become more digestible. It goes without question that animal foods like meat, poultry, eggs, and fish are required to be "well-done" rather than lightly cooked. However, there are places and societies where meat and fish are eaten raw. The Eskimos and Siberian Yakuts--who eat frozen raw meat and fat--and the Japanese--who eat raw fish known as sushi and sashimi--are just a few examples, but it does not mean that other people should eat their meat or fish uncooked. Raw meat may have parasites and viruses, which can cause many health hazards. The majority of meat- and fish-eaters throughout the world cooks their meat and fish.

As with virtually any process in life, cooking is a double-edged sword, with positive and negative sides. We need it, and we pay for it with our health. The more cooking that is involved, the higher the price. The problem with "cooking well done," with the use of high temperature, is that it destroys not only viruses and parasites, but also digestive enzymes and most vitamins present in raw food. The benefits of cooking food include the following:

• Cooking with herbs, spices, and salt makes food tasty.
• Cooking kills parasites, molds, viruses, and bacteria in food.
• Cooking softens firm legumes and grains.
• Cooking makes some vegetables, such as broccoli, cauliflower, pumpkin, and turnips, more digestible.
• Cooking makes it easier to obtain all the essential amino acids from meat or fish of one kind only.
• Cooking activates chemical compounds in some herbs like garlic, which--when subjected to baking, boiling, or frying--reacts by releasing a certain amount of sulfur compounds that account for biological effects.

The downfalls of cooking include but not limited to the following:

• Cooking and eating animal products increase the ratio of protein and fat in food.
• Cooking destroys 85 percent of the nutritional value of food (according to Viktoras Kulvinskas).
• Cooking destroys food enzymes and most vitamins present in raw food.
• Cooking alters organic molecules, converting them into inorganic molecules, which are not assimilated by the cells.
• Cooking alters fats, making them heavy and thick, and deforms their structure.
• Cooking deprives fats and oils of the enzyme lipase, thereby making them difficult to digest.
• Cooking alters protein molecules in meat, destroys the enzyme protease (i.e., the natural protein-digesting enzyme in raw meat), and makes it difficult to digest.
• Cooking alters organic carbohydrate molecules, destroys the enzyme amylase protease (i.e., the natural carbohydrate-digesting enzyme), and destroys life force in grains, vegetables, and fruits.
• Cooking techniques such as boiling lead to a significant loss of vitamins and other water-soluble nutrients.
• Cooking destroys about 90 percent of the heat-sensitive vitamin B_{12}.
• Cooking with common table salt (i.e., sodium chloride, an inorganic compound) causes high blood pressure and a host of diseases of the heart, kidneys, bladder, arteries, and veins.
• Cooking diminishes the vital sun energy that is absorbed and accumulated by plants.

Contrary to a widely accepted belief that cooking makes foods more digestible, the digestion of cooked food deprives the body of energy more than any other activity. It takes energy to the extent that after a good dinner of meat, potatoes, and cheesecake for dessert, a person has no energy to raise his/her drooping eyelids to watch TV.

We rarely escape from addiction of one kind or another. Endorphins released during exercise make us feel euphoric and people can become addicted to exercise. This is an example of a healthy addiction, provided that the exercise is done in moderation. However, eating cooked food can easily become an uncontrolled and unhealthy addiction. People rarely have cravings for apples or carrots; most cravings are for ice cream, sugary cookies, french fries, fried chicken, and potato chips--all cooked foods.

Raw-Food Diet

A raw-food diet is based on a raw-vegetable dietary philosophy, which holds that plants must be eaten raw with no cooking allowed. The main components of this diet are sweet and fatty fruits and green leafy vegetables, including wild edible plants. With 100 percent raw plant food, this diet is stricter than low-heat cooking, yoga, or macrobiotic regimes. The latter two diets consider love while cooking as a means to make food vital on a subtle level. However, raw foods provide the vital essence of plant food to the body, mind, and spirit through a complete denial of cooking.

Many people perceive it as an extreme diet, even as a kind of revolt against established customs. However, the impact of a raw-food diet on health and longevity is also astonishing. No other dietary, exercise, or supplementary plan claims that people with serious heart disease, whose doctors give them no hope to survive more than a few months, can become vibrantly healthy again and live another forty to fifty years. This claim comes from a heart-disease survivor who was doomed to die at the age of fifty-two and who, turning to a raw-food diet, enjoyed superior health at ninety.

Arshavir Ter-Avanesyan is an Armenian from Iran and author of the book, *On the Track of Raw Food Diet* (the translation of the title into English is this author's), which was first published in the Armenian language in 1960. (I have a Russian edition of this book, but a footnote in it stated that there is also an English edition).

The idea of a raw-food diet came to Ter-Avanesyan when he was trying to find out the cause of death of his two children: a ten-year-old son and a fourteen-year-old daughter. Many medical tests in Iran, France, Germany, and Switzerland failed to diagnose their disease, although doctors had administered enormous amounts of drugs and antibiotics. Being in the deepest grief, their father started to study medicine himself and finally came to the conclusion that his children died because of an unnatural, detrimental eating pattern in his family and drug abuse. His own health deteriorated and, because of progressive heart failure and a host of other diseases, he anticipated an inevitable death before long--although he was only fifty-two years old at the time. One day, he abruptly stopped eating cooked food and turned to a raw-food diet, which actually snatched him from the jaws of death. Soon after, he was cured of all his illnesses and he became strong and healthy again. After eight years on this diet, a profound change came over Ter-Avanesyan, not only physically, but also mentally and spiritually. He was eager to share his discoveries, insights, and experiences and wrote the book that has inspired many people around the world.

Among people who was inspired by that book is Dr. Souren Arakelyan, a biologist from Moscow, Russia. In his research, he studies the methods to prolong the life span of domestic animals, such as hens, pigs, cows, and horses. The most striking results were obtained when he fasted these animals for as long as one week, giving them just water with the addition of sedative anti-stress herbs. As a result of this experiment, Dr. Arakelyan's hens (with an average life span of five to six years) lived as long as eighteen years--their life span was tripled. It is worth noting that caloric restriction, tested on many groups of animals, accounts for doubling the life span. He explained that during a fast, sodium chloride, which acts as a conserving agent of wastes inside cells, is released and replaced with potassium from the inter-cellular liquids. Thus, cleansing the cells of wastes increased life duration and rejuvenated his animals.

Dr. Arakelyan also experiments on himself. His premises are based on two main principles: eliminating dead cells from the body and taking inside the body live cells from food. According to Dr. Arakelyan, 30 billion cells die each minute in our body. Once dead, the cells start to decompose and excrete ptomaine, which is poisonous to body systems. Therefore, detoxification through fasting enables the body to get rid of dead cells. The other principle is to not take dead cells from food inside the body.

This philosophy allows Dr. Arakelyan to anticipate a significant life extension, which he is going to prove by making himself an experimental subject. In 1985, after nineteen years on a raw-food/fasting regime, he announced that he is going to live to be 125 years old. His life-extension program is built on four columns: a raw-food diet, caloric restriction, short-term fasting, and moderate exercise. The raw fruits, vegetables, grains, and legumes that he eats supply his cells with live enzymes and vitamin-rich material. Fasting once a month for three days, when he drinks only water, cleanses his cells and eliminates dead cells. For their proper elimination, he insists on exercise during the fast, which helps to fully burn out dead cells.

His calorie intake gradually decreased within the period of thirty-five years that he lived on raw foods alone. For the first ten years on this regime, it was 2,000 kcal a day; for the next five years, it was 1,500 kcal; and the following twenty years, it was 1,000 kcal. Dr. Arakelyan is seventy-two years old now and enjoys superior health and fitness.

The raw-food diet approach is well-rooted in Europe and the United States, where many prominent scientists conducted research and physicians and natural healers applied it with great success in curing an array of diseases. The famous American "drugless physician," Henry Lindlahr, M.D., was cured himself of a progressive form of diabetes by the German natural healer, Father Kneipp, with a diet consisting of only fruits, greens, and vegetables. Later, Dr. Lindlahr became a physician and established the Lindlahr Sanitarium, a well-known "nature-cure" hospital. He is regarded as one of America's pioneers of natural methods in the modern prevention and treatment of disease.

Dr. Norman W. Walker, a prominent researcher of a person's ability to live a healthier and longer life, wrote eight books that advocated the need to provide the body with vital, life-giving enzymes for three quarters of a century. Dr. Walker lived to the age of 109 years, and is proof that the enzymes-rich raw-food diet that he ate is the key to achieving exceptional longevity.

Another enzyme researcher and self-experimenting scientist is the venerable Dr. Edward Howell, whose book *Enzyme Nutrition* is regarded as the bible among raw-food dieters. He researched food enzymes and their implications for human health for more than fifty years. In 1918, at the age of twenty, Dr. Howell started to avoid cooked food, replacing it with vital raw foods. His major contribution to nutrition science is the discovery of the importance of food enzymes for fighting diseases and slowing down the aging processes. Dr. Howell equated the internal enzyme potential of the body with the life force, which has limited reserves. The best way to spare internal metabolic enzymes is to eat enzyme-rich raw fruits and vegetables. He believed that food enzymes play a key role in unlocking secrets of longevity. When *Enzyme Nutrition* was published in 1985, Dr. Howell was eighty-eight years old, enjoying good health and continuing his research and writings.

The raw-food diet movement in the 1970s in the United States was much enhanced by its prominent advocates, including Dr. Ann Wigmore (author of *The Hippocrates Diet* and *The Sprouting Book*) and Viktoras Kulvinskas (author of *Survival into the 21st Century*), and more recently by David Wolfe (author of *The Sunfood Diet Success System*), Stephen Arlin (author of *Raw*

Power), and others.

Dr. Wigmore was a colon-cancer survivor and she attributed her remarkable recovery to drinking the raw juices of alfalfa sprouts, beets, carrots, dandelion greens, lamb's quarter, and watercress. Her story of suffering from terminal disease and being revived to youthful health through a raw-food diet is reminiscent of the story of Arshavir Ter-Avanesyan. She recalled, "My eating habits were very indiscriminate. And I paid the price for it—by the time I was fifty, my hair had turned completely white, and I suffered from arthritis, asthma, colon cancer, and migraine headaches," according to John Heinerman, Ph.D., in his book, *Heinerman's Encyclopedia of Anti-Aging Remedies*.

By eating fermented (i.e., sprouted), grains, nuts, and seeds and by drinking raw juices, Dr. Wigmore not only completely recovered from cancer and other diseases, but also described herself twenty-five years later as "a feisty seventy-five-year-old" who was "a ball of energy." Dr. Heinerman recalled her saying, "I could easily live to be ninety-five if I wanted to." She probably would have, but she died from accidental smoke inhalation in February 1994 at the age of nearly eighty-five. Two years before her death, when Dr. Heinerman met with her for the last time, her hair was as dark as it was a decade ago. The restoration of her hair from white at the age of fifty to its natural dark color at eighty-five shows the enormous rejuvenation effect of the enzyme-rich live foods she ate.

Viktoras Kulvinskas, M.S., N.D., D.D., who is regarded as one of the world's foremost and most experienced researchers on enzyme nutrition, started his raw-food journey at the age of twenty-nine, when he suffered from a type of angina attack. He was overweight at 195 pounds and described his living and eating habits at that time as deadly. Chronic overeating, fifteen cups of coffee, two packs of cigarettes per day, and plenty of alcohol were disastrous for his delicate body constitution, as he has put it. Lots of bakery products and protein, and bad food combining resulted in many ailments, including a tumor on his left wrist. Over a period of six months on a cleansing diet, his weight dropped to 95 pounds; five years later, together with rebuilding the body, he gained weight and weighed 135 pounds. He claims that his tumor disappeared within one week of eating raw food and juices. He joined the Hippocrates Health Institute in Boston, established by Ann Wigmore, where he was the Director of Research. His book, *Survival into the 21st Century*, published in 1975, is considered a raw-food movement classic and has sold more than one million copies. Currently, he is the director of The

Survival Foundation. For more than two decades, he has been lecturing and teaching about the survival and healing arts.

The premise of eating raw food implies that the live, enzymes-rich plant food built of organic molecules can only be assimilated by our cells to give us health and vitality. We are granted these benefits because by eating plant foods, we do not interfere with the laws of nature. Metaphysically speaking, plants readily sacrifice themselves to become food for humans and animals-- God created them this way. Sages of all nations who know the language of plants teach us this truth. Have you ever had that feeling that you can't stop picking wild blueberries or raspberries? Your time is over, but you are stuck– it's as if the berries are screaming, "Pick me! Pick me! And me, too! I am good for you." They want you to eat them; they are happy to give you health.

The raw-food diet is of great importance for people with blood type A, who are created to be vegetarians. Their weak immune system and susceptibility to major degenerative diseases such as heart disease, stroke, and cancer does not allow them to waste energy on processing enzyme-deprived cooked food; there are too few vital nutrients and too many residual wastes to handle. Optimal nutrition--that is, providing the body with all fifty necessary nutrients in the proper amounts--which is absolutely necessary for proper body functioning and no more than that, is the only way for a blood type A people, especially in their fifties or older, to survive and extend their life.

The raw-food diet movement recently received powerful support when David Wolfe released his book, *The Sunfood Diet Success System*. Wolfe has been a 100 percent raw foodist for more than five years and he attributes his becoming tremendously healthy to this diet. In his book, along with sharing his own experiences, he provides all the information necessary for the transition from an ordinary diet to eating 80 to 100 percent raw plant foods. Showing how abundant raw plant foods are, he defines the following fourteen major categories:

1. Fruits	2. Leaves
3. Nuts	4. Seeds and grains
5. Legumes	6. Flowers
7. Green sprouts	8. Roots
9. Shoots	10. Bark
11. Sap	12. Stems
13. Water (sea) vegetation	14. Mushroom

All these foods are divided into three classes that provide the three main macronutrients: green-leafed vegetables or chlorophyll (protein), sweet fruits (carbohydrates), and fatty plant foods (fat). According to Wolfe, a diet with a specific ratio of each of the three classes enables a person to overcome certain disorders and achieve different physical, mental, and spiritual effects (the following figures represent dry-weight ratio):

- For weight loss: Chlorophyll 50, Sugar 50, Fat 0
- For weight gain: Chlorophyll 42, Sugar 16, Fat 42
- For detoxification: Chlorophyll 45-50, Sugar 45-50, Fat 0-10
- For the elderly: Chlorophyll 40, Sugar 20, Fat 40
- To overcome hypoglycemia and diabetes: Chlorophyll 33, Sugar 33, Fat 33
- To overcome candida: Chlorophyll 45, Sugar 10, Fat 45
- For mental clarity: Chlorophyll 33 or 0, Sugar 33 or 100, Fat 33 or 0
- For athletes and endurance: Chlorophyll 33, Sugar 33, Fat 33
- To warm the body: Chlorophyll 20, Sugar 40, Fat 40
- To cool the body: Chlorophyll 60, Sugar 20, Fat 20
- To ground the body: Chlorophyll 50, Sugar 0, Fat 50
- For spirituality: Chlorophyll 50, Sugar 50, Fat 0

If you are inclined to radically improve your health, heal, achieve full personal and spiritual potential, rejuvenate, and lengthen your life, your right choice will be the raw-food diet, according to Wolfe. All blood types will benefit from introducing more enzyme-abundant raw plant foods into their diet, but especially people with blood type A. I highly recommend reading this excellent book, which some people regard as the new "bible" of the raw-food movement. Converting to a vegetarian raw foodist is a serious life commitment and only greatly determined individuals are able to make this decision. Do not expect quick results on a raw-food diet, though. Detoxification, cleansing, and rebuilding of the body take time, which equates to one month for each year on cooked food, according to Wolfe. For example, if you are sixty years old, regeneration and rejuvenation signs can be expected in five years with a 100 percent raw-food diet.

Advocates of this diet have stronger support from the extraordinary long-living people who have lived on raw plant food, than any other diet designers. The most striking example is a famous Chinese herbalist, Li Chung Yun, who allegedly lived to be 256 years of age. He died in 1933. His food consisted entirely of raw mountain herbs and herb teas. To confirm his unbelievable age, the head of Chang-Tu University undertook a thorough investigation, which allowed the Chinese government to conclude that it was true. Dr. Norman Walker, who lived to be 109 years old, is another example.

Elderly people trying to change to the raw-food diet must be very careful.

If large amounts of a raw material are suddenly eaten, it may put a physiological stress on the digestive system. A smooth and long transition period of six months to one year, or even longer, is necessary to increase the digestive "fire." David Wolfe's book provides helpful transition guidelines. "Going raw" entails detoxification of the system, and the blood becomes thicker as it is loaded with toxins. People with blood type A, with their inherent thick blood, are put at increased risk. Adding raw garlic and onions-- reputed blood thinners--to the diet helps overcome the problem.

Protein-Restricted Diet

"Proteins can be body killers, if we are not watchful of our diet."
--Henry G. Bieler, M.D., *Food Is Your Best Medicine*

A protein-restricted diet is usually associated with kidney (renal) disease and cancer. In the treatment of renal disease, protein restriction usually implies a protein intake of 0.7 gram/kilogram/day, as compared with 1.5 grams/kilogram/day in an average American diet. A recent analysis of ten studies showed that protein restriction can retard the progression of kidney disease in patients with and without diabetes. Researchers at the University of California in Irvine (headed by Dr. Ping Wang) and at the New England Medical Center in Boston arrived at this conclusion after analyzing five studies involving 108 insulin-dependent diabetic patients with kidney disease and 1,413 non-diabetic patients. Diabetic patients were followed for nine to thirty-six months and non-diabetic patients for eighteen to thirty-six months.

It was shown earlier in this chapter that the death rate from cancer is proportional to protein consumption. Cancer cells need amino acids for growth. Back in 1950, Drs. W. Dunning, M. Curtis, and M. Moun "...showed that added dietary tryptophane (an essential amino acid that can be as much as twenty times more concentrated in animal meat than in protein from vegetarian sources) increased the incidence of induced mammary-gland and liver cancer and appeared to be a decisive factor in the etiology of bladder cancer," as reviewed by Victoras Kulvinskas in his book, *Survival into the 21st Century*. Dr. Otto Warburg, a Nobel Prize winner and Director of the Max Planck Institute for Cell Physiology in Berlin, Germany, is well known for his discovery that a cancerous tumor may develop if the oxygen supply to tissues is reduced by 35 percent. The August 21, 1971, issue of *Science News* quoted Dr. John Gainer as saying, "Slight protein increases reduce oxygen transport by as much as 60 percent, even though the amount of protein in the fluid would be considered within the normal range for human blood."

Extensive review of these and many other sources allowed Viktoras Kulvinskas to state, "Thus, a high protein diet can reduce the oxygen-carrying capacity of the blood, which produces oxygen starvation, leading to mutation and cancer." The remedy can be found in a protein-restricted diet. Many cancer survivors found a low-protein diet--in conjunction with raw juices and enzyme-rich plant foods--to be helpful in the successful treatment of different cancers. Dr. Ann Wigmore, a colon-cancer survivor, used live fruit and vegetable juices, fresh fruits, sprouts, and wheat-grass therapy for self-curing.

Protein is a double-edge sword. On the one hand, it is absolutely necessary for our health and survival itself by providing essential amino acids. Every cell in our body contains protein and their division--that is, production of new cells during growth--is impossible without protein. Blood cells, enzymes, hormones, antibodies, nerves, and body tissues are all protein. Normal growth, proper physical and mental functioning, and the sense of well-being suffer if the protein supply is inadequate--that is how powerful protein is.

On the other hand, protein is the only macronutrient that leaves the harmful metabolic residues--uric acid and urea--which, if accumulated, are a potential danger for the liver, kidneys, and joints. After metabolism, carbohydrates and fats leave carbon dioxide and water, which are expelled through the lungs and bladder, doing no harm to the body. However, uric acid and urea, being harmful, require detoxification and excretion, which taxes the eliminative organs. Also, amino acids derived from proteins--if produced in excess--acidify the whole system and deplete the body of calcium, which is extracted from bones to neutralize them, leading to osteoporosis. Undigested protein trapped in the intracellular fluid between the cells is a primary cause of this disease, according to Dr. C. Samuel West, author of the book, *The Golden Seven plus One*.

We already know that protein, with its 58 percent utilization, is inefficient and expensive fuel for energy. People with blood type A cannot afford the luxury of running on an expensive fuel that leaves toxic wastes. Their naturally thick blood becomes even thicker because of these wastes, and their naturally thin stomach acid is weak in digesting proteins. What the meat-eating blood type O's and B's can get away with, the blood type A's cannot afford. Their way is a carefully planned *optimal nutrition*. The long-living people in communities such as Hunza, Vilcabamba, and Abkhasia, and individuals such as Dr. Norman Walker and Dr. Galina Shatalova--with their

very low protein intake--are very good examples for blood type A's. Not only is it better for them to keep close to a vegetarian diet, but also to limit protein (including plant sources) as much as possible. Just as it is advised to watch salt or sugar in your food, so it is better to also watch your protein.

What is true for long-living populations and individuals is also confirmed in animal studies. Animals that consumed high protein when they matured and low protein and restricted calories thereafter had the longest life span, as McCay and his co-workers found in their classic studies back in the 1930s. In the short term, it was shown in a study by Dr. L.H. Newberg of Ann Arbor University that test animals that were fed large quantities of meat grew bigger and more alert than those on a vegetarian diet. However, three months later, those animals died from kidney failure, while the control vegetarian animals stayed healthy and lived disease-free.

In determining how much protein is enough for bodily needs, it is better to consider essential amino acid requirements. Daily amino acid requirements for adults are shown in Table 17-1. We can see from Table 17-1 that the requirements for an individual with a body weight of 160 pounds (73 kilograms) range from 219 milligrams of tryptophan to 1,168 milligrams of both leucine and phenylalanine. The particular amino acids can be derived from 16 (phenylalaline) to 28 (methionine) grams of high-quality protein. The requirements for all eight essential amino acids can be met with 28 grams of protein in the diet.

Table 17-1.   Daily Amino Acid Requirements for Adults

Nos.	Amino Acid	Mg/kg of Body Weight	Mg for a Body Weight of 160 pounds (73 kg)	Amino Acid Pattern for High Quality Proteins	
				mg/g	Grams of protein*
1	Tryptophan	3	219	11	20
2	Threonine	8	584	35	17
3	Methionine	10	730	26	28
4	Isoleucine	13	935	42	23
5	Lysine	13	935	42	23
6	Valine	14	1,022	48	21
7	Leucine	16	1,168	70	17
8	Phenylalanine	16	1,168	73	16

*For an individual weighing 160 pounds (73 kilograms).
Source: National Academy of Sciences, *Recommended Dietary Allowances*, 9th Edition, 1980, p.43.

High-quality proteins are found not only in animal foods such as eggs, meat, milk, cheese, and fish, but also in vegetable sources such as quinoa (i.e., a South American grain, a staple food of the ancient Incas and Aztecs), brown rice, wheat germ, tofu, soybeans, broccoli, pumpkin, and sunflower seeds. The quality of soy protein is as high as that of animal protein, and it is free of cholesterol. Although beans and lentils are regarded as low-quality proteins (i.e., the usable protein comprises only about half the total protein), they are rich in methionine, which requires the greatest amount of protein to be satisfied. Brazil nuts are also very rich in methionine. Beans and lentils complemented with quinoa (which can be bought in natural food stores) or brown rice provide an excellent combination that makes complete protein.

The amino-acid requirements are usually met very easily, as shown in the following example. One cup of cooked soybeans (172 grams, 298 kcal, protein 28.6 grams, fat 15.4 grams, carbohydrates 17 grams) contains more than adequate amounts of all the essential amino acids, except for methionine. If one half cup of soybeans (149 kcal, 14.3 grams protein) is complemented with one cup of rolled oats (311 kcal, 13 grams protein), 1 ounce of Brazil nuts (186 kcal, 4.1 grams protein), and half a piece of avocado (162 kcal, 2 grams protein), the methionine also becomes adequate. The total protein amount and calorie value of these four foods is 33.4 grams and 808 kcal, respectively, which is much less than the average person eats. Therefore, a calorie intake of more than 2,000 kcal will definitely provide the necessary amounts of amino acids, even with a (properly planned) vegetarian diet. That is why many authors believe that the fear of not getting enough protein is exaggerated. As Patrick Holford, author of *The Optimum Nutrition Bible*, puts it: "...if you are eating enough calories, you are almost certainly getting enough protein, unless you are living off high-sugar, high-fat junk food." The real menace, especially for people with blood type A, is not an under-eating but rather an over-eating of protein.

Essential amino acids--although of great importance–can be harmful if taken in excess. One of the causes of "over-acidity" in the body is excess protein stored in the cells, which disturbs nitrogen balance, according to Henry Bieler, M.D., author of the book, *Food Is Your Best Medicine*. He stated that: "...the presence of too many amino acids upsets the acid-case equilibrium in the body. Disastrous consequences follow." Just twice the daily requirements of certain amino acids in the diet can be toxic to the cells, according to Dr. C.L. Elvehjem, author of the "Amino Acid Supplementation of Cereal."

The restriction of two essential amino acids, phenylalanine and tyrosine (non-essential amino acid), was found to be beneficial to the immune system by increasing the number of cancer-fighting T-helper cells and T-cytotoxic cells, as shown in a 1990 study by Norris, Meadows, et al., in healthy human volunteers. Neil Nedley, M.D., author of the book, *Proof Positive: How to Reliably Combat Disease and Achieve Optimal Health through Nutrition and Lifestyle*, reviewed this study and several studies in mice, and stated, "There is now evidence that restricting certain essential amino acids, such as phenylalanine and tyrosine, may help to treat certain deadly cancers that have already spread or metastasized." Phenylalanine and tyrosine are abundant in animal sources such as meats, chicken breasts, tuna, and crabs, and in vegetable sources such as lentils. Fruits and vegetables are low in these amino acids.

Is it possible to survive if some essential amino acids are taken in lesser amounts than the RDA requirements? The answer is "yes," as the case of Dr. Norman Walker, who lived to the age of 109, shows. His diet--cited in his book *Become Younger*--consisted of raw fruits, vegetables, nuts, and juices. Following is a typical menu:

> • Breakfast: bananas (1 or 2), ground carrots (2 or 3 teaspoons), raisins (2 or 3 teaspoons), figs (4 to 6), nuts (4 to 6 tablespoons), and carrot juice (1 glass)
> • Lunch: ground carrots (2 or 3 teaspoons); celery, green onion, cabbage or lettuce, and green pepper; shredded beets (2 teaspoons); green peas (1 tablespoon); cauliflower (a small piece); and vegetable juice (1 glass)
> • Dinner: celery (2 tablespoons), lettuce (2 tablespoons), tomato (1 piece), ground carrots (2 to 4 teaspoons), green onion (3 to 5), cucumber (1 tablespoon), green pepper (2 tablespoons), cabbage (3 to 5 tablespoons), ground apple (1 or 2 tablespoons), beets (1 or 2 tablespoons), lemon juice (1 teaspoon), red radish (1 piece), and dressing made of olive oil, lemon juice, tomato, vegetable oil, and honey

I analyzed the nutritional value of Dr. Walker's diet and estimated that it was equal to 1,280 kcal, comprised of 27 grams of protein, 184 grams of carbohydrates, and 49 grams of fats. It was a very low-calorie and low-protein diet similar to that of the long-living people of Vilcabamba. In Dr. Walker's diet, of the eight essential amino acids, four exceeded RDA requirements, three reached the 80 to 99 percent level, and one--methionine--was a mere 34 percent. Because Dr. Walker survived to the age of 109, we may conclude that either the RDA requirements are overestimated or eating raw enzyme-rich food makes a person less dependent on proper proportions of amino acids; it is most likely that both options are true.

Another raw–food advocate, thirty-year-old David Wolfe, consumes much greater amounts of nutrients than Dr. Walker did. As he describes in his book, *The Sunfood Diet Success System*, in a typical day he eats the following:

- 2 avocados, 30 to 40 ripe olives, and/or 25 to 30 macadamia nuts
- 1 papaya, or 1 melon, or 2 to 30 figs (if in season)
- 2 pounds of kale and/or wild green food from his gardens or canyons near his house
- 4 to 5 pieces of citrus fruit, apples, or another juicy fruit in season (e.g., peaches, plums, nectarines, mangoes)
- 2 to 4 ripe hot peppers (usually jalapeno or habanero)
- 2 to 4 strips of dulce seaweed

The nutritional value of Wolfe's daily food, as compared with Dr. Walker's diet, is 3,590 kcal (280 percent), 78 grams of protein (290 percent), 585 grams of carbohydrates (320 percent), and 123 grams of fats (250 percent). Wolfe's diet is very high in calories, protein, carbohydrates, and fat, although he looks slim. David Wolfe is blood type O, thirty years old, very active, and has been on a raw-food diet only five years. If he continues this way, he will probably need fewer calories and amounts of nutrients, as indicated in the previously mentioned case of Dr. Arakelyan, who has eaten raw food for the last thirty-four years.

A low-protein diet is important for people with blood type A because their internal energy resources necessary for protein processing are limited. Drs. Weissberg and Christiano warn blood type A's that a typical American diet rich in meat, potatoes, and saturated fat can kill them. In their book, *The Answer Is in Your Blood Type*, they suggest a diet plan for blood type A's, which is actually a high-protein diet. For example, daily protein foods (for a physically inactive person, Day 3) include a two-egg omelet (12 grams); one slice of toasted sprouted wheat bread (3 grams); albacore tuna (48 grams); two scoops of Personal Protein (30 grams?); and nuts, vegetables, fruits, and rice cakes (the amount is not specified). The total protein intake will probably exceed 100 grams, which I think is too high. I would suggest that people with blood type A try to find a lower limit of protein intake, at which one's weight is maintained unchanged. Just as you watch your salt or sugar intake, also watch your protein intake. This will put you in an optimum nutrition mode, which can help prevent a host of degenerative diseases associated with excessive protein intake.

Food Combining

It is not unusual for a person to eat a vegetable salad, chicken, rice, and cheesecake or fruit for dessert at one meal. However, protein, carbohydrates, and fat in these foods need different environments and enzymes for their proper digestion, and they pass through the digestive tract at different speeds. Sugar and starch begin to digest in the mouth in an alkaline environment with the aid of the enzyme amylase, which is present in saliva when we chew our food. Protein digestion starts in the stomach in a high-acid environment, where hydrochloric acid activates the protein-digesting enzyme pepsin and deactivates amylase. The enzyme lipase is necessary for fat digestion, which begins in the stomach and continues in the duodenum (i.e., the first part of the small intestine), where the environment becomes more alkaline than in the stomach due to the bile released by the gallbladder and the pancreatic digestive juices.

Digestion of carbohydrates continues in the small intestine, where amylase from the saliva is reactivated and amylase secreted by the pancreas is added. Protein is broken up into peptides (i.e., clusters of amino acids) in the stomach, and further broken up into individual amino acids in the small intestine with the aid of the pancreatic enzyme peptidase. Digestive processes end up in the small and large intestines, where glucose, amino acids, and fatty acids--the end products of carbohydrate, protein, and fat digestion, respectively--are prepared for assimilation.

The time required for digestion of protein, carbohydrates, and fat is also different. Fruits are easy to digest and they pass through the stomach within half an hour, whereas meat requires more digestive efforts and may stay in the stomach for 3 to 4 hours. Fat is also difficult to digest: it takes 1 hour to emulsify 10 grams of fat in the duodenum, with the aid of bile salts, before the next portion of fat is discharged from the stomach. Therefore, if meat and sweet fruit are eaten together, the fruit will be halted and will start to ferment in the warm, high-acid environment of the stomach. Alkaline fruit will neutralize the acids in the stomach, and the meat may eventually leave the stomach partly digested, and then be putrefied in the intestine. Fermented and putrefied foods produce toxic acids and cause heartburn, gas, flatulence, and diarrhea or constipation.

Food combining is known from ancient times. Hippocrates taught in his book *Hygiene* that eating food in a certain order is essential for a disease-free and long life. The tenth-century Persian physician Avicenna warned that digestion of different foods occurs at different times, and that mixing incompatible foods is dangerous for the health. Food combining has a strong scientific background of a century-long research. Ivan Pavlov, a famous Russian physiologist known by his research on conditional reflexes, published *The Work of the Digestive Glands in 1902*. In this book, he stated that secretions of digestive juices are specific and vary for different foods eaten, to the degree that one can talk about "milk juice," "bread juice," and "meat juice." Dr. Herbert Shelton, who is regarded as the father of food combining, and Dr. Howard Hay did extensive research in the 1920s and 1930s, establishing the fundamentals of proper food combining. They discovered that protein- and carbohydrate-rich foods must be eaten separately.

Arthur Cason, M.D., showed in his experiments in 1945 that digestion is retarded and even prevented if protein and carbohydrates are eaten at the same meal. Professor Y.D. Vitebsky of Russia discovered and emphasized the role of four inner openings (i.e., valves) that divide the digestive tract into five separate and tightly closed chambers, each having a different environment and specific function in food digestion, as follows:

1. Mouth and esophagus: alkaline environment, cardiac opening into the stomach
2. Stomach: acid environment, pyloric opening into the duodenum
3. Duodenum: alkaline environment, duodenal opening into the small intestine
4. Small intestine: alkaline environment, ileocecal opening into the large intestine
5. Large intestine: alkaline environment, anus

The proper functioning of all openings (valves) depends on an adequate supply of germanium, a mineral that is found in garlic, wild barley, knob of wisteria, and herbs such as ginseng, kashi, sanzukon, and hishi. Despite serious scientific support, mainstream medicine does not acknowledge food combining so far. The primary rules of food combining and good combinations are as follows:

- protein and non-starchy vegetables
- protein and leafy greens
- one concentrated protein per meal
- starches and vegetables, including leafy greens
- oil and leafy greens

• oil and acid or subacid fruits
• one concentrated carbohydrate per meal
• milk must be eaten alone or not at all
• sweet fruits must be eaten alone
• melons must be eaten alone with a time margin of 2 hours before and
after.

Green leafy vegetables comprise the only group that combines well with
proteins, carbohydrates, and fats. Among the bad combinations are protein
and carbohydrates, protein and fat, protein and acid fruits, carbohydrates and
acid fruits, sugar and carbohydrates, animal fat and starch, and sweet fruit and
starch. Proper food combining results in the following benefits:

• reduces stress on the digestive organs
• minimizes toxicity induced by indigestion
• spares the body's energy used for digestion and assimilation

Food combining is most beneficial for people with a weak digestion
system. Some people have such a strong digestion that they do well paying no
attention to food combining. A good example is John Beatty of Woburn,
Massachusetts, who lived to the age of 100 eating beef, mashed potatoes with
milk, and coffee with cream and sugar at one meal. However, John had blood
type O and a "cast-iron stomach." People with blood type A or those with
weak digestion cannot afford such a luxury, but they can improve their health
following the food-combining rules.

Longevity Food

If there are foods that really promote longevity, why doesn't everyone eat
them? First of all, food around the world is not universal. Although the food
in different countries differs very broadly, each country has centenarians who
achieved their super-long age eating local food. There are some claims that
certain centenarians attribute their longevity to a habit of eating specific--even
exotic--foods; for example, Dorah Ramothibe, 116, from South Africa who
eats locusts and turtle meat; and Kin Narita (died in January 2000 at the age of
107) of Japan who ate eel twice a day. However, in most cases, the diet of
centenarians is nothing special, just common food that ordinary people eat.

Some experts say that there are no specific longevity foods and that
genetic and environmental factors, rather than diet, play a major role in
longevity. On the other hand, a few authors--both Western and Oriental--
claim that some foods promote longevity. I am inclined to think that some
foods have healing properties and are more beneficial for our health than

others, especially if a person's blood type is considered. The editors of *Prevention Magazine* in their book, *The Visual Encyclopedia of Natural Healing,* list the following fifty best healing foods. I arranged them into seven groups and highlighted in bold the **foods to avoid** for people of blood type A:

• Fruits and Berries – apples, apricots, avocados, **bananas**, **cantaloupe**, grapefruit, **honeydew melon**, nectarines, **oranges**, peaches, prunes, raisins, strawberries, watermelon

• Vegetables and Legumes – asparagus, broccoli, **cabbage**, carrots, cauliflower, celery, **eggplant**, green peas, **green peppers**, kale, lentils, onions, **potatoes**, spinach, **sweet potatoes**, Swiss chard, tofu, **tomatoes**, winter squash

    • Nuts and Seeds – almonds, peanuts (unsalted), sunflower seeds

    • Grains – barley, brown rice, corn, oat bran, whole-grain cereal

    • Oils – olive oil, **safflower oil**

    • Fish and Poultry – mackerel, salmon, sardines, tuna, turkey (white meat)

    • Dairy – **skim milk**, yogurt

Safflower oil, however, is very controversial. It contains 77 percent of omega-6 polyunsaturated fatty acid, which attracts oxygen from air and rapidly becomes rancid or "peroxidized." In this case, it will be saturated with "lipid hydroperoxide" molecules, the most dangerous free radicals that cause a host of diseases and accelerate the aging process. The pioneering free-radical researcher Dr. Denham Harman, when asked what is the most dangerous fat that people eat, answered, "Corn oil and safflower oil." You do not want to speed up the aging process rather than retarding it by eating these oils, do you? Safflower oil is also a food to avoid for all four blood types, so do not take it inside your body.

The previous list of fifty longevity foods omits garlic; however, I rank *garlic* as a number-one food for achieving longevity. Garlic and onion are two preferred foods that stand out in the diet of long-living people, as found by a prominent American sociologist from the National Institute of Aging, who surveyed more than 8,500 centenarians in the 1980s. It proves once again that the major attitude of long-living people of paying little attention to what others say or think about them works pretty well. We can draw from that one more rule for longevity: *do not feel that you are a burden to others if they don't like how you smell.* We need to be a little selfish to survive and if we want to live a long life. In the case of eating garlic, by trying to please those around us, we shorten our own life.

Among other longevity foods are *cabbage, olive oil,* and *yogurt.* In her book *The Food Pharmacy,* Jean Carper calls them "life-extenders." There are some Chinese mushrooms such as *black fungus* that also allow you to live longer.

Sweet potatoes are appreciated as a longevity food in China and Japan. Ji Han, a Chinese physician of the past, attributed the longevity of people who lived high in the mountains to their custom of eating sweet potatoes, the main ingredient in their diet. The white sweet potatoes that people in this region eat are very rich in *collagen* (i.e., a protein representing about 30 percent of the protein in the body) and other *polysaccharoses* that are believed to help maintain elasticity of blood vessels, lubricate the joints, and prevent atrophy of the connective tissues in the liver and kidneys, according to Henry C. Lu in his book, *The Art of Long Life, Chinese Foods for Longevity.* In other words, sweet potatoes provide us with the substances that help fight the major degenerative diseases of aging, which affect the body's circulation and elimination systems and joints.

The Kochi prefecture of Japan is second after the Okinawa region in its fame for the high ratio of long-living people. According to Japanese scientists, the secret of their longevity is in eating sweet potatoes. Sweet potatoes are listed among the "ten best" longevity foods in Japan too, according to Nagayama Hisao, author of the book, *Food Encyclopedia of Centenarians.* The other nine longevity foods are *soybeans, vinegar, seaweed, vegetables, fish, fruit, tea, milk, and pickled plums.*

In China, *walnuts* are called "longevity fruit" for two reasons: first, walnut trees live a few hundred years; and second, walnuts can strengthen the kidneys, heart, muscles, and brain, all necessary systems for a long life. Other longevity foods of China are *dates, sealwort, black sesame, red beans, tofu, chili, pickles (e.g., turnips, cucumbers, and tomatoes), fish, tea, refined cane sugar, seaweed, and rice* and *fruit wine* and *other liquors* in small amounts.

The Essenes, a religious group that has been living since ancient times in the Dead Sea region of Israel, considered eight fruits as the most important for health and promoting longevity: *apricots, dates, figs, olives, grapes, pomegranates, carob,* and *small yellow apples.*

Many American centenarians attribute their longevity to the food they ate throughout their long lives. The foods of people who achieved 100 and more in the United States are *buttermilk, carrots, catfish, codfish, coffee, cornmeal, eggs, fish, fruit, greens, ham, lamb, meat, milk, olive oil, orange juice, peas, potatoes, prunes, turnips, and whiskey* or *brandy* in moderate amounts.

The list can be continued further, but we must keep in mind that just as there is no universal diet that fits all, there also is no universal kind of food that promotes longevity in everyone. Centenarians around the world who benefited from specific foods are all very different relative to biochemical individuality, ethnic and cultural heritage, ancestral dietary needs, geography and climate, environments they live in, and lifestyle. Some of the American centenarians were born in this country; others are of Anglo-Saxon, Mediterranean, Asian, or other descent. What they have in common with other people is biochemical and physiological diversity among individuals. Without considering their enormous diversity, it is difficult to learn a longevity lesson from their food preferences.

Still, there are universal foods with high health potential that undoubtedly can be regarded as longevity foods. These are vegetables, fruits and their juices, and teas *with a high antioxidant capacity,* which can effectively fight the harmful free radicals that cause heart disease and cancer--the two major killers of people in developed countries. Recent studies at Tufts University conducted by Wang, Cao, Prior, et al., found that among fruits, the richest source of antioxidant phytonutrients is the *blueberry,* followed by *strawberry, plum, orange, red grape, kiwit, pink grapefruit, white grape, banana, apple, tomato, pear,* and *honeydew melon.* At the top of the vegetable list is *garlic,* followed by *kale, spinach, Brussels sprouts, alfalfa sprouts, broccoli florets, beets, red bell pepper, onion, corn, eggplant, cauliflower, potato, sweet potato, cabbage, leaf lettuce, string beans, carrot, yellow squash, iceberg lettuce, celery,* and *cucumber.* The *green* and *black teas* were found to have much higher antioxidant capacities than all the preceding vegetables.

At least one lesson that we can definitely derive from these lists of longevity foods is that the centenarians ate natural foods and produce rather than refined and processed food. Fruits, vegetables, and berries are on the longevity food lists most often, and are universally acknowledged to be the best foods for a longevity seeker.

Author's Diet

My diet has been dramatically changed at least three times in the last ten years. In Russia, up to the age of fifty, I ate a traditional Russian diet based on bread, potatoes, buckwheat, meat, chicken, fish, and eggs. My parents fed me well-cooked meat and fish, beans, raw vegetable salads, and fruits in season. The biggest meal of the day was lunch, and it consisted of three to four dishes: vegetable salad, soup, main dish, and hot drink. Russian bortsch, a soup with beets, potatoes, and cabbage for the major ingredients, was served at least two times a week. My grandmother was a great cook and I can still taste her unrepeatable bean soup, pirozhki (i.e., pastry stuffed with potatoes or fried cabbage), ground-meat rolls, chicken soup with homemade vermicelli, and stewed fish with parsnips. I never was a big dairy-food eater, but I was fond of my grandmother's homemade buttermilk.

For five years in college, I never cooked and mostly ate my meals out in the students' dormitory. Mostly, it was a typical three-dish meal, but sometimes I simply had a half dozen potato pastries and a bottle of milk.

During my life in Moscow, I cooked for myself for about three decades. Quite often, my meals were rice and potato soup, buckwheat with chicken or cheese, and fried potatoes with some green vegetables. I learned, however, to cook some serious dishes such as beaten and press-fried chicken stuffed with garlic, and even exotic dishes like Asian-style pilaf with lamb.

Having cooked for myself for many years, I continued cooking in Israel too. I ate there a lot of raw vegetables and fruits. Fish-head soup and herring with boiled potatoes were among my favorite dishes. If I had a snack when eating out, I often chose pita stuffed with olives and other pickled vegetables.

In Japan, I ate my lunch--which also was the biggest meal of the day-- nearly every day at restaurants. I enjoyed the typical Japanese foods of sushi, miso soup, tempura, and chanko nabe. I still cooked my own breakfast and dinner, but these were quite simple meals. Rice began to be a staple food for me, but I also ate a lot of fruits and vegetables.

In the United States, I have learned more about my type while working on this book and have adjusted my diet to it. I am retired now and can afford to eat garlic without insulting my co-workers. Upon awakening, I grind one clove of garlic and swallow it. Then I work for about an hour on the computer, or go for a walk or swim in the summer time. Next, I grind raw ginger root, make a tea from it, and drink it warm with vitamin C. Then I do a 1-hour set of yoga exercises, or knee bends on alternate days, and have my breakfast around 10 or 11 a.m. My breakfast is late, and I earn it with work and exercises. I start with fruits, then nuts with a piece of chocolate, followed by oatmeal porridge with olive oil. After breakfast, I work or read for about 3 hours. I eat my lunch at 3 or 4 p.m. Until recently, it included green and red salad, stewed chicken or fish with vegetables, and buckwheat, millet, or rice as a side dish. While preparing lunch, I do a few strength exercises with dumbbells or with my own weight.

My dinner is quite late – around 9 p.m. It consisted of two peanut-butter and jelly sandwiches with oatmeal bread and a cup of green tea. I have provided my recipe for green and red salad later in this chapter. It may seem like a whole meal for someone because it contains protein and fat. It also seems to be quite a large portion for only one person; however, I always eat this amount before my dinner and it does not impair my appetite for the main dish. If you are a beginner in raw-salad eating, use only about half of it--you definitely will have a good bowel movement the next morning.

Recently, after learning that blood type A's (sub-type AI, or the most distant from type O)--where I belong--have the shortest life span (averaging sixty-two years), I took it seriously and once again adjusted my diet. I found salvation for myself in the vegetarian raw-food diet. The life-extensionists and raw–foodists, Dr. Souren Arakelyan of Moscow, Russia, and Dr. Norman Walker, who lived to the age of 109, gave me examples to follow. I am trying now to include more raw vital plant foods and reduce the cooking and eating of animal products. I am not totally converted to a raw-foodist yet, but I am in the transition period now. Following is the recipe for the green and red vegetable salad that I eat every day:

Green & Red Salad	
	Yield: 1 portion
1. Redishes (2 pieces)	6. Kale (3 oz)
2. Red Onion (1/8 of a medium bulb)	7. Avocado (1/2 of a piece)
	8. Olive Oil (1 tablespoon)
3. Cranberries (1 oz)	9. Bragg Liquid Aminos
4. Alfalfa sprouts (1 oz)	(1 teaspoon)
5. Spinach (1 oz)	10. Soy Sauce (1 teaspoon)

1. Chop vegetables into small pieces.

2. Put into salad bowl; add soy sauce, Bragg Liquid Aminos, and olive oil; blend well.

This salad is tasteful and very nutritious and satisfying; however, after 2 hours, I feel real hunger again.

Eating Right

If we fall sick, we go to a doctor who is an expert in medical knowledge. He/She prescribes the drugs, which he/she, as a professional, knows will help us fight the sickness. But even having received this highly professional prescription, we are often concerned about drugs, whether they are right or not. We also worry about their side effects, which are predictable if our doctor gave the right prescription, or if it can cause adverse effects if he/she made a mistake. Nowadays, many people realize that food can cure us like a drug, the so-called "pharmacy foods," or it can be harmful to our health. Usually people know next to nothing about chemical reactions of particular foods in their bodies and, if there is no stomach pain or discomfort, they rely mostly on their likes and dislikes. However, if we were starving, we would rush to eat anything that first came to us, even if the food were among our dislikes. "Our flesh is a fool," said Dr. Paul Bragg.

Who can give us advice about diet and proper food? Doctors definitely can't because their business is drugs, not diets. Nutritionists are the professionals in the field of food; they are the people trained to know about diets. But we also cannot expect to hear from nutritionists all we need to know. They surely know about the nutritional value of proteins, carbohydrates, and fats; about enzymes; and about vitamin and mineral supplements--but we need much more than that. Do they know about diets for different blood types, metabolic types, Yin-Yang types, and horoscope types; about food combination, diuretics, gas-forming foods, and the heating or cooling properties of food? Definitely they do not. Then what are we supposed to do?

The only way is to become a nutritionist yourself, to design your own unique diet. Actually, our diets are designed already for us with our constitutional type, blood type, metabolic type, Yin-Yang type, and horoscope type. We can't choose a proper diet because it has already been chosen for us by our genes, nationality, geography, and the culture to which we belong. Our choice is to know about our unique biochemical individuality and to adjust the diet to our type and specific needs. This book gives you some useful information both about yourself and your proper diet. It encourages you to undertake a research study in which the life-long subject is you. The investment of your time and money in this project undoubtedly will be rewarded with healthier and longer years.

Let me share with you a few more considerations, the first of which is about how much we depend on food. The major idea is that we can have more or less freedom with food depending on the level of vibrations with which we live. The higher level our consciousness is, the more freedom we have with regard to food. People who live mostly on a physical level (i.e., the lower chakras) need to feed their body with the full set of macro- and micronutrients. Biological transmutation of elements in their body does not take place--they need to take all elements with food. Any lack in a specific nutrient, vitamin, or mineral in their diet puts them into deficiency. On the other hand, people who operate on the upper level of consciousness (i.e., the upper chakras)--those who are deeply devoted to religious beliefs, occupied with ideas, involved with mental and spiritual activities--are less dependent on food. The thermonuclear reactors of their cells work with high capacities and the biological transmutation of chemical elements is happening in their body. They can live with limited food, both in diversity and in amount, just on bread or Holy Communion. Their upper chakras are more open and they can receive the cosmic energies from the universe--to the extent that they do not need food at all, like the non-eating people and saints.

The next consideration for discussion is the taste of food. People prefer tasteful food, and gratifying their palate is a big motivation in life for many. The taste in food is often achieved with salt, spices, and additives that are not always good for health, and are even harmful in excess. The question is, what is food for--to maintain health and sustain life, or for pleasure? But remember the Balzacian "shagreen skin," we have to pay for any pleasure that comes from outside. Many centenarians are reputed to have no likes and dislikes in food; this is a good lesson. I do not advocate for tasteless food, but I choose the healthy taste enhancers such as gomashio (i.e., eight parts of sesame seed powder and one part of sea salt blend), seaweed (i.e., wakame, kombu, and hijiki), dried parsley and dill, sour cream, pickles, umeboshi (i.e., pickled plums), and others.

Food has a nutritional value, taste, and smell, but also an invisible emanation--an aura. In its subtle level, food has magical qualities to fix the emotional and mental states that we are in when we eat. The advice about skipping a meal if a person is upset means to avoid this negative state to be consolidated on a subtle energy level.

Our thoughts while having a meal affect both physical processes of body chemistry and unconsciousness. For instance, if we think about our problems, losses, or failures during a meal, they will be fastened in our memory and the possibility that they will return to our mind during the next lunch or dinner is increased. Therefore, thought control during mealtime is even more important than at any other time. The best thought pattern when we eat is to think gratefully about the people who grew, harvested, and prepared the food. If you eat bread, imagine a wheat field and the people who harvest, mill, and bake the bread.

It is better to start each meal with a prayer, sending thanks to God for giving us our daily bread. Food must be beautifully served on the table. Use your best plates for your meal, with the silver spoons, forks, and knives; silver kills any bacteria and germs. If you have fruit to eat, eat it first, on an empty stomach. Drinking juices or tea before ingesting food increases the flow of saliva and pancreas and stomach secretions. Raw green salads also must be eaten before cooked food because they provide the enzymes necessary for proper digestion.

Thorough chewing, at least thirty times for each mouthful, is absolutely necessary for good health and longevity. If the food contains little water or is dry, it is better to have small sips of water with it. Try to avoid desserts after the meal. If you have a craving for them, eat them as a separate meal. As a rule, desserts combine badly with the proteins and fats in your food. To spare your stomach, try to avoid drinking ice water or drinks after food. After your meal, walk at least 100 yards for better digestion; then brush and floss your teeth. Do not snack between meals.

Leftovers

Although it may sound wasteful from the ecological and home economy standpoints, never eat leftovers because they promote the growth of yeast. It is better for your health to throw them away than to store them in the refrigerator. If you don't get rid of them, they will somehow find their way to your stomach. Long-living people in Abkhasia traditionally do not eat leftovers; food is prepared and eaten the same day. No one would think of serving warmed-over food to a guest, even if it had been cooked only a few hours earlier. Most Abkhasians shun day-old food as not healthful, and even poor families dispose of uneaten food by giving it to the animals, according to an American researcher.

The gypsy people who live in Romania (about 460,000 people), Albania, and the southern part of Ukraine also avoid eating leftovers. I remember the time I came across a gypsy woman in the Rostov region of Russia. She was my neighbor on the long bus ride and we talked about fortune-telling, which is a quite common means of earning money among gypsies. She mentioned her grandmother, who was keen in fortune-telling and was 103 years old. Her abilities were so great that she was even able to foretell the name of a strange client, but she needed to look into magic books, as my bus neighbor portrayed. I was curious to know the secret of her grandmother's longevity and asked about her eating habits. "Gypsies never eat leftovers, eat many cooked vegetables, and drink plenty of tea," she said. In their nomadic life, they do not use refrigerators and, therefore, eat just freshly cooked food.

The previous food-intake discussion allows us to draw the following conclusions:

• The calorie content of food profoundly affects longevity, which is the greatest if the daily calorie intake ranges from 1,000 to 1,600 kcal. *Calorie rule*: 10 kcal per day per pound of standard body weight

• Protein, although an important component of food, is necessary for the body in very small amounts. The efficiency of its utilization is low. Consumed in excess, protein takes most of the body's energy for its assimilation, toxifies the system with its residue, causes a host of degenerative diseases, accelerates aging, and shortens life. Calories from protein must comprise about 5 percent of the daily value. *Protein rule*: 0.2 gram per day per pound of standard body weight

• Carbohydrates are the best fuel for the body, and the efficiency of their utilization is the highest. They do not leave any residue; rather, the end product of their metabolism is water and carbon dioxide, two extremely good substances for the body. The diets of long-living people consist mostly of carbohydrates, and so must your diet. Calories from carbohydrates must comprise 65 to 70 percent of your daily calorie intake.

• Fats are absolutely necessary for numerous body functions and as a source of energy. Compared with carbohydrates, they require a much larger amount of oxygen for their metabolism, which is accompanied by free radicals that are hazardous to our health and longevity. The efficiency of fat utilization is lower than that of carbohydrates, too. Calories from fats must comprise 25 to 30 percent of your daily calorie intake. The best fats are from plant sources, such as olive oil, avocado, olives, nuts, and seeds.

• A raw-food diet supplies the body with the live, enzyme-rich, highest-quality nutrients; allows the reduction of calorie intake; and significantly promotes longevity. Raw food is essential for each body and blood type, but especially for people with blood type A. Type A's may dramatically improve their health and achieve their longevity goals by including 80 percent or more raw food in their diet. Raw fruits and vegetables and their juices, sprouted grains, beans, and lentils are alkaline-forming foods, which must comprise about 80 percent of the blood type A's diet. Acid-forming foods such as meat, fish, eggs, dairy products, animal fats, sugar, and refined starch must not exceed 20 percent.

• Antioxidant-rich fruits, vegetables, and teas must be included in your diet. Green and black tea, blueberries, strawberries, cranberries, plums, oranges, red grapes, kiwi, pink grapefruit, garlic, kale, spinach, Brussels sprouts, alfalfa sprouts, broccoli florets, beets, red bell peppers, and onions all have a high antioxidant capacity.

• Food combining is the means to achieve optimal nutrition, which is essential for blood type A's and people with weak digestion. Green leafy vegetables comprise the only group that combines well with protein, carbohydrates, and fat.

18

TEN DAYS WITH THE CHINESE MYSTERY, XU FANG

Xu Fang, thirty-one, of China has not eaten in the last thirteen years. The December 1996 issue of the Japanese magazine *Borderland*, based on a report by Pung Chung, published an article (in Japanese) about her mysterious ability to stay healthy without food for nine years (at the time of publication). Fuji TV of Japan showed her in its program after the TV team stayed with her for three days, in an attempt to prove whether or not she eats. The Chinese best-selling author, Ka Un Ro, wrote about her in a few of his books. I first heard about Xu Fang from a Japanese family, Jiro and Masako Tokawa, a retired noble couple who invited me to stay in their home for two months at the beginning of 1998. They helped me get in touch with Fuji TV and Mr. Shirakawa sent me an article and videotape about Xu Fang.

After having learned more about Xu Fang from these materials, I was eager to meet a living, non-eating human being. There are cases in history in which a few people, most deeply religious, abstained from food for years and even decades. Paramahansa Yogananda interviewed two of them--Theresa Neumann of Germany and Giri Bala of India--and wrote about them in his book, *Autobiography of a Yogi*. However, these non-eaters were no longer alive; therefore, I was very excited to meet with Xu Fang. Mr. Shirakawa from Fuji TV gave me Xu Fang's fax number and I sent her a letter with general information about myself. I also explained that I am conducting research about long-living people and requested a meeting with her. She promptly replied in a fax letter, dated February 19, 1998, and quoted as follows:

> Valery Mamonov,
> Meeting with you is my pleasure. I hope to learn from your research for many people's high quality life. I'm sorry I just speak a little English and Japanese. Welcome to China.
> Xu Fang

I was very happy to receive this letter. I started preparations for a visit, acquiring a Chinese visa and buying an airplane ticket to Beijing. In the article I read about Xu Fang, it stated that she does not eat, yet she likes to smell apples. As a gift, I wanted to bring her Japanese apples. There were very beautiful apples in Tokyo, but in the beginning of March many types of apples, harvested about a half-year ago, had already lost most of their fragrance. Jiro Tokawa went with me to a specialty shop, whose owner is an expert on apples. He explained that there is only one kind that still maintains a distinct smell. He ordered a few of those apples and in a couple of days they were delivered to me. They were green in color, quite big, and smelled very nice.

I exchanged faxes with the mother of Xu Fang's boyfriend, Mrs. Huo Huiying, who lives in Shanghai and who helped me arrange my meeting with Xu Fang. She booked me a good, inexpensive hotel and informed me that Xu Fang and her friends would meet me at the airport on my arrival in Beijing.

Arrival; March 6, 1998; Friday

My flight was quite late, not arriving until about 9 p.m., and I worried that this was too late for Xu Fang to come to the airport. I expected her and perhaps one of her friends, but I was surprised to find six people awaiting me: Xu Fang; her younger sister Xu Fung; Ryu Sin Tyu, a researcher who has been studying Xu Fang; his wife; their friend; and the driver. I greeted them and thanked them for coming to meet me.

In the car on the way to Beijing, I sat beside Xu Fang. She was wearing white jeans and a white jacket, looking slim and pretty. Her sister and Ryu were sitting in front of us and his wife and their friend were behind us. Xu Fang's sister graduated from the Russian University and is fluent in Russian. She now works with Russians in an export-import company and they call her by a Russian name, Nadya. She assisted us as an interpreter. Ryu asked me about my work and I told him about my research on life extension. Speaking about extraordinary people and cases, they mentioned a Chinese woman who died long ago, but her body remains fresh, without any signs of decay. They said that if I were interested, they would show me the body. Nadya also told me that recently Xu Fang started to eat a little--an ice cream once a week or so. The reason was that she just wants to be like others.

After about a half-hour drive, we arrived at the hotel and Xu Fang signed the guest register for me in Chinese. We gathered in my room and talked for about a half-hour. First, Xu Fang asked me the purpose of my visit. I told her I did not come to verify whether or not she eats; rather, I came to meet her, talk to her, and write about her. I told her my interest in her is purely private, and nobody supports me. I also hoped that the results of my research on long-living people might be interesting to Xu Fang and her friends. "If so, I'll be feeling more relaxed," said Xu Fang.

I had some souvenirs from Japan that I gave to Xu Fang and the others: the apples, konnyaku jelly, umeboshi (pickled plums), and an electronic English-Japanese dictionary (speaking edition). She smelled an apple and said it was good. The researcher, Dr. Ryu, said there is another Chinese woman who has eaten nothing for a long time. He also mentioned that he included some data about Xu Fang in his two books and that he would show them to me next time. He also compiled an entire book about her, but it is not published yet. I asked whether there were English publications about her--they replied no.

I touched Xu Fang's hand; it was warm--warmer than mine. Her sister's hand was similarly warm, and they said that all their family has warm hands. As Nadya said, Xu Fang does not wear many warm clothes in winter--she does not feel the cold much. Explaining her body warmth, Dr. Ryu said that the source of her energy is in her kindness. Trying to find a possible physiological explanation, I asked about her rate of breathing. Dr. Ryu replied that she does not need to breathe at all! But she was definitely breathing and, seeing my surprised expression, Dr. Ryu said that she can breathe with her skin. I mentioned my alternate dry fasting, when I lost about 18 pounds (8 kilograms) of my weight. He said that if I continued the fast longer, I could probably increase my weight again, after the primary loss of it. To fast for a long time, I must learn to breathe through my skin, he added.

No food, now no air--it's a real mystery. What about water? She drinks some water when she is out with her friends. Sometimes, especially when it rains, she goes without water for days. She drinks more water when she stays in Beijing, where the air is dry, and in the summer when it is hot. However, in Shanghai--with its humid air--she drinks a little and sometimes not at all. She occasionally drinks mineral water too. Her blood type is A; her sister's is B. I showed her the chart of foods for blood type A, in which cola is listed as a drink to avoid; she said she feels bad after drinking cola.

Dr. Ryu, his wife, and their friend left around 11 p.m., but Xu Fang and her sister stayed that night at the hotel, in the room next to mine. So, the two sisters and I continued to talk until midnight. It was time to sleep and we talked about dreams for a while. Xu Fang dreamt until the age of eighteen, when she was still eating. However, since her non-eating state began, she cannot recall her dreams. Perhaps Xu Fang's non-dreaming is a way to not expend the energy that is necessary for her daily activities. Nadya said she had a dream the night before that water burst out of the ground like a fountain. I later found in the *Encyclopedia of Dreams* under the word "fountain" that if a young woman sees a sparkling fountain in the moonlight, it signifies ill-advised pleasure that may result in a desertion. I regret that I did not warn her then about a possible disappointment, but did she see her fountain in the moonlight? Next time I meet Nadya, I'll ask her.

Xu Fang likes to meditate and in her meditations she sees Buddha in her third-eye region. She was never taught about Buddha because her parents are communists and the children were brought up in the atheistic way. After one year in her non-eating state, she began to tell her two sisters and brother about Buddha and God. She was enthusiastic when I mentioned exercises that I wanted to exchange with her. I proposed to take photographs of her exercising and to put them in my book; she agreed. We all said good night and the sisters went to their room.

First Day; March 7; Saturday

In the morning, Xu Fang and her sister came to my room. After a few minutes, Nadya said, "See you later," and went to her job. Xu Fang told me that she wanted to introduce me to her friends. We took a taxi and, after 15 minutes, arrived at her office, a small one-room apartment that she was renting in the Chinese Academy of Culture building. This apartment is her office as well as where she lives with her boyfriend and business companion, twenty-nine-year-old Le Jun Luo.

When we arrived, there were five people waiting for us: her boyfriend Luo and a family--Yue Hui Xiang, his wife Wei Bo Sieng, their daughter Yue Xin, and her husband Lu Huan. After brief greetings, they said everyone was hungry, so we went to a nearby restaurant for lunch. It was served in a separate room where we sat around a big round table with a rotating part made of glass, the type I have seen in many eateries in Singapore. Three or four waitresses served the food for us. The number of dishes was enormous: fried meat, duck, and tofu; steamed carp fish; fish-head soup; many kinds of stewed and fried vegetables; and rice. Everything was delicious, but Xu Fang drank only a small cup of leaf tea--a type of green tea, light yellow in color.

Communication among the group was difficult because I do not speak Chinese and only Xu Fang could speak a word in English. She had a hard time interpreting among her friends and me. From what I could understand, some of them worked for the military and the younger girl occasionally helped Xu Fang in her business of designing and selling fashion garments.

All the members of this family were also her spiritual followers. They came to Xu Fang's place to study the teachings of Buddha. They usually prayed before a small Buddha statue that had been placed on the windowsill because of the lack of space. Near the statue of Buddha were oranges and apples, including one that I brought from Japan. Xu Fang and Luo were preparing to move from Beijing to Shanghai, where his parents live. Their small living room/office with a computer in one corner was overloaded with clothes piled everywhere. Her friends perceived Xu Fang as above ordinary people--like a goddess--and they worshipped a picture of her placed on the piano in the room. Xu Fang told me that she plays the piano a little.

Regarding the Japanese apples, Xu Fang told me that Nadya ate three of them and liked them very much. The two remaining apples she brought to her office and Luo ate one of them. Xu Fang said they had a dispute about the apple smell. She claimed that the Japanese apples smell better than domestic ones, but Luo--being a patriot of his country--insisted that Chinese apples smell better.

Xu Fang's friends became interested in Traditional Chinese Medicine, learning it from her. When we went back to her office after lunch, Wei Bo Sieng, fifty-three, touched both of my hands at the thumbs--exactly at the wrist pits--and told me that my blood pressure is low, not high. She was correct--my blood pressure has always been a little lower than normal. Then she examined the first and second joints of my thumbs. She discovered a small lump on the first joint of my left thumb, then pointed to my left knee and said there is a problem with it. She was right again: my left knee cracks when I stand up--a consequence of my left leg being broken twenty years ago and having my knee in a fixed position in a plaster cast for about five months. Afterwards, I easily found this lump myself.

I was curious to compare the heart rates of Xu Fang and her friends. First, I checked Xu Fang's pulse using a pulse monitor that I brought from Japan; it was 68 to 72 beats/minute in a sitting position. Xu Fang said that usually her heart rate is 58 to 60, but if she sleeps less than her usual 6 to 7 hours, it increases to 70. Wei Bo Sieng's heart rate was 77, her husband's was 82, their daughter's was the highest at 86, and their son-in-law's was 76. My own heart rate was 75.

The family of four soon left and we three--Xu Fang, Luo, and myself-- remained in their room until dinner. Xu Fang told me that Luo wants to learn how to meditate and she asked me to teach him. As a preparation to meditation, I first showed him six acupressure points on the head, which I had learned from the book, *Bring Back Health and Youth*, by Mirzakarim Norbekov and Larisa Fotina. The six points are as follows:

1. One point on the forehead, between the eyebrows ("third eye")
2. A pair of points on both sides at the wings of the nose
3. One point on the middle line between the lower lip and the chin
4. A pair of points at the hollows of both temples
5. Three points on the neck, a little higher than the hairline: one at the middle line and the other two about 1 inch from it on both sides
6. A pair of points between the ear canal and the jaw joints

These points should be pressed with the cushions of the middle fingers or thumbs twenty to twenty-five times each. Next is a massage of the ears with five kinds of pulling and turning movements: down, up, backward, clockwise, and counterclockwise. Each movement should be repeated twenty to twenty- five times. Next, I suggested that Luo proceed with the following two breathing exercises:

1. Diaphragm breathing for 5 minutes using this sequence: inhale (4 seconds), exhale (4 seconds), and hold breath (8 seconds).
2. Sitting in a comfortable position, put hands on the knees with palms facing up. Imagine a cool sensation in the palms while inhaling and a warm sensation while exhaling. This breathing exercise also should be repeated for 5 minutes.

For his meditation, I proposed the following seven themes on which Luo could meditate:

1. Candle flame (12 minutes): 1 minute to see a flame with open eyes; 1 minute with closed eyes trying to visualize the image of the flame on the screen in the forehead region, seeing with the mind
2. Yin-Yang mandala (12 minutes): in the same order, alternating open and closed eyes for 1 minute
3. Buddha statue (12 minutes)
4. Travel inside the body (12 minutes): imagine visiting stomach and digestive tract, heart, liver, kidneys, and so on

5. Pictures of his parents (12 minutes)

6. Picture of Xu Fang (30 minutes)

7. Self-treatment with imagery of his health concern--the growth on his right wrist, about 15 millimeters in diameter (30 minutes): he should imagine that with each exhale going through this growth, it becomes smaller and smaller.

I also suggested that he apply Xu Fang's urine to the growth on his hand. He laughed a lot at my suggestion; Xu Fang was also excited when we talked about her urine. I explained that because she is so special and is close to God, I believed that her urine is a medicine. She said that Traditional Chinese Medicine uses urine as a remedy, and she had heard that in Japan some people drink it. I had heard about that too, in Japan and in Russia.

We did a meditation for about a half–hour. Xu Fang said that when she meditates with the Yin-Yang mandala, she sees with her inner sight the curling movement in her forehead. Luo said he felt very good after our meditation and thanked me for teaching him to meditate.

It was evening already and both Luo and I felt hungry, but not Xu Fang-- she has not felt hungry in the last ten years. We took a taxi and went to a restaurant near my hotel. In the taxi, Luo sat in the front seat beside the driver, and Xu Fang and I sat in the back seat. I asked her about cutting her fingernails; she cuts them twice a month, about 2 millimeters. The shape of her nails is quite long, narrow, and rounded, and they are not manicured; she likes them cut short. At the restaurant, Luo ordered three kinds of dumplings stuffed with meat and vegetables, steamed peanuts, combu (thick seaweed) with steamed carrots, and stewed green vegetables.

I ordered mutton with celery and coffee. After we started to eat, I suffered from tooth pain while eating the combu. Luo was eating very fast, putting the dumplings on a small plate with dressing, a kind of thin soy sauce. Xu Fang drank a small cup of leaf tea, very thin--perhaps common in all Chinese restaurants. She took a small piece of steamed carrot with chopsticks, bit off half of it, chewed a few times, and then spit it out without swallowing. Luo finished eating very soon, but I ate very slowly as always, and they patiently waited for me finish the meal.

Then we talked for some time and I showed them the sketches of the Ayurvedic, Yin-Yang, chakra, and other profiles that I had developed to assess the personality of an individual. On the chakra profile, there was a line for my profile, and I drew in the profile of Xu Fang as I thought it might be. It is shown in Figure 12-3 in the chapter entitled *Chakra System*.

After dinner, they showed me Ti An Men Square, which was about a 1-hour walk to get there. It was not cold but quite cool, and we walked fast. Because of the meeting of the Chinese Communist Party leaders currently being held in Beijing, there were many security guards standing on the streets and in the underground passes. In front of the big portrait of Mao Tse-tung, we took a few photographs of Xu Fang and me. It was around 10 p.m. and we took a taxi to my hotel. In spite of the late hour and a quite active day, Xu Fang did not seem at all tired.

Second Day; March 8; Sunday

It was a sunny morning when I woke up at 7 a.m.; I felt well rested and did a few yoga exercises. Xu Fang and Luo showed up 2 hours later and brought apples, bananas, raisin bread, and soymilk for me.

Luo complained about back strain, so I showed Xu Fang how she could massage his back with her feet. We put a woolen blanket on the floor and Luo laid flat on it; Xu Fang stepped on his buttocks first, then on his middle and upper back. I asked her to do it for me as well and she did (Figure 18-1, see p. 271).

She was interested in the exercises and I showed them my morning yoga set. She had also started doing them and repeated after me the "Greeting the Sun," rocking on the back, and shoulder-stand exercises. She tried to do the buttocks-walk exercise as well, but her jeans were not appropriate for it. She also practices some yoga exercises, and when she demonstrated the headstand pose, it was perfect.

Growing fingernails and hair and dead skin cells are all made of protein that she, like everyone else, loses every day. Trying to assess how rapidly her nails grow, I asked whether she would allow me to take photographs of her fingernails and toenails now and before my departure. She replied it would be better to photograph them tomorrow, after she polishes them. She wanted everything on her body to look attractive in the pictures.

Luo said he already had his breakfast, so I ate the apple, bananas, and bread for my breakfast, and then we left for the Imperial Palace. In the taxi, I asked Xu Fang how she feels in the polluted environment in Beijing. She replied, "It's bad. Sometimes I feel pain in my lungs. In Shanghai, the air is not so bad and I feel better there." Because of the contaminated air in Beijing, the skin on her face itches sometimes; she showed me an irritation on her right cheek. I gave her some *Oronineh*, a Japanese ointment, and she applied it to the spot. Her hair was not oily, just normal, but I noticed a few tiny scales of dandruff on her head. She said that she usually has more dandruff when staying in Beijing, because the air is dry. She does not typically feel thirsty and forgets to drink water. Because the dry air in Beijing is bad for her skin, Luo reminds her to drink a glass of warm water when she gets up. She washes her hair only about twice a week. A few times a day, she combs her long straight hair quite vigorously, but I did not notice any loose hairs on her comb; her hair is strong.

The Imperial Palace is spread over a vast area and gives an absolutely great impression, with several majestic palaces of the Chinese emperors from 1421 to 1911, wide squares, and long gentle stairways. The walled area is called the "Forbidden City" because entry into it was forbidden to all except the imperial family and its servants. At the square near every big palace, there are copper sculptures of turtles and cranes, the symbols of eternity. It was sunny Sunday morning and many visitors came to the Imperial Palace. I took a picture of Luo and Xu Fang with the historical tree at the background (Figure 18-2, see p. 271).

Luo took some pictures of Xu Fang and me too. We were posing on the broad squares with the palaces in the background, near the sculptures. We stood in the corner with a few people beside us, but in a very crowded space with numerous people in sight. I saw the many different nationalities of the Chinese people in the faces of the folks from distant provinces, who came for sightseeing at the Imperial Palace today. Xu Fang was excited while having her picture taken, and tried to be as tall as I am, sometimes standing on her tiptoes.

After the Imperial Palace, we went to Ti An Men Square and walked among people launching kites in the sky. It was quite bright from the sun and I offered my sunglasses to Xu Fang, but she refused. When we sat to rest for a while, she mentioned Ka Un Ro, a best-selling author in China, who wrote about her in some of his books. She said that although he is now famous, many criticize him because he secretly tapes what people say in the buses, on the streets, and in other public places. He thus reveals the peoples' concerns and writes about them in his books, but his method is not good, she judged.

On a huge panoramic painting installed at one corner of Ti An Men Square, the people of major nationalities of China were depicted. I was particularly interested in the "old" man with a white beard but also with a young face and rosy cheeks--perhaps a representative of one of the Silk Road nationalities. Xu Fang warned me that I am not supposed to stop at this place, glancing toward the security guards equipped with portable phones, standing here and there. The great meeting was continuing and security was tight, all too familiar to me after forty-nine years of living in Communist Russia. I felt ashamed for being a cause of possible trouble, apologized, and hurried after them. Actually, she was not afraid at all, and two or three times she silently indicated to me the guards dressed in ordinary clothes.

We walked for about 1 kilometer, then took a taxi and went to my hotel. I was suffering from an overfilled bladder and rushed into the bathroom in the hotel. After a while, we went out to have lunch in a nearby restaurant. This time Luo ordered mabodofu (i.e., tofu with ground meat stewed in a hot sauce) and stewed vegetables for himself, and fish and shrimp for me. We each also ate two small bowls of rice, but again, Xu Fang just drank leaf tea. She told me that Luo does not eat meat because he wants his third eye to be opened, although it seemed to me that last night he had eaten dumplings stuffed with meat. Perhaps those he ate were stuffed only with vegetables.

Xu Fang helped him pick up with chopsticks the pieces of tofu, clean of meat, and put them on top of his rice. She put a few pieces on my plate, too, although I also ate the ground meat. The small fried pieces of fish had lots of bones and were difficult to eat. I usually finish everything on my plate, but this time half of the fish was left. The shrimp was served on a small plate; it was one medium-size shrimp in a red sauce and decorated with sprigs of parsley. It looked so nice, especially the shrimp, that we took a picture of our lunch!

There was a small fruit market on the street and I was curious to know how much the pineapples, pears, and kiwis cost--they were cheap, 2 yuan for pineapple. Xu Fang bought seven pears for me for 7 yuan; however, Luo, who had just joined us, did not approve and he argued with the vendor. I wanted to buy some kiwi too but he stopped me. Later, when we were back at my hotel, he went to the market alone and bought kiwi. He wanted to save my money because as soon as the vendors see a foreigner, they raise the price.

When Luo was out at the market, Xu Fang sat in the room and talked with her sister Nadya using her cellular phone. I brushed my teeth and when I went back in the room, I found her in tears after she finished talking to her sister. I asked her what happened, but she replied that she felt tired. I attributed her tiredness to the difficulties of communicating in English with me. I felt sorry that I could not speak Chinese and had put this burden on her. Later, I understood that she had major problems with her sisters. She was upset that time because of what was said between them.

Luo came back and they soon went back to their place, telling me that Xu Fang would come tomorrow at 10 a.m. Luo had to work tomorrow, and when we said good bye in the corridor, they seemed glad to be going home. I thought they both were tired, especially Xu Fang, having the stress of speaking to me in English all day long.

Third Day; March 9; Monday

I was making notes when Xu Fang knocked at the door; she came with her girlfriend Lung Lung, a clothing designer. They wanted to do yoga exercises so we started with the rocking on the back exercise. Xu Fang brought pink trousers and felt comfortable exercising in them. We did the "Greeting of the Sun," boat pose, cobra, and the other exercises from my morning program. Then we did stretching, including the alternate leg-pull and knee bends as a preparation for the padmasana pose. Lung Lung was slim with a good shape and beautiful legs. She seemed to be a little out of breath and needed to rest after some of the exercises, but Xu Fang showed no sign of being tired at all. I also showed them finger massage and bends, and then we meditated for 15 minutes.

As a theme for meditation, I suggested that they imagine their favorite flowers placed on one line going from the heart to the bottom of the spine. Xu Fang said that her favorite flowers are lotuses; to confirm this, Lung Lung showed them to me on a postcard. Lung Lung finished meditating first; then I opened my eyes. Xu Fang was sitting in the padmasana pose with her eyes closed, still in meditation.

She was breathing shallowly with her chest slightly moving up and down. The collar of her shirt was rising and falling against her neck. I took Lung Lung's watch with a second hand and counted the number of her breaths per minute. Her breathing rate in three measurements was 21, 20, and 21 per minute. I was surprised to find that it was more rapid than the usual rate of 12 to 15 times a minute for an average person; Dr. Ryu had said her respiration rate is slower than that of ordinary people. She had been sitting calmly for 20 minutes and still her breathing rate was faster. My observation seemed to contradict Dr. Ryu's data.

After exercises and meditation, we changed our clothes and each of us had a drink. Xu Fang brought for me a 1-liter bottle of Yellow Peach Nectar. Its label stated, "Yellow peach nectar provides plenty of fruit fiber, gelatin, and other fruit nutrition." Its ingredients included water, yellow peach pulp, aspartame, and sorbic acid. I poured out about three-quarters of a 150-milliliter cup of it for Xu Fang and she drank it; I estimated it to be about 70 kcal. We were going to visit Dr. Rungi, Xu Fang's friend; as a souvenir from Japan, I took for him the nori (dried seaweed) and umeboshi (pickled plums). Xu Fang and Lung Lung each tasted an umeboshi and ate them up, although they are very sour and are usually eaten with rice in Japan. I took the pit from the umeboshi that Xu Fang had eaten as a souvenir for myself.

We went in Lung Lung's car and Xu Fang sat in the back seat beside me. During the 40-minute drive, the girls spoke non-stop in Chinese about the financial problems that Xu Fang has with her sister Nadya and other relatives, as she told me later. She told me more than once, "My sisters, my brother, my father, my mother--they are bad. I lost lots of money because of Nadya and my brother last year, and my apartment is shrinking smaller and smaller. I had a car but I sold it because of them. Now I want to move to Shanghai to be far away from them." About Luo and herself, she told me that they are "boyfriend and girlfriend."

On the way to Dr. Rungi's house, we stopped to have lunch in a classy restaurant, for the new rich Chinese, I guess. There was even an English-speaking waitress assisting me in choosing the dishes. We ordered soup with shrimp, steamed fish, fried noodles with meat, lotus seeds with celery, carrots (a rose made of carrots) and cucumbers, artificial crabmeat, and shrimp. Lung Lung was hungry and ate quickly; I ate slowly but a lot and was still only able to eat half of the big fish.

After lunch, we went to Dr. Rungi's apartment. He lives on the sixth floor of a building in a rather small three-room apartment. Dr. Guobulio Rungi is a practicing Traditional Chinese Medicine doctor; his diploma is displayed on the wall and he showed it to me with pride. A young woman, his assistant, helps him with his patients. The assistant took a photograph of the four of us, shown in Figure 18-3 (see p. 272).

Dr. Rungi is eighty-six years old but he is in great shape and looks twenty-five years younger. However, it was even more surprising to me to learn that Dr. Rungi was related to the imperial family–his older sister was an empress, the wife of the last Emperor of China. He showed us historical books with many pictures of him as a teenager and as a young man playing with the prince. He also showed us a videotape of an Australian TV program in which he acts as a guide at the Imperial Palace. When the civil war started in 1927 in China, he was in exile in Manchuria, and after WWII, in Japan for six years (1951-1957). He speaks fluent Japanese and we could communicate with him without problems. One of the books that he showed us was about the Dauer nationality, a Chinese national minority with only a hundred thousand people. Both he and Xu Fang belong to this nationality; he is the President and Xu Fang is the Vice President of the Assembly of Dauer Nationality.

I wanted to show a video about Xu Fang that I had brought from Japan but we were not able to watch it because the TV system in China is different. Dr. Rungi uses acupuncture in his practice and at the time of our visit, he had a patient in another room that he was treating with needles. The patient was a young man who happened to be a TV and video expert, so Dr. Rungi asked him to try to convert my videotape. He took the tape but was unable to convert it; after a few days, Dr. Rungi returned my copy to me.

We talked at length with Dr. Rungi and he asked me about my work. I showed him the Yin-Yang, Ayurvedic doshas, chakra, and other charts and the graph with calorie intake related to longevity that I developed for my book. He translated my explanations into Chinese for Xu Fang and Lung Lung. I asked him what was his idea on how Xu Fang can live without food; he said he did not know how it is possible. In return, he asked me my opinion about whether she is able to have children. As far as I knew, all women who had been in a non-eating state for a long time could not have children.

I expressed my hope that "theoretically" it would be possible for Xu Fang. Because her body temperature is maintained, all her vital organs function normally; and because she has protein loss (i.e., nails, hair, and dead skin cells), she must have the protein-synthesis mechanism too. I think she has the ability to utilize nitrogen from the air, as well as oxygen, to produce amino acids. My idea is that she also perfectly utilizes her dead body cells; they are not a waste expelled from her body as in ordinary people, but rather a building material and fuel for her body's metabolism. Oxygen in her body, together with its common role of burning fuel (dead cells) for energy, is also used in amino-acid synthesis, a function specifically in Xu Fang and other non-eating people. We need oxygen--it is vital for us--but it burns us alive, slowly and steadily. Actually, oxygen is our number–one killer, but it is friendlier to Xu Fang than to the rest of us. To prove this hypothesis, I wanted to know the contents of the air that Xu Fang exhales. Dr. Rungi said there is a hospital with American equipment for analyzing exhaled air. He had never heard of such a thing about oxygen and he was very surprised, but said he thought it sounded reasonable.

Dr. Rungi is interested in unusual phenomena in people and he showed us the picture of a young woman who is able to read Chinese characters sealed in a neighboring room. I also recalled a case of a Russian woman named Kulagina, who could read the words with her elbow while her eyes were covered with a blindfold. It is said that people with a perfectly opened "third eye" can do these things.

Because Dr. Rungi looks so young, I asked him what was his secret. He said he does nothing special for his own health, just keeps busy with his patients. He eats everything; sometimes he drinks strong Chinese rice wine (62% proof) and feels better than when he drinks ordinary grape wine.

We thanked Dr. Rungi for his warm hospitality and said good-bye. He came out of his apartment and saw us to the elevator. Lung Lung had other things to do and she went home. Xu Fang and I went to the McDonald's restaurant nearby to continue talking for a while. She still seemed upset about the problems with her family members.

The Chinese McDonald's looked like everywhere else, except that it was very cheap. I got a cheeseburger and hot chocolate for 3.8 yuan--about nine times cheaper than in Japan. Xu Fang had cold liquid ice cream and hot tea with milk. After we finished our drinks and food (me), she asked me to write the Japanese equivalents of simple English words: yes, no, good morning, good evening, right, wrong, good-bye, see you tomorrow, I am sorry. Then I asked her to write the same words in Chinese, both in characters and their spelling in English letters. She read the words in a loud voice so I could tape-record them. Then she tried to memorize the following children's poem, "Little Gray Mouse," that I taught her and which my granddaughter Liza likes very much:

> Little gray mouse, where is your house?
> I can show you my flat, if you don't tell the cat,
> My flat has no door; I live under the floor,
> I come out in the night and go back when it's light.

While we were having our English, Japanese, and Chinese lesson, two girls--university students--were sitting at the table next to ours and studying English. Xu Fang started talking to them, asking for explanations of certain words and phrases such as "up to you." It got quite late so we took a taxi and went to my hotel, where Nadya was already waiting for us. She had brought some food in plastic boxes: meat, fried potatoes, and noodles with sour cabbage. Nadya and I ate some of the food, but Xu Fang didn't eat or drink. Nadya wanted to stay overnight again in the hotel and she invited Xu Fang to stay with her. After some hesitation, Xu Fang decided to go home. She had complained about a stomachache after we left McDonald's and were in the taxi; however, before going home, she said she felt better.

Nadya stayed in my room until midnight and we talked a lot. She told me how the non-eating state of her older sister had started. When she was a teenager, Xu Fang ate a lot; she was the greatest eater of all four children in the family. She was well fed, even plump--she even got fat in her adolescence. Xu Fang started to attend Qigong lessons with her two other sisters. During their fourth lesson, Xu Fang had a vision of a woman (i.e., the Goddess of Mercy) who appeared between her and the Qigong teacher. I have already described this episode in the chapter entitled *Food Intake Control*; the point is that the vision of the woman also appeared to Xu Dung, Nadya's identical twin sister, but Nadya saw nothing. Her twin sister also did not eat for a few days, but then started to eat again; only Xu Fang continued to abstain from food.

When it all started with Xu Fang, her parents were very worried about her. In the first three days, they thought perhaps she had eaten too much of her favorite fish during a recent dinner. But when she continued to not eat, they suspected that something was wrong with their oldest daughter. They were very concerned and afraid that she would die because she lost weight and grew skinny. But she stayed alive, looked healthy, and was full of energy; gradually, they grew used to her new condition.

After a few months, still without food, Xu Fang gained weight again and even became fat. Xu Fang told me that when she is engaged in exercises like aerobic dancing or swimming, she gains weight, but if she does not exercise she loses weight--just the opposite of what usually happens to ordinary people. During the ten years (in 1998) that she has been in the non-eating state, her weight has fluctuated from 50 to 55 kilograms (110 to 120 pounds).

Although not eating, Xu Fang brushes her teeth; because of this, the Japanese Fuji TV team became suspicious that perhaps she eats secretly at night. Xu Fang told me that she brushes her teeth after she drinks cola or eats an ice cream. But on the days when she drinks just water, she does not brush her teeth. Her teeth are white and look good. According to Nadya, she and Xu Fang and their brother all have good teeth inherited from their father. The teeth of Xu Dung, Nadya's twin sister, are not so good and her teeth genes come perhaps from their mother.

After a few months in her non-eating condition, Xu Fang started talking about the previous lives of her sisters and other relatives. According to her, Nadya died in her former life at the age of seven, in order to be reborn as a twin with her sister. About herself, she said that she was a firebird and then a swan many, many lives ago. She also was able to foresee the future of people. Nadya's twin sister is married and has a three-year-old son, who is now staying with her parents. Before the child was born, Xu Dung asked Xu Fang about the sex of the child to come and she replied, "A boy."

Although not eating food, Xu Fang enjoyed the smell of apples and fresh bread. But after she smelled them, those foods seemed to lose their smell completely; the bread even became dry. It was a kind of game for her sisters and brother: they smelled the apples or bread before Xu Fang; after she smelled them, there usually was no smell left in them.

At first she was enthusiastic about teaching other people not to eat, but gradually her interests have changed. Now she thinks that more important than not eating is the state of mind. She also started to heal people. A woman had a huge belly due to water retention, but the water was released from her body after Xu Fang treated her. Another woman could not become pregnant for many years, but after Xu Fang's treatment, she gave birth to twin boys. Every year on the boys' birthday, this family visits her to say "thank you." However, as a consequence of healing, Xu Fang was losing her own energy and feeling bad herself, so her mother convinced her to stop healing. She seemed to acquire a cosmic knowledge and started to teach her sisters and brother about Buddha. Her father is a communist, although her mother is not, and the children had never heard about Buddha from their parents.

Interest in Xu Fang arose in Japan and in the United States. Last year, the Japanese TV invited her to visit Japan; most of the arrangements, including visas and tickets, were taken care of for her. People from the TV station were waiting at the airport in Tokyo for her and Nadya to arrive, but at the last moment, Xu Fang forgot to prepare one necessary document and the flight to Japan was cancelled. Also a Chinese American researcher invited Xu Fang to visit the United States. They started the preparations, but eventually gave up and postponed this visit as well.

Fourth Day; March 10; Tuesday

Although it was quite late when I went to bed last night, I woke up around 7 a.m. I feel good in the mornings these days, refreshed after a night's sleep even though I do not sleep much--about 6 to 6.5 hours. Is this the invigorating influence of Xu Fang? For breakfast, I had ginger tea, a banana, a pear, soymilk, and a roll.

Nadya knocked on my door at 11 a.m. while I was making notes. She had stayed overnight in the room next to mine and hurried to her job. I continued to make notes until Xu Fang arrived around 1 p.m. She looked pale and refused to drink the green tea that I offered her. She sat for a while and asked me whether I had already had my breakfast. I said yes, and then I asked her to teach me not to eat. "Some people can go without food, others cannot," she replied. Regarding myself, she said she wants to look in her third eye first, then she will tell me. She continued, saying that in some regions of China people couldn't live without food. She even drew a map of China and wrote the names of those provinces. About myself, she told me that I think too much--that is my biggest problem. Amazingly, it was the same thing that an eighty-two-year-old Japanese man told me. I was so surprised that I exclaimed, "Absolutely." "If you think less, you will feel better," she continued. "You even will be able to do the things that you could not do before." "How does one not think?" I asked. "Become a child," she replied. Again, I was amazed--Xu Fang told me similar words that another non-eating woman, Theresa Neumann of Germany, had heard when the voice of the Holy Spirit sounded in her head: "Always remain childlike and simple." Xu Fang continued, "You work on your book now, you are thinking and working too much, it is not good for you. Also, you are too concerned about your health and food; you would be better to take it easier," she added.

The two students we met last night called Xu Fang (she had given them her number) and asked her to bring me again; they wanted to speak with me in English. We took a taxi and met them at the McDonald's restaurant near Dr. Rungi's house. She called Dr. Rungi, but the videotape was not ready yet, so we postponed our second visit to him. This time, it was a white taxi and I noticed that the fare was more than 25 yuan--although yesterday, going from the same place to my hotel, it was only 15 yuan. I said nothing, but Xu Fang seemed to read my thoughts because she told me that the white taxi is bigger, with a higher roof, and is more expensive than the yellow taxi that we used before. Is Xu Fang able to read thoughts? I know people with channeling abilities who can read thoughts. My yoga teacher, Eugene Bazh, is even able to see thoughts, which he demonstrated for me. If so, I have to be careful with my thoughts so that I do not upset her, I told myself.

After we met the girls, they decided to show me the bookstore. On our way there we passed a market where they were selling live animals including cats, dogs, rabbits, and birds such as canaries and parrots. Xu Fang and the students were excited to see white kittens and tried to pet them. Xu Fang said Luo calls her "cat."

While walking toward the bookstore, I exchanged phrases with the girls about everything that was in sight. They were not as shy as they were yesterday and tried to speak in English too. As best as I could understand, they do not have many chances to speak English with foreigners. There were mostly Chinese books in the bookstore, and I saw one about longevity. Another book that was scheduled for publishing in six months had an advertising pamphlet. I bought the Oxford English-Chinese dictionary for myself. When we left the bookstore, it was about 5 p.m. and Xu Fang had some things to do. We did not have much time and we were obliged to part with these nice girls.

Xu Fang and I took a taxi and went to pay her taxes. We had an appointment with Dr. Ryu for tonight and, in the same taxi, we went to my hotel. When we arrived, Dr. Ryu was already waiting for us in the lobby. In a few minutes we were in my room and began talking with him. Dr. Ryu brought some materials related to Xu Fang and his research on the people who practice Qigong. First, he showed me the color brain-scan pictures of Xu Fang and alfa- wave records of her and other people. The scan pictures and α-waves of Xu Fang were different than those of other people, but this field was out of my scope. Shifting from neurophysiology to physiology, I wanted to clarify about the breathing rate. I wrote for Dr. Ryu on a sheet of paper that the breathing rate of ordinary people is 12 to 15 times per minute. I asked him again what was Xu Fang's breathing rate. His reply was 10 breaths per minute in her usual condition, 5 when she sleeps, and close to zero when she meditates. This was very different from the 20 to 21 breaths per minute that I counted yesterday when she sat quietly with closed eyes, although perhaps it wasn't her deepest meditation state. Anyway, this sounded somewhat strange.

Next, I asked him about the contents of the air she inhales. Again, I wrote down the contents of atmospheric air that comes into the lungs: 78% N_2, 21% O_2, 0.03% CO_2, and ~1% inert gases. Dr. Ryu's reply was ~0% O_2, which also sounded very strange to me. Nevertheless, we continued to discuss this matter and I asked about the contents of the air that she exhales; he replied that N_2 doesn't change, O_2 is 10%, and CO_2 is ~0%. My mind refused to understand these figures. He added, however, that they did not study her exhaled air in detail. He agreed with my opinion that O_2 is necessary for us but it kills us, and that many long-living people live high in the mountains with air that is thin in oxygen.

Dr. Ryu himself had been fasting since Saturday, the day after my arrival, and he had not yet decided how long his fast would last. Within these 3.5 days of fasting, he was just drinking water and he had lost 2 to 3 kilograms of his weight.

Nadya came to the hotel after work and helped us with interpreting. Xu Fang wanted a drink and had a cup of peach nectar, about 150 milliliters. Dr. Ryu showed me two of his books in Chinese, in which there is some data about Xu Fang; I bought them from him for 15 yuan each. He also showed me the December 20, 1996, issue of the Chinese journal *Human Body Science*, with his three papers in it. The graph of human brain power with the full range from dead to saint (i.e., near Buddha state) attracted me so much that I bought the journal from him, although it cost $20 (160 yuan). According to Dr. Ryu, the brain power of Xu Fang is about fifty times higher than that of ordinary people. She is in the middle of the graph, but ordinary people are one-fifth from its lower point.

Telling about my book, I showed Dr. Ryu the Yin-Yang and Ayurvedic doshas questionnaires and my chart linking calorie intake and longevity. He said that the chart was interesting, but I need ten thousand dots on it to find the proper relationship. I agreed that the data array for this chart is too small. Xu Fang commented that she was surprised about how much I know, and I was pleased to hear it from her. Because of the language barrier, I could not express what I know in our previous conversations.

Xu Fang went home by taxi and we three--Nadya, Dr. Ryu, and I--went to a nearby restaurant for dinner. Nadya said she was very hungry and ordered syabu-syabu, the Chinese style of a popular dish in Japan, with thick slices of frozen pig blood. Nadya and I ate a lot, but Dr. Ryu--because of his fast--just drank water. I had more opportunity to talk to Dr. Ryu and I asked him about the speed of blood in Xu Fang's capillaries. According to his test results, mentioned in the Japanese magazine *Borderland*, it is more rapid than in ordinary people. My question was whether it is due to thinner blood or broader capillaries. He said that the blood also flows through the walls of her blood vessels. He demonstrated this effect of permeability by pouring water on a paper napkin. He added that she is different from other people; her body and organs are absolutely different--again, it was beyond my understanding. He also told me that there is a Buddha statue in one of the temples, with two more statues of a small boy and a small girl in sitting poses in front of the Buddha. The girl's face looks very much like Xu Fang's when she was five years old.

After dinner, I said, "Thank you for coming and goodbye" to Dr. Ryu and he went home. Nadya and I went back to the hotel. She said she was too tired to go back to her place, which is far away and she preferred to stay in the hotel again.

Fifth Day; March 11; Wednesday

In the morning, Nadya helped me communicate with a clerk at the reception desk when I paid for the remaining five days of my stay in the hotel. Then she left for work; soon after, Xu Fang came to pick me up and we went to her office. She told me that Luo was angry with Dr. Ryu, who charged me "big money for his small book." I tried to explain to her that it was OK and I consider it as a small support for Dr. Ryu's research. Actually, I was somewhat surprised too, but Xu Fang and Luo's reaction was much more severe: "It is bad of Ryu," they said.

In the taxi on the way, Xu Fang complained to me, saying that the husband of Nadya's twin sister poisoned her and Luo one year ago. She was even in the hospital for a few days--blood came out of her gums and stomach, and she had a severe headache. Luo also suffered so much that Mrs. Huo Huiying, his mother, came from Shanghai because of their illness. The reason why they poisoned them is the money that Nadya and her sister took from her and Luo. They think that Luo has a lot of money, she added. Her relationship with Nadya was very friendly two years ago when the picture of them--smiling and embracing each other--had been taken. I saw this picture in the *Borderland* magazine. At the present time, she prefers to avoid speaking and staying with Nadya because she thinks it is dangerous; she is afraid that Nadya can hurt her. She continued that these three days, Nadya--although having an apartment--was staying in the hotel, paying 232 yuan ($29) per night, which was Xu Fang's money. Xu Fang pays 3,000 yuan ($375) a month to rent her office in Beijing, and she must move to Shanghai because she cannot afford to pay that much. Luo's parents have a big apartment in Shanghai, and they invited her to come and stay with them. This would significantly decrease her living and business expenses in Shanghai. She also said that because of the money issue, all her family is against her--but she loves them all.

Luo's family is ranked high in China and his uncle was a top Communist Party official--he was even placed in a mausoleum after his death. Mrs. Huo Huiying was a classmate of the daughter of Marshall Lin Byao, a former Minister of Defense in China; they even shared the same class desk.

Being concerned about my cold hands, I asked Xu Fang if she knew the reason. She replied that it is because of my weak kidneys. That was true, my urinary system does not work well. Remembering yesterday's question about whether she could teach me to not eat, she said no. "You do not belong to the people who can live without food, you are not prepared yet," she told me. "You have to eat, fasting is not good for your health," she added.

In the office, I met Luo again. He has been very friendly to me and treats me nicely, protecting my interests. He gave me the developed film and printed photographs. We looked through them and Xu Fang marked a few pictures to print some more copies of them. Luo and I were hungry and we went downstairs to have lunch in the restaurant on the first floor of the same building in which they live. Luo had rice and stewed vegetables with tofu. A big bowl of fish soup was ordered for me. It was tasteful, but had many small bones in the fish, and it took a long time for me to eat it. Luo was very quick with his meal and he went back to the office to work. Xu Fang sat beside me and waited for me to finish my lunch. I foolishly asked her whether the fish is good for my kidneys. She seemed to become angry with me for talking instead of concentrating on eating to quickly finish my lunch. She said, "I do not speak English," and silently read the English textbook. I hurried with my food because it was really not fair to keep her waiting. Also the restaurant closed at 2 p.m. and it was already 1:30. When we went back to her room, Luo was out and she sat at the computer--still angry with me, I thought. I was in a panic, feeling that I had spoiled everything and was expecting a complete failure.

Once again, however, I was wrong about her feelings. When Luo came back, she made a friendly suggestion that we go together to do the following errands:
• buy her clothes for yoga exercises in order to take pictures of her exercising
• copy the floppy disk for her
• distribute the advertisement sheets about selling her garments that they wanted to get rid of before moving to Shanghai
• go to the Shangri-la Hotel to see if there are any English books in its bookshop

In the clothing shop, she asked me what color shirt and pants would be better for exercises. She likes green, yellow and blue, but the shop was very small and there was not a big selection. From what we could see, I suggested a classic red and black combination: a red T-shirt with a black character on it and black pants; she agreed and we bought them. We also bought for her a dark-blue hair clip. Later I realized that black is bad for photographs because it hides all the folds and the details of movements are shaded. Luo did not approve of the T-shirt because its short sleeves did not cover her arms, which he thought were too thin to be revealed in pictures. After shopping, we went to the computer service company to copy the floppy disk. However, the person in charge said it could not be done any sooner than the day after tomorrow.

Next, we went to the shopping mall, and while we were walking there, Xu Fang said she wanted a drink of water. In the stall, there were a few kinds of cold drinks but no water. I bought an apple juice for myself, but she refused to buy any drink, saying that she likes hot drinks.

In the shopping mall, Xu Fang became excited. She distributed her ads among dozens of small shops that sell clothes. She explained the matter to some sellers or left the ads if the seller was not in sight.

When we were outside, we enjoyed the fresh air. It was quite hot in the basement where the shops were located; sweat appeared on my forehead. She agreed that it was hot, but no sweat was on her face. At one stall, I bought water for Xu Fang and a pineapple drink for myself; she took two small swallows.

Our last place to go was the Shangri-la Hotel where there is a bookshop for foreigners. On our way, we crossed a wide avenue using the bridge that arched over the road. The bridge had no stairs, just gentle slopes covered with Teflon. We passed the National Library, the bamboo garden, and then turned onto the street leading to the hotel. Although our destination was within walking distance, the street was full of cars and the air was so severely polluted in this rush hour that I was afraid Xu Fang would get sick after the 20-minute walk in the poisonous atmosphere. We took a taxi and arrived at the hotel in a few minutes. The atmosphere in this luxurious hotel was different than outside, with big vases of flowers and an air conditioner. A man was playing the piano in the restaurant. In the bookshop, there were just a few English books about sightseeing in Beijing, Qigong exercises, and martial arts, but they were so expensive that we gave up and bought nothing. I took a few pictures of Xu Fang standing in the middle of a huge round carpet, touching a huge bottle of wine displayed in the lobby.

It was time to go home, so we took a taxi and were in her office in 10 minutes. Luo waited for us for dinner and we went together to a nearby restaurant. It was the dinner hour, but the place was empty and we were the only patrons in the restaurant. The food was good as always, and we ate soup with tofu and shrimp, stewed vegetables, and rice. Again, Xu Fang drank only a little leaf tea.

After dinner, I insisted on going back alone to the hotel, but they would not allow me. We took a taxi and went to my hotel; then they went back to their office. I was feeling a little embarrassed to be causing many troubles for them. I thanked them for such nice treatment and paid for the taxi to the hotel and back to their office. Every time that Xu Fang--either alone or with Luo-- came to my hotel to pick me up, I paid for her taxi too. I knew they had financial problems and I did not want them to have additional expenses.

Sixth Day; March 12; Thursday

Last night I was very sleepy and fell asleep at 10:30 p.m. I then woke up in the middle of night, around 1:30 a.m. and made notes for 2 hours. I took a warm shower, but could not sleep for some time. When I fell asleep again, I had a dream that I was in the house staying with Tokawa's family in Japan. I came back home but the house was dismantled and my room was in another house. There was no bathroom in that house, but I needed to void and I started looking for a place outside the house. However, there were many people in sight and I was in trouble. At the corner of the house, I saw myself naked and tried to cover my genitals with my hands, feeling ashamed. At that moment, I awakened and went to the bathroom to void, then again fell asleep.

I got up early, at 6:45 a.m., and started to get ready because Luo was scheduled to come at 8 a.m. to pick me up. Because I did not sleep long enough, I felt a little tired and seemed to be catching a cold. My dream was coming true: when I see myself in a dream naked and in public, it is always a warning to me that I will catch a cold. Perhaps yesterday I became sweaty in the shopping mall and then when we went out, there was a cool wind. This is not good; I have to train myself to the cold in order to avoid catching colds so easily.

I was making notes and Luo still had not come when Nadya called me. She said that Xu Dung (also called Munya), her twin sister, would come to my room to pick up the shampoo and some other items that she left the other day. Munya looked very similar to Nadya--round face, straight hair, slim, and rather tall. She was dressed in pants and a short shirt that revealed her stomach. She smiled and said in Russian, "Pokhozha?," which means, "Do I look like my sister?" and then she picked up the shampoo and left.

Xu Fang soon came in, pale and a little out of breath after climbing upstairs to the third floor. She said that now she wants to do yoga exercises, but around 2 p.m., we are scheduled to go to the Chinese University of Geosciences and the Academy of Somatic Science. I told Xu Fang that both of her sisters stayed last night in the hotel and that now they are in the room next to mine. She seemed upset and sat on the bed silently.

Soon her twin sisters came in and they exchanged a few phrases in Chinese with Xu Fang; she replied to their questions with her head down. When the twins stood beside each other, Nadya appeared to be somewhat taller. When Xu Fang did not seem inclined to talk to them, the twins looked at each other, raised their eyebrows, shrugged their shoulders, and left for their jobs. The two sisters and their younger brother all work with Russians doing some trading business.

Xu Fang was definitely upset and tears were in her eyes. I tried to calm her by saying that the best way for her to treat them is to continue to love them. She said their faces are smiling and glowing, but their hearts are black. Again, she said they tried to kill her by giving her and Luo a tea with poison in it. In the future, they will understand how badly they treated her and they will surely regret what they did, I said, but she seemed not to understand my words.

Meanwhile, Xu Fang still wanted to exercise and she went to the bathroom to put on the clothes for exercising. We started with the rocking on the back exercise and she became excited when I counted the repetitions in Japanese. If I shifted into English, she insisted that I go back to Japanese. Someone called her and she said it was a high school classmate who had come down to Beijing and wanted to meet with her. She mentioned that Ling fell in love with her during their time in school. Ling soon came in and after greetings, he sat down in the chair and read the newspaper while we continued to exercise.

Of the yoga exercises, I showed them the abdominal-lift (i.e., Uddiyana bandha) breathing exercise. This exercise stimulates the functioning of the visceral organs and glands. To show them how the muscles move, I took off my shirt and pulled up my T-shirt, revealing my belly. Xu Fang tried to repeat the exercise after me. Then, to show them the rotation of the abdominal muscles (i.e., the Nauli exercise), I pulled off my T-shirt. Xu Fang exclaimed in surprise when I started to rotate my abdominal muscles, moving them to the left side and to the right. I demonstrated a proper pose for both the Uddiyana bandha and the Nauli exercises, with the knees slightly bent and hands resting on the legs just above the knees. She assumed this pose and I stressed the importance of pressing the chin against the chest while exhaling at the end of exercise. Without this throat lock, a person's bronchi can be overstrained and he or she can start coughing.

Proceeding with the yoga exercises, I demonstrated for them the peacock pose, which needs special training and is difficult for women to perform. In this pose, one must balance his body parallel to the floor, supporting it with his forearms resting on the floor, and elbows conjoined and placed against the abdomen. Xu Fang tried to take this pose, but I stopped her from doing it because she could have hurt her arms. She said she likes the challenge of difficult endeavors. Ling also tried to take this pose and seemed a little ashamed of not being able to perform it.

Next, we did flexibility exercises for all the body joints, beginning at the neck and going down to the toes. Ling also joined us and he managed to grasp the asynchronous rotation of the shoulders; that is, the left shoulder rotates forward and the right one backward in a simultaneous motion. Xu Fang tried to do this rotation a few times, each time without success.

After the exercises were finished, we went to have lunch at a restaurant that had a tree growing inside near the entrance. On our way, we passed a fruit market and Ling bought some ginseng fruits, with the red cover and transparent eatable part. While we were eating our food, Xu Fang took one piece, peeled it with her fingers, and ate about half of it. She obviously did not like it and a grimace of disgust appeared on her face. I tried to taste this fruit from the remains of her piece and found it slightly sour, sweet, and pungent.

After lunch, the three of us took a taxi and went to the China University of Geosciences. Professor Liu Xue-Cheng, the vice-director of the experimental center, met us outside. He introduced us to Professor Shen Jinchuan, who spent a few years in the United States and speaks fluent English. Their research is centered on parapsychological aspects, such as the influence of the human hand and mind power on plants, the ability to move objects with hand power, and so on. Their research assistant, Sun Chulin, possesses a strong hand power. In one experiment, she applied her hand power to roasted beans--the beans became alive again and sprouted. They showed me an album with pictures of people who can read characters with their ears and move objects with their hand power. Professor Shen also showed me the laboratory equipment used in their experiments. I asked him whether they are able to measure the energy of chakras in people; he said no. I also asked whether Sun Chulin, a beautiful woman about thirty years old, who is a bit plump and rosy, knows previous lives or could see auras. No, she cannot, was the reply.

As far as I know, there have been many research works in this field in the United States, Russia, and other countries. However, this research still remains confined to laboratories and has not yet gotten much practical application. I believe, however, that in the future science will have a deeper understanding of human nature and will be able to take pictures of people's auras or chakras with a technique like Kirlian photography. Anyway, the research center in China does its studies in this very interesting and promising field, and needs financial support to continue its research. This research center has difficulties in finding funds and Professor Shen asked me to write about them to attract the attention of investors. If my dear readers are interested in obtaining more information about this research, the contact address is as follows:

Professor Shen Jinchuan
China University of Geosciences, Institution of Somatic Sciences
Xueyuan Road No. 29, Beijing 100083, China
Telephone: (010) 6202-2244-3173

They showed me a promotional videotape that cost $60 and offered to sell it to me, but I couldn't afford it. It was already 5 p.m. and the working day in the research center was finished. Ling had left earlier, Xu Fang and I said thank you and good-bye to the bio-energy researchers, and we went to visit Dr. Rungi. The ride by taxi took a long time; we were stopped in a traffic jam that was caused by the Communist Party representatives going back after their meeting. All public transportation was stopped for about a half-hour.

It was a friend of Dr. Rungi who opened the door. Xu Fang talked to Dr. Rungi, telling him about her troubles with her sisters and family. He was listening to her with great sympathy, with his hands on his knees. He told me in Japanese that she is upset about the family problems.

Dr. Rungi's female assistant and his friend, a tall man in his early fifties, began serving dinner and we were invited to join them. Xu Fang agreed but told me to hurry because she had one more errand to accomplish tonight. Dr. Rungi offered me a strong Chinese rice vodka and the three men clinked our glasses, saying "Kampeyn." Dinner was dumplings with pork and beef, sausages, pickled beets, and boiled cauliflower; all was delicious and I enjoyed the food, wine, and company. Xu Fang did not sit with us; she stood near the table. Whether it was an effect of the vodka I don't know, but Dr. Rungi suddenly addressed me using a Russian oath. It was so unexpected that I burst out laughing and laughed for a minute or two. He remembered it from when he stayed in Russia for two years, he said. In the middle of dinner, three patients came in and Dr. Rungi and his assistant went with them to another room. We finished the meal with his friend, who put various foods on my plate.

After dinner, we picked up the copy of the videotape about Xu Fang, which a patient of Dr. Rungi unfortunately was unable to convert to the Chinese TV system. Then we took a taxi to do Xu Fang's errands. It was quite late when we got back to my hotel. We agreed with Xu Fang to go tomorrow to the Great Wall of China by bus. After Xu Fang went home, I called Professor Zhang Chang Chun, who is working at the Institute of High Energies and who speaks fluent English. He just came back to China after a one-year joint research project in Japan; Professor Abe of Japan, a relative of Mr. Tokawa, had given me his telephone number. He agreed to meet Xu Fang and me and to help with the translating.

Seventh Day; March 13; Friday

In the morning, I had just started to make notes of yesterday's events when Luo came to pick me up and we went to the office. Xu Fang was pale and said it was because she drank cola in the morning with Luo.

They are preparing to move to Shanghai and Xu Fang and I went to the service company to do some computer work on their processor. I carried the processor in my arms for about 1 kilometer. There was a pain in my right biceps, but it was tolerable and I managed to carry it there and then back to Xu Fang's office after the work was done. It took more than an hour to copy the files.

Meanwhile, Xu Fang and I went outside to breathe the fresh air. The sun was shining brightly and there were no clouds in the sky. There was a construction site nearby and we stood near a fence that enclosed a deep excavation, about 6 to 7 meters deep. Its retaining walls were covered with cement cork. She was in a good mood and asked me to say different words in English, Russian, and Japanese. She liked how the Russian word "lyagushka," which means "frog," sounded and she pronounced it quite clearly.

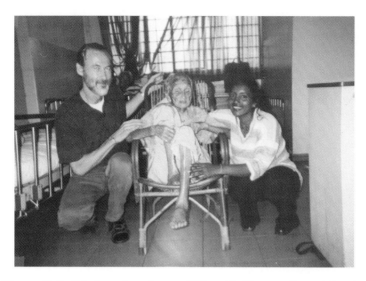

Figure 2-2. Madam Ang Leng, 106, with Vennes S. and the Author

Figure 2-3. Lydia P. Vesselovzorova, 102, with Professor Okuyama and
        the Author

Figure 2-4. The Author Surrounded by a Bouquet of Russian Beauties
            Left to right: Nina (interpreter), Galina (typist), the author,
            Natalie (engineer), and Lilly (interpreter)

Figure 2-5. Nataliya Ya. Yusova, 100, with her Family Members and the
            Author
            Left to right: Victoria, the Author, Nataliya Yusova, and Vera

Figure 18-1. Xu Fang Provides Author with Feet Massage.

Figure 18-2. Luo and Xu Fang in the Imperial Palace

Figure 18-3.   Visit to Dr. Guobuluo Rungi
(From right to left: Dr. Rungi, Lung Lung, Xu Fang, and the author)

Figure 18-4.   Xu Fang Poses on the Great Wall of China

Figure 18-5. Xu Fang Jumps downstairs on the Great Wall of China

Figure 18-6. Xya and Xu Fang in the Buddha Temple

Figure 18-7.   Xu Fang Enjoys the Aroma and Aura of Food

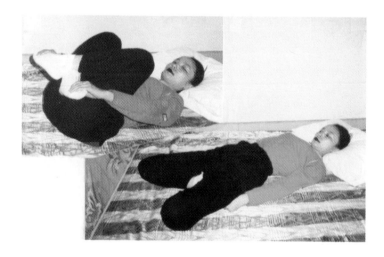

Figure 21-2.   The Pose for Breathing Exercise to Overcome Insomnia

a)   b)

c)   d)

Figure 22-9. Buttocks Walking

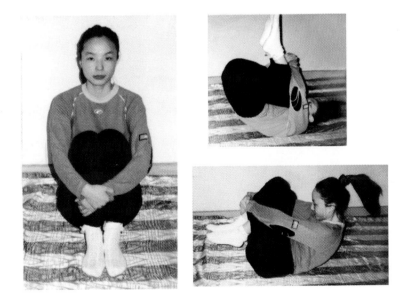

Figure 22-10.   Rocking on the Back

Figure 22-11.   Forward-Backward Bend

Figure 22-12.   Cat Pose

When the job was finished, we went back to her office. After a while, Xu Fang went out to buy lunch for us. From outside, she called me and asked me to come meet her near the shop. I found her feeding a cat with some sausage that she had bought for it. She is very compassionate, I thought. For us she bought rice, mabodofu, stewed long green vegetables for Luo, and some meat for me.

Luo rapidly ate his meal and went back to the computer. This time there was no rush for me and I chewed slowly and ate everything. The other day when we were talking about the pictures of her exercising, Xu Fang suggested that we could take them in Bamboo Park, about a 20-minute walk. But it was windy today and she said she felt sleepy and wanted to take a nap. Actually, I wanted to go to the National Library that is next to Bamboo Park. I said I would go alone, but Luo insisted that Xu Fang accompany me--he was afraid I might get lost. She looked very sleepy, though, and I asked them to draw a map for me, so then he agreed to let me go alone.

It was nearly 5 p.m. when I reached the library and many people were leaving. Among them I saw an American girl and she told me that the library is open from 9 a.m. till 5 p.m. every day. I was too late so I went to the Bamboo Park nearby. The entrance fee was equal to 0.3 yuan, very cheap. In the park, young couples sat on the benches kissing. A middle-aged couple was performing the Qigong exercises; the fat woman with her bulging belly appeared to be more adept in the body movements than the man. In another place, a man in his forties, quite well fed, was practicing the body-wave exercise. I climbed a couple of small hills and enjoyed walking around. A teenage girl approached me and offered to sell me roses; one rose in a vinyl cone cost 5 yuan, so I bought two for Xu Fang. Looking for a place where the pictures of her exercising could be taken, I noticed a round concrete bench in the form of a lotus flower. It was built near the lakeshore as if flowing in the water. This is a nice place for pictures, I thought. I stopped and performed the bridge, a back-bending exercise.

Although we agreed that I would be back at 7 p.m., it was only 6:40 p.m. when I arrived at their place. I knocked on the door and soon Xu Fang opened it. When I came in, I realized that I had wakened her--her face was still sleepy-looking. I apologized for the interruption of her sleep. Luo was washing his hair in the bathroom, and soon entered the room. She invited me to sit on the couch, then took my wrists and did a pulse diagnosis on both of my hands. She told me about the projection of internal organs on the face: lungs, on the nose; liver, on the eyes; kidneys, on the ears; heart, on the tongue; and stomach, on the skin. She said that my lungs need more blood.

My hands are cold because my kidneys are weak. I have gastritis in my stomach, and a wide area of its middle and lower parts is covered with ulcers, caused by the tense, over-cautious, and stressed state of my mind. I was doubtful about the ulcers--I know they are very painful, but I did not feel any pain. To avoid misunderstanding, I found the word "ulcer" in the dictionary and showed her, and she confirmed it. "Why do I not feel pain?" I asked. "That is due to your habit of chewing thoroughly and of doing yoga exercises that shade the pain. If not, you would feel pain," she replied. To cure my stomach, I need to relax, to loosen up for a long time. Think less, was her advice. I was grateful to her--she was absolutely right. I felt the same way.

Luo was ready to go for dinner, but he seemed to have a strain in his shoulders. I showed Xu Fang how to massage and she massaged his upper back and shoulders. She did a similar massage on me too, just long enough for Luo to take a photograph.

We went to a nearby restaurant and had a dinner of rice, mabodofu, and stewed vegetables. As always, Xu Fang ate nothing and just had a few sips of leaf tea. The sour soup with eggs and fried meat was ordered for me too, but I had eaten meat at lunch and I refused to eat it again. Xu Fang suggested I take it to the hotel and eat it for my breakfast. However, I refused because there was no refrigerator in my room. After dinner, they accompanied me to the main street, caught a taxi for me, and I went back this time to my hotel alone.

Eighth Day; March 14; Saturday

Early in the morning, Xu Fang called and told me to go outside the hotel. She and her friend Xu Dao were waiting for me. He came in his car to give us a ride to the Great Wall of China. It was cold and windy, and I rushed back to my room to take a woolen jacket that Kawasaki, my Japanese friend, had given me. Xu Fang was wearing a white vest, green sweater with high collar, and dark green pants. She had sent most of her clothes to Shanghai, so she wore almost the same clothes every day.

After we left Beijing, we passed through the tollgate and drove along the speedway. I was surprised how broad and good the new road was. We arrived in less than an hour, and after the car was parked, Xu Fang and I went to the shop and drank green tea. The day was sunny but the wind was strong and cold. I asked Xu Fang whether Xu Dao would come with us. She said, "No, he will wait for us in the car until we finish our excursion." Because of the cold wind and to prevent Xu Fang and myself from catching cold, I bought fur hats, one for each of us. We put on the hats and started to climb, with Xu Fang always going ahead; she seemed to enjoy the hiking.

Sometimes Xu Fang climbed too fast and was breathing rapidly, but we stopped often to take pictures, so she could have a rest (Figure 18-4, see p. 272). It was my dream for many years to go to the Great Wall of China and it was on the list of items that I planned to achieve in my life. And now I was here, not just for sightseeing, but also accompanied by the pretty Chinese mystery, Xu Fang! I felt really great and became excited, exclaiming in a loud voice, "Great Chinese Wall" and "Banrina Tyo Jo" in Japanese.

With many visitors and foreign tourists, it was quite crowded everywhere. A woman from a Slovenian group bumped into me and asked me whether I am here alone or not. I pointed to Xu Fang--tall, slim, and beautiful in her white jacket and yellowish-gray fur hat. She said, "Lucky man." Tat'yana, her name, was a teacher of Qigong in her country and she was studying Chinese medicine in Beijing. She was very interested to learn that Xu Fang also practices Qigong and is a doctor of Traditional Chinese Medicine. We all exchanged business cards and telephone numbers and took a photograph. Then Tat'yana rejoined her group and we continued to climb up the stairs. When we reached the top of the wall, Xu Fang did not seem tired at all. I needed a toilet and when we started to descend, I found one. Xu Fang waited for me in a quiet corner. A local vendor approached me and offered to sell me silver coins. I bought one for 21 yuan, although Xu Fang was making "no, no" gestures. Another man approached me and demanded "Money," and he was very insistent about getting it from me. Xu Fang told him to go away, but he did not pay any attention to her and tried to grab my sleeve. There was no other way to get rid of him so she said, "Run," and ran ahead. I followed her and we ran for some distance, but the beggar was chasing us, shouting, "Money, money." Eventually, we escaped from him and I took it as fun. She also did not look very embarrassed, but told me apologetically that some Chinese guys have a bad habit of demanding money from foreigners.

Xu Fang was wearing athletic shoes that were too big for her feet and descending induced pain in her toes. She had complained before that she feels uncomfortable in them, but all her other shoes had already been sent to Shanghai. Yesterday she had worn low leather boots, having discovered them by chance in one of the boxes. Unfortunately, today she did not put them on and was now in trouble. I suggested that she descend going backward, especially on the slopes. She tried this while I supported her above the elbow and she grasped the rail with her other hand. She seemed to be unstable on the steps and I repeatedly told her to be careful and to watch her feet. She jumped down the stairs a few times while holding onto both the rail and my forearm (Figure 18-5, see p. 273).

Soon we descended without problems and went looking for souvenirs in a few shops. I bought a T-shirt with the Great Wall of China on it and Chinese copper balls. On our way to the parking lots, there was a group of black soldiers sitting on the stone steps and taking pictures; I took a picture of Xu Fang with them in the background.

We found Xu Dao sleeping in the back seat of his car and soon we started for Beijing. In the car I was curious about rolling the Chinese balls that had a charm inside and a nice sound. Xu Fang got a call on her cellular phone from her sister Nadya. After she finished talking, I suggested teaching her a finger massage. She agreed and I did it on her hands, which were warm and dry.

Back in Beijing, Xu Dao went to the hotel to meet with Dr. Xuan, the Chinese Traditional Medicine doctor. Dr. Xuan appeared to be about thirty-five years old--a well-fed, nice-looking man. He sat in the front seat and talked to Xu Fang over his shoulder. He said that her complexion is better than the last time he saw her. She said it is because she does yoga exercises with me. She did not talk much, just nodded while Dr. Xuan was telling her something in Chinese. Dr. Xuan said good-bye to us near the five-story apartment building. We continued our way back to my hotel, when Xu Fang complained of having heart pain. I showed her a finger lock, which stimulates the Chinese channels of energy flow and is useful in relieving heart pain. She was sitting for a while with both hands cross-fingered. I also showed her the hands lock: both hands clasped together and resting on the heart region, and she assumed this pose too.

Near my hotel, we thanked Xu Dao for a wonderful trip and he left. We had an appointment with Professor Zhung Chan Chun; Xu Fang had called him from the car. He soon came to my room. Xu Fang went out and bought lunch for me: fried tofu, stewed vegetables, and rice. I first showed him an article about Xu Fang from the Japanese *Borderland* magazine. He asked her a few questions in Chinese and they talked for a few minutes.

Then I asked whether the content of the air she exhales had ever been tested. She answered and Professor Zhung translated that one year after she stopped eating, the military researchers investigated her exhaled air, but she never knew the results. It was a secret project because military chiefs were eager to know if soldiers could possibly fight without eating food. For a detailed checkup, they requested that Xu Fang stay in their research center for ten days and nights without going home, but she refused--she thought it would be too big an intrusion on her privacy.

Next, I asked for an explanation of the details on how she started her non-eating state. At that moment, I asked for her permission to tape-record her replies; she asked how I intended to use the recordings. Just for myself, for better understanding, nothing more--I explained--and she agreed. I asked her if she is afraid to die from not eating. She replied that she does not think much about death. Her boyfriend Luo arrived and joined us. He sat on the bed cross-legged and tried rolling the Chinese balls that I bought in his hands.

I then asked if we could determine the Ying-Yang type of each of them, using the questionnaire that I compiled. They agreed and it took more than an hour to complete the test. According to their assessment, Xu Fang was in a very balanced state (51 percent Yang, 49 percent Yin), Luo was 63 percent Yang and 37 percent Yin, and Professor Zhung was 56 percent Yang and 44 percent Yin--also quite well balanced. There was one more questionnaire on Ayurvedic doshas type that I wanted to check, but everybody was tired after the first questionnaire so I gave up.

It was dinnertime already and we went to a nearby restaurant. We had fried chicken, tofu, stewed vegetables, egg soup, and rice. While we three men were eating, Xu Fang went outside and walked around for 15 minutes or so. After dinner, we came back to the hotel and talked some more. I asked Professor Zhung to explain to Xu Fang that I want to take pictures of her doing exercises and use them in my book. He translated and Xu Fang agreed that I could use her photographs in my book.

We finished talking about 9 p.m. and Xu Fang and Luo went back home. "Tomorrow we will go to the bookstore--be ready," Xu Fang said before they left. Professor Zhung was also going to go home. He came by subway and it took him about an hour to get here from his place. I accompanied him to the subway station and, as we walked, I asked him his impression of the non-eating Xu Fang. He said it's difficult to say anything definite until you know her for a long time.

Our mutual friends in Japan had informed me that he is working in a very important research institute and is involved in studies of new elementary particles in nuclear physics. It is way beyond my scope, so instead of objective questions about his work, I asked him what the monthly salary of his co-workers was. His reply was 1,200 yuan (US $142) on average, but his salary is larger. From my Russian experience, I knew that a professor's salary was about four times higher than that of ordinary engineers. If the same proportion works in China, it is still only $570, not much money at all. He lives with his wife and an adult daughter who has already graduated from the university. I thanked him with all my heart for coming and helping me with the interpreting.

Ninth Day; March 15; Sunday

Since I retired two and a half years ago, I often sleep till 8 or even 8:30 a.m., but I was busy these days in China and I got up around 7 a.m. I took a shower and had my breakfast of fruits. Then I was starting to make notes when Xu Fang, Xu Dao, and his daughter Xu Du came in to visit me.

They brought the fur hats that I forgot in the car yesterday. Xu Du, fourteen, is a middle-school student; she studies English and said she was glad to talk to me. I asked her a few questions about her studies, and then I showed them five exercises for the lower back. I started to do them with the girl; after some hesitation, her father joined us too. Xu Fang was busy talking on the telephone and did not participate.

After a half-hour drive, we got to the street with a few bookstores on it. We said thank you and good-bye to Xu Dao and his daughter. In the bookstore, there were a few books in English and I found the book that I was looking for: "*The Mystery of Longevity*," by Liu Zhengcai. There was a good choice of textbooks with tapes for studying foreign languages. I bought English, Japanese, and Russian courses for Xu Fang and a Chinese course for myself. I was delighted with Xu Fang's enthusiasm to learn all three languages and we agreed to exchange the lessons in letters.

Both of us will be very busy from now on learning all these languages. For me, the Chinese language will definitely be a challenge. First, it will allow me to communicate with Xu Fang in the future; and second, I thought it will be a good exercise for my brain to prevent it from deterioration and Alzheimer's disease.

There was a department store on our way and we went there to buy a long-sleeved shirt for Xu Fang's exercises. We were looking around many stalls and had a difficult time finding a proper one. Eventually, we bought a yellow and black shirt, although Xu Fang did not seem to like it much.

It was about 2 p.m. already and my stomach was rumbling with hunger, so we went into a restaurant and I had fish, vegetables, and rice for my lunch. The fish dish happened to be a whole steamed carp decorated with the vegetables. It was a tasteful but bony fish and I had to eat very slowly, extracting small sharp bones. Xu Fang was patient and did not hurry me. She drank some leaf tea. She opened the Russian textbook that we bought and started to read and write the ABCs. Sometimes I corrected her handwriting. She did well and her letters were very similar to those in the textbook. Xu Fang again mentioned her sister Nadya and complained about how much trouble she has with her. I advised her to start sending love from her heart to Nadya, which could have a pacifying effect on her. Also she said that Luo is off from work today and he is lonely without her. I felt really sorry for being the cause of their separation. I suggested that she send Luo a thought message--"I love you"--and to call him often. My other suggestion was a new theme for Luo's meditation: to imagine a row of lotus flowers going from the heart to the bottom of the spine, with Xu Fang sitting in the Padmasana pose on the top of each flower. She said she liked that image.

In another four-story bookstore, I bought a dozen books on longevity, Qigong, and diet, most of them in English. While I was looking through the books, Xu Fang told me she needs to buy medicine for Luo and we agreed to meet on the first floor. Meanwhile, I found some more books on longevity in Chinese. When Xu Fang came back, we went upstairs to the fourth floor and she found two books for me: one on longevity in Chinese and another on health preservation in both Chinese and English, with parallel texts. She went up the stairs so quickly that I asked her if she felt tired; she was not. However, I could not say the same about myself; perhaps much of my energy was spent on digesting the food I had eaten, while Xu Fang saved all hers.

She called Luo from a public phone and he asked her to come back as soon as possible. We hurried by taxi to my hotel and she called him again from my room. She asked me about my dinner, but I thanked her and refused. I did not feel hungry for a big dinner after that fish lunch. But after she left for her office, I went to the nearby shops to buy something simple; I bought cocoa milk, bread, and dried pumpkin, which I soaked in water overnight to make it soft.

Tomorrow is the last day of my visit to China and the last chance to take pictures of Xu Fang performing the exercises. To be prepared, I made a list of exercises that I wanted to photograph.

Tenth Day; March 16; Monday

Despite the polluted air in Beijing, I have been sleeping well these days. This morning I again got up early and, after a breakfast of fruits, continued to make a list of exercises, which took about 3 hours to complete. I was still making notes when Luo knocked on my door around 1 p.m. We said "Ni hao" to each other and he said his version of "Let's go." We took a taxi and went to the shrine where we met Xu Fang, her friend from Shanghai, Xyu, and her girlfriend, Chang Lung Lung.

Everyone except Xu Fang was hungry so we went for lunch. Both Luo and Xyu seemed to eat vegetarian food, but Lung and I had sour soup with chicken and shrimp with steamed vegetables. Xu Fang went to a shop to buy incense sticks for the temple, then she joined us. As usual, I was the slowest with my meal and she told me to hurry. We were going to visit Xya, her Buddhist guru, and the sticks were bought for his temple.

In Lung's car, Xu Fang sat in the front seat and the three men sat in the back seat, with me in the middle. Xu Fang complained that she had a headache after smelling some kind of wood in the shop. To relieve her pain, I showed her the He Gu point on her hand to be pressed, and massaged her left hand for a while. The pain was located in her temples and I showed Luo how to massage her temples and the points on the back of her neck. He gave her the massage for a few minutes, while I continued to press the point on her hand. She said her pain was lessened.

Our direction was to the west from Beijing and it took an hour and a half to reach our destination. We drove through the gate and parked the car in the yard of a big four-story building, Xya's house. The landscape nearby was picturesque with surrounding hills. Nobody was in sight so we went to the living room on the second floor. It was very large, furnished with a wide bed made of carved black wood with inlaid shells, and two bronze cranes on either side--very luxurious. The bathroom next to this room was also very large. All the furniture and interior decorations were indicative of luxury and wealth.

Xya came in and after introductions, we sat on leather couches around a low table. He is seventy-five years old but looks at least fifteen years younger. His wife and five children live in California (United States) and he lived there for about twenty years too. He built this huge house with his own money and established a sort of art school in it. His young students paint Buddha paintings. He speaks some English and seemed to understand me when I talked to him, but he preferred to speak Chinese.

Xya spoke first with Xu Fang and Luo. Xu Fang told me the other day that Xya likes Luo because of his long nose. Then he asked me about my work and I described the idea of my book, referring to a person's chakra profile. He seemed to be interested in it and commented that it made sense; I was encouraged by his appreciation of my work.

He and Xu Fang told me that, unfortunately, people in China do not know much about Buddha. I suggested that the spiritual development of the upper chakras according to Buddha's teachings and the restriction on a physical plane are keys to a long and healthy life. I also showed Xya my graph correlating calorie intake and longevity, with its peak at 1,100 to 1,300 kcal and a much shorter life span for non-eating or overeating people. When I expressed my concern about Xu Fang's future, Xya mentioned that there are a few other people in China who have practiced the "Pi Gu," or non-eating state, for many years. One woman, a nanny in the temple, is now eighty years old and she started to live without food many years ago, he said.

Xya's assistant, Xin, a young and beautiful lady, came in. She speaks fluent English and started to interpret for Xya and me. They mentioned a woman in the nearby village who had died a few years ago, but her body is still fresh and not decaying at all. They even offered to take me to see her so I could take photographs. That was an exclusive chance, but unfortunately there was no time left in my visit. Continuing to talk about my work, I showed them the tables of foods for people with blood types A and O. Xya is type A type and was very interested in this information. He asked his assistant to make a copy for him, and one for Luo as well.

We were invited to see and to pray at the temple built on the fourth floor of the house. In a wide hall there was a statue of Buddha and all the attributes of Buddhist worship. Everyone lit incense sticks, made the namaste pose with their hands, and bowed while kneeling on cushions. I watched how Xu Fang did the bows and repeated after her. When everyone finished the prayers, I took a picture of Xu Fang and Xya in the temple (Figure 18-6, see p. 273).

Back in the sitting room, the conversation continued and Xin told me that Xya is highly respected for his channeling abilities, namely Feng Shui—the art of balancing energies of people, buildings, and landscapes. Xu Fang said she believes that Xya is close to Buddha. According to Xin, while in the United States, Xya was invited many times to consult with companies about the layout of equipment in their factories and plants. For his advice to change the layout, which usually resulted in increased production efficiency, he was paid US $10,000 or $20,000 for each visit.

Now everyone was eager to ask Xya to foresee his or her destiny. He told Lung that with her short, curved-up nose, she is too Yang and she tortured her husband, which was a cause of their divorce.

Looking at a picture of me when I was twenty-two years old, Xya told me that at the age of thirty, I was a big success, but at the age of fifty, I lost everything. This was absolutely true. He predicted that I would become rich in two years. I showed him photographs of my Japanese friend Kawasaki and of Stephen Mourousas, my son-in-law. He said that Kawasaki is a sincere friend of mine, a kind person. He also said that Stephen had financial difficulties last year and that he will find a good job with a good income later this year, after his birthday (in May).

About myself, Xya added that because I was divorced from my first wife, I had better not engage in a second marriage, which would also end in divorce. He saw the picture of my A-frame house in Rome, Maine, and asked me in what direction it is oriented. I answered "to the north" and he advised me to turn it 45 degrees to the northeast. He told me to build inside the house a wall to the ceiling, about 1.5 meters away from the front wall. He also said that it must be built on a firm foundation, and the space below the floor must be closed up to the ground; otherwise, all my wealth will be blown out. I thought his advice sounded very reasonable and convincing.

All of us were gathered around Xya and asking questions about our future. Meanwhile, dinner was served and we were invited into the dining room. We sat around a big round table with a rotating middle part made of dark glass. The food was vegetarian and very delicious, about ten different dishes. Xya is vegetarian, and the dinner had many kinds of vegetable proteins: mushrooms, tofu, and rice. Mushrooms were in many dishes with fried potatoes, carrots, and rice. The seaweed soup was good, as were the other dishes; I would love to eat that kind of food until I am a hundred years old. That was my last dinner in China and definitely the best one. I guess Xu Fang, although not eating, enjoyed the aroma of the food and took in its aura (Figure 18-7, see p. 274).

Soon after the dinner, we said our thank yous and good byes to Xya and hurried back to Beijing. It was already 7:40 p.m. and dark outside. The outside lights were not on, so I held Xu Fang by her arm when we went down the stairs. The ride in the darkness was even more dangerous than in the daytime. Suddenly, people crossing the road would appear close to our car, or a car was stopped right in the road without any lights on. On the way, we were stopped by the road police, who were armed with automatic guns. When they signaled our car to stop, Lung did not seem to understand at first and went on driving, but the men told her to stop. She stopped the car and then backed up. We got out of the car and the police officer checked everyone's ID. When I showed my Israeli passport, the officer looked at the first page briefly and then gave it back to me without a word or any expression, as if he meets an Israeli citizen every day.

Back in the car, everybody continued to talk about Xya's fortune–telling. He told Lung that because she tortured her first husband, if she marries again, her second husband will torture her. The root of the problem was in her short, curved-up nose. I advised her to pull on her nose every day to make it longer. Everybody laughed about the noses, short in Lung's case and long in Luo's.

We got back to the hotel quite late and still we had one more important commitment to accomplish: taking photographs of Xu Fang doing the exercises. Luo and I moved the furniture in my room and arranged the space. I was afraid that Xu Fang might be tired and unable to exercise, but she was full of energy and I took all the pictures I had planned. This took about 2 hours and when we finished, it was already 1 a.m. I was very grateful to them both and felt sorry about pushing Xu Fang to work hard until such a late hour. Xu Fang and Luo went back to their place. I packed my luggage, took a shower, and fell asleep.

Departure; March 17; Tuesday

My flight was early in the morning, and they were back at my hotel at 6:30 a.m. We agreed that they would take me to the bus station and I would go by bus to the airport alone. We took a taxi and in 5 minutes arrived at the bus station. Luo bought the bus ticket for me and warned me not to pay any extra money to the driver.

Before we said good-bye to each other, Xu Fang told me that last night Xya also did fortune-telling about her and Luo. Xya advised them to continue their relationship but not to marry, because they both like to meditate more than other things. I wondered why she told me such a private thing, and I attributed it to her extraordinary generosity. I thanked them for the time they devoted to me, their hospitality, and their warm hearts. They invited me to come to Shanghai next year--after they became rich, as they said. Then Xu Fang said she felt very sleepy and Luo had to work as well, so they left first. In a few minutes, my bus also departed. It was an early hour and I saw dozens of people doing gentle Qigong exercises in the parks as we passed by. The Chinese people accumulate the Qi energy and make it flow in their bodies for their health and longevity. Probably this energy also has allowed Xu Fang to abstain from food and be healthy, fit, and vigorous for ten years.

19

WATER INTAKE CONTROL

In our quest for a healthy and long life, water is equally as important as proper food intake, sufficient sleep, and exercise. Water accounts for approximately 70 percent of our body weight. It is an important component of body cells and, in the form of plasma in the blood, transports substances around the body delivering nutrients and carrying out wastes. Water is not considered a food for ordinary people in ordinary conditions; however, during prolonged fasting or for people like Teresa Neumann or the Chinese mystery Xu Fang, who abstain from solid food for years, it becomes a food.

In the future, perhaps science will discover nutritional properties of water. The hypothesis supporting this idea is that aliens from UFOs, who allegedly have mastered thermonuclear processes, take water from Earth and use it as a food for themselves and a fuel for their spaceships as well. Another hypothesis holds that our body cells are tiny bio-thermonuclear reactors, and they can release energy by the process of nuclear fusion. Although it is not yet evident and sounds too good to be true, I believe that science in the future will prove this hypothesis. The fusion process is known to be a basis of the hydrogen bomb, although the controlled thermonuclear reactor is unsuccessful so far and is a subject of current research.

Water Balance

The water balance in the body very much influences our steady weight and continuing good health. It is regulated with various hormones and food-derived minerals that act on the kidneys--the filtering and eliminating organ. The water balance consists of its input and output. The input water is obtained from water or beverages consumed as a component of liquid foods such as soup or porridge, from solid foods, as an end product of metabolism, and from water vapor in the air, especially in high-humidity climates. The output water is lost in the urine and feces, through the lungs, by evaporation from the body surface, and through perspiring. People who cry a lot and lose water through tears are not common; a runny nose is also not a loss to consider. In human adults, the amounts of different forms of input and output water (in milliliters) are as follows:

Input		Output	
Drinks and liquid food	1,100-1,200	Urine	1,000-1,400
Solid food	500-1,000	Evaporation	550-1,000
Metabolic water	300-500	Feces	80-200
		Lungs	370-400
Total	1,900-2,700	Total	2,000-3,000

The amount of water we need depends on many factors, including the kinds of food we consume, temperature of the environment, level of physical activity, metabolic type, age, and body constitution. When excess protein is consumed, water needs are greater because it is needed to flush out the nitrogenous end products of protein metabolism.

Just as food intake is ruled by a sense of hunger, water intake similarly is controlled by a sense of thirst. If the amount of water in the blood drops to the lower limit, the cells send a signal to the thirst center of the brain, and we feel thirsty. However, the water-regulation system in humans is not dependent on thirst alone, but is also influenced by the concentration of sodium in the extracellular fluid, the anti-diuretic hormone (ADH) called vasopressin, and other hormones. The hypothalamus contains osmo-receptors--cells that are sensitive to the density of blood--and when it becomes low, ADH is produced and released through the pituitary gland.

Because of these factors, we can feel no thirst even if the water content in the body is reduced to below the normal level. What are the body's reactions if water is lost in excess? A loss of water less than 2 percent of body weight normally causes a feeling of thirst--a sign of dehydration, the symptoms of which include dry lips and reduced urination. A water loss of 6 to 8 percent causes a semi-fainting-fit state to set in; a 10 percent causes possible hallucinations; and more than 12 percent can cause death. This shows how hazardous excessive water loss can be and how important it is to regulate water balance for maintenance of good health and survival itself.

The sense of thirst declines as we age, and we do not feel thirsty even if there is borderline water loss in the body. "Not drinking enough water every day is one of the most common conditions in old age, and although it has received almost no publicity, chronic dehydration is a major cause of premature aging. Some authorities go so far as to count dehydration among the leading causes of death in old age," says Dr. Deepak Chopra in his best-selling book, *Ageless Body, Timeless Mind*. The elderly often have fluid and electrolyte disturbances in their bodies, and dehydration is the most common cause of this condition. As we age, our kidneys lose their ability to perform proper conservation of water and, along with reduced thirst sensation and reduced fluid intake, this adds to imbalances of water in the body.

Along with the decreased sensation of thirst in elderly people and their forgetfulness about drinking enough fluids, dehydration can be caused by the intake of diuretics, both medicinal and natural. Diuretics act as an agent that increases the secretion and discharge of urine. If you are fortunate not to suffer from high blood pressure and do not take prescription diuretic drugs, they are found in abundance in fruits, vegetables, and herbs.

Water is the number-one natural diuretic because the more we drink, the more we urinate. Examples of diuretics include mineral water and alcohol such as beer, wine, and whiskey. Common natural foods and substances such as sugar, table salt, sea salt, sodium bicarbonate, urea, and other salts are also taken as diuretics. But the salts are known for their fluid retention, you will probably remark. Yes, if they are taken in large quantities; however, in small amounts, they work as diuretics. They work by osmosis, attracting the stronger solution of the intracellular liquid to pass through the membrane. Therefore, increased salts are released into the urine with a certain amount of fluid. This confirms once again that our body chemistry is very complex.

Beverages that contain caffeine--such as coffee, teas, and soft drinks--act as diuretics. They directly affect the kidneys, increasing the rate of blood filtration and reducing the ability to reabsorb salt necessary for blood homeostasis. Among fruits and berries, lemons, plums, melons, watermelon, fresh grape juice, currants, alpine cranberries, and wild strawberries have diuretic properties. Many common vegetables, including artichokes, asparagus, carrots, celery, chicory, cucumbers, fennel, garlic, onions, parsley, radishes, and watercress, all act as diuretics. Beans have the diuretic properties as well. Diuretics also are found among the spices, such as chervil, dill, horseradish, mint, savory, and wintergreen. A plentiful number of herbs, about 142 of them, have the diuretic action; the fifteen most common herbs are alfalfa, burdock, dandelion, elder, goldenrod, goldenseal, hops, horehound, horsetail, juniper berries, mugwort, mullein, sarsaparilla, sienna, and shepherd's purse. The other 127 herbs are listed in *The Herb Book*, by John Lust.

The question arises: How do we possibly manage to retain some fluid in our bodies if so many common foods and beverages are eager to expel it? The answer may be in vasopressin, or ADH, which regulates the conservation of water in the body. As people age, ADH is not produced in the same quantity as in younger people. As a result, water-balance disorders become more common with age. In severe cases, the diminished production of ADH leads to Diabetes Insipidus, a disease that is accompanied by watery urine. The urinary water loss in this disease can be as high as 30 liters a day, and the person feels extreme thirst. The administration of ADH in this case helps to control the water loss.

Another opposite abnormality of water balance is excessive retention of fluid in the body, which is called *edema*. Urine volume becomes very low and concentrated. The limbs become swollen and fluid accumulates in the abdominal region. Most often, this disorder is caused by high blood pressure and heart disease. Weight reduction, salt-intake restriction, and diuretics help to lower high blood pressure and reduce edema.

Fluid Intake Requirements

The amount of water we need varies considerably from person to person. It can be dependent on age, gender, types of food we eat, level of activity, climate, and other factors. The recommended amount of water for daily intake ranges broadly from one expert to another and the advice is very controversial. There are both proponents and opponents of large and small amounts of water to be consumed; east and west, south and north, all consider their own philosophy the best.

For the climatic conditions in Russia, people who live in the middle zone need to drink 2.2 to 2.5 liters of water, including the water in soups, says Dr. I.P. Nehumyvakin, a medical academician. "A resting man needs somewhere about 3 pints of water a day; a man taking considerable physical exercise, much more," say H.G. Wells, et al., in their book, *The Science of Life*. The authors are Englishmen, and they surely mean an English pint, which is equal to 0.57 liter, so 3 pints is equal to 1.71 liters. Although the climate in Russia is not more arid than in England, the amount of water is larger, perhaps because of the soups that Russians always eat. What about the United States?

The range is quite large. At the lower end are Harvey and Marilyn Diamond, who advocate for eating 70 percent high-water-content foods (fruits and vegetables) and 30 percent concentrated foods (everything else). In their best-selling book, *Fit for Life,* they say, "You will find that you will have much less thirst if you eat high-water-content food rather than eating foods devoid of water and then drinking the water separately." Vikroras Kulvinskas, N.D., in his best-selling book, *Survival into the 21st Century,* supports the idea of obtaining fluids from water-rich fruits and vegetables. He says, "Drinking water is completely unnatural and is necessitated only by a concentrated acid-forming diet. Our natural foods, fresh fruits and vegetables, contain at least 90 percent energy-charged tasty fluid. This is all the water we need." Yet another best-selling author, Gennady Malakhov of Russia, says that the body does not need water if vegetables and fruits count for 40 to 60 percent of the diet.

However, the majority of authors do not deny drinking water. "Depending on weight and physical activity, you should drink six to eight glasses of water every day," says Dr. Hans J. Kugler in his book, *The Anti-Aging Weight Loss Program.* Dr. Paul C. Bragg, an American health pioneer, praised water very highly for health and longevity and called it "Doctor Pure Water." In his famous book, *The Miracle of Fasting,* he stated, "Pure water is important for health.

> *"To the days of the aged it addeth length,*
> *To the might of the strong it added strength,*
> *It freshens the heart, it brings the sight,*
> *'Tis like quaffing a goblet of morning light.*

"The body is 65 percent water and pure, steam-distilled (chemical-free) water is important for total health. Seven to nine glasses of pure liquids a day are best."

Regarding the amount needed for elderly people, Agatha Thrash, M.D., of Uchee Pines Institute in Seale, Alabama, says that our water needs increase with age. She recommends a minimum of six to eight 8-ounce glasses of water a day for people under age fifty, eight to ten 8-ounce glasses for those in their fifties, and ten to twelve 8-ounce glasses for active people sixty and over. "An adequate water intake consists of 30 to 35 milliliters per kilogram of ideal body weight," says Neil A. Campbell in his book, *Biology* (4th edition). In another source, we find that the minimum daily requirement for adults of all forms of water is estimated at 35 to 40 grams of water per kilogram of body weight; that is, 2,800 to 3,200 grams for a person weighing 80 kilograms. According to *The Human Body,* a book published by Running Press GEM, for a man who weighs 70 kilograms (154 pounds), the daily input of water is 2,145 grams and output is 2,480 grams.

For people engaged in a fitness program, drinking 1 to 2 gallons (3.78 to 7.56 liters) a day is advised by Rick Villasenor, the president of Fitness Media, Inc., in Los Angeles, California. Athletes sweat a lot and they must drink more to replenish water loss. A long-distance runner loses 8 pounds of water (3.6 liters) and football players lose almost 14 pounds of water (6.35 liters) in about an hour's time, stated Paul Bragg in his book, *The Miracle of Fasting*. Bob Delmonteque, America's number-one senior fitness expert and a seventy-three-year-old muscular athlete pictured on the front cover of his book, *Lifelong Fitness*, advises people to drink 0.5 ounce per pound of body weight, or ten 8-ounce glasses if your weight is 160 pounds. This is probably the right amount for his high-intensity strength workouts that involve profuse perspiration.

Drink more water, at least 3 liters a day, says Yogi Ramacharaka. If you do not drink enough water, many health problems--ranging from constipation to heart disease--may arise, he adds. Although the climate in India is more arid than in the United States, the amount in question is about the same. This is interesting because it was in India that Giri Bala abstained from food and water for fifty-six years, until she died at the age of sixty-eight. Perhaps she could take water from the air, which is very humid in the Calcutta region where she lived. Regarding this possibility, Xu Fang, thirty-one, who has lived without food for the last thirteen years, told me that on rainy days she does not drink either.

The macrobiotic school and its founder, George Ohsawa, hold that the less one drinks, the better. We have enough water intake with food; cooked rice has 60 to 70 percent water and vegetables have 80 to 90 percent. Drinking water, which is Yin, just increases the Yin-Yang imbalance in our body. "For best results from macrobiotic cures, we must drink less, so that we could urinate just two times a day for women and three times for men," according to Ohsawa in his book, *Zen Macrobiotics: The Art of Rejuvenation and Longevity*. Ohsawa himself lived only to the age of seventy-four, not that great an age that could be called impressive longevity. It is important for the proponents of longevity to live long lives; otherwise, no one will believe them. When Elie Metchnikoff, a renowned Russian microbiologist and a Nobel Prize winner who introduced yogurt as a longevity drink, died at the age of seventy-one, disbelief about his theory quickly arose in the public.

According to Oriental medicine, the kidneys suffer the most from excessive water intake. If you want to spare your kidneys, cut down on the amount of fluid taken into your body, says Edward Obaidey in his article, *Reducing Fluids to Spare the Kidneys*, which was published in *The Japan*

Times newspaper, March 2, 1996, issue. "In Oriental medicine, excess fluid makes the body too Yin and causes the kidneys to overwork. The heart then also overworks as it tries to compensate by providing more Yang energy to maintain balance," he explained.

Exactly the opposite recommendation is found in the West. Dr. Linus Pauling, also a Nobel Prize winner, said in his book, *How to Live Longer and Feel Better*: "Water...is required for life in the amount of about 1 liter per day...A larger intake of water, preferably about 3 liters (more than 3 quarts) per day, is needed for the best of health...One reason for a high intake of water is that it leads to a high volume of urine; this reduces the burden on the kidneys, which excrete a dilute urine with less work than they do a concentrated urine. That is especially important for persons with impaired kidney function."

Among the tips on healthy dieting, Tracy C. Semler in her book, *All About Eve,* advises that people do drink lots of fluids while restricting calories. She says, "The more you drink—ideally, water—the more full you'll feel (and the happier your kidneys will be)...you *need* water, and there's pretty much no limit to the amount you can have safely, so drink before, during, and after meals."

Dr. S.A. Borodin of Russia is not included in *The Guinness Book of World Records*, but he claims that he cured himself of ankylosing spondylitis disease, a rarely curable illness, by drinking up to 40 liters of warm water a day during a seven-day fast. He also took enemas of a beet concoction.

On the other end of the spectrum is the complete cessation of water intake with the alternate dry-fasting therapy introduced by V.P. Lavrova of Russia. She claims that this method can cure cancer, AIDS, and other incurable diseases. The reason for this is that during a dry fast, the cells get rid of *deuterium water*--or heavy water--a highly destructive substance that is in the water we drink and is accumulated in the body during the course of life. The biological effects of deuterium water are such that seeds do not germinate in it and animals cannot live in it. In biological systems, the heavy water inhibits cell division and interrupts reproductive processes.

It sounds like a myth, but a man named Schroth, who was a German peasant in the eighteenth century, is known for his successful cures of cancer, sarcoma, and tuberculosis by keeping his patients from drinking water for a few weeks; they were given one or two glasses of homemade light wine instead. Schroth is known as a naturopath who was also successful in curing rheumatism. "The Schroth Cure: also used in the treatment of rheumatism, this method alternates dry days (of fast) with liquid days over a period of two or three weeks," according to *The Complete Family Guide to Alternative Medicine*, edited by C. Norman Shealy, M.D., Ph.D.

Body constitution affects water intake. It has been observed that slim people drink less water than well-fed people. Plump people have a thicker layer of fat under the skin and look "juicier" than skinny people, who look "dried."

Water Intake Differences

It seems that people are born with different requirements of water for their bodies. People with a low metabolic rate produce less metabolic water in their bodies so they need more water from outside the body. Their counterparts with a high metabolic rate have lower water requirements.

Under equal conditions, even in arid climates, water intake is different in people with different body constitutions. I made another observation when I rented a room for two months in the apartment of a young Malaysian family in Singapore. The wife, Riza, was plump and definitely overweight, while her husband, Nahmud, was very slim. Of their two children, Liana, an eleven-year-old girl, was quite slim, and Haze, a three-year-old boy, appeared well fed. I asked Riza how much water she drinks and her answer was about six glasses a day. Her husband, instead of water, drinks four or five cups of hot tea with milk. This seemed typical because it is very hot in Singapore all year long, and people drink more water than those in countries with cooler climates. Their children also were very opposite in the amount of water they drank. The small boy, quite short for his age, often reached for the cold water from the refrigerator; his older sister drank little, much less than her brother.

Fluid Intake in Centenarians

Centenarians are authorities in every aspect of life, including drinking water; therefore, we should take notice. Again, there is a rather wide range in the amount of fluid intake. Alice Wei of Singapore, who lived to 107, drank seven glasses of water a day, always had her lunch at noon, and ate a special wheat and soybean porridge for dinner. If we assume that her porridge was cooked with one glass of water, then she had a total of eight glasses of fluid daily. One glass contains 220 grams of water, which results in 1,760 grams a day. This is a very large amount, but the climate in Singapore is arid all year long; therefore, water intake is probably increased.

The diet of George Burns, 100, a famous American comedian, included soups, low-fat milk, black coffee (up to four cups a day), orange juice, tea with lemon, and a martini. The intake estimate shows that his daily fluids totaled about 800 to 900 grams. There was also some liquid content in the green salads, cooked vegetables, and rice that he ate.

Many centenarians attribute their longevity to a proper diet, but two secrets of longevity of Nina Amanda Rust, 106, from Roseburg, Oregon, are about drinks and medicine: "Don't drink water. Stay away from doctors," she says. She shares the first secret with the macrobiotic school and those who warn about deuterium water. However, she probably never heard about those ideas, being very busy raising twelve children.

Figure 19-1 illustrates the range of fluid intake discussed to this point.

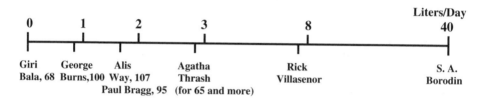

Figure 19-1. Daily Fluid Intake of Different People

Certainly, this scale has many conditions, but its aim is to show just how broad the range is. On the high extreme is Dr. Borodin; he did not drink 40 liters a day his entire life, but rather for just one week and only for therapeutic purposes. Rick Villasenor's recommendations are for younger people involved in fitness programs. Paul Bragg is a great authority because he was living proof of the workability of his health system. He died at the age of ninety-five in an accident during surfing practice. George Burns is also legendary proof--he achieved 100 years of age and wrote his book *How to Live to Be 100 - Or More* when he was eighty-six.

Water That Is Good for the Body

There are many kinds of water and beverages that are called longevity, rejuvenation, and healing liquids and teas. People drink either pure water or water with various flavorings, colorings, and/or nourishing or stimulating additives. Spring, deep-well, and distilled waters are considered pure. I would add **metabolic water** to this list–it is the purest because it is produced in the cells, those chemical factories inside our body. Neither contaminants nor pollutants are involved in the production process. In the previous water-balance table, the minimum amount of water intake is 1,900 milliliters, the maximum is 3,000 milliliters. For metabolic water, the range is from 300 to 500 milliliters; let's use the mean value of 400 milliliters. If we limit water intake to the minimum, the ratio of metabolic water in the total amount is 21 percent; if we consume the maximum amount, it is 15 percent. Isn't it better to have more than one fifth of the purest water rather than less than one sixth?

One other consideration is that metabolic water is our innate water, just as any fluid taken from outside our body is alien water, which needs energy to be adjusted to our tissues. Nothing that is taken from outside is given to us free of charge, and every satisfying thing has a price attached to it--this is a universal law and water is not excluded. Some people say why not take advantage of a nutritional element (water) that has been around since the beginning of time and costs almost nothing? Because the more we consume, the higher will be the bill--the same as when a water supply company charges us as a customer. However, with the water taken inside, the price is the health that is requested and the body has to pay this deadly bill.

There are warning signs that not everything is so clear with water. Deuterium, or heavy water, which is poisonous and has an adverse effect on our body, was discussed previously. Just **as free radicals are attached to the oxygen we inhale, deuterium water is similarly attached to the water we drink**. "Water, by the way, is particularly unstable around body temperature (36.2 - 36.7° C). Since chemical reactions are taking place all the time inside us, keeping us alive, it is not fantasy to suggest that to some extent we are regulated by cosmic forces in our most fundamental processes," say Guy L. Playfair and Scott Hill in their book, *The Cycles of Heaven*. We do not know all the properties of water yet; the scientists of the future will make many discoveries about water, both its healing and harmful characteristics.

Many centenarians who are living proof of their wisdom say that moderation is the key. In the case of water, if we assume that a daily intake of **1 liter of fluids is moderate and that half of that is the minimum, my preference is somewhere between the two.** Certainly, it should be a different amount for each individual. We are all different and factors such as body constitution, metabolic type, Yin-Yang type, the food we eat, activity level, and climate must be considered--especially the Yin-Yang difference. Water is Yin and Yang people will more easily tolerate the increased water intake than their Yin counterparts.

Water plays a crucial role in the condition of our skin. When the water content in the outer layer of the skin is less than 10 percent, our skin becomes dry, flaky, and rough. Water helps reduce wrinkles and well-hydrated skin is smoother and less prone to develop fine wrinkles. A lifestyle that involves a lot of outside work and exposure to the sun also dries the body and the skin. The face and hands look older with more signs of aging, such as toughening, roughening, and wrinkling of the skin. Dr. Stuart M. Berger in his book, *Forever Young,* displays photographs of a sixty-two-year-old American Indian women and a ninety-one-year-old Tibetan monk. The woman, who has had extensive exposure to the sun, appears to have rough skin on her face, which is covered with deep wrinkles, and she looks very old. The man, about thirty years older, who stayed indoors most of his life, has a soft, young-looking face without any visible wrinkles. A sufficient intake of water increases water content in the skin--nourishing it from the inside; moisturizers applied on the exterior help achieve the same results. Water is probably the best anti-aging "vitamin" available for the skin. It is the only "medicine" that has no side effects, states John H. Bland, M.D., in his book, *Live Long, Die Fast.*

Under normal conditions (i.e., no inflammation or excessive protein intake), the color of urine is a good indicator of whether the amount of water we drink is sufficient. If the urine is light yellow in color, we are drinking enough; if it is yellow or even darker, we need to drink more water.

Longevity Drinks

One of the world's earliest scientific inquiries in the field of health and longevity is traced to China. The ancient sages and scholars of China created many recipes for tonic drinks that promoted health and longevity. Of the few in the following list, one of the most familiar is **green tea**. A Chinese legend says that the emperor Shen-Nung first brewed tea in 2737 BC, when a few tea leaves accidentally fell into some boiling water--that was green tea. Today, it has been proven that this ancient herbal tea blocks *cancer*, heals *heart disease*, reverses *aging,* and even lowers *cholesterol*. At present, it is known that green tea has at least the following three undeniably potent healing properties:

1. *Antioxidant protection.* Green tea has strong antioxidant powers-- stronger than blueberries, strawberries, garlic, and kale, which are the antioxidant champions among fruits and vegetables. It has more anti-cancer and anti-heart-disease power than even vitamins C and E.

2. *Anti-tumor protection.* The *Journal of the National Cancer Institute* recently reported on a study that showed how green tea reduced cancer risk 57 percent for men and 60 percent for women.

3. *Lowers cholesterol and cuts stroke risk in half.*

To get the most of green tea's healing properties, do not use boiling water to make it; use lukewarm distilled water instead. After soaking for 10 minutes, the well-done tea is ready. Distilled water free of inorganic salts perfectly extracts the soluble components from the tea leaves. When eaten, the leaves of green tea help to lower blood pressure. The leaves are very nutritious, so don't discard the tea grounds after pouring the tea. Eat them or grind up the leaves and sprinkle the powder on rice. Elementary and middle schools in Tokyo use it in school lunches. Eating black tea and oolong tea, however, has little effect, as a Japanese study showed.

The Chinese super-centenarian, Li Ching-Yun (1677-1933), who allegedly lived for 256 years, was a Taoist master and herbalist. Although his extremely old age is doubtful in light of recent age-exaggeration disclaimers, there are notes that his age has been verified. "After his death, modern scholars confirmed his identity, traced his life all the way back to the year of his birth, and conclusively verified his lifespan," according to Daniel Reid in his book, *The Complete Book of Chinese Health and Healing.* Li Ching-Yun used **Fo-ti-Tieng** and **ginseng**, two powerful rejuvenating herbs prepared as teas. For promoting health and prolonging life, he recommended tonics made from **ginseng**, **gotu kola**, **Polygonum multiflorum**, and **garlic**.

Ginseng may be used as a single herb tea or in a formula with other herbs. Ginseng powder is available in natural food stores such as Bread & Circus. One teaspoon of ginseng in a glass of hot water with honey makes a pleasant and warming drink, although it is a little bitter and pungent.

Chinese Longevity Tonic. According to Reid, the following longevity formula, which includes ginseng, "boosts vital energy and tones the liver and kidneys," and can be prepared at home.

The ingredients include 8 grams each of *Panax ginseng*, *Polygonum mlutifloru*, *Lycium chinensis*, *Schizandrae chinensis*, and *Asparagus lucidus*. To make a one-day dosage of the concoction, the mixture of these herbs should be boiled in 3 cups of water until the volume is reduced to 1 cup. The remaining herbs are used in a second boiling with 2 cups of water reduced to 1 cup. Two doses daily are recommended for three to six months. If the tonic is prepared with spirits, 48 grams of each ingredient must be used to make 6 liters. The ingredients are available at traditional Chinese pharmacies in

Chinatowns. When sick with cold, fever, and respiratory ailments, it is better to suspend drinking this formula.

Lao-jan Longevity Liquid. For those who prefer a ready-made patent formula, natural food stores sell the Lao-jan tonic made of many kinds of roots, flowers, leaves, stems, and fruits. It originated in Li's family in China and was handed down from generation to generation for more than a thousand years. The tonic comes from China in a package of twenty-four 10-milliliter bottles.

Longevitea. Bread & Circus offers a blend of herbs called Longevitea, which includes *Siberian ginseng, sarsaparilla, Fo Ti, hawthorn, nettles, ginkgo, gotu kola, licorice, alfalfa, oat straw,* and *violet*. To make a concoction, put 1 teaspoon of the blend in 1 cup of water and then boil it for 10 minutes. With 1 teaspoon of honey, it becomes a very flavorful and tasteful tonic.

There is a pitfall, however, in using hot water for teas. Paul Kouchakoff, M.D., found that cooking food and boiling water is responsible for leukocytosis, an excessive number of white blood cells in the blood. "Critical temperatures at which food became 'pathological' producing symptoms of leukocytosis, varied with the food: carrots at 206 degrees F, potatoes at 200 degrees F, and even water heated above 191 degrees F. Considering the toxic reaction of water when heated should discourage the use of herb teas in favor of live juices of greater biochemical potency and anti-leukocytosis properties," stated Victoras Kulvinskas, N.D., in his best-selling book, *Survival into the 21st Century*." Actually, it is not necessary to use water at boiling temperature to get a good concoction; using lukewarm water poured over green tea or ground ginger root makes a good drink.

Other well-known longevity drinks are **yogurt, buttermilk, red grape wine**, and **fresh juices** of greens, vegetables, and fruits. Freshly squeezed juices made of greens such as clover, alfalfa, reddish sprouts, wheat grass, kale, parsley, dill, spinach, cabbage, and dandelion greens are particularly potent because they are rich in chlorophyll. Chlorophyll--one of nature's best cleansers and detoxifiers--is the real elixir of youth. It performs many miracles for the body: purifies the blood; builds red blood cells; neutralizes toxins; helps keep the body's vital fluids pure, such as enzymes, hormones, and neurotransmitters; and provides the body with fast energy. A person benefits most from fresh juices if the greens, vegetables, and fruits chosen are appropriate for blood, Ayurvedic dosha, and Yin-Yang types.

Following is a recipe for a juice of greens, vegetables, and fruits that is appropriate for people of most blood, Ayurvedic dosha, and Yin-Yang types (the portion is for two servings):

Longevijuice	
1-2 carrots	1 medium kale leaf
1-2 apples	1 beet, including leaves
¼ papaya	1 clove garlic, peeled;
3 sprigs fresh parsley	or
1 handful spinach	1 ounce horseradish

If they were not grown organically, all ingredients must be peeled and thoroughly washed. After they are processed in the juicer, drink the juice cocktail immediately. The beet juice ingredient of the cocktail is a perfect blood builder; a splendid regulator of peristalsis; and a good therapy for the kidneys, gallbladder and liver stones, and sexual weakness. Although the iron content in beets is not the highest among other foods, in raw beets it is present in a form easily assimilated by the body. In terms of Yin-Yang, beets have a cooling effect on the blood. The healing qualities of other ingredients in the Longevijuice cocktail are discussed in other chapters of this book.

The basic guidelines for fluid intake are as follows:

• Start your day with a glass of freshly squeezed, organically grown fruit or vegetable juice. Use fruits and vegetables appropriate to your blood, dosha, and Yin-Yang types. Sprouts (e.g., alfalfa, garlic, bean) and grass (e.g., wheat, barley, rye) juices are the best. Have another glass or two of juice during the day. Let your juicer make your best medicine.

• Get the fluids for your system by eating plenty of fresh water-rich fruits and vegetables and juicing them in your mouth.

• Drink green, black, and herb tea made with distilled water or drink distilled water alone. Avoid milk, coffee, and alcoholic beverages or drink them sparingly. Buttermilk and yogurt, a source of acidophilus, are good for your intestines.

• Regulate your fluid intake according to your sense of thirst, the color of your urine, and the condition of your skin.

20

OXYGEN INTAKE CONTROL (BREATHING)

All living creatures need oxygen to maintain their health and sustain life itself. Oxygen is taken from the air through the process of respiration and delivered by blood to the cells. It is used there in chemical reactions with food molecules for release of the energy that has been stored in their chemical bonds. Cells need this energy to carry out their basic functions, including synthesis of nucleic acids and proteins, reproduction, and division of the cells. Fish and aquatic animals use gills for respiration; insects use tracheae. Most air-breathing animals and humans use their lungs, where the oxygen (O_2) taken from the air is passed into the bloodstream and the carbon dioxide (CO_2) produced in the cells is released back into the air. Thus, respiration is the fundamental process of life and the reason we need to breathe.

For centuries, physicians of all countries were unanimous in their belief about oxygen giving us health and vitality--and life itself. The more oxygen we take in, the healthier we are is widely assumed as conventional wisdom. Until now, a majority of doctors and sports and health experts believed in magic oxygen. The advice, "Breathe deeply," can be heard on morning exercise radio programs around the world. "For health and longevity, you don't want to stop oxidation. You want to maximize it. Oxidation is the basic process of life," according to Dr. Michael Colgan in the August 1977 issue of *Man's Fitness* magazine.

America's health pioneers, Dr. Paul C. Bragg and his daughter Dr. Patricia Bragg, say the following about the benefits of oxygen intake for health and fitness: "...high vibration people...display seemingly inexhaustible vitality and stamina, creative power, and/or athletic ability of the highest quality. What is their secret? How do they live at a superior rate of high vibration? The answer is really very simple. Such people consume large amounts of oxygen. They breathe deeply and fully, utilizing every square inch of their lung capacity. The more oxygen you can breathe into your lungs, the more energy you will have and the higher will be your rate of vibration."

We can clearly learn from this quotation that increased oxygen intake is highly beneficial for our health; it is common sense knowledge with which we are raised. Dr. Paul Bragg called air "Doctor Fresh Air" because of its oxygen value and praised oxygen to the extreme. Dr. Patricia Bragg attributed her father's high level of fitness and extraordinary vitality to his breathing exercises, which involved increased oxygen intake. It has been noted previously that Paul Bragg died at the age of ninety-five in an accident while practicing *surfing*–he drowned in a very high wave. At the age of ninety-five, he was engaged in a sport that many twenty-year-olds are unable to do. This was an incredible achievement and his belief of living a long and healthy life to its highest strikes me deeply and encourages me tremendously.

Breathing Rate and Longevity

I am a big fan of Dr. Paul Bragg and share many of his ideas, including the one regarding the role of deep, slow breathing for our health and longevity. In his book, *Building Powerful Nerve Force,* Dr. Bragg equates diaphragmatic breathing that enables one to intake more oxygen to a source of longevity. Diaphragmatic breathing combined with rare breathing creates miracles. "Animals that breathe fast live short lives; long-living animals breathe slowly." Dr. Bragg learned this secret from a 126-year-old holy man (who looked only seventy years old) who he met in the foothills of the Himalayan Mountains in India. He had sharp eyesight, a bright mind, and good spirits. He inhaled just once a minute and experienced a continuous bliss, according to Dr. Bragg. In his other book, *The Miracle of Fasting*, Dr. Bragg said, "For over seventy years, I have done extensive research on long-lived people and I find one common denominator among all of them. They are deep breathers. I have found that deeper, and therefore fewer, breaths a person takes in one minute, the longer they live, and the rapid breathers are the short-lived people." A breathing rate of once a minute is thought to be a secret of longevity in Indian yogis. Although it is difficult to verify the holy man's advanced age, Dr. Bragg explained, "This man had no reason to lie to me, because his whole life was spent in getting closer to God."

Having heard that the Indian yogis can do miracles, I can believe that the age of the holy man was not exaggerated, although 126 years is beyond the proven cases of superior longevity in humans. What impressed me most was the possibility of extending life by changing breathing patterns. Until now, the science that studies aging and life extension did not link human longevity to oxygen intake or rate of breathing. There were a few centenarians, however, who attributed their longevity to a special breathing technique. I recall the case of Shirali Muslinov, a peasant from Azerbaidzhan in the former USSR, who was proclaimed the oldest man on earth when he died at the alleged age of 168 years. He was once even included in *The Guinness Book of World Records* as the oldest man on earth. Now, in light of many cases of age exaggeration, no one takes these claims seriously; recently, the researchers from the Azerbaidzhan Academy of Sciences disregarded the claim of Muslinov's age.

Nevertheless, he definitely achieved a very ripe old age and his case can be used for our purpose. When once asked what was the secret of his longevity, Muslinov replied: "All people try to inhale as much air as they can; on the contrary, throughout my life I tried to *exhale* as much air as I could." In his efforts to exhale more air, he used a kind of prolonged exhalation--like in the *zazen* breathing technique--or he held his breath after an exhalation. Because the exhaling phase of breathing in this case is longer than usual, it leads to a reduction of the breathing rate. In other words, Muslinov's secret of longevity was in a lower rate of breathing. Although we do not know how many times a minute his breathing pattern was, what is important is that he attributed his longevity not to diet, exercise, or a healthy lifestyle, but rather to the habit of breathing more slowly than usual.

Two more cases are from the book, *The Miracle of Fasting*, by Dr. Bragg: "I had a friend for many years named Amos Stagg, the famous football and athletic coach. Mr. Stagg lived to be over 100 years of age. I asked him his secret of long life and his answer was, 'I have the greater part of my life indulged in running and other vigorous exercise that forced large amounts of oxygen into my body."

"I had a friend in New York, James Hocking, who was one of the greatest long-distance walking champions this country has ever had. I asked Mr. Hocking, on his hundredth birthday, the secret of his long, active life and super-health. His answer was, 'I have always walked vigorously and breathed deeply.'" Exercise involves large O_2 intake along with a large production of CO_2. The role of these two gases for our health is discussed later in this chapter.

Although not yet a hundred years old, Nakagawa Masamichi, ninety, of Japan, also considers his breathing exercise as one of the secrets of his sound fitness and vitality. He uses a breathing technique of forceful exhaling as much air from his lungs as he can. Each exhalation lasts up to 45 seconds. Sitting on his heels on the floor in a zazen posture, he swings his upper body from side to side and raises his voice while exhaling. He appeared on the *Diet for Longevity*, the Japanese NHK TV program on January 22, 1998.

In Japan, the prominent scholars and researchers who promote deep diaphragm breathing are long-living people themselves, says Fujibayashi Toshihiro in his book, *Health Savings in Preparing for the Aging Society*. The Tokyo University professor who originated the breathing method is ninety-four years old.

The case of the Indian yogi who breathed once a minute was so striking that I attempted to check out his words about rapidly and slowly breathing animals and their life span. Searching for information, I realized that the data on maximum life span can be found easily and covers about a hundred species of animals and insects. The data on the maximum life span of animals used in the following figure was obtained primarily from *The Guinness Book of Animal Facts and Feats*. Although data on breathing rate is more rare, I was able to find matching figures for humans and for eighteen species of animals. Some data on breathing rate was adapted from the *Chronological Table of Natural Sciences*, 1996 issue (in Japanese). The relationship between rate of breathing and maximum life span is shown in Figure 20-1.

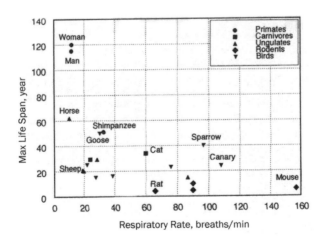

Figure 20-1. Maximum Life Span versus Breathing Rate for
Five Groups of Animals

The dots in this figure represent five groups of animals: primates (humans and monkeys), carnivores (flesh-eating mammals), ungulates (hoofed or horny-foot mammals), rodents (mammals with strong incisors and no canine teeth, such as the rat, mouse, squirrel, and beaver), and birds. Although the scatter of data is quite large, the inverse relationship can be seen clearly: the *faster the respiratory rate, the shorter the life span* is. This proves the theory of the Indian yogi, and from this we can draw the conclusion that by reducing the breathing rate, we can increase our chances to live longer.

Air that we inhale, or atmospheric air, is a composition of fourteen gases, but just four of those gases--nitrogen, oxygen, argon, and CO_2--constitute 99.99 percent of the atmospheric air. The other ten gases--known as inert--are found in trace amounts.

The presence of water vapor in the air varies depending on climate and determines the air humidity. Of the four gases, only oxygen and CO_2 can be utilized by plants, animals, and humans. Although nitrogen gas constitutes 78 percent of air, it cannot be utilized directly by higher organisms; it must be fixed or converted into useable form. Cyano-bacteria and some other bacteria are capable of nitrogen fixation, which extracts nitrogen from air and converts it into compounds such as ammonia and nitrates, which other organisms can use. Tiny amounts of dinitrogen oxide (N_2O), which can be utilized by animals and plants, also are found in the atmospheric air.

Now let's look at how the air is absorbed in our bodies. Atmospheric air inhaled into the lungs mixes with the water vapor that is always present in the lungs. Therefore, the contents of all gases from the air that fill the lungs, called *inspired air*, are reduced because they are "diluted" in the water vapor. Furthermore, air in the lungs undergoes the gas exchange in the *alveoli*--tiny air sacs numbering many millions. The content of alveolar air is different than inspired air because O_2 is continuously removed from inspired air and CO_2 is added. Finally, expired air has its own gas-content package, which is enriched in CO_2 and reduced in O_2.

Although the basic knowledge of the physiology of respiration was established long ago, there is still controversial data on the content of expired air in humans, primarily about nitrogen content, although the O_2 and CO_2 figures do not differ significantly. Some authors show larger nitrogen content in the expired air than in the inspired air, meaning that nitrogen loss takes place--but others show a nitrogen gain. For example, in his book, *Mountain Medicine,* Dr. Michael Ward provides the changes in the composition of air during respiration at sea level. The figures in Table 9 of his book represent the partial pressures of gases in air in mmHg; I have converted them to percentages of gas content in order to compare them with findings from other authors. For example, Dr. Ward gives the partial pressure of oxygen in atmospheric air as 159 mmHg. Because the total atmospheric pressure is 760 mmHg at sea level and it corresponds to 100 percent of gases, the content of oxygen is calculated as follows:

$$(159 / 760) \times 100\% = 20.92\%$$

The percentages of gases are presented in Table 20-1. For comparison, some data from the book, *Human Anatomy & Physiology*, by Dr. Elaine N. Marieb (shown in parentheses), and from *Human Physiology*, a textbook for medical students in Russia (shown in brackets), are also shown.

Dr. Ward explains the difference in oxygen content in the atmospheric and inspired air this way: "As air is inhaled into the lungs, it becomes saturated with water vapor at body temperature. The partial pressure of water vapor is 47 mmHg. Therefore, the PO_2 of inspired air is 20.9 percent of 760-47 mmHg = 149 mmHg." This results in the following equation:

$$(149 / 760) \times 100\% = 19.6\%$$

Table 20-1. Exchange of Gases During Respiration

Gas	Atmospheric Air	Inspired Air	Alveolar Air	Expired Air
(Contents by volume in %)				
Nitrogen (N_2)	78.55 (78.6)	74.13	74.87 (74.9)	74.47
Oxygen (O_2)	20.92 (20.9) [21]	19.64	13.68 (13.7) [14.6]	15.79 [16.6]
CO_2	0.04 (0.04) [0.03]	0.04	5.26 (5.2) [5.4]	3.55 [3.7]
Water (H_2O)	0.48 (0.46)	6.18	6.18 (6.2)	6.18

According to Dr. Ward, a further decrease of oxygen in alveolar air occurs because of the continuous process of oxygen removal from inspired air and the addition of CO_2 from blood. It is interesting to note that expired air contains more O_2 than alveolar air because it is mixed with residual air in the lungs. Also, expired air contains 0.34 percent more nitrogen than inspired air; that is, nitrogen loss takes place. This excessive nitrogen may come from protein-rich foods.

In the textbook, *College Zoology*, the following table shows concentration changes of atmospheric gases during respiration.

Table 20-2. Concentration Changes of Gases during Respiration

Gas	Inspired Air	Expired Air	Net Difference
Oxygen (O_2)	21.00%	16.02%	Gain: 5.80%
CO_2	00.05%	03.60%	Loss: 3.55%
Nitrogen (N_2)	78.30%	75.00%	Gain: 3.30%

Adapted from *College Zoology.*

In the table, the oxygen gain of 5.80 percent is a mistaken overestimate; that is, if 16.02 is subtracted from 21.00, the result is 4.98 percent. Also, this table shows a gain in nitrogen; however, in the previous table, a nitrogen loss occurred. Therefore, the data from these two sources is contradictory regarding nitrogen, so we will review some other sources.

Two Japanese sources and one American source--*Encyclopedia of Medical Sciences, Biological Encyclopedia,* and *Inquiry into Life* (5th edition by Sylvia S. Mader)--provide the following data on inspired and expired air (Table 20-3).

Table 20-3. Contents of Gases in Inspired and Expired Air

Gas	Encyclopedia of Medical Sciences		Biological Encyclopedia		Inquiry into Life	
	Inspired Air	Expired Air	Inspired Air	Expired Air	Inspired Air	Expired Air
Oxygen (O_2) %	20.93	16.23	20.94	16.44	20.96	16.02
CO_2 %	00.03	04.05	00.03	03.84	00.04	04.38
Nitrogen (N_2) %	79.04	79.72	79.03	79.03	79.00	79.60
N_2, mmHg	563.6	568.0	596.0	565.0	–	–
Water vapor (H_2O) mmHg	47	47	5.7	47	–	–

As shown in this table, the oxygen gain in expired air ranges from 4.50 to 4.94 percent, CO_2 loss is from 3.81 to 4.34 percent, and nitrogen is either lost by 0.60 to 0.68 percent or remains unchanged. Although the figures on O_2 and CO_2 content are quite stable, the biggest discrepancy is found in nitrogen content. With the data from Table 20-2, we have all three cases: gain, loss, and unchanged amount of nitrogen. A different interpretation is also given to both partial pressure of water vapor (H_2O) and nitrogen (N_2). The *Encyclopedia of Medical Sciences* shows the same partial pressure of 47 mmHg for H_2O in both inspired and expired air; however, another source gives 5.7 and 4.7 mmHg for the inspired and expired air, respectively.

Nitrogen partial pressure in expired air is larger in the *Encyclopedia of Medical Sciences* and smaller in the other Japanese source.

Even atmospheric air is interpreted in different ways. *The New Encyclopedia Britannica* defines dry atmospheric air as composed of nitrogen and inert gases (79.02 percent), O_2 (20.94 percent), and CO_2 (0.03 percent). Therefore, nitrogen and the inert gases, such as argon, neon, krypton, and xenon, are combined into one group. Finally, I want to note that *The Big Soviet Encyclopedia* of the USSR says that the O_2 content in the expired air as compared with inspired air is reduced to 15.0 – 18.0 percent and the CO_2 is increased to 2.5 – 5.5 percent; however, the nitrogen content remains about the same. This is a much bigger range in the two major gases involved in respiration—O_2 and CO_2—in the expired air.

Of the three gases (i.e., nitrogen, O_2, and CO_2), nitrogen is probably the most mysterious. In his book, *Biological Transmutations,* Professor C. Louis Kervran (1901-1983), who was a member of the New York Academy of Sciences and the director of the Conference of the Paris University, gave an "audacious explanation" of the nitrogen metabolism: nitrogen is converted into carbon monoxide. Animal experiments showed that nitrogen production occurs in the inside wall of the intestines. Under a normal eating regimen, however, one ingests more nitrogen than one excretes. Carnivorous animals, which eat nitrogen-rich meat, do not produce it and excrete very little of it. Herbivorous animals, whose nourishment is poor in nitrogen, produce a lot of nitrogen. In one experiment, a man put on a complete fast excreted 11.9 grams of nitrogen per day. When he was given sugar (i.e., no nitrogen food), he excreted only 6.3 grams of nitrogen per day. This experiment showed that with the carbohydrates available from food, the conversion of body protein into carbohydrates decreased and nitrogen was produced in smaller quantities. The endogenous metabolism of nitrogen in these examples is related to food. Professor Kervran, however, did not support the idea of atmospheric nitrogen metabolism.

This discussion shows that the physiology of respiration is still a developing science and some problems--such as the content of expired air and the possible utilization of nitrogen--have to be clarified. We can anticipate many discoveries in this field in the future, especially regarding the extraordinary condition of people like the Indian yogi breathing once a minute and the Chinese mystery Xu Fang, who has not eaten for thirteen years.

Oxygen Uptake

Now let us analyze the amount of oxygen that the yogi master took in while breathing once a minute and compare it with an average man. First, we will look at how much oxygen a healthy individual inhales in a normal breathing pattern and then compare it with the intake of the slowly breathing yogi. We need to know the following:

1. *Rate of respiration,* or number of breaths per minute
2. *Oxygen gain* in one breath, or difference in oxygen content between inspired and expired air
3. *Volume of air* that is exchanged in the lungs with one inhale-exhale cycle, or alveolar ventilation volume

We can assume that a typical young person primarily uses his rib cage for breathing, expanding it outward, and does not use diaphragm breathing. According to Dr. Elaine N. Marieb, author of the book, *Human Anatomy & Physiology*, the lung tidal volume (TV) for a healthy twenty-year-old male is 500 milliliters and the dead space volume (DV) (i.e., air in the passageways from the throat to the lungs) is 150 milliliters.

Rate of respiration depends on age, sex, profession, environment, health condition, activity level, and other factors. In healthy adults at rest, it ranges from 11 to 18 breaths per minute. Many Japanese sources indicate a breathing rate for adults to be on average 12 to 16 breaths per minute, although some give higher figures. According to the Japanese source, *Illustration Anatomical & Physiological Basis of Human Body*, newborn babies breathe 40 to 50 times per minute; children at the age of five, 26 to 28 times per minute; and adults, 16 to 20 times per minute. The *Standard Values of Japanese, Book 4,* shows a graph of respiration-rate changes with age. At the age of four, the rate is at the maximum, with 26 to 26.5 times per minute. As children grow, it decreases; in non-trained males, the respiration rate achieves its minimum value of about 18 breaths per minute by eighteen or nineteen years; in females, it is 20 breaths per minute by twenty-one to twenty-three years. Then, with continued aging, the respiration rate gradually increases to 21.7 and 22.4 breaths per minute in males and females, respectively, by the age of seventy.

The Japanese source *Encyclopedia of Medical Sciences* provides the following respiration rates:

At rest: Average 11.7 (range 10.1 to 13.1) per minute
Light work: Average 17.1 (range 15.7 to 18.2) per minute
Heavy work: Average 21.2 (range 18.6 to 23.3) per minute

All three Japanese sources give somewhat different values for the average breathing rate. Respiration rate reduces with increased fitness level--well-trained athletes breathe 7 to 9 times per minute—while non-fit obese people breathe 22 to 24 times per minute. According to Dr. Marieb, for healthy American males, the average is 12 breaths per minute. In her book, *Inquiry into Life,* Sylvia S. Mader gives 14 to 20 times per minute as a normal breathing rate. For our purposes, we will use 16 breaths per minute as the average.

Oxygen gain is the amount absorbed by the body within one breath; determining a mean value from the data in Tables 3-3 through 3-5 results in 4.6 percent. The *volume of air* that passes through the lungs into the bloodstream and back is assumed to be 350 milliliters in one breath. The volume of air per minute in a typical breathing individual is calculated to be:

$$(500 - 150) \times 16 = 5{,}600 \text{ milliliters per minute}$$

This equation results in an oxygen intake of $5{,}600 \times 0.046 = 257.6$ milliliters per minute. As stated in both *Inquiry into Life*, by Sylvia S. Mader, and the *Japanese Biological Encyclopedia*, this figure is in good agreement with 250 milliliters per minute of oxygen absorbed by the lungs of an adult male in a restful state.

Now let's analyze the corresponding values for an infrequently breathing yogi. Because he uses deep diaphragm breathing, we can assume that his breathing pattern, or proportional duration of inhalation, breath–holding, and exhale, is 1:4:2, which is common in the yoga Pranayama breathing exercise. His respiratory rate is 1 breath per minute; so, using the previous assumption, he inhales for 8.5 seconds, holds his breath after inhalation for 34 seconds, and then exhales for 17.5 seconds--which totals 60 seconds for one breathing cycle. During his prolonged inhalation and breath-holding after inhalation, he fills his lungs using not only the TV of 500 milliliters, but also the inspiratory reserve volume (IRV), which is equal to 3,100 milliliters--if not 100 percent of it--but let's assume it is 70 percent. Because of his prolonged exhale, the yogi also uses about 70 percent or more of his expiratory reserve volume (ERV). His total TV is calculated as follows:

$$0.7 \times 3{,}100 + 0.7 \times 1{,}200 + 500 = 3{,}510 \text{ milliliters}$$

This is approximately the same amount of air typically inhaled in one breath by trained athletes in strenuous exercise.

For comparison, in the Japanese zazen religion, which uses a breathing technique that also utilizes diaphragm breathing, the maximum breathing volume is thought to be 1,700 milliliters, which is equal to the sum of the 500-milliliter TV and the 1,200–milliliter ERV. In zazen breathing, however, the depth of breathing is achieved only by deeper expiration (i.e., up to 100 percent of the ERV), although the inspiration does not go higher than an average TV.

Obtaining the *volume of air* absorbed by the yogi's lungs is calculated using the following equation:

$$(0.7 \times 3{,}100 + 0.7 \times 1{,}200 + 500 - 150) \times 1 = 3{,}360 \text{ milliliters per minute}$$

Next, we will consider how much oxygen the yogi absorbs with each breath. The amount of oxygen in his expired air must be less than that of other people. If we assume that the *oxygen gain* of a yogi master is 5 percent (i.e., close to the 4.94 percent maximum in Table 3-5), then his oxygen intake is calculated as follows:

$$3{,}360 \times 0.05 = 168.0 \text{ milliliters per minute}$$

Compared to 257.6 milliliters per minute for an average man, the yogi master consumes only 65 percent of the average amount of oxygen. *Lung Ventilation Efficiency.* By breathing deeply once a minute, the yogi uses his lung ventilation more efficiently than an ordinary man, as the following comparison shows. The percentage of lung ventilation efficiency (LVE) is calculated by subtracting the DV from the TV, and then divided by total lung capacity (TLC), which is equal to 6,000 milliliters. The calculation for an average individual breathing at rest is as follows:

$$LVE = [(TV - DV) / TLC] \times 100\% = [(500 - 150) / 6000] \times 100\% = 5.8\%$$

For the Indian yogi, the LVE is calculated in the following equation:

$$[(0.7 \times IRV + 0.7 \times ERV + TV - DV) / TLC] \times 100\% =$$
$$[(0.7 \times 3{,}100 + 0.7 \times 1{,}200 + 500 - 150) / 6{,}000] \times 100\% = 56.0\%$$

Isn't it amazing that, with his once-a-minute deep diaphragm-breathing pattern, the yogi's LVE is about ten times more efficient than that of an ordinary breathing person who breathes 16 times per minute.

It is known from the physiology of respiration, and was confirmed in the previous calculation, that increasing the depth of breathing enhances alveolar ventilation and gas exchange more than raising the breathing rate. This is because the proportion of TV to DV is larger in deep breathing. In shallow breathing, the proportion becomes smaller and the alveolar ventilation decreases because only a little fresh air reaches the alveoli, where the gas exchange takes place. Increasing the breathing rate while shallow breathing does not help much because of the low efficiency of alveolar ventilation.

The previous calculation of oxygen intake shows that, for the assumptions made, the per-minute oxygen intake of a yogi master is about two-thirds that of an average man. From common sense and without any calculations, it seems evident that a person inhaling once a minute--even with the deepest breathing--could not consume more oxygen than a person inhaling 16 times per minute. Therefore, was it really oxygen that gave the Indian yogi a super long life and vitality, or was it something else? In this case, oxygen does not seem to play a major role. Then what else does?

Another gas involved in respiration needs to be discussed--CO_2, which is usually regarded as a waste. Modern medical science holds that our respiratory system is mostly concerned with obtaining O_2 and ridding the body of CO_2. In contrast with oxygen, CO_2 was always a culprit, happy to be expelled as soon as possible. Plants are designed to consume CO_2 and excrete O_2, which is a waste for them; however, animals and humans are CO_2 expellers and O_2 consumers. Actually, although we eliminate the excess, CO_2 is an important element for our bodies; it constitutes 18.5 percent of our body mass--second only to O_2, which constitutes 65 percent. Our muscles contain 6 percent CO_2, and the CO_2/O_2 ratio of the blood is an important factor to maintain a normal environment for all body systems.

A rapid loss of CO_2 induced with fast and deep breathing causes muscle rigidity, stupor, and cataleptic coma. Shallow and slow breathing increases the CO_2 content of the blood. If CO_2 accumulates in the blood due to infrequent breathing, the bronchi, small blood vessels, and capillaries of the lungs widen and the blood (and eventually the body cells) receives more oxygen. This is because the alveoli--with the increased blood flow in the capillaries--can absorb more oxygen. Therefore, the point is not the amount of oxygen in the lungs, but rather how much of it reaches the cells.

In the case of a yogi master who exhales only once per minute, the accumulated amounts of CO_2 in his blood cause the bronchiole and capillaries to open widely for larger amounts of oxygen to be absorbed. His cells and tissues will also have a sufficient amount of oxygen if he can maintain an extremely infrequent breathing rate. He has achieved this body condition by decades of breathing exercises, resulting in a change in the physiology of his body: the O_2/CO_2 ratio of his blood is different than in an ordinary man because of the higher CO_2 content.

It is understood that breathing is an automatic process that goes on without our conscious attention. This automatic breathing is governed by the "respiratory center" in our brain, which in turn is regulated by the contents of CO_2 in the blood. An increase in CO_2 content induces faster and deeper breathing; a decrease causes shallow and slow breathing. Is it possible to change the natural breathing pattern and make infrequent breathing an automatic process? It appears to be so. Training results in miracles. The yogi master was able to control his respiratory center and, despite the high CO_2 content in his blood, his breathing is slow and deep. This new pattern is automatic and continues both in the day and at night when he sleeps.

The abilities of Indian yogis to regulate the body's automatic processes such as breathing rate and even heart rate are well known. I recall another yoga guru who came to Moscow about fifteen years ago and appeared on a TV program. Newspapers reported afterwards that among his extreme vitality, flexibility, and other demonstrated miracles was the ability to control his breathing rate: he was able to reduce his daytime breathing pattern of a few breaths per minute to 1 breath per minute when he slept.

Lifetime Oxygen Consumption

Some people believe that many physiological functions–including number of heartbeats, number of breaths, calorie intake, and oxygen consumption--have limited value within our life span. That idea was originated in 1908 by the German physiologist Max Rubner, who discovered that the longevity of animals is related to their metabolic rate and body size. This idea is known as the *"rate of living" theory of aging*. According to Rubner, small animals (e.g., mice and guinea pigs) as well as large animals (e.g., horses and elephants) expend about the same number of kilocalories (200 to 280) per gram of tissue during their lifetime. Small and short-lived mice expend larger amounts of calories per gram of tissue per year than the bigger and long-lived elephants. Humans are different--they metabolize about 800 kcal, or three to four times more than animals.

Oxygen consumption is greater in small animals and decreases progressively with the increase in an animal's weight. An animal's life span is also related to its body weight; therefore, the bigger the animal, the longer is its life span. Thus, oxygen consumption divided by body weight is inversely related to an animal's life span. The life span and many physiological functions, such as heart and breathing rate, can be calculated based on the body weight of animals. In his book, *Time of Elephant, Time of Mouse,* the

Japanese author Tomokawa Tatsuo gives the following formula for the breathing cycle duration--or breathing interval (BI)--in seconds, depending on the animal's weight (W) in kilograms:

$$BI = 1.1 \; W^{0.26}$$

The BI for a mouse with a weight of 0.035 kilogram is 0.46 second; for a horse weighing 703 kilograms, it is 6.0 seconds—therefore, the breathing rate is 130 and 10 times per minute for a mouse and a horse, respectively. These figures correspond well with the data plotted on Figure 20-1. The lifetime oxygen consumption in animals depends on their weight and ranges from 3,000 L for a mouse (maximum life span of six years) to 55,400,000 L for a horse (maximum life span of sixty-two years).

In humans, the lifetime oxygen consumption is limited to 21 million L, according to the Japanese best-selling author Shigeo Haruyama in his book, *The Wellness Revolution for Happiness*. A person dies as soon as he/she has consumed this amount of oxygen, he adds. Another Japanese source indicates that the average amount of air that we inhale throughout our life is 200 million L. Because we gain 4.6 percent of oxygen with each breath, this results in 9,200,000 L of oxygen, or 44 percent of the lifetime oxygen limit determined by Haruyama.

We can also analyze lifetime oxygen consumption based on a study of energy, protein, fat, and carbohydrate consumption among seventy-two elderly men and eighty-nine elderly women. The results of the study, which was conducted in 1995 in Japan, were published in the *Data Book, 1995,* released by the Ra • Ra Society. The daily consumption by men was 1,940 ± 325 kcal; by women, it was 1,697 ± 381 kcal. These data are shown in Table 20-4.

Table 20-4. Daily Oxygen Consumption by Elderly Japanese

Food	Amount, grams		O_2 Consumption, L per 1 gram	O_2 Consumption, L per total amount	
	Men	Women		Men	Women
Protein	72.6	66.5	0.950	69.0	63.2
Carbohydrates	264.0	235.0	0.745	196.7	175.1
Fat	54.6	52.0	2.020	110.3	105.0
			Total	376.0	343.3

Using these daily amounts of food consumption throughout life, a centenarians' lifetime (i.e., 100 years) oxygen consumption to metabolize this food is calculated as follows:

For men: 376 x 365.25 x 100 = 13,733,400 L
For women: 343.3 x 365.25 x 100 = 12,539,032 L

For an average life span, which in Japan is seventy-nine years for men and eighty-four years for women, the following calculations are used:

For men: 376 x 365.25 x 79 = 10,849,386 L
For women: 343.3 x 365.25 x 84 = 10,532,787 L

Isn't it amazing that in terms of oxygen consumption, men and women use the same amount within their average life span? Women eat less, consume less oxygen, and live an average of five years longer than men. Furthermore, the latter figures are fairly close to the 10 million quarts (9,454,550 L) of oxygen that each person consumes in a lifetime, according to the estimate of Jules Hirsch, M.D., of the Rockefeller University Hospital.

The previous calculations also show that either the limit of 21 million L of O_2 is overestimated or the maximum human life span can be about 150 to160 years. For comparison, the sumo wrestlers of Japan--who consume about 5,500 kcal per day throughout their life--need 1,100 L of O_2 to metabolize this food, reaching the limit when they are just fifty-two years old. It is clear from these considerations that the more we eat, the more oxygen we consume--and the sooner it burns out our food and us as well, thereby shortening our life span.

Oxygen consumption is very dependent on our level of daily activities–that is, how fast we burn the food and stored calories. For a person weighing 70 kilograms, O_2 consumption in L/minute is 0.21 when sleeping; 0.33 when sitting; 0.66 when walking; 1.87 when jogging; 1.63 when swimming; and 3.62 when stair–climbing. Oxygen consumption also is greatly influenced by a person's fitness level.

Fitness implies one's ability to sustain high-intensity exercise for longer than 4 or 5 minutes and is measured by *maximal oxygen uptake* ($VO_{2\,max}$). The higher the fitness level, the higher is the $VO_{2\,max}$ value. According to Arthur T. Johnson and Cathryn R. Dooly of the University of Maryland, typical values of $VO_{2\,max}$ are 2.5 L/minute for young male non-athletes and 5.0 L/minute for well-trained athletes; the women's values are about 70 to 80 percent of those for men. Maximal oxygen uptake achieves its peak at approximately twenty-two to twenty-four years, and then steadily declines with age at 1 percent per year. With one kind of exercise, it increases from about 0.3 L/minute in a young healthy male weighing 60 kilograms at rest, to its maximum value of 3.2 L/minute when exercise progresses from rest through light, moderate, heavy, and maximal stages.

If exercise progresses from rest to maximum exertion through all these stages, the oxygen concentration in the expired air gradually decreases from 17 percent to its minimum of 14.3 percent in 10 to 12 minutes, and then increases gradually again to 17 percent in the next 13 minutes. At the same time, the CO_2 concentration in the expired air increases from 3.3 percent at rest to its maximum value of 5.0 percent within the first 18 minutes of exercise, and then decreases to 4 percent in the next 7 minutes. It should be emphasized that the contents of expired air is not constant and changes depending on the fitness level of a person, including activity level, exercise, and other conditions.

Carbon Dioxide Production

Carbon dioxide (CO_2) usually attracts less attention than oxygen (O_2), although its role is of great importance for the body's homeostasis. *Homeostasis* is defined as a tendency toward a relatively stable equilibrium between interdependent physiological processes in our body. For example, there is an acid-alkaline balance in our blood, expressed by a pH value typically ranging from 7.35 to 7.45. Any fluctuation beyond this narrow range is dangerous for our health. CO_2 plays a crucial role in maintaining this pH balance.

The content of CO_2 in blood is related to respiratory rate. Respiratory rate is controlled by the respiratory control center located in the medulla of the brain. The rate of breathing is under two kinds of control: neural and chemical. The concentration of CO_2 in the blood influences the chemical control directly and the neural control indirectly, through nerve impulses. A high concentration of CO_2 increases the respiratory rate; a low concentration decreases it. A slow or rapid breathing rate raises or lowers the concentration of CO_2 in the blood. What is a *normal* rate of breathing?

According to the *Pocket Guide to Respiratory Care* by P.B. Weilitz, a normal, rhythmic breathing rate of 16 to 20 breaths per minute at rest is called *eupnea.* Infrequent breathing, at a rate of less than 12 breaths per minute, is considered abnormally slow. A rate of less than 10 breaths per minute, called *bradypnea,* occurs during sleep or in a hypnotic state. It also can be caused by the suppression of respiratory reflexes with drug overdose, narcotics, sedatives, and central nervous system (CNS) lesions.

A condition of hypoventilation inhibits the excretion of CO_2, which is accumulated in the arterial blood in a concentration above the normal 45 mmHg. Increased CO_2 combined with water produces excessive carbonic acid, which leads to a reduced blood pH--less than 7.35--and an increased plasma hydrogen-ion concentration. This condition, considered abnormal, is called respiratory or CO_2 *acidosis*.

On the other hand, rapid breathing in adults at rest at a rate of 25 breaths per minute is considered accelerated. A breathing rate of 40 or more breaths per minute leads to another abnormal condition called respiratory *alkalosis*, which is manifested in CO_2 loss and decreased PCO_2, decreased plasma hydrogen-ion concentration, and increased blood pH--that is, more than the normal range of 7.35 to 7.45. Alkalosis can be caused by aspirin toxicity, air pollution, diseases such as asthma, and often an extreme anxiety.

A sharp loss in CO_2 and respiratory alkalosis can also be induced with *deep and fast breathing* at rest. Alveolar air, which is usually quite stable (i.e., 14.6 percent O_2 and 5.4 percent CO_2), changes depending on the depth of breathing. Deep and fast breathing vastly decreases the CO_2 concentration, but does not greatly increase the O_2 concentration. It was Dr. Buteyko who discovered this physiological paradox in his respiratory tests. On the other hand, *shallow and slow breathing* increases the CO_2 content in alveolar air.

Exercise involves an increased production of CO_2 and a higher uptake of oxygen. The plot in Figure 20-2 shows the CO_2 production and O_2 uptake for different stages of exercise and walking/running speed. I adapted the data for this plot from the chapter entitled *Exercise Physiology*, by Arthur T. Johnson and Cathryn R. Dooly, in their book *Biomechanics* (CRC Press, Inc., 1995).

This plot shows that the production of CO_2 at rest is less than the O_2 uptake; however, for light, moderate, and maximal exercise, CO_2 production exceeds O_2 uptake. This is a very important point because it demonstrates that the super health, vitality, and longevity of runners and exercisers discussed previously were achieved due to **the CO_2 accumulated in their bodies, which enhances an increased oxygen supply to body cells**. Apparently, not all the benefits of CO_2 for our bodies are known yet and science will continue to discover its properties--and probably its *antioxidant* powers among them.

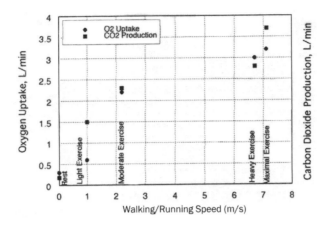

Figure 20-2.   Carbon Dioxide Production and Oxygen Uptake in Exercise

CO_2 is produced in the body during the process of food metabolism; different foods require different amounts of oxygen for combustion and end up with different amounts of CO_2. In the following table, protein, fat, and carbohydrates (1 gram) are shown with corresponding values of O_2, CO_2 (L), and respiratory quotient (RQ), which is the ratio of CO_2 production and O_2 consumption.

	O_2 Consumption	CO_2 Production	RQ
Protein	0.95	0.76	0.8
Fat	2.02	1.40	0.7
Carbohydrates	0.83	0.83	1.0

As shown in this data, carbohydrates are the most efficient and fat is the least efficient in terms of CO_2 production and O_2 consumption. The more O_2 we consume, the sooner we die, and the more CO_2 that is produced in our body, the healthier and longer life we can live. This is why the diet of long-living people and centenarians is mostly composed of carbohydrates, with little fat in it. Of course, if people live in cold climates and in the wintertime in other climates, they need more fat to provide energy. Under equal conditions, a higher percentage of carbohydrates seems to be more beneficial for health and longevity.

Breath-holding

CO_2 concentration in the alveolar air is closely related to the *breath-holding ability*, which is thought to be an indicator of overall health, fitness, and vitality. People are quite weak in breath-holding because the body stores very little oxygen and we need to continuously supply it from the outside. Brain cells are the most sensitive to oxygen shortage; they start to die within 8 minutes if they do not receive oxygen. Average men can hold their breath for 1 to 1.5 minutes, women for 0.5 to 1 minute. An exception are the ama, the female Japanese pearl divers, are reputed as great breath-holders, being able to continue diving for 1.5 to 2 minutes.

The longer the breath can be held after exhalation, the healthier an individual is. Only very healthy and specially trained people like Jeaque Maerou, Harry Houdini, and the ama pearl divers with their legendary breath-holding abilities could challenge their commitments. According to data obtained by Dr. Buteyko, if the breath is held (called "control pause") for 30 seconds, the CO_2 content in alveolar air is 5.0 percent; for 40 seconds, it is 5.5 percent; for 50 seconds, it is 6.0 percent; and for 60 seconds, it is 6.5 percent. The *control pause* is defined as the duration of breath-holding after exhaling up to the moment when the first uneasiness and urge to inhale is felt.

The relationship between duration of breath-holding and CO_2 content in alveolar air is shown in Figure 20-3.

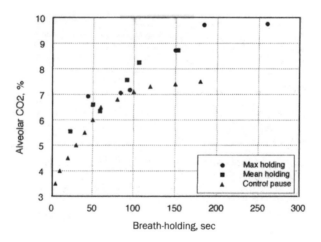

Figure 20-3.   Breath-holding versus CO_2 Content in Alveolar Air

There are three groups of dots on this plot. The round and square dots represent the findings of A.B. Otis, H. Rahn, and W.O. Fenn (1948) on the measurements of alveolar CO_2 during the breath-holding of men at sea level; the alveolar pressures were measured at the breaking point. I converted the pressures into percentages by dividing them by 760 mmHg. Round dots represent maximum values for both duration of breath-holding and the alveolar CO_2 obtained in measurements; squares display the mean values of a series of measurements. Triangles represent the findings of Dr. Buteyko, which were published in *Healing Powers, Biosynthesis, and Bioenergetics* by G.P. Malakhov.

Jocelyn Oliver, director and founder of Alive and Well, The Institution of Conscious Bodywork in San Anselmo, California, gives the same figures as Dr. Buteyko for holding breath and the CO_2 content in the alveolar air. She gives the following explanation of how to determine the breath hold: "Inhale normally for 2 seconds. Exhale for 3 seconds softly. Hold your nose to hold your breath until you feel a distinct desire to breathe. Count the seconds as you hold your breath."

The duration of breath-holding affects the respiration rate: a control pause of 30 seconds usually corresponds to 15 breaths per minute, 40 seconds to 12 breaths per minute, 50 seconds to 10 breaths per minute, and 60 seconds to 8 breaths per minute. From these figures, it can be concluded that the fittest breathe slowly. Although contemporary medicine considers a slow respiration rate as abnormal, the fittest are in some sense abnormally healthy when compared to average people. What is important is that slow breathing promotes vitality and, therefore, longevity because of CO_2 buildup. Of the two gases in question, it is **CO_2 that enhances longevity, not O_2**--the evidence is very clear.

CO_2 does not burn itself and, like a fire extinguisher, it regulates the speed of burning processes in our cells. In other words, it is responsible for our rate of living. The more intensive burning process in the cells, the sooner they get worn out and the sooner we die.

Oxygen and Carbon Dioxide: Which Is Friend and Which Is Foe?

No one doubts that oxygen is essential for our health and for survival itself. We need it, we depend on it, and we can't live even a few minutes without it. The cells of our body require about 250 milliliters of oxygen per minute in a sitting position; during exercise, the demand is much greater. In healthy individuals, an "oxygen debt" can occur if the lungs and blood circulation deliver less oxygen than the muscles consume during exercise. Chronic oxygen deficit in the body causes many severe diseases, including asthma and pneumonia, and heart diseases such as angina pectoris.

Is oxygen really so good for us that the formula "the more the better" should be applied? Every one has heard about oxygen tanks that are used by mountaineers in high altitudes or by patients with emphysema, pneumonia, or respiratory failure caused by carbon monoxide poisoning. They are helpful in emergency cases, but 100 percent oxygen is poisonous and its prolonged inhalation for just a few hours can lead to death. Hyperbaric oxygen--that is, oxygen at a pressure of more than 1 atmosphere--is even more harmful. Hyperbaric-oxygen chambers are used to administer larger amounts of oxygen to a patient's body in emergency cases such as carbon monoxide poisoning and circulatory shock. Breathing oxygen at 2 atmospheres for a short time is said to not present many problems, but it can be harmful if prolonged significantly.

Oxygen is a double-edged sword. Giving us life with one hand, it takes our life with the other hand--slowly and steadily. An increasing understanding among experts about the harmful properties of oxygen is evidenced in the following quotations:

• Raj S. Sohal, a researcher from Southern Methodist University in Dallas, Texas, who found that his experimental fruit flies had shorter life spans when they consumed more oxygen, said: "Oxygen gives life. Oxygen is killing us."

• Durk Pearson and Sandy Show in their best-selling book, *Life Extension,* state: "Oxygen is a poison, as well as a necessity, for most animals and plants. Organisms exposed to excessive oxygen can suffer severe damage or even die."

• Leonard Hayflick, Ph.D., says in his book, *How and Why We Age:* "...when oxygen is used in metabolic processes, highly reactive free radicals are produced.... Antioxidants in the body prevent oxygen from producing free radicals that might, in turn, damage important molecules."

• David Heber, M.D., Ph.D., in his book, *Natural Remedies for a Healthy Heart* says: "...it is the oxidized form of cholesterol that is most likely to settle in the arterial walls and cause trouble. This oxidation, or rancidity, is caused by molecules called *free radicals.* Free-radical production is related to the body's use of oxygen."

• Jeffrey S. Bland, Ph.D., in his book, *The 20-Day Rejuvenation Diet Program*, says: "Beneficial though oxygen is, however, it is not without hazard. Oxygen has a dark side. It is a reactive chemical substance, and in certain forms it can be harmful to the body." He adds: "Although our bodies don't rust, they undergo a process called biological rancidification, in which oxygen causes damage by combining with the fats (lipids), structural proteins and enzymes, and genetic material (DNA) that make up cells, tissues, and organs."

• Thomas J. Moore, author of the book, *Lifespan*, says: "The essential and ubiquitous element oxygen...is potentially toxic because of its chemical capacity to transform either a block of unpainted iron or a fragile cell membrane. In the 1940s, physicians were puzzled by the damaged eyes found in many premature babies. The eye lenses, they discovered, were being oxidized by excessive concentrations of oxygen provided in the incubators."

• Carol Orlock in her book, *The End of Aging*, says: "Oxygen takes its reactive toll on all that it touches, burning through delicate cell membranes, injuring tissue, and even damaging DNA. Life needs to marshal defenses against it."

As demonstrated by these quotes, the situation with oxygen is similar to that with calorie or protein intake—the correct amount--not more or less. Many researchers until recently believed that one of the causes of an oxygen deficit in cells is an insufficient supply of oxygen from air. Inspired air at sea level is typically rich in oxygen, containing a concentration of 21 percent oxygen at a pressure of 1 atmosphere. Sometimes, however, the oxygen supply is less than adequate; examples are breathing an oxygen-poor mixture from gas tanks and ascent to high altitude, is a quite common way of thinking. In other words, a content of oxygen in air less than 21 percent is considered inadequate. If this is true, then people who were born and live in high altitudes would all suffer from diseases related to oxygen deficit. However, they are very healthy and most of the world's longevity valleys–including Hunza, Vilcabamba, and Abkhasia--are located in high altitudes of 1,500 to 1,800 meters above sea level.

Health problems like asthma arise not from the small content of oxygen in the air, but rather because it cannot be properly delivered to the cells. A CO_2 deficit in the body caused by deep breathing and hyperventilation is responsible for that condition, according to the theory of Dr. Buteyko. He conducted numerous respiration tests in the research institute in Novosibirsk, Russia, measuring the contents of gases in inspired, alveolar, and expired air, and in blood. He proved that hyperventilation does not increase the amount of oxygen in the blood and in the cells above the level that is achieved by normal respiration, but rather that it vastly decreases CO_2 content in the blood, which leads to respiratory alkalosis and its harmful consequences. The amount of 21 percent oxygen in the air is too large, says Dr. Buteyko; he claims that for our health and vitality, 12-percent oxygen content is the best concentration.

Buteyko Method

The primary idea of this method is that CO_2 plays a highly beneficial role in our body and its depletion due to deep, fast breathing (i.e., hyperventilation) causes numerous illnesses. A shallow breathing technique was developed to increase the CO_2 content in the blood. The history of the discovery of this method is the story of the recovery of its author from a deadly disease. In 1952, Dr. Buteyko, then a medical school student, suffered from malignant hypertension. Although a young man, he had high blood pressure (i.e., 220/120), headaches, heart pain, insomnia, and many other disorders. Because he was involved in research on this disease, he knew that it was incurable with existing medicine. He estimated that only 1.5 years remained for him to live-- and he probably would have died if he hadn't fortunately recalled the role of CO_2. He started to experiment on himself: when he breathed rapidly and deeply, it resulted in dizziness, compressed temples, heart discomfort, palpitation, and weakness. The voluntary slowing down of his breathing rate and depth gave him immediate relief and after 1 minute, he felt much better. Thus, on September 10, 1952, he created a revolutionary theory that he later proved experimentally.

Buteyko's theory saved his own life and the lives of thousands of other people. According to official statistics, by January 1, 1967, more than a thousand people suffering from asthma, hypertension, and other heart diseases had been completely cured. In September 1983, Dr. Buteyko received the USSR state certificate of invention called "*A Method of Curing the Hemohypocarbia*"; that is, the curing of a number of diseases caused by a decreased CO_2 level in blood. An increased level of CO_2 broadens the bronchi, allowing the air passages to the alveoli to bring oxygen more freely, thereby enabling people suffering from asthma to overcome their breathlessness and wheezing.

According to Dr. Buteyko, a prolonged decrease in the CO_2 level results in a shift of the blood acidity-alkalinity balance--which is very important for the body's overall health--to the alkaline edge. This deranges the cell's biochemical reactions, which leads to the disruption of homeostasis and deterioration of the immune system. One of the major contributors to the CO_2 depletion in blood is hyperventilation caused by deep, fast breathing. To accumulate CO_2, he recommends shallow breathing and gradually increasing breath holds on a daily basis.

In Russia, the Buteyko Method is called "Volitional Liquidation of Deep Breathing" and has been taught in that country for forty years. In Sweden, this method became known after the book, *The Russian Revolution in Medicine,* was published. This method was also tested and used in Australia for seven years and in England for two years, where it is called the "Buteyko Method." In these countries, this method helped more than a hundred thousand asthmatics to gain a sense of control over their condition without drugs, according to Rosalba Courtney in the March – April 1998 issue of *Health* magazine.

Hyperventilation

Hyperventilation is defined as breathing at an abnormally rapid rate, resulting in an increased loss of CO_2. Hyperventilation can be caused voluntarily or involuntarily. Involuntarily, breathing tends to be rapid under stress, when the top half of the lungs is primarily used. Stress-induced hyperventilation leads to tiredness and anxiety, and creates tension in the neck, shoulders, and upper back. Also, hyperventilation stimulates the production of histamine, a substance that causes inflammation and breathing difficulties. Other causes of histamine release from the body tissues are injury and allergic reactions, such as asthma or hay fever.

Hyperventilation can be common among athletes and pearl divers. Before leaving the surface, they breathe deeply and rapidly, taking as many as 60 to 100 non-stop deep breaths in an attempt to saturate their blood with oxygen. Just before going into the water, divers fill their lungs as fully as possible. Sometimes they lose consciousness or even drown because of the under-depletion of CO_2 in their blood. During descent, the increasing water pressure reduces the lung volume, while partial pressure of oxygen increases. At 40 meters underwater, the partial pressure of oxygen is 1 kilogram per square centimeter, which is five times greater than on the surface. This increasing partial pressure imposes additional harm to divers because oxygen under pressure is *toxic*.

What is the greatest diving depth achieved by humans without equipment? In 1983, Frenchman Jeaque Maerou has set a world record diving to a depth of 105 meters. He reached this depth in 104 seconds and then ascended to the surface in about 90 seconds. He held his breath for a total of 3 minutes, 23 seconds. Even greater depths were conquered eleven years later. According to *The 1999 Guinness Book of World Records*, Francisco "Pipin" Ferreras from Cuba set a world record for the deepest breath-held dive to a depth of 428 feet (130 meters) on March 10, 1996. He was underwater for 2 minutes, 11 seconds. Pipin's previous diving record had been set in 1994 at 417 feet and 2 minutes, 22 seconds, underwater. His lungs and his entire body experienced water pressure that no other human had ever experienced.

These two people proved what the human lungs could achieve. Considering that they were strenuously moving during the long breath–holding, we can only imagine how extremely healthy these people are. Actually, it is an ill-advised and very dangerous breath-holding activity; but some people risk their lives to challenge existing records. However, it is definitely hazardous to their health and totally ignores the moderation motto of centenarians.

Pearl divers do not hold records for diving depths, but they have great achievements in breath-holding. It is known that pearl divers in the Pacific Ocean can hold their breath for more than 10 minutes. Porphiry Ivanov from Russia possessed legendary breath-holding abilities, although his story may sound like a fairy tale. The rumors are that once he submerged himself underwater at a Black Sea beach and stayed there for about 20 minutes.

Hyperventilation followed by breath-holding was a technique of Harry Houdini (1874-1926), the American escape artist and magician. He became famous for his ability to escape from handcuffs, straitjackets, and locked containers that were put under water. He thrilled audiences with his miracle escapes, often risking injury or death during a performance. To escape from an underwater container before suffocation, he hyperventilated using *pure oxygen* just before being locked in. This allowed him to hold his breath much longer than he had usually been able to do because the oxygen content in his blood was vastly increased. At the same time, the concentration of CO_2, which chemically stimulates breathing, was greatly decreased in his blood. Some of his stunts that involved the highest exertions were harmful to his health, and breathing pure oxygen possibly shortened his life. He died at the early age of fifty-two--although that was the average life span in the United States at the beginning of the twentieth century. To avoid any misunderstanding, it must be emphasized that deep breathing and hyperventilation that occurs naturally during hard work, mountain climbing, or strenuous exercise (e.g., running or swimming) should be distinguished from hyperventilation in a *motionless* condition. The principal difference is that during physical exertion, a lot of CO_2 is produced in skeletal muscles and its loss caused by hyperventilation is replenished with higher production, which maintains the CO_2/O_2 balance in the body. This balance can be easily disturbed if vast amounts of CO_2 are lost, as in the case of motionless hyperventilation.

The most common adverse effect of hyperventilation is found in asthma patients. This severe disease is often linked with over-breathing, which causes the excessive loss of CO_2 in the alveoli air and in the blood. With the loss of CO_2, our ability to utilize oxygen is also decreased. This is known as the *Bohr effect*, which holds that the ability of hemoglobin to release oxygen is dependent on the CO_2 concentration in the blood. Asthmatics who chronically hyperventilate have constricted airways that are also caused by the reduced CO_2 content in their blood. In the asthma condition, the additional over-breathing makes the sufferers breathless. Herbert Herxheimer reported in his article, "Hyperventilation Asthma," in the 1946 issue of *The Lancet* that if asthmatics were forced to hyperventilate, four out of five people would have an asthma attack within just 2 minutes.

Hypoventilation

Hypoventilation is defined as breathing at an abnormally slow rate, resulting in an increased amount of CO_2 in the blood. Too much CO_2 in the body has an adverse effect too; however, in a condition such as asthma, hypoventilation helps significantly. "Asthmatics feel as if they don't have enough oxygen. In fact, they don't have enough CO_2," says Jocelyn Oliver in her article entitled, "Mothering," in the March-April 1998 issue of *Health* magazine. She promotes Eucapnic Breathing in the United States--a breathing technique that normalizes CO_2 levels by reducing lung ventilation. This technique was developed by Dr. Buteyko of Russia and was tested in several clinics in that country for more than forty years.

Explaining the benefits of hypoventilation in Eucapnic Breathing, Oliver further states, "Deep breathing–taught by yogis and breath-work teachers– destabilizes the autonomic nervous system to generate altered states. Eucapnic Breathing–exactly the opposite of this–is a rhythmic shallower breathing pattern. In Eucapnic Breathing, you learn a variety of ways to hypo ventilate. You practice shorter and longer breath holdings designed to raise the carbon dioxide in your blood. The result is healthier endocrine, autonomic, nervous, and immune systems."

Deep breathing does not necessarily lead to hyperventilation. If it is deep but very *slow* breathing like that of the Indian holy man (i.e., breathing once a minute), it will induce hypoventilation. In a lecture in February 1970 in Moscow, Dr. Buteyko said that he discovered the secret of deep breathing taught in yoga. Indian yogis do deep breathing exercises for 3 minutes a day, but during the remaining 23 hours and 57 minutes, they breathe shallowly. This is why they need to occasionally hyperventilate their lungs, explained Dr. Buteyko.

Deep and slow breathing is used in many religions to induce a trance-like state. Prolonged chanting, singing, shouting, and dancing all lead to an excessive increase of CO_2, which is accompanied by a decrease of oxygen. This condition leads to *anoxia*, or a feeling of euphoria and/or lightheadedness, in which individual experiences altered states of consciousness and mystical states.

Buteyko Eucapnic (Shallow) Breathing Method

The main objective of this method is to eliminate the habit of deep breathing and to develop an automatic breath-holding ability after exhaling. It can be achieved after two or three years of breathing exercises and continuous control of current breathing, when the deep breaths induced by physical activities are consciously suppressed. To develop this habit, even a thin corset-type undergarment that tightly fits the chest--like the swaddling of newborn babies--can be helpful. As a result of the exercises, a diaphragm-breathing pattern is developed. Diaphragm breathing is usually associated with deep breaths; however, in this method, it is *shallow diaphragm breathing*, when the thoracic cage is not used much in the process of respiration.

This method of breathing brings about a curing effect. Dr. Buyteko claimed that in addition to pulmonary diseases such as asthma and bronchitis, high blood pressure and many diseases of the circulation system, nervous system, digestive tract, skin, and sexual organs could be successfully cured.

The exercises should be done six times a day every 4 hours, starting at midnight. The duration of breath holds, or *control pause* and *maximum pause* measurements, done at each exercise session must be recorded in a notebook. "Control pause" is defined as the time to that moment when a person starts to feel difficulty in continuing the breath holds. "Maximum pause" is when no further breath-holding can be tolerated. The date and time of each exercise session and the heart rate before exercise also must be recorded.

The exercise is done in a relaxed sitting position. Shallow breathing is achieved more easily if the back is kept straight, the pelvis is thrust forward, the abdomen and diaphragm are relaxed, the knees are spread apart, the eyes are raised upward, the lips are pouting, and the mouth is closed. The depth of breaths is gradually lowered to make breathing as silent as possible, like a mouse trying to keep its breath from being heard by the cat. After some time, a light shortage of air will be felt. Five minutes after starting, the control and maximum pauses should be measured followed by five more minutes of shallow silent breathing with pause measurements afterwards. This sequence should be repeated five times in each exercise session. After a few months, the length of each exercise should be extended to 10 minutes until it takes 50 minutes for one session. For people who have difficulty with breath-holding, pinching the nose with the fingers may help. After an inhalation, the nose is pinched, the breath is held as long as possible, and then the nose is released-- slowly allowing the air to expel through it.

With regular exercise, a person will notice that his/her breath-holding ability is growing and miraculous changes are occurring in the body. These changes are accompanied by the so-called "quarry"–that is, aches and discomfort in different parts of the body when ailing internal organs cleanse themselves of wastes and toxins. When the cleansing process starts, the body feels a lack of salt; therefore, Dr. Buteyko advises drinking hot water with an orotat potassium tablet, a magnesium tablet, and a half-teaspoon of table salt.

After the exercises are continued for a year or so, the control pause becomes 1 minute long; this means that a person has a sufficient buildup of CO_2 in the body. When this has been achieved, the exercises can be reduced to two times a day and should be continued for one more year. Then, if further progress is obtained, the exercises can be done once a day for one more year.

To enhance the healing effect of shallow breathing, Dr. Buteyko also advises the following:

1. Restrict food intake.
2. Eat more vegetables, fruits, and greens.
3. Do physical exercises, particularly jogging and running, that enhance CO_2 release in working muscles.
4. Avoid smoking and drinking.
5. Train the body to the cold.

6. Get plenty of fresh air.
7. Use a sauna.
8. Learn to cope with stress.
9. Take cold showers or baths.
10. Sleep on the stomach on a hard bed.

Breathing Exercises

Why do we need breathing exercises? It is common knowledge that breathing is the process of the exchange of O_2 and CO_2 in the lungs. In the lungs, the gas exchange occurs in the alveoli--the tiny sacs about 0.1 mm in size and 750 million in numbers. Some sources say that during the inhale-exhale process, their diameter changes from 0.15 to 0.3 mm. In the elderly, some walls between adjacent alveoli sacs can be broken and two sacs become one, thereby decreasing their inner surface and, therefore, the gas-exchange area in the lungs.

Breathing exercises help maintain the vital capacity of our lungs. Without deep but slow breathing exercises, certain alveoli and muscles involved in respiration become weak and even can be replaced with connective tissue, which leads to a decrease in lung capacity. The law of nature that states, "Use it or lose it, " applies to the lungs too. Indian yogis know this law and train their lungs with pranayama breathing exercises throughout their lives.

The necessity of breathing exercises increases with the increase of meat or other protein-rich food in the diet. An increase in blood-plasma protein reduces oxygen transport in the blood by as much as 60 percent, according to Dr. John Gainer. Breathing exercises help increase CO_2 accumulation in the tissues, thereby widening the airways and facilitating oxygen penetration to the blood, which can offset the decreased transport.

Actually, the aim of all existing breathing exercises is to achieve an optimal balance of O_2 and CO_2 in the blood. Most of the exercises target increasing the CO_2 content in the blood using slow-breathing or breath-holding techniques. There are hundreds of breathing techniques; it would be impossible to review all of them, so we will concentrate on just a few of them, keeping in mind people of various constitutional types to enhance their vitality and longevity in the long term. Breathing exercises that involve abdominal breathing are discussed in detail in the *Activity Control (Exercise)* chapter.

Among the best exercises that allow a rapid increase in the level of CO_2 are diving and swimming with the face held in the water between breaths. The number of strokes per breath in swimming can be gradually increased to three or four. Before swimming, I like to do knee bends with breath-holding after exhaling. After twelve knee bends without breathing, I feel very warmed; then, after my breathing returns to normal, I go into the water. I also do push-ups combined with breath–holding; twelve push-ups without breathing warms me up for the one-hand push ups that I do every other day. When I still lived in Russia, I read an article in the newspaper about a man from the city of Ul'yanovsk who cured his severe arthritis and firmness of the spine with an exercise that involved breath holds. Because I am also vulnerable to arthritis due to my Vata Type constitution, I experimented on myself and found that these exercises are helpful in maintaining flexibility of the spine and joints.

This breath-holding exercise raises the blood pressure and it suits me well, because my blood pressure is somewhat low. However, it is very strenuous and should be done with extreme caution. I practiced almost every day for fifteen years and built up very gradually to the twelve knee bends or push-ups. This exercise should be started with just two or three repetitions for a month; then add one more repetition and continue for another month. It is better not to try this if you have high blood pressure.

Breath-holding exercises can be done easily while walking. My preference is 4 footsteps per inhalation, and then 4 footsteps per exhalation, followed by 8 footsteps while breath-holding--and then repeat the whole sequence. If the speed of walking is 96 steps per minute, one cycle of inhalation, exhalation, and breath-holding takes 10 seconds. With this exercise, the breathing rate can be reduced to six times per minute. When doing breath holds as I walk, I usually do abdominal breathing as well—that is, bulging the belly wall while inhaling and contracting the abdominal muscles while exhaling.

Deep and slow abdominal breathing is considered to be the key to relaxation, increased vitality, and longevity. It creates an optimal balance of O_2 and CO_2 in the bloodstream and helps accelerate the flow of lymph, thereby enhancing the elimination process. Emotional states affect the breathing pattern: when we are calm and relaxed, our breathing is deep and slow; in a stressful situation, our breathing becomes fast. Conversely, by changing the breathing pattern, we can alter our emotional states. "Breathe deeper, you are agitated," an expression originated by the Russian writers Ilf and Petrov, has now became a national saying.

The Ayurveda, traditional Indian medicine, uses breathing techniques extensively for healing and health-enhancing purposes. Special attention is given to alternate-nostril breathing and to reducing the rate of breathing. Breathing through the left nostril is considered to be Yin--feminine, cool, soothing, and passive; breathing through the right nostril is Yang--masculine, warm, energizing, and active. The left nostril breath is believed to promote creativity and visualization, to calm the emotions, and to silence the nerves and mind--even **longevity can be increased with left-nostril breaths**. The Ayurveda teaches us to use left-nostril breathing during the day and right-nostril breathing at night.

It is clearly evident that respiration is an important process that affects all vital organs and their functioning. With a change in just the breathing pattern, many benefits for health and longevity that cannot be obtained with diet or medicine are possible. Getting breathing patterns under control is definitely a worthwhile activity to pursue. Just as with the intake of food, water, and other life–supports, **moderation in O_2 consumption and the enhancement of CO_2 production** is the best way to achieve good health and increase the length and quality of life.

The previous discussion about the role of oxygen and carbon dioxide enables us to arrive at the following two conclusions:

1. Oxygen is necessary for our survival; however, it burns us up slowly yet steadily. Oxygen is our foe; it is a silent killer--not because of free radicals that come with it, but rather because of its own destructive nature. **The formula for a healthy and long life should be "Only a minimal, absolutely necessary amount of oxygen and no more."**

2. Carbon dioxide is our real healer, friend, and helper. **Carbon dioxide is life itself and it helps make us healthy and fit while prolonging our life.** Science has yet to discover its additional healing and probable antioxidant properties. Accumulating it in our body (ensuring the delivery of the needed amounts of oxygen to our cells) to the level that we could do breath-holding for 60 seconds must become our first priority in our goal to become fit and healthy.

21

SLEEP CONTROL

Sleep is another basic physiological need that is absolutely necessary for our survival. Sufficient and sound sleep provides health and a sense of well-being, and promotes longevity. In a 1995 study of 548 male and 2,303 female centenarians in Japan, 42 percent of the men and 31.5 percent of the women attributed their longevity to the fact that they always had good sleep and rest throughout their lives.

Quantity of Sleep

The recommendation for 7 to 8 hours of sleep every night is one of the seven guidelines for a long and healthful life drawn from a previously mentioned study in Southern California. In his book, *The Centenarians of the Andes,* David Davies considers sleep as a factor of longevity among inhabitants of Vilcabamba in Ecuador and the world's other longevity valleys: "The majority of the communities where we find the centenarians throughout the world live in technologically primitive areas. They go to bed with the sun and get up with the sun, to the degree unknown in developed parts of the world. Those that are living on the Equator, or near the equatorial line, therefore have much the same amount of sleep each day of the year. This regularity may aid their longevity, whether by accident or not. They have few clocks or radios to let them know the time of day, and depend almost entirely on their observations of the sun's movements. Many doctors believe that this regular sleep pattern is an aid to longevity, especially in Western countries. Western centenarians rarely suffer from insomnia. Many people have asked me, when discussing the centenarians of the Andes, if they sleep much of their lives away, and this is so--about half their lives are spent in sleeping."

The case of John Hilton, 103, from Ft. Lauderdale, Florida, confirms that sleeping long hours is also a feature of centenarians in the United States.

"John Hilton keeps regular hours, getting up at about 7:00 or 7:30 and retiring at about the same time in the evening," reported Jim Heynen in his book, *One Hundred over One Hundred*. For all of her life, Matsuo Todome, 100, of Japan liked to eat sweets and to sleep. A former primary-school teacher, she laughs a lot and sleeps for 13 hours at night. Another Japanese centenarian, To Megoro, 100, also likes to eat and sleep. He looks quite well fed and sleeps for 10 hours. Also getting 10 hours of sleep is Donato DiMatteo, another American centenarian. "In his life today, he keeps a regular schedule, getting up at 8:30 and going to bed at 10:30," reported Jim Heynen.

These are all cases of people one hundred years and older who sleep 10 to 13 hours in their present life; however, it does not mean that they followed that sleeping pattern all their lives, especially in their working years. It was surely impossible for To Megoro, who raised eleven children, to sleep that long, but now, in his own words, there is nothing left in his life except eating and sleeping. You can sometimes hear as others say that older people don't sleep long hours. The previous cases are either exceptions or these centenarians are not old enough yet.

In addition to night sleep, many people take a nap in the daytime. In countries with an arid climate, especially in the hot summer season, a nap is part of the daily routine of people who can afford this luxury. In many Mediterranean countries–such as Greece, Spain, and Israel--some people enjoy an after-lunch snooze called a "siesta." The small private shops in Israel are closed from 1 to 4 p.m. for the siesta break all year long, not just in the summer. I had occasion once to enjoy the siesta, but not in Israel, where I was quite busy with my work. It was in Vietnam twenty years ago, when I worked for three months at the Bim Shon cement-plant construction site. Our working hours were from 8 to 11 a.m., and then from 2 to 5 p.m. After lunch at 11:30, I usually had a nap for about 1 hour. For the first time, I was leading such a luxury life, and I enjoyed this custom very much. The experts argue about whether a nap taken in the daytime interferes with sleep at night; from my own experience, I would say no--I slept well at night too.

Later I learned that a nap after a meal can be harmful to the health, but in those days, I did not think much about health--I was just quite healthy. Although there is a Russian proverb, "Lunch is gilded with a nap," Dr. I.P. Nehumyvakin, an academician of medicine and a health expert from Russia, disclaims it, saying: "It is difficult to think of a more harmful effect on the body than a nap after lunch." As an illustration of the adverse effect of a nap on the health, consider the case of sumo wrestlers in Japan who eat a gigantic lunch and then take a 2-hour nap. Their average life span is sixty-two to sixty-three years, about sixteen to seventeen years shorter than that of average Japanese men--mostly because of overeating, but partly because of napping on a full stomach.

However, if the nap is taken correctly, it is beneficial to health. In Greece, people traditionally enjoy the after-lunch snooze and it has been found to be good for health. In a study conducted by the University of Athens Medical School, it was found that the risk of developing heart disease in men who had a daily 30-minute nap was 30 percent less. My American friend, Demetrios, whose father came to America from Greece in the 1920s, explained the details to me about the Greek nap. He told me that lunch is not usually a big meal and, afterwards, people have fruit for dessert, eating it slowly while they enjoy conversation. This takes time; therefore, they do not take nap immediately after the meal. His father, Spiros Antonopoulos, of Lorain, Ohio, who lived ninety-nine years and eight months, developed the habit of taking a 2-hour nap after he retired at age sixty-four.

Another important feature about a nap is the proper napping position. Lying on the back with a full stomach may cause a discomfort, but a nap sitting at the desk may not. One American health advocate wrote that his afternoon productivity was better if he had a 10-minute nap after lunch. He had a small pillow in a drawer of his desk, and he would put it on the desk to rest his head. The pillow is not important for true nappers. A Japanese colleague who also took a 10-minute after-lunch nap used to pile several reports on his desk to substitute for a pillow.

At the other extreme, there are long-living people who sleep short hours-- not because of sleeplessness, but rather because they trained themselves to take this pleasure with moderation. Teresa Hsu, 100, of Singapore sleeps only 4 hours, and is known among the local people for her yoga exercises and Spartan lifestyle. As reported in the November 7, 1997, issue of *The Straits Times* newspaper, "She starts her day at 4 a.m. with calisthenics, meditation, and an hour of yoga exercises. At night, she does yoga again, then reads until midnight." Toshio Doko, president of Toshiba Corporation of Japan from 1965 to 1974, lived to the age of ninety-two and did not allow himself to sleep more than 4 hours a night for the last forty-five years of his life. He usually took a very hot bath for just a few minutes at midnight, woke up at 4 a.m. with the help of an alarm clock, and read Buddhist texts for 1 hour. Edward M. Yashin, Ph.D., seventy, of Russia--who announced that he is going to live forever--trained himself to sleep 4 or 5 hours a night. At the core of his regimen is a 25-minute-long, strenuous morning exercise routine that involves major muscles of the body.

However, both too much and too little sleep is considered to be not good for longevity. If you sleep more than 10 or less than 5 hours a night, you can subtract two years from your average life span, according to Kathleen Stassen Berger in her book, *The Developing Person Through the Life Span*. A study of a million elderly people showed that the lowest death rate was among those who slept 7 hours a night. The death rate was higher if sleeping time was both fewer and more hours. Some doctors believe that oversleeping is as bad as overeating; therefore, the principle of moderation applies to sleep as well.

On average, we spend about one third of our lives sleeping and unconscious. This mysterious state was often compared in folk proverbs to a temporary death. "You fell asleep, you died, and in the morning you revived again," says a Russian proverb. A saying related to the theory of rebirth goes like this: "Sleep is a death when one changes his clothes, coming back into his own body the next morning; death is when one changes the body." Sleep is perhaps oblivion for the consciousness, but not for the controlling mind and the body. All physiological processes slow down in this state: the muscles relax and the blood pressure, heart rate, and metabolic rate decrease by about 20 percent.

For ordinary people, the loss of sleep for more than 24 hours produces a general disturbance of the body and any normal performance demands an increased amount of effort, according to researchers at the University of Georgia who studied the effects of sleep deprivation for 100 consecutive hours. They also found that going 48 hours without sleep impaired the ability to read. The volunteers involved in this study experienced difficulties in maintaining balance and could stagger. Some people suffered severe headaches; some had the sensation of a band pressing on their head. There were people who saw flashes of light. The ability to be certain about one's location or destination while walking was also found to be impaired.

There are rare cases of people who do not sleep at all. I remember when the newspapers in Russia reported the case of a Bulgarian soldier who never slept. His officers took advantage of him by giving him guard duty every night because he did not need to sleep. Another case, reported by the Russian newspaper "Trud" (Labor) in the April 29, 1997, issue, was of Yakov Tseperovitch from Minsk, Belorussia, who did not sleep for seventeen years. At the age of twenty-six, he died from drinking too much wine, but he was revived by doctors in the hospital. Since that experience, he never sleeps, feels enormous energy, and his body temperature has been as low as 34°C. "I have a feeling that time does not exist for me anymore. I do not feel the passed years. These years turned into one day, which is endlessly lasting, without breaks or intervals. It seems to me that I will live forever," he was reported as saying. Medical examinations have not found any abnormalities in his health condition. People who know him say that he has not changed at all in the last seventeen years, as if time really stopped for him.

A few individuals have been reported to require very little sleep--as little as 15 minutes a night was enough. Commenting on these cases, Durk Pearson and Sandy Shaw state in their best-selling book, *Life Extension:* "We have no explanation for this as yet, but they probably have an alternative mechanism of growth hormone release. We would like to see studies of the pituitary temporal release patterns and biochemical releasing mechanism of the growth hormone and vasopressin (the release of which triggers REM sleep) in these people. Since we spend a third of our lives unconscious while asleep, finding ways to get along without sleep or even cutting it down is a way to extend subjective life span. Although living without sleep would not increase the number of years we live, it would seem to us that we lived many years longer because we would be able to spend the extra time enjoying life rather than being unconscious. We have been able to cut our sleep time down by about an hour by using Deaner" (Ricker)." Well, these two life-extensionists found a drug solution to reducing sleeping hours and it sounds like their motivation was merely to get more pleasure from life. However, they humbly omitted to say that they needed the extra time for their work as well. They proved themselves to be hard workers by doing all that major research and writing an eight-hundred-page book.

As shown in the previous discussion, the length of sleep ranges quite broadly from one person to another. Regarding sleep length, all human beings are very different. Many researchers have tried but failed to suggest how long an adult should sleep. The range of sleeping hours of the people mentioned previously is shown in a one-axis diagram in Figure 21-1.

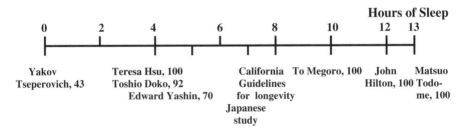

Figure 21-1. Range of Sleeping Hours of Certain People

As shown in this graph, sleeping more than the optimal 7 to 8 hours was not an obstacle for some American and Japanese centenarians.

Quality of Sleep

Everyone wants to have good sleep at night and to awaken fresh and full of energy. No one likes sleepless or interrupted sleep at night, waking up moody and mean. To get sound, restful sleep, it helps to understand the causes of sleep disturbances and the ways to overcome them. Knowing one's personal sleep type also may be useful for the development of good sleep.

There are three types of sleepers. People of the first type can go to bed early or late at night, but they wake up at a certain hour without any problem, provided they slept enough. They have equal productivity in the morning, during the daytime, and in the evening. They are called "pigeons" and they comprise about half of all sleepers. Most of them are engaged in physical labor. Individuals of the second type are alert in the evening, do not fall asleep easily, reach their deepest sleep early in the morning, and wake up late, often feeling tired. They are called "owls"--their most productive hours are in the afternoon, and they account for 30 percent of all people. As a rule, they are the intellectual workers. The people of the last group are "larks," who are tired in the evening, go to bed early, and wake up early in the morning, refreshed and well rested. They work better in the morning and comprise about 20 percent of the population. This division into three groups is not exact and people usually have a difficult time deciding to which type they belong. To assist them, G. Hildebrandt, a German researcher, suggested a simple test: upon awakening, measure the resting heart rate and breathing rate. The ratio of these two values shows what type of sleeper the person is. The pigeons usually have a ratio of 4:1; the larks, 5:1 or 6:1. The breathing rate of the owls is often increased and the ratio is smaller.

Sleep is not only a necessity for restoration after the fatigue and tiredness of the day, it is also a great pleasure. Some people enjoy sleeping so much that they become sleep addicts. Among the famous sleep amateurs was Sancho Panza, who accompanied Don Quixote on his travels, and who is known for saying: "God bless the man who first invented sleep." One Russian count of the nineteenth century was known for his habit of ordering his servant to wake him up every 2 hours at night. When asked by friends why he is torturing himself, he replied: "You don't understand how sweet it is to fall asleep again." Lucky count--he certainly did not suffer from insomnia. During the six years of her university studies, a friend of mine used to sleep nearly all the time--perhaps 15 to 16 hours a day--except during the study hours. She likely slept away the best years of her youth. She is now sixty, but she looks much younger; maybe the extra sleep preserved her from the normal pace of aging.

Actually, sleep is more vulnerable to disturbances than, for instance, appetite. Many factors affect the soundness and restfulness of sleep, including level of tiredness, kind of activity during the day, emotional state, amount and types of food eaten and time passed since the meal, noise, type of house in which one lives, and sleeping position. Valery A. Ivanchenko, M.D., in his book, *The Secrets of Your Good Spirits* (in Russian), considers the following five groups of factors:

1. External factors that over-stimulate the nervous system such as stresses at work and at home, as well as light-, noise-, and temperature-related disturbances.

2. Disturbance of blood supply to the brain, which continues its work during sleep, can be caused by prolonged bad posture in the evening while typing, reading, writing, watching TV, and so on.

3. Excessive signals from internal organs and glands caused by foods eaten, which act as diuretics, laxatives, or gas–producers. A long talk about sex in the evening can also interfere with sleep.

4. Type and quality of the bed; width of the bed if a couple sleeps together; material of the sheets, blankets, and pillows; direction of the bed toward the magnetic field of the Earth; and others.

5. Disturbances of the habitual sleep-awakening rhythm, such as watching TV or visiting with friends until late in the night, late swimming or taking a sauna, and night flights in an airplane. A lifestyle that lacks physical activity resulting in a body that is not tired by the end of the day is also related to this group of disturbances.

To sleep just after a meal is bad, but an empty stomach is irritable and also interrupts sound sleep. If there are physical problems and pain, it is difficult to fall asleep. Sleep comes more quickly after an active day, when the body and mind are very tired.

People who live in wooden, stone, or brick houses have better quality sleep than city dwellers who live in concrete buildings, according to a study conducted in Moscow by the Central Research Institute of Housing Estate. One possible explanation about why we feel refreshed after a good sleep is that the growth hormone (GH) is released during sleep. Sufficient GH is necessary for the proper functioning of the immune system and its T-cells, which are natural killers of bacteria, viruses, cancer cells, atherosclerotic plaques, and autoimmune self-attacks such as in rheumatoid arthritis. "If sleep is delayed or interrupted, GH release can be eliminated, reduced, or aborted. And without a healthy T-cell system, aged persons are susceptible to disease and cancer," state Durk Pearson and Sandy Shaw. It seems to me that in the release of GH, a cosmic radiation that penetrates our relaxed body plays an important role. Concrete has steel-reinforcement inside that deflects these cosmic rays and deprives us of them. Perhaps because of this effect, I feel better when I sleep in a wooden house, without being surrounded by a steel cage.

The direction of the body during sleep also influences its soundness. When the body is positioned with the head toward the north and the feet toward the south, it is coaxial with the magnetic field of the Earth--this direction promotes better sleep. Sleeping posture for a comfortable sleep has attracted some attention among the experts. Most people feel well when they are lying on their backs. "A healthy sleeping posture is flat on the back with arms relaxed at the sides. Generally, sleeping on the sides or on the stomach shows problems," according to Shizuko Yamamoto and Patrick McCarty in their book, *Whole Health Shiatsu*. On the contrary, Dr. Konstantin P. Buteyko recommends sleeping on the stomach on a hard bed in order to avoid deep breathing, which he believes is the cause of dozens of ailments and disorders. My favorite sleeping posture is on my right side with my right leg outstretched and my left leg bent at the knee. Xu Fang, the Chinese mystery, also sleeps on her right side, but with her left leg outstretched and her right leg bent.

The inability to sleep or habitual sleeplessness, called insomnia, that many older people suffer, may be a sign of depression. In this state, sleep cannot come, or it is frequently interrupted during the night, or waking occurs in the early morning--all interfering with normal sleep. Quite often, we cannot fall asleep because of the internal dialogue going on and on in our mind. It may be induced by worrying, excitement from a movie or late show, or accumulated stress from recent days. To start sleeping, we have to stop this internal dialogue. The imagery that Don Juan taught to Carlos Castaneda can help: Imagine that you leave your body from your feet and keep going in that direction. You then leave the room, house, street, city, state, country, continent, Earth, and solar system, traveling farther into space. Sometimes I use that imagery; other times, instead of worrying that I will be drowsy the next day because of restless sleep, I try to remember a day in my life when I was very happy. I recall as many details as possible and live in that day again emotionally. However, when I cannot sleep, a breathing exercise works the best for me. Lying on my back, I bend my knees and grasp my toes with my hands, as shown in Figure 21-2 (see p. 274). Xu Fang demonstrates the position of the legs and hands for the sleep-promoting breathing exercise.

In this pose, I do diaphragm breathing with a sequence of inhale, exhale, and breath-holding after the exhale. All the focus in this exercise is brought to the breath-holding. I start with 10 counts for breath-holding and repeat three times; then I increase the breath-holding to 12 counts with three repetitions; then 14 counts and so on. When I reach 24 counts, it is quite difficult to continue and I stop holding my breath. Then I stretch my legs, turn onto my right side, and soon fall asleep. During this exercise, which lasts about 10 minutes, the carbon dioxide content of the blood has increased and it acts like a sleeping pill--but without side effects.

Sleep has a great healing power, especially if we become sick with a cold or flu. The GH released during deep sleep enhances the immune system and many of its functions. Sometimes, just the good sleep alone, without any medications, is enough to feel recovered by the next morning.

Regarding sleep, as with everything else in life, people are so different that one general rule cannot be established. Some people sleep well wherever they are: in a hotel, in a camp, while traveling, or when visiting friends and relatives. However, many find it difficult to sleep in such places, especially during travel by plane or train. I am in the latter group, and am particularly uncomfortable when traveling by train. The beds in all the Russian trains were just a little shorter than necessary for stretching out my long legs; they were not designed for a long-legged boy like me. I won't even mention the ventilation or quality of the mattresses and pillows. Train trips in Russia could last a few days; for example, the trip from Moscow to Krasnoyarsk in Siberia took four days. By the end of the trip, if not exhausted, I felt quite tired. I also can't sleep on planes because of the lack of space for my knees in the economy class; after the sleepless 14-hour flight from Boston to Tokyo, I need a couple of days to recover and to adjust to the time difference.

Trying to find a way to sleep while flying, I asked a Japanese acquaintance who is a pharmacist whether he would advise a sleeping pill. "No, I never take sleeping pills myself and I do not advise you to try. The best thing is a shot of brandy before sleep," he replied. I tried the brandy, but it did not work for me either. For some people, it works perfectly; perhaps the answer is in the dose. It definitely worked for a friend of mine when we were traveling by train together with two other friends from Tashkent in Uzbekistan to Moscow twenty years ago. At the start of our trip, we had a rich dinner that included local delicacies such as sausages made of horsemeat, nun (flat local bread), fresh vegetables, pickles, and many other foods--all washed down with a couple of glasses of vodka by my friend. After that difficult-to-survive dinner, he slept so soundly (he snored very loudly) that when he fell to the floor from his bed, he did not even wake up and slept there until the next morning. We laughed a lot the next morning while he had a few shots of vodka to recover from the effects of his hangover.

Considering the amount and quality of sleep, my preference is for less than a moderate duration of sleep--I would say **6 to 7 hours of sound, good-quality sleep--**after which one awakens refreshed and in the best spirits.

As can be seen from this discussion, sleep control can be accomplished in a few ways. The main goal is to get a sound, refreshing, high-quality sleep in a sufficient amount. This is possible if every one understands their own sleeping type and finds the best ways to improve it. Sleep should be a means to achieve good health and to extend life, not shorten it.

22

ACTIVITY CONTROL (EXERCISE)

Recent gerontological studies in the United States, Japan, France, and other countries have shown that centenarians lead active, healthy lives; rather, I should say, they are healthy because they are active. A few centenarians confirm this very distinctly.

> Jeanne Calment of Arles, France--the world's oldest person, who died in August 1997 at the age of 122--rode a bicycle at 100 and released a rap CD at 121. She never felt bored and stayed interested throughout all her long life. Herbert Kirk, 101, graduated in 1993 from Montana State University with a bachelor's degree in art as a sculptor. Kirk attributes his longevity to exercising: he played tennis into his eighties and still loves to run. At the age of ninety-five, Kirk won two gold medals in 800-meter and 5-kilometer races, and one silver medal in a 200-meter race at an international seniors' track meet in Helsinki, Finland. Kubo Kotaro, 101, who is called the "Japanese tennis boy," is a three-time champion in tennis competitions among centenarians. When asked how long he expects to live, he replied: "At least to 110."

There are other examples of exercising centenarians. In her book, *Bragg Apple Cider Vinegar,* Dr. Patricia Bragg includes photographs of her father, Dr. Paul C. Bragg, a physical therapist and America's health pioneer, and Roy White, 106, with dumbbells in his raised hands, who practiced weight training for health and fitness. Long-distance runner Toraichi Okuyama, 103, of Japan, who enjoys running in good spirits, is another centenarian exerciser.

Matniaz Ollobergenov, 107, of Uzbekistan--who at his age is as flexible as a young man and who attributes his longevity to spine flexibility exercises-- is one more striking example. George Burns, 100, a famous American comedian and actor, practiced stretching exercises similar to yoga and walked for exercise. On the cover of his book, *How to Live to 100 and More*, he appears with a dumbbell in one hand and a cigar in the other.

"Exercise is the means to an alert, vigorous, and lengthy life. Inactivity will kill you," stated Laurence E. Morehouse, Ph.D., professor of exercise physiology and founder and director of the Human Performance Laboratory at the University of California in Los Angeles.

It seems to be clear to many that exercise is essential for our health and vigor; nevertheless, many of us are uncomfortable with the process of becoming a regular exerciser. When we are overwhelmed with stressful work or family problems, exercise is usually the first thing we stop doing. To many, "exercise" is still a dirty word because they feel they have to force themselves to do it, according to Edward J. Jackowski, in his book, *Hold It! You're Exercising Wrong*. It is because we haven't made it a habit, like brushing our teeth or shaving.

To make exercise a habit, you have to feel an inner eagerness for it. It starts from believing that exercise can be beneficial to you; followed by selecting the type of exercise that fits your constitutional individuality, lifestyle, and preferences; and, finally, by implementing an exercise regimen. To incorporate exercise into your daily routine, you need discipline and time. The only time resource available is leisure activities and inactivity; that is why I call *inactivity control* a means to include exercise in your daily routine. Taking control of the time available for exercise is one more "control" game that we are playing in this book; therefore, I am sorry to say, nothing can be done without control in the case of exercise as well. I am sure you will not regret investing some time in exercise; let me illustrate the kind of benefits you will reap from exercising regularly.

Exercise and Activity

Benefits of Exercise. Exercise is widely recognized nowadays as beneficial for our health and well-being. The *Time Medical Dictionary* defines *exercise* as "physical exertion for health improvement; voluntary muscle activity." There is much evidence strongly suggesting that exercise vastly improves both quality and duration of life--that is, you feel better, look better, perform better, and enjoy life more. Following are some of the benefits of exercise and its positive effect on health, vigor, rejuvenation, and longevity:

1. Exercise provides **freedom** from diseases and enables you to achieve life **goals**--to make your **dreams** come true.

2. Exercise makes you **younger** and improves the **quality** of your life. It adds years to your life, making it **happier** and **longer**.

3. You feel radiantly alive due to the **endorphins, growth hormone (GH),** dehydroepiandrosterone **(DHEA),** and other good hormones produced in your body during exercise.

4. Exercise increases **metabolic rate** and enhances the burning of body fat, which is especially beneficial for slow oxidizers. Exercising on a completely empty stomach decreases metabolic rate and keeps it lowered during the day, thus enhancing longevity.

5. An elevated production of **carbon dioxide** thins the blood and keeps the bloods vessels wide open, thereby improving circulation, which allows better blood flow in the capillaries.

6. Exercise conditions the heart, lowers the cholesterol level and triglyceride counts, and--if done regularly and with moderation--decreases the resting high blood pressure. Exercise also improves the condition of other vital organs, muscles, bones, joints, and tissue.

7. Exercise improves digestion, promotes **assimilation** of food, and facilitates **elimination** of waste from the body, thereby stimulating the lymphatic system, which is responsible for the removal of toxins from the body.

8. Exercise controls insulin production, helps control blood-sugar levels, and increases the glucose-tolerance level.

9. Exercise adds vitality to your **chakras (i.e., energy centers).**

10. Exercise is one of the best **investments** of your time: it costs you nothing and produces a big profit.

11. Exercise allows you to forget yourself while enjoying fresh air, sun, and nature.

12. Exercise reduces tension and increases mental clarity and cognitive ability.

A Customized Approach to Exercise

Although the benefits of exercise are many and well documented, it is not free of downfalls. Not everyone is fond of exercise and there are its opponents, who maintain that exercise increases the metabolic rate, thereby accelerating the aging processes through wear and tear on the body's systems. Proponents of exercise, however, believe that the metabolic rate can be lowered if exercise is done on a completely empty stomach. In this case, the metabolic rate allegedly is kept low throughout the rest of the day. As with the French Paradox relative to diet, here we have the *Exercise Paradox*: both the speeding up and the slowing down of the "rate of living" that both shortens and lengthens the life span, depending on the conditions under which the exercise is performed. When exercise is done correctly, its training effect improves the cardiovascular system and other vital organs, which increases the life span. When the exercise is being performed, we live faster; however, in the resting time, because of the decreased rate of the conditioned heart and respiratory system, we live more slowly. Because the resting time is much longer than the workout time, we have a positive outcome regarding longevity.

Again, like with a diet, an "exercise program that fits all" approach does not seem to work. Any exercise program, although beneficial for someone else, may produce ill effects if it does not fit a person's type. In the same way as with food, people will benefit most if they adjust the kind and level of exercise to their individual blueprint. From the variety of exercises, everyone must choose those that are appropriate to their particular type and needs. Those who need to raise their low metabolism will benefit from a certain level of exercise; those with fast metabolism may have some problems.

Slow oxidizers need a faster metabolic rate; therefore, they need fast-paced exercises that stimulate metabolism, such as strenuous exercises with weights or brisk walking and jogging. Fast oxidizers already have intensive internal workouts that burn starch and fat; they need to pacify their metabolism. The best forms of exercise for fast oxidizers include yoga, Qigong, hiking, slow-paced swimming, and bicycle rides.

Ayurvedic dosha types are also advised to engage in different forms of exercise. Vata types calm their mind and Pitta types strive for peace with self-practicing meditation on a regular basis; however, Kapha types need stimulating aerobic exercises.

The various blood types get different effects from exercise too. Those with blood type O need frequent vigorous exercise, such as aerobics, to increase their energy and ward off fatigue, as suggested by Dr. D'Adamo. Ann L. Gittleman found that for people with blood type O, exercise is even more important that correct diet. For those with blood type A, light exercise is the best, including stretching, yoga, walking, and slow–paced swimming. The range of exercises for those with blood type B is broader--from strenuous and heavy exercise to yoga, Qigong, and meditation. People with blood type AB have features similar to those with blood type A, and do better with slower, less strenuous workouts.

Exercise of any kind affects the endocrine glands and, if performed incorrectly, may strain them. Most important for the thyroid type is endurance and stamina, followed by muscular strength, as suggested by Dr. Abravanel.

His advice is to engage in sustained swimming and rowing for endurance and Nautilus-type workouts for strength. Being naturally quite flexible, thyroid types may pay less attention to flexibility exercises. Adrenal types need coordination, cardiovascular conditioning, and flexibility; their best bet includes tennis, basketball, and ping-pong--which require quickness and sharp focus--followed by jogging, swimming, and martial arts. Compulsive, repetitive, or exhaustive exercises are not good for the pituitary type, according to Dr. Abravanel. What they greatly need is mind integration and involvement in what they are doing; aerobic dancing, martial arts, and Nautilus-type workouts fit them perfectly. Therefore, the knee-bend exercise-- with many advantages but being repetitive–does not suit the pituitary type. However, I am a thyroid type, and it works well for me; I believe it also works for cardiovascular conditioning of the adrenal type too. This example confirms once again that no one exercise fits all.

An active lifestyle that involves a lot of body movement is as beneficial as exercise. The following centenarians give us some examples. Frank Shomo of Robinson, Pennsylvania, who died in 1997 at the age of 108, was very active: he walked 15 miles every day for forty years in his job as a line foreman on a railroad. He also worked hard in his gardens, but he never did any special exercise. Alice Wei from Singapore, who lived to the age of 107, was reportedly quite active--giving music classes to kindergarten children at the age of ninety-four--but she didn't do any regular exercise. Her son, John Wei, sixty-three, when asked what his mother's longevity secret was, replied that it was her healthy diet, but nothing was said about exercise. Long-living people in Hunza, Vilcabamba, Abkhasia, Okinawa, and Bama are active in their daily life, but they don't exercise.

In my opinion, I think everyone can benefit from moderate exercise appropriate for their body constitution, personality type, blood type, gender, age, lifestyle, goals, and other conditions. Exercise can also be harmful and even lead to a sudden death if it is too strenuous and taxes the heart beyond its limits. Again, control of the workout adjusted to the level of fitness, body condition, and mood is absolutely necessary to improve rather than deteriorate our health condition through exercise. We need to be tuned in to what our body tells us during exercise; that is, how we are feeling, not being locked in to a preplanned schedule. If you reduce a number of repetitions or sessions, don't feel guilty--be happy that God gave you wisdom to slow down a little and to not overstrain yourself. Moderation--once again, dear reader--it is moderation. We are eternal and, in time, we will meet all our commitments.

"Don't bend the elbow too much," as Frank Shomo used to say, a wise man who lived to 108 years old.

Exercise and Aging

If there is an anti-aging remedy, its name is exercise. If a person's lifestyle involves a lot of physical activity, his/her heart is probably strong enough, but certainly not as strong as it was forty years ago. In the case of a sedentary lifestyle, a person's heart condition is probably much worse: climbing one flight of stairs makes him/her breathe in great gasps. Aerobic exercise is the best medicine for heart-strengthening. The following discussion mentions certain factors of health deterioration associated with aging and how they can be stopped or even reversed with exercise. Through exercise, joints will stay flexible longer, the bones will become denser, lower-back pain can be diminished, the digestive process will work more smoothly, and insomnia will be less frequent. You can delay or eliminate many common signs of advanced age with exercise, says Jim Glenn in his book, *Exercise & Fitness*. For these reasons, you're never too old to begin a conditioning program--with your doctor's okay. Even if you spent six decades in relative inactivity, fitness exercise will work, and work well, to improve the quality of your life.

At all ages, an ideal workout program takes no more than 30 minutes three times a week: a 5-minute warm-up, brisk walking or jogging for 2 or 3 minutes, recovery intervals between them, and a final cool-down. Nothing more is required; however, as your condition improves, your appetite for physical activity may increase.

In many studies, the physiological data of exercisers was compared with that of non-exercisers. "Heart and lung performance, blood pressure, muscle control, flexibility, strength, even mental acuity, have all been measured, usually with the same result: exercisers are ten to fifteen years 'younger' than non-exercisers. This finally disposes of the myths that exercise somehow wears out your body. The opposite is true. Regular, moderate activity rejuvenates your body and mind," says Jim Glenn about the benefits of exercise for elderly people.

Exercise and Longevity

One of the major contributions to longevity is fitness. Fit people live longer than "couch potatoes." Those who exercise for about 3 hours a week, starting at age of forty, outlive their sedentary peers by about thirteen months. And, more important, a fit person's last years are often more enjoyable than an inactive person's, because regular exercise helps blunt the effects of aging. As physical activity increases, death rates decrease up to a plateau of 3,500 calories a week (i.e., about 6 hours of jogging). Even a small amount of exercise is better than none at all; in fact, a recent study showed a more than 50 percent reduction in death rate between those who were completely sedentary and those who were only slightly more fit. Of course, the people who were the most active had the best chance for longevity.

There are even life-extensionists who believe that longevity can be achieved solely by exercise. Edward M. Yashin, Ph.D., a Russian scientist in physics and mathematics, and who developed the original life-extension program for living up to 120 years, believes that strenuous exercise is the cornerstone. Every morning he does a peak–output, 25-minute exercise routine that involves all the muscles of the body. He starts by running around the room, followed by knee bends and jumping jacks. These are followed by 10 repetitions each of push-ups against the floor, pull-ups on a steel bar, lifting 73-pound (32-kilogram) weights with each arm, leg scissors lying face up on the floor, and finally lifting the legs over the head in the same position. This set of exercises is then repeated in the same order.

The point is that there is no rest between exercises--he rushes immediately from one to the next. It is interesting to note that the idea of moving immediately from one exercise to the next is also proposed in the article "Ultimate Heart-Building Program," by Joe Kita in the April 1997 issue of the *Men's Health Journal*. He suggests keeping the heart rate at 60 to 85 percent of its maximum level (i.e., 220 minus your age).

Because Dr. Yashin does the entire set of exercises on a completely empty stomach, he probably decreases his metabolic rate and thus promotes longevity. He further slows down his metabolism by skipping breakfast and restricting his daily calorie intake by eating only one meal a day. Dr. Paul Bragg utilized a similar approach; he used to say that we have to earn our breakfast with exercise (on an empty stomach).

Dr. Yashin's strenuous exercise approach to longevity was supported by E.C. Hammond (1964), who studied the physical complaints of 1,064,004 men and women, following them for two years. Hammond found that the death rates for the 461,440 men between the ages of forty-five and ninety were the lowest for those engaged in heavy exercise. Progressively higher were death rates for men exercising moderately, lightly, and not at all. The difference in life expectancy between heavy exercising and non-exercising groups was estimated to be from ten to twenty years.

Regular Exercise. Eating healthy foods combined with regular exercising enables one to get the full benefit of each. Regular exercise keeps us toned up, trim, and looking good due to the endorphins produced in our body. It also keeps the heart muscle strong. "Regular exercise benefits the heart and lungs, improves the blood vessels, increases muscular strength, tightens the ligaments, and helps control body weight," said Dr. Linus Pauling, the two-time Nobel laureate, in his book, *How to Live Longer and Feel Better*. What is the ideal frequency of regular exercise? Four or five times a week will enable us to reap the benefits in no time.

Types of Exercise

A long and healthy life is hardly possible without fitness, which is achieved through activity and exercise. All systems of the human body decline steadily throughout a lifetime. Each and every day, no matter what we do, we spend our health more or less--drop by drop, our health supply is drained. Therefore, our body needs steady attention and care. We need to make efforts to restore our health, to maintain it in good condition. Good health is not just the absence of illness, but rather a state of vitality that gives us a sense of muscle tone, self-awareness, and readiness, making us feel more secure and comfortable. Good health gives us freedom and the sense of control to handle emergency situations if and when they occur.

The way to achieve good health and fitness is to have a healthy lifestyle: good diet, proper rest, hygiene, and fitness can make many positive contributions to our health. Most of us do not wish to be as fit as a competitive athlete, but rather strive for a more general kind of fitness--that is, the so-called health-related fitness. Fit individuals complete their daily tasks without being exhausted at the end of the day; moreover, they have energy to spare. Fitness implies the appropriate body weight, blood pressure, and heart rate; sufficient energy; the ability to handle stress; a better appearance; and an improved sex life--all features of a quality life.

Fitness typically is considered to entail the following five major components (other components sometimes included are agility, balance, coordination, and speed):

1. *Body composition*: Shape, proportions, fat content, and weight/height ratio (partly inherited, partly developed by lifestyle, diet, and exercise).

2. *Cardiovascular and respiratory fitness*: The ability of the heart and lungs to supply oxygen to the muscles and to remove waste products. Arguably, cardiovascular and respiratory fitness matters more than all the rest.

3. *Endurance*: How long specific muscles can perform a task before fatigue sets in.

4. *Strength*: The force that contracting muscles can apply to move a load.

5. *Flexibility*: Range of joint movements.

The classification of exercises used in this book is different from those mentioned previously. It relies on the chakra system, with exercises divided into the following five groups that match the major chakras:

1. *Survival exercises:* Aerobic (i.e., cardiovascular and respiratory), muscle endurance, strength, and flexibility

2. *Exercises for healthier sexual organs*

3. *Yoga exercises*

4. *Breathing exercises*

5. *Meditation*

The higher the chakra (i.e., level of consciousness) is, the thinner is the energy involved and the calmer is the exercise. At the survival level (i.e., the first chakra), the "fight or flight" need is fulfilled with dynamic exercises that train the body systems to be physically fit. Yoga and breathing exercises train both mind and body and they are more static; meditation, being the most static, influences mind and spirit in the first place. If you are a singer or want to learn to sing (i.e., the fifth chakra), mastering diaphragm breathing is more essential for you than other exercises such as strength or endurance.

Younger people, who have good stamina and do not feel stiffness yet, might be more interested in building up strength than in endurance and flexibility. However, people in their fifties might be more focused on maintaining or improving flexibility and endurance. As discussed previously, different types may choose a form of exercise that fits their biochemical individuality. The description of exercises that follows is based on my own experience and the teachings of my guru, Eugene Bazh, as well as the works of the following authors: James Glenn, *Exercise & Fitness*; J. Connors with N. Gorgon, *Don't Count Yourself Out*; Kenneth H. Cooper, M.D., M.P.H., *The Aerobics Program for Total Well Being;* L.E. Morehouse and L. Gross, *Total Fitness in 30 Minutes*; Edward J. Jackowski, *Hold It! You're Exercising Wrong;* and Running Press Gem, *The Human Body*.

1. SURVIVAL EXERCISES

Endurance (Aerobic) Exercise

Aerobic exercise improves the efficiency of the cardiovascular and respiratory systems and of our muscles. Dr. Kenneth H. Cooper, who introduced the term in 1968, defines "aerobic exercises" as the activities that require oxygen for prolonged periods and place such demands on the body that it is required to improve its capacity to handle oxygen. In other words, these exercises last long enough to require the muscles to burn oxygen for energy production.

Among the muscles that benefit most from aerobic exercise is the heart. The heart muscles are the best-developed fibers in the body because they do the heaviest work. However, the heart is a muscle and, like other muscles, if we don't use it, we'll lose it. As a result of exercise, the heart, like all muscles, becomes stronger and larger, enabling it to pump blood to the exercising muscles more easily, carry more oxygen to all the muscles--including the heart itself--and remove muscle wastes faster. Aerobic exercises stimulate both the respiratory and circulatory systems.

All aerobic exercises--even walking–must start with stretching exercises to warm up the body and prepare the muscles and joints for work. Although the main objective of stretching exercises is to prevent injuries and strains, they also help reduce muscle strains, thereby increasing blood flow through the vessels and capillaries. A study conducted in Japan showed how the heart benefits from stretching exercises: the resting heart rate in a group doing stretching exercises decreased to 52 beats per minute compared to 59 beats per minute in the control group–the stretching exercises alone also have an aerobic effect.

Regular aerobic exercise can enhance cardiac function, improve blood cholesterol levels, strengthen bones, and lower the risk of heart attacks, high blood pressure, strokes, diabetes, and even some forms of cancer, as stated in Report #29 of *the* Harvard Medical School. Another study in Japan showed that in a regularly exercising group, the amount of calcium in the bones increased within one year, while in the same period, the calcium content decreased in the non-exercising control group.

The prime examples of aerobic exercise are *walking, jogging, running, cross-country skiing, swimming,* and *cycling.* Dr. Cooper ranks *cross-country skiing* first for aerobic value, *swimming* ranks second, *jogging* ranks third, *cycling* fourth, and *walking* fifth.

For indoor workouts, the results can be achieved utilizing such common gym equipment as the Lifecycle, Concept II Ergometer, and Nordic track. Exercises such as *knee bends, stair-climbing, jumping rope, and aerobic dancing* are good aerobic activities if they are performed for at least 20 minutes. The important thing is to do some kind of exercise that keeps your heart rate at 60 to 85 percent of its maximum rate (i.e., 220 minus your age) three times a week--strenuous enough to make you pant and perspire for 20 to 30 minutes.

Heart Rate and Longevity

If there were an absolute truth, it would be this: "Only people with healthy and strong hearts can live the longest." Other than exercise, there is no other medical means or method that can make the heart strong--no medicine, no drug, no herb, no therapy exists that can achieve heart miracles--only exercise can.

There are cases of people who inherited their strong heart and they enjoyed long lives while seemingly doing nothing to strengthen their heart. They are fortunate not to have to work hard to have and maintain a healthy heart, as most of us must do. Another truth is: "The healthy hearts of long-living people beat slowly." The following discussion shows how the heart rate can be lowered with exercise and how this can prolong our life.

In a normal condition, the heart beats 72 times a minute for men and about 80 times for women. According to *The Popular Medical Encyclopedia*, by Morris Fishbein, M.D., at birth the heart beats about 130 times a minute; at six years, it beats 100 times a minute; at ten years, about 90 times, and at fifteen years, about 85 times. Among adults, a heart rate from 65 to 80 beats per minute may well be within the normal range. During an average lifetime, the heart beats 2.5 billion times and pumps a total of nearly 15 million gallons, according to Dr. Fishbein.

Henry S. Cabin, M.D., states in the *Yale University School of Medicine Heart Book* that in 1 minute in an average adult, the heart completes the full cardiac cycle seventy times. The same heart-rate figure is stated in the book, *The Aerobics Program for Total Well-Being* by Dr. Kenneth H. Cooper, who is also the author of the best-selling book, *Running Without Fear*. He says that the average American male who is not in condition has a resting heart rate of about 70 beats per minute; the average American woman's rate is about 75 to 80 beats per minute.

Paul D. Thompson, M.D., a professor of medicine at the University of Pittsburgh, provides approximately the same figure--he says that the average American has a resting heart rate of 66 to 72 beats per minute. The number of times an average person's heart beats in a day is about 100,000. In one year, the human heart beats 36.5 million times--the heart of a seventy-year-old has beaten more than 2.5 billion times. These figures were presented in an article entitled "Strong at Heart," by Joe Kita, in the April 1997 issue of the *Men's Health Magazine.*

Athletes have larger and stronger hearts that can deliver an adequate supply of blood while beating slower than the hearts of untrained individuals. Generally, the greater the physical fitness of an individual, the slower is the heart rate at rest. Some well-trained athletes are known to have a pulse rate of 35 beats per minute, which is half the average rate for the general population. According to Dr. Thompson, a famous New Zealand distance runner named Jack Lovelock had a resting pulse of 32 beats per minute. The slowest resting heart rate that Dr. Cooper has ever seen documented was in Hal Higdon, a marathon runner: 28 beats per minute.

It is obvious that athletes train their hearts to be suited for elite-level performance. However, a low heart rate is beneficial for the overall health, well-being, and longevity of ordinary people as well. "I think a slow heart rate is absolutely beneficial for health. In fact, there are about nine studies showing that people with the slowest heart rates live the longest," says Dr. Thompson.

Even minimal aerobic conditioning results in a significant decrease of the average resting heart rate, which indicates that the heart is more efficient and can work harder and longer with less strain. In one study involving middle-aged men (i.e., forty-five to fifty-five years old), there was a decrease from 72 to 55 beats per minute after only three months of aerobic conditioning.

Harvey Diamond achieved the same result in decreasing his heart rate even faster, within just one month. In the book, *Fit for Life,* by Harvey and Marilyn Diamond, he says, "When I first started exercising regularly (10-mile bike ride), my resting heartbeat was 72 beats per minute. One month later, it was 54! In one month, I had strengthened and improved the function of my heart by 18 beats per minute. That's more than 15,000 fewer beats per day! This translates to millions fewer beats per year. We're talking about longevity. Lessening the burden on the heart by several million beats a year can't help but lengthen one's life." Let's do some simple calculations to see how many years we can add to our life with a stronger heart by including regular exercise in our daily routine.

Effect of Exercise on Life Extension

According to the "rate of living" theory of aging, the number of heartbeats within a life span is limited. Aerobic exercise produces a conditioning effect on the heart, which leads to a reduction of the resting heart rate. The estimate of the training effect on heartbeats is based on the following assumptions:

1. The number of heartbeats within a person's life span is limited to 3.5 billion.

2. The person adheres to regular exercise at the age of fifty-five and continues it as long as he/she is alive; as a result of the training, the heart rate decreases from 72 to 60 beats per minute.

3. The person exercises four times a week for 20 minutes at a time.

4. Exercise brings the heart rate to 120 beats and it takes 10 more minutes for the heart to subside to its new normal rate of 60 beats per minute.

5. The person sleeps 8 hours at night and the resting heart rate during the sleeping hours and upon awakening is 64 beats if he/she is not exercising.

6. The resting heart rate of a trained person during sleep is decreased to 54 beats per minute.

7. In the daytime, the heart rate increases by 20 percent (to 86 and 72 beats, respectively, for untrained and trained people) for 1 hour due to daily activities such as stair-climbing, brisk walking, and lifting and carrying objects.

The *life span for* many people *is determined by a definite number of heartbeats.* Leonard Hayflick, Ph.D., in his book, *How and Why We Age,* says that a human heart beats about 3 billion times in a seventy-five-year period, and a centenarian's heart has beaten about 4 billion times.

In my estimation, the lifetime limit for the number of heartbeats is assumed to be 3.5 billion. This number is about 10 percent larger than the number of seconds in a 100-year period, assuming that a 100-year-old person from the age of eighteen had an average heart rate of 60 beats per minute. The basis for this assumption is that long-living people are usually very fit and their heart rate is somewhat lower than that of ordinary old people. The assumption also is supported with data that I obtained directly from long-living people themselves.

While traveling in Iceland in June 1997, I came across the American artist and writer, Morris J. Spivack, at the hotel in Reykjavik. He was ninety-five years old and had been living in Iceland for the last thirty years. He was very small and thin, and he was definitely not an exerciser and not very fit, but he moved around by himself. We talked a few times and I was interested to learn that his heart rate was among his other longevity secrets. He allowed me to measure it, which was 60 beats per minute in a sitting position. I can't say that his heart was beating very strongly, but the beats were quite distinct and regular. In his case, it was not a personal achievement; rather, he just enjoyed good heredity. He was a highly intellectual person, artist, and writer, but he was not engaged in any type of exercise.

The coefficient that considers the slowed-down heart rate at sleep and the accelerated rate during daily activities and exercise is equal to the following:

- For an untrained, non-exercising person:
$$(8 \times 64 / 72 + 15 \times 1.0 + 1 \times 1.2) / 24 = 0.972$$
- For a trained, exercising person: $(8 \times 54 / 60 + 1.0 \times 14.5 + 1.2 \times 1 + 2.0 \times 1 / 3 + (2.0 + 1.0) \times 0.5 \times 1 / 6) / 24 = 0.992$

The heartbeats of a non-exercising person in an average life span. First, let's calculate how many times a person's heart beats within an average life span. According to U.S. Statistics for 1993, Americans currently fifty-five years old have a life expectancy of 24.9 years; that is, they can achieve an age of 79.9 years. Considering the previous assumptions about different heart rates at birth and at various periods of life, as well as the reduction coefficient of 0.972 for an untrained person, we obtain the following:

$60 \times 24 \times 365.25 \times [(130+100) \times 0.5 \times 6+(100+90) \times 0.5 \times 4+(90+85) \times 0.5 \times 5+(85+72) \times 0.5 \times 3+ 72 \times 61.9] \times 0.972 = 3,169,560,593$ or 3.17 billion beats

The heartbeats of an exercising person in an average life span. Now let's look at the case of a person who started exercising regularly at the age of fifty-five. In the average life expectancy of 79.9 years, the heart will beat:

$60 \times 24 \times 365.25 \times [(130+100) \times 0.5 \times 6+(100+90) \times 0.5 \times 4+(90+85) \times 0.5 \times 5+(85+72) \times 0.5 \times 3+72 \times 37+60 \times 24.9] = 3,103,689,960$ beats

In this case, both reduction coefficients have to be applied: 0.972 for the fifty-five-year period and 0.992 for the 24.9-year period. Then we obtain the following:

$3,103,689,960 \times (0.972 \times 55 + 0.992 \times 24.9) / 79.9 = 3.04$ billion beats

Compared to his non-exercising counterpart, our hero has 3.17 - 3.04 = 0.13 billion heartbeats as a reserve, which allow him to live an additional:

$$130,000,000 / 60 \times 60 \times 24 \times 365.25 = 4.1 \text{ years}$$

By exercising for 20 minutes four times a week, he spent 5,919 hours, or 0.67 year, on exercise alone in 24.9 years. Therefore, the **benefit in life**

prolongation results in 4.1 - 0.67 = **3.43 years.** Three and a half years of quality life is worth playing the game, don't you think?

Now let's calculate how many years he can live with the 3.5-billion-heartbeat limit if, like centenarians, he happened to have good heredity and was wise enough to avoid self-destructive habits and behaviors throughout his life:

$$460,000,000 / 60 \times 60 \times 24 \times 365.25 = 14.6 \text{ years}$$

Can you believe that after he **started exercising at age fifty-five, he had a chance to live to ninety-five years** because of his improved heart condition! I don't about you, but I am excited by this.

Heartbeats in 100-year-olds. As discussed previously, we consider healthy centenarians as fit (trained) people. Therefore, the number of heartbeats of a 100-year-old person whose average heart rate after the age of eighteen was 60 beats, with the reduction coefficient of 0.992 for a trained (fit) and exercising person, is as follows:

$$60 \times 24 \times 365.25 \times [(130+100) \times 0.5 \times 6+(100+90) \times 0.5 \times 4+(90+85) \times 0.5 \times 5 + (85+60) \times 0.5 \times 3 + 60 \times 82] \times 0.992 = 3,467,044,166,$$
$$\text{or } 3.47 \text{ billion beats}$$

This figure tells us that a 100-year-old person has not yet used his limit and still has 0.03 billion heartbeats left.

Heartbeats in the longest life of 122 years. Finally, let us see how many times the heart of Jeanne Calment, 122 (February 21, 1875 – August 4, 1997) beat in her super-long life. She definitely had a strong heart and never suffered from heart disease. Although she never worked, she did enough exercising. She was physically active throughout her life, starting as a "turbulent child, ever in motion," as Dr. Michel Allard, Dr. Victor Lebre, and Jean-Marrie Robine wrote about her in their book, Jeanne Calment: *From Van Gogh's Time to Ours: 122 Extraordinary Years.* Her physical activities included fencing, walking (long hikes, even trips to the glaciers of Mont-Blanc in the Alps), hunting, and occasionally sports such as tennis, ice- and roller-skating, cycling, and swimming. She did exercises every morning and throughout the day too; flexibility exercises for keeping her joints supple were her favorite. Until she was 100, she occasionally rode a bicycle around Arles where she lived, although this was not her regular cycling exercise. With these activities and lifestyle, she was fit enough and had a rather well-trained heart.

Her heredity was very good: even though the average life span in France at the end of the nineteenth century was fifty years, her maternal grandfather died in 1898 at the age of eighty-eight, her father lived till ninety-three, her mother till eighty-six, and her older brother died at ninety-seven. Her heart was definitely healthy, but her brother--who lived to the very old age of ninety-seven--had heart problems, and even had a heart attack at the age of thirty-six. From these considerations, we can assume that her average heart rate was 66 beats per minute in the daytime. Taking into account the reduction coefficient for night sleep and that she lived 122 years and 164 days, we calculate the following:

$$60 \times 24 \times 365.25 \times [(130+100) \times 0.5 \times 6+(100+90) \times 0.5 \times 4+(90+85) \times 0.5 \times 5+(85+66) \times 0.5 \times 3+ 66 \times 104.45] \times 0.972 = 4{,}410{,}765{,}989,$$
$$\text{or } 4.41 \text{ billion beats}$$

The case of "Queen Jeanne," as she was called, shows that the human heart probably has the ability to beat more than 3.5 or 4 billion times--at least in queens.

Walking

The sovereign invigorator of the body is exercise,
and of all exercises, walking is the best.
--Thomas Jefferson

Walking is one of the best exercises anyone can do, and it is especially beneficial if you are out of shape at the outset. Dr. Paul Bragg, an American health pioneer, says in his well-known book, *The Miracle of Fasting:*"Of all forms of exercise, walking is the one that brings most of the body into action...Walking is the king of exercise, and ideal for you."

Many people value walking and benefit greatly from it. One friend of mine, Romain Vallas from Switzerland, walks for 4 hours every day. He is now fifty-seven years old and in sound condition, and he believes that walking allows him to stay healthy even under extreme circumstances. He is a professional teacher who teaches six languages: French, German, English, Italian, Spanish, and Portuguese. He is a quite remarkable person; he has lived in twelve countries and traveled to 135. I met him in the Japanese language school in Tokyo. He did not use the train to get to the school from the district where he lived. One evening after school, I joined him and it took us an hour and a half to walk to his home. For me, it was a one-way trial walk; for him, it was routine to walk roundtrip to the school and back home. He also walked to all his classes in the daytime; in total, he actually walked more than 4 hours a day.

In reality, 4 hours is too much time to devote to exercise and I do not think that many busy people, for whom time is precious, can afford that luxury. So what is the minimum time that works? Harvey and Marilyn Diamond say in their best-selling book, *Fit for Life,* that the minimum is a 20-minute *brisk* walk every day. John Evans of Swansea, Wales, who lived to age 112, walked at least a mile a day--about the same walking distance for Maudie Ryder of Holladay, Utah, who was 106 when she was interviewed by Dr. John Heinerman, author of *Heinerman's Encyclopedia of Anti-Aging Remedies.* Both centenarians walked more in a strolling pace, taking about 40 minutes to cover a mile. George Burns, the famous American comedian who died at the age of 100, usually walked for an hour and a half in the morning.

Frank Shomo, 108, of Robinson, Pennsylvania, who died in March 1997, gives us an excellent example of the impact of walking on longevity. His job involved checking for fractures in the rail and other railroad problems, and for forty years he walked 15 miles a day. That is more than half a marathon distance--and every day! "Just imagine how much of an affect that forty years of walking 100-plus miles a week has on the cardiovascular system. Sure, he was not running. He was walking swiftly, which would elevate the heart rate enough to have a positive influence on his life," says his grandson, Brent Hawkins, who is a coach at Litchfield High School in Maine.

According to Dr. Kenneth H. Cooper, brisk walking is defined as walking at a speed of 14 minutes per mile. This means that Frank Shomo walked on the job for $14 \times 15 = 210$ minutes, or 3.5 hours, every day. "He must have walked a million miles," said his granddaughter Adda Lee Hoskinson-Seifert. Actually, we can calculate how many miles Frank walked in those forty years. Let's assume that he walked 350 days a year, because there were days when he was out of town. "Every Saturday and Sunday off, Frank walked his entire section of track to check for broken rails. If he couldn't, he'd ask one of his men to do it. He always said he couldn't live with himself if an accident happened because of a broken rail," his granddaughter explained. Therefore, this gives us 15 miles x 350 days x 40 years = 210,000 miles. During his long life, he probably walked a quarter of a million miles--or about sixty times around the world--incredible!

Walking, combined with good genes and a healthy lifestyle, is a longevity secret of Gin Kanie, 108, of Japan. Her identical twin sister, Kin Narita died in

January 2000 at the age of 107. They attributed their longevity to physical activity. "At this age, I walk 2 hours each morning for exercise," said Gin Kanie at the celebration of their 105th birthday.

I like walking very much and use every possible opportunity to walk instead of taking a bus or train. If my destination is within walking distance-- that is, about an hour or so--I usually walk. Last year in the fall, I walked around the lake near Horn Pond Mountain in Woburn, Massachusetts. Actually, it was a combination of walking and jogging. It took about 2 hours to go up the mountain, including a few exercises at the top. While I walked, I also did the breathing exercise--four steps to each inhale, four steps to each exhale, eight steps holding my breath--described in the *Oxygen Intake Control* chapter. The walking times of the people discussed herein are shown in Figure 22-1.

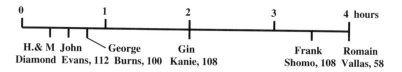

Figure 22-1. Walking Times of Fit and Long-Living People

This time axis shows a rather broad range of time spent on walking exercise by these people. Many do not limit their exercise plan merely to walking; they add half an hour of stretching or yoga exercises, as George Burns did. The total exercise time is about 2 hours, which is quite a significant commitment; you can find the time if you are a retired person, but it is difficult if you still work.

Jogging

Among aerobic exercises that develop the cardiovascular capacity, fast and deep jogging is one of the best. The advantage with jogging is that it is about three times faster in getting the same aerobic benefit from walking. Dr. Cooper ranks *jogging* third for aerobic value, with *cross-country skiing* first and *swimming* second; in the fourth and fifth places are cycling and walking. He also makes a distinction between jogging and running by the speed: running slower than 9 minutes per mile is jogging, faster than 9 minutes is running.

Some experts value running as the best life-extending exercise. Bill Rodgers, the only runner to win the Boston and New York marathons four times each, calls running "the fountain of youth." In his book, *Bill Rodgers' Lifetime Running Plan,* he says: "Past thirty, your aerobic capacity drops about 1 percent a year. But the more aerobic exercise you get, the longer your capacity will take to decline. If you start running past the age of thirty-five, it will even increase for several years, regardless of aging. When runners are in shape, they can be better lovers." Running is very popular in the United States--one in eleven Americans is an active runner, and half of them are over the age of thirty-five.

This does not mean that running cannot be started after age thirty-five. Whatever one's age, it is never too late to start running, and there are several encouraging examples. Rikichi Shimizu, eighty-eight, of Japan, who started running at the age of sixty-five, participates in 10-kilometer races among world veterans. He is also determined to run in the Honolulu marathon in two years, when he is ninety. Even more striking is the case of Kazuhito Tsutsumi, ninety-five, of Japan. He broke the world record in the 100-meter race for ninety-five- to ninety-nine-year-old runners. Tsutsumi started running at sixty-two, being inspired by Abebe Bikila, a marathon runner from Ethiopia. He jogged in the mornings and then took part in a local mini-marathon. However, at the age of forty-four, he was so sick that he could not continue and had to quit his job. Doctors were unable to help him, but he cured himself by beating himself with bamboo sticks and taking cold baths in a nearby river.

Actually, long-living people usually do not jog or run--they just stay active, mostly with their every day tasks. However, there are examples of marathon runners among people of very advanced age. In the September 1994 issue of *The Japan Times* newspaper, there was a photograph showing 103-year-old Toraichi Okuyama of Shimabara, in the Nagasaki Prefecture of Japan, as he began the marathon run on Amakusa Island.

Keeping in mind our goal of life extension, it seems practical to consider jogging as an exercise for fitness conditioning. However, I would limit the age to start jogging to sixty-five or seventy because it is a strenuous exercise. Before starting to jog, elderly people should have a medical checkup and their doctor's approval.

Cycling

Cycling causes less wear and tear on the leg joints and muscles than jogging, so older people who have joint problems can benefit from this exercise. According to Dr. Cooper, a cycling speed of about 15 miles per hour is the optimum rate for a good training effect for the average person. For elderly people, a much slower speed will also be effective.

To strengthen the muscles and heart and to get the training effect, cycling must be done correctly. The trouble spot with cycling is the knees, and cycling incorrectly can easily overstrain them. To reduce knee strain, one must know how to use the gears of the bicycle properly, especially on hills. Brakes and other safety features must also be working properly. For safe riding, one should know and follow the rules of the road and wear a helmet. To avoid dehydration while cycling, always bring a water bottle along.

Some elderly people prefer cycling as their routine exercise. The world-famous Russian writer Leo Tolstoy was known to ride his bicycle when he was in his eighties in the last decade of the nineteenth century. The longevity champion, Jeanne Calment of France, who lived to 122, rode a bicycle until she was 100.

Swimming and Water Workouts

Swimming involves all major muscles in the body; as a result, it is considered to have more of an aerobic effect than other exercises, according to Dr. Cooper. Furthermore, there is less pressure on joints and muscles while swimming due to the buoyancy effect of the water. However, the drawbacks of swimming, including weather constraints in natural swimming areas or an inconvenient location of an indoor pool, can make swimmers inconsistent. There are also proper techniques for swimming; otherwise, you can be exhausted after just one lap in the pool. To really get an aerobic effect, 20 minutes is the minimum, but if swimming incorrectly, it's difficult to last even 2 minutes. Because it takes a lot of time to build up to swimming any distance, people usually start out by swimming a short distance, then stopping to rest. Therefore, the initial stages of swimming are anaerobic for many people, according to Edward J. Jackowski.

When elderly people begin swimming for exercise, there might be a problem with tightness or weak muscles in their shoulders. In this case, flexibility exercises and some strength training with free weights might be necessary. Some people choose swimming as exercise and benefit from it despite their old age, as the example of Tom Lane shows. In 1995, he was 100 years old and still swimming. Moreover, he raced in the 100-meter backstroke event of the Senior Olympics, held in September 1994 near San Diego, California.

Considered as effective as jogging or brisk walking, water workouts are becoming increasingly popular in the United States, Japan, and European countries. People suffering from arthritis or osteoporosis, heart-attack survivors, mastectomy patients, and people recovering from injuries all benefit from warm-water exercises. The classes, which usually last an hour, involve aerobic exercises such as walking in the shallow water with hand weights, stepping on and off an underwater platform, and running in deep water. Because elderly people are vulnerable to falls, which often result in hip fractures, water workouts can be especially beneficial for older people for improving balance. My grandmother never recovered from a fall and hip fracture, and died after being confined to bed for eight years.

Cross-Country Skiing

In cross-country skiing, not only are the leg muscles involved, but also many other muscles of the body, which provides excellent aerobic conditioning. However, cross-country skiing is a more strenuous exercise than jogging, and elderly people must be cautious not to strain their heart. I was thirty-two years old when I experienced almost pre-heart-attack exhaustion while cross-country skiing in the suburbs of Moscow. It was a cold, windy day but many people were skiing. Although I was not a trained skier, I was trying to race faster than my usual pace. After skiing, I felt very weak and my face was so pale that my friend was frightened and wondered whether he should call for a doctor.

I also remember when a senior colleague of mine, who worked with me at the research institute, died after cross-country skiing. He was seventy-nine years old, very active and exercised regularly, including brisk walking and often cross country skiing in the winter. On that day, he felt terrific and skied 10 miles instead of his usual 6 or 7 miles. He came back home, lay down on his bed, and died of a heart attack.

Knee-Bend Exercise

Unlike sports experts who merely mention it, I rank knee bends as the number-one low-impact aerobic exercise. I first learned about this exercise and its miracle effect on health from an article by Henrich Epp of Novosibirsk, Russia, that was published in 1985 in the Russian magazine *Physical Culture and Sports*. In it, the author described his own experience. He was sixty-four and his heart condition was so bad that just climbing two flights of stairs left him short-winded. A number of accompanying diseases made his life miserable. When he decided to try knee bends, at first he could do only five repetitions before becoming short of breath. However, he was very determined to exercise and the next day he did six repetitions, then continued to add just one more repetition each day.

After a month, he found himself able to add two more repetitions each day; by the time he reached a hundred repetitions, he was adding three repetitions in each session. He was very consistent about doing the knee bends every day; after eight months, he had built up to a thousand repetitions in one session, at a speed of a hundred knee bends in 5 minutes. All his diseases fell away like leaves in the autumn, and his heart strength was so improved that he included running in his exercise routine. At the age of seventy, he participated in a super-long 60-mile marathon. This remarkable experience encouraged him to write the article to share his successful experiment on himself with others.

His article was followed by the comments of a physician. He recommended the knee-bend exercise, emphasizing its safety for elderly people because increasing the number of repetitions in the workout occurred very gradually. Unlike with jogging or running, the heart can hardly be overstrained by knee bends.

While staying in Japan, I once mentioned this article to one of my coworkers and about the thousand-knee-bend buildup. He replied that some young Japanese people could do as many as ten thousand repetitions at a time. Although it sounds incredulous, I do not think it is impossible. It is known that prisoners of war during the Vietnam War, particularly those captured by the Viet Cong, survived their ordeal because they exercised a lot. One of the prisoners set a record of three hundred push-ups and *up to seven hundred knee bends*. These numbers are very impressive, but it is **most important to start with just a few knee bends and then build up gradually**.

Epp considered the aerobic effect of a hundred knee bends to be equal to 1 kilometer of running. For elderly beginners, he advises ten repetitions within the first six weeks, exercising three times a week. Then gradually the number of repetitions can be increased, by one or two knee bends, up to a total of fifty repetitions in one session by the second six weeks. In the following twelve weeks, untrained people may add five to ten repetitions every week, for a total of 110 repetitions. Advanced exercisers may progressively increase the number of repetitions by ten to fifty--for a maximum of 450 knee bends in one session. In the beginning, the exercise must be done slowly--5 to 6 seconds per repetition. Then the speed is increased to fifty repetitions per 5.5 minutes, and finally, a hundred repetitions per 5 minutes. However, the best way is for people to follow their own rhythm.

Currently, I do 1,200 knee bends in one session and it takes exactly 1 hour to complete the entire set. The one-thousand mark was my millenium resolution, which I achieved on December 20, 1999. Ten years ago, before emigrating from Russia and when I had just started doing this exercise, my buildup was eighty knee bends. Many times since then I could gain as many as two hundred to three hundred knee bends, but after a few months break, I would have to start from forty again. It took me about one year of doing it on a regular basis to hit the thousand mark. For the last half year, I have been doing the knee bends every other day, but previously it had been usually three times a week.

I rank the knee-bend exercise so high because it provides a good aerobic effect without a sharp increase in the breathing rate, as with other aerobic exercises. My rate in this exercise is twenty knee bends per minute, adjusting one breathing cycle to one down-up body movement. Compared with my resting breathing rate of about fifteen times per minute, it is only a 33 percent increase.

The slow breathing rate allows me to do diaphragm breathing; that is, exhaling and contracting the abdomen wall while going down, and inhaling and expanding the belly while moving up. This breathing pattern is the opposite of what all exercise experts advise: exhaling during the exertion part of the movement. However, when the body goes down, the abdomen (and chest, to some degree) is bent and compressed, and it is more natural to exhale at that moment. During the upward movement, the abdomen and chest are released, so their expansion while inhaling occurs more easily. Also, because the exertion in raising the body is so little, it is not difficult to inhale during the exertion. The heart rate achieved after the first 3 to 4 minutes is 135 to 140 beats and doesn't increase any farther. Figure 22-2 shows my heart rate measured with a heart monitor during the knee-bend exercise in May 1998.

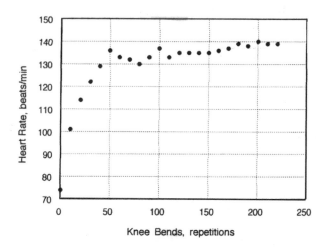

Figure 22-2. Author's Heart Rate versus Number of Knee Bends

As with other prolonged aerobic exercises that induce sweating, knee bends provide an excellent detoxifying effect for the body. After two or three hundred knee bends, and depending on whether it is warm or cool weather, I start to sweat and lose about a pound of my weight by the time the 1,200 knee bends are done. This is like going to a sauna three times a week, but my internal sauna that raises my body temperature is even better. To avoid dehydration, I drink a big cup of green tea or water before exercising. I sweat profusely during the workouts, but other people probably would not sweat as much.

Believe it or not, together with warming the body, doing the knee bends has a calming effect on my mind. While counting the number of knee bends in my mind, I practice imagery meditation. With each ten-knee-bend cycle, I imagine a rainbow in the sky with seven major colors and three white colors. Each section of my imaginary rainbow has a relevant gem incorporated in it: ruby in the red; topaz in the orange; yellow sapphire in the yellow; emerald in the green; sapphire in the blue; amethyst in the purple; iolite in the violet; and moonstone, pearl, and jade in the three white sections. When I go down, one of the gems is activated; as I raise up, it sparkles and radiates a beam of healing light that showers my body. Sometimes a flow of thoughts distracts my mind from concentrating on the rainbow, but as soon as I catch myself wandering, I go back to the color play.

This exercise not only supplies a sufficient amount of oxygen to the tissues, but also prevents an excessive elimination of carbon dioxide. As a result, the blood vessels are kept wide open and the blood pressure doesn't increase much. Actually, the knee-bend exercise does not need warming up because the first twenty repetitions have a warming effect on the body and joints. **In addition to its excellent training effect, the knee-bend exercise does not tax the heart to its limit.** However, it does aggravate the knees and people who have arthritis should do it with caution, limiting the depth of the bend and the number of repetitions.

1. Stand with your feet shoulder-width apart and your toes pointed somewhat outward; inhale.

2. Keep your back straight and lower yourself as far down as it is comfortable for your knees. Keep both heels and toes flat on the floor, stretching your arms forward for balance. Keep your mouth closed and exhale while bending your knees.

3. Lower your arms while standing up to the straight-knee position; inhale while rising up.

Start with six repetitions and build up gradually, within twenty-four weeks, to a hundred knee bends a day. While counting the repetitions in your mind, concentrate on rhythmic breathing. After you have acquired some experience, try diaphragmatic breathing: bulge your belly when you inhale and contract your abdominal muscles when you exhale. Count the number of heartbeats both before exercising and afterwards. Walk around and continue the abdominal breathing to cool down after exercising.

The modified version of this exercise may work well for those with problem knees. Clutch your hands behind the lower back for balance and do not fully bend your knees when squatting down--that is, avoid deep sitting. This way can spare your knees and prevent the cartilage from wearing out. I have done the knee bends this way for the last two years. Doing a thousand repetitions each session for one year and currently doing 1,200 for six months, I have not had any knee problems so far.

Flexibility Exercises

Flexibility exercises involve stretching the muscles and tissues, thereby helping extend our range of motion in the joints. Disuse restricts joint flexibility at any age. Of all parts of the body, flexibility of the spine is the most crucial for our health, fitness, and longevity. The spinal cord is a bunch of nerve fibers that run from the brain down the spine through the channel in the vertebrae. Body parts and internal organs are connected to the brain through thirty-one pairs of nerves that branch out from the spinal cord. If the nerves are compressed somewhere in the spine, many disorders result. There is a saying that "we are as young as our spine is flexible."

For me, the most impressive sign of backbone flexibility is someone's ability to assume a full bridge pose with straight legs and arms. When I was in the ninth grade, a schoolmate of mine easily assumed the full bridge pose during a gymnastics lesson. He was so flexible that he could keep his legs and arms almost straight in this pose, with his hands flat on the floor near his heels. Another boy jumped on him and sat as if on a bench. I was very envious and impressed to such a degree that I can still visualize this picture in my mind now, more than forty years later.

Throughout my life, I have given most attention to the people able to do this exercise. One of them was a circus performer, Tamara Flyagina of Russia, who was very famous for her acrobatic art. She was so perfect in the bridge pose that she could lower her arms 1 foot lower than the level of her feet. At the age of thirty-six she was still performing, mostly in Soviet circus trips abroad. When asked what was the secret of her spine flexibility, she replied that every day she does as many as two hundred repetitions of the full bridge exercise. Tamara Flyagina proved that a high level of flexibility can be maintained even as we grow older.

Richard L. Hittleman, a famous yoga instructor on American TV, is wholly convinced of that. In his book, *Yoga for Physical Fitness,* he stated, "I have proved to hundreds of thousands of people through my books, classes, and television programs that they can regain the youthful flexibility of the spine practically regardless of age or physical condition. Many yoga students who are so-called 'senior citizens' possess greater flexibility than their grandchildren!"

Flexibility requires a lot of work to achieve a certain level and also to maintain it. If the exercises are not done for a week or two, one will soon find that some joints have become more rigid. Only regular exercise--preferably every day--is the key to achieve a desired degree of flexibility.

The super flexibility demonstrated by circus performers is definitely a gift and it cannot be achieved, regardless of how much time one devotes to the exercises. It is beyond human limits when a fourteen-year-old Chinese circus performer, whom I watched in a performance in Tokyo, does a backward body bend with her head resting on her thigh below her buttocks. I was also very impressed with three contortionists--the Yagaansetseg "snake-girls" from Mongolia--when I saw them performing with the Shrine Circus in Wilmington, Massachusetts.

In a recent American TV program about Guinness-record challengers, there was shown a yogi from France who apparently was in his fifties. He looked quite well fed and was a large man, but he managed to put himself into a clear Plexiglas box. He filled the box with his body to the full, displaying a thorough flexibility. A photograph of him inside the box was published in *The 1999 Guinness Book of World Records.*

My yoga teacher, Eugene Bazh, who at forty is very flexible, can assume the pose called "a child's spine." He grasps the toes of his feet with his hands behind his head and brings them up to touch his head and even his shoulders. Actually, this pose involves great spine flexibility and few children can do it. However, each of us has the potential to make his/her spine and joints more supple.

There were times when flexibility was crucial for the survival of our ancestors. In his book, *Khan Bateau,* the Russian author Yan describes the torture that Mongolian invaders inflicted on their victims in Russia and Central Asia. They bent the backs of the captured people to bring their feet in contact with their head; the victim's back usually was broken and he/she would die. However, when they invaded India and tried to torture a local man this way, it did not hurt him at all. He stood up on his feet and tried to flee; they were so impressed by his supple back that they released him.

The flexibility of our body changes throughout the day: we are more rigid on awakening each morning and then become more flexible in the afternoon, provided we have had enough body movement. An inactive life of watching TV and excessive food consumption can also result in decreased flexibility. Therefore, regular exercise is important for maintaining flexibility. The following discussion describes two sets of flexibility exercises: the ***backbone-joints*** exercises and the ***muscle-tissue*** exercises.

Backbone-Joints Exercises

This set of exercises is designed to work out the backbone and all major joints of the body. Most of these exercises I learned from my yoga teacher, Eugene Bazh; others I learned from the book, *Bring Back Health and Youth*, by Mirzakarim Norbekov and Larisa Fotina, M.D., who in turn learned them from 107-year-old Matniaz Ollobergenov of Uzbekistan. The exercises start at the neck and proceed down the body to the feet. Each exercise has to be repeated six to twelve times at the beginning and can be doubled with the buildup.

Neck Exercises

Head roll. Stand with your feet apart and your hands hanging at your sides. Drop your head. With your chin moving toward your right shoulder, slowly roll your head clockwise. Imagine that you are rolling the ball of your head on the platform of your shoulders. Do six rotations, relaxing your neck muscles more deeply with each rotation. Then do the same number of head rotations in a counterclockwise direction. Actually, this exercise is a warm-up for the other neck exercises.

Head up/down bend. Let your head down gently as far as possible, as if trying to reach your chest with your chin; then, from that position, draw your chin farther downward as if trying to reach your abdomen. Then raise your head and bend it back as far as you can. From that position, draw your head farther downward, as if trying to lay it on your buttocks like a turtle does. Repeat six times up and down, trying each time to go a little farther.

Head side bend. Keep your spine straight and shoulders fixed. Let your head fall gently to the left side in an attempt to touch your left shoulder with your left ear; then bend your head to your right shoulder. Repeat six times on both sides, trying each time to come closer to the shoulders. This exercise is quite common among office workers in Japan–the tired company workers are often seen doing head side bends at their desk and in the subway on the commuter trains. They do just a few bends until a neck-cracking sound is heard.

Head side twist. Stand with your feet slightly apart, making a straight line with your spine and head. Imagine that you are a chicken. Slowly twist your head to the left as far as you can. From that extreme head position, although you feel you have reached your limit, try to gently strain your neck muscles to go a few millimeters more. Do not overstrain. Then do the same on the right side. Repeat six times on both sides, trying each time to go farther to the side with your chin.

Chin over the shoulder. The starting position is with your head bent forward and your chin attempting to touch your chest. Turn your head in a sideways-upward motion and raise your chin over your left shoulder. Come back to the starting position and do the same over your right shoulder. Repeat six times on both sides, trying each time to raise your chin higher over the shoulders.

Chin on the shoulder. The starting position is with your head bent backward with the chin pointing up. Turn your head in a sideways-downward motion and lay your chin on your left shoulder. Come back to the starting position and do the same movement to your right shoulder. Repeat six times on both sides, trying each time to reach your shoulders with your chin.

Chin in a horizontal circle. Imagine you are a snake. From a straight-head position, move your chin horizontally to your left shoulder, then forward, to your right shoulder, and then back again in a circular motion such as a cobra snake does. Do the same in the opposite direction. Repeat six times in both directions, trying each time to make a wider circle with your chin.

Shoulder (Upper Spine) Exercises

Shoulder up/down move. Stand with your feet together and your hands hanging relaxed at your sides. Lift both shoulders as high as you can, then drop them down. With some straining, pull them farther down--as low as you can. Repeat twelve times, counting the up-and-down movement as one repetition.

Shoulder forward/backward move. Stand with your feet slightly apart and your arms hanging at your sides. Bring your shoulders forward and your chin down to your chest. Try to further draw your chin downward toward your abdomen and your shoulders to meet each other. The upper part of your spine will bend like a bow. Then bring your shoulders and head backward and pull, with some straining, your head farther toward your buttocks and your shoulder blades toward each other. Each forward and backward movement should take 6 seconds. Repeat twelve times in both directions.

Shoulder rotation. Stand with your feet together and arms hanging relaxed at your sides. The shoulder rotation exercise involves six kinds of rotations, each done in six repetitions. First, rotate both shoulders forward with your arms hanging heavily, in an up-forward-down-backward circle.

Second, rotate both shoulders backwards, in up-backward-down-forward circles. Third, rotate forward each shoulder in turn, similar to a swimming crawl stroke, but using your shoulders, not your arms. Fourth, rotate backward each shoulder in turn, like a swimming backstroke. Fifth, rotate asynchronously your left shoulder forward while your right shoulder is rotating backward. In the beginning, it will probably be difficult to rotate each shoulder in the opposite direction. Try to rotate just your left shoulder forward with your right shoulder motionless; then switch to your right shoulder. Try to combine the rotations; after a few attempts, you should be able to master it. Finally, rotate your right shoulder forward while your left shoulder rotates backward. This asynchronous shoulder rotation is very beneficial for the upper spine.

Upper-spine side bends. Stand with your feet together and your hands, arms, and forearms tightly clasped to your sides. Bend your body to the left, sliding your palms along your sides as you reach for the sides of your knees, all the time keeping your arms in tight contact with your body. Then straighten and bend to the right in a similar motion. Repeat the entire sequence six times on both sides.

Upper-body rotation. Place the palms of your hands on your sides close to the armpits, with your fingers toward the chest and your thumbs toward the back. Clasp your upper sides with your hands as if fixing the spine in a steady position below the level of your hands. Rotate the upper part of your body above the level of your hands in a clockwise direction six times. Then repeat the rotation in a counterclockwise direction six times.

Elbow Exercises

Hanging-elbow rotation. Stand straight with your elbows spread at shoulder level with your forearms hanging down. Keeping the elbows fixed at shoulder level, rotate your hands and forearms in a plane parallel to your body, with your hands moving in opposite directions. Repeat the rotation six times in both directions.

Fixed-elbow rotation. Stand straight with your elbows pressed to your sides and your forearms hanging down. Keeping your elbows fixed at your sides, rotate your hands and forearms in a plane parallel to your body, with your hands moving in opposite directions. Alternate the movement of your hands closer to or farther from the body when they meet in the front. Repeat the rotation six times in one direction and then six times in the opposite direction.

Figure 22-3. Dumbbell Curls

Figure 22-4. Front Dumbbell Raises

Figure 22-5.   Lateral Dumbbell Raises

Figure 22-6.   Bent Torso Lateral Dumbbell Raises

Figure 22-7.   Lateral Dumbbell Stretch

Figure 22-8. Dumbbell Upward Press

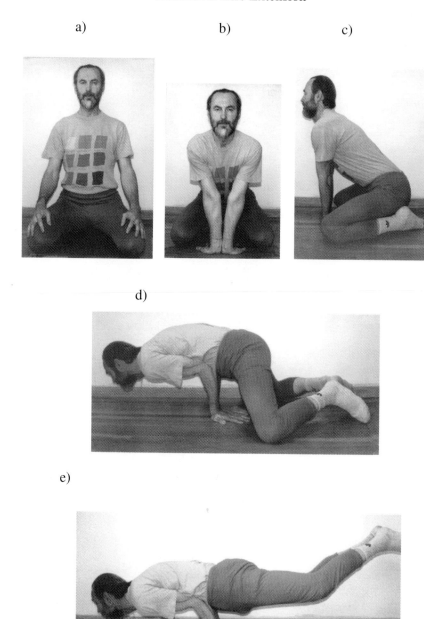

Figure 22-13.   Peacock Pose

a)   b)

c)

d)

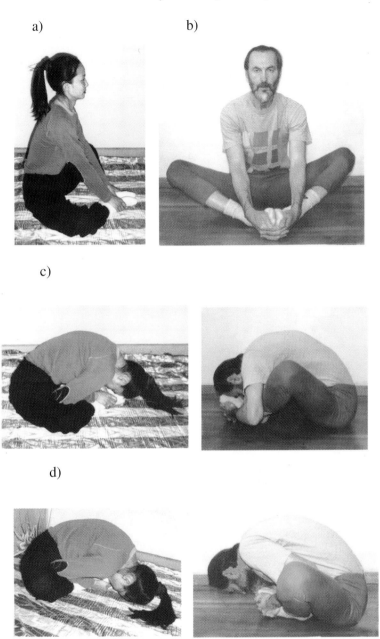

Figure 22-14.   Head to Instep Exercise

a)

b)   c)

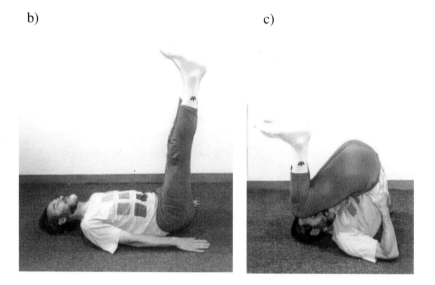

Figure 22-15.   Shoulder Stand

d)

e)

Figure 22-15.   Shoulder Stand

Figure 22-16.   Exhale through Water

Figure 22-17.   Xu Fang in the Meditation Pose

Fixed-elbow wrist rotation. Stand straight and press your palms together at heart level--like in the Indian *namaste* position--with your fingers pointed up and your elbows spread apart. Keeping your elbows fixed, turn both palms in a forward-down-backward motion. When your fingers are pointed downward, turn your hands so their backs are touching. Repeat twelve times in each direction.

Wrist Exercises

Hand up/down bend. Stand straight with your hands stretched forward at shoulder level. With your wrists fixed, bend your hands to point your fingers upward; then throw your hands and fingers downward. Repeat twelve times.

Hand rotation. From the same starting position, rotate your palms inward, then outward. Repeat twelve times.

Finger grips. From the same starting position, stretch your fingers as much as you can, then grip them into fists. Repeat twenty-four times, gradually increasing the speed.

Middle-Spine Exercises

Forward/backward bends. Sit straight on a chair and hold the chair's seat with your hands. Exhale; then bend your head downward, pulling it toward your navel. Keep pulling your head down with some straining for 5 to 6 seconds. Release the tension, inhale, and raise your head. Bend your head backward as if you were trying to reach your buttocks with your head. Arch your spine and pull your head backward with some straining, but do not overstrain. Repeat the entire sequence six times.

Side bends. This exercise resembles the upper-spine side-bend exercise except that only your palms touch your sides, which allows you to work on the middle part of the spine. Bend your body to the left, with the left palm sliding down to reach the side of your left knee while the right palm slides up to your hip. Then straighten and bend to the right in a similar motion. Repeat the entire sequence six times.

Torso twist. Sit in a chair with your head and spine in a straight line.

Twist your shoulders and head as far to the left as you can. When you reach your limit, that is the starting position. Exhale, hold your breath, and start twist bounces, with your shoulders gripping a little more with each bounce. It helps to grasp your left leg above the knee with your right hand. While bouncing, do additional short exhales. Do twelve bounces, then inhale and twist to the right. Repeat the same sequence to the right.

Waist (Lower-Spine) Exercises

The following five waist exercises should be done from the same starting position. Stand with your feet well apart, about two widths of your shoulders. Keep your knees absolutely straight and still, with your heels spread wider than your toes. Experience the steadiness of this stance as if you were rooted to the floor. Occasionally correct this starting position of your legs and feet while you do the waist exercises.

Torso side bends. Put your hands on your hips with your thumbs facing forward. Bend your body to the left, holding it in a strict vertical plane. While bending, your left hand should be pressed against your left hip, sliding down your left leg in a massage pass and reaching for your left knee and as far below it as you can. Your right hand slides up your right leg, hip, and the long muscle of your lower back, also in a massage pass. When you straighten and then bend to the right, your left hand massages the side of your left leg, hip, and the other long muscle of your lower back, while your right hand slides down toward your right knee and below it. Repeat six times on both sides, then gradually build up to twelve times.

Torso forward/backward bend. In the leg starting position, place your hands on your chest. Bend forward, with your hands sliding down your chest, abdomen, and legs in a massage pass, and reaching for your toes. Unbend gradually with your hands massaging your legs and torso up to your shoulders. Continue to move, bending backwards with your hands reaching as low as you can toward your buttocks, legs, and calves. Repeat the entire sequence six times, then gradually build up to twelve times. Each time, try to reach an inch lower both forward and backward.

Torso side twist. From the starting leg and feet position, with your arms extended out at shoulder level and palms down, swing your relaxed arms to the left, and turn your head and shoulders to the left far enough to see your left heel behind your left shoulder. While looking at your heel, do not bend your neck--keep your head high. Then swing your arms to the right and repeat the entire movement on the right side. Repeat the sequence twelve times.

Torso rotation. Clasp your hands behind your head and bring your chest forward and your elbows backward as far as they will go. Rotate your body clockwise, bending the torso and touching your left knee with your left elbow, then your right knee with your right elbow, and finally raise your torso and stand straight. Rotate your body counterclockwise, touching first your right knee with your right elbow, and so on. Repeat the entire sequence twelve times.

Combined torso bend and twist. From the starting position, twist your body to the left and place your right palm on your left side below the armpit. Put your left hand on the right one and bend your body toward your left foot while your hands rub down along your sides, thighs, and legs in a massage pass. Unbend and massage your left leg, hip, and side back to the armpit. Then twist your body to the right and do the same massage and bending for the right leg. Repeat the entire sequence six times, gradually building up to twelve times.

Hip rotation. Stand with your feet well apart. Place your hands on your thighs and push them with your hands rotating in a clockwise direction. Try to draw a circle with your hips. Then rotate your hips in the opposite direction. Repeat twelve times in both directions.

Thigh rotation. Stand with your feet together and put your hands on your hips. Raise your right knee to hip level. Balancing your body weight on your left leg, turn your right knee outward as far as you can and then let it down. Rotate your right knee backward, raise it up to hip level, point it forward, and then let it down. Do the same rotations with your left leg. Repeat six times in both directions for both legs, and gradually build up to twelve times.

Hip swinging. Stand with your feet well apart and your knees slightly bent. Place your hands on your hips and thrust your seat backwards, arching your back. Bring your seat under and the pelvis forward, as in a lovemaking motion. Then move your seat in a down-backward-up motion. Repeat the pelvic tilt six times in the first few weeks, and then gradually work up to twelve times.

Knee Exercises

Knee synchronous rotation. Stand with your feet together and place your hands on slightly bent knees. Using your hands to keep your knees close together, rotate both knees in circles in a clockwise direction. Then rotate in a counterclockwise direction. Repeat twelve times in both directions.

Knee asynchronous rotation. Stand with your feet shoulder-width apart and place your hands on slightly bent knees. Using your hands, rotate both knees in circles in an inward direction, first touching each other and then apart. Then rotate your knees in an outward direction. Repeat twelve times in both directions.

Knee-hanging and rotation. Stand with your feet together and place your hands on your hips. Raise your right knee up to hip level, and balance your body weight on your left leg. Keeping the knee fixed, rotate your heel in clockwise circles, and then rotate it in a counterclockwise direction. Repeat twelve times in both directions.

Ankle Exercises

Free-ankle rotation. Stand with your feet together and hands resting on your hips. Raise your right foot a few inches above the floor and balance your weight on your left leg. Keeping the knee stretched and the ankle motionless, rotate the toes of your right foot in clockwise circles; then rotate them in a counterclockwise direction. Do the same toe rotations with your left foot. Repeat twelve times in both directions.

Fixed-ankle rotation. Stand with your feet slightly apart and place your hands on your hips. Lift the heel of your right foot a few inches above the floor with your toes still resting on the floor. Keeping the tips of your toes fixed on the floor, rotate the ankle of your right foot in clockwise circles, followed by counterclockwise circles. Do the same ankle rotations with your left foot. Repeat twelve times in both directions.

Toe bend. Stand with your feet together and hands resting on your hips. Raise your right foot a few inches above the floor and balance your weight on your left leg. Keeping your knee stretched and your ankle motionless, bend the toes of your right foot up and down. Do the same toe bends with your left foot. Repeat twelve times with both feet.

Strength Exercises

In our daily life, we need muscular strength to carry, lift, push, and pull weighty objects. This strength is necessary even to pick up children and play with them. Children often like to be lifted high in your arms, put down, and lifted again. If we don't have enough strength, we can't please them.

Muscle strength, coordination, and balance deteriorate with age. Muscle weakness is a problem for elderly people and, as some studies show, it leads to recurrent falls, a major cause of immobility and death among the American elderly population. When my own grandmother was eighty-five years old, she fell down, injured her hip, and became immobile. After that accident, she was confined to bed, suffered a lot, and became a burden for my mother who took care of her. She died at the age of ninety-three, spending her last miserable eight years in bed. To avoid this kind of misfortune, we need to be fit-- strength capacity is necessary not only for sports, but also for the normal pursuits of daily life.

Strength exercises improve the efficiency of both muscular strength and endurance. Many experts recommend moderate strength exercises for elderly people. In a 1990 study at Tufts University in Boston, a group of frail nursing-home residents--men aged eighty-six to ninety-six--participated in a weight-lifting program. Under the close supervision of researchers, the elderly weightlifters increased their muscle strength from three-fold to four-fold in eight weeks. Strength training can also do miracles for aging women. According to Miriam E. Nelson, Ph.D., a researcher at Tufts and author of the book, *Strong Women Stay Young*, strength training results in the following benefits:

- halts bone loss and even restores bones
- improves balance
- helps prevent bone fractures from osteoporosis
- energizes and revitalizes
- helps control weight, trims, and tightens
- improves flexibility
- acts as a health tonic

The results of the Tufts University research are impressive and leave no doubt that it is beneficial to include strength exercises in your regimen. Smiling from the cover of his book, *Lifelong Fitness*, Bob Delmonteque, eighty, a former bodybuilder and America's #1 senior fitness expert, is a shining example of just how muscular one can be in the golden years by doing strength exercises. Another example of a lifelong strength exerciser is Jack LaLanne, eighty-seven.

If you are going to exercise at home, invest in two sets of hand weights. For building strength, the experts suggest a weight that can be lifted eight to twelve times.

Dumbbell curls. Stand upright with your feet slightly apart or sit in a chair. Hold a dumbbell in each hand next to your thighs with your palms facing in. Bend your arms and curl the weights up to shoulder level, twisting your wrists so the palms face your body at the top (Figure 22-3, see p. 373).

Pause to flex your biceps, and then lower the weights back down slowly. Repeat the entire sequence twelve times for one or two sets.

Front dumbbell lifts. Stand upright with your feet together or sit on a chair. Hold a dumbbell in each hand next to your thighs in an overhand grip. Keeping your back straight and elbows slightly bent, lift both arms forward until they reach shoulder level and then farther up overhead (Figure 22-4, see p. 373). Pause briefly and then lower the weights back down, using your back to assist. Repeat the entire sequence six times for one or two sets.

Lateral dumbbell lifts. Stand upright with your feet together or sit on a chair. Hold a dumbbell in each hand at your sides in an overhand grip. Keeping your elbows bent slightly, lift the weights laterally to shoulder level and then farther up overhead (Figure 22-5, see p. 374). Pause briefly and then lower the weights back down under control. Repeat the entire sequence six times for one or two sets.

Bent-torso lateral dumbbell lifts. Bend forward at the lower back so that your upper body is parallel to the floor. Hold a dumbbell in each hand in an overhand grip with your arms hanging relaxed from the shoulders. Keeping your elbows bent slightly, lift the weights laterally as high as you can (Figure 22-6, see p. 374). Lower the weights back down under control. Repeat six times for one or two sets.

Lateral dumbbell stretch. Lie on your back with your knees bent and feet flat on the floor. Hold a dumbbell in each hand in an overhand grip, with your arms extended and palms up. Keeping your elbows bent slightly, lift the dumbbells and bring your hands together overhead (Figure 22-7, see p. 375). Lower the weights back down to your sides. Repeat twelve times for one or two sets.

Dumbbell upward press. Stand straight with your feet slightly apart, holding a dumbbell in each hand at shoulder height. Press the weights directly overhead (Figure 22-8, see p. 375). Lower them back down and repeat twelve times for one or two sets.

If performed with little or even no rest between them, these six strength exercises using dumbbells of an appropriate weight also have an aerobic effect. If I rush from one exercise to the next without a break, it takes me about 6 minutes to perform them. With this approach, we can get some continuous carbon dioxide production in our muscles, thereby increasing our fitness and even extending our life, according to the theory and practice of Dr. E. Yashin of Russia.

On alternate days of the week, I also do some strength exercises involving my body's own weight: *push-ups* against the floor and *pull-ups (chin–ups)* to a steel bar (or a branch of a tree).

The pull-up (chin-up) exercise can be done with the hands gripping at shoulder width, at one and a half shoulders width, or together. With a narrow hand grip, you can bring your chin over the bar; with a wider grip, you can touch the bar to the back of your neck. In this case, both biceps and your side back muscles are involved. To warm up for the pull-ups, I usually do twelve dumbbell curls.

Pull-ups. Hang on the steel bar with your hands shoulder-width apart; inhale. Bend your elbows while you inhale and bring your chin over the bar. Lower your body and inhale. Repeat four or six times.

2. EXERCISES FOR HEALTHIER SEXUAL ORGANS

Any exercise involving the legs and repeated and prolonged movements in the sacral area can be beneficial for healthier sexual organs in both men and women. Walking, jogging, running, cross-country skiing, and cycling are all helpful in this respect. Aerobic exercise may help boost a man's sexual performance. According to Tom Monte and the editors of *Prevention Magazine's* "Staying Young," a group of seventy-eight previously inactive but healthy men jogged or bicycled at 75 to 80 percent of their aerobic capacity for 1 hour a day, 3.5 days a week; the control group of seventeen men did not exercise. After nine months, the exercisers reported a 30 percent increase in frequency of intercourse, with 26 percent more orgasms and more caressing and passionate kissing. In contrast, the non-exercisers had sex slightly less often. Regular walking is also effective because it strengthens the lower part of the abdomen.

Specific exercises such as yoga and stretching can improve the condition of the arteries in the abdominal area, including arteries that rush blood to the sacral area, thereby preventing prostate-gland problems in men and uterus and vaginal problems in women. The reproductive organs of both men and women will be healthier as a result of these exercises. In my opinion, the most effective among them is the *buttocks-walking* exercise.

Buttocks Walking

1. Sit on the floor, bend your knees, grasp your legs with your hands just below the knees, and lift your feet off the floor. Keeping your body balanced, walk forward on your buttocks as far as 10 feet (Figure 22-9 a, b, see p. 275). Gradually increase the distance or double the number of walks.

2. Stretch your legs, put your hands on your legs just above the knees, and walk backwards on your buttocks to the starting point (Figure 22-9 c, d, see p. 275).

3. If walking forward with your feet raised is difficult, then move both forward and backward with outstretched legs. After you have grasped this motion, try it as described in Step 1.

I learned this exercise about twenty five years ago from my friend Vladimir Samol, who was an advanced yogi. Just recently, I found a reference to it in *The Edgar Cayce Handbook for Health,* by Harold J. Reilly and Ruth Hagy Brod. Edgar Cayce, a famous American prophet gifted with channeling abilities, described the buttocks walk in the following words: "a movement as if sitting on the floor and walking across or swinging the limbs one in front of the other for three or four movements."

There was a time when I did the buttocks-walking exercise every day, recording the distances I covered. In 1984-85 in Moscow, I moved nearly 20 feet each day; within two years, I had walked on my buttocks as far as 9,200 feet (2.8 kilometers). Quite a distance, isn't it? I wonder whether there were attempts to win the Guinness record doing the buttocks walk. Later on, however, I was not very consistent in doing this exercise. Recently, since I am retired and have more time for myself, I again included this exercise in my morning yoga exercises. Usually I do two runs back and forth, covering a distance of 20 feet.

Other useful exercises that I include in my morning yoga program to increase circulation in the genital area and strengthen the lower back muscles are the *boat* and *back leg-lift* exercises.

Boat Exercise

1. Lie flat on the floor on your stomach with your hands stretched over your head. Your forehead should be touching the floor, the palms facing down, and the tops of your toes touching the floor.

2. Breathe out completely, then inhale and raise your arms and legs as

high as you can, also lifting your head and looking up. Then exhale and lower your arms and legs back to the resting position. Make sure you keep your arms straight, with no bending at the elbows or wrists. Your knees should also be straight and your toes pointed. Repeat from six to twelve times.

Back Leg-Lift Exercise

1. Lie on the floor on your stomach and place your hands at your sides with the tops of your fists facing the floor. Bend your elbows slightly and press your fists against the floor.

2. Lift your left leg as high as you can, keeping your knee stiff; hold this position for a few seconds, then lower your leg to the floor. Repeat with your right leg and then with both legs held together. Do the entire sequence three times.

3. YOGA EXERCISES

Yoga exercises combine flexibility, stretching, strengthening joints and muscles, improving circulation and functioning of the endocrine system, breathing, and relaxation exercises. Yoga is widely accepted as an alternative therapy for normalizing physical disorders such as high blood pressure, asthma, digestive problems, arthritis and rheumatism, back and neck pain, and emotional and mental disorders such as anxiety, depression, fatigue, insomnia, stress-related disorders, and many others.

The proponents of yoga are many, some of them believe that yoga brings about a rejuvenating effect and promotes longevity. Russian author Victor I. Belov in his book, *Health Encyclopedia,* considers a daily set of yoga asanas (for 50 to 60 minutes every morning) to be a powerful means for achieving longevity. Yoga exercises are the central theme of the health and longevity systems of both Victor F. Vostokov (called the "white lama") and yoga instructor Polkovnikov, who are both from Russia. The Japanese author Gomi Masayoshi in his book, *The Aging Weak Point Is Found,* holds that the sacroiliac joint, located at the hipbones where they are attached to the bottom of the spine, is responsible for aging. With yoga exercises, he significantly improved the health and vitality of seventy thousand of his patients.

Yoga is suited to most blood types and it is highly recommended for people with blood type A, B, and AB to include it in their exercise regimen. A regular and gentle exercise like yoga is appropriate for people of the Vata constitution who can become exhausted by vigorous exercise. However, the Pitta and Kapha constitutions also can benefit from yoga asanas. Yoga exercises are perfectly appropriate for people who start regular exercises after the age of forty. They should avoid strong exertions and quick movements, especially harsh body and head bends that can dramatically increase blood pressure.

Some centenarians attribute their longevity to yoga exercises.

The sisters Sarah, 107, and Elizabeth (who died at 104) Delany from New York City did yoga exercises every morning. The comedian George Burns, who lived to 100, regularly performed yoga exercises. Teresa Hsu, 100, of Singapore, who is strong, supple, and looks thirty years younger, also practices yoga every morning.

However, some sports experts are skeptical about yoga benefits. "Although I think yoga has advantages, it is still passive exercising. If you combine a sound fitness program with yoga, then it will add to your fitness level. But yoga alone will not get or keep you fit. It is also very time-consuming," according to Edward J. Jackowski in his book, *Hold It! You're Exercising Wrong.* Time spent on yoga exercises may be considered as a concern or a merit, depending on your viewpoint. "Spending time on the body is the key to being a healthy, contented human being," says TV yoga instructor Lilias Folan.

Rocking on the Back

1. Sit on a floor mat with your legs bent at the knees. With your left hand, grasp your right leg just above the ankle. Grasp the wrist of your left hand with your right hand. Bring your chin close to your knees and arch your back.

2. Rock backward until you touch the floor with your head, then forward back to a sitting position (Figure 22-10, see p. 275). While rocking forward, keep your chin near your knees. Do not allow your back to straighten; keep it arched. Repeat twelve times, then gradually build up to thirty times.

Hip Rotation

1. Stand straight with your feet together and place your palms on the

kidney region near the lower ribs on your back.

2. Rotate your hips in small circles in a clockwise direction. Feel the pumping action under your palms while the muscles of your spine are working.

3. Do the same hip rotation in a counterclockwise direction. Repeat twenty-four times in each direction, gradually building up to sixty rotations.

According to Edward Obaidey, this exercise gives the kidneys--a seat of longevity in Oriental medicine--an internal massage and increases their energy.

Forward-backward Bend

1. Sit on your heels, feet together with your hands on your knees. As you exhale, drop your head, pull in the abdomen, and hump your back.

2. On your inhale, raise your head looking upward, push your chest forward, and arch your back (Figure 22-11, see p. 276). Repeat the entire sequence twelve times.

Cat Pose

1. Assume an all-fours position with your hands shoulder-width apart and your knees less than that apart. Inhale, bend your head down, and hump your back like an angry cat.

2. Exhale, drop your chest, and sag your back. Raise your head and look upward (Figure 22-12, see p. 276). Repeat the entire sequence twelve times.

Easy Bridge Pose

1. Lie on the floor or on a mat. Your knees should be bent. Place your feet flat on the floor and as close to your buttocks as possible. Your hands should be at your sides, with palms facing down.

2. Breathe out slowly as you relax your head, neck, and shoulders. As you start, breathe in, and slowly lift your buttocks and then your lower and upper back off the floor. Arch your back, with your shoulders and neck remaining on the floor. Hold this position for one or two breaths, then slowly lower your hips to the floor as you exhale. Repeat two more times.

3. Advanced version: Grab your ankles with your hands and proceed as described previously.

Peacock Pose

1. Kneel on the floor and sit on your heels with the knees spread wide in the "hero" pose (Figure 22-13 a, see p. 376).

2. Join your arms together and place both hands on the floor at the knee line with your fingers pointed inward and arms straight (Figure 22-13 b, c, see p. 376).

3. Exhale and holding breath bent your elbows while you lean your upper body forward, and bring your elbows together. Place the conjoined elbows into the pit of your upper abdomen, lea the upper body farther forward and down (Figure 22-13 d, see p. 376), raise your knees off the floor, and balance your whole body on your forearms.

4. Stretch your legs and straighten your back to keep your body parallel to the floor (Figure 22-13 e, see p. 376), and hold this pose for six seconds.

5. Keeping balance, lower your head close to the floor while you bend and lower your knees until they reach the floor, inhale. Unfold your elbows, raise your head, and sit in the starting pose, breathe evenly.

Head to Instep Exercise

1. Sit on the floor and bring your feet close to your body, with the soles facing each other (Figure 22-14 a, b, see p. 377).

2. Grasp your toes with your hands and try to bring your forehead (Figure 22-14 c, see p. 377) down to touch the insteps in short, easy bounces. Bring your feet closer and reach the toes with your nose, then with your chin (Figure 22-14 d, see p. 377). Start with twelve and work up to twenty-four repetitions.

Butterfly (Crotch Stretch)

1. Sit on the floor with your back straight. Place your feet sole to sole and grasp your toes with your hands. Raise and lower your knees in a bouncing movement, as if your legs were the wings of a butterfly. Repeat 12 to 24 times. It helps to place your hands on your knees to press them down.

2. Grasp your ankles firmly with your hands. Place your elbows on your knees and press them down toward the floor as far as possible. Repeat twelve times, always trying to get nearer to the floor.

The last yoga exercise that I do in the morning is the *shoulder stand*, which has many benefits. The inverted body position increases blood circulation in the neck, head, and brain, while the legs and organs that are usually below the heart are relieved of blood pressure. Improved vision and hearing, a healthier complexion, alertness, improved thyroid-gland functioning, and less loss of hair are just a few merits of the shoulder stand.

The thyroid gland is thought to govern other glands that are responsible for proper functioning of the immune system and also to affect body metabolism. "Some people seem to be fireballs of energy, able to eat what they like without putting on weight, while others need a lighter pace and easily gain weight. Such differences are largely due to the thyroid gland in the neck. If it is overactive, you burn up energy, tend to lose weight, and may be excitable and nervous. A healthy thyroid is vital to wellbeing. In the shoulder-stand, your concentration and circulation are entirely directed to the thyroid, as it is massaged and stimulated, restoring a healthy metabolism," according to *The Book of Yoga*, published by The Shivananda Yoga Center.

At the same time, because of the bent neck, the shoulder stand does not impose too much pressure on the blood vessels of the brain and does not overload the neck vertebrae, as the headstand pose does, which is why it is more suitable for elderly people. Teresa Hsu, 100, of Singapore, who has all her own teeth and looks at least thirty years younger, has been practicing yoga for the last thirty-four years. She does yoga exercises, including the shoulder stand, twice a day.

Shoulder Stand

1. Lie flat on your back on the floor or a mat with your legs extended and your arms by your sides, palms on the floor (Figure 22-15 a, see p. 378). Do six breaths to adjust to the horizontal position.

2. Pressing with your hands against the floor, tense your legs and abdominal muscles, and raise your straight legs to the vertical position (Figure 22-15 b, see p. 378). Hold them upright while you do six more breaths to adjust the blood circulation to the changed position.

3. Again using your hands to raise your hips off the floor, bend your knees and bring them up to touch your forehead. Bend your elbows and rest them

firmly on the floor. Support your trunk with your hands placed at the lower back against your hipbones (Figure 22-15 c, see p. 378). Do six more breaths.

4. Straighten your legs upward and balance your body, which is resting on the back of your head, the back of your neck, your shoulders, and partly on your elbows (Figure 22-15 d, see p. 379). Now become motionless, close your eyes, do abdominal breathing, and concentrate on the thyroid gland. Hold this pose for 3 minutes, gradually increasing up to 6 minutes.

5. To come out of the pose, bend your knees and bring them up to your head; lower your toes to the floor behind your head (Figure 22-15 e, see p. 379). Relax in this position and do six breaths. Then place your palms on the floor and, using your hands to brace yourself, lower your hips slowly to the floor without raising your head. Straighten your legs and relax for 1 minute or so.

6. Turn your head to both sides a few times and then turn over and lie on your stomach. Raise your head and turn it to both sides. Raise your shoulders off the floor and support your upper body with your elbows. Bend your head upward and turn it to both sides. Then unfold your elbows and assume the cobra pose. Again, bend your head up and turn it to both sides. Finally, lie down on the floor and relax for a while.

4. BREATHING EXERCISES

The necessity of the breathing exercises, especially for elderly people, was discussed in the *Oxygen Intake Control* chapter. The following three exercises help to strengthen the lungs, increase blood circulation in the lungs, and accumulate carbon dioxide in the body. The exercises are *exhaling through water*, *breathing while walking,* and *breathing in the shoulder stand.*

Exhaling Through Water

1. Sit on the floor cross-legged in the lotus pose or in a chair. Hold in your hands a three-quarters filled bottle of water with a straw in it. Raise your eyes and put the straw in your mouth (Figure 22-16, see p. 380).

2. Inhale through your nose and slowly exhale the air from your lungs through the straw, keeping its lower end in the water about 5 centimeters deep. Keep

exhaling for 15 seconds; then exhale the remaining air through your nose. Repeat twelve times at the beginning; then gradually increase the duration of each exhalation, the depth of the straw in the water, and the number of breathing repetitions.

Breathing Exercise While Walking. Normal-pace walking does not tax the respiratory system much, which makes it possible to perform the breathing exercises while walking. If it is hard for you, try slow-pace walking so you can sustain the breathing for a few minutes.

1. Inhale for four steps and exhale for four steps.

2. Hold your breath for four steps. Repeat the inhale-exhale-hold-the-breath pattern while walking for 5 minutes. Gradually increase the breath-holding up to eight steps and the duration of the breathing exercise to 10 minutes.

Breathing in the Shoulder-Stand Pose

1. Assume the shoulder-stand pose. Inhale for 4 seconds, then exhale for 4 seconds.

2. Hold your breath for 6 seconds. Repeat the inhale-exhale-hold-the-breath pattern for 5 minutes. Gradually increase the breath-holding for up to 8 seconds and the duration of the breathing exercise in the shoulder-stand pose to 6 minutes.

5. MEDITATION (IMAGERY EXERCISES)

Meditation is a blessing because it allows the functioning of the upper chakras, thereby reminding us of our divine nature. When meditating, all earthly affairs can be forgotten, freeing one's mind of judging and decision-making for a while. It is a chance to steer one's attention away from stormy, racing thoughts--to stop the endless internal dialogue. In a meditation state, one lives "here and now," which brings a most profound effect on the physical, emotional, mental, and spiritual wellbeing. What happened yesterday and what might happen tomorrow can be put aside during meditation. Living in the moments of the meditation state, one belongs to himself, devoting the time to reach a deep level of consciousness and to become acquainted with the inner self.

In addition to deep relaxation and stress reduction, meditation promotes openness and alertness of mind. Meditation results in many physiological and psychological benefits for our body. According to C. Norman Shealy, M.D. Ph.D., in his book, *The Complete Family Guide to Alternative Medicine,* the benefits include the following:

- decreased anxiety, feelings of anger and aggression, depression, nervousness, and physical tension

- increased awareness and concentration, mental clarity and resilience, creative intuitive powers, emotional stability and control, and overall health and well-being

It has been found in many studies that meditation produces positive body responses: the heart and breathing rates decrease, oxygen consumption decreases, the metabolic rate decreases, blood pressure normalizes, and muscle tension decreases. The hormonal imbalance associated with stress is reversed. As discussed previously, all these changes in the body retard the aging process and promote longevity. "From my experience with studies on people using meditation, it has been established that long-term meditators can have a biological age between five and twelve years younger than their chronological age," says Deepak Chopra, M.D., in his best-selling book, *Ageless Body, Timeless Mind.*

The connection between anti-aging and life extension as a result of meditation is linked to production of the hormone DHEA. This all-important hormone, which is secreted by the adrenal cortex, is thought to produce stress hormones such as adrenaline and cortisol. Each time these hormones are produced in the body, the amount of DHEA is depleted. DHEA drops dramatically as we age: a typical seventy-five-year-old person has only 10 percent of the DHEA that a twenty-five-year-old has. High levels of DHEA are associated with better brain function, immunity, good sleep, and a lower risk of coronary artery disease, breast cancer, and osteoporosis. DHEA is also found to promote longer life in the elderly and reduced death rates from various diseases.

In a study by Dr. Jay Glaser, the effect of DHEA production was compared between 328 experienced meditators and 1,462 non-meditators. He found that meditating men and women aged forty-five and older had 23 and 47 percent more DHEA, respectively, than non-meditators. According to Dr.

Glaser's estimation, the levels of DHEA in people who regularly meditated were similar to those of people five to ten years younger. This result seems to establish the **connection between meditation and anti-aging and life extension.**

DHEA was so broadly advertised as a supplement for fighting insomnia, memory loss, and even blocking cancers that you may wonder if the synthetic hormone is better than meditation. The data obtained so far is controversial. A prominent French researcher, Etienne-Emile Baulieu of the College de France, found a positive effect. In his tests, elderly people were given low doses of synthetic DHEA; as a result, many health improvements were reported, including decreased muscle fatigue and bone fragility and better brain functioning.

However, the editors of Ronin Publishing in their book, *Fountain of Youth,* say that the oral supplementation of DHEA does not seem to increase the maximum life span. "The supplementation of growth hormone, estrogen, testosterone, and the adrenal hormone DHEA, all of which decline with age, does not seem to significantly improve the normal curve," they stated. Therefore, meditation, which enhances the internal factory's production of DHEA, seems to have advantages over DHEA supplements.

To practice meditation, one should find a quiet place, assume a comfortable posture, and devote 15 to 20 minutes in the morning or before going to bed. Helpful enhancers of meditation include relaxation music or a *mantra* (i.e., chanting words or sounds) for Vata types, a steadily burning candle flame or a Yin/Yang symbol for Pitta types, and sandalwood or other wood and flower incense for Kapha types. The best postures for meditation are the *corpse pose* and the *lotus (padmasana)* pose. Meditation can also be done in a *shoulder-stand* pose, which is how I practice in the mornings.

Meditation in the Corpse Pose. Lie on your back on the floor on a carpet or a mat with your legs straight. Place your arms along your sides, contract the muscles of the entire body for a second, and then relax them all. Close your eyes and take slow, shallow breaths. To achieve a deeper relaxation of your muscles, imagine that you are breathing in the prana, which comes from the most distant universe beyond the solar system. While you exhale, imagine that your feet become rapidly larger and lighter: first, as big as your room, then as your house, city, country, the planet Earth, the Sun, and the Milky Way. Then, they become less and less solid, then as thin as air--like ether--and eventually disappear. Again, breathe in the prana from the universe where your feet were dissolved. With your next exhalation, enlarge your ankles. With each following exhalation, dissolve your shins, knees, thighs, hips, abdomen, chest, hands, arms, shoulders, neck, and head. This imagery of dissolving the body parts is preparation for the main meditation, although in itself it is a kind of meditation too.

Medusa (Jellyfish) Meditation. Imagine that you are floating like a medusa on the surface of shallow water close to a beach. The sky is blue and cloudless, the water is warm, and sweet music is heard coming from the beach. Your body is a large thin layer of transparent jelly and it feels all the small waves rippling on the surface of the water. Feel as if the wave runs from your feet toward your head, from your left foot to your right shoulder, then from your right foot to your left shoulder. You enjoy the pleasant fluctuations of your absolutely flexible body. Your body is carried on the waves of the pretty blue water accompanied by the waves of sweet-sounding music.

Free-Fall Meditation. Imagine that you have jumped out of an airplane with a parachute. The land is far below and at first you are falling with the parachute closed. You will open it when the land gets closer, but now you are enjoying a free-fall. The sky is blue, the air is fresh after a big rain, and you feel the streams of thin air flowing around your body. You see a rainbow arching across the sky; it is so close to you that you can almost touch it. Its colors are so beautiful and bright, it sparkles and smiles at you, and it is all yours. Your body is light, nearly weightless; you stretch your arms and legs wide apart. You hear sweet music coming from somewhere and you like it. You are filled with joy--you are having a great time in this free-fall and you want it to last longer.

Flower Meditation. Close your eyes and imagine that your favorite flowers are aligned from your heart through the abdomen to the lowest point of your spine. You smell the flowers; you touch and feel the softness of their petals. Xu Fang's favorite flower is the lotus; mine is a deep red rose. With every beat of your heart, imagine a wave running along the line and shaking the flowers a little. You feel quiet and relaxed, and enjoy playing with the flowers.

Candle-Flame Meditation. Place a candle 6 to 7 feet from you at the eye level. Stare at the steadily burning flame and try not to blink. After half a minute or so, you will see an emanation of light sparkling around the contours of the candle, table, and other objects within sight. Watch the play of light and let your thoughts flow freely in your mind. Stare until your eyes start to fill with tears; then close them and see the reflection of the flame and candle on the inner screen in your forehead. Enjoy the bright beautiful colors of the flame--red like a ruby, and the candle--green like an emerald. After their images in your inner sight became vague, open your eyes and stare at the candle again.

Listen to relaxation music while you stare at the candle flame. My favorite musical themes are a vocal flight of a woman's voice from the composition *Equinox*, by Jean Michael Jarre; the *Chakra Sounds* from the "World of Osho Meditations" with music by Karunesh; and the *Shaman's Call*, music of a *Zazen* shrine.

Incense sticks or cones with their fragrance of cinnamon, eucalyptus, jasmine, musk, patchouli, sandalwood, and others are also good meditation enhancers. They create an atmosphere of an Oriental shrine, with its image of meditation as an essential part of attaining God.

Meditation in a Shoulder-Stand Pose. After some time of practicing, the shoulder-stand pose can be mastered to a degree that one can relax all the muscles except those supporting the body in the inverse position. Duration of the shoulder-stand pose of up to 12 minutes is long enough to accomplish one or two meditations. I usually do two meditations: *prana healing* and *opening the chakra lotuses*.

"Healing with Prana" Meditation. With an inhalation, I imagine that my lungs are filled with air rich in prana. After the inhalation, I hold my breath for 2 to 3 seconds and imagine that, along with the penetration of oxygen into the tiny alveoli sacs, my lungs become balloons filled with a golden prana. With the first exhalation, I release a stream of prana from my lungs and send it into my stomach, where it penetrates the lining and heals all disorders. Then I hold my breath and do the Kegel exercise (i.e., contracting the muscles so that the urine flow can be voluntarily stopped) six times, then I also contract the muscles of the anus six times. I continue to imagine that each muscle contraction pulls a string that opens an outlet and releases a portion of the prana from my lungs. After 12 Kegel contractions and all the prana is released, I inhale and repeat the entire sequence for the stomach three more times. Then I do the same healing with my knees and imagine that the cartilage becomes thick, clean, and with a firm transparent outer layer.

Finally, I send the prana streams into my brain to cleanse the blood vessels (to prevent stroke). All this healing meditation takes about 5 minutes.

"Opening the Chakra Lotuses" Meditation. While breathing in, I visualize that the stream of golden prana flows into my body from space via two cones open outside—one above my head and another below my feet. While breathing out, I direct the stream of prana flowing into the Muladhara chakra, where it opens one petal of its previously closed four-petal red lotus flower, as if I gently touched it with my finger. With the next exhale, the second petal is opened, and so on. Then six orange petals of the Svadhisthana chakra lotus are opened one by one, followed by ten yellow petals of the Manipura chakra lotus, twelve green petals of the Anahata chakra lotus, sixteen blue petals of the Vishuddha chakra lotus, two large purple petals of the Ajna chakra, and finally two big layers--one dark violet and the other white--of the thousand-petal Sahasrara chakra lotus. In Figure 22-17 (see p. 380), Xu Fang is shown in the meditation pose.

As a closing remark to this chapter, I note that although this is not an exercise book, I have included many exercises (some of them unique) that you may choose according to your type, goals, personal preferences, and time available. I believe that exercise is a loss-free investment of your time and efforts, and that you will reap from it improved health, fitness, and quality years ahead. Visualize yourself becoming stronger, more supple, and younger with each exercise session. Make it your belief that on the day you exercise, you do not age. Earn the right to live your disease-free day by exercising. Include exercise in your daily routine, practice it, and arrive at the stage when exercise becomes second nature, bringing pleasant sensations rather than just pain. Anticipate the exercise time with eagerness and joy; don't force yourself. I know from my own experience that it is possible.

23

SEX CONTROL

If I started this chapter with words such as, "Sex is a natural instinct and basic physiological need, and its gratification is very important for health and longevity," you would probably want to kill me, or at least be very disappointed. No, I have other words to start this chapter about sex: "Sex is abso-loving-lutely great"--these are the appropriate words. It is difficult for me to imagine there are people who refute George Sand's great words about sex: "Sex is the most respectable and holy thing in all creation, the most serious act in life." Still, there are people who think differently. As discussed often throughout this book, people are so different in various ways that it is not a surprise that some of them do not love sex.

"There is a distinction between love and sex. Sexual desire by itself is lust; it is universally regarded as immoral. But for true lovers, the act of physical union is motivated not merely by a desire for pleasure, but also for the transcendent sense of total union which it can bring," according to Julian Huxley in his book, *All About Love*. In many religions, sex is prohibited and many societies are too strict about it. Once again, we have a wide range of opinions; however, I believe the centenarians know the truth about sex. Let's listen to what they have to say.

Sex and Longevity

When asked what was the secret of her old age, Geraldine Pringle, 101, from Oakland, California, replied, "Men and brandy. Men are never too old."

Donato DiMatteo, 100, says his earlier days were always good too, especially when he was old enough to dance and court women. "He's always had an eye for women," says his niece. On his last visit to Italy at ninety-six, he disappeared several times--only to be found visiting a woman down the street, reported Jim Heynen in his book, *One Hundred Over 100*.

George Burns, one of America's best-loved comedians, who lived to 100, recalled in his book *How to Live to Be 100 - Or More* that during his regular medical checkup, he was asked by the doctor when his sex life had ended. "At 3 a.m. this morning," Burns replied, who was eighty-six at the time.

> One of my friends, Vladimir M. Kuznetsov, eighty-nine, from Zelenograd (a suburb of Moscow), is one of the health pioneers in Russia and an instructor at a health club. He created his own original health system and was in a sound condition himself. He married twice but divorced from both his wives. In 1989, at the age of seventy-eight, he wanted to find a woman through advertisement, but he had no telephone for replies. I agreed to let him use my number. On the first day after publication of his advertisement, the telephone calls were non-stop all day long--dozens of women called and he had a difficult time arranging dates with many of them. Eventually, he married a woman from his health club who was fifty-two years old. Men are never old, especially if they do not think they are.

Long-living people in Abkhasia consider the continuation of sex life into old age as natural as maintaining a healthy appetite or sound sleep. They think that increased years are no reason to deny so human a function. Sex in Abkhasia is considered a good and pleasurable thing to be regulated for the sake of one's health--like a good wine.

There is a significant difference in the nature of the male and female orgasms, which reflects the fundamental inequality of the two sexes. When a man reaches orgasm, he ejaculates and his semen essence is cast out of his body; thus, he loses it. When a woman achieves orgasm, she secretes ova, the sexual essence that remains in her body--nothing is lost. Moreover, she receives an injection of the man's semen and partly absorbs it. Semen is a great source of vital energy; the immune system and all other systems and functions of the body are nourished with it.

Sexual intercourse followed by orgasm induces a great burden on the man's body. All physiological functions and psychological reactions are altered at this time: muscle tone increases, calories are burned as quickly as in sprint running, the heart and breathing rates increase to supply more oxygen, blood pressure is elevated, and all the senses become sharp. All these strains on the body and mind peak during the pre-orgasm state and then, together with orgasm and ejaculation, they collapse like a building that imploded. A man feels the greatest pleasure at this time, to the extent that he can lose control over his emotions and often screams and moans. A woman at the time of orgasm similarly feels intense pleasure and enjoyment, but afterwards does not feel as exhausted as a man because she does not lose her vital essence. After intercourse, the man's greatest desire is to sleep (unless he is a teenage boy who is ready for another orgasm in a few minutes), but the woman is still excited and wants to continue lovemaking.

The next day, especially after more than one orgasm, some men experience a weakness in their legs and lower back, impaired vision (e.g., double vision), moments of an accelerated heartbeat, and imbalance with possible staggering. This minor discomfort is payment for the previous night's pleasure--pleasure never comes without a price tag. Old men are warned about the possible hazardous effects of sex for their health because overdoing it can cause a heart attack. There are cases when even young men died at the peak of sex; the well known is that of Raphael Santi, a famous Italian artist. There is even an expression sometimes used in medicine, "Raphael death," meaning a sex-induced death.

If a man ejaculates and loses his semen every time he has sex, this weakens his immune system and deprives him of vital energy. He eventually becomes physically and mentally exhausted, and falls into depression. The weakened immunity cannot resist diseases, which shortens the man's life. This is one reason why men live shorter lives than women, need more calories and sleep to survive, get sick more often and need more time to recover from illness, have less endurance, and are more vulnerable to stress.

A few decades ago when the first information about world centenarians started to appear, researchers shared the view that most of the extremely old people were men. "Generally, it has been found that the very oldest people in the world--i.e., those over 110--are male. Then come spinster females; it is supposed that the lack of stress in their lives is an aid to longevity, especially the lack of hazards of childbearing," wrote David Davies in his 1975 book, *The Centenarians of the Andes.* Twenty-six years later, there are changes in this view regarding both centenarians and their gender. There are many doubts among experts that all the centenarians in Hunza, Vilcabamba, and Abkhasia-- the three world-famous valleys of longevity--are not as old as they claim to be. Also, in countries with reliable information about people's ages–such as Japan, Iceland, the Scandinavian countries, and the United States--80 percent of the centenarians are women; they also predominate among people aged 110 or more. The world longevity champions reported in the *The Guinness Book of World Records* in the 1990s were all women: Jeanne Calment, 122, of France; Felicie Young Cormier, 118, and Marie-Louise Febronie Meilleur, 117, both of Canada; and Sarah Knauss, 117, of the United States.

After the death of Jeanne Calment in August 1997, the leading claimants to the title of oldest in the world were Rodoma Dahmani, 116, of Algeria;

Anitica Butuariu, 116, of Romania; and Christian Mortensen, 115, of the United States. Christian Mortensen, the oldest man among these people, died in 1998. "He is also atypical, being a man. Most of the oldest people in the world are female since women generally outlive their male counterparts by several years," commented *The Straits Times*, the newspaper of Singapore, in the August 8, 1997, issue.

The great doctors and scholars of ancient India and China, who first understood how crucial the semen essence is for men's health, developed the practice of having frequent sex without the harmful consequences. By natural processes, the sevenfold generation of bodily elements--including semen--is taking place in the human body. The major Indian medical text, entitled the *Sushruta Samhita*, describes the stages of the transformation of elements as follows, "Life-essence produces blood, from blood is produced flesh, from flesh originates fat, which gives rise to bones. From bones originates marrow, which in turn goes to semen or ovum." The Chinese treatise entitled *Tao of Sex* (Way or Path of Sex) teaches men how to have sex without the usual ejaculation, thereby conserving their semen. The Taoist master Yang-Sheng-Yao-Chi said, "A man should learn to control his ejaculation. To be greedy for feminine beauty and emit beyond one's vigor injures every vein, nerve, and organ in the body, and gives rise to every illness. Correct practice of sexual intercourse can cure every ailment and at the same time, open the doors to Liberation."

This practice involves training to regulate breathing and to move Yang energy internally so that a man can maintain a peak drive and high performance level. According to the ancient texts, if a man learns to control and regulate his ejaculation without the loss of semen, his body will become stronger, his mental abilities will increase, and his sight and hearing will improve. "One of the greatest promises (of ancient Chinese texts) is that his love for his woman will greatly increase. He will feel as if he can never get enough of her. And, importantly, he will have the capacity to act on this love," according to Shizuko Yamamoto and Patrick McCarty in their book, *Whole Health Shiatsu*.

The Taoist philosophical system teaches that there are four techniques for increasing longevity: (1) breathing exercises; (2) diet with emphasis on small amounts of food; (3) Kung Fu exercises; and (4) sex with avoidance of the man's orgasm, for which the medical term is *coitus reservatus*. In the medical text, *Precious Recipes*, the Chinese doctor Sun Simiao stated, "A man can live a healthy and long life if he carries out an emission frequency of two times monthly or twenty-four times yearly. If at the same time he also pays attention to wholesome food and exercises, he may attain longevity." Dr. Sun applied this knowledge to himself and he lived to the age of 101. During sex in his own life, he followed the regimen of only ejaculating once in every hundred sexual acts; however, for the average man, he believed this was too strict.

The role of sex in achieving a long life is a theme of the Japanese classic, *Yojokun* (*The Secret of Health Preservation*), written by Kaibara Ekiken (1630-1714). According to Kaibara, if a man follows the Tao of Yin and Yang, there is no limitation for him to enjoy sex regularly. He advised preserving the vital essence by controlling the frequency of ejaculation. With regard to age, the man's physical condition, and season of the year, the emission of semen varies. The older a man is, the less frequent his semen release should be. A strong man, whose body is able to tolerate the loss of vital essence, can afford to ejaculate more often than a weaker man. In the winter, ejaculation must be infrequent; in the summer, it can be more often.

The beginning of regular sexual relations later in life is regarded as another factor that promotes longevity. The long-living people in Abkhasia believe that postponing sexual satisfaction in early life will prolong sexual potency later in life, resulting in the enjoyment of sex for a longer time. Many of the Abkhasians get married between the ages of forty and fifty; they are called "late bloomers."

Ejaculation Control

I first heard about semen retention about twenty years ago from my yogi friend, Vladimir Samol, who was very knowledgeable of yogic texts. "Father (he called me father, although he was nine years older than me), one portion of semen is worth forty boxes of pearls. We are not that rich to throw out such a wealth," he used to say. He was experimenting on himself with diets, fasting, marathon running, meditation, and sex. At the age of forty-six, almost every day he went out with twenty-year-old women. He told me that during long fasts, he could feel the energy spontaneously moving from his sacral region upward along the spine. Then, he felt that his entire body became light. He believed that his semen fueled his body and mind during fasts.

His semen-preservation technique involved diaphragm breathing, the tongue's position in the mouth, and constriction of certain muscles in the anus region, which should be used at the moment when orgasm is imminent. The man should stop his movements for a while; deeply exhale, contracting the abdominal muscles; and bend his tongue to allow the tip to reach the soft palate as far back as possible. While inhaling, he should strain his tongue and pull an imaginary string attached to the root of his penis in an upward movement. At this moment, the muscles in the region between the anus and the root of the penis must be strongly clenched. In a few moments, he will feel that his orgasm has receded, and he can continue his movements to satisfy his partner. At the beginning of this learning process, there will be inevitable failures, with the attempts to constrict the sacral muscles inducing ejaculation. However, with persistence, this technique can be mastered.

This technique is somewhat complicated and requires perseverance to be mastered. Wu Hsien, a master of the Han Dynasty, had a simpler method for ejaculation control. It is described as follows by Nik Douglas and Penny Slinger in their book, *Sexual Secrets*: "He (Wu Hsien) first advises the man not to get too excited while making love so as not to lose control. He suggests that a man first learn to regulate his rhythm, trying one deep followed by three shallow love-strokes, for eighty-one total cycles. He next advises the man to follow this rhythm with one deep and five shallow love-strokes, again for eighty-one repetitions. Finally, the man should try one deep and nine shallow love-strokes. The master adds that if the man feels he is about to ejaculate, he should stop his movements and withdraw his Jade Stalk so that only the tip remains within his partner's Jade Gate. After his passions have calmed, he can begin to resume deep insertion. He stresses that the man's main concern should be that the woman reach orgasm quickly and frequently."

Knowledge of the ancient Chinese Tao of Sex and Indian Tantra-yoga, kept secret for many centuries, is now available in the United States, and the technique of semen preservation is taught in some yoga centers. One center in California teaches men to contract certain muscles very hard just as they are about to ejaculate. This supposedly prevents ejaculation while still allowing orgasm, as reported in the January/February 1997 issue of *Men's Health* magazine. The author of this article is very angry with "certain misguided Hollywood types" who "have stumbled blindly into yet another dumb and painful practice: seminal conservation." He calls them "these numbskulls" captured by the "dry" orgasm craze and is full of sarcasm when he says, "It's also supposed to help you preserve your creative and physical energy. But if that were true, wouldn't there be better movies coming out of Hollywood?" As we can see, semen retention is helpful in preserving the creative energy as well. The author of this short article is definitely exaggerating when he calls the semen-retention technique a "dumb and painful practice." I have never heard from people who use this practice that it is painful.

Well, it seems that in the East, they know how to not ejaculate for health and longevity, but in the West, they do not like this idea and prefer to ejaculate for health and longevity. As Rudyard Kipling said, "East is East and West is West, and never the twain shall meet"--at least on the ejaculation path. It's true that some men ejaculate often and still achieve strength and vitality in advanced age. The long-living people in Abkhasia certainly are not aware of the Chinese and Indian secrets, and they do it naturally, with proper ejaculation. An American researcher reports that "one of the relatives" of Kutzba Murat, 101, "married eight times and had nine children, the youngest of whom was born when he had reached one hundred. The doctors obtained sperm from him when he was 119, in 1963, and he still retained his libido and sexual potency." Everyone now doubts the super age of the Abkhasian people since detailed scientific investigations found that the majority of the reported centenarians were actually in their seventies and eighties. However, being sexually potent at this age is still not bad!

Fortunately, we have fairly reliable information about two famous Americans, screen actor Anthony Quinn and TV exercise guru Jack LaLanne, both eighty-four years old. Anthony Quinn reportedly has twelve children by five women, and he claims that there are more of his children scattered around the world. Six years ago, at the age of seventy-eight, he fathered his last child. One of the secrets of his sexual activity is his diet rich in natural foods, supplements, and herbs. When Jack LaLanne appeared in the May 1997 *Details* magazine--the sex issue--he stated that he started his sex life at the age of fourteen. At the time of the interview, Elaine, his wife of more than forty years, said that they have sex nearly every day: "nearly on Monday, nearly on Tuesday, nearly on Wednesday..." but "Elaine always said how well hung I am," added Jack. His secret is in a healthy diet and exercise. Every day, he gets up at 5 a.m. and exercises with weights for an hour. Then he does water exercises, such as tying himself in place in his pool and doing the butterfly stroke for an hour. "Sex and exercise are synonymous," says Jack. In this interview, there was no specific mention of ejaculation, except from this quote: "Sex is about giving, giving, giving! If you've got nothing to give, how the hell are you gonna be any good in the sack?" This giving attitude probably gave Jack a long sex life.

Semen Quality Control with Foods

To ejaculate or not to ejaculate, that is a problem. The point is that it is the quality of semen or sperm that influences an ejaculation. Sperm of varying quality is produced in a man's bodies depending on what kind of food he eats. According to yoga teachings, all food is divided into three groups, called *sattvic, rajasic,* and *tamasic* foods. Each group has a different effect on the body, mind, and spirit. Traditional Indian medicine implies that the taste essence of food is transformed into all the body's constituents, including men's semen and women's ovum. Some women claim that they can tell what kind of food and drink their lovers had just from the taste of their semen.

The sattvic foods are considered nourishment for a person's attitude and creative force, and they include fresh vegetables that grow above the ground; fresh and dried fruits; salads; lentils; yogurt, milk, fresh butter, and other dairy products; whole grains such as buckwheat, rice (especially brown rice), wheat, rye, and barley; nuts such as walnuts, hazelnuts, and almonds; and honey. All these foods--sometimes called "ambrosia" or "food of the Gods"--are perfect nourishment for the whole body, but are especially good for the upper, creative charkas, and they promote creativity and spiritual growth. The sattvic foods are associated primarily with a "sweet" taste, one of the six major tastes listed in the Ayurveda, the traditional Indian medicine. If a man eats sattvic foods, his sperm is of the highest quality--sweet, non-irritating, relatively thin in texture, and transparent in appearance. The body needs it as a source of strength, vitality, and mental and spiritual vigor. It can be easily sublimated by higher energy centers; this sperm tends to be kept in the body, not wanting to leave it.

The rajasic foods heat the body and stimulate the senses, and they include root vegetables; animal products such as red meat, chicken, and turkey; and many kinds of fish, salts, and spices. Their nature is of salty and pungent tastes, but the sweet taste is also present in taste combinations. Animal proteins and fats of the rajasic foods can be digested by people with blood type O, but they are difficult to digest for people with blood type A. If a man eats rajasic foods, his semen becomes slimy, salty in taste, and unpleasant. This low-quality sperm is not very welcomed by the body systems and tends to leave the body, which is why a man who has eaten rajasic foods is eager to have sex.

The tamasic foods are particularly strong, gas-forming, sense–destructive, and create excessive body odors. They include garlic, onions, chili peppers, heavier meats such as steak, eggs, deep-fried foods such as fried chicken, and fish or foods cooked in heavy oil. These foods have excessively pungent, bitter, or astringent tastes. They make the body fat and heavy, and bring about the mucus stored in the intestines and lungs. Heavy workers and athletes crave this kind of food because they need to replenish the energy lost in extreme physical exertion. The semen of a man who eats tamasic foods is of the worst quality--thick and sticky, irritating, bitter in taste, and smelly. This type of semen tends to leave the body too. Sexual intercourse becomes a striving for just physical satisfaction, rather than sensitive lovemaking as when sattvic foods are eaten.

Whatever the truth, it is clear that the loss of vital energy becomes even more critical when we age. Fortunately, most elderly men do not ejaculate every time they have sex. "By ejaculating only once for every two or three times they make love, older men can extend intercourse for the enjoyment of themselves and their partners," according to David H. Solomon, M.D., et al., in their book, *A Consumer's Guide to Aging*. It seems apparent that nature equipped elderly men with another protective mechanism: the loss of erection during the sexual act, which makes them unable to go to the "victorious end." Nature prefers to preserve the old man's life rather than his dignity when he feels ashamed of being impotent. "There wouldn't be happiness, but unhappiness helped," says the Russian proverb.

Sexual Disorders

Impaired Sexual Desire, Impotence. With aging, our sexual activity slows down somewhat. The problem for older men is not premature ejaculation; rather, the erection may be the most common problem. Many older men say their natural sex drive has diminished and in some cases vanished. Scientists estimate that in the United States more than 30 million men suffer from erectile dysfunction, erective senility, and impotency--but this certainly doesn't mean that our love life is over with retirement. Duke University researchers have found that eight out of ten men in their late sixties continue to be sexually active, while one in four men aged seventy-eight and older continues to be sexually involved. Dr. Michael T. Murray, of Bastyr University in Seattle, also points out that men are capable of retaining their sexual virility and libido well into their eighties.

Impotence occurs when men cannot achieve or maintain an erection firm enough to engage in satisfactory sexual intercourse. An erection naturally occurs when blood flow into internal areas of the penis, induced by sexual desire, is increased. Potency problems may have psychological, physiological, and even environmental origins. Erections are controlled by nerve centers in the brain that react to erotic stimulation. Stress and anxiety about performance are common reasons for impotence. Often, it is caused by diseases that block the blood flow essential for erections: vascular disease, clogged arteries, prostate disorders, low thyroid function, high blood pressure, arteriosclerosis, diabetes--or by lack of exercise, lack of sexual activity, and other problems. Current research suggests that in older men, levels of the male sex hormones-- testosterone and androgen--remain equal to those of their sons--even their grandsons--and the levels remain highest among men who keep their *sexual activity* on the highest level, says Stuart M. Berger, M.D., in his book *Forever Young*. The heart, mind, muscles, and sex organs operate on the same "use it or lose it" principle. If you are sexually active throughout your early and middle years, you have the best chance of staying sexually active into old age. This means that you have to find ways to be as sharp, vital, and alive in your sixties as you were in your thirties.

Interestingly, even the fabric of underwear may be responsible for inhibiting erections. According to Egyptian researchers, a buildup of static electricity due to wearing polyester underwear may cause erection problems.

For improving potency of a physiological nature, the health industry offers some medications (or recommends ceasing certain medications), "vacuum pumps," surgery, and the implantation of special devices. To solve psychological problems, honest discussion with one's sex partner or even consultation with a sex counselor may be helpful. Stress-reducing therapies such as exercise, yoga postures, and meditation may also be useful.

For married couples, especially if they are in their fifties or sixties, when the husband loses his erection, the wife may blame herself, feeling that she failed as a woman because she cannot keep him aroused. However, in many cases, it just means that more foreplay is needed for the man to be aroused again. Quite often, lovemaking lasts longer, as if to compensate for slower arousal time.

Sex Control with Diet

Food and sex are two basic natural needs absolutely necessary for survival and reproduction of the species. Confucius said, "Food and sex are natural." Proper eating is crucial to a healthy sex life, according to Lynn Fischer, author of *The Better Sex Diet*. Men need clear arteries for erections, and if the arteries are clogged with fatty deposits from unhealthy foods, the sexual response is ultimately shut down, she states. If a man can find no disease-related causes for a low sex drive, he needs to review his current lifestyle and diet.

Mahatma Gandhi had this to say regarding diet and its influence on sex: "Yes, diet is important in the *Satyagraha* movement--as everywhere else. One must conquer the palate (taste) before he can control the procreative instinct.

After overcoming the inward *greed* for food, a *satyagrahi* (nonviolence movement fellow) must continue to follow a rational vegetarian diet with all necessary vitamins, minerals, calories, and so forth. By inward and outward wisdom in regard to eating, the *satyagrahi*'s sexual fluid is easily turned into vital energy for the whole body." Oriental medicine believes that the kidneys control the sexual organs, according to Naboru Muramoto in his book, *Healing Ourselves*. "Balance is necessary for a healthy sexual appetite. There is a Japanese saying that states, 'Men who like carrots like women.' In America and in Russia, people believe that parsley increases sexual appetite, that it is men's food. "Carrots are a *Yang*-quality vegetable, while parsley is Yin. Most Americans have a very *Yang* condition; they need *Yin* to restore the balance that will release sexual appetite and power. Thus, red peppers and onions, beer, and whisky are included among American folk remedies for impotency. Orientals, whose problems stem from a *Yin*-quality condition, need *Yang* to provide balance," according to Naboru Muramoto.

He continues, "Now we can see why ginseng enjoys such renown as a rejuvenator of sexual prowess. Ginseng is a very *Yang* root. But one man's medicine is not necessarily another's. With strong, Yang-type people, ginseng will probably have no effect. One possibility for such people is to take Yin food, as mentioned before. Another is to combine ginseng with Yin herbs. This will actually increase the ginseng's effectiveness. But the best remedy of all is to follow a healthy, balanced diet and to chew the food very well. Chewing strengthens the sexual organs since they are connected to the jaw muscles. Regular exercise, such as walking, strengthens the lower parts of the abdomen. Yang persons with a weak sexual appetite may take Day Lily Tea. Weak people with a weak sexual appetite may try one of the following teas: Small Saikoto, Black Warrior, Heavenly Root, Ginseng Herb, or Hachimigan. The last is especially effective for diabetics, who are prone to loosing their Yang force suddenly and, along with that, their sexual appetite."

Supplements

Substances that help combat an erectile disfunction ED and enhance the sex drive are *dopamine, zinc, and vitamin E,* as well as those that increase testosterone release.

Dopamine. Dopamine, which plays a central role in the overall neuromuscular condition, has recently received a lot of scientific and public attention. Durk Pearson and Sandy Shaw, in their book *Life Extension,* define dopamine as an important brain neurotransmitter (i.e., a chemical that enables nerve cells to communicate with each other), which plays a role in body movement, motivation, primitive drives and emotions including sexual behavior, and immune system function. The dopaminergic system is one of the systems that declines most in the aging brain. L-Dopa, an amino acid the brain uses to make dopamine, can increase the life span of experimental animals by as much as 50 percent. Some patients state than while on L-Dopa, they experienced an increase in sex drive. Dopamine (Intropin) is known also as cardiac stimulant that enhances the contraction capacity of the heart muscle. The lack of dopamine leads to Parkinson's disease, which causes muscle tremors that ultimately escalate into extreme muscular rigidity and immobilization.

Our brain produces dopamine from nutrient substances in the food we eat. Excellent sources of dopamine include coffee beans and soybeans, says Julian Whitaker, M.D., founder and president of the Whitaker Wellness Center in Newport Beach, California. Vitamin C plays a key role in the production and release of dopamine.

Zinc and Vitamin E. Zinc can help older men suffering from some forms of "crippled sexuality." According to Dr. Heinerman, 50 milligrams of zinc (sucked on as a lozenge) and 55 international units (IU) of vitamin E (in a gelatin capsule) every day seem to be an optimal and safe intake. He also recommends the following substances.

L-arginine is an amino acid that dramatically increases male sperm counts and may prevent premature ejaculation. It is available in health food stores in 500-milligram capsules. Double or triple this amount may be necessary for desired effects.

Ginseng is one of the most popular herbs of all times. It is used extensively throughout the Orient by millions of men to increase their sexual prowess. The best kind typically sold in most health food stores goes under the brand name of Ginsana. Two or three capsules taken an hour before lovemaking begins are advisable. Also, sipping one or two cups of hot ginseng tea a few minutes before intercourse often encourages penile erections in older men.

Certain products from the *beehive* may be efficacious as well. Two capsules of *bee pollen* and an equal amount of royal jelly have helped some men and women with their impotency and frigidity problems.

The prescription drug *Viagra* (sildenafil citrate) is widely advertised as a perfect solution for men with erectile dysfunction. Viagra is found to increase blood flow to the penis, thereby helping with erections and increasing the sex drive. It is distributed in 25-, 50-, and 100-milligram pills, at a cost of $10 per pill. Cardiac patients taking nitroglycerin are warned, however, that Viagra may cause an abrupt drop in blood pressure. Other side effects of Viagra are flushing, headache, stomachache, blurred vision, and temporary color- and light-perception changes. Other prescription drugs include Zyban, Valtrex, Xenical, and Propecia. *Progenis*, which is advertised as an all-natural breakthrough, is acclaimed to help boost sex drive and sexual stamina.

Herbs for better sex. Panax *ginseng* root, a type of Asiatic ginseng, is a favorite among athletes, business people, and active individuals. Studies have indicated that ginsengosides are responsible for ginseng's long-standing reputation as a health and vitality herb. Ginseng is an extremely *Yang* root; therefore, it is very effective for a *Yin* person, according to Naboru Muramoto. For a Yang person, it will be either ineffective or cause high blood pressure. Ginseng contains germanium, which has recently been discovered to be effective in curing *cancer*. When the heart or the digestive organs become weak, ginseng can be used; it is also effective in cases of anemia, thin urine, and cold feet. However, it is rarely used alone and preferably should be mixed with some other herb--a *Yin* herb, of course. Ginseng promotes appetite and may be helpful for digestive disturbances. It is mildly stimulating to the central nervous system and to various glands, perhaps accounting for its reputation as a rejuvenator, says John Lust in his book, *The Herb Book*. Ginseng is rather effective in eliminating dizziness and also helpful for coughs, colds, and various chest problems. Lust considers the following herbs to have *aphrodisiac* (i.e., arousing or increasing sexual desire or potency) properties: artichoke, carline thistle, celery, clove, coriander, common lettuce, common plantain, English walnut, European vervain, fenugreek, galangal, jasmine, jimson weed, lovage, matico, Mexican damiana, mint, onion, pride of China, queen of the meadow, saffron, savory, saw palmetto, sea cucumber, sundew, and water eryngo.

Gingko. Dozens of scientific research studies have documented the ability of ginkgo to increase peripheral circulation, thereby enhancing blood flow to the arms, legs, and brain. Millions of people use ginkgo daily for its unique effects on the circulatory system and its natural antioxidant properties.

Among available dietary supplements for better sex is *Summetry Botanicals Male Balance* available in a tablet form. Its ingredients include Vitamin E (10.5 IU), zinc (arginate and citrate, 20 milligrams), and 500 milligrams of a blend of the following herbs: ho shou wu, Chinese ginseng, saw palmetto, hoelen sclerotium, astragaius root, angelica root, peony root, rehmania root, lovage root, toasted licorice root, cinnamon bark, red dates, and pygeum.

While Viagra is working on erections, *yohimbe*, the bark of the African yohimbe tree used for centuries as an aphrodisiac, and *yohimbine*, a drug approved by the U.S. Food and Drug Administration, can enhance both sexual desire and performance. Yohimbine, however, has side effects including dizziness and fluctuations in blood pressure; people with heart disease and kidney disorder are advised against taking it.

Sex Control with Exercise

Exercise is reputed to greatly improve sex life. According to Julian Whitaker, M.D., author of the book, *Shed 10 Years in 10 Weeks*, a study of 160 master swimmers between the ages of forty and eighty, showed that the sex life of those engaged in vigorous exercise was typical of people twenty to forty years their junior. "Sex and exercise are synonymous," says Jack LaLanne, eighty-five. Yoga exercises, both dynamic and static, are helpful in preventing prostate problems in men, improving vaginal muscle tone in women, and increasing men's potency. These exercises, described in detail in the *Exercise* chapter, are the buttocks walk, pelvic circles, full spine stretch, boat, rocking boat, reverse back bend, back leg lift, knee-squeeze pose, easy-bridge pose, and cobra pose.

Gomi Masayoshi, eighty-six, of Japan, suggests in his book, *Understanding Weak Points of Aging* (in Japanese), an exercise to improve blood circulation in the penis. A man should hold his penis with both hands and twist it as if wringing a wet washcloth. While holding this twisted position for a while, he should contract the anus muscles. This exercise must be performed gently and with great precaution to avoid injuries to the tissues and skin.

Vaginal muscle tone can be maintained by sexual activity, masturbation, and Kegel exercises. The buttocks-walk exercise described previously is very beneficial for both women and men. Exercises that strengthen muscles and improve circulation, as well as herbs including yohimbe and aphrodisiac foods, may provide a holistic alternative to Viagra, Zyban, Valtrex, Xenical, Propecia, and Progenis-those widely advertised formulas for men--but without the side effects.

Our thoughts are the language of the mind,
And they are energy and they are matter.
If they are obedient, controlled, and kind,
You have peace and joy and feel better.

Thoughts always flow; they arrive and disappear.
They drag you into the past from now and here,
They pull you into the future, can act upon you tougher,
The draught of disturbing thoughts makes you suffer.

Emotions like hate, fear, anger, and greed
Harm your body, your mind, and your spirit.
Be here and now, use breathing, observe: with all it
You'll master your thoughts and emotions indeed.

Raw foods in your diet and fasts will increase creativity,
And mind exercises give your brain health and longevity.

24

EMOTION CONTROL

To feel or not to feel, there is no such question. No one can deny that our life would be flavorless and flat without emotions. An unemotional person is often given the non-appealing nickname "robot." Humans and their emotions are inseparable, and a lack of emotions, feelings, and sensations is abnormal. Feeling to the full is the essence of life. The history of humanity from the beginning of time is the interplay of emotions. Emotions have been a never-ending field of research from ancient to modern times. Philosophers, thinkers, psychics, and psychologists--to name just a few categories--have always been concerned with people's emotions. In the discussion of human emotions and thoughts (see the next chapter) and some approaches to control them, I employ both psychological and metaphysical resources.

It is universally accepted that emotions play an important role in our overall health, well-being, and longevity. The *Oxford English Dictionary* defines *emotion* as "any agitation or disturbance of mind, feeling, passion; any vehement or excited mental state." Deepak Chopra, M.D., in his best-selling book, *Ageless Body, Timeless Mind,* also connects emotion with thought: "An emotion is a thought linked to a sensation." L. Atkinson, et al., in their book, *Introduction to Psychology,* define *emotion* as a condition of the organism during affectively toned experience, whether mild or intense. Daniel Goleman, author of the best-selling book, *Emotional Intelligence*, refers emotion "to a feeling and its distinctive thoughts, psychological and biological states, and range of propensities to act." He adds, "There are hundreds of emotions, along with their blends, variations, mutations, and nuances." Thus, emotions being acute, immediate responses and lasting a short time (e.g., short bouts of anger) are distinguished from moods that are more muted and last longer (e.g., a "blue" mood that can last one or more days). People of different temperaments tend to evoke certain emotions or moods more readily than others.

Researchers trying to classify emotions consider primary, derivative, and basic families of emotions. The primary emotions seem to be *anger*, *fear*, *sadness*, *enjoyment*, *love*, *surprise*, *disgust*, and *shame*. According to Plutchik, a psychology researcher, a fundamental life situation is associated with one of the primary emotions. These are grief (sorrow) that is triggered by the loss of a loved one, fear that is elicited by a threat, and anger that is evoked from an obstacle, as well as joy induced by a potential mate, trust among group members, disgust with a gruesome object, anticipation from a new territory, and surprise with a sudden, novel object.

These primary emotions also can be considered as heads of the family of emotions. Each family has a few or even a dozen variations and blends as family members. For example, Goleman lists acceptance, friendliness, trust, kindness, affinity, devotion, adoration, and infatuation as members of the *love* family of emotions. All this emotional complexity has two basic drives at its core—pain and pleasure. Emotions associated with pain that we all try to avoid are negative emotions, and those associated with pleasure that we all pursue are positive emotions. Examples of positive emotions include love, enjoyment (happiness), contentment, joy, surprise (pleasant), and sexual excitement; the negative emotions include anger, depression, fear, grief, sadness, disgust, and shame.

The psychologist Roseman associates specific emotions with situational aspects. We experience joy when a desired event occurs, sorrow when a desired event does not occur, distress when an undesired event occurs, and relief when an undesired event does not occur. As an example, if a young man loves and marries a nice woman who is ten years older than him, he would probably feel joy; his rival would feel sorrow; his parents, distress; and her parents, relief.

What are the causes of various emotions? They are our instantaneous reactions to and evaluation of other people, outside objects, places, and events. Our likes and dislikes, and our judgment play a dominant role. Everything we perceive, we evaluate as either *good* or *bad*. Adults know that "*no*" means we must resist and restrict our instinctive impulses. Mature people have less freedom in expressing immediate reactions than children, who freely cry if they are scared, hungry, wet, or lonely. Unexpressed negative emotions lead to a *stored hurt* and a host of psychological distresses. According to psychiatrist David Viscott, the deposited hurt disguises itself as anger, anxiety, guilt, and depression.

Emotions and Physiology

Emotions affect the functions of the vital organs and endocrine glands of the body. In this respect, there are at least two approaches: scientific and metaphysical. Psychological science gives us a few examples. It maintains that emotions induce an increase in the heart and respiration rates, a "jittery" feeling, and muscle tremors. When we turn pale with fear, the withdrawal of blood from the skin to the internal organs and muscles--mostly the legs-- prepares us to run away, and our circulation quickens. In moments of horror, when our hair stands on end and our heart beats fast, the intense nerve impulses from the brain and released stress hormones from the adrenal glands do their job. "Emotions play a powerful role in affecting your body and especially your heart," says Dean Ornish, M.D., director of the Preventative Medicine Research Institute in Sausalito, California, and author of *Dr. Dean Ornish's Program for Reversing Heart Disease*.

The heart rate is very sensitive to the emotions, especially to negative emotions: a 1983 study by Ekman, Levenson, & Frieson showed that anger, fear, and sadness increased the heart rate by 7 to 8 beats per minute, but happiness, surprise, and disgust –increased it by only zero to 2 beats per minute. A much greater heart-rate increase was recorded when a twenty-two-year-old actor of the Noh Theater in Japan was monitored. According to videotape that I saw in Tokyo, because of the intense internal emotions that he generated while his body was nearly motionless, the actor's heart rate soared to 205 beats per minute.

Among the vital organs, our heart is the most sensitive and can be badly damaged by emotions such as anger, fear, and hostility. In his book, *Emotional Intelligence,* Goleman states: "...the strongest scientific links between emotions and heart disease are to anger: a Harvard Medical School study asked more than fifteen hundred men and women who had suffered heart attacks to describe their emotional state in the hours before the attack. Being angry more than doubled the risk of cardiac arrest in people who already had heart disease; the heightened risk lasted for about two hours after the anger was aroused." Many other studies also show that being frequently angry, enraged, and hostile is suicidal.

Anger or fear--which is the most harmful to our heart? It seems that fear is the most influential emotion. In his book, *Timeless Healing,* Herbert Benson, M.D., states: "Fear appears to be a particularly strong emotion, and we often feel the effects of fear in marked physiologic ways...Fear appears to be a major contributor to the mysterious sudden-death phenomenon among Hmong refugees, members of the Laotian ethnic group who fled Southeast Asia for the United States during the Vietnam War." Most often, it occurs among male refugees between the ages of twenty-five and forty-four years. Researchers who studied the sudden-death syndrome concluded that emotional reactions to a fierce combination of "fear, awe, and abasement" result in disturbances in cardiac electrical conduction, usually during sleep, which leads to cardiac arrest and sudden death. Victims that were revived from cardiac arrest described their experience as a horrific nightmare and felt that an evil spirit recognized in their culture visited them at night and suffocated them. My aunt in Russia told me that she experienced such a nightmare while sleeping, when she felt that the devil was sitting on her chest, making it difficult for her to breathe. Fortunately, she survived without fatal consequences.

According to metaphysical tradition, emotions fall somewhere midway between thinking on one side and acting on the other. If the thinking process is going on in the brain, where the upper chakras are located, the actions are given forth by the lower chakras. Therefore, emotions might be seated somewhere in the heart region. The seat of intense emotions such as anger, joy, and laughter is the Manipura (third) chakra; for love and compassion, it is the Anahata (fourth) chakra, according to Naomi Ozaniec in her book, *The Elements of the Chakras.*

A more sophisticated connection between emotions and chakras is in the book entitled *Chakras,* by Harish Johari. According to Johari, greed and patience are attributed to the Muladhara (first) chakra. The sensual desires and associated emotions such as satisfaction, moodiness, jealousy, nervousness, and false display of emotions are linked to the Svadhisthana (second) chakra. Anger and sorrow are linked to the Manipura (third) chakra. Love, hate, anger, cruelty, contentment, happiness, and joy are all assigned to the Anahata (fourth) chakra. Enmity, shyness, fear, and attachment are related to the Vishuddha (fifth) chakra. Mercy, honesty, forgiveness, and firmness are the features of the Ajna and Svadhisthana, the two upper chakras. In contrast with other emotions, anger and love are so powerful that they are each present in two chakras.

People whose third eye is open and who are able to see the aura report that anger, envy, irritability, and other negative emotions interrupt the balance of chakra energy and the energy flow between chakras, which leads to many disorders and ailments.

Emotions and psychological reasons have medical significance and play a dominant role as a cause of virtually all diseases, according to some authors. In her book, *You Can Heal Your Life,* Louise L. Hay states that the cause of constipation is "Refusing to release old ideas. Stuck in the past. Sometimes stinginess." The cause of cancer she finds in "Deep hurt. Longstanding resentment. Deep secret of grief eating away at the self. Carrying hatreds. 'What's the use?'" Hay claims that the forgiveness, joy, and love states that she puts herself in, as well as imagery together with diet and alternate therapies, helped her to cure her own cancer.

A cancer expert, Dr. G. Hamer of Munich, Germany, maintains that severe stress imposed by a long-term conflict is the only cause of any cancer. He even located cancer in the body depending on the form of conflict. Thus, cancer of the left breast is linked to a deep-seated conflict between a mother and her child, cancer of the right breast with her husband. Stomach cancer is induced by domestic violence, prostate cancer by self-disappointment, and lung cancer by fear of death. According to Dr. Hamer, the only treatment that helps is the character of the psyche; that is, the psyche is the software, the brain is a computer, and the diseased organ is a machine. Under the guidance of effective software, the computer reprograms the organ and puts it into healing mode. He claims that twelve thousand of his patients were cured using this method.

Definitely, there are certain hereditary, lifestyle, and environmental causes of various diseases such as a predisposition to heart disease in the family, lack of physical activity, and fiber in the diet that can lead to constipation and even colon cancer, or work at an asbestos mill that may cause lung cancer. Nonetheless, negative emotions seem to be a high risk factor in development of these and other illnesses.

Positive Emotions

Affection, bliss, compassion, confidence, contentment, faith, forgiveness, hope, joy, love, peace, sentiment, and trust are examples of positive emotions. These are the pleasures of life and they are usually attained if a person does right, thinks right, and feels right. It is important to treat the body right, to have a good lifestyle, to rest, and to exercise. By thinking positively, people treat their mind right too. Attaining a wonderful state of joy and peace of mind is the aim of a positive thinker. If a person persistently seeks joy and fun in life and is joy-oriented, he/she will find them sooner or later. It is helpful in this path to enjoyment to throw out envy, hate, and selfishness; to avoid being sarcastic and cynical; and to stop saying and even thinking mean things.

The curative effect of positive emotions is widely recognized. Norman Cousins, author of the best-selling book, *Anatomy of an Illness*, attributed his complete recovery from a severe form of ankylosing spondylitis to an enormous will to live, laughter, and mega-doses of vitamin C. With this disease, which leads to disintegration of the connective tissue in the spine, his doctors assessed that he had one chance in five hundred for recovery. According to Herbert Benson, M.D., "faith healing" that evokes one's internal healing resources is reported to have positive effects on physical problems such as backaches, chronic pain, and arthritis in 67 percent of those surveyed in Baltimore, Maryland. In his book, *Timeless Healing,* Dr. Benson indicated that the rate of healing was even higher--77 percent--for psychological problems including anger, anxiety, depression, and fear.

The moderation principle is fully applicable to positive emotions as well. This does not necessarily mean that if they are positive and good that more is even better. The disruptive effect of intense emotions, both positive and negative, is real. The over-expression of positive emotion can be harmful to both humans and animals--it is known that a dog can die of intense joy from meeting its master after a long separation.

Negative Emotions

Negative emotions such as anger, fear, hate, sadness, and greed are found to badly affect internal organs of the body. In one study, the exhaled air of people who expressed anger was analyzed and poisonous substances were found. This means that angry people are harmful to themselves as well as the people around them. "The heart is destroyed with fear, liver with anger, and stomach with sadness and depression," said Dr. Emmanuel, a Russian academician in medicine. Repressed emotions and stress are widely believed to be strong contributive factors in the development of stomach and duodenum ulcers. Several psychological studies have shown that a person's reaction to stress, rather than simply the amount of stress, is what counts in ulcer development.

If you experience positive emotions, you will benefit in terms of health and a pleasant life; however, being occupied with negative emotions results in nothing but harm. Their influence affects how one perceives life and the world in general. The ancient Indian texts depict what the God Shiva said when replying to the Goddess Parvati about the role of emotions: "The emotions are feelings of ecstasy, love, hate, and so forth. When an awareness of the nature of emotions is present in the consciousness, nine sentiments manifest. From the original tranquil sentiment, the amorous, humorous, compassionate, furious, heroic, awesome, wondrous, and repugnant sentiments arise. Of these, the amorous, humorous, compassionate, and wondrous sentiments are naturally uplifting and potentially liberating. The furious, heroic, and awesome sentiments play a major role in Tantric evolution because they transcend convention. As for the repugnant sentiment, it serves to repel undesirable influences."

Modern mind/body research arrived at conclusions that sound at least partly similar to the wisdom of the God Shiva. "*Positive feelings invite unity. Negative feelings invite isolation,*" says Joan Borisenko, Ph.D., in her book, *Minding the Body, Mending the Mind.*

Ayurvedic medicine teaches that the negative emotions are harmful to certain internal organs. According to Dr. Vasant Lad, the negative emotions and organs that they affect are as follows:

Negative Emotion	**Organ**
Sense of lack of love, feelings of deep hurt	Heart
Anger	Liver
Hate	Gallbladder
Fear	Kidney
Sadness and grief	Lungs
Lack of fulfillment, lack of contentment	Stomach
Greed, attachment, possessiveness	Spleen
Sense of failure	Small intestine
Nervousness	Colon
Insecurity	Bladder
Anxiety, sense of lack of support	Adrenals

Negative emotions are classified in Ayurveda depending on the person's excess doshic energy, which affects feelings and the mind. According to Judith H. Morrison, excess doshas are associated with the following negative emotions:

Excess Vata: anxiety, confusion, fear, grief, insecurity, lack of communication, lack of integrity, loss of creativity, moodiness, nervousness, sadness

Excess Pitta: ambition, anger, envy, fear of failure, frustration, hate, jealousy, judgmental or critical tendencies, pride, and skepticism

Excess Kapha: boredom, carelessness, feeling lack of love, feeling lack of support, greed, lack of compassion, lack of interest, lack of discernment, obsessive behavior, unkindness

Actually, most of us have the features of all doshas present in us more or less; therefore, we can feel any of these emotions. For instance, I belong to the Vata type with Pitta as a second dosha. When the Vata dosha in me is increased due to some aggravating lifestyle changes, I can still feel, let's say, greed. Although greed is associated with excess Kapha, which cannot be excessive in me, it is increased from its usual low level.

According to Ayurveda, there is a food and emotion connection: rajasic food stimulates the passionate sentiments, tamasic food induces the furious and destructive emotions, and sattvic foods evoke the creative and erotic sentiments. Negative emotions deprive food of its prana, the live force attached to it. Blood loaded with bad hormones released in a state of negativity cannot provide the best conditions for food digestion at that time, which is why people are advised to skip a meal if they feel anxiety or anger. If food is eaten at the time when one is overloaded with negative emotions, it reinforces them in the body on a subtle level and makes it more difficult to overcome and get rid of them. The same is true for disturbing thoughts while you eat–eating fortifies the negative thoughts and imprints them on the subconscious, and they recur easily the next time you eat, which has a detrimental effect on your system.

Emotional Disorders

Emotional problems are numerous, so listed here are only those that occur most frequently: anxiety, anger, burnout (i.e., mental and physical exhaustion), depression, eating disorders (e.g., anorexia nervosa and bulimia nervosa), fear, grief, irritability, jealousy, mood swings, panic attacks, phobias (e.g., fear of enclosed spaces, of flying, of being alone, of heights, of insects), shyness, and schizophrenia. According to Matthew M. Burg, Ph.D., the author of the article, "Stress, Behavior, and Heart Disease," published in the *Yale University School of Medicine Heart Book*, the emotional indicators induced by mental *stress* are anger, anxiety, confusion, depression, difficulty concentrating, excessive crying--especially without obvious cause--excessive talking or inability to express self, fears, feeling of time pressure, forgetfulness, frustration, impatience, irritability, overreaction to events, phobias, panic attacks, withdrawal, and lack of emotional feeling.

There are a few more or less common emotional problems such as taking drugs, gambling, sex addiction, obsessions (e.g., the urge to check closed doors or count things or to wash hands frequently), and loss of the sense of smell. Just a few are discussed herein.

Anxiety. A threatened or real loss is often a source of anxiety, which is a common emotional disorder in elderly people. Medical treatment includes medication, psychotherapy such as professional counseling, and advice to find a support group. If anxiety is caused by ordinary life situations, such as having to wait to see a doctor, it is better to ask the reason for the delay--understanding the reason in this case might reduce the anxiety felt.

Millions of people all around the world are afflicted with *depression*, a condition characterized by feeling down, sad, and drained of energy. Especially during attacks of depression, people feel lasting fatigue and weakness, lose the ability to enjoy life, often lose their appetite, and experience anxiety and insomnia. If a person suffers frequent and long bouts of depression, the condition can become so bad that even the desire to live can be impaired. Depression reduces the protective strength of the immune system and a depressed person becomes vulnerable to many diseases.

Another psychological disorder is *schizophrenia*. A person with this illness loses the sense of reality and can suffer delusion–including delusions of grandeur--hallucinations, disordered thinking, scattered speaking, and other dramatic symptoms. Here is how schizophrenia patient Casey (pseudonym), thirty-seven, described his sufferings, as reported by David Phung in the July/August 1997 issue of the Singapore magazine *Health Digest*: "I have seen light in the sky, heard choruses of people inside me--taunting, tormenting me, pinning me against the wall, and driving me crazy. The 'drama' is endless, and the agony and terror are even more detrimental." Most schizophrenia patients are treated with drugs, but Casey was lucky to establish a relationship of long-term cooperation and even friendship with his therapist. He said that it was the help of his therapist that nearly cured him and supported him in his journey back to reality.

What kind of life is it if a person suffers from the pain and agony of this disease for many decades? Endlessly miserable; however, fortunately schizophrenics know good times too. If they did not, they could not live a long life, as shown in the case of Madam Tan (not her real name), 100, a chronic schizophrenic at Woodbridge Hospital in Singapore. She was first diagnosed with this disease in 1949, more than fifty years ago. She has resided in this hospital since 1971; a few years later, her son stopped visiting her because he said he could not cope with her. She is still very strong physically and she spends her days sitting quietly in her chair. "Beyond spitting out food she dislikes, such as watermelon and bananas, she is no trouble," said a staff nurse. "But she has a quick temper, and may hit us sometimes with her arms or legs," she added, sounding more amused than annoyed, as reported by Lea Wee in the April 26, 1998, issue of *The Sunday Times* of Singapore.

As mentioned in the *Chakra System* chapter regarding drunken people who can descend from the mind to the lower levels of consciousness, the forms of schizophrenia look somewhat alike: patients with violent behavior drop to the Muladhara (first) chakra and become dangerous to others, expressing self-destructiveness most intensely; sex maniacs fall to the Svadhisthana (second) chakra; and patients with delusions of grandeur–fall to the Manipura (third) chakra. In severe cases, these patients are confined to an asylum and treated with medications that have severe side effects, as depicted in the famous movie, *One Flew over the Cuckoo's Nest*.

In some schizophrenics, creativity is increased and they, for example, start to paint.

> A friend of mine, Vladimir Strelkov, who was murdered by the Mafia, was a journalist with the Russian magazine, *Man and Law*. He told me that he happened to attend an exhibition of paintings of schizophrenic patients. He said that many paintings, which depicted the visions and hallucinations of their creators, were very bright and impressive.
>
> Another friend, Nina Yakovlevna, told me that she is happy to be a psychiatrist by profession--the most interesting people she has met have been her patients. Some of them sometimes express themselves using a "word medley," or a set of words without sense or even unknown words. "However, I could understand that they live in a few of their previous lives simultaneously at this moment," she said. In order to understand this, I think a person must at least be acquainted with the reincarnation theory.

Alternative medicine offers about two-dozen natural-healing remedies that were found to be helpful in treatment and for taking control over emotional problems. Aromatherapy, Bach flower/essence therapy, food therapy, homeopathy, imagery, relaxation and meditation, and yoga may be helpful in the treatment of most emotional problems. To control stress, Dr. Ornish advises yoga exercises, relaxation techniques, and imaging routines.

Are negative emotions universally bad? Let's consider how the use of negative emotions can be for good. First, negative emotions are a means to know yourself better. When we are in trouble and overwhelmed by bad feelings, even losing sleep, we think a lot and work hard to find the solution. At these moments, we move forward in our mental and spiritual growth, we progress in our evolution. We are really awakened during hard times. In contrast, when nothing is bothering us, we regress both mentally and spiritually. It is said that God gives us trouble because He remembers us and wants to train us. He loses interest in us if everything is okay in our life, and goes somewhere else.

Second, negative emotions are an energetic phenomenon and one can even enjoy dealing with them, according to Osho, known also as Bhagwan Shree Rajneesh. To release anger, he advised hitting a pillow. If one feels so angry that he could hit somebody, he can express his anger by hitting a pillow--he can even kill it with a knife if his anger is so great that he feels the urge to kill. This expression of anger does harm to no one and a person feels relaxed after this fighting exercise; moreover, the desire to hurt a real person subsides as well. I have read that some companies use a similar psychological approach by displaying a dummy of the boss and letting the employees hit it, thereby releasing their anger.

Handling Emotions

The ability of taking control over an outburst of emotions has been praised as a human's virtue since ancient times in both the West and the Orient. Temperance, the restrain of excessive emotions, was much valued by Plato, Aristotle, Shakespeare, Benjamin Franklin, and in Shaolin and samurai traditions, to name just a few. Self-mastery has always been appealing, but a passion's slave image was not. Uncontrollable anger, chronic anxiety, and depression are considered illnesses and, in severe cases, are treated with medication or psychotherapy.

Handling, managing, or mastering negative emotions is a difficult task. The instrument for taking control over emotions is our rational mind. However, emotions originate in the emotional mind, which is different from the rational mind. There are two groups of emotions: pre- and after-thought emotions. Those emotions that erupt in the face of danger are much faster and less accurate than subsequent thoughts and are called "quick-and-dirty" emotional responses. In an emergency, when we must react instantaneously and when there is no time for thoughtful analysis, accuracy is sacrificed for speed. The quick-response emotions are not our choice; rather, they are chosen for us by the situation or our perception of it. Emotions such as anger and fear in their full heat are very brief and last only a few seconds. They are ordinarily out of control of the rational mind, although it can control the course of emotional responses. People often justify their inappropriate actions by being in the grip of emotion.

Another group of emotions induced by thoughts is potentially more controllable by the rational mind than emergency emotions. Embarrassment about being late to a meeting, regret about not selling stocks when they were high, and apprehension over an upcoming road test are examples of emotions that originate from reflective thoughts. Because thoughts depend on perceptions that can be changed, and because we can choose what to think about, we can change (i.e., through good memories) the thoughts and emotions that bring us down into those that cheer us up.

There are five ways that people handle emotions: denial, expression, over-expression, repression, and understanding. People who *deny* emotions always say that they feel fine, regardless of what is happening in their lives in reality. They seem to be non-emotional, but if their emotions do not affect the conscious mind, they surely put a burden on the unconscious mind. As a result, they suffer many psychosomatic illnesses. Free *expression* of emotions that are under control of the intellect is the best way to handle emotions. There is nothing bad about emotions--they are natural and normal; moreover, they are the essence of life. There is even a saying, "I live because I feel." Emotions are attributes of human beings, and people without emotions would look like automatons. There are rumors that the extraterrestrial beings known as aliens are intellectually superior to humans but emotionally inferior to us because they are unemotional.

Overdoing of any kind is never good in one way or another, but the *over-expression* of emotions is simply dangerous. In a state when a person is not just angry but is the embodiment of anger, he/she loses control and can behave like a furious animal. At the other extreme, some people think that it is disgrace to be angry and they suppress it internally, without letting it go. The overall control of their mind over emotions--especially negative emotions--results in harming all body systems. Research shows that people who demonstrate personality C behavior--that is, those who *repress* emotions--are vulnerable to cancer, heart disease, and other diseases. The Japanese sumo wrestlers who are trained in the best samurai traditions to never display their emotions regardless of whether they win or lose are a good example. I became a fan of Takanonami ozeki (a high-ranked sumo master) whose handsome face never showed a sign of "triumph or disaster." However, this habit is not healthy and, together with extreme obesity due to overeating, significantly shortens the lives of sumo wrestlers.

The *understanding* of emotions rather than expressing or repressing them is the best way, teaches the Ayurveda. Understanding has a power to transform emotions and then to release them. If one were depressed, he/she would do better to search for the reasons of the depression. Nothing happens without a reason, and the reason for depression, anxiety, anger, or guilt can be a stored hurt that one tries to silence. If the hurt is understood, then conscious efforts and time may heal it, allowing one to move on.

Knowing one's emotions is the keystone of "personal" or emotional intelligence, according to Peter Salovey, a Yale psychologist, and Goleman. Other features of emotional intelligence are as follows:

• managing emotions
• motivating oneself; an ability to persist in the face of frustrations
• regulating one's moods and keeping distress from swamping the ability to think
• recognizing emotions in others, being tuned to others' needs and wants, an antidote to being emotionally tone-deaf
• handling relationships, an ability to manage emotions in others, the skill

of social politics-- (this skill is extremely important in emergency situations when one becomes a leader of a group)

The ability to handle relationships is important in contests such as the TV show "Survivor." The show's host, Jeff Probst, and the contestants say that it is more the interpersonal survival of each member of the group than physical survival. I want to emphasize that emotional control, mental flexibility, and nonattachment to preplanned ideas are absolutely necessary among the survivors on these shows. These qualities were demonstrated by the winner of the first "Survivor" show: Richard Hatch, thirty-nine, a corporate trainer from Rhode Island. He is a professional in interpersonal relationships and he applied his skills with success. A contestant who lacks these qualities risks being eliminated.

Some contestants have the idea of finding someone in the tribe whom they can trust. Although it is necessary to build an alliance to be secure, the "trust" idea is a weak point, especially when applied to a complete stranger. In this game, everyone tries to undermine you and if you trust someone, it takes you away from the "on-the-alert" state. Trusting ties you up, ties up the trusted one--particularly if you announced it to him or her--and confines the freedom of both. It is also an attempt to buy someone so that they won't vote you out.

Here are examples of how it happened on "Survivor2," the TV show filmed in the Australian outback. In the second tribal council, Kel Gleason, thirty-two, an Army Intelligence officer, was voted out from the Ogakor tribe of eight. He allegedly fell prey to false allegations originated by Jerry Manthey, a thirty-year-old actress who accused him of secretly eating beef jerky. He explained that he was chewing grass and bark, but doubt and distrust of him arose among the other contestants. Marilyn "Mad Dog" Hershey, fifty-one, a retired police inspector, whom Kel trusted the most in the tribe (he had a plan to find someone to trust in the first three days), also voted him out, although she did not believe that Kel broke the rules--and even apologized to him for the misconduct of the other members of the tribe. Three days later, in the third tribal council, Marilyn herself failed to perform a physical challenge in a contest with the Kucha tribe, which resulted in a loss of immunity (i.e., voting out of one of the contestants) for her tribe. Tina Wesson, forty, a nurse whom Marilyn trusted the most, calling her "my constellation," also voted her out. I felt I was witnessing proof of the old adage: "Don't dig a pit for others, you will fall in it yourself."

These two cases proved that inappropriate trust (or the extra efforts of Kel to catch fish and of Debb Eaton, forty-five, a corrections officer, to procure fire for the benefit of their tribes) works against those who are blindly attached to those or any particular idea. What was necessary was being attuned to the emotions of others, not to stand out, not to be a "white raven"-- but instead to "go with the flow," as Probst put it. Being stuck to a preplanned idea looks somewhat childish and makes people rigid, keeping them closed to possibilities not only in a game such as "Survivor," but also in life situations. People who trust are usually left with the feeling that their trusted ones betrayed them; they never blame themselves. False ideas entail a negative way of thinking that in turn induces bitter feelings. I know this from my own experience, learning this tough nonattachment rule from my own failures.

Understanding one's emotions is the first stage of mastering them, according to Dr. Chopra. He advises making a list of basic positive and negative emotions and abstract feelings such as discovery, faith, or forgiveness, and taking the list wherever one goes as a reminder. If a person checks his or her feelings with the list during the day, they can gain an insight into the origin of emotions, particularly if they are negative. Knowing where a negative emotion comes from helps to dissipate its energy that yields letting it go. For more details on this technique, I refer you to Dr. Chopra's landmark book, *Ageless Body, Timeless Mind*.

In most **emotional disorders, practicing to be in the *"here and now"* state is a very helpful vehicle**. It means that all of a person's attention, thoughts, and feelings must be focused on doing something now that he/she likes to do. Hobbies are the best, but any kind of activity that can capture the attention entirely is okay. To live in the present is one of the most fundamental universal laws and we often are punished for violating it. To live in the present moment is absolutely necessary in extreme situations and conditions such as war or even driving on a highway.

> My colleague at the research institute in Moscow, Vladimir Galitsky, Ph.D., who survived WWII, told me that he followed certain rules. One was to attentively look around every passing moment, not allowing himself to be occupied with remembering the past or dreaming about the future. Another person, a journalist to whom I happened to give a ride, told me that he sold his own car after two accidents. They happened because of his own fault--he used to daydream about the past or the future too much while driving. The rule, "Be here and now" is crucial in these situations for survival itself.

There is a Russian saying, "Imaginary fears are much worse than real ones." Everyone has moments in their life when they are occupied with imaginary fears. This drains the energy, causes anxiety, and results in the unpleasant experience of insomnia. On the contrary, "here and now" is a place where one might feel good, and there is no doubt that everyone wants to feel good. In his book, *The Only Dance There Is,* Ram Dass describes how he cured his father of severe depression caused by the death of his wife. He returned from India and found his father in the deepest depression, feeling that he was a failure as a human being and saying that he was approaching death. Instead of dwelling on his father's "it's all over" attitude and "we'll look through the old photographs tonight," they made raspberry jam, one of his father's hobbies. The state of being here and now while making the jam worked so perfectly that by the time they finished it, his father was smiling and feeling happy. Ram Dass continued to stay with him and, as a result of living in the here and now, his father happily remarried eight months later.

Why does this work so perfectly? Because emotions are the most present-centered thing one has. "An emotion is a thought linked to a sensation. The thought is usually about the past or the future, but the sensation is in the present. Your mind quickly links sensations with thoughts, but when we were infants, our first experiences and emotions were much closer to physical sensations," says Deepak Chopra, M.D., in *Ageless Body, Timeless Mind.* "To feel an emotion fully and completely, to experience it and then release it, is to be in the present, the only moment that never ages," he adds. If this is true, then handling emotional problems with the "here and now" approach is doubly beneficial: one can control the negative emotions and retard the aging process.

Another powerful vehicle for handling emotions is to become an observer, a witness of what is happening around you. Many emotional problems arise when two forces act--active and passive--and we identify with one of them, according to Peter Damien Ouspensky in his book, *The Fourth Way.* For example, a demanding person is an active force and one who resists is a passive force. These dual forces cannot often resolve the problem, but a triad of forces is able to do the job, maintains Ouspensky. The third, a *neutral* force, is the one from which we have to detach ourselves. It is our intellectual self, the observer that allows us to see ourselves from the outside. The Russian proverb, "Don't be stuck with your heart all in it," says about the same thing. It means that, in dealing with difficulties, don't identify your whole being with your involved actions--leave a part of you, your heart, as the seat of emotions, to be a nonjudgmental observer.

Actually, this is easy to say but much more difficult to do. The problem is that when a critical situation arises, we are all in it, with all of our self, and we forget to detach as an observer. Emotions can outrage the mind, the intellect becomes clouded, and the primitive instincts come into play. It takes time to train oneself to stay calm and to remember the neutral force. Rudyard Kipling, in his famous poetry "If," wrote the following line: "If you can keep your head when all around you are losing theirs and blaming it on you." Only a calm mind can make a proper decision. The ability to become an observer, to single out the neutral force, is the key to keeping the mind calm.

No one denies that physiology and psychology in us are closely interrelated. In this respect, breathing has been proven to be a very powerful tool in taking control over emotions, because it supplies us not only with oxygen, but with prana as well. "Four negative emotions—fear, anger, greed, and envy—throw Prana out of balance and are to be avoided. Positive emotions, particularly love, increase Prana," says Deepak Chopra, M.D., in *Ageless Body, Timeless Mind*. When we are filled with prana, we may experience a state of euphoria, which athletes call being "in the zone." This state is dream-like when time is slowed and everything seems to be done without effort. I experienced this state during the presentation of my Ph.D. thesis. It was induced by the extreme stress of the event, and I felt that I was observing from outside my body how someone else (me) correctly answered the questions of the scientists' panel.

Everyone knows that different emotions alter the rate and depth of breathing. "Anger produces shallow inhalation and strong, panting exhalation. Fear creates rapid, shallow, ragged breathing. Sorrow creates spasmodic, broken breathing--the kind that arises when you are sobbing. On the other hand, positive emotions such as joy induce more regular breathing as the chest relaxes," says Deepak Chopra, M.D., in *Ageless Body, Timeless Mind*.

"This phenomenon also works in reverse–changing the breathing pattern also causes altered emotions. As a young intern on duty in the emergency room, I was taught to calm down agitated patients just by sitting next to them and asking them to breathe slowly, deeply, and regularly with me. As we fell into a relaxed breathing rhythm, our bodies spontaneously followed suit, and their agitated emotions were stilled," he adds. "Breathe deeper, you are agitated," said the famous Russian writers Ilf and Pertov, and their words became a national saying.

Breathing to calm down is even more effective when it is done with full attention. In any psychological phenomenon, the power of attention is enormous. No learning or mental work is possible without paying attention to a particular subject. An increased lack of attention, such as in Attention Deficit Disorder (ADD) in some children, is regarded as an illness and treated with medications. The more we pay attention to any specific task we perform, the better the outcome. Because attention is one of the aspects of awareness, we can dramatically change our life with just shifting our attention. As Dr. Chopra states, "...*the quality of one's life depends on the quality of attention.* Whatever you pay attention to will grow more important in your life." Psychologist Ellen Langer at Harvard showed in her 1979 study that even the aging process can be retarded if people focus their attention on reviving the events that happened twenty years ago. Followers of the "physical immortality" theory assign to attention--which involves visualizing the prana inflow with each inhalation (i.e., pranic nourishment)--one of the major roles in achieving their goal.

The following breathing exercise can help reduce negative emotions. Sit calmly in a chair or lie flat on your back on the floor. Exhale deeply, then inhale and imagine that your lungs are filled with the prana that came in with the air. Visualize it as hazy gold in color. Hold your breath for a second, and then slowly exhale. Send the flow of that golden prana from your lungs to the internal organ that is wounded by the negative emotion. If your feel angry, it is your liver; if you are fearful, it is your kidneys (refer to the previous list that links negative emotions with specific internal organs). It is not that deep of a life-threatening wound, but it is significant enough to cause pain in your organ and in your soul. Imagine that the flow of golden haze--prana--heals this wound with each exhalation. Continue for five or six minutes and imagine that together with the wound, which becomes shallower and then disappears, the emotion that caused it is gradually released too.

In our stressful life, an emotional imbalance can be reduced with a shot or two of an *alcoholic* beverage. Anxiety, fear, guilt, and depression do not feel as pressing in a slightly drunken state when one can relax and forget for a while about the problems that induced the emotions. "The sea is only up to the knees to a drunk," says a Russian proverb. Although alcoholism is a big issue in Russia, some Russian doctors say that there is no better antidepressant than vodka. In my own experience, it was helpful for me sometimes to have a shot of vodka or cognac to reduce stress and fears while working in Russia and later in Japan. Alcohol eliminates the blocks in the Chinese channels caused by negative emotions, and the energy flows more freely in them. As a result, one feels relaxed and the mood improves.

As a remedy for emotions such as guilt, repentance, or regret about hurting someone, a *confession* can serve well. This is one of the most efficient tools of handling negative emotions and acts as a spiritual cure that people have used from the beginning of time. When a person addresses his thoughts to God and begs His forgiveness for bad deeds, his/her body and soul are profoundly cured. *The Jesus prayer* was a powerful spiritual remedy in the Orthodox Christian religion for centuries. *The Jesus prayer* is: "Good Lord, Jesus Christ, the Son of God, forgive me, for I am sinful." The sainted Russian hermits, who combined the Jesus prayer with breathing exercises and repeated this prayer all day long, were able to abstain from food and sleep for many days. With this prayer, they established a connection to the highest spiritual energies that fed them, according to Valentina Efimova-Yaraeva in her book, *Encyclopedia of Your Health* (in Russian).

In handling the negative emotions, *laughter* may be very useful too. Laughter helps reduce physical pain in the body and raises the mood as well. It is natural to laugh when we are happy, but when we are unhappy, laughter heals due to the feedback effect. Earnest Hemingway laughed in the hospital when he felt intolerable pain from being badly injured and having two hundred pieces of metal in his body after a mine explosion during WWI.

> In my own experience, I happened to get an inflammation of the nerves in my left leg. The pain was so severe that I could not concentrate on anything. I was twenty-seven years old then and came from Moscow to the city of Novotcherkassk in the Rostov region for a class reunion, five years after graduation from the college. I could not really enjoy the celebration because of the severe pain. One day I was walking with my friend, Vyacheslav Kleimyonov, a fellow who laughed easily, and we began to laugh for some insignificant reason. Then we purposely started to escalate our laughing and, after a few minutes, we found ourselves laughing almost hysterically. Five more minutes or so passed and we were still laughing, but when we tried to slow down, it was difficult to stop this intense laughing. We managed to end it somehow and I suddenly found myself with the thought that I had forgotten the pain--it had disappeared. After some time, it came back again, but it was distinct proof for me that laughter can relieve pain.

When I was working at the research institute in Moscow, our working day quite often started with laughter from telling anecdotes. The most popular were political jokes. In the Stalin era, telling political anecdotes could be life-threatening, but during the Brezhnev and Gorbachev eras, it was not that dangerous. People in the office or in the smoking areas were often seen telling anecdotes and laughing. Arnold Fine in *The Jewish Press* published the following joke with a Russian theme:

A Russian was awakened at four in the morning by a loud knock at his door.
"Who is it?" he cried.
"The mailmen," two KGB agents answered. "Are you Comrade Boris?"
"Y-y-y-y-es."

"Is it true, comrade, that you've requested permission to leave our wonderful country? Aren't you happy here?"

"Of course I am."

"Then why is it that you want to leave?"

"Because," Boris answered, "I just want to see what it's like to live in a country where they don't deliver mail at four in the morning!"

This could have happened in the 1970s, in the middle of Brezhnev's rule, I suppose, but it was impossible to say something like that and get away with it in the "Joe the Terrible" times. Merely saying that one wanted to leave the country could result in twenty-five years in jail. Fortunately, the times have changed and nobody came to my door at four in the morning when I requested permission to emigrate from the USSR in 1989.

There are centenarians who consider laughter as an important factor in achieving a long life.

One of them is a Japanese woman, Matsuo Todome, 100, who possesses a light character and is called a "ha-ha-ha" centenarian. She attributes their longevity to the sweets that she likes, good sleep, and frequent laughter.

Two others are American comedians Hal Roach and George Burns, the laughter centenarians. "The barrel-chested and very robust Hal Roach (January 14, 1892 - November 2, 1992) and the diminutive, soft-spoken George Burns (January 20, 1896 - March 9, 1996) couldn't have been more different from each other in terms of physical appearance, stature, and achievements. For what they lacked in differences, they easily made up for in a shared trait: they loved to laugh and enjoyed making others laugh as well. It has been said of them that 'laughter made them the kings of longevity' in a ruthless and highly competitive place (Hollywood), not known for having too many centenarians around," wrote John Heinermann, Ph.D., in his book *Heinerman's Encyclopedia of Anti-Aging Remedies*.

Do the oldest people experience stresses in their lives? Of course they do. Consider, for example, the Caucasian shepherds who encounter fear and anxiety when a wolf attacks the sheep they pasture. The first time, it is a great stress, but when it occurs for the second and third time, they feel much less fear--they are already used to this ordeal. Thus, their lives are low-stress for most of the time.

Among the physical exercises that are useful in handling emotions, the "Rocking on the Back" exercise is found to be helpful when one feels down. It is described in detail in the *Activity Control (Exercise)* chapter.

There are many ways to handle emotions, but I want to emphasize *meditation* as an incredibly profound method. By meditating for just a few minutes a day, one can achieve health, pacify emotions, and grow spiritually. Because of its still nature, meditation suits elderly people perfectly, especially during recovery from an illness. In dealing with stress-related disorders and diseases such as depression, insomnia, asthma, and eczema, meditation is found to be very effective. A few meditation techniques were discussed in the *Activity Control (Exercise)* chapter; here, I want to add that the meditation technique is different depending on the Ayurvedic dosha type of a person. "*Vata* types need chanting or mantras. *Pitta* types are visually oriented and should meditate with visualization techniques. *Kapha* types are smell- and taste-oriented and should use incense or flowers," says Dr. Sodhi. With my predominant Vata dosha, I start my day by listening to and singing "Credo" (Prayer), by the Russian composer Gretchaninov, which I believe would please my deceased mother.

25

THOUGHT CONTROL

There is nothing either good or bad, but thinking makes it so.
--William Shakespeare

Do we control our thoughts or do our thoughts control us?--that is the question. Certainly, everyone wants to be a master of his/her thoughts--why be a slave if it is possible to be a king or queen. Thoughts have great power, and to become the ruler of that power is an attractive motive for everyone. Whether one's mind is his/her true friend, companion, and interpreter in life or his/her tyrant and torturer depends on the attitude one takes toward it--on how hard they worked to inform it, train it, and make it clear, obedient, and decisive. The true attitude toward the mind is to perceive and make it one's flexible tool and instrument. The ideal relationship with the mind can be compared to the master who walks ahead and the dog (i.e., mind)--trained, obedient, and cute--follows behind.

This does not mean that we have to take away all the power from any kind of thought. We have a wide spectrum of thoughts during a day, ranging sometimes from tyrannous and demanding to little funny fancies, fears, and worries. Immediately after awakening, we think about what we have to do and what is the first task. While doing it, we will probably remember that we promised to call somebody, or we have to pay a bill, write a letter, and so on. Perhaps we have a problem and we will think about how to solve it. We turn on the TV, where the "Juice Man" is advertising a new juice machine, exclaiming how healthy and robust he is from drinking carrot juice, and we will think, "I should start the juice therapy too." We then may remember a pleasant event associated with carrots, and smile to ourselves. Or if the crime news reaches our ears, we may think about the dangerous surroundings and worry about our daughter who will take a late commuter train tonight--and so on without end. Hundreds if not thousands of thoughts arise in our minds every day.

Modern psychology holds that the mind, which is responsible for thought, feelings, and volition, is associated with the functional aspect of the brain. The brain is a tool of the mind, which is a mode of how the thoughts are organized. *The Concise Oxford Dictionary's* definition of "thought" is the process or power of thinking; the faculty of reason. "Mind" is defined as a seat of consciousness, thought, volition, and feeling. Also, the mind is associated with the intellect, intellectual powers, memory, and remembrance. Furthermore, the mind is defined as a way of thinking or feeling, the focus of one's thoughts or desires, and the state of normal mental functioning. The definition of "brain" is an organ of soft nervous tissue contained in the skull, functioning as the coordination center of sensation and of intellectual and nervous activity.

Psychologists Bruner, Oliver, and Greenfield say that thought can be considered as a "language of the brain." They distinguish three modes of thought: (1) prepositional thought in the form of the stream of sentences like an audible language, that we seem to "hear in our mind"; (2) imaginable thought that is associated with images, a sort of visual language, which we are able to "see in our mind"; and (3) motor thought, which is assigned to sequences of "mental movements." These modes of thought are reflections of internal representations derived from our auditory, visual, and kinesthetic sensations, with which we experience the world. They are fed by three of the five senses—sound, sight, and touch.

Why do we need to control our thoughts? Because uncontrolled thoughts, such as wishing for life to be different, condemning others or our destiny of miseries, regrets, sadness of losing, and so on, lead us to nothing but suffering. Uncontrolled thoughts tend also to shift to negative thinking about events and other people. "Now, if we let our thinking go uncontrolled, we can find much to dislike in almost anyone. By the same token, if we manage our thinking properly, if we think right toward people, we can find many qualities to like and admire in the same person," according to David J. Schwartz, Ph.D., in his best-selling book, *The Magic of Thinking Big*.

However, just as we find it difficult to control our bodywork and movements, thought control is a much more difficult and challenging task in our lives. "Control of physical actions begins in infancy. As the physical body increasingly comes under control, so the role of the mind is enhanced. Yet people all too easily assume that they cannot control their thoughts, although learning to control the brain and to use the mind constructively is the greatest adventure in life," says Howard Kent in his book, *The Complete Yoga Course*. As far as I know, a Hatha yogi apprentice devotes the first fifteen to twenty years of his life to master and control his body; then the Raja yoga or mind control starts for him. "Because the karmic slavery of human beings is rooted in the desires of maya-darkened minds, it is with mind control that yogi concerns himself," said Paramahansa Yogananda.

The point of interest is whether our mind is a thought broadcasting station or receiving device. Dr. Schwartz holds that our mind is a mental broadcasting station that transmits messages to us on two equally powerful channels: Channel P (positive) and Channel N (negative). It seems to me that both functions--thought generation and thought receiving--are present in our mind. Most people in most cases receive thoughts, but some people generate thoughts, and are known as generators of ideas.

The American artist and writer, Morris J. Spivak, who was ninety-five when I met him in Iceland in 1997, said the following in his manuscript, *The Vital Correlations Classification System,* about thought generation: "Thought radiates in the mind in all directions, from stimulation centers--each thought (sensation) is thus given an opportunity to explore the entire range of memory (impaired impressions of previous impacts)." Our brain can both receive and generate not only thoughts but also emotions.

Is our brain the only organ in which thinking or feeling activity takes place? Where does the "physiology of thoughts or emotions"occur? Experts in brain research distinguish between the "thinking brain" (i.e., the neocortex, a thin outer layer of the brain) and the "feeling brain" (i.e., the limbic system, which rests on top of the brain stem). Most of us, together with experts, believe that it is the brain, but some think that the heart, liver, or blood cells also may be involved. "Your immune cells and endocrine glands are outfitted with the same receptors for brain signals as your neurons are; therefore, they are like an extended brain," says Dr. Deepak Chopra in his book, *Ageless Body, Timeless Mind.* Our eyes also are the extended brain, brought outside and displayed on our face.

Thoughts are material bodies and--like radio and TV waves--they flow inside us, through us, and everywhere in the space around us. We cannot see them, but there are people with channeling abilities who can see thoughts.

One of them is my yoga teacher, Eugene Bazh, who now resides in Moscow. It was about twelve years ago when he happened to visit me at the research institute where I worked. I had a separate room, so we sat and talked. I do not remember the exact theme of our conversation, but I was about to ask him a tricky question when he said, "You're about to ask me a bad question; I just saw an unpleasant-looking thought, brown in color, fly into your head." I was startled because it was the absolute truth. I confessed that I was going to ask him a ticklish question.

There are numerous energy fields, including magnetic, ultrasound, and infrared, that vibrate in the environment and are hidden from us; the thought field is one of them. According to a theory by Professor M. Nalimov, of Moscow University, thoughts are the *continual flows of consciousness,* which exists outside of us somewhere in the environment. Rupert Sheldrake, a biological scientist, suggested for a wide range of living organisms--from slime molds to people--"an existence of interwoven fields of influence." They are "pervading the whole universe, which record all the subtle shades of form and behavior pattern ever adopted anywhere by individuals of every species and variant of organism," as Dr. Peter Mansfield describes them. Sheldrake called them *fields of formative causation;* Dr. Mansfield called them interwoven *fields of influence.*

Our thinking mechanism, our memory, is just some special pattern of vibrations that attracts thoughts from these flows, due to the law of resonance. Edgar Cayce, the American "sleeping prophet of Virginia Beach," called them *river of thoughts.* That is what Carl Jung called the *collective unconscious,* meaning a level of the mind where all people were one, and that it was impersonal, transpersonal, and the source of all that evolves in the conscious mind. In her book, *The Power of Your Dreams,* Soozi Holbeche says that the writer and explorer Laurens van der Post, who knew Jung well, described the unconscious as "a great area of unknown spirit and awareness in man which remains the same for all, regardless of race or creed. In all human beings, there is such an area in which the whole of life participates, as it were, mystically."

Carl Jung formulated his idea of the collective unconscious based on his observations of schizophrenic patients in the hospital where he worked. He discovered that many hallucinations and delusions of people suffering from this mental illness had similar themes--in most cases, they corresponded to the major world religions, ancient myths, and legends. "To Jung, the collective unconscious contained the wisdom of the ages. He believed that the more attuned to it man was, through dreams, visions, and active imagination, the more balanced, integrated, and happy his life and personality would be," according to Holbeche. Jung's collective unconsciousness, Nalimov's continual flows of consciousness, Cayce's river of thought, and Sheldrake's fields of formative causation are all similar to the Akashic Records--the nebulous vibrational archives on which everything, including each person's deeds and thoughts and feelings from the beginning of time, are recorded. They are not merely figments of a fertile imagination, although they are "quite incomprehensible as material quantities. They need to be explored, lived by, and checked for validity in your personal experience; there is no other way you can prove or believe in them," according to Dr. Mansfield. One kind of fascinating vibration structures, which can make useful sense if someone believes in them, is the concept of the *egregore*.

Egregore (Egrigor)

The term "egregore" may sound disturbing to some people. Some recent Internet occult contributors colored it with dark colors. I do not consider myself to be New Age adept, but I do not see anything fearful in egregores. However, if this is the case for you, please take it as a metaphor.

Egregore is a thought form, often created in magical ceremonies by the combined "will" or visualization powers of the participants. A similar definition is found in the *Encyclopedia of Occultism and Parapsychology*, by Leslie A. Shepard, Ed., where egregore is explained as a folklore term denoting a collective ritual of primitive societies in order to accumulate group magical energy for successful hunting, rain–making, or harvests. Occultists have used the term to denote an astral entity evoked by group energies.

Eliphas Levi calls the egregores "the chiefs of the souls who are the spirits of energy and action." The Oriental Occultists describe the egregores as beings whose bodies and essence comprise a tissue of so-called astral light. They are the shadows of the higher planetary spirits whose bodies and essence consist of the higher divine light, as described by H.P. Blavatsky in her book, *Theosophical Glossary*. According to the psychic Ted Serious, if thought forms are projected forcibly enough, they can leave an image on photographic film.

The simplified definition of egregores assigns them a role of distinctive energy expanses (niche, reservoir) that are formed due to mental (energetic) bonds of the similar mentalities of people concentrated on the same image. For this discussion, we will use egregore as meaning the *energy-information structure* that is built by people's accumulated *thoughts* intensified due to the resonance law to form the "thought cloud."

For example, physicians and folk healers of all times and nations have thought about how to cure and prevent the diseases of people in the best way: remedies, drugs, surgeries, herbs, healthy food, lifestyle, and so on. Their thoughts have formed the "medical egregore," which exists in an astral plane. In a physical plane, the World Health Organization was established in 1948 with the purpose of helping all people to attain the highest possible level of health. However, the medical thought on earth has existed from the beginning of time and its body is the "medical egregore." Doctors and healers around the world are its members, although the overwhelming majority of them have not the slightest idea about that. Nevertheless, each member of this invisible organization exchanges energy and information with an egregore.

Similarly, there are egregores regarding various professions, religions, nations, peoples' beliefs, skills, interests, habits, states, emotions, desires, and so forth. For instance, a person is a carpenter, Christian, Italian, believes that a glass of red wine with his meal is good for his health, is skillful in playing the accordion, is interested in women, has a habit of smoking, and likes to joke and laugh. This person belongs to the corresponding egregores and participates in an energy exchange with these thought structures. Let's say, for example, his doctor said his gout ailment is due to red wine and he should quit drinking. He tries, but after a few days he goes back to his habit because the egregore of drinking opposes his attempt to stop supplying it with energy. He will find many excuses to fall back into the addiction, but all of them were induced by the egregore, which keeps him tight and not willing to release and let go.

When we age, we often find the annoying and disappointing signs on our face and body: another wrinkle, more gray hair, the skin on our elbows is flabby and not elastic anymore, and so on. The chain of other unpleasant thoughts begins: we are becoming unattractive, the opposite sex will never love us again, we are becoming really old, and so on. These self-humiliating thoughts actually have little in common with reality. Attitude is what is really important. The American comedian, George Burns, who lived to be 100 years old, was asked about the secrets of his vigor, prosperity, and longevity. He answered in one word, "Attitude. If you have a problem getting a twenty-two-year-old girl, get a twenty-four-year-old," he wrote when he was eighty-six years young.

Many kinds of negative as well as positive thinking have corresponding egregores, and we can belong to certain kinds of them. Let us discuss first the egregores of negative thinking, such as dependence, worry, internal dialogue, and unrealistic desires. The egregores of positive thinking and attitude include happiness, joy, love, and friendship.

Egregore of Dependence

If we think for ourselves, we are free and independent. Unfortunately, most of us are dependent on others throughout our lives. As a child, we are dependent on our parents and tutors; as a teenager, on teachers; as an adult, on bosses, spouses, children, and family members; as we grow older, on doctors, accountants, club leaders, and whoever's advice we follow. Nothing is wrong with moderate dependence, which is valid in this case being the reality of life; what is bad is overdependence.

Now imagine that there is a thought-form organization, an egregore of dependence, with all the necessary hierarchy: president; general managers; departments of parents, bosses, and doctors; and managers in each department. You are an active member of this organization and donate your thought energy to it together with other dependents like yourself. It was established thousands of years ago and there was a master (for slaves and serfs) department too, but it gradually shrank and recently was abolished. The egregore of dependence was small at first, but now it is a huge corporation and the number of its members is increasing. What kind of payback can you get in return for your donations? It would be a box of dependence, nicely packaged with a bright ribbon. This is because each of the egregore's departments also has production and distribution units, and their products are various sorts of dependence. A good deal, isn't it? The more you pay, the more dependent you become--a sad story, actually.

Now you are grown up and want to decrease your donations to the parents department of this egregore. However, the egregore feels quite comfortable to regularly receive your energy and opposes your decision. In some families, people are dependent on their parents their entire life. When the parents grow old and lose their decisive powers, they could try to influence you with their advice. To shorten this story, it is simply not wise to be stuck to the egregore of dependence and to be its perpetual victim.

What is the possible escape? Take a one- or three-day fast. By this time, you will have joined the egregore of fasting (for a novice)--a very powerful egregore--which helps cut ties to undesirable egregores. More than that, it will send you a parcel containing a health-improvement kit, where you will find items to cleanse vital organs, increase digestive powers, and strengthen the immune and other systems. Or just send your thought-energy donation to the *egregore of laughter*, watching your favorite comedies.

I do not expect you to believe in the concept of egregore; this information is probably too sudden for you and you cannot accept it at once. Even if you are inclined to, the *egregore of doubt* will not allow you. However, if the idea of an egregore were helpful in lessening your dependence, I would feel happy (and would readily pay the bill of the *egregore of happiness*).

Do centenarians belong to the egregore of dependence? Not many, really. Certainly those who are disabled, wheelchair-bound, and with impaired sight and hearing depend on their relatives or nurses who take care of them. The world's oldest woman, Jeanne Calment who lived to 122 years old, and oldest man, Christian Mortensen who died at the age of 115, lived their final years in a nursing home or sheltered home and were dependent on their doctors and nurses. However, Frank Shomo, who died at the age of 108, and the Japanese twin sisters Kin Narita (who died in January 2000 at the age of 107) and Gin Kanie, 108, were self-sufficient in their major life-supporting activities. Moreover, the Japanese twins said that one of their mottos is to avoid paying much attention to what other people say. If we give a lot of attention to the opinions of others around us, we automatically become dependent on them.

Egregore of Worry

Perhaps there is no one who does not worry at all. Because we live in a society, many of our worries are caused by relationships with others. We doubt whether we acted or treated people right; we worry about our children, security, and financial problems; we are afraid to lose face, love, or friendship; and so on. We also worry about our health and are fearful of becoming ill and dying. Most of the national proverbs have something to say about worries. A Russian proverb says, "The anticipated fears are worse than real ones." The great thinkers, writers, and sages also expressed their thoughts about worries and fears. "The only thing we have to fear is fear itself," said Franklin D. Roosevelt. "Fear destroys the winged life," wrote Anne Morrow Lindberg in her book, *Gift from the Sea*. According to Joan Borysenko, the great sage who writes teabag aphorisms, "Worry is the interest paid on a debt before it comes due."

We mostly worry about past or future events--often anguishing about things that have happened, we keep saying to ourselves, "I shouldn't have said those foolish words, what a disgrace" or "If only I had fully focused on it." Or perhaps we fret about things that could happen: "My boss will be disappointed after he has found that I know little about this matter." Why do these upsetting thoughts invade our mind? It is because we do not live here and now. When we worry about the past or future, God punishes us because we violate the major principle of the Universe: "Be here and now." So He sentences us to be attached to the *egregore of worry* and to pay its bills. This egregore has the departments of fear, doubt, hesitation, regret, loss, humiliation, trouble, problems, and others. Like any other egregore, the egregore of worry in return pays us back with the bags of worry. We repeat the vicious cycle.

How can we break down this cycle, to detach from being chained to the egregore of worry? There are a few ways to do that; one of the best ways is to leave the problem alone and let it solve itself. Most problems are self-created, we create them for ourselves, but they also tend to be solved on their own. We sometimes just need to *wait* and let their energy dissipate. "If you can wait and not be tired by waiting..." says Rudyard Kipling in his poem "If." So, you readdress your thought donation to the *egregore of waiting,* right? It is not easy but if you are persistent, you'll succeed. Another great *egregore, the egregore of faith,* is ready to accept you as a permanent member.

There is the saying, "Faith can move mountains." In any of your problems--health, the well-being of your loved ones, security, financial troubles--you can rely on God as well as on yourself. God created us, took care of and maintained us to this day, and He will take care of our health, our problems, and every detail of our life in the future. God is loving, friendly, trustworthy, and blissful, and helps us in all our moments. With faith in God, all difficult moments can be turned into blessings and joy. Faith and prayer are the paths to God.

There are many examples of when God took care of the health of the oldest people. I was deeply impressed by the interview with Edna Olson, 100, which was described in the book, *Ageless Body, Timeless Mind*, by Dr. Deepak Chopra. She said, "I was only about two years old when God spoke to me. He told me he was God and He wanted me to believe in Him, and He said, 'I will take care of you.' And He has. He said, 'Don't tell your mother yet. She'll just say you're a silly child and you don't know what you're talking about. I will send you dreams.' And God did send me dreams in the morning--before I woke up--and they would always be true dreams. They would tell me what I should do. That's how I've lived my whole life."

Many centenarians believe that they achieved their age because they deeply believed in God.

> Trust in God, honesty, and hard work are the secrets of longevity, according to Lee Ying, 100, from Ipoh, Malaysia, as reported in the April 3, 1998, issue of the *Sun Newspaper*.

> Lula Bell Mack, 100, from Selma, Alabama, told how she got so old, "Treating people right, and having good thoughts of people, and trust in God," reports Jim Heynen in his book, *One Hundred over 100*.

> Another centenarian interviewed in this book was Julia Preston, 101, from Oakland, California, who said, "The Lord let me live. When I was 100, I asked the Lord to let me live to get another one. Now I ask for one more."

When asked for advice, the third centenarian, Bessie Hubbard, answered, "But the only advice that's worthwhile is about Jesus. I obey Jesus. He tells what to do and where to go. Living with Jesus, I never got tired."

A Japanese American, Sadaichi Kuzuhara, 100, told Jim Heynen during the interview, "I am a happy man. Wherever I go, the Lord has guided me." He converted from Buddhism to Christianity and founded eleven churches in Los Angeles and other places.

"God helped me," said Philip Eastburg, 100. "I believe in guardian angels. They have watched over me and kept me alive," reports Jim Heynen. Two other centenarians in this book attributed their longevity to their faith in God too.

"Trust in the Lord, and don't drink alcohol--it ruins your system," were the wise words of Jackson Pollard, 100. "When young people ask me for advice, I tell them to get in touch with the Lord," said Jack Goodenough, 100, from Boise, Idaho.

There are many other centenarians who allegedly rely on God.

However, back to the discussion of worry--it seems that everything is not so plain with worry. It is not universally bad and even can be used for good. If this is so, how can worrying help? The point is that worry can be of two types: conscious and unconscious. With unconscious worry, you are stuck to the egregore of worry, to its harmful part. With conscious worry, you do not burden your body and mind any more, you just play with worry. In this case, the worrying becomes beneficial. Paula Levine, Ph.D., says, "You don't really want to keep worrying, but you think you can't help it. Some people believe that their worrying keeps awful things from happening. They really think that if they were to stop worrying, awful things would happen. The worriers feel...like they're doing something about it." Joan Borysenko, Ph.D., in her book, *Minding the Body, Mending the Mind,* acknowledges this phenomenon, saying, "Some become superstitious, with worrying becoming a talisman that prevents bad things from happening."

Theory of Destruction of an Unwanted Event

Actually, I feel that I am that kind of superstitious worrier myself. I will try to explain how this *something* works in my understanding. I call it the *Theory of Destruction of an Unwanted Event.* This speculation implies that each and every event or thing that happens has its unseen reason, latent form, and apparent material shape. The whole event needs a certain amount of energy for its embodiment, which is designed somewhere in the upper spheres. There is also a sequence of five stages in which the event is prepared, developed, and cast on the scene to occur:

1. intention (of a Super Mind or Supreme Power) for that thing/event to happen

2. thought images on the future event

3. words discussing an idea and putting it on paper

4. detailed plan with involvement of place, schedule, participating parties, and so forth

5. implementation of the event

Each stage consumes its own portion of energy. Along the way, the energy thickens, starting from a very thin form at the intention stage and becoming denser up to the appearance of the event itself in a thick material form. If the energy was distributed properly among these stages and suitably used at each stage, the thing/event happens smoothly. However, too much energy could be wasted at any of the earlier stages. Then, the later stages are left lacking or without any energy, and the entire enterprise fails to occur. Nothing was born, the event did not happen. It's interesting to note that there are Russian proverbs related to this explanation. One proverb says, "Many words but little deeds"; another is similar: "All the energy was used up in a whistle" (like in a steam engine). Whistle means empty words--many words were said in vain, but nothing has been done.

However, it is the thought-image stage and dissipation of energy that is employed in conscious worrying.

> For example, I stood in line to buy a ticket to the Bolshoi Theatre in Moscow. The seller announced that not many tickets were left and my chances of getting one became obscure. However, I was eager to see this performance because it was "Aida," my favorite opera by Verdi. In previous experiences, many times tickets were sold out just before my turn and I considered myself unlucky with tickets. However, that time I pushed my mind to work in conscious worrying. On the screen in my forehead I imagined myself going back home by subway a few minutes later having failed to get into the theatre and greatly disappointed. Meanwhile, in the current reality, I was getting closer to the window and I was able to buy the much-wanted ticket. I was lucky that night and I enjoyed the arias, music, and scenes of the opera. The difference was that I prevented the undesired event–my failure to buy the concert ticket–from happening.
>
> This technique worked for me many times. My friend David Michalev, a prominent Russian dissident, once asked me how I managed so smoothly in a multi-step procedure to get an entry visa to Israel for my emigration. I replied, "I worked on it." He knew it was impossible "to work" on a visa and he insisted that I explain. I explained but he just shrugged his shoulders--he did not believe me. It sounded like nonsense to him.

Although this kind of "negative meditation" works for me, it does not mean that it will work for everybody. I asked many people how it happened in their case; some said that they get what they pictured, the desired event, in their imagination directly. Perhaps for most people, "positive meditation" might be more helpful. For myself and some others, the opposite works. My daughter Victoria asked me once to explain why reality is sometimes different than what she expected. If she imagines all the details of an anticipated meeting with someone, a trip, or another event, it does not happen as she wanted. Something has been interrupted and something goes wrong. She noticed, however, that if she does not allow herself to think about the desired event, immediately shifting her thoughts to other things, the actual event happens in a way that she wanted. When I explained to her in terms of the *Theory of Destruction of an Unwanted Event*, she seemed to agree with it and to accept that her working method is probably the "negative meditation" too.

> While working in Tokyo for a Japanese company for five years, I proved the workability of this approach many times. If I anticipated the worst scenario happening, it actually was not so bad. On the contrary, if I relaxed and told myself, "Everything is okay, all is under control, you are doing better than you expected, don't worry in vain," immediately--as if I tested God's patience--events could turn on me. There were times when the pressure of the work was so intense that I had to work until midnight and even half the night. I lost a lot of weight, looked ugly, and really worried about my health. To cheer myself up, I remember I wrote the following words on a poster hanging on the wall in my room: "Don't crash under the pressure, Valery, don't crash." In my usual manner, I imagined then how I could collapse soon and go to the hospital and my Japanese friends would visit me. Soon after, however, the job was somehow simplified and then completed; I survived without going to the hospital.

Another kind of thought work in which my mind is engaged is a "firm decision." As soon as I decide to do something on a regular basis, be it another set of exercises, self-massage, or before-sleep meditation, dozens of reasons immediately arise about why I cannot fit these new practices into my routine--as if my body, my other selves, all resist against the firm decision, whatever it is. So, I avoid announcing to myself a strict verdict, and rather try to implement it quietly, step by step, without noisy internal debates. In this case, I somehow manage to force my mind to accept it "de facto." Although I was very busy last summer with this book, I gradually included into my morning routine going barefooted to the nearby lake to swim, then morning yoga exercises and a short meditation, before lunch a couple of strength or aerobic exercises, and before dinner flexibility exercises. Because there were plenty of raspberries and blueberries in the woods near the town of Rome,

Maine--"tons" as the local people say--I also went to pick them two or three times a week after lunch. Nobody picked them but me, so they were all mine. My mind does not object to berries, although there were lots of mosquitoes and I was bitten repeatedly. Mixed berries with a tablespoon of sour cream is a favorite dish before breakfast and before dinner.

Egregore of Internal Dialogue

An internal dialogue is going on in our heads non-stop all seventeen or eighteen hours that we are awake. It is the most intense when we are doing something automatically, like cooking, washing the dishes, walking, and so on. Even when we are talking with other people, it is spinning in our minds. Many times we are embarrassed because of its interruption, such as forgetting someone's name right after we are introduced, forgetting the names of locations soon after they were told to us, having trouble remembering the items we were asked to buy on our errands, just to name a few. Each time our attention was drawn away because of an internal dialogue going on at that particular moment. "This thinking goes on without our awareness; you are 'lost in thought' and are not 'present' with what is actually going on," according to Joan Borysenko.

This can become a real issue, especially while dealing with other people. We actually do not know how to hear our counterparts when we talk to them. Half or more of their words we do not hear because we are just waiting for a pause in their speech to insert our own comment. It's not that severe when we are alone, but is still troubling if we cannot fall asleep because of our thoughts participating in a noisy internal dialogue.

The relationship with the egregore of internal dialogue is similar to what we discussed previously: we send him our thought energy, part of our life force obtained from our "humanly impossible efforts"; in return, we receive more themes for internal dialogue. We will be busy again, engaged in this daydreaming and missing the life that is passing by. How can we put ourselves into "here and now" with all that distraction?

To start with, we first have to become aware that the internal dialogue is going on in our mind. If you manage to catch it and start to listen to what these thoughts say to each other, they fall silent as if their conversation is secret from you. Following are a few more methods to stop the internal dialogue:

• Yoga teachers advise meditation; according to Harish Johari, the visualization of the god Ganesha helps to stop the internal dialogue.

• Don Juan advised Carlos Castaneda to watch the horizon, not focusing on any particular object.

• In a quiet place, bring all your attention to the surroundings available to your vision, at the top, bottom, and both sides. Try to see all the details and not concentrate your sight on any particular object; at the same time try to hear all the sounds around you, loud and soft, whispers, rustles, any ringing in your ears, and so on.

• Become physically tired before going to bed.

• Bring your breathing to the center of your attention, counting the seconds for inhaling, exhaling, and breath holds.

• The success philosopher Anthony Robbins suggests turning down the volume of voices heard in your head, making them softer, weaker, and farther away.

• Travel inside your body--along the digestive tract and the respiration and circulation systems, and so forth.

• Use meditation and especially the visualization exercise mentioned in the chapter about Xu Fang (first day), also described in the *Activity Control (Exercise)* chapter.

Egregore of Unrealistic Desires

Many sufferings come from dissatisfaction with our present life, with our health, with what we have or do not have. It is in human nature to not value what we have now, to envy others, to think that if we were in their place we would feel better. Alexander Pushkin, a great Russian poet, expressed this human nature in one of his verses: "...The heart lives in the future, the present is boring." Dissatisfaction and discontent are the engines of progress; it is a good side of them. However, we are talking now on how we perceive our life, family, surroundings, and so on. Are we realistic or not? "Proper assessment of reality can be as crucial to life as oxygen. To try to make it through this world without reasonable understanding of reality is like stumbling around in a dark room laden with land mines," according to Robert J. Ringer in his best-selling book, *Looking Out for #1.* He defines a realist as a person who believes in basing his life on facts and who dislikes anything that seems imaginary, impractical, theoretical, or utopian. However, I think imagery can be realistic as a meditation technique and theoretical exercises may actually help in enhancing the brain against deterioration.

The root of suffering is in desires, say the philosophies of Yoga and Buddhism. However, we live in the Western world, where desires are welcomed. The only problem is that we are impatient and, like children, we want our dreams to become true immediately. This is a part of my nature too; my mother called me the "take it out and put it on" boy. When I was a schoolboy, if I wanted something, I wanted it furiously and immediately.

Impatience with health problems is another root of unhappiness. A person violates the laws of nature for decades by overeating, drinking, smoking, a sedentary lifestyle, and getting angry or fearful. When he/she inevitably becomes sick, he/she wants an immediate cure. That is why Western medicine--with its operations and magic pills--is so popular. In a few days or weeks, one can rush back to his/her pleasures and enjoy life in that way until the next illness. Natural healing methods need effort and time; therefore, they are regarded as somewhat exclusive.

To be on the loose end of the egregore of unrealistic desires, one has to become aware of a few universal laws of nature and then follow them:

• The Law of Patience: Be patient; it took time for you to get into trouble, it will take time to get rid of the trouble. Nature has its own schedule and waiting list.

• The Conformity Law: Everyone deserves his/her conditions, his/her relationships, his/her treatment. Children deserve their parents and parents deserve their children; a wife deserves her husband and vice versa; people deserve their government, the government deserves its people; one deserves conditions he/she lives in and the conditions deserve him/her; and so on. If a person wants to radically change his/her life, he/she has to make extra efforts such as remarriage, second divorce, selling the yacht and buying the plane, retirement, or immigration.

• The Law of Payment: Every pleasure in life has a price tag attached to it. More than money, health is often involved. We often pay with our health for the minute pleasures; however, we cannot buy it. The only way to gain health is to earn it with conscious, regular, and steady efforts. This law is profoundly expressed in *The Wild Ass's Skin*, a novel by Honore de Balzac. The Balzacian idea of human will is expressed by the symbol of the magic piece of chagrin. This is a drama of the choice between ruthless self-satisfaction and moderation, between vice and virtue, between the waste of life force and restraint.

• The Law of Teaching Troubles: Any trouble gives us the chance to become more conscious and aware and to take another step on our path of mental and spiritual evolution. This does not mean that we have to seek troubles. "Don't trouble troubles until troubles trouble you," says a wise proverb. However, when they happen in our life, we should better take them as a challenge. "Blessed is the man whom the Lord doth test! He has remembered, now and then, to put a burden on me," said Paramahansa Yogananda.

Another helpful instrument is understanding one's true role in the world and in his/her own life. People tend to exaggerate their role in their own destiny, relying on their will power. However, free will and predestation are proportioned in most people as one to four. Some metaphysical traditions associate free will with the thumb and predestination with the other four fingers of the hand. For the most part, our lives are largely predetermined, whether or not we deny it. Here is the proof. Vanga, a famous Bulgarian fortuneteller, was known to foretell future events in a person's life, sometimes years ahead, with an accuracy greater than 80 percent that was documented many times by researchers. During her fortune telling for more than sixty years, more than a hundred thousand people worldwide visited her (up to thirty people a day). For events to occur, each of these individual's lives is influenced by the dozens of other people with whom they interact. Other people, in their turn, are connected with yet dozens more, and so on. To accurately predict one individual's future events, Vanga would have be able to foresee the future of all mankind. And she did. This means that the destiny book for mankind that she was reading is already written. The insights, discoveries, or prophetic dreams that many of us have also confirm that our lives are largely predetermined.

Does this mean that we can do nothing, just sit and wait for our destiny to unfold? Not at all, there is a great deal we can do. The higher the level of consciousness on which we operate, the greater proportion is our free will. We can make our average 20 percent of free will equal to 100 percent and acquire the freedom of gods, or we can lose them and turn ourselves into slaves (or prisoners). Thus, the solution is in understanding our real place in the universe, the power of the unseen, the limits set for us, and the conscious efforts needed to progress on the path of intellectual and spiritual growth.

Egregore of Happiness

Egregores of positive thinking such as happiness and satisfaction do not need much to campaign, because the problem is to loosen your ties with the negative egregores. As soon as you manage to achieve that, you enter almost automatically into the egregore of happiness. Many centenarians love this egregore. This is what David Kane, 102, a painter from New York City, said during his interview with Jim Heynen: "Enjoy whatever you see of nature that we didn't create. Look at the sky! Look at the clouds! Look at the water! Look at the trees! I say, 'Be grateful.'"

Mind Tricks

The human mind is very creative, either working as our ally or trying to take advantage of us. A Russian proverb says, "The clever man will not climb the mountain, the clever man will make a detour around the mountain." This folk wisdom means that a clever or intelligent person will search for an easier way to get to the other side of the mountain, rather than burden the body, to steam up in vain. It follows from this saying that it is not wise to climb uphill and then descend the mountain. At the time this proverb was created, perhaps many centuries ago, the people led a heavy labored life. They were so tired with their field or site work that they would consider one a fool who did unnecessary physical exertions, which are unpleasant and cause discomfort to the body. Times have changed and nowadays many people are engaged in hiking, mountaineering, and even rock-climbing. These are good aerobic exercises that train the heart, lungs, and circulation system; cleanse the body of toxins through sweating; strengthen the immune system; and enhance the senses by seeing nice views of nature, listening to bird songs, and smelling the aromas of greenery. However, the point is that the mind rejects any activities that lead to body exertion and fatigue.

It is said that the entire technological progress in the world for the last two thousand years occurred due to the desire of the mind for comfort and pleasures. This is due to the mind's urge to have tasteful food, sleep, and sex in abundance while also avoiding troubles by decreasing and even eliminating physical strains. Currently, in highly developed countries, most labors are put on the shoulders of machines and the only thing people have to do is push buttons. This is a sure victory of the intellect, which now can enjoy the pleasures of life with minimal unpleasant body efforts. However, nothing in this life, pleasures included, is acquired without a price. Everything that we get from the world has a price tag attached to it. The worst thing is that we must pay for mind tricks with our health and years of our life.

The Yoga Approach to Thought Control and Purification

• *Yama* includes nonviolence, truth, honesty, sexual continence, forbearance, fortitude, kindness, straightforwardness, moderation in diet, and purity (cleansing of the body)

• *Niyama* includes austerity, contentment, belief in God, charity, worship of God, listening to explanations of doctrines/scriptures, modesty, having a discerning mind, repetition of prayers, and sacrifice/performing religious sacrifices

• *Asana,* or the seated posture in which the spine is kept straight, and the neck and head are aligned with the spine. The mind becomes steady if one can sit still and comfortably, without pain, for twenty to thirty minutes. "Posture helps to make the mind calm," says the *Tantrarajatantra* 27, 59. The lotus posture (padmasana) is highly recommended, though it is difficult to attain.

• *Pranayama,* or breathing exercises, means control of prana, which is regarded as a vehicle of the mind. Prana is a vital force and both mind and body cannot function without it. Alternate breathing through the right and left nostrils suspends activities of the brain and mind, and temporarily stops the internal dialogue. "There are two causes that make the mind wander around: (1) Vasanas--desires that are produced by the latent impressions of feelings; and (2) breathing. If one is controlled, the other automatically gets controlled. Of these two, breath should be controlled first," says *Yogakundalyupanishad*, 1, 1-2. The breathing exercises are described in detail in *the Activity Control (Exercise)* chapter.

Mental and Brain Degenerative Diseases

Among the mental diseases are obsessions, phobias, schizophrenia, and manic depression. Recurring thoughts and ideas, which are frightening and distressing, are characteristic of obsessions. Uncontrollable and irrational fear of a situation or an object, such as a fear of heights, the dark, or being alone, is a feature of phobias. Schizophrenia is defined as a mental disease marked by a breakdown in the relationship between thoughts, feelings, and actions, frequently accompanied by delusions and a retreat from social life. In the Middle Ages and among superstitious people nowadays, an insane person is thought to be possessed by evil or, more rarely, good spirits. Perhaps these spirits can enter our body through the gaps in the aura caused by drugs or alcohol. The Kirlian photography of the body parts showed how the aura, which in a normal condition surrounds our body like a protecting shell, can be broken and the gaps appear in it. The cases of sudden violence after alcohol or narcotics use might be explained by this phenomenon. These individuals often do not understand afterward why they behaved violently or even committed crimes against innocent people.

Many elderly people suffer from brain-degenerative diseases including senile dementia, Alzheimer's disease, and Parkinson's disease. Disuse can lead to degeneration of the mind and may be more rapid and hazardous than the disuse of muscles and tendons.

Brain-Enhancing Methods

To prevent brain-degenerative diseases, the following approaches that stimulate the brain or push it to work might be helpful:

• Any kind of activity or skill that involves the fingertips, such as playing the piano or violin, painting, and sculpting. According to the science of hand reflexology, the fingertips are connected to the brain through Chinese channels of energy flow. Thus, pressing the fingertips stimulates the brain. People who play the piano will never have Alzheimer's disease, as was said on a Japanese TV program. Playing the piano stimulates the brain in another way too, since it controls the movements of both hands simultaneously. One Japanese life-extensionist has a pipe organ in his house and plays it regularly. This is even better because controlling the movements of both the hands and feet is a great exercise for the brain.

• Finger massage will do the same job: first massage the fingers of your left hand with the right hand, and then switch. Finger massage is described in detail in the exercise chapter. You can also massage the toes of your feet with your hands, which doubles the stimulating effect because the tips of the toes are also connected to the brain.

• Rolling Chinese copper balls or golf balls in the hands provides a good effect. You can do a variety of finger works by rolling the balls with both hands clockwise and counterclockwise, synchronically and asynchronously.

• Asynchronous body movements are very stimulating for the brain. These include rotating the left shoulder forward and the right shoulder backward and vice versa. Another exercise is moving the legs as if trying to draw circles, with the feet on the floor. The elbows are fixed at the sides and the hands draw circles in the vertical plane. The feet may move in and the hands out and vice versa. If you try some of these movements, you will probably notice in the beginning that something in your brain resists asynchronous movement. If you persist, you will grasp the movement all of a sudden and you will feel as if something in your brain gave up resisting.

• Learning a new foreign language or a new branch of science. In a seminar on successful aging held in December 1997 in Japan, one of the guests advocated studying mathematics as a good mental exercise.

• Exploring a new habit or skill. Each of us has a dream to master something. It is never too late to start and learning a new skill is an interesting and challenging task.

Singing songs is a very promising tool in thought control and achieving longevity. The benefits for the body, emotions, and mind are many; only a few will be discussed herein, including training the lungs, decreasing the respiration rate, accumulating carbon dioxide in the body, and feeling great that you are healthy enough to enjoy the challenge of singing, which includes the vibration of your voice and expecting the applause of your listeners if you are not alone. Be here and now and in harmony with your inner self while training your memory and remembering and reciting the words. Push your brain to work at synchronizing the words, melody, and rhythm, thereby preventing its deterioration. The song or aria for those who love opera music should be your favorite, and is even better if it is from your younger days. Consider the great song "My Way" by Frank Sinatra; I think of this song as a hymn of longevity. Many centenarians would probably find that the lyrics of this song describe their own lives. However, to eliminate some sadness from the beginning of the song, I would rewrite the first two lines as follows:

"And now the end is near"   to   "And I'm living now and here"
"And so I face a final curtain" to   "I do believe in my great fortune."

Also, I would change all the past-tense verbs to the present tense, like "I live," "I travel," "I love," and so on. This revised version seems to me to be entirely optimistic and cheerful. However, to spare the feelings of others who may consider it a violation of the classical text, I would advise singing the new version in private.

Intuition. "Intuition" is defined as immediate comprehension by the mind or by a sense (perception) without reasoning or immediate insight. In *You Are Smarter Than You Think,* John Kord Lagemann says, "Intuition is a way of thinking without words--a shortcut to the truth, and in matters of emotion, the only way of getting there at all. Dr. Carl Jung defines it as 'a basic psychological function that transmits perceptions in an unconscious way.' This perception is based on the evidence of our physical senses. But because it taps knowledge and experience of which we aren't aware, it is often confused with telepathy, clairvoyance, or extrasensory perception."

The unconscious part of our brain never stops working; therefore, when you're faced with a perplexing job, work on it as hard as you can. Then, if you can't overcome it, try sleeping on it or taking a walk or relaxing with friends. If you have primed yourself with all available facts, the answer is likely to "dawn" on you while your mind is seemingly at rest.

In the case of a purely personal decision, the important facts are your own deep feelings, and you know intuitively what to do without preliminary deliberations. Dr. Sigmund Freud once told a friend, "When making a decision of minor importance, I have always found it advantageous to consider all the pros and cons. In vital matters, however, such as the choice of a mate or a profession, the decision should come from the unconscious, from somewhere within us. In the important decisions of our personal lives, we should be governed, I think, by the deep inner needs or our nature." I can attest to this truth from my own experience. There were situations when I acted instantaneously, without giving it a thought, knowing unconsciously that I am doing the right thing--and it was.

Our instinctual reactions to other people, known as first impressions, are also based on intuition. This keen sensibility, which is usually quick and often precise, was developed in the course of evolution to distinguish between friend and foe. I would call it emotional intuition--if there is such a thing--and its sensual point is located in the very center of our chest. My teacher, Eugene Bazh, calls it the "golden center," which, like personal radar, is the most precise instrument in our possession, if we are sensitive enough to it. If we meet a new person who is destined to affect our life, something will stir, pleasant or not, in our golden center. If the sensation is unpleasant, it is our warning to keep away from that person. From my own experience, I know that months later, I would recall this sensation after a business deal or a new relationship has fallen apart.

Intuition is affected with physiology and becomes stronger if the body is detoxified through fasting, cleansing therapies, and a raw-food diet. "When you eat raw plant foods, your instincts become stronger. Your intuition becomes more reliable—clearer—and decision-making becomes effortless," according to David Wolfe in his book, *The Sunfood Diet Success System*.

Forgiveness. Forgiveness of oneself and others is a strong soul-healing therapy, and comes together with the release of hurts stored inside. Hurt is usually caused by other people to whom we are related or with whom we interact. No one, including ourselves, is perfect and other people are often driven by negative emotions when they hurt you. "One should forgive, under any injury," says the Mahabharata. "Forgiveness is holiness; by forgiveness the universe is held together. Forgiveness is the might of the mighty;

forgiveness is sacrifice; forgiveness is quiet of mind. Forgiveness and gentleness are the qualities of the self-possessed. They represent eternal virtue." To hold grudges and carry them around makes your mind uneasy, poisoning your system with bad hormones and causing harm yourself; therefore, not forgiving is actually an irrational and self-harming act. "My reason for being forgiving is pragmatic in nature: it's simply not in my best interest to harbor grudges, particularly toward those from whom I derive pleasure. Forgiving is a rationally selfish action on my part," says Robert J. Ringer in his best-selling book, *Looking Out for # 1.*

In his book, *Something in This Book Is True,"* Bob Frissell equates forgiveness to the art of elimination. As we periodically clean the house, discarding unnecessary garbage, similarly we need to clean our soul through forgiveness. A person overloaded with hurt and resentments resembles a trash box in which others dispose of their negative emotions; there is no room for anything good then. Getting rid of old resentments gives way to let goodness in. The aspiration to offend, punish, or humiliate someone, and hatred of any sort leaves scars in the soul and leads to illnesses of the body. If you are in pain, in trouble, or in debt, forgive. Forgiveness heals any evil. The mind in the state of forgiveness possesses a magnetic power to attract goodness. Forgiveness is almighty; let it in.

You can hear "forgive and forget" advice from many authors of self-help and self-improvement books, including Louise Hay, Bob Frissell, and Katherine Ponder. Although in complete agreement with the forgiving part, I have a somewhat different opinion on forgetting. It depends on with whom you are dealing; if it is a relative or close friend and we cannot eliminate them from our life, we have to make efforts to forget. If they are not, you have to ask yourself whether you value the relationship (love or friendship) so highly that you are prepared to tolerate even greater irritations in future. If you are not, get out of the relationship--to blindly forget is to throw your valuable experience out the window, which is irrational. To avoid possible regrets, your decision must be made with deliberate consideration, not with an outburst of emotions such as anger or resentment. I learned this tough but rational rule from Arthur Schopenhauer, a prominent German philosopher, about four decades ago and have applied it a few times in my life. Robert Ringer, a great social politician, offers similar advice.

Love. It is the rare person who does not dream of a great love. Literature, poetry, music, and other arts of all nations and times are marked with great love stories.

I have also had my share of love dreams. It began in my late teens when I read the *Letter from an Unknown Woman*, a novella by the Austrian writer, Stefan Zweig. The young heroine, Lisa Berndle of Vienna, falls in love with the celebrated novelist R. She devotes all her life to him, but he hardly knows her. She was just one in the long line of women with whom he made love. Their son dies and then she dies soon after writing him a letter. I was a romantic fellow and this sad story of undying love struck a chord in my innermost soul: it highlighted many years of my youth. Imagine my delight when a few years later I saw the movie based on this novella, directed by Max Ohuls. In the movie, Lisa loves Stefan Brand, a musician who plays a piano etude by Franz Liszt ("Un sospiro" or "Sigh," No. 3 in D flat major). This etude, which reflects all the hopelessness, submission, and intensity of her love, is repeated as a love theme many times, and has become one of my favorites ever since.

Another love story that left a deep imprint on my heart is *The Garnet Bracelet*, a novella by Russian writer Alexander Kuprin. In this equally hopeless and sad love story, Georgy Zheltkov, an employee of the Board of Control in a small resort town on the Black Sea, falls in love with the princess Vera Sheyina, wife of the marshal of nobility. She loves her husband and does not know him at all. Her marital and high social status leaves absolutely no hope to the innocent fellow, but his love from the first glance is so enormous that it destroys him: he commits suicide. In a letter written in his last hour, he wrote (translated by Stepan Apresyan): "I am immensely grateful to you just because you exist. I have examined myself, and I know it is not a disease, not the obsession of a maniac—it is love with which God has chosen to reward me for some reason...As I depart I say in ecstasy, '*Hallowed be thy name.*' Eight years ago I saw you in a circus box, and from the very first second I said to myself: I love her because there is nothing on earth like her, nothing better--no animal, no plant, no star--because no human being is more beautiful than her, or more delicate. The whole beauty of the earth seemed to be embodied in you." The only thing he asked her for was: "If you do—I know you are very musical, for I saw you mostly at performances of the Beethoven quartets—if you do think of me, please play, or get someone else to play, the Sonata in D Major No. 2, Opus 2." A movie was also made based on this novella, and when my heart is longing for love, I like to watch both movies and listen to their love themes.

Life without love is mere existence, but an immense love such as in these and other world-famous stories does not leave room for any existence too. Immense love quickly burns up its bearer. God gives tremendous love as a gift to some people and takes their life in return. Love, being a positive emotion but experienced in excess, is as destructive as negative emotions are. This is paradox and a sad reality of life.

Love at first sight is familiar to me too, and not long ago I fell in love with a woman, being attracted by her looks. When I got to know her better, however, and discovered that she is excessively stubborn, irrational, stupid, undereducated, obsessed, and has self-destructive tendencies, I was very disappointed and my love for her vanished. This happened because I did not properly employ my "golden center," discussed previously. Attractiveness and sex appeal is not enough for me to be in a serious relationship any more, probably because of the unconscious demanding of a grown man like myself. However, too much mind and too little heart do not yield a long-lasting love.

Each individual, myself included, has the potential for unconditional love in them. "Let unselfishness, goodness, mercy, justice, health, holiness, love—the kingdom of heaven—reign within us, and sin, disease, and death will diminish until they finally disappear," says the Holy Scripture. This is the sure way to a golden age when people are perfect and enjoy immortality. In the observable future, however, while we strive to improve the quality and increase the duration of our lives, love and forgiveness are our great aides. It is in our power to make our life like a paradise, and if there is a password for entering the forthcoming paradise on earth, its name is probably "unconditional love."

Hormones That Affect Brain Longevity

Our body, including the brain, is subject to aging processes, which seem to be inevitable yet can be retarded. Among the major causes of brain aging are the following:

 • free-radical damage from fatty acids leading to an accumulation of age-associated pigmentation (i.e., lipofuscin) deposits in the brain
  • disruption of glucose metabolism in the brain
  • calcification and atrophy of the pineal gland
  • impairment of cerebral blood flow
 • underproduction of ATP (adenosine tri-phosphate), the primary energy source, in the energy centers of the brain cells

For their effective function, brain cells need proper nourishment and supply of oxygen and relevant hormones. They are extremely vulnerable to damage and death if certain hormones are produced in excess. Of more than 100 hormones produced in our body, the bad hormone cortisol and the good hormones serotonin, melatonin, growth hormone (GH), DHEA, and endorphins seem to affect the brain the most.

Cortisol. Cortisol is a hormone secreted by the adrenal glands in response to stress. Cortisol acts directly on the brain, increasing general arousal and aggressive behavior. It is not harmful in moderate amounts. "But when produced in excess, day after day—as a result of chronic, unrelenting stress—*this hormone is so toxic to the brain that it kills and injures brain cells by the billions,*" states Dharma Singh Khalsa, M.D., in his book, *Brain Longevity.* He believes that cortisol toxicity is one of the primary causes of Alzheimer's disease, a mental condition characterized by immense death of brain cells.

Serotonin. Serotonin is a neurotransmitter that is responsible for the maintenance of our good mood and is sometimes called the "contentment chemical." It promotes well-being during our waking hours (i.e., the hormone of the daytime) and also controls our sensitivity to pain. Its lack contributes to frequent negative moods and depression. The well-known drug Prozac, a magic bullet for treating depression, increases serotonin secretion.

Melatonin. The hormone melatonin is released by the pineal gland. It plays an important role in the functioning of the immune system and other biological functions. It also regulates our sleep by controlling the "circadian rhythms," which determine our sleep-arousal cycles. As we grow older, the pineal gland secretes decreasing amounts of melatonin due to gradual calcification and withering.

Growth Hormone. GH is released by the pituitary gland and called is "growth" because it is abundant in growing children and teenagers. In adults it is less accessible, but its production is encouraged by exercise, fasting, stable blood sugar, adequate sleep, trauma, dopaminergic stimulants, and other factors. According to some scientists, exercising on an empty stomach greatly enhances the release of GH. It is believed to help retard many degenerative diseases associated with aging.

DHEA. The so-called "youth hormone," DHEA (de-hydro-epi-androsterone) is secreted by the adrenal glands. High levels of DHEA are associated with better brain function, immunity, good sleep, and lower risk of coronary artery disease, breast cancer, and osteoporosis. DHEA is also found to promote longer life in the elderly and fewer deaths from various diseases. Stress depletes the amount of DHEA in the bloodstream, increasing the levels of cortisol. These two hormones compensate each other—the higher the levels of cortisol, the lower the levels of DHEA.

Endorphins. Endorphins are recently discovered natural morphine-like chemical substances that are secreted and used by our brain. Endorphins enhance the immune system, reduce the experience of pain, and help overcome depression by acting as a natural tranquilizer. They give us the feeling of optimism and well-being. On the contrary, depressed people show a severe lack of endorphins. Science shows that a positive attitude and optimistic thinking produces endorphins. In their book, *The Joy of Working,* Dr. Denis Waitley and Reni L. Witt state that, according to behavioral researchers, *we can actually stimulate the production of endorphins through optimistic thoughts and a positive attitude.* In one study, actors were wired to electrodes and connected to blood catheters. They were then asked to perform various scenes. When they portrayed characters that were angry or depressed or without hope, their endorphin levels dropped; when the scene called for emoting joy, confidence, and love, their endorphin levels shot up.

Vigorous exercise and endurance triggers the release of endorphins. Jogging releases endorphins and enkephalins (i.e., other natural short-acting heroin-like compounds), giving many joggers a euphoric feeling. Most regular runners report that after a workout, they experience a tremendous sense of relaxation and well-being, according to Dr. Kenneth H. Cooper. I experience a similar euphoric feeling after I finish my thousand-knee-bend workout.

Both body and mental health are equally important in achieving longevity. What we need is an increased production of good hormones and a reduced release of bad hormones. For brain longevity, many researchers recommend hormone supplementation; however, most of them are concerned about possible harmful effects. With the wide advertisement of "wonder drugs," many elderly people take melatonin, DHEA, human growth hormone, and amino acids to enhance the secretion of these hormones.

Hormone-replacement therapies, although popular due to their immediate positive effects, may vastly and negatively interfere with the body's hormone secretion mechanisms. Personally, I take the cautious side of Richard M. Restak, M.D., a brain researcher who, in his book *Older and Wiser,* says in regard to melatonin: "Melatonin may make sense for nighttime sleep disturbances, but no convincing research exists that it exerts any possible effect on longevity." Rather than taking DHEA, which looks promising as an anti-aging agent, he advises to follow research findings over the next several years. Dr. Khalsa, who combines in his research and practice both Western and Eastern medical traditions, developed an integrated program of combating brain aging, Alzheimer's disease, and revitalizing and regenerating the mind and memory. His plan includes the right diet, stress-relieving techniques, mind-body exercises, meditation, and supplements. His diet guideline is eating about 50 percent whole grains and about 25 percent fruits and vegetables. With its 15 to 20 percent of fat and emphasis on non-animal protein, it is virtually a low-protein, low-fat, and high-carbohydrate, "one-size-fits-all" therapeutic diet. I refer you to his excellent book, *Brain Longevity*, which Andrew Weil, M.D., regards as a must-read book.

My own approach to longevity discussed in this book has much to do with brain longevity as well. The personalized approach to diet, supplements, exercise, and lifestyle that I promote has the potential to improve both the body and the brain. For instance, a proper supply of brain cells with nutrients--especially glucose, their primary fuel--can best be achieved if one eats right for his/her type. The aerobic, strength, flexibility, and yoga exercises together with heart, muscle, and joint conditioning greatly improves blood circulation in the entire body, including the brain. The inverted poses of yoga exercises, such as the shoulder stand, increase blood flow to the brain directly. My breathing exercises that are aimed to accumulate carbon dioxide in the cells and bloodstream make the capillaries wider, thereby increasing blood flow and oxygen delivery to the brain cells.

At this point, I want to mention the "Breath of Fire" exercise, which Dr. Khalsa advocates for increasing oxygen delivery to brain. This is **fast and deep** abdominal breathing performed for three minutes. "To do the Breath of Fire, breathe through your nostrils rapidly—more than one inhalation per second. Do not pause between inhaling and exhaling," says Dr. Khalsa in describing the technique. Regarding its effect, he says, "This exercise may cause a mild feeling of lightheadedness, which may feel like hyperventilation (a decrease in blood carbon dioxide), but this is probably not the case. Clinical studies have indicated, in fact, that while the carbon dioxide level in the blood remains normal, the oxygen level actually increases during the 'Breath of Fire.'"

That carbon dioxide does not decrease during the hyperventilation condition sounds paradoxical to me. The feeling of lightheadedness is already an indication of carbon-dioxide depletion. I would like to examine these clinical studies. If carbon dioxide decreases, as I expect, then the Breath of Fire exercise--at least at the time of its performance--will not do any good for the brain. This is because the depletion of carbon dioxide leads to a constriction of blood vessels and capillaries in the brain, thereby aggravating oxygen delivery. In this case, the blood pressure would soar and this may be why one experiences mild perspiration on the forehead during this exercise, as Dr. Khalsa notes.

Regarding hormones, aerobic exercises like the knee bends that I promote reduce cortisol and, therefore, elevate the DHEA levels, while anaerobic exercises such as push-ups, pull-ups, and dumbbell exercises described previously enhance a release of the growth hormone. Meditation helps release more melatonin and DHEA. Some researchers believe that meditation significantly retards the aging process, increasing both life span and "health span," as Dr. Khalsa puts it.

Furthermore, I emphasize fasting--especially dry fasting--for decalcification of the brain glands and cleansing of the brain's blood vessels, capillaries, and cells. Short-term, one- or two-day fasts are by no means dangerous to the brain cells because the body uses its reserves of carbohydrates, fat, and even muscle protein to produce glucose, the fuel for brain cells. Animal experiments in Russia with fasting dogs to death showed that muscle tissue and some organs like the liver lost more than half their weight, while the most important vital organs—the heart and the brain—lost just 3 percent of their weight. If caloric restriction was found to be helpful in keeping the brain from deterioration during the aging process, fasting is even more powerful in this respect. Dr. Paul Bragg (who died at ninety-five due to an accident), Dr. Herbert Shelton (who lived to ninety), American comedian George Burns (who lived to 100), and others who practiced fasting to the last days of their lives enjoyed perfect overall and mental health. They have proven that fasting increases both body and brain longevity.

PART FOUR: REJUVENATION

It's really possible to grow younger,
The fountain of youth is not a farfetched tale.
What's necessary is your inner hunger,
To become young again and sing like a nightingale.

You need the energy to have this desire,
You need all your systems to get vital fire.
Your body and cells cry for detoxification,
With cleansing and fasting comes rejuvenation.

The best purifying is from the dry fast,
And a diet of raw plants bathed in sun shower.
Laughter and imagery has rejuvenating power,
When you try to make the happiest day of your life last.

Stop aging now, take action steps, don't wait,
Get super health and the fullest life--rejuvenate.

A review of the lifestyles and health habits of long-living people shows that-- as a matter of fact--they do not do anything special for life extension or rejuvenation. Many enjoy longevity genes inherited from their parents; however, regarding lifestyle, they just live, usually a busy life--and, in many cases, they are surprised that they managed to live so long. It seems to me that centenarians are gifted people who avoided all the odds of life and spontaneously found a way of living that was not harmful to their health. They can be thought of as long-living personalities with special features that allow them to follow the laws of nature.

What about the majority of us who do not have longevity genes, but rather are predisposed to life-threatening diseases such as heart disease, cancer, and stroke? Regardless, we can do a lot to stay fit and healthy and to increase the quality and quantity of life. To achieve that goal, we must take control of our diet and lifestyle in the same way that these life-extensionists have. Control implies discipline; that is the will to eliminate bad habits and replace them with healthy ones, to actually change our life.

We all know how difficult it is to change habits. The reason is that all our energy is distributed among our daily tasks and no energy is left for change, even if we have the desire. The point is that few people consider their health their number-one priority; they have so many other important things to do, ideas to implement, and desires to fulfill. In their busy schedule, no time is left to improve health. Health is considered an endless resource, taken for granted and rarely thought of. However, it is not endless, and the time comes when we see the signs of our health deterioration.

Why do we need a blow in the form of a serious illness as motivation to start investing in our health? Is this wise? I don't think so. However, many more persuasive words can be written about health being one of the most important concerns of our life, but they will not convince. What really works is an inner eagerness to stay healthy, to prevent the loss of health. That eagerness appears if we can manage to accumulate some energy. The best method of increasing the body's energy level is *fasting*. Fasting, however, can be harmful if vital organs are overloaded with the waste buildup. Fasting by itself is a powerful cleansing process, which helps rid the body of toxins and wastes. However, this elimination process can cause physiological stress to the body, which can be reduced by a transition period of preparing for fasting; that is, *cleansing* the major organs and systems.

26

FOUNDATIONS OF REJUVENATION

Rejuvenation has always been a dream of aging folks of all nations and times. Sages, healers, physicians, and health enthusiasts elaborated upon a handful of methods that aim to reverse the aging process. Most of them do not work because they rely on some therapy, substance, or technology advances that you take in from the outside. I believe that the process must go in the opposite direction—from the inside to the outside—and that the human body created in the image of God has great healing and rejuvenating powers hidden within it. To unseal and make them work, however, one needs determination, strong belief, self-discipline, and great deal of effort. A few of these methods that require hard personal work are discussed in this chapter.

Specific rejuvenating effects may be achieved on virtually all levels of consciousness, or chakras. Lifestyle, diet, exercise, sex, social life, love, arts, intellectual activities, and spiritual devoutness all have a rejuvenating potential, as follows:

• a healthy lifestyle that prevents the body from accumulating toxins and wearing out, and that uses body cleansing and detoxification therapies, including fasting and saunas
• a raw-food diet with emphasis on green leafy vegetables, sprouts, and fruits and their juices
• breathing exercises combined with meditation techniques and pranic nourishment
• sex with controlled ejaculation; sex with a much younger partner
• creative work; doing what one loves to do; the joy of working
• love of and caring about loved ones, children and parents
• filling life with arts, joy, and laughter; surrounding oneself with beauty
• the joy of mental work and exercises; sharing ideas with loved ones and friends
• affirmations

Affirmations are positive statements made in a loud voice and addressed to your subconscious mind to convince it of something. Georgy N. Sytin, Ph.D., a Russian psychologist and author of the book, *Real Rejuvenation of Men* (in Russian), developed a method called "control of emotional states through volitional word-image affirmations." His method is based on the theory of Ivan Pavlov, a world-famous Russian physiologist, about the connection between speech and the subconscious, which governs both psychological and physiological processes. Words are employed to act upon the psyche, which is believed to be able to affect physiology and thus improve functions of the body's vital organs and systems.

Dr. Sytin claims that his method helped not only himself recover from physical and mental disabilities due to body and memory injuries during World War II, but also many other people. Eighty-year-old Dr. Sytin is now healthy, fit and robust, and he fathered a child at the age of sixty-nine. Examples of his affirmations, which cover various aspects of the body, mind, and spirit, include "A tremendous, colossal creative force flows into my head. All my intellectual abilities are developing very, very quickly, and my will is rapidly growing. A young soul of an enormous power in me gives birth to a joyful healthy youth at 100 years of age and far beyond. With every passing second, my head grows full of hair."

Louise L. Hay, a popular self-improvement motivator, uses affirmations such as these: "I am worth loving. Loving others is easy when I love and accept myself. I am in the process of positive change. My unique and creative talents and abilities flow through me and are expressed in deeply satisfying ways. My creativity is always in demand." Affirmations are definitely more difficult to incorporate into one's lifestyle. As a reminder to do them, I post on the walls of my room affirmations such as "I love myself as I am. I approve of myself. I am learning how to be happy. I love my freedom the most. I am a healthy and long-living person."

Rejuvenation through Cleansing and Detoxification

On the physical level, rejuvenation can be achieved with diet, exercise, cleansing of vital organs, and detoxification by fasting. The laws of rejuvenation sound sometimes paradoxical and need a certain degree of open-mindedness. For example, according to the Hungarian scientist Bauer, when the number of destroyed body cells prevails over regenerated cells, the rejuvenation process occurs. Cells may be destroyed by strenuous exercise, which Dr. Edward M. Yashin uses as a means to achieve longevity, or during fasting, especially dry fasting. The disintegration of cells is necessary for their replacement by new cells and, therefore, for rejuvenation.

This process affects the color of one's urine. Turbid urine (except in the case of a high-protein and high-chlorophyll diet or a medical condition) indicates that you are in the detoxification and rejuvenation process. It occurs after hard work or endurance *exercises* in cold weather, with prolonged physical exertion but little sweating, during *illnesses* such as fever (except dark urine, which is caused by liver diseases such as hepatitis, cirrhosis or lupus, and immune system diseases), or during *dry fasting*. During a sickness, the body's immune system is enhanced and, together with a virus and bacteria, it may accomplish some of the dead-cell destruction, which would otherwise have to be accomplished by internal lytic processes (*lysis* is the destruction of a cell or substance by an influencing agent). In some sense, the illness evokes cleansing, thereby exerting a rejuvenating effect.

These are extraordinary conditions. Under normal conditions, urine darker than the color of beer--say, brownish in color--indicates that an excess of meat, fish, grains, green leafy vegetables, or salt was eaten the previous day. However, when induced by exercise, a brief illness such as the flu, or dry fasting, dark urine indicates that the kidneys are functioning perfectly, that they did a good job in filtering and cleansing the blood of waste products that passed out in the urine. These waste products are dead cells; their toxins and wastes resulted from the metabolic breakdown of body fat and some tissue protein, if the fat supply is limited.

During dry fasting, dark urine also indicates that the kidneys are in a contracted (Yang) condition; they are spared because not too much water passes through them. This contraction of the kidneys is totally different from the one induced by high animal protein and too much salt in the diet, when the heart is forced to beat harder and the blood pressure increases to help the kidneys push down the liquid. This results in high blood pressure that stems from kidneys in trouble. Eating and drinking sparingly or not at all is a good method for healing diseased kidneys, as well as leg and general body swelling, which is a related condition, according to Naboru Muramoto in his book, *Healing Ourselves*.

During dry fasting or sickness, the majority of the body's energy is used for elimination. Dark urine indicates that dead cells and waste deposits, such as heavy metals from drugs and environment pollution, stored in the bones and connective tissues are being eliminated from the body. Children with no waste buildup in their bodies have urine that is lighter in color than adults' urine.

Cleansing and Body Cycles

Good cleansing effects of all body systems can be achieved quite simply. We don't need to change our diet, we can continue eating what we like. The only factors to adjust are the times for eating and for abstaining from eating. Actually, it does involve some changes in lifestyle, but the regimen is easy to follow. This cleansing regimen relies on *body cycles*, which are described in the book *Fit for Life,* by Harvey and Marilyn Diamond; however, my guru Eugene Bazh taught me almost the same information a decade earlier—the difference is minimal.

I first came across the concept of body cycles about thirty-five years ago, when I happened to read the book by Likhanov entitled *Magician's Scripts* (in Russian). Published at the beginning of the twentieth century, it was devoted to raja (i.e., mastering mind) yoga. According to Oriental medicine and proven by modern research, a human's ability to deal with food is not the same at different hours of the day. Among others, there are three regular daily cycles: we take in food (*appropriation*), we absorb and use some of that food (*assimilation*), and we get rid of wastes (*elimination*). Actually, each of these three functions is always occurring to some extent, but each is more intense during certain hours of the day.

Noon to 8 p.m.: *Appropriation* (eating and digestion)
8 p.m. to 4 a.m.: *Assimilation* (absorption and use)
4 a.m. to noon: *Elimination* (of body wastes and food debris)

If we look closer at our body in action, our body cycles can become apparent to us. During our waking hours, we eat (*appropriate*); digestion starts after we put the food in our stomach, or even earlier. At night, we don't eat or drink for 7 to 8 hours, which is actually a short dry fast. At that time, the body utilizes what was taken in during the day (*assimilates*) and produces wastes and urine (*eliminates*). When we awaken in the morning, we have a bowel movement and empty the bladder. Night fasting results in what is called "morning breath" and perhaps a coated tongue because our body is in the midst of eliminating wastes. When we first awaken in the morning, we usually don't want to eat and we can skip breakfast; however, going without food later than lunch-time would be uncomfortable because our body has entered the appropriation cycle and is prepared to take in food.

How about you, my dear reader, do you feel hungry when you get up in the morning? I doubt that you do, although some people insist they are starving. Let's see what the cleansing regimen coupled with the body cycles looks like. If we cannot skip breakfast, we should eat just water-rich fruits, appropriate for our blood type, or drink fresh fruit juice. From noon, we can eat what we want two or three times, but after 8 p.m., it is better to avoid solid food, only drink tea or coffee without dessert. Leading a lifestyle based on our natural body cycles allows overweight people to lose weight without changing their typical diet. It also involves a natural *cleansing* of the body without special procedures. I know people who have tried it for two weeks and they found that it works quite well. The flexibility of their body increased and their eyes looked brighter than before. I would say they rejuvenated themselves somewhat.

A more significant rejuvenation effect can be achieved if the body's major elimination organs and systems go through a cleansing. The cleansing of the entire body described herein takes about three months: (1) colon (enema, five weeks); (2) small intestine (garlic, two weeks); (3) joints (laurel, two weeks); (4) liver (apple juice and olive oil, one week); and (5) the kidneys (melon, two weeks). Sounds like quite a job, doesn't it? First, let me explain why a serious cleansing is necessary.

Why Do We Need Cleansing?

It would not be an exaggeration to say that we are overloaded with toxins. To start with, toxins are in the air we inhale, in the water we drink or bathe in, and in the food we eat. Millions of people live in urban areas with environmental pollution, often near roads with the air full of exhaust fumes (containing lead and aldehydes) from passing cars. They drink tap water disinfected with chlorine, which is carcinogenic. They eat meat treated for botulism with nitrates and nitrites, which form carcinogenic nitrosamines, and vegetables and fruits sprayed with DDT, pesticides, and herbicides. Dr. Paul Bragg describes in his book, *The Miracle of Fasting,* how on the nineteenth day of his complete water fast, he passed red urine. It was analyzed and found to contain DDT and other pesticides. "In my personal opinion, fasting is the only way to rid the body of commercial poisons found in our fruits and vegetables," he concluded.

Environmental contamination due to industry contaminates us with heavy metals such as lead, mercury, arsenic, strontium, aluminum, cadmium, and nickel. They accumulate primarily in the kidneys and the brain, and are linked to many diseases including coronary heart disease, a few types of cancer, and an impaired nervous system. In our jobs and at home, we are exposed to toxic chemicals, solvents, formaldehyde, pesticides, herbicides, alcohol, drugs, and food additives that accumulate in the liver, placing a tremendous load on it. The metabolism of protein in our body results in the formation of toxic waste products such as urea, ammonia, and others accumulated in the kidneys. Bacteria and yeast in our intestines produce microbial toxins that are absorbed by the intestinal lining and then the bloodstream, causing liver diseases, pancreatitis, allergies, asthma, and skin diseases such as psoriasis. People taking medications are loaded with toxins and poisons from the drugs.

An individual's health is significantly determined by his/her ability to get rid of all these toxins, to detoxify the body. You need strong, healthy elimination organs and energy for detoxification and cleansing. Even if you were born with the greatest liver, kidneys, and intestines in the world, they will eventually cease to function properly if they are overwhelmed with poisons and toxins. All those mouth-watering fried, smoked, and roasted food delight our taste buds, but they also contain substances that clog and poison our bodies. This is another example of the universal law that says every pleasurable thing in life has a price tag. We must pay for pleasure and the price is both money and our health. My stomach is not oversensitive, but I remember a few occasions when it took me weeks to recover from an extremely upset stomach and a gastritis bout after eating delicious foods in an expensive restaurant.

I realize how tough this statement is, but I think that "Food is our number-two killer." As with oxygen (the number-one killer), we can't live without it, but because we are absolutely dependent on it, it slowly kills us, just as a snake kills a hypnotized and helpless mouse. You probably know the old saying that "we dig our grave with our own teeth." "Delicious food ruined mankind," stated Dr. N. Amosov, a Russian academician of medicine. This is because most of the delicious dishes of all the world's cuisines clog our bodies, rather than cleanse them. Let me remind you of these words of Mark Twain: "The only way to keep your health is to eat what you don't want, drink what you don't like, and do what you'd rather not." I am not saying that you have to give up enjoying your food--no, not at all! Just keep in mind that if you eat food that clogs your organs and systems, you will need a cleansing. Moreover, if you wish to feel and look younger, cleanse your body on a regular basis.

The body-cleansing (i.e., detoxification) procedure described herein is accomplished in five stages, as suggested by Nadezhda A. Semenova, a chemist at a food-processing factory in Shakhty, Russia. She cured herself of heart disease, rheumatoid arthritis, gastritis, and many other ailments with body cleansing and food-combining. After restoring her health, she started marathon running and became well known in Russia in the late 1980s. This five-stage procedure involves the cleansing of the large intestine, small intestine, joints, liver, and kidneys. I have supplemented it with the cleansing of blood vessels, which is crucial for overall health.

Stage 1. Large Intestine Cleansing

The large intestine is a muscular tube that continuously digests food (primarily in the small intestine), absorbs water from chyme, forms solid wastes, and expels them from the body. It is one of the major elimination organs. An old proverb says that death resides in the intestines. A Russian scientist, physiologist Ivan I. Metchnikov, stated that the "major obstacle to achieve longevity is auto-intoxication from the intestines," a condition very common in millions of people suffering from constipation. Professor Elie Metchnikov of the Pasteur Institute called the large intestine the "murderer of men." Thus, the healing process and body cleansing also has to start with the large intestine, which is the temporary storage area for waste products of the digestive system. Modern man knows about the exceptional role of the large intestine in our health and well-being. However, the sages of ancient times; the healers of China, Tibet, and Egypt; and the Indian yogi knew that the large intestine must be kept clean if a person wants to be vigorous and healthy. Maintaining the health of the large intestine is very dependent on the types of food we eat; dietary fiber is thought to be of particular importance. Various colon-cleansing methods, including laxatives and enemas, are known from ancient times. The following list varies from smooth and comfortable to very difficult because of their action on the body:

1. Detoxification by eating raw fruits and vegetables (70 percent) and concentrated foods (30 percent) and proper food combining, suggested by Harvey and Marilyn Diamond in their best-selling book, *Fit for Life*.

2. A detoxification diet consisting of steamed vegetables, whole grains, and fresh fruits, and, after the initial three-week period, legumes, nuts, and other whole foods, recommended by Dr. Elson Haas, the author of *Staying Healthy with Nutrition*.

3. A three-week cleansing diet starting with a two-day fast of barley water, freshly squeezed fruit juices diluted with mineral water, or filtered tap

water, advised by Dr. Peter Mansfield in his book, *The Good Health Handbook*. The diet includes herb teas, fresh fruits, fresh coleslaw, raw and baked vegetables, whole-wheat bread, nuts, and raisins.

4. Laxatives, herbal or artificial, are typically lubricants, irritants, or diarrhea-inducers and peristaltic stimulants. They range from soft-acting like prune juice and sienna leaves, to strong ones involving discomfort and abdominal pain like castor oil, large doses of vitamin B-5, and Glauber's salt. Although providing only temporary relief, laxatives are used so often that some people complain that they have spent a small fortune on them. Dr. Max Bircher-Benner, an acknowledged pioneer in prevention medicine, warned against the wide use of laxatives: "The quantities of laxatives that are so largely used by millions of constipated people are by no means harmless. They will never remove the dangers inherent in all constipation—auto-intoxication and its incurable sequels. The convenience of their use prevents doctors and patients from applying drastic measures that would really cure."

5. Enemas, from the tiny 30-milliliter glycerin enema sold in Japan and the United States, to as much as the 2-quart water enema advised by Dr. Agatha Thrash. Enemas inject water into the colon to cleanse it of impacted feces. Many constipated people who easily use laxatives are frightened of administering an enema. I saw horror in the eyes of one of my friends to whom I advised applying the 30-milliliter bottle; "It's so big," he said. Many consider the enema a means to cleanse only the lower part of the colon; however, I combine the enema with specific positions of the body that allow water to penetrate deeper and to cleanse the colon up to its ascending part. For people of the Vata dosha, who are underweight, have dry skin, and suffer from dehydration, Ayurveda advises a 100-milliliter warm milk enema with 20 grams of ghee (i.e., clarified butter) dissolved in it. This helps cure constipation and excessive gas formation, and restores good intestinal bacteria.

6. Colonic irrigation, or colonics, is a type of hydrotherapy, which--like the enema--flushes out impacted feces. Water at body temperature is flushed into the rectum through one tube; the softened colonic debris mixed with the water is carried out of the body through another tube. Colonic irrigation enables the removal of feces from farther up in the bowel, and is thought to be more effective than an enema. However, the procedure is dangerous and can have side effects. Edgar Cayce, a medical diagnostician and healer who was called the "sleeping prophet of Virginia Beach," was a great advocate of colonics. "Take a colonic irrigation occasionally, or have one administered, scientifically. One colonic irrigation will be worth about four to six enemas,"

he said in one of his readings. Unfortunately, a colonic irrigation cannot be administered at home either to one's self or to another person, according to Dr. Harold J. Reilly and Ruth Hagy Brod in their book, *The Edgar Cayce Handbook for Health*. For this treatment, you must visit a professional, and many communities do not offer this service, they add. The amount of water used in colonics is between 6 and 10 gallons: 3 gallons go in and out of the patient, the rest siphon out the other water. It is quite a drastic treatment.

I want to mention that the modified enema procedure described in the next chapter, which can be administered at home, also can achieve the deep colon-cleansing effect. I agree, however, that both colonics and enemas have negative side effects including the overexpansion of the colon and the flushing out of good bowel bacteria along with the bad. Fortunately, these side effects are not serious; in time, the colon returns to its original size and the good bacteria are renewed. To quickly repopulate the bowel with good bacteria, acidophilus and bifidus supplements are essential afterwards, advises C. Norman Shealy, M.D., Ph.D., in *The Complete Family Guide to Alternative Medicine*. The advantages of homemade acidophilus, which uses a cabbage recipe, are described in *The Complete Book of Chinese Health & Healing*, by Daniel Reid.

7. Shank Prakshalana, which is a yogic cleansing procedure, involves drinking salty water and special exercises to let the water flow from the stomach down to the duodenum, then to the small intestine, farther through the large intestine, and finally out the anus. One should drink ten to fourteen glasses of water with 5 to 6 grams of table salt in 1 liter of water. After each glass of salty water, four types of body movements should be performed: side bends, torso twists, side bends from the cobra pose, and twists from the low bent-knee pose. These exercises help open the sphincters and promote the advancement of the water along the gastrointestinal tract. The procedure is continued until relatively clean water comes out of the anus.

In my own experience, I have tried most of these procedures except colonics, but my favorite one that I have used many times is the five-week–long, 2-liter enema cleansing procedure recommended by Semenova. In the first week, an enema is administered every day, about 3 hours before going to bed. In the second week, an enema is administered every other day; in the third week, every third day; in the fourth week, every fourth day; and in the fifth week, once. It is also advised to continue taking the enemas one more week after the fifth week.

You may think that 2 liters--the volume of a large soda bottle--is too much water and it can overextend the colon. However, the large intestine is a broad tube about 5 feet long; to rinse it all the way up to the ascending part, we need that amount. Also, the smooth muscles of the intestinal wall are flexible enough and will gradually shrink to normal size and peristaltic function will be restored after the procedure. I modified the procedure to minimize the overextension. Fill an enema bag with a mixture made from the juice of half a lemon added to 2 liters of boiled water, cooled to a lukewarm temperature. Hang the bag on a hook 3 to 4 feet above the floor. Using a finger of your left hand, lubricate the end of the enema tubing and the anus with Vaseline or oil. Lie on your back on the floor with your buttocks and feet against the wall and your knees bent at a right angle. Press your feet against the wall and raise your hips about 1 foot off the floor. With your left hand, gently insert the tubing into the anus about 2 inches deep. Then use your right hand to release the valve to let the water enter the colon.

To prevent cramping, control the speed at which the water enters the colon. If you feel that you cannot hold any more water, relax your abdomen, take slow deep diaphragmatic breaths with your mouth open, and close the valve until the intense feeling subsides. Continue to let all the water in, then close the valve. Carefully remove the tubing and put it in an empty jar prepared beforehand. Lower your back to the floor, roll on your right side, and keep this position for 1 minute to let the water go through the colon and farther up the ascending part of the intestine. Then assume the same position as for taking in the water, raising your hips for 1 minute to let the water flow back into the transverse part of the intestine. Next, turn to your left side and lie for 1 more minute to allow the water to accumulate in the descending part of the intestine. Finally, stand up and sit on the toilet until all the contents of the intestine are expelled and gas is released.

Because you held the water for only 3 minutes, very little water contaminated with diluted feces will be absorbed through the intestinal lining and enter the bloodstream. To spare your blood from this polluted water, you can use your fresh *urine* instead of water, which--being salted--remains inside the intestine somewhat unabsorbed. You may collect urine from the previous day and night and keep it in a bottle in the refrigerator; be sure to warm it to a lukewarm temperature before use. Urine is very good for the mucous lining of the intestine and it can heal small scratches on the walls. It also provides a more thorough cleansing of the entire large intestine. When using urine, a smaller amount is needed--the same cleansing effect can be achieved with just 1 liter; therefore, you spare your intestine from overextension as well. I tried a urine enema and found that the expelling goes more smoothly and fully. If you are squeamish, you can use salty water (2 tablespoons of salt in 1 liter of water) in place of urine.

The diet in the course of colon cleansing should be rich in fiber derived from vegetables and whole-wheat bread and porridge. The intestines must be filled with bulky material to stimulate the colon muscles to restore peristaltic movements, thereby returning the expanded intestine to its original size.

Stage 2. Killing Bad Bacteria in the Small Intestine

Bacteria parasites including the fungus *Candida albicans*, coliform bacteria, and yeasts are abandoned in our intestines, especially if we eat lots of sugar, meat, and yeast products such as breads and other baked goods. They spread if the intestine lacks the acids and its environment turns alkaline. This is often the case with people of blood type A because of their low levels of stomach acid. Bad bacteria and yeast produce nitrogenous gases and harmful substances, which irritate the intestines and enter the bloodstream. Chronic irritation may cause colitis, constipation, and even colon cancer. To reduce the harm from bad bacteria, many experts recommend a diet rich in fiber. Fiber in oat bran and vegetables, especially raw cabbage, can bind to toxins and excrete them from the intestines; medicinal charcoal tablets, preferably the homeopathic Carbo Veg (vegetable charcoal), also work.

One of the best methods to destroy bad bacteria is to eat *raw garlic*. Raw garlic is a powerful natural antibiotic without the side effects of medicinal antibiotics. Many studies have established that it is effective on bacteria, viruses, fungi, and parasites. "Raw fresh garlic deters *Candida* very strongly," says Dr. Peter Mansfield in his *The Good Health Handbook*. Garlic therapy involves eating one clove of garlic twice a day: in the morning, 1 hour before breakfast, and at night, 2 hours after the last meal. Just garlic, nothing more-- washing it down the throat with water is not allowed. I have tried the garlic therapy many times and find it very beneficial. I grind a clove of garlic using a fine grinder and swallow the mass. The first time is really painful--a strong burning sensation in the mouth, pharynx, and esophagus, and down to stomach--but it is bearable and one has to tolerate it for the sake of curing. The pain lasts for a couple of minutes, then subsides. After the garlic is swallowed, I quickly rinse my mouth to avoid irritation of the mucous membranes by the strong garlic acids. With each succeeding session, it becomes less painful.

The entire procedure may take a week or two, depending on the degree of one's bacterial contamination. I continue eating garlic until it does not cause the painful sensation, a sign that the bad bacteria is destroyed and does not irritate the mucous in the gastrointestinal tract anymore. It may sound unbelievable, but after a week or so, I can eat garlic like an apple and it does not bother me; however, my bad breath bothers the people around me, which is the real inconvenience of garlic therapy. Before going out, I chew a sprig of parsley.

Stage 3. Cleansing the Joints

Many people suffer from sore joints that are sensitive to changing weather and rain, and they cannot sleep well because of joint pain. Nutritional imbalance, misuse, and other causes may trigger joint pain. Millions of Americans have osteoarthritis and rheumatoid arthritis, which attack the cartilage and lining of the joints. Many studies link the over-consumption of meat and dairy products to joint diseases. Vegetarian food and detoxification diets have been found to be helpful in relieving arthritis and other joint pain.

The joint-cleansing procedure involves drinking a concoction of laurel leaf for three days. Laurel leaf, or bay leaf, is a famous ancient plant that is aromatic in cookery and a healing herb. For centuries, a laurel wreath was associated with fame and achievement, and was conferred to emperors and statesmen, poets and athletes. It adds subtle flavor to vegetable, meat, game, fish, and other dishes, and is used in soups and sauces. Laurel oil added to salves and liniments is beneficial in the treatment of rheumatoid arthritis, bruises, and skin disorders.

To prepare the concoction, I use 5 grams of laurel leaves with 300 milliliters of water boiled for 5 minutes and steeped in a thermos for 3 hours. I drink this in small portions over 12 hours; drinking the entire amount all at once may be harmful. The diet doesn't change. I continue to drink this concoction for three days, then repeat the entire procedure in one week. It is advised to cleanse the joints with the laurel concoction once every quarter-year, then once a year.

Under no circumstances should you drink the laurel concoction without cleansing your intestines because it could cause a bad allergy, skin reactions, increased eye fluid pressure, and many other problems. Therefore, it is important to administer the cleansing stage by stage.

Stage 4. Cleansing the Liver

The liver serves simultaneously as an organ of digestion, circulation, and elimination. It is responsible for the metabolism of proteins, carbohydrates, fats, vitamins, minerals, and hormones. The liver stores proteins, fats, and sugars, releasing them into the bloodstream when they are in demand. It produces bile, which is extremely important in the digestion of fats and fat-soluble vitamins. About 1 liter of bile a day is secreted into the small intestine; some of it (about 2 ounces, or 60 milliliters) is stored in the gallbladder. The liver also produces certain blood proteins. Protein metabolism results in uric acid, which is also manufactured by the liver and then eliminated through the kidneys. The liver also controls glucose--the body's major fuel supply--storing any excess as glycogen and converting it back to glucose when required. It is the major laboratory for detoxifying toxins and drugs in the blood.

Proper liver functioning is vital to the body's ability to maintain overall health. The liver is quite sensitive to the food we eat and many foods, including meat, poultry, eggs, sugars, dairy products, nuts, caffeine-containing drinks, alcohol, chocolate, and fried foods, are believed to be liver-unfriendly. In a liver-supporting diet, these foods should be avoided. Unfortunately, our lifestyle and diet are far removed from liver–supporting, which leaves many people with overburdened--even toxic--livers. Using foods and supplements to support and stimulate the liver, and flushing and cleansing it of toxins and congestion, can restore its proper functioning. That is why we need to periodically cleanse the liver.

Two of the quite frequent liver and gallbladder disorders are gallstones and liver stones, which are hard deposits that develop from cholesterol and bile salts. Their size can range from a grain of sand to golf ball or even egg size. Risk factors for developing gallstones include heredity, being overweight, a high-fat diet, and even significant weight loss in a short time. Gallstone attacks are extremely painful and the standard treatment is surgery to remove the gallbladder.

A few of my friends have suffered from gallstones and went through surgery. One of them showed me the stones that were removed with the gallbladder--there were five or six and they resembled hazelnuts in the shell in size, color, and texture of the surface. This happened about fifteen years ago and I remember regretting that I couldn't help my friend spare his gallbladder. A few weeks before, I had undertaken the cleansing of my gallbladder using olive oil, and I had expelled naturally many green soft stones. I had had no gallstone disease, no pain at all--I was just trying to master the cleansing procedure to have it for an emergency. I fasted for four days and then took 600 milliliters of olive oil. The last time that I administered the liver/gallbladder cleansing was in August 1997; I will describe it in detail.

First, in the morning I administered a 1.5-liter enema of boiled lukewarm water with 1 tablespoon of lemon juice. To soften the stones, I started two days of apple-juice fasting. Both days, I drank 1.5 liters of the freshly squeezed juice of three large, sweet apples. I drank it four times a day, every 3.5 to 4 hours, 380 milliliters each time. Within 24 hours, my weight dropped from 165 to 159 pounds. On the second day in the morning, I administered another 1.5-liter enema, this time of chamomile infusion with 1 tablespoon of lemon juice. The apple-juice intake was the same four drinks, the first at 8 a.m. and the last at 6:30 p.m.

Then I prepared 300 milliliters of freshly squeezed lemon juice and 300 milliliters of olive oil for the cleansing procedure. Lemon juice helps to further soften the stones and olive oil induces an intensive bile flush by the gallbladder. I also prepared two hot-water bottles. Warmth applied to the liver region helps open up the ducts that connect the liver, gallbladder, and small intestine, thus promoting the gallbladder's cleansing reaction.

The olive-oil intake procedure started at 7 p.m., the hour of the liver's biological relaxation. The entire amount of olive oil and lemon juice must be divided into six portions, with one portion taken every 15 minutes. A portion is 3 tablespoons of lemon juice and 3 tablespoons of olive oil poured into a glass. The olive oil is difficult to drink and the lemon juice helps avoid the spit-out reflex. After I drank the first portion of the olive-oil/lemon-juice cocktail, I went to bed, laid on my right side, and applied the hot-water bottle to the liver region. Then, 15 minutes later, I drank the second portion and again went to bed with the hot-water bottle on my right side. I repeated the entire procedure four more times every 15 minutes, with the last one at 8:15 p.m. To maintain warmth on the liver region overnight, I re-warmed the water bottles and fell asleep around 10 p.m.

The first bowel movement occurred about 5 a.m. A dozen green pale-colored soft stones up to a half-inch (12 millimeters) in size and a few dozen grains of sand were eliminated. At 7 a.m., there was a second bowel movement and then another at 9:15 a.m.; more stones were eliminated each time. After starting the juice fasting, my weight dropped 8 pounds, from 165 to 157 pounds, within 48 hours.

The next day, I drank carrot juice and beet-leaf juice, which are highly beneficial for people of my blood type A. My food was vegetarian and I gradually increased the portions with each meal. Late in the evening, I had one more chamomile enema, after which the five biggest stones--up to 3/4-inch--were expelled from my gallbladder. They were mixed green and pale in color, rounded, and quite soft. I kept them on a plastic plate for two weeks at room temperature. The green stones formed of bile gradually melted down and lost their shape, the pale stones containing calcium salts did not change their shape, and the mixed-colored ones partly deteriorated due to the green part. I ate vegetarian food for two more days and my weight returned to 165 pounds.

Actually, I had considered my diet for the last ten months to be quite healthy and I was surprised to observe stones that big. I cannot say that I felt a big difference, but the thought of the gallbladder and liver being freed of stones encouraged me. It was not a case of gallstone disease; nevertheless, it is better to have these stones, even the soft ones, out of the system. Once more, as fifteen years before, I confirmed for myself that liver cleansing with olive oil works for me, even after two days of fasting. This time, I had undertaken the liver cleansing to prepare my body for the alternative dry fasting for one month, which I describe in detail later in this chapter. For Yin people, *licorice tea* has a cleansing effect on the liver. It aids the liver in discharging the poisons it filters from the blood. Once the liver releases the poisons, the licorice further helps the kidneys to eject them from the blood.

Stage 5. Cleansing the Kidneys

The urinary system, composed of the kidneys and the bladder, maintains the body's internal balance of salts and water. The kidneys filter waste and waste products from the blood, and remove toxins and poisons to prevent their accumulation in the body. The kidneys are two organs located behind the stomach, one on each side of the spine, about half the size of the heart. Approximately 150 liters of blood passes through the kidneys every day and about 1 liter of urine is produced in them. Urine is an amber liquid largely composed of water, uric acid, urea, and inorganic salts. From the kidneys, the urine passes through the urethra to the bladder and then is expelled. Together with the large intestine and the liver, the kidneys function as an important elimination organ.

Kidney stones--that is, hard deposits of chemical salts--are a quite frequent kidney disorder. A diet with too much animal protein, calcium-rich foods such as dairy products, and inadequate water intake may be the cause of kidney stones. Meat eaters often develop creatinine crystals in their kidneys. Foods containing calcium oxalate, including spinach, rhubarb, beets, grapes, blueberries, strawberries, and chocolate, also are linked to the formation of kidney stones. Foods that contain sulfur, such as eggs, beans, peas, lentils, and radishes, may lead to the formation of sulfuric crystals.

Whatever the cause of these stones, cleansing the kidneys of them is essential for our health and rejuvenation. Among the many options available for flushing the kidneys, the following watermelon flushing procedure gets rid of kidney stones. A good cleansing effect can be achieved with a diet consisting solely of watermelon and dark whole-wheat bread for one week. These are delicious foods and we are not restricted in the amount--we may eat as much as we want. Don't you think this is the most pleasurable cleansing procedure of all those discussed previously?

If there are stones in the kidneys, it will be indicated by mild pain in the lower back on one side; in this case, we need other efforts in addition to the simple procedure described earlier. We need to use the kidney's biological hour, which is from 2 a.m. to 3 a.m. At that late night hour, sit in the bathtub filled with pleasantly warm water and eat watermelon. The warmth promotes a flushing of urine together with the stones.

In one case history, Semyenova profiles a woman marathon runner, a strong-willed person. She had kidney disease and after surgery twelve years ago, she was left with one kidney. However, the remaining kidney also suffered from kidney stones and bothered her very much. She tried various treatments, including mineral water from Truskavets--the reputed kidney-curing health resort in the Ukraine--but without any success. She was afraid of another surgery on her last kidney. On the advice of her doctor, she stopped eating meat and ate cottage cheese instead. Semyenova warned her against eating cottage cheese because it also causes kidney stones.

Eventually, she came under the care of Semyenova and went through all four previous stages of body cleansing. Then she ate watermelons for three weeks and a big stone was expelled; her last kidney was spared. She had that stone made into a ring and she wore it on her finger like a precious gem.

As an alternative to the watermelon therapy, there are some herbs that have the ability to dissolve kidney stones. One of them is rubia, the root of the madder, which provides an excellent effect, says Dr. A. Vogel in his book, *Swiss Nature Doctor*. Rubiasan treatment involves ingesting a box of pills in one week, combined with a restriction of liquids. The following week, as many liquids as possible should be drunk for a thorough flushing of the kidneys. This sequence must be repeated three times: three weeks of medication alternating with three weeks of flushing. During treatment, refined foods containing white flour, sugar, pork, cold cuts, spinach, asparagus, rhubarb, and Brussels sprouts should be avoided. A diet consisting of wild rice, vegetables, salads, and lots of carrots to provide vitamin A is recommended. Hot hip baths and warm, moist compresses made with hay flowers and chamomile and applied to the kidney area, are also beneficial. It is interesting to note that Dr. Vogel recommends water restriction while taking the root pills, which is similar in approach to the dry-fasting treatment, in which liquids are not taken for a day or a few days, enabling just metabolic water to exert a cleansing effect on all body organs, including the kidneys.

6. Cleansing the Blood Vessels

Tibetan method of blood-vessel cleansing and rejuvenation.

Process 200 grams of fresh, juicy garlic in a meat grinder and steep with 200 milliliters of pure alcohol. Seal the mixture in a jar and store it in a cool place for ten days, then filter and squeeze the infusion. Drink the infusion diluted in 50 milliliters of milk three times daily, 20 minutes before a meal, in the following amounts:

- First day: 1 drop before breakfast, 2 drops before lunch, 3 drops before dinner
- Second day: 4, 5, and 6 drops before breakfast, lunch, and dinner, respectively
- Third day: 7, 8, and 9 drops
- Fourth day: 10, 11, and 12 drops
- Fifth day: 13, 14, and 15 drops
- Then in reverse; that is, the sixth day: 15, 14, and 13 drops, and so on until the tenth day
- In the following days, take 25 drops with 50 milliliters of milk before each meal as long as it lasts

Tibetan method of blood-vessel cleansing with herbs (dating from the fourth century BC).

Blend 100 grams each of the flowers of chamomile, St. John's-wort, immortal and birch buds, and seal in a jar. In the evening, steep 1 tablespoon of the blend with a half liter of boiling water for 20 minutes. Filter the mixture through a tissue and squeeze. Dissolve 1 teaspoon of honey in a glass of the concoction and drink it before going to bed, abstain from food and drink afterwards. The next morning, steam the remaining concoction, add 1 teaspoon of honey, and drink it 15 to 20 minutes before breakfast. Drink the tea until the blend is finished. Repeat this vessel-cleansing procedure in five years.

The Tibetan text, in which this recipe is found, says that the treatment improves metabolism and cleanses the blood vessels of fatty and calciferous deposits, making them elastic, which prevents atherosclerosis, high blood pressure, and myocardial infarction; cures dizziness and ringing in the ears; and restores sight.

Semyenova method of cleansing the blood vessels.

Place 2 tablespoons of ground valerian root, 1 ounce of ground dill seed, and 2 ounces of honey in a thermos, and steep with enough boiled water to yield 2 liters; leave it for one day. Drink one glass of the concoction a half-hour before meals until it is finished.

Kurennoy method of strengthening the blood vessels and rejuvenation.

Grind 1 pound of garlic and mix it with the freshly squeezed juice of twenty-four lemons; leave it to infuse for twenty-four days. Shake before using. Take 1 teaspoon of the infusion diluted with a half glass of water once a day before sleeping. This recipe is attractive because the lemon kills the bad smell of the garlic.

27

FASTING

Fasting is defined in the *Academic American Encyclopedia* as "the practice of abstaining from food, either completely or partially, for a specified period." The *Encyclopedia Americana* defines it somewhat differently, as "a ritual abstention from *food* and *drink* observed by either individuals or communities for varying lengths of time." This latter definition implies the total restriction of both food and drink intake; in other words, *dry fasting*.

Fasting is a practice known from ancient times and found in most religions of the world. It was widely used throughout history not only in religions, but also in whole nations. The restriction of not eating certain foods, such as meat, fat, or eggs, is called fasting. Going without food during the daytime, as Muslims do during the Ramadan month, is also considered fasting. Traditionally, as a form of asceticism and penitential practice, fasting was observed for the purpose of purifying a person, mostly spiritually, and of atonement for sins and wrongdoing. Recent scientific research, however, suggests that fasting also may be beneficial for the therapeutic cleansing of the body and for resisting many diseases.

During fasting, the digestive tract and all body systems receive a rest. The metabolism, body temperature, breathing rate, heartbeat rate, and blood pressure are reduced during fasting and the "heart and arteries are also relieved of a burden and secure rest," says Dr. Herbert M. Shelton in his book, *Fasting Can Save Your Life.* "A heart that is pulsating 80 times a minute will fall to 60 or even fewer beats a minute...Another restful factor is the fall of blood pressure. If the pressure is 160 mm, it will speedily fall to 140, 130, even 115, where it will remain for the rest of the period of fasting. I saw one case of a woman who had a systolic pressure of 295 mm in which the pressure was reduced in less than two weeks to 115. ...Today we are forced to recognize the fact that instead of fasting weakening the heart, it results in strengthening this wonderful organ," according to Dr. Shelton.

This is true--I know of the case of Vladimir P. Voronov, sixty-four, from the city of Volgodonsk, Russia, whose life was saved twice by fasting. He had two severe heart attacks (i.e., myocardial infarctions) and he was rushed by ambulance to the hospital. His doctor had no hope of him surviving when she saw his bad electrocardiogram. However, he fasted after each infarction and was able to recover and continue his busy work as a workshop manager. I remember him as being a very large man weighing 285 pounds (130 kilograms) and eating in excess. However, once a year he fasted for thirty days, not while on vacation but rather while continuing his work. Despite his unhealthy eating habits, his healthy fasts kept him alive.

The blood-cleansing effect of fasting can be easily understood, since fatty deposits in the vessels are burned for energy. "Fasting is the great system renovator. Three fast days a year will purify the blood and eradicate the poison diathesis more effectively than a hundred bottles of expurgative bitters," says Felix L. Oswald, M.D. A great authority on fasting, American physician and naturopath Dr. Paul C. Bragg used to say: "You are as old as your arteries." In his book, *The Miracle of Fasting,* he considers fasting as a means of internal purification and the purification of the arteries. "In my opinion, we can add years to our hearts with a systematic program of fasting, coupled with a program of natural food, which reduces the waxy substance that forms in the arteries," says Dr. Bragg. The Fasting Center International holds also that the most important benefit of fasting is that it thoroughly cleans and purifies the bloodstream. Fasting also restores the natural alkaline/acidity balance of the blood.

Fasting is perhaps the oldest therapy known to humankind for curing even cancer. The first time I heard about fasting was the case of a forty-two year old Russian man who cured himself of sarcoma--bone cancer in his case--with two sessions of month-long fasts. It was about twenty-five years ago, soon after Dr. Bragg's book, *The Miracle of Fasting,* won great popularity in Russia. My own experience of trying this therapy was liquid fasts "after Bragg." It involved a gradual, step-by-step self-curing remedy: twelve sessions of one-day fasts, seven sessions of three-day fasts, and three sessions of ten-day fasts. In subsequent years, I also tried dry fasts "after Ivanov," starting with 42 hours and building up within a few sessions to 72 hours. My goal was to master fasting as a possible self-cure for future illnesses.

An immune system that is activated and enhanced due to fasting can overcome tumor growth. Curing people suffering from cancer involves long and disciplined fasts. Case histories show that if the growth has not diminished, its further progress can be stopped or retarded by fasting. A complete change of diet is deemed necessary in addition to fasting, involving the complete elimination of animal proteins, including meat, eggs, fish, cheese, curd, milk, butter, and oils; as well as refined carbohydrates, yeast products such as sugar and yeast breads, coffee, cola, black tea and other stimulants, alcohol, and tobacco.

To return the body's metabolism to normal, fasting has been found to be a very effective method. In *The Miracle of Fasting,* Dr. Bragg describes the case of his sister, who was very thin and could not gain a pound despite the cakes and other rich foods that her mother fed her. Under Bragg's supervision, she twice fasted for seven days; afterwards, her metabolism had improved and she gained weight. Her body filled out, she became very attractive, and was married successfully to a young businessman.

There is a Russian saying: "Wedge is chucked out with a wedge." Therefore, for slim people, fasting also works in the same way--they lose weight during a fast and then increase it beyond their starting weight in the rehabilitation period. Some diet experts call this effect a "starvation response."

Fasts with full abstinence from solid food range from juice (fruit or vegetable), water, distilled water fasting to dry fasting.

Juice Fasting. Juice fasting entails drinking freshly squeezed or prepared fruit and vegetable juices. Some call it "juice therapy" because the body receives various nutrients in an easy-to-digest form. Juice fasting has great healing power. Dr. Norman Walker recommended raw vegetable and fruit juices for curing several diseases. Dr. Ann Wigmore claimed that she cured herself of colon cancer with wheat-grass and vegetable juices. Some patients of Roe Gallo, a natural healer and the author of *The Perfect Body*, claim that juice fasting helped them heal breast cancer, according to David Wolfe in his book, *The Sunfood Diet Success System.*

Juice fasting is widely used in European health sanatoriums. Dr. Otto H.F. Buchiger, Jr., of Germany, and his father, also a medical doctor, supervised more than eighty thousand fasts during their fifty years of combined practice. Dr. Paavo Airola describes in his book, *How to Keep Slim, Healthy, and Young with Juice Fasting*, the case of a fifty-four year old woman suffering from arthritis who was put on a liquid fast for 249 days. She lost 74 of her 262 pounds and her arthritis cleared up completely. In addition to various curative effects, Dr. Airola stresses the rejuvenation effect of juice fasting when he states, "...fasting has such a profound rejuvenation effect on the functions of all the vital organs, including the functions of the all-important endocrine glands, which are so decidedly responsible for how young or how old you feel and look." In his book, he gives detailed instructions for successful juice fasting. People who have active lifestyles with fast food a large proportion of their diet--for whom regular fasting would be impractical--can attain a cleansing effect with raw-juice therapy or fasting. A three-day fast of only freshly squeezed apple juice provides a great cleansing effect for the arteries.

Water Fasting. Water fasting is the classic form of fasting in which only pure water is taken. Most practitioners and clinics in the United States use water fasting; in Europe, juice fasting--considered to be superior to water fasting--is more prevalent. Dr. Bragg practiced ***distilled water fasting***, which he believed had a greater cleansing effect, himself and so did his numerous patients. In his book, *The Miracle of Fasting*, he said, "Distilled water helps to dissolve the terrible, morbid, putrid, toxic poisons that collect in civilized men's bodies. It passes through the kidneys without leaving inorganic pebbles and stones."

Dry Fasting. Dry fasting is known as the Schroth procedure and was used by this German naturopath of the eighteenth century to cure many illnesses. In Russia, it became known mostly due to the dry-fasting proponent, Porphiry Ivanov, who advised fasting for health and vigor for 42 hours once a week. The fast should start at 6 p.m. on Friday and continue till noon on Sunday. Ivanov himself fasted without water for one week and longer.

Actually, each of us does dry fasting for 6 to 8 hours during our sleep every night. We feel tired, sometimes nearly sick by the end of the day, but after a good night's sleep, we feel refreshed and full of energy. What is it that returns vitality to our bodies? Together with the relaxation that opens the clamps in our Chinese channels--allowing energy to flow freely through them--it is the dry fasting that cures us. And we have all the signs of fasting in the morning: bad breath and a coated tongue. It is due to this dry fasting that we live our lives as long as we do; if we ate and drank during the day and night, our lives would be shortened by one third.

Animals who pass the winter in a resting state--called hibernation--also go through dry fasting. In a limited number of the small mammals that experience the winter sleep, the body temperature and metabolic rate decrease tremendously and there is no sign of brain activity. For some animals, such as bears in Northern Europe, the winter sleep lasts five months, from November to April. They stay in their lair, slowly burning the fat stored in the summer.

Why is dry fasting more effective than water or juice fasting? In water fasting, the wastes, toxins, and deposits are flushed out with the water we drink. This water must first be processed, which requires the body's energy, in order to penetrate the cell membranes. In dry fasting, there is no water intake and the water that is present in urine, feces, and sweat is metabolic water as an end product of carbohydrates, fat, and protein metabolism. The wastes from inside the cells are flushed out with that metabolic water, which makes the elimination process easier. As fruitarian Arnold Ehret states, "The less you drink, the more aggressive the fast works."

Most alternative practitioners and fasting promoters do not approve of dry fasting, regarding it as too "extreme." Dr. Watanabe of Japan, who cures cancer with holistic therapies including juice and water fasts, said it is dangerous to discuss dry fasting. However, unlike other natural hygienists, Dr. Herbert Shelton actually leaned toward dry fasting when he said, "...don't drink any more water than you really feel like, and that may be better advice."

Dry fasting seems to be the most powerful instrument for cleansing all body systems. As a cleansing therapy, it is deemed to be three times more effective than water fasting. Why is metabolic water better for body cleansing than the external water we drink? Because drinking water contains, together with other contaminants present in tap water, small amounts of deuterium, or heavy water (D_2O). Unlike ordinary water (H_2O), deuterium water includes two ions of heavy hydrogen (D). This water is very harmful and poisonous to all of our systems, and has a tendency to accumulate in our bodies. According to some gerontologists, it is responsible for our aging and degenerative diseases. Some experts believe that dry fasting is the only way to get rid of deuterium water buildup.

Who can benefit from dry fasting the most? Overweight, especially obese, people with extra fat to burn will find it highly beneficial. Thin, slender people of the Vata dosha type (where I belong), for whom it is a problem to gain weight, are not advised to fast by Ayurvedic authors. The same is true for Yin people; traditional Chinese medicine does not recommend fasting for them either. Why is it difficult for slim people to gain weight? Their inherited body constitution and metabolic type are mostly responsible; specifically, the fat-producing capacity of their liver is low or their metabolic rate is too fast.

Another benefit of dry fasting is worth mentioning: the fast goes more smoothly--no rumbling in the stomach, which usually accompanies water fasting--and there are no other discomforts. Except for the minor discomfort of being thirsty, you can cope with it by using imagery to picture yourself drinking cold water.

The common cold and flu can be quickly and effectively cured with dry fasting. Doctors and folk medicine healers typically prescribe drinking lots of herbal tea, such as raspberry tea with lemon. However, abstaining from all drinking and eating works even better. There is a saying that when we eat while ill, we feed the disease and it lasts longer. In the case of the common cold and flu, with mucus being expelled from the body by a runny nose, the mucus is burned more rapidly and we recover quickly if we decrease our water intake. I confirmed this with my own experience. I took a laxative and undertook dry fasting for two days. As a result, my temperature decreased to 37.7° C in one day; the next day, it was normal at 36.7° C and I felt fully recovered.

Dry fasting also helps to get rid of kidney stones. Kidney cells clean not only the blood that passes through them, but also themselves with the metabolic water that flushes out the deposited salts and stones. My own experience proves it. For eight months, I had a back pain in my left side. It did not bother me in a normal sitting or standing position, but when I tried to arch my spine while exercising, I felt a mild pain in the left kidney area. The pain gradually vanished during one month of alternative dry fasting that I underwent in August 1997.

There are even claims that dry fasting is helpful for patients with tumors. If water fasting fails to cure tumors, dry fasting should be undertaken, as recommended by the Russian naturopath, G.P. Malakhov, in his book *Fasting* (in Russian).

In my experience, I tried dry fasting for 42 hours "after Ivanov" a few times during the last ten years, both in winter and in summer. To illustrate the workability of dry fasting for me in gaining weight, let me describe the 42-hour fast that I undertook in Japan in December 1994. In the two weeks before fasting, my weight was quite stable, about 76 kilograms. My diet in Japan at that time consisted of rice with milk and a banana for breakfast, some kind of fish or seafood with miso soup for lunch, and a type of vegetable soup with buckwheat or noodles for dinner.

The last food and water intake was at 10 p.m. and I took a 0.75-liter enema of boiled and then cooled water with the juice of half a lemon at midnight. Because some water was absorbed through the lining of the intestine, the enema actually marked the start of this fast on Friday, December 24, 1994. During the next 40 hours that I abstained from food and water, my weight dropped by 3 kilograms, from 76 to 73 kilograms. I took my first drink--the freshly squeezed juice of carrots, sweet peppers, and celery--at 4 p.m. on Sunday. The fiber of these vegetables mixed with the yogurt that I ate shortly after was my first food. For dinner that day, I cooked noodle soup with potatoes, tofu, and onion. After fasting, I resumed my usual diet and my starting weight of 76 kilograms was restored in two days. I continued to gradually gain weight and within the next month, it increased to 79 kilograms. Within the next two months I gained an additional 3 kilograms, bringing my weight to 82 kilograms.

I undertook the next 42-hour dry fast in March 1995; however, this time it was for body cleansing rather than weight gain. My starting weight was 82 kilograms, which is very close to my standard weight of 82.4 kilograms. By the end of the fasting, I had lost 4.2 kilograms, but again, my weight returned to 82 kilograms within one week.

Weight loss during a dry fast depends on body constitution, metabolic rate, starting weight, weather conditions, stress level, and other factors. In my case, the weight loss of 3 and 4.2 kilograms in previous fasts occurred from the starting weights of 76 and 82 kilograms, respectively, and both fasts were in cold seasons. However, in Tokyo on June 28-29, 1996, I undertook a 42-hour dry fasting in that hot summer and lost 5.2 kilograms, from a starting weight of 79.7 kilograms.

Some people experienced dry fasting when they were involuntarily deprived of food and water.

Elizabeth Choy, 87, of Singapore was interned for about seven months in World War II during the Japanese occupation. "It was a nightmare. I cannot believe it happened. It was two hundred days of starvation, torture, without a comb, toothbrush," she said. There were days that she was left *without food* and *drink*, reported *The Straits Times* in the November 1, 1997, issue. "My waist shrank to 18 inches [45 centimeters] from 25 inches. What saved me were my prayers and faith in God."

The case of Andreas Mihavecz of Bregenz, Austria, was even included in *The 1997 Guinness Book of World Records* as the world's longest deprivation of food and water. Eighteen-year-old Andreas was locked up by the police in a holding cell in a local government building on April 1, 1979, and was totally forgotten until April 18. He was discovered close to death after seventeen days without food and water. There are no details available about how he felt those seventeen days, but one can imagine how stressful and frightening that time was for him. He survived, but the conditions of his compulsory dry fasting were extremely severe psychologically.

Leonid Aleksandrovich of Russia undertook a voluntary dry fasting for rejuvenation and health-enhancing purposes. In March 1981, he fasted for ten days without water. He got some moisture from the night air and through his skin by occasionally submerging himself in a tub of water during the day. He lost 20 kilograms of his weight, but recovered in one week after breaking the fast. His longest fast lasted eighteen days and he claimed that it was longer than the *Guinness Book* of records.

Strictly speaking, his fasts were partial ones because *complete dry fasting* implies total abstinence from contact with water. Of all the other fasting methods, complete dry fasting has the greatest curing effect because it is the only method in which all cells of the body, including the skin, are renewed and repaired. Even washing hands is not recommended. Nevertheless, Leonid's eighteen-day fast was a great personal achievement that also provided beneficial evidence about the practice of dry fasting.

In this country, I thought I was the only person who practiced dry fasts. However, just recently I encountered on the Internet an essay on dry fasting by David Wolfe, a health professional from San Diego, California. He mentions at least four people who have gone seven to nine days without food and water. He writes also about his friend, Joe Alexander, who undertook a twenty-one-day fast, the first seven days of which were dry--no food, no water. Joe described it as a remarkable experience, saying, "Maybe the best thing to do when fasting is go as long as you can without food or water. Could well be that we would be much healthier and live longer if maybe once or twice a year, we'd take a week off, rest, and not eat or drink even water."

28

ALTERNATE DRY FASTING

Recent information about alternate dry fasting appeared in the following Russian books: *The Keys to Life Secrets*, by Valentina Lavrova, *Fasting*, by G. Malakhov, and *Encyclopedia of Your Health*, by Valentina Efimova-Yaraeva. The procedure originally developed by Lavrova is called "cascade fasting," which implies alternating dry fast days and drinking/eating days. There is even an "inventor" of dry fasting–L.A. Stchennikov–who received the USSR Certificate of Invention No. 2028160, called *The Method of Organism Recovery*. Lavrova, who claims that she received this method as an "insight" from "higher forces," describes it in great detail. The following full-length procedure for achieving the maximum curing and rejuvenating effect takes five months:

• First month: Alternating one fast day and one rehabilitation day; that is, one day of dry fasting followed by one day of drinking and eating. This sequence is repeated fifteen times during one month. Only a vegetarian diet is recommended on rehabilitation days.

• Second month: Alternating two fast days and two rehabilitation days; that is, two days in a row of dry fasting, then two days of drinking and eating. This is continued for one month.

• Third month: Alternating three fast days and three rehabilitation days.

• Fourth month: Alternating four fast days and four rehabilitation days.

• Fifth month: Alternating five fast days and five rehabilitation days.

In each of the five months, the total number of dry fast days equals fifteen. The fifth month is the most difficult because going without water and food for five days results in severe thirst. However, if the person has the will and patience, all possible diseases can be cured–**even AIDS, cancer, and diabetes–by alternating five days of fasting**, claims Lavrova.

The Author's One-Month Alternate Dry Fasting

Having had about ten experiences of 42-hour dry fasting, I wanted to test myself on how long I could go without water and food. In those days, back in 1987, in Moscow, I fasted about every two or three months, gradually increasing the dry fast duration from 48 to 54, 60, and 72 hours. The last one was my personal record, but I couldn't see any specific result or health improvement because I had no particular health problem at that time. I strongly believed in dry fasting and considered it an overall curing method, so I tried to master it in order to have it "for emergency." I needed it because I was planning to emigrate from Russia to Israel and wanted to be able to cure myself if necessary. I was preparing myself to face the odds of an immigrant's life, in case I happened to get sick and had no money to see a doctor.

Fortunately, I have been an immigrant for ten years without getting seriously sick, so I have had no opportunity to use the powerful method of dry fasting for self-curing purposes. Three years ago in Japan, after coming back from a six-week vacation trip to the United States and Europe, I got a fever. To cure myself, I stayed in bed, abstained from food for three days, and drank ginger tea; this was water fasting, not dry fasting.

However, I was impressed with the description of cascade (i.e., alternate) dry fasting and its miraculous rejuvenation effects, and I was eager to apply it to myself. I had a few ailments such as pain in my lower back on the left side in the kidney region (kidney stones?); a polyp found in my gallbladder in September 1996 during a medical checkup in Japan; I was underweight by about 5 percent; my vision was changing, and some other minor conditions, which I wanted to eliminate or improve by means of dry fasting. Although I was prepared mentally, the proper conditions did not appear until I moved to Rome, Maine, in July 1997, and I then had an ideal environment. The best conditions for fasting therapy are when you are alone and close to nature. For his seven-day fasts, Dr. Bragg also preferred to seclude himself in a quiet place, staying at a camp near a river. Similarly, my summer camp is near a lake, the weather was fine, and I enjoyed complete solitude.

Dry fasting is an intense therapy and it greatly taxes the vital organs; therefore, a preliminary cleansing of the digestive tract is essential. I first undertook the liver, gallbladder, and large intestine cleansing therapy (i.e., enema) described previously. On the starting day of July 31, my weight at 9 a.m. was 165 pounds. Using a juicer, I squeezed 380 milliliters of fresh juice from three big apples and drank it at 10 a.m. I prepared and drank the same amount three more times that day, at 2 p.m., 6:30 p.m., and 9 p.m. Each time,

I weighed myself and registered the time of urination and the amount expelled. In the first day, I drank a total of 1,550 milliliters of apple juice, and expelled 2,390 milliliters of urine by the next morning; my weight dropped by 6 pounds.

In the morning of the second day, I took a 2,000-milliliter enema of boiled warm water made from chamomile and 1 teaspoon of freshly squeezed lemon juice. Then I drank four equal amounts of apple juice, the first at 8 a.m. and the last at 6:30 p.m. Then I prepared a mixture of freshly squeezed lemon juice and olive oil, 300 milliliters each. This mixture was divided into six portions and I drank one portion every 15 minutes, starting at 7 p.m. In between the olive-oil/lemon-juice drinks and later in the night, I laid on my right side holding a hot-water bottle against my liver. I finished the mixture at 8:15 p.m. and fell asleep.

My first bowel movement occurred at 5 a.m. the next morning, eliminating a few dozen soft green and pale-colored stones up to a half-inch in diameter. I had a second bowel movement at 7 a.m. and a third at 9:15 a.m. I collected and rinsed all the stones, placing them on a plastic plate and periodically observing them. The number of green and pale-colored stones was about the same. Gradually, the green ones--consisting of condensed bile--melted into liquid bile; however, the pale-colored stones, perhaps a mixture of bile and calcium salts, did not lose their shape. Although I had considered my diet to be quite healthy in the last year, I was surprised to see how many stones were in my liver and gallbladder. Three and a half years later, when I again did the liver flush, I expelled about two dozen (half-ounce in weight) pale-colored stones ranging in size from one-quarter to three-quarter inches. This means that I tend to form liver and gallbladder stones and I need to periodically flush my liver.

At 9 a.m., my weight was 157 pounds; I had lost 8 pounds in those two days. I started breaking the fast with a glass of water with 2 tablespoons of sour cream dissolved in it. Then I had fresh juice made of carrots and beets, followed by croquets made from the pulp of those vegetables and flour. That day, I had two more meals of fruit, green salad, and vegetable soup with noodles and tofu. At 10:30 p.m., I took a 1,500-milliliter enema and soon another five large stones up to three-quarter inches in size were expelled. In the next two days, I continued to eat vegetarian food, and did my usual yoga exercises in the morning and 120 knee bends and flexibility exercises in the evening. My weight increased to 165 pounds after two days. The next day, August 5, 1997, was the first day of my one-month alternate dry fasting.

As explained previously, alternate dry fasting involves one day of no food and no water, followed by one day of drinking water and eating vegetarian food; this sequence is repeated for one month. On the fasting days, any contact with water–even a bath or shower--must be avoided. To increase the detoxifying effect of fasting, I modified this therapy by adding daily enemas using all the urine that I collected the previous day and night.

On the first day, I took the 1,500-milliliter urine enema at 7:30 a.m. and abstained from food and water until the next morning. Every 3 hours, I measured my weight, heart rate, body temperature, and amount of urine after each void. I usually kept the bottle of collected urine in the refrigerator, warming it before using it for enemas. On that day, I reduced my usual activity, worked a little on a book, sunbathed for 20 minutes, and napped for 2 hours. I had four urine flows in the daytime and one during the night. The night urine was very dark and became cloudy after a few hours, so I discarded it.

The next day, I measured my weight (159 pounds), body temperature (36.0° C), and resting heart rate (60 beats per minute). I started by drinking 300 milliliters of warm spring water. Then I had a 1,150-milliliter urine enema and, after a bowel movement, I did my morning set of yoga exercises. During the day, I ate three vegetarian meals, drank a few glasses of water and green tea with ginseng, and took vitamin supplements. I recorded all food eaten and the amounts, and took measurements as mentioned previously. I ate my usual amount of food and by the end of the day, my weight was up to 165 pounds.

The following twenty-eight days were dry-fast days with intermittent eating/drinking days. I continued my exercise regimen and usually did morning yoga exercises and two hundred knee bends every day, regardless of whether it was a fast day. On eating days, I also did six exercises with dumbbells and walked for 1 hour after lunch. The amount of urine expelled after fast days averaged 1,000 milliliters; after eating/drinking days, it was 1,400 milliliters. During dry-fast days, my urine became gradually darker in color. As a result, a layer of brown sediment formed on the bottom of the urine bottle. I guess it was the sand that came out of my kidneys; the pain near my left kidney during backward body bends did not bother me anymore.

My diet on eating days consisted of fruit, berries, nuts, green salads, cooked vegetables, oatmeal, buckwheat, rice noodles, tofu, miso, olive oil, and other vegetarian food. I also had peanut butter and grape jelly sandwiches made with oatmeal bread. My drinks were mostly warm boiled water, green tea with ginseng and brown sugar, and instant breakfast diluted with hot water.

My physical condition and mood were good and, despite instances of doubt and self-indulgence, I was determined to continue the fast and to complete the entire program. There were occasional uncomfortable feelings such as a rumbling stomach, excess gas, ringing in the ears, and headache, but these discomforts were minor. I found that the Shoulder Stand inverted pose helped relieve a headache quickly. In some instances, it was my own fault because my dinner on eating days sometimes was as late as 10:30 p.m. and my sleep that night was interrupted.

Most of the time I slept soundly, except for waking up once or twice to void. From my previous experience, dreams during fasts are very bright and lucid. Every night I expected to have interesting dreams, but they were nothing special this time--not nightmares, but not especially pleasant dreams. Only once, after the thirteenth fast day, did I have a frightening dream. In the dream, I saw that the skin on my left shin near the ankle separated and my flesh was revealed. I saw that the skin on the left part of my belly had also separated and I could see a dark red internal organ. Two strangers were nearby and I showed them, trying to explain it. Then I discovered that on the right side of my belly, the skin didn't cover my organs anymore. I was scared and wanted to fix my belly and leg with tape.

In my diary, I recorded all the foods and drinks, as well as their amounts that I ate and drank on the eating days. Based on these records, I compiled a chart of my nutrition, which is shown in Appendix D. This chart also contains an estimate of all nutrients, vitamins, and minerals that I took and how they compared to the RDA. As shown in the chart, although I did not eat animal proteins, the proteins from vegetables, nuts, tofu, and grains were approximately the amount advised by the RDA. Concerning vitamins and minerals, I did not get a sufficient amount from food; therefore, I took some supplements too.

Although I ate enough food on eating days, because of the dry-fast days my weight was steadily decreasing and I was becoming thinner–in fact, by the end of the fast, I was quite skinny. The change in my weight before, during, and after dry fasting–a total of ten months–is shown in Figure 28-1.

As shown in the figure, my weight at the beginning of the fast was a little lower than usual as a result of the liver-cleansing therapy prior to the dry fast. The daily fluctuations of my weight during its overall steady decrease during the one-month alternate dry fast were about 5 to 7 pounds.

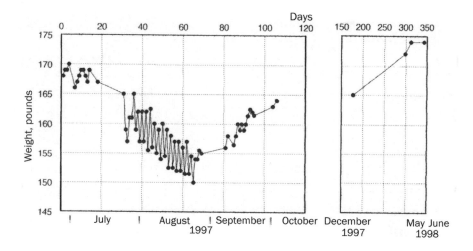

Figure 28-1. Changes in the Author's Weight Induced by Alternate Dry Fast

Restoring the weight after ending the fast was a very slow process for a few reasons. First, because of my body constitution--I am naturally thin and gaining weight has always been difficult for me. Second, after just four rehabilitation days in the United States, I traveled to Japan, where I stayed for one month, followed by a two-month stay in Singapore. Then I went back to Japan for three months and visited China for ten days. The change in continents, climate, and diet resulted in a physiological stress on my body, causing my weight restoration to halt. I was back in the United States for six months before I fully regained my weight. The photographs taken in April 1998 show that I was no longer skinny; my weight was actually about 10 pounds heavier than when I started the dry fast. I am quite certain that I would have regained the weight more quickly if I stayed in the United States for a couple more months. Nonetheless, I conclude that even for my naturally thin body type, the dry-fast therapy enables me to gain some weight because of the detoxification and cleansing effects on my body and all its systems.

My appearance by the end of the fast was so bad that my Japanese friend Yasuko nearly cried when she met me at the airport in Tokyo. She had not seen me for five months and saw such big changes in me that she kept saying, "What did you do to yourself? You look so bad." She was right--I was afraid to see myself in a mirror, and even avoided meeting with some Japanese friends because of how I looked. However, after my weight came back to normal, my appearance also improved. I consider the overall effect of this fast on my health to be positive because I got rid of kidney sand and liver stones, and the pain in my back vanished. More than that, however, I had a valuable experience and gained the confidence that I can use this powerful method in case of a serious disease. However, Xu Fang was very adamant concerning my fasts when she told me, "Fasting is bad for your health. Don't fast." I agree with her to some degree. It seems that such a tough regimen like dry fasting is more appropriate for a person who is robust and vital; because I am not, the physiological stress imposed on my body perhaps exceeds the positive effects of the dry fast.

Thinning and Graying Hair

Hair loss and graying hair are the biomarkers of aging. There are a few observations that stress, which involves an increased production of free radicals and a depletion of antioxidants, is responsible for sudden hair loss and the whitening of hair. Free radicals damage the melanocytes and their enzyme tyrosinase, which produce hair pigment and color our hair. Food preferences can also affect the condition of hair. Another observation shows that eating high-cholesterol food, such as meat in excess, puts a person at higher risk of developing heart disease and turns their hair gray prematurely. Hair thinning and loss in men may also be caused by excessive ejaculation, which drains essential nutrients from the body.

Likewise, hair thickening and restoration of the primary color of graying hair are definite indicators of rejuvenation. Following are a few reported cases:

• In his book, *Eat Right, Live Longer,* Neal Barnard, M.D., describes the case of Ed Huling of Bethesda, Maryland, whose hair became noticeably thin at the age of thirty. It seemed that genetics played a role because his father became bald at about the same age. Ed was overweight and, in trying to lose 40 pounds, he turned to a vegetarian diet consisting mostly of raw vegetables and fruits. He lost the desired pounds and within two years, his hair became full and thick again.

• According to John Heinerman, Ph.D., the white hair of Dr. Ann Wigmore that she had at age fifty was restored to its natural dark color when she was eighty-five by eating fermented (i.e., sprouted) grains, nuts, and seeds and by drinking raw juices, especially wheat-grass juice.

• According to Victoras Kulvinskas, there were reports in Japan about a few men who claimed that their gray hair darkened after they drank wheat-grass juice.

• Charles Hamilton of Thousand Oaks, California, wrote in a testimonial that his previously gray "beard and mustache has gradually changed color until it is nearly black," which resulted from practicing five ancient rites–exercises involving chakra workouts that are described in the book, *Ancient Secret of the Fountain of Youth*, by Peter Kedler.

• There are also references claiming that barley-grass juice, walnuts, and black sesame seeds help darken graying hair.

The rejuvenation methods discussed in this part of the book deal primarily with cleansing, detoxification, and fasting as means to improve the functioning of vital organs. Giving all due credit to fasting for its great cleansing effect, I have to admit that a raw-food diet is superior to it. You cannot fast seven days a week, but you can eat cleansing and detoxifying raw fruits and vegetables every day for years. The most profound effect on body cleansing and rejuvenation can be achieved by the combination of a raw-food diet and juice or water fasts for one day a week. Dry fasting can be used in an emergency to cure a serious disease.

PART FIVE: LONGEVITY

To live on our wonderful Earth longer,
Was always the dream of all humankind.
With passing ages, this urge grew stronger,
And now science is about secrets to find.

Meanwhile, by adhering to a lifestyle's fidelity,
We can become a centenarian personality.
If we follow the paths laid by longevity crusaders,
And open our mind for their wisdom to persuade us.

They will teach you to grasp all your will powers,
To turn to fasting, exercise, and a raw-plant diet.
And doing all things right for your type, if you try it,
Your reward is a long life filled with beautiful flowers,

And the joy of being young in body, mind, and spirit,
And living a life that's full with all the glory that's in it.

Currently, the number of people worldwide who live 100 years and more is probably approaching 100,000. Rich nations have the most centenarians and this sector of the population is faster growing than any other age group. In the United States alone, this number in 1998 was 61,000, although some authors and I as well think this figure is overestimated. We can compare this figure with a little more than 10,000 centenarians in Japan, where a reliable birth-registration system was established almost 130 years ago. It is known that Japan has the longest life expectancy and the highest ratio of centenarians in the world. Because the population of Japan is about half that of the United States, it corresponds to approximately 20,000 in the United States, even if we assume the same centenarian ratio for the two countries. Thousands of the oldest old live also in Canada, Europe, China, and Australia, as well as Asian, South American, and African countries.

Most of us probably would not deny wishing to become a member of this honorable group and live longer, provided we stay in good physical and mental health. Both targets--longer years and a life of health and vigor--are they really achievable? The answer is one word is YES. Examples of centenarians in this book provide evidence for this assurance. Every person, even without great genes, is able to vastly improve the duration and quality of life. If taken under control, lifestyle--as a major component of longevity--can help in achieving life-extension goals.

Regardless of your chronological age, you can start a life-extension program at any time. The sooner the better, but it is never too late, even if you are in your seventies or eighties. There is always room for physical and/or mental improvement.

29

APPROACHES TO LONGEVITY

Every nation has its own ideas about longevity and develops its own methods on how to achieve it. The international community now enjoys the combined wisdom of all nations and modern research, and is informed about all knowledge regarding life extension. Well known are longevity systems of the ancient Ayurveda, Yoga, and traditional Chinese medicine. Yet, there are health enthusiasts and longevity explorers who, through their outstanding achievements, add their unique contributions to the wisdom of humankind and our knowledge about longevity. The approaches to longevity described in this chapter do not cover all existing methods; rather, it is a review of those individuals who left a deep impression on this author.

Raw-Food Diet Approach

Dr. Norman W. Walker, from Arizona, an American enzyme researcher for more than fifty years, lived to the great age of 109. Until his last days, he was healthy, disease-free, completely independent, and leading an active life. He grew his own vegetables and used to eat them raw more often than cooked. In his book, *Natural Weight Control*, Dr. Walker wrote: "Every plant, vegetable, fruit, nut, and seed in its raw natural state is composed of atoms and molecules. Within these atoms and molecules reside the vital elements we know as enzymes." The enzymes in the human body are similar to those in vegetation. However, enzymes are sensitive to heat and, at 130°F, they are dead. Therefore, the best way to get them into the body is to eat raw food, which is "live" food; cooked food has no enzymes and it is "dead" food. To be healthy and to have a slim and vibrant body, one must consume raw and high-water-content food, emphasized Dr. Walker.

Edward Howell, M.D., an American pioneering enzymologist and the author of the raw-food-diet classic, *Enzyme Nutrition*, believed that our longevity depends on the quantity and strength of enzymes present in the body. According to Dr. Howell, the more cooked enzyme-less food we consume, the faster we age. To spare the body's enzyme-producing systems and thus retard the aging process, it is essential to obtain food enzymes from raw fruits and vegetables or from enzyme supplements. In his nineties, Dr. Howell was fit and robust; he attributed his longevity to his habit of eating raw food for many years.

Souren Arakelyan, Ph.D., seventy-one, a Russian biologist, announced that he is going to live to 125. In his longevity system, Dr. Arakelyan combines a vegetarian diet of raw foods, exercise, and short-term fasting. He eats two or three times a day. For the first ten years of his self-experiment, which he began in 1965, he consumed 2,000 kcal a day, then reduced it to 1,500 kcal within the next five years; his current daily consumption is 1,000 kcal. His one meal consists of 50 grams of raisins, two raw carrots, or one orange; or 100 grams of raw cabbage; or 50 grams of peas, kidney beans, or lentils; or 100 grams of raw wheat, pearl barley, buckwheat, and whole grains. He first pours boiling water over grains and dry fruit and then soaks them overnight.

Dr. Arakelyan fasts for the first three days of every month--he eats no food but he drinks water, supplementing it with an "anti-stress" mixture. This mixture consists of 0.005 gram of lemon acid, 0.005 milliliter of mint infusion, 1 gram of honey, and 1 milliliter of water per 1 kilogram of a person's weight; he drinks this on each of the three days of fasting. His exercise regimen includes running about 2 miles every day.

According to Dr. Arakelyan, 30 billion cells die in our body every minute. After a short time, the dead cells become poisonous to our systems; the best way to get rid of these toxins is by fasting. Another way is to avoid ingesting dead cells from cooked food and animal food. Strenuous physical exercise is also necessary to burn the dead cells and cells that are alien to our body; for example, yeast--an accumulation of yeast in the body is responsible for cancerous growths and cardiovascular diseases. When asked what is the real life span for humans, Dr. Arakelyan replied: "Three hundred to five hundred years. It will occur when we learn how to replace the inter-cell sodium with potassium." In his fasting experiments on chickens, he achieved a threefold increase in the life span, the highest yet in biological science.

The recipe for a yeast-free bread is as follows: 1 kilogram of whole wheat flour, 100 grams of vegetable oil, and some water to make the dough. A scone is then baked in the oven at 113 to 118° F (45 to 48°C). To make the bread sweet, add 100 grams of honey to the dough. Dr. Arakelyan usually drinks water with the addition of baking soda (1gram per 3 liters). He also likes soda water with honey with a few grains of lemon acid in it. Eating lemons with honey is a well-known cure and prevention remedy. On fasting days, he drinks about 2 liters of unfiltered tap water.

Balanced Diet Approach

Justine Glass, an English gerontologist, believes a balanced diet is the primary key to achieving the age of 180. Her life-extension system also includes exercise, correct breathing, and the mind/body connection--but proper nutrition for all body systems, she believes, is of primary importance. In her dietary recommendations, she advises against cocoa and chocolate, which deprive the body of calcium, thereby advancing the aging processes and shortening life.

Galina Shatalova, M.D., a Russian scientist in diet and nutrition, thinks that a low-calorie (i.e., 1,000 calories), low-protein (i.e., 18 to 20 grams), well-balanced diet will greatly prolong your life. She was one of the first medical doctors who promoted live food in Russia. She claims that many of her patients who suffered from diabetes were cured by a healthy diet alone. She believes that elderly people who eat bread harm themselves because the baking process entails very high temperatures that destroy the structure of proteins and water, resulting in poor digestion. However, she allows some cooked food, provided the temperature does not exceed the boiling point, and she recommends that the food be boiled for only a few minutes.

To prove the validity of her approach, she and a group of her followers went through the Kara Kum Desert in Central Asia in 1989. Their food consisted of dry fruits, nuts, honey, soup made of rice and herbs, and green tea. All members of her group finished the trek in good condition, although half of the members of another group--who ate a "civilized, normal diet"-- failed to pass through the desert. Dr. Shatalova is now in her nineties, but still is very active and even participates in long-distance runs.

Caloric Restriction Approach

Roy Walford, M.D., an American biogerontologist, has been living on a calorie-restricted diet since 1987. His experiments on many groups of animals have proven that caloric restriction extends the life span twofold. To confirm that caloric restriction also works for humans, Dr. Walford began experimenting on himself. "Walford deserves enormous credit for doing what few humans have attempted, and those of us who know of his efforts to increase our knowledge of human aging wish him well," wrote Leonard Hayflick in his book, *How and Why We Age*. Dr. Walford's diet is nutrient-dense and his daily intake is approximately 1,500 to 2,000 calories, which is about 500 to 1,000 calories per day fewer than most elderly men eat in this country. He is in his seventies now and we need to live another forty to fifty years to know whether he was right.

Natural Health Approach

Dr. Paul Bragg was a reputed American health pioneer who lived to the age of ninety-five and died in an accident: he drowned while practicing surfing in California. His book, *The Miracle of Fasting,* became very popular in Russia in the 1970s and 1980s. He and his daughter, Patricia Bragg, Ph.D., developed a life-extension program to live to 120. Their system includes natural-food diets, exercising in the fresh air and sunshine, drinking distilled water, short-term fasts, and deep diaphragm breathing.

Dr. Alexander A. Mikulin (1895-1985) was an academician, the Soviet designer of jet airplane engines, and author of the book *Active Long Life: My System to Combat Senility*. He was a renowned scientist and engineer, and he designed the best airplane engines in the world. Of 125,000 military airplanes that were produced in the USSR during World War II, 40,000 fighters were equipped with his engines. For his extraordinary achievements, in 1940 he was awarded the order of the "Hero of the Socialist Labor," which was marked No.3 on the reverse side (No.1 belonged to Joseph Stalin). He did not pay much attention to his own health until the age of fifty, when he fell seriously ill with heart disease. As most people, he greatly exploited his body as if its resources were endless. He also was too busy with his work and had no time for himself. However, when he spent a few months in the hospital, he finally had this time.

He started to think about the human organism as an engine that needs to be treated carefully, if one wants to be fit and healthy. This was a turning point in his life and, after recovering from the illness, he began to study physiology and anatomy. He started to experiment on himself by cleansing his body of wastes and doing many kinds of exercises using training machines that he developed. With diaphragm breathing, he learned to stop within a few seconds the cardiac assaults that previously led to his hospitalization. In searching for health and fitness, he studied the influence of biocurrents, negative ions, heat stress, facial and body exercises, and body shakes on the human body. He developed and applied to himself body shakes by striking his heels against the floor (this increased the venous blood flow due to stimulation of the venous valves in the legs), hot steambaths, air ionizer, and rowing machine. As a result of his efforts, he cured himself of heart disease and, until his death at the age of ninety, he was leading an active life playing tennis, mountaineering, and courting women.

Michael M. Kotlyarov, a journalist and famous Russian health enthusiast, lived to the age of almost ninety. He retired at sixty-four, a seriously ill man suffering from ischemic heart disease and tuberculosis, and taking handfuls of medicine. He started a health-restoration program with food restriction, walking and then running exercises, and training to the cold. At seventy-five, he ran a marathon. When he was eighty-three, the All-Union Cardiology Research Center in Moscow found in its medical examination that his physiological functions were similar to those of twenty-five to forty-year-old men. At the age of eighty-six, he won two gold medals at an international championship for athletes/veterans.

He was often seen running in Moscow wearing only a T-shirt and shorts regardless of the season–both in +86°F (30°C) in summer and -58°F (-50°C) in winter. His motto was, "A healthy spirit makes the body healthy too." By overall self-control, he trained both his body and his nervous system to achieve a positive psychological state. In his late eighties, he led the life of a young man, going to different places around the country giving health lectures, participating in ballroom dancing contests, and having all-night discussions with sportsmen. He died from cancer, which caused severe pain and suffering, but he maintained his high spirit and love of life till the end.

Natural Hygiene Approach

Dr. Herbert M. Shelton was a renowned and well-respected American proponent of the natural hygiene philosophy, principles, and practice. For more than half a century, he ran a "health school" in San Antonio, Texas, which included a clinic, laboratory, and teaching program. Natural hygiene teaches that the body has self-healing, self-cleansing, and self-maintaining abilities; and that all the healing power of the universe can be found in the human body, which is directed with an immense intelligence. If a person follows the laws of Nature, he/she will enjoy a healthy, happy, and long high-quality life. The tools of natural hygiene are healthy food and fasting. Dr. Shelton, who lived to the age of ninety, was living proof of the workability of the principles he preached. In his clinic, he healed thousands of people with fasting and proper diet. His book, *Fasting Can Save Your Life,* should be a textbook for anyone who seeks to improve his/her health and to increase vitality and length of life.

Biochemistry Approach

Linus Pauling, a two-time Nobel Prize winner, lived to the age of ninety-four. He took mega-doses (i.e., 18,000 milligrams a day) of vitamin C for a quarter-century, and believed that it helped postpone his prostate cancer (the cause of his death) by a full twenty years. Dr. Pauling also believed that a high intake of vitamin C and other vitamins could increase life expectancy by up to twenty-four years--that means someone who is expected to live to seventy or seventy-five has a good chance of making it to 100.

Durk Pearson and Sandy Shaw, authors of the best-selling book, *Life Extension*, rely on the achievements of current scientific research on aging and life extension. Their approach is not that of natural, holistic, or alternative medicine therapies; rather, they believe that nutrients and pharmaceuticals can extend people's life without the restrictions imposed by diets, vegetarian foods, exercise, and other alternative remedies. According to them, the aging effects that eventually end all athletic careers can be delayed by means of biochemistry for at least several years, and perhaps for decades.

Exercise Approach

Edward M. Yashin, 70, Ph.D., a Russian scientist in physics and mathematics, developed the original life-extension program in his aim to live forever. He belongs to the rare group of people who believe in immortality. He started the longevity experiment on himself twenty-seven years ago. He found a theoretical basis for immortality in the hypothesis of the Hungarian scientist Bauer, who suggested that isolated biological systems under certain conditions might live endlessly.

According to Bauer, the molecules of living organisms are always in a state of "stable non-equilibrium." To maintain the non-equilibrium state, the body does its work using the external energy that comes with food, water, and air. However, the external energy is alien to the organism and cannot be used for its further development unless it is built into its living structure. To be built-in, it must find space and, therefore, destroy a portion of the living organism. Bauer concluded that if the amount of energy produced by the destruction of part of an organism prevails over external energy, the rejuvenation process takes place.

This can be achieved by fasting, food-intake restriction, intense physical work or strenuous exercise, training to the cold, and so on. Dr. Yashin developed a program of lifestyle changes, including very strenuous exercise, fasting, little food, brief sleep, and high-intensity physical and psychological activities.

In the morning, he does an exercise that involves all muscles of his body. He starts by running around the room for 5 minutes, followed by the knee-bend exercise combined with jumping jacks. Then he does push-ups against the floor, pull-ups on a steel bar, and lifts 73 pounds (32 kilograms) with each arm. He follows that with the scissors exercise with his legs while lying face-up on the floor, and then lifting his legs over his head in the same position. Each exercise is done ten times, as fast as he can with increasing strength to the extent that he feels muscle pain. This set of exercises is repeated in the given order, with no rest between exercises; when he finishes one exercise, he rushes immediately to the next.

When he started the program, the duration of his morning exercise was 25 minutes; by 1997, it was 40 minutes. On weekends, he also includes a 15- to 20-minute speed run or marathon run. He eats one meal a day consisting of bread, raw vegetables, milk, and some meat. He sleeps 4 hours a night and leads a high-intensity life working in a research institute, acting as a coach, reading, writing, playing musical instruments, carving wood, learning foreign languages, and so on. His physical condition is remarkable: his resting heart rate is 36 beats per minute and his Harvard step-test ratio is 34 (a ratio of 26 is regarded as the best trained condition). "I feel as if I am twenty years old. I cannot wait to become 100 and thus prove that a person in ripe old age can and must stay healthy and young," Yashin said recently at the age of sixty-seven.

Kazuhiko Tsutsumi, ninety-five, of Japan, attributes his miracle recovery from liver disease to exercise and running. A former navy officer, he came back to Japan from the World War II South Asian front. At the age of forty-four, he experienced such severe pain that he could not work. His liver condition was very bad and incurable by existing means. Doctors told him that they gave up and that medicine was unable to help him. He did not give up, though, and started to apply an "anti-method" to himself: beating his body with a bamboo stick, massaging it, and swimming each morning in the nearby river. Beaten to death, his disease receded in one year.

At the age of sixty-two, he started jogging after being inspired by marathon runner Abebe Bikila of Ethiopia, a medalist at the Olympic Games in Tokyo. After that, he took part every year in a local mini-marathon event and, in 1997, he set a new world record running the 100-meter distance in a competition for ninety-five to ninety-nine-year-olds. "There is no place for repentance in my life" is the motto of Kazuhiko Tsutsumi, who was highly determined to run into the twenty-first century, as reported by *Asahi Shimbun* in the October 1, 1997 issue.

Yoga Approach

B.K.S. Iyengar, eighty-two, is author of *Light on Yoga* and other best-selling books, and a world-famous proponent of yoga. Iyengar has practiced yoga for more than sixty years and reveals an incredible flexibility in the photographs that illustrate his books. He is living proof of the old adage, "You are as young as your spine is flexible." Being vegetarian--which is natural for Indian people, and looking well fed--which is unusual among yogis, his body seems not to have changed for the last forty years.

Iyengar expanded my image of a typical yogi, which is usually very slim or even skinny. It seems that the layer of fat he has may even increase the flexibility of his spine and joints by serving as lubrication. He found an elixir of youth in yoga and invites others to join him. "It is never too late to practice yoga," he says in his book, *The Tree of Yoga*. He warns, however, about the dangers of injury if an elderly student of yoga is impatient and wants quick results.

Indra Devi was born in 1899 in Riga, Russia, and is famous for her best-selling book, *Forever Young, Forever Healthy*. She is a legendary yoga teacher who inspired yoga followers all over the world. She was attracted to India from her childhood days and traveled extensively in India, where she met Mahatma Gandhi and studied yoga with T. Krishnamacharya, Iyengar's yoga teacher. Devi established a yoga school in Hollywood in the late 1940s and Gloria Swanson was among her students.

She lectured worldwide and one of my teachers, Vladimir Kusnetsov, attended her yoga lecture in Moscow. He was impressed with the perfect yoga asanas that the eighty-five-year-old "First Lady of Yoga" demonstrated. When Suza Francina, author of the book, *The New Yoga for People Over 50: A Comprehensive Guide for Midlife and Older Beginners*, interviewed her, the ninety-four-year-old Devi said, "The practice of yoga is invaluable. Yoga affects all of our faculties--physical, mental, and spiritual." Every day she practiced asanas, deep breathing, and deep relaxation.

Restriction-Abundance Approach

The Author, sixty, developed his own system for improving health and fitness and achieving longevity. It is based on twenty years of studying holistic methods under the guidance of yoga teachers and self-experimenting with fasting, diets, and various exercises. The health and longevity seeker must first have the desire and determination to begin this life-long project and start working hard to achieve the goal. He/she must become number one and take control of his/her own life. Next, the person has to do a self-study in order to choose from the many existing recommendations those that fit best. This can be done through understanding the person's unique body constitution and personality peculiarities. The thirteen systems (i.e., eight Western and five Oriental) discussed in this book provide insight about a person, enabling him/her to determine a personality profile. This provides a theoretical basis and direction for achieving a balanced state of physical and emotional health.

Taking into account personality features and peculiarities, one can then apply dietary, exercise, and lifestyle recommendations; everyone has to find their own path to health and longevity. Overall health has the following four major manifestations:

• physical health (i.e., the two lower chakras; basic biological needs), which is influenced by heredity, diet, sleep, sex, breathing, fluid intake, exercise, lifestyle (work, rest, and habits), hygiene, training to cold, massage, and others

• emotional health (i.e., the two middle chakras; emotional needs), which is influenced by upbringing; emotions; desires; love; social, family, and sexual well-being; will power; being in control of body needs and emotional states; and being valued at work and by family and society

• mental health (i.e., the fifth and sixth chakras; intellectual needs), which is influenced by education, intellectual activity, creativity, being in control of mental states, interests, and goals

• spiritual health (i.e., the upper chakra; spiritual needs), which is influenced by altruism; ideal-seeking; self-actualization; intuition; perceiving one's role in Nature, the cosmos, and the universe; and striving for God and a higher Self.

Proper health and longevity may be achieved if one practices restriction regarding basic biological needs; takes control over emotional and mental states; allows talents, creativity, and skills to bloom in abundance; and strives for intellectual development and spiritual growth. In other words, a person leads his/her life with restrictions in the lower chakras and abundance in the upper chakras.

The personalized approach to longevity discussed in this book is a powerful instrument for achieving one's goals in the most effective way. Your time is precious and you do not have to lose it going in circles along the trial and error path. Actually, you will need some corrections and fine-tuning on the way, but that will increase your self-understanding and awareness. This is the direct road to becoming the master of your own life and the guru of your longevity.

30

FACTORS AFFECTING LONGEVITY

Longevity and the postponement of senility are influenced by a number of factors, including heredity; lifestyle; body type; health habits; socioeconomic status; and physical, emotional, mental, and spiritual condition. The interplay of many different factors may result in extreme longevity when people live to 100 years and more. Many centenarian studies show that interactive patterns involving personality, attitude, intelligence, and behavior seem to play a greater role than heredity, diet, and education. When it comes to longevity, especially exceptional longevity, psychological factors seem to prevail over physiology.

In the last decade, more emphasis has been on mental vigor and the interaction between the brain and the body. "Scientists are becoming convinced that longevity depends on a dynamic interplay involving three factors: the health of our brain, our attitudes and thinking patterns, and our general health—in other words, the brain-body connection," according to David Mahoney and Richard Restak, M.D., in their book *The Longevity Strategy*. Their strategy includes three objectives that lead to a healthy and happy longevity: an optimally functioning brain in a sound body, favorable social support systems, and financial security.

As far as physiology is concerned, only two factors have been scientifically determined to actually extend life, at least in animals: caloric restriction and lowering the body's core temperature. Much can be done to prevent the development of changes associated with old age by *diet* and moderation in food and drink, by *relaxation* of the mind through hobbies and vacations, by healthful but moderate *exercise*, and by other practices in the field of body and mind hygiene. In this brief review of longevity factors, we start with heredity and physiology, and continue with psychology and socioeconomic conditions. The groups of factors and individual factors that affect longevity are as follows:

1. Genetic, constitutional, and physiological factors: heredity,

grandparents' ages, parents' ages, height, body weight, teeth, metabolism, breathing, and chronic diseases

2. Lifestyle habits: lifestyle changes, diet, caloric restriction, fasting, exercise, smoking, drinking, and sleep

3. Psychological traits: optimism, devoutness, and attitude toward aging

4. Socioeconomic factors: childhood, education, occupation, and marriage

5. Destiny factors: luck

To avoid repetition, I only describe new factors, omitting those that were previously discussed in relevant chapters of this book.

Longevity and Height. A belief that many share is that only short, thin people live to be 100 years old, and there is enough evidence to ascertain that belief. The oldest living American, Thomas Mortensen, 115, a resident of San Rafael, California, who was born in Denmark, is just 5 feet, 4 inches (162.6 centimeters) tall. "It is common observation that the very long-lived men in our American population tend to be short," says Dr. W. Sheldon in his book, *Atlas of Men.* "Moreover, the shortness is not a result of decrement of stature in old age. These men have been short all their lives," he adds. William James, a Harvard doctor of medicine and a philosopher, suggested an explanation that perhaps being tall imposed an increased strain on the cardiovascular system "in an animal that has recently assumed an upright posture."

The heart of tall people is overstrained, working hard to pump blood to their long limbs. Their lungs, especially in the upper parts, have a poor supply of blood and also become weak. Tall people use most of their energy to move joints and little is left for other activities. They are usually very slow in their movements and less effective than their shorter counterparts.

When I was a college student, there was a fellow in my group, Pavel by name, whose height was about 2 meters, 10 centimeters (7 feet). He was quite thin, with prominent joints and an unattractive appearance. There was something wrong with his skeleton and he soon died, although he was just nineteen years old. The tallest recorded giant in medical history, Robert Wadlow (1918-1940), grew to a height of 2 meters, 72 centimeters (8 feet, 11 inches) and died at the age of twenty-two.

However, there are examples of tall centenarians.

Ciel Boyle, 106, from Randolph, Iowa, was 6 feet, 2 inches tall and he lived longer than many short people. Al Holmgren, 101, from Evanston, Illinois, was not only 6 feet, 2-1/2 inches tall, but he was also obese, weighing 245 pounds most of his life.

Longevity and Body Weight. The majority of long-living people are slim; however, there are exceptions to this rule. Hunza inhabitants, Vilcabambians, and Abkhasians, who are reputed for their longevity, are mostly slim and have no excess weight, especially the elderly. Among Abkhasians, fat people are regarded as ill and overeating is considered dangerous to the health. However, this belief does not find support among scientists and experts, as recent studies have shown.

"In the past few decades, Americans have been getting fatter and fatter, yet life expectancy has continued to increase. If fat were as lethal as many believe, we should see a more striking effect on mortality rates," say Dr. R. Ornstein and Dr. D. Sobel. "Contrary to the findings for a reduced-calorie diet, the finding is that a slight increase in weight during middle age will lengthen life. These conclusions are thought to relate to the poor American diet; the body needs to consume more food to offset the lack of meaningful nutrients. A varied diet of whole fresh foods will eliminate this problem and add years to your life," according to G. Kirschmann and J. Kirschmann.

Recently released data on the largest ever study of obesity and its effects on health show that being overweight increases the risk of premature death only moderately. A study published on January 1, 1998, in the *New England Journal of Medicine* found that the risk declines as people age, becoming negligible by age seventy-four. It appears that obesity is less dangerous than previously was thought. The American Cancer Society analyzed the obesity of 324,135 people of both sexes over a twelve–year period using the "body mass index." This is determined by dividing weight in kilograms by height in meters, squared. In this study, which was conducted by June Stevens with colleagues at the University of North Carolina in Chapel Hill, it was found that people with a body mass index between 19 and 22 lived the longest.

Longevity and Teeth. "Teeth are life," proclaim the smiling Japanese couple with brilliant white teeth on a poster in a Tokyo subway. My dentist in Japan, Dr. Arakawa, advised me to brush my teeth after each meal, first with toothpaste, then with just water, for a total of at least 20 minutes a day. Most Japanese are accustomed to brushing their teeth after each meal; after lunch, my coworkers stood in line in the company restroom waiting to get access to the sink.

Longevity and Body Temperature. Many gerontological studies show that reducing body temperature is one of the most promising ways to increase the lifespan of warm-blooded animals and humans. Decreasing the body temperature can be achieved with a low-calorie or a low-protein diet. With a low-calorie diet, the life span can be increased by 40 to 50 percent and body temperature decreased by 1.5 to 2.5°C; with a low-protein diet, the life span can be increased by 25 to 30 percent and body temperature decreased by 0.2 to 1.2°C, according to V.V. Frolkis in his book, *Aging and Life-Prolonging.* Thus, the main reason that the life span increases in animals on a low-calorie or low-protein diet is the drop in body temperature.

Depending on body constitution and metabolic rate, the body temperature of humans can vary within a few degrees. Do centenarians have a lower body temperature? The example of Lydia Vesselovzorova, who lived to be 103, shows that it may be so. According to *Harrison's Principles of Internal Medicine* (14th edition, 1998), the overall mean normal body temperature for healthy individuals between the ages of eighteen and forty is 36.8 ± 0.4°C (98.2 ± 0.7°F). In her case, it ranged from 35.8 to 36.4°C (96.4 to 97.5°F); that is, it was lower than normal. Actually, it is common for elderly people to have a decreased body temperature–the condition called *hypothermia*–when the core body temperature is lower than 35.0°C. It can be caused by excessive heat loss due to overexposure to a cold environment. Inadequate heat production as a result of decreased metabolism induced by malnutrition and hormonal disorders also may lead to hypothermia. In the case of Lydia Vesselovzorova, it was not hypothermia, just a minor lowering of the body temperature that may have been a characteristic of her body constitution and low metabolic rate. Her case is my only observation; perhaps specific centenarian studies are necessary to clarify this question.

Longevity and Chronic Diseases. A strong immune system with an ability to cope with chronic diseases, acquired from their parents, is one secret of exceptionally long-lived people. Again, Lydia Vesselovzorova, who lived to be 103, is an example of someone who was never seriously sick throughout her long life. She attributed her perfect health entirely to her great heredity.

The diseases most likely to occur in old age are *cancer*, which is particularly a disease of old age, and *enlargement of the prostate gland*, which is said to occur in at least half of all men over the age of seventy. *Arthritis* is another condition especially frequent in people after the age of forty, which cripples and disables many older people. Many centenarians have suffered from these diseases for a part or most of their lives; however, they did not cause their death as they do in other people.

> Nataliya Yusova, who lived to be 101, had a skin cancer that started some twenty years ago, but it progressed very slowly. She underwent radiation treatment at the age of 100. When I visited her in February 1999, the doctors were as surprised as I was about the success of the cure.

Oscar Williams, 101 (in 1987), from Decatur Country, Georgia, had prostate cancer and cobalt treatments ten years earlier. "There still is some cancer in the scrotum, but it doesn't worry him and it doesn't seem to progress," said Jim Heynen in his book, *One Hundred Over 100.*

Frank Flansburg, 101, another centenarian in Heynen's book, said, "I've been sick most of my life. Arthritis has been the worst. Had it my whole life. It's not so bad in my shoulders. But it's my knees, my fingers, and thumbs. I've got arthritis in my face!"

The people, not the diseases, won in these cases, which is what makes centenarians so special. Even if they got sick, they fought the disease successfully by either their great genes, which we could call a "God-made centenarian," or a great personal will, called a "self-made centenarian," like Rosa Mae Wolfe, 101. She said, "But I think I've stayed healthy because I've had arthritis of the spine and I had to exercise to stay well. I've had pain all my life."

In order not to fall victim to disease, the primary and secondary disease discovery and treatment is extremely important. The most developed countries and wealthy nations such as the United States, Western Europe, Japan, and Singapore provide their people with advanced medical diagnostic and cure technologies and techniques. As a result, early detection and curative measures enable people in those countries to enjoy the longest life span and have the highest percentage of centenarians. If the rate is a few individuals per 10,000 in developed countries, then only a few or even fewer than one centenarian per 100,000 in China and Russia is found. For instance, only one centenarian, Nataliya Yusova, lived in Nahkodka, Russia.

Among mental disorders, *dementia* is often found to accompany the last years of old people. However, the New England Centenarian Study, in which the cognitive function of sixty-nine centenarians was tested, revealed surprising results. Although the oldest people frequently have some degree of dementia, 20 percent surveyed in this study survived the years in perfect mental health. "It has been common thinking that dementia is inevitable with old age. That isn't so. We are studying centenarians whose thinking is perfectly clear," concluded Margery Silver, an associate director of the study.

Longevity and Lifestyle Changes. One theory of aging implies that the number of changes in our lifestyle influences our life span. The more often we change our environment and lifestyle, the less we live because each shift causes harmful physiological and psychological stresses on our body. Long-living people typically live in one place their entire life and do not travel much. They are accustomed to their environment, lead a quiet life, and usually are confident and content with their lives. Almost nothing changes around them and time in some sense has stopped for them.

Longevity and Exercise. The world's longevity champion, Jeanne Calment, of France, who lived to be 122; South African, Dorah Ramothibe, 114; and Alice Wei, 107, of Singapore, were reported to be active but they were not known to do any special exercises. Examples of exercising centenarians who confirmed that moderate exercise contributed to their long lives include George Burns, 100 (walking, stretching); the Delaney sisters, Elizabeth, 104, and Sarah, 107 (yoga); Matniaz Olobergenov, 107, (flexibility); Roy White, 106 (weight-lifting); and Toraichi Okuyama, 103, (running).

Longevity and Smoking. The scientific society does not welcome tobacco smoking into the realm of longevity; it warns that a person who smokes two or more packs of cigarettes a day must subtract twelve years from the average life span; between one and two packs, seven years; and less than a pack a day, two years. A forty-year study conducted by physicians in Great Britain showed that smoking is very bad for the health, while moderate drinking can increase longevity. Although statistically the data show adverse effects from smoking, many individual centenarians--including Jeanne Calment, 122, of France--smoked most of their lives.

Longevity and Drinking. In the last decade, American researchers have often discussed the "French paradox."

> The most famous world longevity champion, Jeanne Calment, 122, drank a glass of port wine at each meal. Fritz Muller, from Ipsach, Switzerland, who lived to 104 years, had a habit of starting each day with a glass of apple brandy.
>
> Among American centenarians, the famous comedian George Burns, 100, drank up to four martinis a day and abstained from food on Sundays.
>
> During an interview, Otto Burthus, 100, from Minneola, Minnesota, was asked, "Did you take vitamins?" He replied: "The only thing I took was a good shot of whiskey once in a while but not very often."
>
> Another whiskey lover is Paul Flores, 100, from Denver, Colorado. He believes that his daily shot of whiskey is what made him live so long--coffee with a shot of whiskey in it was his morning drink for years. However, because of a minor heart problem, he recently has given up the whiskey.
>
> Lydia Vesselovzorova, who lived to be 103 and who lived in a nursing home in Yokohama, Japan, also liked wine. She was shown on a Japanese TV program drinking champagne with her Japanese university students who came to visit her. When asked where her longevity originates, she replied that it

came from her grand-grandfather. He lived to the age of ninety-four, but he was not a good man, according to Lydia, because he drank and loved women in excess--he died at a banquet with a glass of wine in his hand.

The older generation knows well Sir Winston Churchill, the United Kingdom Prime Minister during World War II. He was obese, smoked cigars, and every day drank a bottle of Armenian cognac imported from the USSR, as the legend goes. He lived to the ripe old age of eighty-nine. Many believe that drinking a glass of dry red wine that contains antioxidants promotes health and longevity.

Especially among women in Oriental countries, drinking is less prevalent than in the West. A 1993 study of 2,303 women aged 100 years and more in Japan showed that 8.7 percent of them drink alcoholic beverages. Ms. Aki of Japan, 100, is one of the drinking centenarians. She drank beer and smoked when she appeared on a TV program on February 7, 1998. She also drinks sake--a Japanese rice wine--and although she is in a wheelchair, she is in good spirits and likes to sing. Her longevity secret is: "Take it easy." The audience burst into laughter many times when she joked with Mr. Koasa, the comedian who hosts the programs about centenarians. Ms. Aki was married three times, loved four men, and wants to be reborn to marry again. She is popular among city residents and in the nursing home where she has lived for the last twenty-one years. Male Japanese centenarians drink more often; among the 548 men studied in 1993, 23.7 percent replied that they drank sake.

Longevity and Optimism. The white blood cells of optimists may be more effective in defending the body against tumors. An optimistic attitude may become the only factor that helps a person survive under severe circumstances, as in the case of Lola Blonder, 104, a Holocaust survivor. "Many Holocaust victims lost their will to live under similar conditions, or were so emotionally crippled by the experience that their health was permanently damaged...Her resilience and optimism were still evident in her nineties, when she began painting, and even into her 104th year, when she fought back from severe life-threatening infections. As much as her genes, her immune system, or the heart that beats in her chest, her personality seemed to have contributed to her lifelong robust health," wrote Dr. Thomas T. Perls in his book, *Living to 100*.

Longevity and Intelligence. Higher intelligence appears to contribute to longer life. The Supreme Court Justices are among the longest-lived of all Americans. "Justice William Brennan, eighty-three, is continually using his mind on something that is an absolute passion with him," says Betty Friedman in her book, *The Fountain of Age*. He doesn't have a lot of other interests--he watches a little golf on TV, reads a little history, puts in an hour on his exercise bicycle. His world is law and the Court. And the cases--which he chooses personally rather than delegating that to law clerks as some of the other justices do--continually challenge him to grow.

Another such long-lived group is *symphony conductors, artists,* and *writers.* Conductors Arturo Toscanini, Stokowski, and Leonard Bernstein were able to learn entire new symphonies in their seventies and eighties. Viennese *conductor* Herbert Zipper, who died on April 21, 1997, at the age of ninety-two, lived a life full of suffering. During World War II, he "was imprisoned by the Nazis first at Dachau, and later in Buchenwald. After his family in Paris got him a visa and rescued him, Mr. Zipper went to Manila, only to be imprisoned again by the Japanese. In Dachau, Mr. Zipper recruited fellow inmates from Vienna and Munich orchestras to give secret concerts to bolster other prisoners' spirits," as reported in the April 22, 1997, issue of *The Boston Globe.* "I realized in Dachau that the arts in general have the power to keep you not just alive," he told the *Los Angeles Times* a few weeks before his death, "but also to make your life meaningful even under the most dreadful circumstances."

Musicians who play piano and violin and artists who paint never have Alzheimer's disease. One reason is that they force their brains to work hard intellectually; another is that the Chinese channels at the tips of the fingers, which are connected to the brain, are affected when they play or paint. Japanese violinist Shinichi Suzuki, who died on January 26, 1998, at the age of 99, is one example. He became famous by developing the "Suzuki Method" of childhood music instruction. His method, which is used in many countries, encouraged children to learn musical composition through imitation and example rather than by sight-reading scores.

English *writer* Victor S. Pritchett, the author of more than forty books, was ninety-six when he died in March 1997. He wrote short stories, novels, essays, literary criticism, and an autobiography. Among his many honors from British and American universities, he was especially proud of his honorary doctorate of literature from Harvard in 1985. At one time, he also worked as a correspondent for the *Christian Science Monitor.*

Another group that also provides examples of long-living people is *scientists.* "Harvard professors are in the top 1 percent of oldest people in the United States. It can't be the food, the pay, or the exercise," say Robert Ornstein, Ph.D., and David Sobel, M.D., in their book, *Healthy Pleasures.*

Linus Pauling, a prominent biochemist and a two-time Nobel Prize winner, lived to the age of ninety-three.

Medical scientists and *doctors* have professional knowledge that is beneficial to others and also can be applied to themselves. They are fortunate because this knowledge first provides their living and, second, gives them awareness about how to stay healthy. However, in reality, their knowledge doesn't work much for their own wellness. *"Physician, heal thyself"* is a famous saying, but strangely, doctors rarely live long lives.

The reason, in my opinion, is that their task is to teach lay people about a proper lifestyle and which habits they should change in order to prevent and cure diseases. Diseases are thought to be God's punishment, imposed on people for violating the laws of Nature. Back in the Middle Ages, illnesses were considered to be meted out by divine justice, and the bitter medicines originated in those times were part of the punishment. Doctors usually carried a bag full of instruments of torture; even now, their image hasn't changed: they inspire fear in patients. As conductors of divine justice, doctors are destined to explain how people should live in harmony with Nature, to be almost spiritual teachers for the people. In reality, however, doctors do the opposite--they act mostly on a physical plane, giving us pills or performing surgeries in their attempt to correct the consequences of our violations, not their causes. In this way, they interrupt God's affairs and they are punished for the interruption--almost as if God takes them away from His divine business.

However, there are cases of centenarian doctors.

Dr. Terada San, 100, of Japan, is in sound condition and still works in his private clinic for urology and external diseases. He is currently healthy, but four years ago he suffered from a stricture of the heart and was hospitalized for the first time in his life for a week of medical tests. He does not wear glasses and can easily read newspapers, but his hearing is a little impaired. He is most proud of his teeth, which are all his own--not one false tooth. Dr. Terada attributes his longevity to good heredity: his parents each lived more than ninety years and his nine brothers and sisters also lived about that long. In addition to good genes, he names "luck" as another secret of his longevity.

People such as composers and those who read poetry or scrupulously keep a diary--that is, people who use their brain every day--do not become mentally weak. In addition to his work in the hospital, Dr. Terada writes poetry and tends his garden, in which he has 150 types of flowers. Writing a book is another way he keeps his mind busy and, in 1987, he published a book of essays. He also has plans to publish his book, *Introduction to Longevity*, in which his research data will be included. Not much time is left for him, however, and he says that more than life itself, time is what he values the most.

Another case of exceptional longevity among doctors is Dr. Mildred R. Prouty. She was a pediatrician and dermatologist on the staff at Massachusetts General Hospital for forty years, and was ninety-three when she died in April 1997. One American physician, at his 100th birthday party, was asked the secret of his longevity. He replied, "If you spare your stomach for the first fifty years, your stomach in return will spare you for the next fifty years." This doctor certainly shared his secret with his patients, teaching them from more of a spiritual perspective than from a physical plane. In this way, he perhaps managed to avoid being a hindrance to God, who rewarded him with a long life.

World-famous Dr. Benjamin Spock, the childcare expert and author who died a few years ago at the age of ninety-four, is another long-living doctor. His highly influential book, *Baby and Child Care,* was published in 1946 and sold 50 million copies worldwide. In his book, he advised parents to trust their instincts and use common sense while rearing their children. He also encouraged a more flexible and relaxed form of parenting than previous guides. His instructional book was also very popular in Russia, and many families tried to raise their children "after Spock."

Among German centenarians are Margarete Schteinbach, ninety-seven, one of the world's oldest practicing physicians; George Bredtschneider, 103, a gardener who is still actively working; and Ernst Yunger, 102, a writer whose mind is as bright and creative as before.

Longevity and Devoutness. Regular attendance at religious services has been linked to an increase in the immune system function, which promotes longer life. In a study at Duke University involving 1,718 men and women aged sixty-five and older, researchers found that high blood levels of *interleukin-6* among churchgoers are half as likely when compared to non-attendees. Interleukin-6 is a protein that regulates immune and inflammatory functions in the body. Some types of cancers, heart disease, and autoimmune disorders have been associated with increased levels of interleukin-6. Researchers conclude that attending religious services reduces stress, which inhibits the immune function. In religious worship, higher powers are involved and a feeling of belonging enhances well-being and may reduce stress.

Similar results were obtained in a study conducted in Israel and published in the March 1996 issue of the *American Journal of Public Health.* Mortality rates in religious and secular communities (kibbutzim) were compared in the sixteen-year study. Researchers found that the religious Jewish community had consistently lower mortality rates than the secular group, and concluded that a supportive religious environment, a belief in God, and frequent prayer may reduce stress and increase health. Religious prayer or meditation for 10 to 20 minutes a day can decrease blood pressure, the heart rate, and breathing and metabolic rates, according to Dr. Herbert Benson, an associate professor of medicine at the Mind/Body Medical Institute of Harvard. The relaxation response is even more enhanced if it is combined with belief; that is, the union that Dr. Benson calls the "faith factor" in his book, *Timeless Healing*.

"The devout apparently enjoy measurable benefits of faith on earth as well as hereafter; Baptist ministers, Mormons, and Seventh-Day Adventists have mortality rates substantially lower than the comparable general population," says Thomas J. Moore in his book, *Lifespan*. Rabbis also belong to the long-living group.

Here is a good example of a devout person, first to his family and community and later in life to God.

Frank Shomo of Robinson, Pennsylvania, who lived to the age of 108. His niece, Jean Casey, 76, of Belgrade Lakes, Maine, told me about him and provided articles from local newspapers.

Remembering his childhood days, Frank said that even though they were poor, they were rich in love and good times and fun. Frank had two brothers and a sister, and they lived in Lockport, near the railroad. Frank was only 100 days old when he survived the disastrous Johnstown Flood of 1889 that destroyed the dam and killed 2,209 people. He was lucky to safely escape from two other major floods in the Johnstown region, in 1936 and in 1977.

He recalled that as children, they didn't get into much trouble because their parents kept them in line. "My mother was a good baker. She made apple butter and jelly. We had bread and butter and molasses, and buckwheat cakes. My dad was a good role model. He told us kids what we could do and what we couldn't. He wouldn't allow us to swim when the water was high and we couldn't jump on the trains. But we never got licked," said Frank on the eve of his 108th birthday.

Frank started to work very early, at the age of twelve, earning just four cents an hour. Later, he worked as a line foreman for the Pennsylvania Railroad for forty-two years. He married in 1913, at the age of twenty-four, and had four children. "The railroad was his day job, but evenings were spent working too. He planted huge gardens, hand-spaded, so they had fruits and vegetables to put up and can for winter. He helped two men dig the foundation for his house. He worked night and day. He worked just as hard after retirement. If someone infirm needed a roof tarred, he'd carry his wooden extension ladders across town with the tar bucket and do their roof," recalled Shomo's granddaughter Adda Lee Hoskinson-Seifert of Robinson. She said he never owned a car, having driven only once and deciding he didn't like it. He walked everywhere. He used to climb the long stairway to his apartment, and could get to the senior citizens center by counting the telephone poles on the way.

In 1960, at the age of seventy-one, he remarried and lived with his new wife for another fifteen years. "Frank was blind in one eye from a railroad spike injury. He was losing his vision in his good eye from a cataract that he never told anyone about. Later, he had successful eye surgery. He had a dry wit, keeping us all laughing with his observations right up to the end," continued Adda Lee. "We were all around him laughing often. His sense of humor was something special," said his niece, Jean Casey.

"At 104, he had read the complete Bible, Old and New Testaments, fifty-two times. He read for hours at a time." For his last few months, he lived at a personal care home. His favorite snack was "coffee soup"--coffee with sugar and bread cut in cubes and soaked in it, recalled Jean Casey. "As to his longevity, he attributed it to three things: lay firm foundations, don't drink, and above all, believe in the Almighty," she added.

Longevity and Attitude toward Aging. Some scientists and gerontologists believe that the stereotypical thinking now common in most societies--that we can live just seventy to eighty years--confines our lives to that age. If societies of the future expand this stereotype to 100 to 120 years, we will live that long.

Some people, though, are ahead of the societal trend and have a strong determination to live 100 years or more; they believe that their determination helps them achieve the advanced age.

Mr. Sasaki, eighty-three, whom I met in the National Diet Library in Tokyo is that kind of highly determined person. He is a survivor of the Hiroshima atomic bombing and is confident that if God spared him in that disaster, He will also grant him a 100-year-long life. Mr. Sasaki looks vigorous and full of energy, and his round face emits life force. He is engaged in Biblical research and plans to write a few books.

At the coffee shop where we sat for a while, he ordered an ice cream for himself, which indicated to me that he belongs to the Yang type, which is very good for his advanced age. He asked me a few questions about myself, then took a pendulum out of his pocket and suggested that we check my energy level. He placed the fingers of his right hand on my wrist and held the upper end of the pendulum against the "third eye" location on his forehead, allowing it to swing in circles. Referring to a chart on a small card, he told me that I have a lack of vitality. I agreed with him because I had been feeling that my batteries were somewhat discharged.

As for me, I attributed my lack of energy to the alternate dry fasting that I had undertaken the month before and from which I was still not fully recovered. However, Mr. Sasaki's judgment was totally different. "You are taking everything too seriously and thinking too much, that is your problem," he told me. "Keep for yourself 1 percent and leave the remaining 99 percent to God. You have to pray and God will give you energy. Let's pray together," he suggested. Then, keeping both of my hands together, he started the pendulum swinging again. The circular motion across my hands gradually changed to a lengthwise path, and that was a good sign to Mr. Sasaki. "Pray to your God Yehova," he said.

However, some people say that a determination to live long has nothing to do with reaching 100 years of age. "If someone decides to live a long life, the probability to achieve 100 years is close to zero," according to Hajime Mizuno in his book, *Japanese Men Born in 1924-1933 Cannot Live Long.* He adds that whether a person will live to 100 is 80 percent predetermined at his birth. It is not just a matter of longevity genes, but rather one's ability to resist diseases–the strength of the immune system--that matters; the ability to make efforts for one's own health does not help much, in his opinion.

Longevity and Education. College graduates have notably lower mortality rates than those who didn't finish high school. "Many well-educated women and men living so long made us wonder about how worthwhile an investment in education is for a person. Paralleling the great improvement in health and longevity is the increased education of most individuals," according to Robert Ornstein, Ph.D., and David Sobel, M.D., in their book, *Healthy Pleasures.*

Longevity and Occupation. Politicians and statesmen live the longest lives, up to their eighties, while ballet dancers have the shortest lives with many dying in their forties, as shown in one longitudinal study conducted in the former USSR. Prime Minister El Hadji Muhammad el Mokri, the Grand Hadji of Morocco, died on September 16, 1957, at the reputed age of 112.5 years. Former Philippine president Diosdado Macapagal, who was head of state from 1961 to 1965 (followed by Ferdinand Marcos), died in April 1997 at the age of eighty-six.

White-collar professionals in the United States, Europe, and Japan live longer than those with lower skilled jobs, and the longevity difference between social groups is widening.

Longevity and Marriage. Married people tend to live longer than unmarried or divorced people. The longevity icons of Japan, Kin Narita (died in January 2000 at the age of 107) and Gin Kanie, 108, were married and had eleven and five children, respectively. Nataliya Yusova, who lived to be 101, of Nakhodka, Russia, had eleven children. Jeanne Calment, 122, of France, and Lydia Vesselovzorova, 103, were both married but had no children. However, there are many centenarians, both men and women, including the American Delaney sisters Elizabeth, 104, and Sarah, 107, who never married.

Longevity and Luck. Along with the longevity that runs in her family, Della Zieske, 101, considered luck to play a definite role in her life. "My third husband and I were walking along the street one winter day. It was almost Christmas, and I stopped to look at some colored lights. He was just a few feet ahead of me when a car skidded on the ice and killed him. It could have been me, but it wasn't."

Factors affecting longevity can be used to calculate one's life expectancy. Inventories of this kind have been published in books and magazines, with the primary factors about the same, but with slight variations depending on the author. The quiz based on the book *Living to 100*, by Dr. Thomas Perls and Margery Silver, is available on the Internet. It includes twenty-three questions related to heredity, age, gender, body size, kinds and quality of food, exercise, smoking and drinking, environment, hygiene, sexual habits, exposure to the sun, ability to cope with stress, and dietary supplements. This quiz predicted my life expectancy to be 97.4 years--too good to be true--but my thanks to the authors anyway; it sounds good to me. This quiz is definitely reader-friendly.

This discussion does not aim to cover all possible factors that influence longevity or to review all existing data--that is a subject for gerontology research, which conducts many studies in the field. Some of the factors, if not mentioned in this chapter, were discussed in relevant chapters of the book. My task was simpler: to compile information that may be of interest to my readers and to assist those who are planning a health, fitness, and life-extension program.

31

LIFE - EXTENSION PROGRAM

Are there ways for those who are determined to live a long life, but lack an inherited strong immune system, to achieve their goals? Yes, there are dozens of methods that can be used with a self-help approach that could be applied to virtually every individual. Among the methods are well-known health habits and alternative medicine therapies. I have categorized them using the chakra, or level of consciousness (body-mind-spirit), scheme. Some of them have scientific support such as the following twenty-one secrets of super immunity, described by Dorothy Foltz-Gray in the October 1998 issue *of Prevention Magazine*. Other methods were discussed in previous chapters of this book and/or are described in the referenced alternative medicine books.

- *Survival Level (First Chakra): primary biological needs (e.g., food, sleep, exercise)*

1. Sleep well (6 to 8 hours of sound sleep).

2. Avoid antibiotics (excessive antibiotics suppress the immune system).

3. Take herbs (Echinacea, tablet or capsule; ginseng, two 100-milligram capsules) and Maitake mushrooms (2 to 6 grams daily).

4. Avoid drinking wine (a daily glass of wine may threaten the defenses).

5. Take vitamin C (200 to 500 milligrams daily; 1,000 milligrams can cause kidney stones).

6. Take vitamin E--an elixir of youth (200 IU a day).

7. Exercise every day (heart-pumping brisk walk, 30 to 45 minutes; yoga; and stretches).

8. Detoxify your body (water, juice, dry fasting, mono diet, alkaline diet, and colon therapy, chelation therapy, heat stress saunas, deep and slow diaphragmatic breathing).

9. Eat the right food (appropriate to your blood type, Ayurvedic dosha type, Yin-Yang type, horoscope type, lifestyle, and energy needs).

10. Center your diet around raw fruits and vegetables.

- *Sexual Level (Second Chakra): sexual pleasures*

11. Practice sex with controlled ejaculation (avoid frequent loss of semen).

- *Social Level (Third Chakra): relationships with family, at work, with friends*

12. Become friendlier (for extroverts, go out with friends, begin social relationships).

13. Laugh (watch funny videos, read joke books, add humor to life).

14. Get a massage (relaxation effect of massage strengthens the natural killer cells).

15. Be optimistic (positive outlook and good mood when under stress).

- *Emotional Level (Fourth Chakra): feelings and emotions*

16. Keep a diary or talk to a friend (write down stressful and traumatic events; share deepest feelings with friends).

- *Creative Level (Fifth Chakra): talents, skills, hobbies, crafts*

17. Get some culture (concerts, exhibits, games, listening to music).

- *Thought Level (Sixth Chakra): thinking, imagery, meditation*

18. Relax (imagery, daydreaming, and tapes with sounds of ocean waves).

19. Meditate (visual, audio, and fragrance).

20. Learn new skills (play a musical instrument, study new subjects or foreign languages)

- *Faith Level (Seventh Chakra): devotion, prayer*

21. Pray (faith makes one healthier; attend religious services once a week or more often).

If you decide to become a longevity seeker, the following twelve steps may help you achieve your goal:

- **Learn about your heredity**. Knowing your genetic predisposition to certain diseases and taking preventive measures helps to minimize the risk of their development. In my case, my maternal grandmother had varicose veins and so do I. For prevention, I always wear a bandage on both legs. While I was living in Japan, I had minor surgery on one leg, in which the enlarged portion of the vein was blocked, resulting in a much-improved condition. My father died of colon cancer and had prostate enlargement. Therefore, I eat fiber-rich vegetables and fruits, exercise, and monitor my bowel movements. To avoid prostate problems, I walk, hike, and do the buttocks walking and stretching exercises. My mother had weak lungs and died of pneumonia. I take care of my lungs by practicing breathing exercises, keeping my chest and feet warm, and avoiding cold drinks.

• **Determine your body type**. A personalized approach to longevity is the most effective way to move in the right direction. You are unique and will benefit the most if you choose the lifestyle and activities appropriate to your type. Invest your time in understanding your body type using the information in this book and other sources. Answer the questionnaires and compile your personality profile. For a better understanding of your metabolic type, I refer you to the books of W. Wolcott, Dr. E. Abravanel, Dr. G. Cousens, and others cited herein.

• **Assess your health condition**. It is difficult to begin a life-extension program if you are not healthy enough. Evaluate your inherited (if any) and acquired chronic diseases and take measures to cure them. Only after becoming healthy will you have the spirit and intention to find time for further physical and mental improvement. Your starting point will depend on your age, lifestyle, habits, level of wear and tear, and state of mind. Regardless of your present condition and age, there is much you can do. The worse a condition, the harder you have to work. Make your life-extension program your first priority and full-time job, especially if you are retired, free, and have sufficient financial means.

• **Learn about risk factors of major degenerative diseases.** Cardiovascular (heart attack) and cerebrovascular (stroke) diseases and cancer are the leading causes of premature death in industrialized countries. The risk factors for these diseases are as follows:

Cardiovascular Disease: A family history of heart disease; age (high levels of homocysteine); blood type (those with blood type A are at higher risk); somatotype (ectomorphic mesomorphs are at higher risk); Ayurvedic dosha type (Pitta types are at a higher risk); personality type (type A's are at higher risk); lifestyle habits such as drinking and smoking; occupation (intellectuals are at higher risk); medical conditions such as atherosclerosis, high blood pressure, high cholesterol, diabetes, and obesity; high protein, excessive animal fat, salt, and sugar in the diet; lack of carbon dioxide; toxemia; physical inactivity; stress; and anger.

Cerebrovascular Disease: The risk factors are virtually the same as those for heart disease; the three major risk factors for stroke are atherosclerosis, high blood pressure, and diabetes.

Cancer: Genetic vulnerability; blood type (people with blood type A and AB are at higher risk); height (tall people are at higher risk); personality type (types A and C are at higher risk); lifestyle habits such as drinking and smoking; overexposure to sunlight; drinking contaminated tap water; obesity;

bad diet with low fiber, excessive animal fat, refined carbohydrates, high protein, and smoked and cured foods; lack of oxygen; hyperventilation; mechanical and chemical cell irritation; and toxemia.

Avoiding these risk factors will increase your chances to achieve a ripe old age and to enjoy a disease-free life. Regular medical checkups help in the early detection of a disorder and taking measures for its cure. In the near future, science is going to provide genetic information on each person showing the risks for future diseases; therefore, stay informed about ongoing research.

• **Plan your financial security**. Money is freedom. You can afford good living conditions, a car, natural food, supplements, vacations, early retirement, education, entertainment, and other necessities and pleasures of life if you have enough money. Now matter how substantial your income is or isn't, what your assets are, or how much you rely on a pension and Social Security, you can increase your savings through financial self-discipline. Albert Crenshaw, a financial writer for the *Washington Post*, advises keeping track of income and expenses by category. To make income prevail over expenses, write in a notebook your bill payments and every cash expenditure. In my case, house, car, and health insurance payments; telephone; propane gas; and electricity bills comprise most of my expenses. I recently found an inexpensive insurance with the same coverage and I was able to reduce my expenses. You cannot avoid expenses for food and gas, but you can always eliminate unnecessary spending such as credit-card interest, impulse purchases, and frequent dining out. If your surplus money becomes substantial, you can invest it.

• **Adopt a long-living attitude**. Many centenarians and the researchers who study them acknowledge that the right attitude helps most in achieving an advanced age--even more than diet or good education. The point is to always feel "young at heart" and do not pay much attention to your age. Rather than the frustration about aging that usually accompanies the later years in most people, centenarians see new opportunities in every age. Most people had dreams that never came true, probably because of the lack of time or money. Some people dreamt about learning a foreign language, becoming a university graduate, playing a musical instrument, painting, or writing poetry. Especially during retirement, it is a time to fulfill the dreams of your youth. Whatever it is, do it now--it is never late to start a new project regardless of how big and challenging it may be. If you act as a young man or woman, you put yourself in a rejuvenation mode. In doing so, you join a youth egregore and, indeed, you become young--the aging egregore gives up on you.

• **Eat right for your type**. You need most of your food to metabolize it efficiently with maximum energy and for building materials, and minimum wastes. Whatever healthy food you choose, it may not give you this benefit unless you adjust it to your body type and specific needs. A customized approach to nutrition is obviously superior to the "one diet fits all" approach. Learn about the diet of your parents and include the foods they ate in your own diet. Avoid or minimize foods that are inappropriate to your blood and dosha types. Do not rely on popular diet authorities; become your own diet guru. However, even with a customized approach, do not follow each recommendation to the letter--leave room for common sense and moderation in your diet and eating habits.

• **Exercise right for your type**. Physical activity and exercise, although less influential on our body than diet, may help to eliminate imbalances in the body's organs and systems, if they are adjusted to your type. Endomorphs, people with blood type O, slow oxidizers, carbohydrate types, and Kapha dosha types should choose more strenuous and intense exercises such as strength training and aerobics. Ectomorphs; people with blood type A, B, and AB; fast oxidizers; protein types, and Vata dosha types do best with less strenuous, slower-paced workouts and activities that include meditation. Refer to relevant chapters of this book for more details.

• **Choose the lifestyle and entertainment right for your type**. Living conditions, environment, and lifestyle habits, together with diet and exercise, may help to balance your organs and systems, especially if they suit your type. While Vata types are advised to avoid all physical, emotional, and mental stress, Kapha types do better if they lead an active and stimulating physical, emotional, and mental life, trying to interact with the world. A warm, moist, and tranquil environment, which is best for Vata types, transforms into a cool and calming personal, social, and work environment that works well for Pitta types. Watching TV and sitting in front of a computer monitor are bad for Vata and Kapha types and should be minimized, but they are not as detrimental for Pitta-type people.

• **Grow intellectually right for your type**. It is said that within our life span we use less than 10 percent of our brain's potential. We also were taught that our brain continuously loses nerve cells. Brain researchers found, however, that in the thinking areas of the cerebral cortex, the brain does not lose cells. Studies have shown that the metabolic rate of the brain does not decrease between the ages of twenty and eighty, which means that the brain is always alert and ready to do any given job. Its capability is enormous and ready to be revealed upon demand. To keep the brain fit and healthy, we need to exercise it, just as we exercise the body. The brain controls everything in us—our thoughts, dreams, decisions to act, and actions themselves—and it is the brain that we use to train and control the brain itself.

The goal of the individualized approach to brain exercises is to restore balance in some innate traits of certain types. For instance, tall and thin ectomoph and Vata types are naturally inclined to intellectual activities, and they do not need to push themselves for brainwork. Endomorphs and mesomorphs, Kapha and Pitta types need to become more mentally alert. They would benefit from additional efforts to engage the brain in exercises such as learning new subjects or languages, acquiring new professions, and doing creative work. The same seems to apply to slow oxidizers and the carbohydrate type.

A person of any type may develop a plan of intellectual growth by making a list of his/her goals for the rest of their life. For instance, the list of goals that I would like to achieve before I die includes more than fifty big projects involving development on all levels of consciousness. Regarding health, I want to improve my flexibility, strength, endurance, and stamina. Also, I want to try some new professions, get some more education, learn foreign languages, learn to play the piano and to paint, and help people and improve my relationships with them. I have dreams about reading religious texts and world literature, listening to operas and attending plays in world-famous theaters, traveling to places of interest and seeing the wonders of the world, and so forth. You can see that I am ambitious and will need at least fifty years more to accomplish my projects!

- **Improve your physical and mental health**. Good health requires your time, devotion, conscious efforts, and hard work to be achieved. Depending on the level of wear and tear of your body and brain, you have to make health a full-time job, or at least part–time. Do not wait for a magical pill that will cure all diseases, which scientists want to discover. Metaphysically speaking, your inner watcher, who sends you a disease, wants you to understand what you were doing or feeling wrong. He trains you to overcome disease through increased awareness and with your own efforts. He will never allow you to get away without paying the debts by hard physical and mental work--it is a law of Nature. Scientifically speaking, based on centenarian studies, prolonged good health is a more achievable goal than the increased duration of life--but again, through your own efforts rather than achievements of science. Nature does not give up its laws despite the power of science.

Mental health can be dramatically improved if you load your brain with lots of exercises. Memorizing poetry or song lyrics is a good method. A holistic approach to mental health--namely, hand reflexology--advises you to intensively use your fingertips in your daily pursuits because they directly activate the brain through the Chinese channels of energy flow. Those who play the piano do not get Alzheimer's disease, according to Japanese scientists. Playing the organ is even better because both the hands and the feet are engaged, especially if you play with bare feet. Handcrafts of any kind and finger self-massage also improve mental health.

• **Plan your spiritual growth**. Spirituality is an exclusively human need. You want to grow spiritually because you were born with this desire. Whatever you do in your life, you have a deep-seated powerful urge to unfold your full potential and to achieve *self-actualization*, which is the process of mental and spiritual growth. The components of spiritual health are altruism; ideal-seeking; self-actualization; intuition; perceiving one's role in Nature, the cosmos, and the universe; and striving for God and the higher Self. It usually occurs later in life, after the basic needs such as shelter, food, and sleep followed by success and status are fulfilled. Self-actualization is a long process and the longer one's life, the more chances a person has to achieve it.

Our life is an excursion on this beautiful planet. We are allowed to try anything and experience whatever we want. When on an excursion to see an ancient tower or high monument, tourists climb up the stairs to enjoy the view from the top. Similarly, we climb up from the lower to the upper levels of consciousness. How can we leave the Earth without becoming familiar with the wisdom of mankind, without sensing the mental and spiritual insights? If so, we will miss the best of what life can offer. We live between the earth and the sky, and the wiser we grow, the closer we get to the sky. This is the purpose of our life--to progress in the spiritual evolution, to get closer to God. We also are given the opportunity to learn how to love others and, even more important, ourselves. If we follow the rules set by the Universal Mind (they are not the rules created by people), our excursion will last long enough to progress in spiritual growth.

Spiritual practices are not confined to going to church. You alone or together with a spouse or in a group can read religious texts, listen to audiotapes, or watch videos. If you are religious and you are Christian, familiarize yourself with the wisdom of other religions--they have much to offer. A trip to the holy places is a real inspiration. Regularly practice prayer and meditation, which nourish and heal the body, mind, and soul.

The overwhelming majority of centenarians followed these health habits, some of them unaware of these rules. At the beginning of this book, I posed a question: What is it that centenarians do right that the majority of people are doing wrong? The answer is this: They were gifted with or acquired during the course of life a talent for understanding their body language. They intuitively knew what is good for their body, mind, and soul. They followed the rules set by Nature for their biochemical individuality. They were perfect navigators of their lives and did not allow anyone to distract them from their glorious way. Actually--although perhaps randomly and by chance--they applied to themselves the same knowledge in the personalized approach to longevity. You may think that the majority of long-living people did not use a personalized approach, but nevertheless achieved an exceptional longevity. They did, but for these very rare people, it was pure luck (if not great intuition) to survive all the odds of their lives. Because the likelihood of being this lucky and living so long is for most of us similar to the chances of winning a million-dollar lottery, we need to make special efforts to extend our years and fulfill our goals. As this paraphrase advises, "Do not die until the song sounds in you."

Our longevity teachers—the centenarians—were wise enough to live in harmony with the laws of Nature. Certainly, they were lucky to be chosen by God and supported by guardian angels, but their own contribution was also valuable. In many cases, their personalities and attitudes facilitated their struggle against the odds of life and helped them to acquire superior inhibitors of deterioration of their health and vitality, which is associated with aging. Dozens of cases described in this book confirm that each of us--even without great genes--through conscious effort and ongoing hard work may gain great health, achieve life's goals, and prolong enjoyment of our unrepeatable life on our wonderful planet named Earth.

CONCLUSION

Now after you've finished reading this book,
You know yourself much deeper and better.
Most likely, it changed your life outlook
That your aging depends on the lifestyle matter.

Whatever your age and condition of health,
Discover inside you an intelligence wealth.
Unfold potential that you have within
The keys are hard work and self-discipline.

For your body and soul great transformation,
Vehicles must be simple lifestyle and diet
Right for your type, and all making quiet
Your mind, such as prayer and meditation.

Fasts, yoga, and eating raw plants help to quicker
Attain health and long life for a longevity seeker.

It is not an exaggeration to say that now, after you have finished reading this book, you know yourself better than before. We say, "Good to know" in appreciation for acquiring a new piece of knowledge about something. However, knowing more about ourselves increases our consciousness and awareness, and can have a profound effect on our entire life. Your personality profile compiled from answering the questionnaires will allow you to apply the factual information in this book and others of this kind with better understanding. If you feel you need an improvement program, you can design it according to your body constitution, psychological traits, and intellectual and spiritual needs of your unique personality.

Regarding body and personality types and the longevity connection, we now know the following:

Somatotypes. Excessively long-lived people (i.e., centenarians) usually belong to the endomorphic mesomorphs. If a person belongs to the endomorph type and is overweight, he/she would do better to undertake diet and exercise measures to transform his/her body into the mesomorph type. Extremely underweight ectomorphs need to gain weight by doing strength exercises and eating more carbohydrates.

Personality Types. Type B behavior promotes longevity; therefore, Type A and Type C personalities must control their personality traits and move in the Type B direction.

Instincts. The egophylum type, which represents the self-preservation instinct--careful, egocentric, suspicious, non-adventurous, and sober-minded, is often found among centenarians. The reproduction instinct is very strong in most centenarians; many of them had several children. The altruism instinct promoted the longevity of many centenarians. The research instinct, driven by curiosity, is also a characteristic of many centenarians. The freedom instinct is quite strong among long-living people as well. The preservation of dignity, which is aligned with the freedom of thought and speech, definitely manifests itself in some centenarians.

Temperaments. A phlegmatic temperament promotes longevity. Cheerful, inspiring, optimistic, and lively sanguine people are found among centenarians quite often. Aggressive, adventurous, repressive, and stubborn people of the choleric temperament tend to live less than the average life expectancy, although other qualities of this temperament--such as forcefulness, dominance, and self-confidence--are found to be factors that increase longevity. People with a melancholy temperament type and who are faithful and suspicious are some of the qualities of centenarians. However, because they are resentful and unforgiving, they harm their health and decrease their longevity.

Blood Types. Among the many factors affecting longevity, blood type seems to be the most influential, which is why I used it as the dominant factor to determine the personalized diet. Many centenarians in Western countries have blood type O; blood type B is predominant in Japan. People with blood type A have the lowest life expectancy and are vulnerable to cancer and heart diseases; therefore, they must follow a healthy diet and lifestyle. Compared to people with blood type A, type Os and type Bs have more chances to achieve longevity under similar conditions.

Lifestyle. Although many centenarians attribute their longevity to a healthy lifestyle, we cannot say that they lived to the age of 100 or more for that reason alone--their heredity definitely played a role as well. For those who are not granted great genes, a healthy lifestyle plays a predominant role.

Heredity. Heredity definitely plays an important role in people's longevity, although the data on its influence is controversial. The impact of the genetic factor on a person's life span ranges from 25 to 80 percent. Some researchers believe that diet more than heredity influences duration of life.

Ayurvedic Doshas Type. Knowing your dosha type and applying the principles of Ayurveda enables you to become more health-conscious and to increase your chances for living a healthier and longer life.

Yin-Yang Type. Yang-type people seem to burn themselves too fast, while Yin-type people can smolder longer until a ripe old age.

Five Elements. Flexible joints and bones are associated with the strong *Water* element, which prolongs youth and longevity. Sarah Delany, 108, says that she has been a worrier and an optimist at the same time, which are signs that she has a strong *Earth* element in her.

Chakra System. For a better understanding of the whole concept of this book, the chakra system is employed. Basic biological needs such as food, air, water, sleep, and sex, which bind us to the animal world and are associated with the lower chakras, can--if satisfied with *restriction* and *moderation*--result in many noticeable benefits for health and longevity. Gifts, talents, skills, interests, hobbies, intellectual activities, and spiritual devotion such as a belief in God, all of which are associated with the upper chakras, if employed in abundance, also promote longevity and physical and mental health.

The amount of freedom that each person acquires in life is related to the degree of control that he/she managed to gain over different aspects of his/her life. The least freedom is observed in the lower chakras, or levels of consciousness. People such as unskilled manual workers, farmers, the military, policemen, and low-ranked company workers with limited knowledge, interests, and awareness--who are bored with their jobs and need entertainment in their lives (and without an "internal fire")--are examples of lower levels of consciousness. They are entirely dependent on food, water, air, and sleep to maintain their health. They need healthy food with a full range of macro- and micro-nutrients, vitamins, minerals, fiber, and so on. Most of the existing nutritional recommendations in developed countries are actually addressed to this category of people. The biothermonuclear reactors of their cells operate at low capacities, if not already shut down. They have minimal freedom and are fully dependent on importing from the outside everything that constitutes basic biological needs. Can they achieve a very old age? Yes, they can, if they were fortunate to inherit great genes from their parents. They did a good job in choosing their parents and can enjoy a long and disease-free life, even without special efforts to maintain their health--they have a large balance in their health account and just keep withdrawing from it.

Another category could be the same people of these professions and occupations, but who love their work and everything they do, and who have interests, skills, and hobbies that keep them active, busy, and deeply involved. They differ from the previous category mostly by the absence of boredom. They worked very hard all their life, but do not feel exhausted or tired of living. They honestly fulfilled their duties, they are the model of karma-yogi, and they are happy with life. Their love and happiness feed an internal fire and they get energy from both food and in the form of prana from the universe. They are less dependent on a full range of nutrients and have some ability for element transmutation. Although they may not have great heredity, they can achieve an advanced old age if they were physically active, had a healthy lifestyle and habits, were wise enough not to harm their bodies, avoided self-destructive tendencies, and learned to cope with stress. It could happen to them unconsciously, but very rarely, with a likelihood of one centenarian per ten thousand or less--this is the rate of centenarians in many countries, who themselves do not know how they managed to live that long.

People of the third category acquired the most freedom in their lives and are less dependent on importing a variety of nutrients and supplements from the outside. They are artists of all types, thinkers, believers, and religious devotees. They operate on the upper chakras, and the bio-thermonuclear reactors of their cells operate at high capacity. The transmutation of elements is occurring in their bodies and they need little food of a limited variety to maintain their health and life. In the extreme cases such as Theresa Neumann, they need a tiny amount of food or are even able to live without any food at all, as in the cases of Giri Bala, Asanami Toshie, and Xu Fang.

Although there are many cases of achieving very old age among the scientists, artists, writers, philosophers, and religious devotees, the percentage of centenarians among them is low. There are no longevity champions among them; they are in the first two categories. Longevity and number of years are certainly not goals for their own sake; what is valued is both duration and quality of life. A high-quality life is worth living even without quantity. It is good if the person's potential is developed to the fullest; if not, then the quantity of life necessary to achieve self-actualization is more important. A person who is not bored and not tired of living needs time to fulfill all his/her plans and projects.

It seems that the "more the better" principle does not work in any aspect, including freedom. Any extremes do not lead to the best results; the peak of the curve is somewhere in between. If there is a best working principle, it must be *moderation*--in every aspect and in each respect. Specifically, moderation is the secret of longevity that centenarians and the scientists who study them reveal most often. Moderation is like the top of a hill--difficult to achieve and even more difficult to maintain. It is so easy to slip from it that to remain there requires a lot of self-control, discipline, effort, and work. Combined with **restriction** in the lower chakras and **abundance** in the upper chakras, moderation will enable a person to be young, healthy, and fit, and to live a long life to its fullest.

The examples of centenarians who achieved a fulfilling life are many. Here are some of them.

The queen of longevity, Jeanne Calment of France, who lived to 122, always watched her diet, including in it garlic, olive oil, and fish, which are the reputed promoters of health. She exercised (e.g., hunted, rode a bicycle at age 100); enjoyed personal gratification playing the piano, painting, and singing (she released a rap CD at 121); and liked chocolate, port wine, and cigarettes (in small amount just for pleasure). She retained her humor to the end and was "never bored."

Frank Shomo, of Robinson, Pennsylvania, who lived to 108, worked for forty-two years. After retirement, in his seventies, he used his skills to make leather wallets, belts, and handbags. He deeply believed in God, was a member of the Masons Lodge for forty-seven years, and Bible study became a daily ritual in his later years.

The American Delany sisters, Sarah, 108, and Elizabeth, who died at 104 in 1995, did stair-climbing and yoga for exercise; ate garlic; wrote a book entitled, *Having Our Say: The Delany Sisters' First 100 Years*; and enjoyed poetry, literature, art, and music. There are many more examples.

Oriental Horoscope. The majority of centenarians in both the United States and Japan were born in the winter or spring seasons. People born in other seasons can extend their lives by taking control over their diet and lifestyle.

Summary

Results of the research conducted by the author for this book can be summarized as follows:

Food Intake

• The calorie content of food profoundly affects longevity, which is the greatest if the daily calorie intake ranges from 1,000 to 1,600 kcal. *Calorie Rule*: 10 kcal per day per pound of standard body weight.

• Protein, although an important component of food, is necessary for the body only in very small amounts. The efficiency of its utilization is low. Consumed in excess, protein takes most of the body's energy for its assimilation, toxifies the system with its residue, causes a host of degenerative diseases, accelerates aging, and shortens life. Calories from protein must comprise about 5 percent of the daily value. *Protein Rule*: 0.2 gram per day per pound of standard body weight.

• Carbohydrates are the best fuel for the body, and the efficiency of their utilization is the highest. They do not leave any residue; rather, the end product of their metabolism is water and carbon dioxide, two extremely beneficial substances for the body. The diets of long-living people consist mostly of carbohydrates, and so must your diet. Calories from carbohydrates must comprise 65 to 70 percent of the daily calorie intake.

• Fats are absolutely necessary for numerous body functions and as a source of energy. Compared with carbohydrates, they require a much larger amount of oxygen for their metabolism, which is accompanied by free radicals that are hazardous to our health and longevity. The efficiency of fat utilization is also lower than that of carbohydrates. Calories from fats must comprise 25 to 30 percent of the daily calorie intake. The best fats are from plant sources, such as olive oil, avocado, olives, nuts, and seeds.

• A raw-food diet supplies the body with the live, enzyme-rich, highest-quality nutrients; allows the reduction of calorie intake; and significantly promotes longevity. Raw food is essential for each body and blood type, but especially for people with blood type A. Type A's may dramatically improve their health and achieve their longevity goals by including 80 percent or more raw food in their diet. Raw fruits and vegetables and their juices, sprouted grains, beans, and lentils are alkaline-forming foods, which must comprise about 80 percent of the diet of people with blood type A. Acid-forming foods such as meat, fish, eggs, dairy products, animal fats, sugar, and refined starch must not exceed 20 percent.

• Antioxidant-rich fruits, vegetables, and teas must be included in your diet. Green and black tea, blueberries, strawberries, cranberries, plums, oranges, red grapes, kiwi, pink grapefruit, garlic, kale, spinach, Brussels sprouts, alfalfa sprouts, broccoli florets, beets, red bell peppers, and onions all have a high antioxidant capacity.

• Food-combining is the means to achieve optimal nutrition, which is essential for people with blood type A and those with weak digestion. Green leafy vegetables comprise the only group that combines well with protein, carbohydrates, and fat.

A lifelong intake of about 1,000 to 1,600 kcal for both men and women (depending on body size) is the key that opens the gate to the longevity garden. In the United States, 2,000 and 2,670 kcal for women and men, respectively, is recommended between the ages of twenty-three and fifty; however, this is too high and seems to decrease the chances for living more than an average life span. If a person wants to achieve a very old age, it is worth taking control of calorie intake and confining calorie consumption to the level of the longevity champions.

If your digestive system is strong, include plenty of raw vegetables in your diet; if it is not, eat fresh and lightly cooked food, and avoid leftovers. Increase your digestive fire by gradually increasing the proportion of raw food in your diet. Eat plenty of garlic and other longevity foods listed in this book.

Water Intake. Just as free radicals are attached to the oxygen we inhale, similarly deuterium water, a highly harmful substance, is attached to the water we drink. An average 0.5 to 1.0 liter of fluids a day is deemed an optimal water intake. Certainly, it should be a different amount for different individuals. We are all different and factors such as body constitution, metabolic type, Yin-Yang type, foods we eat, activity level, and climate must be considered--especially the Yin-Yang difference because water is Yin and a Yang person can tolerate an increased water intake more easily than his/her Yin counterpart.

Oxygen Intake. At rest, the production of carbon dioxide is less than the oxygen uptake; however, for light, moderate, and maximal exercise, the CO_2 production exceeds the O_2 uptake. This is an important point because it makes clear that the super health, vitality, and longevity of runners and exercisers were achieved due to the carbon dioxide accumulated in their bodies, rather than the increased oxygen supply, as is commonly thought. Of the two gases in question, it is *carbon dioxide* that enhances longevity, not oxygen. Carbon dioxide does not burn itself and, as a fire extinguisher, it regulates the speed of the burning processes in our cells. In other words, it is responsible for our rate of living: the more intensive the burning process in our cells, the sooner they get worn out and the sooner we die.

The formula for a healthy and long life should be: "The less oxygen, the better." Breathing exercises help maintain the vital capacity of our lungs. Among the best exercises that enable us to quickly increase the level of carbon dioxide are diving and swimming (with the face held in the water between breaths). According to Ayurveda, longevity can be increased with left-nostril breaths. Moderation in oxygen consumption and enhancement of carbon dioxide production through physical activity and exercise is the right way to achieve good health and to increase life duration.

Sleep. Duration of sleep may be a bit less than the moderate. I believe that 6 to 7 hours of sound, good-quality sleep, after which one awakens refreshed and in the best spirits, is the best for good health and longevity.

Activity (Exercise). By exercising for 20 minutes four times a week starting at the age of fifty-five, a person can prolong his/her life by 3.43 years; becoming fit, he/she has the chance to achieve ninety-five years. Among aerobic exercises, the knee-bend exercise is one of the best for heart conditioning. Together with an excellent training effect, the knee-bend exercise does not tax the heart to its limits. In addition to supplying a sufficient amount of oxygen to the tissues, this exercise avoids the excessive elimination of carbon dioxide.

Flexibility of the spine is absolutely important for overall health and longevity. Among the best exercises for the spine is the torso forward-backward bend. Strength exercises help prevent hip fractures and other injuries as a result of falls. The most important muscle group to be trained is the long lower-back muscles. The boat exercise is the best for strengthening these muscles. The reproductive organs of both men and women will be healthier as a result of these exercises. I believe that one of the most effective is the *buttocks-walking* exercise.

The inverted body position of the shoulder stand increases blood circulation in the neck, head, and brain, while the legs and organs that are usually below the heart are relieved of blood pressure. Improvements in vision, hearing, complexion, alertness, and thyroid gland functioning, as well as the cessation of hair loss, are just a few benefits of the shoulder stand.

The *exhale-through-water* exercise helps to strengthen the lungs, to increase blood circulation in the lungs, and to accumulate carbon dioxide in the body. There is an indisputable connection between meditation and life extension; the medusa (jellyfish) meditation is highly recommended.

Sex. Ejaculation control using the semen-preservation technique promotes health and longevity. Semen quality and sexual disorders can be controlled with specific foods described in this book.

Emotions. In handling emotions, practicing the *"be here and now"* state, becoming an observer, and laughter may be very helpful vehicles. Among the many techniques for handling emotions, I greatly emphasize *meditation.*

Thoughts. You are probably unfamiliar with egregores, but perhaps you would find them interesting in connection with thought control. Get away from the egregores of dependence, worry, and unrealistic desires, and attach yourself to the egregore of happiness. The technique of conscious worry for influencing future events may help you in your commitments.

Rejuvenation. A rejuvenation effect can be achieved if the body's major elimination organs and systems go through a thorough cleansing. The six-stage procedure of cleansing the large intestine, small intestine, joints, liver, kidneys, and blood is suggested for detoxification of the body. Water and juice fasting, and especially alternate dry fasting, may be used for effective detoxification of the organs and the whole body. There are claims that even AIDS, cancer, and diabetes can be cured with alternate five-day fasting. The overall effect of the one-month alternate dry fast on my health was positive because I got rid of kidney sand and liver stones, and the pain in my back vanished. The most profound effect of body cleansing and rejuvenation can be achieved by the combination of a raw-food diet and juice or water fasts one day a week. Dry fasting can be used in an emergency to cure a serious disease.

Longevity. The approaches to longevity of people who experimented on themselves include the raw-food-diet, balanced–diet, caloric–restriction, natural–hygiene, biochemistry, exercise, yoga, and the author's restriction-abundance approaches.

Factors affecting longevity discussed in this book do not cover all the possible factors, although some unusual ones are included, such as height, fasting, and breathing. All the "valleys of longevity" are located in high altitudes, where the air is thin in oxygen. Low oxygen intake keeps the metabolism of the people who live there at a low level, thereby increasing their longevity. The high content of carbon dioxide in their tissues and blood, which is attributed to increased physical activity, keeps their vessels clean and their hearts strong throughout their advanced age. I believe that air thin in oxygen is a major key to the longevity.

Those people who are determined to live a long life but who lack an inherited strong immune system may enhance it by following the twenty-one rules described in the previous chapter.

In general, awareness, moderation, and restriction gained through control of our own lives are the keys to a healthy and long life. What a few take for granted, the rest must acquire through significant and continuous efforts. To live to 100 and longer is a major undertaking and a great challenge throughout your entire life, and it requires courage to and work hard to implement. It does not allow any kind of laziness or self-indulgence; the body, mind, and soul must work hard day and night, day and night--every day until the end of your time!

Control, another key concept in this book, can unlock the magic box containing all the treasures of health, long life, and happiness. They can be all yours, because you now know what to take under control and how. I hope you fully understand that by "under control," I mean *self-control*. Consciously and with a sober mind, you choose it as a guiding principle in your life. You and only you are in full possession of its power. If you follow someone's recommendations regarding diet, exercise, lifestyle, or personal growth, you put yourself under their control, which confines your freedom of choice and clips your wings. Likewise, I do not want you to become dependent on whatever you found useful in this book.

From my instinct profile, you may remember that I greatly appreciate freedom and value it above everything else. Most likely, you do as well, and I respect your freedom very much. Therefore, my aim is not to restrain your freedom, but rather to provide you with information that I hope will be useful to you. Self-control also gives you confidence and contentment, and attracts people to you with a similar attitude. As far as I know, on a physical level, there is no "self-control" club or society, but I believe it exists on a collective unconscious level. The self-control egregore is a good egregore and it is worth joining as a full–time member.

With all their attractiveness, even control and life extension are not to be undertaken fanatically or excessively. Remember that *moderation* is the motto of many centenarians. Scientific achievements, holistic traditions, and common sense are your trusted supporters. Doing something in excess is always a challenge to Nature--it is better not to compete with Nature, but rather to become aware of its laws and to follow them. Keep in mind that although you made yourself fit and healthy, you still are not as young as you used to be. Behaving according to your age will prevent you from the tough tests of Nature. Be temperate in whatever you do, enjoy your life despite all its problems and odds, and be grateful to God for every additional year, month, or day that He gives you. Be wise about and respectful of the laws of Nature, rely on yourself, and our Earth will be yours, my dear life-extension seeker.

APPENDICES

Charts of Foodstuff for Four Blood Types   Appendix A
Blood Type O: Table A-1, Page 1.

GROUP	CATE-GORY	HIGHLY BENEFICIAL FOODS	NEUTRAL FOOD	FOODS TO AVOID
GRAINS, BREAD & CEREALS	GRAINS	None	Barley flour Buckwheat Kasha Artichoke pasta Rye flour Spelt flour Quinoa Basmati rice Brown rice White rice Wild rice Rice flour	Bulgur wheat flour Couscous flour Graham flour Soba noodles Oat flour Durum wheat flour Gluten flour Whole wheat flour White flour Semolina pasta Spinach pasta Sprouted wheat flour
	BREAD and MUFFINS	Essene bread Ezekiel bread	Rye vita Rice cakes Brown rice bread Fin crisp Rye crisps Spelt bread Wasa bread Ideal flat bread Millet Gluten-free bread Rye bread, 100% Soya flour bread	Wheat bagels Durum wheat Corn muffins Wheat matzos English muffins Multi-grain bread High-protein bread Oat bran muffins Pumpernickel Wheat bran muffins Whole wheat bread Sprouted wheat bread
	CEREALS	None	Amaranth Barley Buckwheat Kasha Cream of rice Kamut Puffed millet Rice bran Puffed rice Spelt	Cornflakes Cornmeal Cream of wheat Familia Grape nuts Farina Wheat germ Seven grain Wheat bran Oatmeal Shredded wheat Oat bran
VEGE-TABLES	VEGE-TABLES	Domestic artichoke Jerusalem artichoke Garlic Beet leaves Leek Kale Broccoli Okra Chicory Parsley Dandelion Pumpkin Spinach Collard greens Parsnips Escarole Horseradish Kohlrabi Romaine lettuce Seaweed Turnips Red onions Spanish onions Yellow onions Swiss chard Red peppers Sweet potatoes	Arugula Beets Dill Asparagus Celery Chervil Bamboo shoots Coriander Daikon Bok choy Carrots Ginger Caraway Cucumber Endive Fiddlehead ferns Fennel Lima beans Bibb lettuce Boston lettuce Tofu Iceberg lettuce Shallots Tempeh Mesclun lettuce Radicchio Radishes Abalone mushroom Tomatoes Enoki mushroom Mung sprouts Portobello mushroom Rappini Tree oyster mushroom Rutabaga Green peppers Radish sprouts Green olives Green onions Jalapeno peppers Yellow peppers Shallots Watercress Snow peas All types of squash Water chestnut Zucchini Scallion All types of yams	Alfalfa sprouts Avocado Brussels sprouts Chinese cabbage Red cabbage White cabbage Cauliflower Yellow corn White corn Eggplant Mustard greens Domestic mushroom Shiitake mushroom Black olives Greek olives Spanish olives Red potatoes White potatoes
FRUITS	FRUITS	Dried figs Fresh figs Dark plums Green plums Red plums Prunes	Apples Apricots Bananas Black currants Blueberries Grapefruit Boysenberries Lemons Cherries Cranberries Red dates Red currants Elderberries Mangoes Gooseberries Black grapes Kiwi Green grapes Red grapes Kumquat Concord grapes Guava Loganberries Canang melon Limes Casaba melon Christmas melon Pears Peaches Crenshaw melon Pineapple Raisins Spanish melon Musk melon Watermelon melon Papayas Nectarines Persimmons Pomegranates Raspberries Prickly pears Carambola star fruit	Blackberries Coconuts Oranges Cantaloupe melon Honeydew melon Plantains Rhubarb Strawberries Tangerines

Blood Type O:　　　Table A-1, Page 2.

GROUP	CATEGORY	HIGHLY BENEFICIAL FOODS	NEUTRAL FOOD	FOODS TO AVOID
MILK, YOGURT & CHEESE	DAIRY FOODS	None	Butter Farmer Feta Goat cheese Soy cheese Soy milk	American cheese　Brie Blue cheese　Casein Buttermilk　Colby Camembert　Cottage Cream cheese　Cheddar Emmenthal　Edam Goat milk　Gouda Ice cream　Gruyere Jarlsberg　Kefir Monterey jack　Munster Parmesan　Provolone Neufchatel　Ricotta Skim or 2% milk　Swiss String cheese　Whey Yogurt, all varieties Whole milk
FATS, OILS & SWEETS	FATS, OILS	Linseed (Flaxseed) oil Olive oil	Canola oil　Sesame oil Cod liver oil	Corn oil　Cottonseed oil Peanut oil　Safflower oil
	SUGARS	None	Barley malt　Molasses Brown rice syrup Chocolate　Honey Maple syrup　Rice syrup Brown sugar　White sugar	Cornstarch Corn syrup
MEAT, POULTRY, FISH, DRY BEANS, EGGS & NUTS	POULTRY & MEAT	Beef　Beef, ground Buffalo　Heart Lamb　Liver　Mutton Veal　Venison	Chicken　Duck Cornish hens　Partridge Pheasant　Quail Rabbit　Turkey	Bacon　Goose Ham　Pork
	FISH & SEAFOOD	Bluefish　Cod Hake　Halibut Herring　Mackerel Pike Red snapper　Salmon Rainbow trout　Sardine Shad　Snapper Sole　Striped bass Sturgeon　Swordfish Tilefish　Whitefish White perch　Yellowtail Yellow perch	Abalone　Anchovy Albacore (Tuna)　Beluga Bluegill bass　Carp Clam　Crab　Crayfish Eel　Flounder　Frog Gray sole Grouper　Haddock Lobster　Mahimahi Monkfish　Mussels Ocean perch　Oysters Pickerel　Porgy Sailfish　Scallop Sea bass　Sea trout Shark　Shrimp Silver perch　Snail Squid (calamari)　Smelt Turtle　Weakfish	Barracuda Catfish Caviar Conch Herring (pickled) Lox (smoked salmon) Octopus
	BEANS, PEAS	Aduke beans Azuki beans Pinto beans Black-eyed peas	Black beans　Green beans Broad beans　Fava beans Cannellini beans　Red beans Garbanzo beans　Lima beans Jicama beans　Snap beans Red soy beans　String beans Northern beans　White beans Green peas　Pods peas	Copper beans Kidney beans Navy beans Tamarind beans Domestic lentils Green lentils Red lentils
	NUTS, SEEDS	Pumpkin seeds Walnuts	Almond butter　Almonds Chestnuts　Filbert Hickory　Litchi nuts Macadamia　Pignola (pine) Sesame seeds Sesame butter (tahini) Sunflower butter Sunflower seeds	Brazil Cashew Litchi Peanuts Peanut butter Pistachios Poppy seeds

Blood Type O: Table A-1, Page 3.

GROUP	CATEGORY	HIGHLY BENEFICIAL FOODS	NEUTRAL FOOD	FOODS TO AVOID
TASTE ADDITIVES & DRINKS	CONDIMENTS, SALAD DRESSINGS, SAUCES, GRAVIES & SPREADS	None	Mayonnaise Mustard Salad dressing (low-fat, from acceptable ingredients) Worcestershire sauce	Dill pickles Ketchup Kosher pickles Relish Sour pickles Sweet pickles
	DRINKS	Club soda Seltzer water	Beer Green tea Red wine White wine	Regular coffee Decaf coffee Distilled liquor Cola soda Diet soda Black regular tea Other soda Black decaf tea
	JUICES	Black cherry Pineapple Prune	Apricot Carrot Celery Cabbage Cucumber Cranberry Grape Grapefruit Papaya Tomato water (with lemon) Vegetable juice (corresponding with highlighted vegetables)	Apple Apple cider Cabbage Orange
	SPICES	Carob Curry Cayenne pepper Dulse Kelp (bladder wrack) Parsley Turmeric	Agar Almond extract Allspice Anise Cream of tartar Arrowroot Cumin Basil Bay leaf Barley malt Dill Garlic Bergamot Brown rice syrup Honey Cardamom Chervil Chives Chocolate Cloves Coriander Plain gelatin Horseradish Maple syrup Marjoram Mint Miso Molasses Mustard (dry) Paprika Peppermint Peppercorn pepper Red flakes pepper Pimiento Rice syrup Rosemary Saffron Sage Salt Savory Spearmint Soy sauce Sucanat Tamari Brown sugar White sugar Tamarind Tapioca Tarragon Thyme Wintergreen	Capers Cinnamon Corn syrup Cornstarch Black ground pepper Nutmeg White pepper Apple cider vinegar Balsamic vinegar Red wine vinegar Vanilla White vinegar
	HERBAL TEAS	Cayenne Ginger Chickweed Dandelion Fenugreek Hops Linden Mulberry Parsley Peppermint Rose hips Sarsaparilla Slippery elm	Catnip Chamomile Dong quai Elder Ginseng Green tea Hawthorn Horehound Licorice root Mullein Raspberry leaf Sage Skullcap Spearmint Thyme Valerian Vervain White birch White oak bark Yarrow	Alfalfa Aloe Burdock Coltsfoot Corn silk Echinacea Gentian Goldenseal Red clover Rhubarb Saint-John's wort Senna Shepherd's purse Strawberry leaf Yellow dock

Blood Type A: Table A-2, Page 1.

GROUP	CATEGORY	HIGHLY BENEFICIAL FOODS	NEUTRAL FOOD	FOODS TO AVOID
GRAINS, BREAD & CEREALS	GRAINS	Buckwheat Kasha Oat flour Rice flour Rye flour Noodles, soba Pasta Artichoke	Couscous Barley flour Bulgur wheat flour Durum wheat flour Gluten flour Graham flour Spelt flour Spelt noodles Sprouted wheat flour Quinoa Basmati rice Brown rice White rice Wild rice	White flour Whole wheat flour Semolina pasta Spinach pasta
	BREAD and MUFFINS	Essene bread Rice cakes Ezekiel bread Soya flour bread Sprouted wheat bread	Wheat bagels Rye vita Corn muffins Millet Brown rice bread Fin crisp Spelt bread Wasa bread Ideal flat bread Rye bread, Gluten-free bread 100% Oat bran muffins Rye crisps	Durum wheat English muffins High-protein bread Wheat matzos Multi-grain bread Pumpernickel Wheat bran muffins Whole wheat bread
	CEREALS	Amaranth Buckwheat Kasha	Barley Cornflakes Cream of rice Cornmeal Puffed millet Oat bran Oatmeal Rice bran Puffed rice Spelt	Cream of wheat Familia Grape nuts Farina Wheat germ Granola Seven grain Wheat bran Shredded wheat
VEGE-TABLES	VEGETABLES	Domestic artichoke Kale Jerusalem artichoke Garlic Beet leaves Leek Broccoli Okra Carrots Parsley Dandelion Pumpkin Collard greens Parsnips Escarole Spinach Horseradish Chicory Alfalfa sprouts Tempeh Romaine lettuce Tofu Red onions Turnips Spanish onions Kohlrabi Yellow onions Swiss chard	Arugula Cauliflower Asparagus Celery Avocado Chervil Bamboo shoots Coriander Beets White corn Yellow corn Bok choy Caraway Cucumber Daikon radish Endive Fiddlehead ferns Fennel Bibb lettuce Boston lettuce Iceberg lettuce Shallots Mesclun lettuce Radicchio Abalone mushroom Enoki mushroom Seaweed Portobello mushroom Tree oyster mushroom Mustard greens Radishes Green olives Rappini Green onions Rutabaga Brussels sprouts Scallion Mung sprouts Watercress All types of squash Water chestnut Zucchini	Chinese cabbage Red cabbage White cabbage Lima beans Eggplant Domestic mushroom Shiitake mushroom Black olives Greek olives Spanish olives Tomatoes Green peppers Jalapeno peppers Red peppers Yellow peppers Sweet potatoes Red potatoes White potatoes Yams
FRUITS	FRUITS	Apricots Dried figs Blackberries Fresh figs Blueberries Grapefruit Boysenberries Lemons Cherries Pineapple Cranberries Dark plums Green plums Red plums Prunes Raisins	Apples Black currants Dates Red currants Pears Elderberries Gooseberries Black grapes Green grapes Red grapes Concord grapes Guava Kiwi Watermelon Kumquat Spanish melon Loganberries Canang melon Casaba melon Nectarines Christmas melon Limes Crenshaw melon Peaches Musk melon Persimmons Pomegranates Raspberries Prickly pears Strawberries Carambola star fruit	Bananas Coconuts Mangoes Oranges Cantaloupe melon Honeydew melon Papayas Plantains Rhubarb Tangerines

Blood Type A: Table A-2, Page 2.

GROUP	CATEGORY	HIGHLY BENEFICIAL FOODS	NEUTRAL FOOD	FOODS TO AVOID
MILK, YOGURT & CHEESE	DAIRY FOODS	Soy cheese Soy milk	Farmer Feta Goat cheese Goat milk Kefir Yogurt Low fat mozzarella Low fat ricotta String cheese Yogurt with fruit Frozen yogurt	Cream cheese Cottage Cheddar Edam Emmenthal Gouda Gruyere Ice cream Jarlsberg Munster Monterey jack Parmesan Provolone Neufchatel Sherbet Swiss Skim or 2% milk Whole milk Whey
FATS, OILS & SWEETS	FATS, OILS	Linseed (Flaxseed) oil Olive oil	Canola oil Cod liver oil	Corn oil Peanut oil Cottonseed oil Sesame oil Safflower oil
	SUGARS	Barley malt Blackstrap molasses	Brown rice syrup Chocolate Cornstarch Corn syrup Honey Maple syrup Rice syrup Brown sugar White sugar Jam (from acceptable fruits) Jelly (from acceptable fruits)	Plain gelatin
MEAT, POULTRY, FISH, DRY BEANS, EGGS & NUTS	POULTRY & MEAT	None	Chicken Cornish hens Turkey	Beef ground Buffalo Pork Duck Goose Heart Lamb Liver Venison Mutton Rabbit Veal Partridge Pheasant Quail
	FISH & SEAFOOD	Carp Cod Grouper Mackerel Monkfish Pickerel Red snapper Salmon Rainbow trout Sardine Sea trout Snail Silver perch Whitefish Yellow perch	Abalone Mahimahi Albacore (Tuna) Pike Ocean perch Porgy Sailfish Sea bass Shark Smelt Snapper Sturgeon Swordfish Weakfish White perch Yellowtail	Anchovy Barracuda Beluga Bluefish Bluegill bass Catfish Caviar Clam Conch Crab Crayfish Eel Flounder Frog Gray sole Haddock Hake Halibut Herring (fresh) Lobster Herring (pickled) Tilefish Lox (smoked salmon) Mussels Octopus Oysters Scallop Shad Shrimp Sole Squid (calamari) Striped bass Turtle
	BEANS, PEAS	Aduke beans Azuki beans Black beans Green beans Pinto beans Green lentils Domestic lentils Red soy beans Red lentils Black-eyed peas	Broad beans Fava beans Cannellini beans Jicama beans Snap beans String beans White beans Green peas Pods peas Snow peas	Red beans Kidney beans Lima beans Navy beans Copper beans Garbanzo beans Tamarind beans
	NUTS, SEEDS	Peanuts Peanut butter Pumpkin seeds	Almond butter Almond nuts Chestnuts nuts Filberts nuts Hickory nuts Litchi nuts Macadamia nuts Pignola (pine) nuts Poppy seeds Sesame seeds Walnuts Sesame butter (tahini) Sunflower butter Sunflower seeds	Brazil nuts Cashews Pistachios

Blood Type A: Table A-2, Page 3.

GROUP	CATEGORY	HIGHLY BENEFICIAL FOODS	NEUTRAL FOOD	FOODS TO AVOID
TASTE ADDITIVES & DRINKS	CONDIMENTS, SALAD DRESSINGS, SAUCES, GRAVIES & SPREADS	Mustard	Dill pickles Kosher pickles Sour pickles Sweet pickles Salad dressing (low-fat, from acceptable ingredients) Relish	Ketchup Mayonnaise Worcestershire sauce
	DRINKS	Decaf coffee Green tea Regular coffee Red wine	White wine	Beer Club soda Distilled liquor Cola soda Seltzer water Diet soda Black decaf tea Other soda Black regular tea
	JUICES	Apricot Carrot Black cherry Celery Grapefruit Pineapple Prune Water (with lemon)	Apple Apple cider Cabbage Cucumber Cranberry Grape Vegetable juice (corresponding to highlighted vegetables)	Orange Papaya Tomato
	SPICES	Barley malt Garlic Blackstrap molasses Ginger Miso Soy sauce Tamari	Agar Almond extract Allspice Corn syrup Anise Cream of tartar Arrowroot Cumin Basil Curry Bay leaf Dill Bergamot Dulse Brown rice syrup Honey Cardamom Carob Chervil Chives Chocolate Cinnamon Cloves Coriander Cornstarch Horseradish Kelp Maple syrup Marjoram Mint Mustard (dry) Nutmeg Oregano Paprika Parsley Peppermint Pimiento Rice syrup Rosemary Saffron Sage Salt Savory Spearmint Brown sugar White sugar Tamarind Tapioca Tarragon Thyme Turmeric Vanilla	Capers Plain gelatin Black ground pepper Cayenne pepper Peppercorn pepper Red flakes pepper White pepper Apple cider vinegar Balsamic vinegar Red wine vinegar White vinegar Wintergreen
	HERBAL TEAS	Alfalfa Ginger Aloe Ginseng Burdock Green tea Chamomile Hawthorn Echinacea Milk thistle Fenugreek Rose hips Saint-John's wort Slippery elm Valerian	Chickweed Hops Coltsfoot Horehound Dandelion Licorice root Dong quai Linden Elder Mulberry Gentian Mullein Goldenseal Parsley Peppermint Raspberry leaf Sage Sarsaparilla Senna Skullcap Shepherd's purse Spearmint Thyme Strawberry leaf Vervain White birch Yarrow White oak bark	Catnip Corn silk Cayenne Red clover Rhubarb Yellow dock

Blood Type B: Table A-3, Page1.

GROUP	CATEGORY	HIGHLY BENEFICIAL FOODS	NEUTRAL FOOD	FOODS TO AVOID
GRAINS, BREAD & CEREALS	GRAINS and PASTA	Oat flour Rice flour	Brown rice Basmati rice Graham flour Quinoa Spinach pasta Spelt flour Semolina pasta White rice White flour	Artichoke pasta Buckwheat Barley flour Couscous Bulgur wheat flour Kasha Durum wheat flour Rye flour Gluten flour Noodles, soba Whole wheat flour Wild rice
	BREAD and MUFFINS	Brown rice bread Essene bread Rice cakes Ezckiel bread Fin crisp Millet Wasa bread	High-protein no-wheat bread Ideal flat bread Gluten-free bread Oat bran muffins Pumpernickel Spelt bread Soya flour bread	Corn muffins Rye vita, crisps Durum wheat bread Wheat Multi-grain bread bagels Rye bread, 100% Whole wheat Wheat bran muffins bread
	CEREALS	Millet Oat bran Oatmeal Puffed rice Rice bran Spelt	Cream of rice Familia Farina Granola Grape nuts	Amaranth Barley Buckwheat Cornmeal Cream of wheat Cornflakes Kamut Kasha Rye Seven grain Shredded wheat Wheat bran Wheat germ
VEGE-TABLES	VEGETABLES	Beets Beet leaves Broccoli Chinese cabbage Collard greens Eggplant Cauliflower Carrots Brussels sprouts Red cabbage Kale White cabbage Lima beans Mustard greens Shiitake mushroom Parsnips Red peppers Green peppers Jalapeno peppers Yellow peppers Parsley Sweet potatoes Yams, all types	Asparagus Arugula Cucumber Water chestnut Bamboo shoots Bok choy Chervil Chicory Ginger Garlic White potatoes Dandelion Endive Fennel Escarole Fiddlehead ferns Bibb lettuce Horseradish Kohlrabi Red potatoes Swiss chard Boston lettuce Seaweed Iceberg lettuce Shallots Mesclun lettuce Radicchio Red & green Onions Romaine lettuce Rutabaga Daikon radish Snow peas Rappini Spanish onions Dill Okra Spinach (cooked) Scallion Alfalfa sprouts Zucchini Abalone mushroom Turnips Enoki mushroom Leek Yellow onions Watercress Domestic mushroom Celery Portobello and Tree oyster mushroom Squash, all types	Avocado Domestic artichoke Jerusalem artichoke Black olives Green olives Greek olives Pumpkin Spanish olives Mung sprouts Radishes White corn Radish sprouts Tempeh Tofu Tomatoes (cooked) Tomatoes (raw) Yellow corn (fresh)
FRUITS	FRUITS	Bananas Cranberries Black grapes Green grapes Red grapes Concord grapes Papaya Green plums Pineapple Dark plums Red plums	Apples Apricots Cherries Boysenberries Blackberries Black currants Fresh figs Cantaloupe melon Dates Grapefruit Dried figs Kiwi Lemons Honeydew melon Peaches Plantains Raisins Red currants Casaba melon Elderberries Gooseberries Mangoes Oranges Guava Kumquat Limes Pears Loganberries Canang melon Christmas & Spanish melon Crenshaw melon Prunes Musk melon Watermelon Nectarines Tangerines Raspberries Strawberries	Coconuts Persimmons Pomegranates Prickly pear Rhubarb Carambola star fruit

Blood Type B: Table A-3, Page2.

GROUP	CATEGORY	HIGHLY BENEFICIAL FOODS	NEUTRAL FOOD	FOODS TO AVOID
MILK, YOGURT & CHEESE	DAIRY FOODS	Cottage cheese Farmer Feta Goat cheese Goat milk Frozen yogurt Kefir Yogurt Mozzarella Ricotta Skim or 2% milk Yogurt with fruit	Brie Butter Buttermilk Casein Camembert Colby Cream cheese Cheddar Edam Emmenthal Gouda Gruyere Jarlsberg Munster Monterey jack Parmesan Provolone Neufchatel Sherbet Swiss Whole milk Whey Soy cheese Soy milk	American cheese Blue cheese Ice cream String cheese
FATS, OILS & SWEETS	FATS, OILS	Olive oil	Cod liver oil Linseed (Flaxseed) oil	Canola oil Corn oil Cottonseed oil Peanut oil Safflower oil Sesame oil
	SUGARS	None	Brown rice syrup Honey Chocolate Molasses Maple syrup Rice syrup Brown sugar White sugar Jam (from acceptable fruits) Jelly (from acceptable fruits)	Barley malt Cornstarch Corn syrup Plain gelatin
MEAT, POULTRY, FISH, DRY BEANS, EGGS & NUTS	POULTRY & MEAT	Lamb Mutton Rabbit Venison	Beef Beef ground Buffalo Liver Turkey Pheasant Veal	Bacon Chicken Ham Cornish hens Duck Goose Heart Pork Partridge Quail
	FISH & SEAFOOD	Cod Flounder Grouper Haddock Hake Halibut Mackerel Mahimahi Monkfish Ocean perch Pickerel Pike Porgy Salmon Sardine Sea trout Shad Sole Sturgeon Sturgeon eggs (Caviar)	Abalone Albacore (Tuna) Bluefish Carp Catfish Herring (fresh) Herring (pickled) Rainbow trout Red snapper Sailfish Scallop Shark Silver perch Smelt Snapper Squid (calamari) Swordfish Tilefish Weakfish White perch Whitefish Yellow perch	Anchovy Barracuda Beluga Bluegill bass Clam Conch Crab Crayfish Eel Frog Lobster Lox (smoked salmon) Mussels Octopus Oysters Sea bass Shrimp Snail Striped bass Turtle Yellowtail
	BEANS, PEAS	Kidney beans Lima beans Navy beans Red soy beans	Broad beans Fava beans Cannellini beans Green beans Copper beans Jicama beans Northern beans Red beans Snap beans String beans Tamarind beans White beans Green peas Pods peas	Aduke beans Azuki beans Black beans Garbanzo beans Pinto beans Domestic lentils Green lentils Red lentils Black-eyed peas
	NUTS, SEEDS	None	Almond nuts Almond butter Brazil nuts Chestnuts Hickory nuts Litchi nuts Macadamia nuts Pecans nuts Walnuts	Cashews Filberts nuts Peanuts Peanut butter Pignola (pine) nuts Pistachios Poppy seeds Pumpkin seeds Sesame seeds Sesame butter (tahini) Sunflower butter Sunflower seeds

Blood Type B: Table A-3, Page 3.

GROUP	CATEGORY	HIGHLY BENEFICIAL FOODS	NEUTRAL FOOD	FOODS TO AVOID
TASTE ADDITIVES & DRINKS	CONDIMENTS, SALAD DRESSINGS, SAUCES, GRAVIES & SPREADS	None	Apple butter Dill pickles Kosher pickles Mustard Sour pickles Relish Sweet pickles Mayonnaise Salad dressing (low-fat, from acceptable ingredients) Worcestershire sauce	Ketchup
	DRINKS	Green tea	Beer Black regular tea Black decaf tea Regular coffee Decaf coffee Red wine White wine	Distilled liquor Cola soda Diet soda Club soda Other soda Seltzer water
	JUICES	Cabbage Cranberry Grape Papaya Pineapple	Apple Apple cider Apricot Black cherry Carrot Celery Cucumber Grapefruit Orange Prune Water (with lemon) Vegetable juice (corresponding with highlighted vegetables)	Tomato
	SPICES	Cayenne pepper Curry Ginger Horseradish Parsley	Agar Anise Arrowroot Basil Bay leaf Bergamot Capers Carob Caraway Chervil Cardamon Chives Cream of tartar Cloves Cumin Coriander Dill Dulse Garlic Kelp (bladder wrack) Marjoram Pimiento Miso Mustard (dry) Nutmeg Oregano Mint Paprika Salt Peppercorn pepper Vanilla Red flakes pepper Saffron Rosemary Sage Savory Spearmint Soy sauce Tamarind Tarragon Thyme Turmeric Wintergreen Apple cider vinegar Balsamic vinegar Red wine & White vinegar	Almond extract Allspice Cinnamon Black pepper Black ground pepper White pepper Tapioca
	HERBAL TEAS	Ginger Ginseng Licorice Peppermint Raspberry leaf Sage Parsley Rose hips	Alfalfa Burdock Cayenne Catnip Chamomile Chickweed Dandelion Dong quai Echinacea Elder Goldenseal Green tea Hawthorn Horehound Licorice root Mulberry Saint-John's wort Valerian Sarsaparilla Slippery elm Spearmint Yarrow Strawberry leaf Thyme Vervain White birch White oak bark Yellow dock	Aloe Coltsfoot Corn silk Fenugreek Hops Gentian Linden Mullein Red clover Rhubarb Senna Skullcap Shepherd's purse

Blood Type AB: Table A-4, Page 1.

GROUP	CATEGORY	HIGHLY BENEFICIAL FOODS	NEUTRAL FOOD		FOODS TO AVOID
GRAINS, BREAD & CEREALS	GRAINS and PASTA	Brown rice Oat flour Basmati rice Rice flour White rice Rye flour Wild rice Sprouted wheat flour	Bulgur wheat flour Spelt flour Durum wheat flour Quinoa Gluten flour Graham flour Spinach pasta Semolina pasta White flour Whole wheat flour		Artichoke pasta Buckwheat Kasha Soba Noodles
	BREAD and MUFFINS	Brown rice bread Millet Essene bread Rice cakes Ezekiel bread Fin crisp Rye bread, 100% Rye crisps Wasa bread Rye vita Sprouted wheat bread Soya flour bread	High-protein bread Ideal flat bread Durum wheat bread Spelt bread Multi-grain bread Wheat bagels Gluten-free bread Wheat matzos Wheat bran muffins Pumpernickel Whole wheat bread Oat bran muffins		Corn muffins
	CEREALS	Millet Oat bran Oatmeal Puffed rice Rice bran Spelt	Amaranth Barley Cream of rice Cream of wheat Familia Farina Granola Grape nuts Seven grain Shredded wheat Soy flakes Soy granules Wheat bran Wheat germ		Buckwheat Cornmeal Cornflakes Kamut Kasha
VEGE-TABLES	VEGETABLES	Beets Beet leaves Broccoli Cauliflower Celery Collard greens Cucumber Dandelion Eggplant Garlic Kale Mustard greens Parsley Parsnips Sweet potatoes Alfalfa sprouts Tempeh Tofu Yams, all types	Asparagus Arugula Bamboo shoots Bok choy Brussels sprouts Pumpkin White cabbage Red cabbage Chinese cabbage Caraway Carrots Chervil Chicory Coriander Daikon Endive Fennel Escarole Fiddlehead ferns Ginger White potatoes Kohlrabi Horseradish Leek Red potatoes Swiss chard Dill Bibb lettuce Boston lettuce Iceberg lettuce Shallots Okra Mesclun lettuce Radicchio Red onions Green onions Romaine lettuce Rutabaga Turnips Spinach Snow peas Rappini Seaweed Spanish onions Green olives Greek olives Spanish olives Enoki mushroom Yellow onions Domestic mushroom Watercress Portobello mushroom Zucchini Tree oyster mushroom Tomatoes All types of squash Scallion Water chestnut		Avocado Domestic artichoke Jerusalem artichoke Black olives Lima beans Mung sprouts Red peppers Green peppers Jalapeno peppers Yellow peppers Radishes Abalone mushroom Shiitake mushrooms White corn Radish sprouts Yellow corn
FRUITS	FRUITS	Cherries Cranberries Figs fresh Figs dried Gooseberries Black grapes Green grapes Red grapes Concord grapes Grapefruit Kiwi Lemons Loganberries Pineapple Green plums Dark plums Red plums	Apples Apricots Boysenberries Blackberries Blueberries Black currants Cantaloupe melon Dates Honeydew melon Peaches Plantains Raisins Limes Red currants Casaba melon Elderberries Kumquat Nectarines Canang melon Pears Papaya Christmas & Crenshaw melon Spanish & Musk melon Prunes Watermelon Tangerines Raspberries Strawberries		Bananas Coconuts Guava Mangoes Oranges Persimmons Pomegranates Prickly pear Rhubarb Carambola star fruit

Blood Type AB: Table A-4, Page 2.

GROUP	CATEGORY	HIGHLY BENEFICIAL FOODS	NEUTRAL FOOD	FOODS TO AVOID
MILK, YOGURT & CHEESE	DAIRY FOODS	Cottage cheese Farmer Feta Goat cheese Goat milk Kefir Mozzarella Ricotta Sour cream (non fat) Yogurt	Casein Cheddar Colby Cream cheese Edam Emmenthal Gouda Gruyere Jarlsberg Munster Monterey jack Neufchatel Skim or 2% milk Swiss Soy cheese Soy milk String cheese Whey	American cheese Blue cheese Brie Butter Buttermilk Camembert Ice cream Parmesan Provolone Sherbet Whole milk
FATS, OILS & SWEETS	FATS, OILS	Olive oil	Canola oil Cod liver oil Peanut oil Linseed (Flaxseed) oil	Corn oil Cottonseed oil Safflower oil Sesame oil Sunflower oil
	SUGARS	None	Brown rice syrup Honey Chocolate Molasses Maple syrup Rice syrup Brown sugar White sugar Jam (from acceptable fruits) Jelly (from acceptable fruits)	Barley malt Cornstarch Corn syrup Plain, ground gelatin
MEAT, POULTRY, FISH, DRY BEANS, EGGS & NUTS	POULTRY & MEAT	Lamb Mutton Rabbit Turkey	Liver Pheasant	Bacon Beef Buffalo Beef ground Chicken Ham Cornish hens Duck Goose Heart Pork Partridge Veal Quail Venison
	FISH & SEAFOOD	Albacore (Tuna) Cod Grouper Hake Mackerel Mahimahi Monkfish Ocean perch Pickerel Pike Porgy Rainbow trout Red snapper Sailfish Salmon Sardine Sea trout Shad Snail Sturgeon	Abalone Bluefish Carp Catfish Caviar Herring (fresh) Mussels Scallop Shark Silver perch Smelt Snapper Sole Squid (calamari) Swordfish Tilefish Weakfish White perch Whitefish Yellow perch	Anchovy Barracuda Beluga Bluegill Bass Clam Conch Crab Crayfish Eel Flounder Frog Gray sole Halibut Haddock Herring (pickled) Lobster Octopus Lox (smoked salmon) Oysters Sea bass Shrimp Striped bass Turtle Yellowtail
	BEANS, PEAS	Navy beans Pinto beans Red beans Red soy beans Green lentils	Broad beans Copper beans Cannellini beans Green beans Jicama beans Northern beans Snap beans String beans Tamarind beans White beans Green peas Pods peas Domestic lentils Red lentils	Aduke beans Azuki beans Black beans Fava beans Garbanzo beans Lima beans Kidney beans Black-eyed peas
	NUTS, SEEDS	Chestnuts Peanuts Peanut butter Walnuts	Almond nuts Almond butter Brazil nuts Cashews Hickory nuts Litchi nuts Macadamia nuts Pignola (pine) nuts Pistachios	Filberts nuts Poppy seeds Pumpkin seeds Sesame seeds Sesame butter (tahini) Sunflower butter Sunflower seeds

Blood Type AB: Table A-4, Page 3.

GROUP	CATEGORY	HIGHLY BENEFICIAL FOODS	NEUTRAL FOOD	FOODS TO AVOID
TASTE ADDITIVES & DRINKS	CONDIMENTS, SALAD DRESSINGS, SAUCES, GRAVIES & SPREADS	None	Apple butter Mustard Mayonnaise Salad dressing (low-fat, from acceptable ingredients)	Ketchup Dill pickles Kosher pickles Relish Sour pickles Sweet pickles Worcestershire sauce
	DRINKS	Regular coffee Decaf coffee Green tea	Beer Seltzer water Red wine White wine Club soda	Distilled liquor Cola soda Diet soda Other soda Black regular tea Black decaf tea
	JUICES	Cabbage Carrot Celery Cranberry Black cherry Grape Papaya	Apple Apple cider Apricot Cucumber Grapefruit Pineapple Prune Tomato Water (with lemon) Vegetable juice (corresponding with highlighted vegetables)	Orange
	SPICES	Curry Garlic Horseradish Miso Parsley	Agar Arrowroot Bay leaf Bergamot Cardamon Carob Chervil Chive Cinnamon Clove Coriander Cream of tartar Cumin Dill Dulse Ginger Kelp (bladder wrack) Marjoram Mint Mustard (dry) Nutmeg Paprika Peppermint Pimiento Saffron Sage Salt Savory Soy sauce Spearmint Tamarind Tarragon Thyme Turmeric Vanilla Wintergreen	Almond extract Anise Allspice Capers Black pepper Black ground pepper Cayenne pepper Peppercorn pepper Red flakes pepper White pepper Plain, ground gelatine Tapioca Apple cider vinegar Balsamic vinegar Red wine vinegar White vinegar
	HERBAL TEAS	Alfalfa Burdock Chamomile Echinacea Ginger Ginseng Green tea Hawthorn Licorice root Rose hips Strawberry leaf	Catnip Cayenne Chickweed Dandelion Dong quai Elder Goldenseal Horehound Mulberry Raspberry leaf Sage Saint-John's wort Sarsaparilla Slippery elm Spearmint Yarrow Thyme Valerian Vervain White birch White oak bark Yellow dock	Aloe Coltsfoot Corn silk Fenugreek Hops Gentian Linden Mullein Red clover Rhubarb Senna Skullcap Shepherd's purse

Chart of Foodstuff for Blood Type A, Vata Dosha (diminant),
Yin-Yang type (Author's case):   Table B-1, Page 1.

GROUP	CATEGORY	HIGHLY BENEFICIAL FOODS		NEUTRAL FOOD		FOODS TO AVOID	
		Super	Very Good	Good	So so	Bad	Very Bad
GRAINS, BREAD & CEREALS	GRAINS / BREAD and MUFFINS	Rice (all kinds)	Buckwheat	Brown & wild rice	Gluten flour	Wheat	Semolina pasta
		Rice flour	Kasha	White rice	Couscous	White flour	Spinach pasta
		Oats (cooked)	Noodles	Basmati rice	Graham flour	Whole wheat	
		Oat flour	Soba	Durum wheat flour	Spelt flour	flour	
		Pasta		Bulgur wheat flour	Spelt noodles		
		Artichoke	Rye flour	Sprouted wheat flour	Barley flour	Durum wheat	Wheat bran
			Oats (dry)	Quinoa	Millet	Wheat matzos	muffins
						English muffins	Bread (with
		Essene bread	Rice cakes	Brown rice bread	Spelt bread	High-protein bread	yeast)
		Ezekiel bread	Soya flour	Wheat bagels	Rye vita & crisps	Multi-grain bread	
		Sprouted wheat	bread	Gluten-free bread	Wasa bread		Pumpernickel
		bread (Essene)		Ideal flat bread	Rye bread, 100%	Whole wheat bread	
				Fin crisp	Oat bran muffins		
					Corn muffins	Cream of wheat	Familia
	CEREALS	Amaranth	Buckwheat	Rice bran	Puffed millet	Shredded wheat	Farina Granola
			Kasha	Cream of rice	Barley Spelt	Grape nuts	Wheat bran, germ
				Puffed rice	Oat bran	Seven grain	
				Oatmeal	Cornmeal Cornflakes		
VEGE-TABLES	VEGETABLES	**Carrots**	Beet leaves	Daikon radish	Chervil		
		Cilantro	Broccoli	**Avocado**	Radishes (raw)		
		Red onions (cooked)		**Beets**	Radicchio	Chinese cabbage (cooked)	
		Spanish onion	Chicory	Yellow corn	Bok choy		Red cabbage (raw)
		Yellow onions	Alfalfa	Water chestnut	Green onions		White cabbage
		Leeks	sprouts	Arugula	Endive		
			Turnips	Fiddlehead ferns	Iceberg lettuce	Black olives	
		Horseradish	Collard greens	Fennel	Boston lettuce	Greek olives	
		Parsnip	Parsley	Mustard greens	Mesclun lettuce	Spanish olives	
			Dandelion greens	All types of squash	Bibb lettuce	Lima beans	Green peppers
		Pumpkin	Spinach (raw)	Coriander	Green olives		Jalapeno peppers
		Garlic	Kale	Asparagus	Celery	Sweet potatoes	Red peppers
		Escarole	Tempeh	Cauliflower (cooked)	White corn		Yellow peppers
			Romaine lettuce	Cucumber	Shallots Rappini		Domestic mushroom
		Okra	**Jerusalem**	**Watercress**	Cauliflower (raw)		Shiitake mushroom
			artichoke	Rutabaga	Abalone mushroom	**Tomatoes (cooked)**	
		Domestic artichoke		Seaweed	Tree oyster mushroom		
		Spinach (cooked)		Caraway	Enoki mushroom	Red potatoes	White potatoes
			Kohlrabi	Zucchini	Portobello mushroom	Yams	Eggplant
			Swiss chard	Scallion	Mung sprouts		
			Tofu	Bamboo shoots	Brussels sprouts		
FRUITS	FRUITS	Apricots	Figs	Apples (cooked)	Apples (raw)		
		(dry)		Strawberries			
		Blackberries		Raspberries			
		Cranberries		Loganberries			
		Blueberries		Gooseberries	Dates (dry)		
		Boysenberries		Elderberries	Black currants		
		Cherries		Guava **Kiwi**	Red currants	Coconuts	
		Dark plums		Dates (fresh)		Cantaloupe melon	
		Green plums		Kumquat **Limes**		Honeydew melon	
		Red plum		**Peaches**	Carambola star fruit	Bananas	
		Prunes (soaked)		Black & red grapes		**Oranges**	
		Raisins (soaked)		**Green grapes**	Watermelon	Mangoes	
		Lemons	Prunes	**Concord grapes**		Papaya	Plantains
		(dry)		Casaba melon		Rhubarb	Tangerines
		Grapefruit	Raisins	Christmas melon	Pears		
		(dry)		Crenshaw melon	Prickly pears		
		Figs (fresh)		Spanish melon	Persimmons		
		Pineapple		Musk melon	Pomegranates		
				Nectarines			

Table B-1, Page 2.

GROUP	CATEGORY	HIGHLY BENEFICIAL FOODS		NEUTRAL FOOD		FOODS TO AVOID	
		Super	Very Good	Good	So So	Bad	Very Bad
MILK, YOGURT & CHEESE	DAIRY FOODS	Soy cheese Soy milk		String cheese Goat cheese Low fat ricotta Low fat mozzarella Yogurt (spiced) Goat milk	Farmer Goat milk (powdered) Feta Frozen yogurt Yogurt with fruit Kefir	American cheese Blue cheese Cottage Cream cheese Sherbet Butter Emmenthal Provolone Jarlsberg Monterey jack Buttermilk Skim or 2% milk Whole milk	Brie Cheddar Camembert Casein Colby Gruyere Edam Gouda Ice cream Munster Parmesan Neufchatel Swiss Whey
FATS, OILS & SWEETS	FATS, OILS	Linseed (Flaxseed) oil Olive oil		Canola oil Cod liver oil		Peanut oil Sesame oil	Corn oil Cottonseed oil Safflower oil
	SUGARS	Barley malt Blackstrap molasses		Brown rice syrup Maple syrup Corn syrup Brown sugar Jam & Jelly (from acceptable fruits)	Rice syrup Cornstarch White sugar Chocolate Honey	Plain gelatin	
MEAT, POULTRY, FISH, DRY BEANS, EGGS & NUTS	POULTRY & MEAT	None		Turkey (dark) Cornish hens Chicken (dark)	Turkey (white) Chicken (white)	Duck Goose Partridge Heart Liver Veal Beef Beef ground	Pheasant Quail Rabbit Lamb Mutton Pork Ham Bacon Buffalo Venison
	FISH & SEAFOOD	Salmon Sardine Cod Red snapper Rainbow trout Monkfish Sea trout Whitefish Carp	Mackerel Pickerel Grouper Silver perch Yellow perch Snail	Abalone Albacore (Tuna) Sturgeon Sailfish Snapper Swordfish Ocean perch White perch	Mahimahi Shark Porgy Sea bass Smelt Pike Weakfish Yellowtail	Caviar Anchovy Beluga Herring (fresh) Herring (pickled) Crab Lobster Shrimp Turtle Hake Gray sole Lox (smoked salmon) Frog Sole Eel Striped bass Oysters	Catfish Barracuda Bluefish Flounder Halibut Bluegill bass Crayfish Conch Shad Haddock Clam Scallop Tilefish Octopus Squid (calamari) Mussels
	BEANS, PEAS	Red lentils Red soy beans Domestic Pinto beans Lentils Azuki beans Green lentils Black beans & beans Black-eyed peas		Green peas Broad beans Cannellini beans Jicama beans String beans	White beans Fava beans Snow peas Snap beans Pods peas	Red beans Copper beans Tamarind beans Garbanzo beans	Kidney beans Navy beans Lima beans
	NUTS, SEEDS	Peanuts Peanut butter Pumpkin seeds		Chestnuts nuts Hickory nuts Walnuts Pignola (pine) nuts Sesame seeds Sesame butter (tahini) Almonds Almond butter	Filberts nuts Poppy seeds Macadamia nuts Litchi nuts Sunflower butter & seeds	Brazil nuts Cashews Pistachios	

Table B-1, Page 3.

GROUP	CATEGORY	HIGHLY BENEFICIAL FOODS	NEUTRAL FOOD		FOODS TO AVOID
	CONDIMENTS, SALAD DRESSINGS, SAUCES, GRAVIES & SPREADS	Super Very Good Mustard	Good Dill pickles Kosher pickles Sour pickles Sweet pickles	So So Salad dressing (low-fat, from acceptable ingredients) Relish	Bad Very Bad Worcestershire sauce Mayonnaise Ketchup
TASTE ADDITIVES & DRINKS	DRINKS	Green tea Decaf coffee Red wine Regular coffee	White wine		Black regular tea Seltzer water Black decaf tea Beer Diet & club soda
	JUICES	Apricot Black cherry Celery Grapefruit Prune Pineapple Carrot Water (with lemon)	Cabbage Apple Grape Apple cider Cucumber Cranberry Vegetable juice (corresponding to appropriate vegetables)		Distilled liquor Club soda Other soda Orange Tomatos Papaya
	SPICES	Barley malt Blackstrap molasses Miso Garlic Soy sauce Tamari Ginger	Coarse sea salt Horseradish Saffron Parsley Thyme Rosemary Chervil Agar Almond extract Allspice Salt Cream of tartar Arrowroot Cumin Basil Curry Bay leaf Dill Cinnamon Nutmeg Anise Vanilla Cloves Coriander Bergamot Dulse Brown rice syrup Cardamom Carob Chives Oregano Chocolate Kelp Peppermint Marjoram Mint Mustard (dry) Maple syrup Paprika Pimiento Rice syrup Sage Corn syrup Savory Spearmint Turmeric Cornstarch Tamarind Tapioca Brown sugar White sugar Tarragon Honey		Capers Plain gelatin Apple cider vinegar Balsamic vinegar Red wine vinegar White vinegar Wintergreen Black ground pepper Cayenne pepper Peppercorn pepper White pepper Red flakes pepper

	HERBAL TEAS	Chamomile Ginseng
		Echinacea Burdock
		Hawthorn Alfalfa
		Rosehip Milk thistle
		Fenugreek
		Aloe
		Saint-John's wort
		Green tea
		Slippery elm
		Valerian
		Ginger
			Parsley Mulberry
			Coltsfoot Strawberry leaf
			Licorice root Dandelion
			Dong quai Linden
			Elder Senna Horehound
			Gentian Mullein
			Goldenseal Sage
			White birch Vervain
			White oak bark Skullcap
			Raspberry leaf Hops
			Sarsaparilla Yarrow
			Shepherd's purse
			Spearmint Thyme
			Chickweed
			Peppermint
					Cayenne Catnip
					Rhubarb Red clover
					                Yellow dock
					                Corn silk

Charts of Foodstuff for Horoscope Types: Table C-1, Page 1.

Sign of Zodiac	Nouri-ture	Grains	Vege-tables	Fruits	Herbs and Spices		
					First Decan	Second Decan	Third Decan
Oven (Aries)	Lamb Mutton Goat	–	Carrots Hops Onions Peppers Pimentos Radishes Shallots	Grapefruit Watermelon	Allspice Anise Basil Chili pepper Cloves Coriander Cumin Curry Garlic Ginger Horseradish Maple Mustard Nutmeg Pepper Peppermint Sage Sarsaparilla Sassafras	Bay leaves Chamomile Chicory Cinnamon Citron Ginseng Rosemary Saffron Sesame	Anise Cloves Maples Nutmeg Sage Sarsaparilla Sassafras Cardamon Licorice Spearmint Thyme Vanila
Taurus	Beef	Barley Corn Oats Rye Wheat	Peas Spinach Tomatoes	Apples Avocados Bananas Blackberries Cherries Huckle-berries Peaches Pears Plums Persimons Raspberries Rhubarb Strawberries	Allspice Basil Bittersweet Chili pepper Caraway Clover Coriander Cumin Curry Garlic Dill Fennel Ginger Mint Horseradish Mustard Parsley Pepper Peppermint	Bittersweet Caraway Clover Dill Fennel Mint Parsley Peppermint Wintergreen	Tamarind Tarragon
Gemini	Fowl	Almond Brazil nuts Filberts Pecans Pistachios	Beans Broccoli Cauli-flower Celery	Apricots Pomegranate	Anise Cardamon Cloves Licorice Maple Nutmeg Sage Spearmint Thyme Vanila Sarsaparilla Sassafras	Cardamon Licorice Sage Spearmint Thyme Vanila	Bay leaves Chamomile Chicory Cinnamon Citron Ginseng Rosemary Saffron Sesame
Cancer	Crab	–	Cabbage Cucumbers Gourds Lettuce Potatoes Turnips	Coconuts Grapes Lemons Papayas	Cardamon Lemon peel Licorice Sage Spearmint Thyme Vanila Wintergreen	Allspice Basil Bittersweet Chili pepper Caraway Clover Coriander Cumin Curry Dill Garlic Fennel Ginger Mint Horseradish Mustard Parsley Pepper Peppermint	Anise Cloves Lemon peel Maple Nutmeg Sage Sarsaparilla Sassafras Wintergreen

Table C-1, Page 2.

Sign of Zodiac	Nouriture	Grains or nuts	Vegetables	Fruits	Herbs and Spices		
					First Decan	Second Decan	Third Decan
Leo	Wild game	Cashews Sunflower seeds Walnuts	Okra Olives Squash	Limes Oranges Pineapples Tangerins	Tamarind Tarragon	Anise Cloves Maples Nutmeg Sage Sarsaparilla Sassafras	Allspice Basil Chili pepper Coriander Cumin Curry Garlic Ginger Horseradish Mustard Pepper Peppermint
Virgo	Veal	Almond Brazil nuts Filberts Pecans Pistachios	Beans Broccoli Cauliflower Celery	Apricots Pomegranate	Bay leaves Chamomile Chicory Cinnamon Citron Ginseng Rosemary Saffron Sesame	Cardamon Licorice Sage Spearmint Thyme Vanila	Cardamon Licorice Sage Spearmint Thyme Vanila
Libra	Cornuopia	Barley Corn Oats Rye Wheat	Peas Spinach Tomatoes	Apples Avocado Bananas Blackberries Cherries Huchleberries Peaches Pears Persimons Plums Raspberries Rhubarb Strawberries	Wintergreens and the oils extracted from the peels of citrus fruits, particularly Lemons and Limes	Tamarind Tarragon	Anise Bittersweet Cloves Caraway Clover Dill Fennel Mint Maple Nutmeg Parsley Peppermint Sage Sarsaparilla Sassafras
Scorpio	Shell-fish	–	Carrots Hops Onions Peppers Pimentos Pumpkin Radishes Shallots	Grapefruit Watermelon	Allspice Basil Cardamon Chili pepper Coriander Cumin Curry Garlic Ginger Horseradish Licorice Mustard Pepper Peppermint Sage Thyme Spearmint Vanila	Bay leaves Chamomile Chicory Cinnamon Citron Ginseng Rosemary Saffron Sesame Anise Cloves Maple Nutmeg Sage Sarsaparilla Sassafras	Cardamon Lemon peel Licorice Sage Spearmint Thyme Vanila Wintergreen

Table C-1, Page 3.

Sign of Zodiac	Nouri-ture	Grains or nuts	Vege-tables	Fruits	Herbs and Spices		
					First Decan	Second Decan	Third Decan
Sigitta-rius	Ham Pork Sausages	Chestnuts	Artichokes Brussel sprouts Endives	Dates Figs Mangos	Bittersweet Caraway Clover Dill Fennel Mint Parsley Peppermint	Allspice Basil Chili pepper Coriander Cumin Curry Garlic Ginger Lemon peel Horseradish Mustard Pepper Peppermint Wintergreen	Bay leaves Chamomile Chicory Cinnamon Citron Ginseng Rosemary Saffron Sesame
Capri-corn	Lamb	–	Beets Eggplant Zuccini	Cantaloupe Honeydew melons Quinces	Anise Cloves Maple Nutmeg Sage Sarsaparilla Sassafras	Allspice Basil Cardamon Chili pepper Coriander Cumin Curry Garlic Ginger Horseradish Licorice Mustard Pepper Peppermint Sage Spearmint Thyme Vanila	Bittersweet Caraway Clover Dill Fennel Mint Parsley Peppermint Bay leaves Chamomile Chicory Cinnamon Citron Ginseng Rosemary Saffron Sesame
Aquarius	Seafood	–	Beets Eggplant Zuccini	Cantaloupe Honeydew melons Quinces	Cardamon Licorice Sage Spearmint Thyme Vanila	Bittersweet Caraway Clover Dill Fennel Mint Parsley Peppermint	Cardamon Lemon peel Licorice Sage Spearmint Thyme Vanila Wintergreen
Pisces	Fish	Chest nuts	Artichokes Brussel sprouts Endives Kale	Dates Figs Mangos	Tamarind Tarragon	Lemon peel Wintergreen	Allspice Basil Chili pepper Coriander Cumin Curry Garlic Ginger Horseradish Mustard Pepper Peppermint

Appendix D

Nutrition Value of Daily Food Taken by the Author during His Alternate Dry Fasting: Table D-1, Page 1.

Valery Marmonov
56 years old
Fasting started: Aug 6, 1997

Height: 192 cm (6'4")
Body Mass Index: 20

August 8, 1997

Daily Nutrition on Eating Days During One Month Alternate Dry Fasting

Diet	Food	Serving Size Amount		Calories	Calories from Fat	Protein(g)	Carbohydrates(g)	Fat(g)	Cholesterol(mg)	Fiber(g)	Vitamin A(%)	Vitamin C(%)	Thiamin - B1(mg)	Riboflavin(%)	Niacin - B3(mg)	Vitamin B6(%)	Folacin(%)	Vitamin B12(%)
Daily Value*				2000	600	63	300	66	300	23	1000	60	1.2	1.4	15	2.0	200	2.0
Fats, Oils & Sweets Group	Olive oil	1 Tbsp(14ml.)	1	130	130	0	0	14	0	0	0	0	0	0	0	0	0	0
	Peanut butter	2 Tbsp(32g)	0.5	95	70	3.5	3.5	8	0	1	0	0	0	0	2	0	0	0
	Butter	1 Tbsp(14g)	1	180	180	0.0	0	10	0	2	100	0	0	0	0	0	0	0
	Dark brown sugar	1 teasp(4g)	2	30	0	0.0	8	0	0	0	0	0	0	0	0	0	0	0
	Grape jelly	1 Tbsp(20g)	2	100	0	0.0	26	0	0	0	0	0	0	0	0	0	0	0
Subtotal				535	380	4	38	32	0	3	100	0	0	0	2	0	0	0
Protein Group	Tofu	1/5 block(91 g)	0.6	56	28	5.6	0.6	3.1	0	3.0	0	0.0	0.1	0.1	0.2	0.0	11	0.2
	Miso	1 Tbsp(18g)	0.8	23	8	1.5	2.3	0.8	0	0.4	0	0.0	0.0	0.0	0.1	0.0	2	0.2
	Instant Breakfast (choco)	1 Envlp(37.5g)	1	130	13	4.0	26.0	1.5	3	0.9	250	15	0.2	0.2	3.8	0.4	50	0.2
	Almonds	1 oz(28.3g)	0.4	76	58	2.8	0.4	6.4	0	1.6	10	0.6	0.0	0.0	0.2	0.0	2	0.0
	Brazil Nuts	1 oz(28.3g)	2	53	46	1.3	0.9	1.4	0	0.6	50	3.0	0.1	0.1	0.8	0.1	10	0.1
	Walnuts	1 oz(14 halves)	1	91	37	0.3	3.0	1.3	6	0.5	20	1.2	0.0	0.0	0.3	0.0	4	0.0
	Hazelnuts	1 oz(30 nuts)	0.25	42	34	1.0	0	3.8	0	0.6	150	9.0	0.2	0.2	2.3	0.3	30	0.3
	Black beans	1/2 cup(95 g)	0.5	45	0	14	27	0.3	0	10	0	0	0.1	0.0	0.2	0.1	0	0
Subtotal				516	223	30	60	19	9	18	480	29	0.7	0.6	7.7	0.9	110	1.0
Milk, Yogurt & Cheese Group	Sour Cream	2 Tbsp(30g)	1	50	45	1	1	5	15	0	4	0	0	0	0	0	0	0
Subtotal				50	45	1	1	5	15	0	4	0	0	0	0	0	0	0
Daily Value*				2000	600	63	300	66	300	23	1000	60	1.2	1.4	15	2.0	200	2.0

* Daily Values are for males, of age 51+, and of weight 170 lbs.

Table D-1, Page 2.

Diet	Food	Serving Size	Amount	Calories	Calories from Fat	Protein(g)	Carbohydrates(g)	Fat(g)	Cholesterol(mg)	Fiber(g)	Vitamin A(IU)	Vitamin C(mg)	Thiamin - B1(mg)	Riboflavin(mg)	Niacin - B3(mg)	Vitamin B6(mg)	Folic acid(mcg)	Vitamin B12(mcg)
Fruits Group	Dates	10 small	4 dates	98	0	0.8	26	0	0	2.6	0	72	0.02	0.03	0.60	0	2	0
	Apricots	5 medium	6 apric.	120	0	1.2	35	0	0	4.8	24	1.4	0.14	0.17	2.6	0	0	0
	Figs	2 large		150	0	1.5	39	0	0	6.0	0	0.0	0.09	0.11	0.7	0	6	0
	Raisins	1/4 cup	0.5	65	0	0.5	16	0	0	1.0	0	0.0	0.05	0.11	0	0	0	0
	Prunes	1/2 cup	0.3	58	0	2.5	12	0	0	6.0	320	2.4	0.05	0.03	1.2	0	0	0
	Kiwi	1 fruit	1	46	0	0.0	12	0	0	3	30	74.4	0.05	0.03	0.3	0	0	0
Subtotal				537	0	6	140	0	0	23	374	150	0.35	0.44	5	0	8	0
Vegetables Group	Carrots 3	1 medium	1	31	0	0	6	0	0	2	4050	7	0.06	0.06	0.5	0	6	0
	Potato	1 medium	1	116	0	3	27	0	0	2	0	10	0.11	0.13	1.4	0	6	0
	Onion	1/2 cup chopped	0.5	30	0	1	3	0	0	2	0	2	0.00	0.00	0.0	0	0	0
	Garlic	3 cloves	2 cloves	9	0	0	0	0.1	0	0	0	0	0.00	0.00	0.0	0	0	0
	Shiitake mushrooms	4 mushrooms	3 mushr	33	1	1.8	6	1	0	3	0	0	0.00	0.00	0.0	0	0	0
Subtotal				219	1	5	42	41	0	5	4050	19	0.0	0.27	3	0	21	0
Grains Group	Buckwheat	1/4 cup	1	120	0	0	0	0	0	0	0	0	0	0	0.0	0	0	0
	Oat Bran	1/2 cup(40g)	1/7	43	7	2	7	1	0	2	0	0	0.1	0.02	0.0	0	0	0
	Oatmeal	1/2 cup(39g)	2	280	50	10	52	6	0	8	0	0	0.00	0.00	0.0	0	0	0
	Rice vermicelli	55 grams	1	209	10	4	18	2	0	2	0	0	0.00	0.00	0.0	0	0	0
	Oatmeal bread	1 slice (25g)	4	60	5	2	12	1	0	2	0	0	0.05	0.02	0.0	0	0	0
Subtotal				712	72	18	89	9	24	16	0	0	0.48	0.34	4.8	0	9	0
	Vitamins & minerals	Tablet, caplet	1	0	0	0	0	0	0	0	8000	1620	55	55	80	55	500	60
Subtotal				712	72	18	89	9	24	16	8000	1620	55	55	80	55	500	60
Total				2569	721	64	370	106	24	64	13008	1818	56.8	56.7	102	56	639	62
Daily Value*				2000	600	63	300	66	0	23	1000	60	1.2	1.4	15	2.0	400	2.0

* Daily Values are for males, of age 51+, and of weight 170 lbs.

Table D-1, Page 3.

Daily Nutrition on Eating Days During One Month Alternate Dry Fasting

Valery Mamonov
56 years old
Fasting started: Aug 6, 1997

Height: 192 cm (64)
Body Mass Index: 20

August 8, 1997

Diet	Food	Serving Size	Amount	Vitamin D (IU)	Vitamin E (IU)	Sodium (mg)	Potassium (mg)	Calcium (mg)	Iron (mg)	Magnesium (mg)	Phosphorus (mg)	Zinc (mg)	Copper (mg)	Manganese (mg)	Selenium (mg)	Chromium (mg)	Iodine (mcg)	Germanium (mg)
Daily Value*				400	30	2400	3500	800	18	350	800	15	2.0	5.0	70	250	150	150
Fats, Oils & Sweets Group	Olive oil	1 Tbsp(14ml.)	2	0	0	0	0	0	0	0	0	0	0	0	0	0	0	0
	Peanut butter	2 Tbsp(32g)	0.5	0	0	75	0	0	0.2	0	0	0	0	0	0	0	0	0
	Butter	1 Tbsp(14g)	1	0	0	90	0	0	0	0	0	0	0	0	0	0	0	0
	Dark brown sugar	1 teasp(4g)	2	0	0.5	10	0	0	0	0	0	0	0	0	0	0	0	0
	Grape jelly	1 Tbsp(20g)	2	0	0	175	0	0	0.2	0	0	0	0	0	0	0	0	0
Subtotal				0	0.5	350	0	0	0.4	0	0	0	0	0	0	0	0	0
Protein Group	Tofu	1/5 block(91g)	0.6	0	0	6	197	20	0.9	39	0	1.2	0	0	0	0	0	0
	Miso	1 Tbsp(18g)	0.8	0	0	653	26	6	0.3	4	0	0.4	0	0	0	0	0	0
	Instant Breakfast (choco)	1 Envlp(37.5g)	1	0	8	160	250	560	4.5	70	120	3.0	0.5	0	0	0	23	0
	Almonds	1 oz(28.3g)	0.4	0	4	0	25.6	0.6	0.0	0	0	0	0	0	0	0	0	0
	Brazil Nuts	1 oz(28.3g)	0.3	0	0	0	175	40.0	0.9	11	0	1.1	0	0	175	0	0	0
	Walnuts	1 oz(14 halves)	0.25	0	0	0	0	6.9	0.2	0	0	0	0	0	0	0	0	0
	Hazelnuts	1 oz(30 nuts)	0.6	0	0	0	0	6.9	0.2	0	0	0	0	0	0	0	0	0
	Black beans	1/2 cup(95 g)	0.4	0	0	289	158	16.0	0.7	32	0	1.0	0	0	0	0	0	0
Subtotal				0	12	1108	831	656	8	155	120	7	1	0	175	0	23	0
Milk, Yogurt & Cheese Group	Sour Cream	2 Tbsp(30g)	0.5	0	0	35	385	64	1	0	0	0	0	0	0	0	23	0
Subtotal				0	0	35	385	64	1	0	0	0	0	0	0	0	0	0
Daily Value*				400	30	2400	3500	800	18	350	800	15	2.0	5.0	70	250	150	150

* Daily Values are for males, of age 51+, and of weight 170 lbs.

Table D-1, Page 4.

Diet	Food	Serving Size	Amount	Vitamin D(IU)	Vitamin E(IU)	Sodium(mg)	Potassium(mg)	Calcium(mg)	Iron(mg)	Magnesium(mg)	Phosphorus(mg)	Zinc(g)	Copper(mg)	Manganese(mg)	Selenium(mcg)	Chromium(mcg)	Iodine(mcg)	Germanium(mg)
Fruits Group	Dates	10 small	4 dates	0	0	0	238	10	0.4	11.2	0	0.12	0	0	0	0	0	0
	Apricots	5 medium	6 apric	0	0	0	600	38	1.3	0	0	0.00	0	0	0	0	0	0
	Figs	2 large	3 figs	0	0	0	525	144	2	158	0	1.35	0	0	0	0	0	0
	Raisins	1/4 cup	0.5	0	0	0	158	8	0.5	0	0	0.00	0	0	0	0	0	0
	Prunes	1/2 cup	0.5	0	0	0	245	16	1.0	16	0	0.23	0	0	0	0	0	0
	Kiwi	1 fruit	1	0	0	0	245	16	0.4	21	0	0.00	0	0	0	0	0	0
Subtotal				0	0	0	2011	232	6	205	0	1.70	0	0	0	0	0	0
Vegetables Group	Carrots	1 medium	1	0	0	0	245	16	0.4	11	0	0.0	0	0	0	0	0	0
	Potato	1 medium	1	0	0	0	455	0	0.4	25	0	0.3	0	0	0	0	0	0
	Onion	1/2 cup chopped	0.5	0	0	0	70	8	0.0	4	0	0.0	0	0	0	0	0	0
	Garlic	3 cloves	2	0	0	0	11	11	0.0	0	0	0.0	0	0	0	0	0	0
	Shiitake mushrooms	6 oz(70 pieces)	3 mushr	0	0	192	184	0	0.0	13	57	0.9	0	0	0	0	0	0
Subtotal				0	0	192	954	35	0.8	52	57	1.2	0	0	0	0	0	0
Grains Group	Buckwheat	1/4 cup	1	0	0	0	0	0	0.8	20	0	0.43	0	0	0	0	0	0
	Oat Bran	1/2 cup(40g)	1/7	0	0	0	15	5	0.8	100	135	0.00	0	0	0	0	0	0
	Oatmeal	1/2 cup(39g)	2	0	0	0	0	0	3.6	0	0	0.00	0	0	0	0	0	0
	Rice vermicelli	55 grams	1	0	0	190	0	0	2.9	0	0	0.00	0	0	0	0	0	0
	Oatmeal bread	1 slice(25g)	4	0	0	100	20	64	0.0	0	0	0.00	0	0	0	0	0	0
Subtotal				0	0	290	35	169	25	120	135	15.4	2	0	0	0	0	0
	Vitamins & minerals	Tablet, caplet	1	400	60	0	15	100	18	100	78	15.0	2	0	0	0	150	0
Subtotal				400	60	0	15	100	18	100	78	15.0	2	0	0	0	150	0
Total				400	72	2400	4215	1156	40	532	255	25	3	0	175	0	173	0
Daily Value*				400	30	2400	3500	800	18	350	800	15	2.0	5.0	70	250	150	150

* Daily Values are for males, of age 51+, and of weight 170 lbs.

SELECTED BIBLIOGRAPHY

Abravanel, Elliot D., M.D. *Dr. Abravanel's Body Type Program for Health, Fitness, And Nutrition*. New York: Bantam Books, 1985.

Allard Michel, Victor, Dr. and Jean-Marrie Robine. *Jeanne Calment: From Van Gogh's Time to Ours 122 Extraordinary Years*. Thorndike, Me.: Thorndike Press, 1999.

Aronne, Louis J., M.D. *Weigh Less, Live Longer*. New York: John Wiley & Sons, 1996.

Atkins, Robert C., M.D. *Dr. Atkins' New Diet Revolution*. New York: An Avon Book, 1999.

Atkins, Robert C., M.D. with Sheila Buff. *Dr. Atkins' Age-Defying Diet Revolution*. New York: St. Martin's Press, 2000.

Atkinson, Rita L., et al. *Introduction to Psychology*. San Diego: Harcourt Brace Jovanovich, 1987.

Austad, Steven N., Ph.D. *Why We Age*. New York: John Wiley & Sons, 1997.

Balch, James F., M.D. and Balch, Phyllis A., C.N.C. *Prescription for Natural Healing*. New York: Avery Publishing Group, Inc., 1990.

Barnard, Neal, M.D. *Eat Right, Live Longer*, New York: Harmony Books, 1995.

Benson, Herbert, M.D. with Stark, Marg. *Timeless Healing*. New York: Scribner, 1996.

Berger, Kathleen S. *The Developing Person Through the Life Span*, New York: Worth Publishers, 1988.

Berger, Stuart M. *Forever Young*. New York: William Morrow and Company, Inc., 1998.

Bland, Jeffrey S., Ph.D. *The 20-Day Rejuvenation Diet Program*. New Canaan, Conn.: Keats Publishing, Inc., 1997.

Blavatsky, Helen P. *Theosophical Glossary*. New Delhi, India, 1986.

Boolootian, Richard A. *College Zoology. 10th Ed.* New York: Macmillan, 1981.

Borisenko, Joan, Ph.D. *Minding the Body, Mending the Mind*. New York: Simon & Schuster, 1988.

Bragg, Paul C., N.D., Ph.D. and Bragg, Patricia C., N.D., Ph.D. *The Miracle of Fasting*. Santa Barbara, Ca.: Health Science, ~

Brennan, Barbara Ann. *Hands of Light*. New York: Bantam Books, 1987.

Burns, George. *How to Live to Be 100 — Or More: The Ultimate Diet, Sex and Exercise Book*. Boston: G.K.Hall & Co., 1985.

Burton Goldberg Group. *Alternative medicine: The Definitive Guide*. Puyallup, Wash.: Future Medicine Publishing, 1993.

Cantor, Alfred J., M.D. *Dr. Cantor's Longevity Diet: How to Slow down Aging and Prolong Youth and Vigor*. West Nyack, N.Y.: Parker Publishing Company, Inc., 1967.

Carper, Jean. *Stop Aging Now!* New York: Harper Perennial, 1995.

Castaneda, Carlos. *Art of Dreaming.* London: HarperCollins *Publishers,* 1994.

Chopra, Deepak, M.D. *Ageless Body, Timeless Mind: The Quantum Alternative to Growing Old.* New York: Harmony Books, 1993.

Collins Pocket Reference Astrology. The Diagram Group. Glasgow: HarperCollins *Publishers,* 1996.

Connors, Jimmy. *Don't Count Yourself Out.* New York: Hyperion, 1981.

Cooper, Kenneth H., *The Aerobics Program for Total Well-Being: Exercise, Diet, Emotional Balance.* Toronto, New York: Bantam Books, 1983.

Dass, Ram. *The Only Dance There Is.* New York: J. Aronson, 1976.

D'Adamo, Peter J., M.D. with Catherine Whitney. *Eat Right for 4 Your Type.* New York: G. P. Putnam's Sons, 1996.

Davies, David. *The Centenarians of the Andes.* Garden City, N.Y.: Anchor Press, 1975.

Delany, Sarah L., with Hearth, Amy Hill. *On My Own At 107, Reflections on Life Without Bessie.* San Fransisco: Harper, 1997.

Delmonteque, Bob with Hays, Scott. *Lifelong Fitness.* New York: Warner Books, Inc., 1993.

The Diagram Group. *The Human Body: A Complete Guide.* Philadelphia, Pen.: Running Press, 1994.

Diamond, Harvey and Marilyn. *Fit For Life.* New York: Warner Books, Inc., 1985.

Douglas, Nik and Slinger, Penny. *Sexual Secrets.* Rochester: Destiny Books, 1989.

Fishbein, Morris, MD, *Illustrated Medical and Health Encyclopedia.* New York: H. S. Stuttman Co., 1957.

Fountain of Youth: How To Live Longer & Healthier. The Editors of Ronin Publishing Berkeley, Ca.: Ronin Publishing, Inc., 1996.

Friedan, Betty. *The Fountain of Age.* New York: Simon & Schuster, 1993.

Frolkis, V. V. *Aging and Life-Prolonging Processes.* Wien: Springer-Verlag, 1982.

Fuhrman, Joel, M.D. *Fasting and Eating for Health.* New York: St. Martin's Press, 1995.

Gittleman, Ann Louise, M.S. *Your Body Knows Best.* New York: Pocket Books, 1996.

Glass, Justine. *Live To Be 180.* Moscow: Fizkultura & Sport, 1991.

Glenn, Jim. *Exercise & Fitness.* Springhouse, Pa.: Springhouse Corp., 1986.

Godagama, Shantha, Dr. *The Handbook of Ayurveda.* Great Britain: Kyle Cathie Ltd., 1997.

Goldschneider, Gary and Elffers, Joost. *The Secret Language of Birthdays.* London: Penguin Studio Books, 1994.

Goleman, Daniel. *Emotional Intelligence.* New York: Bantam Books, 1995.

The 1999 Guinness Book of Records. Guinness Publishing Ltd., New York: Bantam Books, 1999.

Hadady, Letha. *Asian Health Secrets: The Complete Guide to Asian Herbal Medicine.* New York: Crown Publishers, 1996.

Haas, Elson, Dr. *Staying Healthy with Nutrition: The Complete Guide to Diet and Nutritional Medicine.* Berkeley, Calif.: Celestial Arts, 1991.

Haruyama, Shigeo. *A Great Revolution in the Brain World*, (in Japanese). Tokyo: Kodansha, 1995.

Hay, Louse L. *You Can Heal Your Life.* Carlsbad, Calif.: Hay House, Inc., 1987.

Hay, Louse L. *The Power Is Within You.* Carlsbad, Calif.: Hay House, Inc., 1991.

Hayflick, Leonard, Ph.D. *How and Why We Age.* New York: Ballantine Books, 1994.

Heber, David, M.D., Ph.D. *Natural Remedies for a Healthy Heart.* Garden City Park, N.Y.: Avery Publishing Group, 1998.

Heinerman, John, Ph.D. *Heinerman's Encyclopedia of Anti-Aging Remedies.* Englewood Cliffs, New Jersey: Prentice Hall, Inc., 1996.

Heller, Richard F. and Heller, Rachael F., Dr. *Healthy for Life.* New York: Dutton,1995.

Heynen, Jim. *One Hundred Over 100: Moments with One Hundred North American Centenarians.* Golden, Colo.: Fulcrum Pub., 1990.

Hittleman, Richard L. *Yoga for Physical Fitness.* New York: Warner Books, Inc., 1964.

Holford, Patric. *The Optimum Nutrition Bible.* Freedom, CA: The Crossing Press, 1999.

Jackowski, Edward J. *Hold it! You're Exercising Wrong.* New York: Simon & Schuster, 1995.

Keane, Maureen, M.S. and Chace, Daniella., M.S. *What to Eat if You Have Cancer.* Chicago, Ill.: Contemporary Books,1996.

Keanne, Jerryl L., Ph.D. *Practical Astrology: How to Make it Work for You.* Delhi: Vikas Publishing House PVT Ltd., 1997.

Kelder, Peter. *Ancient Secret of the Fountain of Youth.* Gig Harbor, Wash.: Harbor Press, Inc., 1989.

Kent, Howard. *The Complete Yoga Course.* New Burlington Books, 1993.

Kervran, Louis C. *Biological Transmutations.* Magalia, CA: Hapiness Press, 1998.

Khalsa, Dharma Singh, M.D. with Stauth, Cameron. *Brain Longevity.* New York: Warner Books, Inc., 1997.

Kirschmann, Gayla J. and Kirschmann, John D. *Nutrition Almanac.* New York: McGraw Hill, 1996.

Koop, Everett C., M.D., *Dr. Koop's Self-Care Advisor.* Time Inc Health, 1996.

Kulvinskas, Viktoras. *Survival into the 21-st Century: Planetary Healers Manual.* Wetherfield, Conn.: Omangod Press, 1975.

Kushi, Michio and Jack, A. *The Cancer Prevention Diet*. New York: St. Martin's, 1983.

Lad, Vasant. *Ayurveda, The Science of Self-Healing: A Practical Guide*. Twin Lakes, Wis.: Lotus Press, 1984.

Langone, John. *Long Life*. Boston: Little, Brown and Company, 1978.

Lewis, Frederick and Johnson, Dick. *Young at Heart*. Waco, Tex.: WRS Pub., 1992.

Life Span Plus. The Editors of Prevention Magazine. New York: Berkley Books, 1996.

Lindlahr, Victor H. *The Natural Way to Health*. New York: National Nutrition Society, Inc., 1939.

Littauer, Florence. *How to Understand Others by Understanding Yourself Personality Plus*. New York, Fleming H. Revell Company, 1983.

Lu, Henri C. *The Art of Long Life. Chinese Foods for Longevity*. Selangor Darul Ehsan, Malaysia: Pelanduk Publications (M) Sdn. Bhd., 1996.

Lust, John. *The Herb Book*. New York: Bantam Books, 1974.

Mader, Sylvia S. *Inquiry Into Life*, 3th ed., Dubuque, Iowa: W.C. Brown Co., 1982.

Mahoney, David and Restak, Richard. *The Longevity Strategy*. New York: John Wiley & Sons, 1998.

Mansfield, Peter, Dr. *The Good Health Handbook*. London: Grafton Books, 1994.

Marieb, Elaine N., Dr. *Human Anatomy & Physiology*, 4th Ed., New York: Addison Wesley Publishing Company, 1998.

Mindel, Earl, R.Ph., Ph.D. *Earl Mindel's Vitamin Bible*. New York: Warner Books, 1991.

Mindel, Earl, R.Ph., Ph.D. *Earl Mindel's Anti-Aging Bible*. New York: Fireside Books, 1996.

Moore, Thomas J. *Lifespan: Who Lives Longer—and Why*. New York: Simon & Schuster, 1993.

Morehouse, L. E. and Gross, Leonard. *Total Fitness in 30 Minutes a Week*. New York: Simon & Schuster, 1993.

Morningstar, Amadea with Desai, Urmila. *The Ayurvedic Cookbook*. Lotus Press, 1990.

Morrison, Judith H. *The Book of Ayurveda: A Holistic Approach to Health and Longevity*. New York: A Fireside Book, 1995.

Muramoto, Naboru. *Healing Ourselves*. New York: Avon Books, 1973.

Murray, Michael T., N.D., and Pizzorno, Joseph E., N.D. *Encyclopedia of Natural Medicine*. Rocklin, CA: Prima Publishing, 1991.

NAVIX, Encyclopedia of Current Knowledge. Tokyo: Kodansha, 1997.

Nedley, Neil, M.D. *Proof Positive: How to Reliably Combat Disease and Achieve Optimal Health through Nutrition and Lifestyle*. Ardmore, OK: Neil Nedley, M.D., 1998.

Netzer, Corinne T. *Corinne T. Netzer's Big Book of Miracle Cures*. New York: A Dell Book, 1999.

Ozaniec, Naomi. *The Elements of the Chakras*. London: Hodder & Stoughton, 1994.

Ornish, Dean, M.D., *Dr. Dean Ornish's Program for Reversing Heart Disease*. New York: Random House, 1990.

Ornstein, Robert, Ph.D. and Sobel, David, M.D. *Healthy Pleasures*. Reading, Mass.: Addison–Wesley Publishing Company, 1989.

Ouspensky, Petr D. *The Forth Way*. London: Routledge & Kegan Paul, 1957.

Pauling, Linus, Ph.D., *How to Live Longer and Feel Better*. New York: W. H. Freeman and Company, 1986.

Pearson, Durk and Show, Sandy. *Life Extension: A Practical Scientific Approach*. New York: Warner Books, Inc., 1982.

Perls, Thomas T., M.D. and Silver, Margery H., Ed.D. with Laurman, John F. *Living to 100*. New York: Basic Books, 1999.

Rao, Ramachandra S. K., Prof., Ed. *Encyclopedia of Indian Medicine*. Bangalore, 1987.

Reid, Daniel. *The Complete Book of Chinese Health & Healing*. New York: Barnes & Noble, 1994.

Reid, Daniel. *The Tao of Health, Sex, and Longevity*. New York and London: Simon & Schuster, 1989.

Reilly, Harold J. and Hagy, Brod Ruth. *The Edgar Cayce Handbook for Health*. New York: Macmillan, 1975.

Restak, Richard M., M.D. *Older and Wiser*. New York: Berkley Books, 1997.

Ringer, Robert J. *Looking Out For #1*. New York: Fawcett Crest, 1977.

Ronin Publishing, Editors. *Fountains of Youth: How To Live Longer & Healthier*. Berkeley, Ca.: Ronin Publishing, Inc., 1996.

Roy, Hampton, M.D. and Russel, Charles, M.D. *The Encyclopedia of Aging and The Elderly*, Facts on File, 1992.

Schwartz, David J. *The Magic of Thinking Big*. Prentice Hall, 1990.

Sears, Barry, Ph.D. with Lawren, Bill. *The Zone: A Dietary Road Map*. New York: Regan Books, 1995.

Sears, Barry, Ph.D. *The Age-Free Zone*. New York: Regan Books, 1999.

Shealy, C. Norman, M.D. Ph.D., *The Complete Family Guide to Alternative Medicine*. Element Books, 1996.

Sheldon, William. *Atlas of Men; a Guide for Somatotyping the Adult Male at All Ages*. Hafner Publishing Co., 1970.

Shelton, Herbert M., Dr. *Fasting Can Save Your Life*. Tampa, Flor.: American Natural Hygiene Society, Inc., 1996.

Shepard, Leslie A., Ed. *Encyclopedia of Occultism and Parapsychology*. Detroit, New York: Gale Research, Inc., 1991.

Solomon, David H., M.D., et al. *A Consumer's Guide to Aging*. Baltimore: Johns Hopkins University Press, 1992.

Sonberg, Lynn. *The Health Nutrient Bible*. New York: Simon & Schuster, 1995.

Staying Young. By Editors of Prevention Magazine. New York: Berkley Books, 1996.

Taylor, Renee. *The Hunza-Yoga Way to Health and Long Life*. New York: Costellation International, 1969.

Temoshok, Lydia, Ph.D., and Dreher, Henry. *The Type C Connection: The Behavioral Links to Cancer and Your Health*. New York: Random House, 1991.

Tiwari, Maya. *Ayurveda Secrets of Healing*. Twin Lakes, Wis.: Lotus Press, 1995.

Thorsons Editorial Board. *The Complete Raw Juice* Therapy.Glasgow: Thorsoms, 1989.

Vogel, Alfred, Dr.h.c. *The Nature Doctor*. New Canaan, Conn.: Keats Pub., 1991.

Walford, R.L. and Walford, L. *The Anti-Aging Plan: Strategies and Recipes for Extending Your Healthy Years*, Four Walls, Eight Windows, 1994.

Ward, Michael. *Mountain Medicine: A Clinical Study of Cold and High Altitudes*. New York: Vahnostrand Reihold, 1976.

Waitley, Denis, Dr. and Witt, Reni L. *The Joy of Working*. New York: Dodd, Mead, 1985.

Walker, Norman W., D.Sc. *Become Younger*. Prescott, AZ: Norwalk Press, 1995.

William, Tom, Ph.D. *Chinese Medicine*. Australia: Element Books Ltd., 1995.

Whitaker, Julian, M.D. and Colman, Carol. *Shed 10 Years in 10 Weeks*. New York: Fireside, 1997.

Weissberg, Steven M., M.D. and Christiano, Joseph, A.P.P.T. *The Answer is in Your Bloodtype*. Lake Mary, FL: Personal Nutrition USA, Inc., 1999.

Wells, Herbert G., Huxley, Julian S. and Wells, G.P. *The Science of Life*. Garden City, N.Y.: Doubleday, Doran & Company, Inc., 1931.

Wolcott, William L. and Fahey, Trish. *The Metabolic Typing Diet*. New York: Doubleday, 2000.

Wolfe, David. *The Sunfood Diet Success System*. San Diego, CA: Maul Brothers Publishing, 2000.

Yamamoto, Shizuko. *Barefoot Shiatsu*. Tokyo: Japan Publications, Inc., 1990.

Yamamoto, Shizuko and McCarty, Patrick. *Whole Health Shiatsu*. Tokyo and New York: Japan Publications, Inc., 1993.

Yogananda, Paramahansa. *Autobiography of a Yogi*. Los Angeles, Self Realization Fellowship, 1955.

Zhengcai, Liu. *The Mistery of Longevity*. Singapore: An Asiapac Publication, 1991.

Index

D

L

Index

Testimonials

Mamonov's *Control for Life Extension* is a perfect balance of scientific ...oration into the field of longevity and interesting personal experience. ...nyone interested in improving their own quality of life will find this book to be a thorough and holistic discussion of all aspects of health: physical, mental, emotional, and spiritual. The various questionnaires used to determine an individualized approach to diet, exercise, and stress management--combined with traditional philosophies and practices from other cultures--result in specific guidelines for achieving better health and enhancing the odds for living a long life. The author incorporates not only his own experiences to illustrate various techniques, but also the fascinating stories of centenarians and health proponents he interviewed in several countries. His technical explanations of how the systems of the body function validate his recommendations for lifestyle changes—and he practices what he preaches. Readers at all life stages will benefit from his unique approach.

--Constance Burt, Editing Consultant, TechEdit Services, Topsham, Maine

Valery Mamonov shares his own extensive cross-disciplinary experiences and original research to create a book, which shows the reader many ways to improve the quality and length of life. Readers are shown how to determine their own physical and psychological state. The author also guides them to the particular changes in diet, attitude, and activities, which would be the most beneficial in a quest for longevity and better health.

--Curtis Gifford, Former Bio-Medical Reference Librarian at Dartmouth College, Reference Librarian at Colorado State University, and a Visiting Scholar at Cambridge University. He now lives in Monte Carlo, Monaco.

Having lived and worked in different parts of the world and among different cultures for over 20 years, I was impressed to see how the author is approaching the issue of "Control for Live Extension." It is a holistic research work comparing and clarifying different approaches in various cultures, which all have essential elements in common. Mr. Valery Mamonov describes in a practical way—based on his own experience and observations—how to choose among the various methods and approaches, what will work for you to maintain good health. I find it an enriching and personally stimulating work.

--Eugene Boelens, Esq., a United Nations official, New York.